John Knox Laughton

Letters and Despatches of Horatio

Viscount Nelson, duke of Bronte, vice admiral of the White squadron

John Knox Laughton

Letters and Despatches of Horatio
Viscount Nelson, duke of Bronte, vice admiral of the White squadron

ISBN/EAN: 9783337319168

Printed in Europe, USA, Canada, Australia, Japan

Cover: Foto ©ninafisch / pixelio.de

More available books at **www.hansebooks.com**

NELSON'S
LETTERS AND DESPATCHES

PRINTED BY
SPOTTISWOODE AND CO., NEW-STREET SQUARE
LONDON

LETTERS AND DESPATCHES

OF

HORATIO, VISCOUNT NELSON, K.B.

DUKE OF BRONTE

VICE-ADMIRAL OF THE WHITE SQUADRON

SELECTED AND ARRANGED
BY
JOHN KNOX LAUGHTON, M.A.

PROFESSOR OF MODERN HISTORY AT KING'S COLLEGE, LONDON, AND LECTURER
ON NAVAL HISTORY AT THE ROYAL NAVAL COLLEGE, GREENWICH

TO

ADMIRAL

SIR GEOFFREY PHIPPS HORNBY, G.C.B.

Dear Sir Geoffrey,

Those of us who have had the privilege of attending your lectures, and of listening to your private exposition of some of the questions raised, know how you, more distinctly perhaps than most of our admirals, have recognised in Nelson not only the national hero but the consummate tactician; and how emphatically you have insisted that the principles which he enunciated and illustrated are, in spite of all changes, as true now as they were eighty or ninety years ago.

It seems, therefore, especially fitting that your name should be associated with this endeavour to set forth, as far as possible in Nelson's own words, the exact story of Nelson's professional life; and, in accordance with your permission, I have now the very great pleasure of dedicating it to you.

Believe me,
Dear Sir Geoffrey,
Your faithful and obedient servant,
J. K. LAUGHTON.

2 *April* 1886.

INTRODUCTION.

THIS selection of Nelson's letters and despatches has been made with the view of bringing within a moderate compass Nelson's own exposition of his professional life. The materials were ready to hand in Sir N. Harris Nicolas's great work, for permission to quarry in which, I am indebted to the courtesy of the author's son, Mr. Harris Nicolas of the Audit Office, and of Messrs. Chatto & Windus, the representatives of his publishers. I have indeed been fortunately able to correct some errors of transcription and to add a few letters or minutes of interest. Had merely new letters been an object, it was in my power to have included several on matters of everyday routine, which the more systematic arrangement of the Admiralty Records has brought to light; as also some which have been published in the 'Athenæum.' But I was not in search of mere novelty of this kind; and with very few exceptions, I found enough for my purpose in Nicolas's seven portly volumes, the value of which to the naval student has been somewhat lessened by their great bulk, and even, perhaps, by the very completeness of the collection. Letters to different correspondents often repeat the same story, in nearly the same words; and numerous others, on trivial or commonplace subjects, choke, to some extent, the more important. Still, even putting these on one side, the number of those of naval interest was so great that the utmost rigour of compression and excision was absolutely necessary. In exercising this, I have cut off the beginnings and endings of the letters, giving the address and date in a marginal note, which I have, to some extent, amplified in the index. I have cut out whatever seemed to have no naval or personal importance; have avoided repetitions as much as possible, and have sometimes given the narrative in a mosaic of paragraphs from different letters: very few of the letters are given in full. Explanatory or connecting matter, and letters or narratives by other hands are printed in smaller type. Whatever is in the larger type is Nelson's, though I have occasionally summarised the matter or corrected obvious mistakes of haste, but always within square brackets. It must be remembered that a large proportion of the letters are taken from a rough draft, the language of which was, sometimes at least, modified in making the fair copy. Spelling of names of places I have generally altered in accordance with the usage of our modern maps and charts.

I may say, once for all, that it has been no part of my plan to supersede Nicolas's most valuable work; but rather, on the contrary, to induce the reader of this selection to refer to it for fuller details. It is the only work on Nelson's life which may be implicitly trusted. Clarke and McArthur had great opportunities, but had neither the judgment nor the tact rightly to use them, and published two enormous volumes, containing indeed much of interest and importance, but much also that is contradictory, puerile, or ridiculous, and stuffed with galley yarns and reported conversations, of which many are certainly false, and few can be relied on as true. The earlier lives—and more especially Harrison's—are worthless; written with a purpose, not exactly that of presenting a faithful view of Nelson's career. Southey's is simply an enlargement of an article in the 'Quarterly Review' (February 1810), written, without any special knowledge or research, from the materials readiest to hand, as supplied by the different biographers just referred to, selected with the skill of a literary artist and spiced from the mendacious pages of Miss Williams's 'Sketches.' The easy style of the writing has given the book a long-continued popularity, which as an historical record it is very far from deserving. Pettigrew's bulky work is mainly filled with the story of Nelson's supposed amour with Lady Hamilton, and is better suited for the society of the 'School for Scandal' than for the student of naval history. I repeat then, that the one work which gives a full and accurate account of Nelson's career is the collection of his 'Dispatches and Letters' by Sir Harris Nicolas; and to that, and to that alone, I refer those of my readers whom I have induced to seek for further and more minute details on some of the points which I have been compelled to slur over.

For with every care in arrangement and compression, it was impossible to find room for all that I wished to include. I can only hope that the selection I have made will put in a fair light Nelson's professional character—his method of carrying on the duty of the fleet, his untiring attention to detail; his geniality, his cordiality and yet his strictness; his passionate and enthusiastic zeal for the service, which will sound strange in these days when enthusiasm or zeal is derided as 'bad form;' his feminine affection and yearning for affection, his childlike vanity, his masculine courage, honour, and integrity; and above all, his tactical studies. It has been too much the custom to attribute his remarkable achievements to dash, to the magic of his name, to the eager and loving co-operation of all his officers; and to quote expressions—said to be his—to the effect that the whole secret of naval war is contained in three words: 'Go at 'em.' The evidence of these is often doubtful, and the context always wanting. Lord Dundonald, writing sixty years after date, has recorded his impression that one of Nelson's frequent injunctions was 'Never mind manœuvres; always go at them;'[1] but he has not recorded and probably did not know that Nelson's lifelong study was as to the proper way of 'going at them.'

It was the thoroughness of this study and the constant readiness for battle resulting from it that permitted the almost total absence of preliminary manœuvres when the enemy was actually in sight, and gave to the attack an appearance of dash, of utter recklessness, which has misled many. But Sir Edward Berry, who—as his flag-captain in the Vanguard—was behind the scenes, has told us that, in preparing for that meeting with the French, which actually took place off the mouth of the Nile—'There was no possible position in which they could be found, that he did not take into his

[1] *Autobiography of a Seaman*, vol. i. p. 88.

calculation, and for the most advantageous attack of which he had not digested and arranged the best possible disposition of the force which he commanded. With the masterly ideas of their admiral, therefore, on the subject of naval tactics, every one of the captains of his squadron was most thoroughly acquainted; and upon surveying the situation of the enemy, they could ascertain with precision what were the ideas and intentions of their commander, without the aid of any further instructions; by which means signals became almost unnecessary, much time was saved, and the attention of every captain could almost undistractedly be paid to the conduct of his own particular ship, a circumstance from which, upon this occasion, the advantages to the general service were almost incalculable' (p. 150). And Nelson's own letter to Lord Howe (p. 180) shows, in a few words, how clearly and distinctly he understood what he was doing. 'By attacking'—he wrote—'the enemy's van and centre, the wind blowing directly along their line, I was enabled to throw what force I pleased on a few ships.' So also when he wrote twelve days before the battle of Trafalgar, detailing the mode of attack, and saying—'The whole impression of the British fleet must be to overpower from two or three ships ahead of their commander-in-chief, supposed to be in the centre, to the rear of their fleet. I will suppose twenty sail of the enemy's line to be untouched. . . . The enemy's fleet is supposed to consist of forty-six sail of the line, British fleet of forty. If either is less, only a proportionate number of enemy's ships are to be cut off; British to be one-fourth superior to the enemy cut off' (p. 421). Similarly, in the memorandum on p. 383, careful provision for the manner of attack under different circumstances is detailed.

Does all this agree with the received idea of ' Go at 'em ' tactics? Is it not rather the refinement, the perfection of forethought and arrangement, which permitted the fleet to ' go at 'em ' with wildering impetuosity directed by the most approved science? If we admit that there is a right way and a wrong way of doing everything, then there is a right way and a wrong way of ' going at 'em.' Our history offers many examples of the wrong way, and of failure. Nelson's papers show what extreme care he took to decide on the right way, and how that care was rewarded with the most brilliant successes. And more than that, they show also how utterly he was opposed to anything that savoured of recklessness or rashness: there was very little of the rude 'go at 'em' in his head when he wrote, on 2 July 1804, 'I think the fleet will be ordered out to fight close to Toulon, that they may get their crippled ships in again, and that we must then quit the coast to repair our damages, and thus leave the coast clear; but my mind is fixed not to fight them, unless with a westerly wind, outside the Hières, and with an easterly wind to the westward of Sicie' (p. 257): or when he wrote to Admiral Campbell, on 24 May 1804, 'I am more obliged to you than I can express, for your not allowing the very superior force of the enemy to bring you to action. Whatever credit would have accrued to your own and your gallant companions' exertions, no sound advantages could have arisen to our country; for so close to their own harbour they could always have returned, and left your ships unfit, probably, to keep the sea' (p. 348); or when he urged the necessity of due caution to Sir Richard Strachan (p. 321), to Captain Mowbray (p. 346), to Captain Donnelly (p. 357), and in many other letters not included in this selection. We are not to judge the teaching of such a man as Nelson from the partially remembered conversations, passed along from mouth to mouth and recorded many years afterwards, separate from context or circumstance; and it is as an emphatic protest against this much too common error that I have collected in this volume his exact teaching as written down by himself at the time, illustrating it by the exact record of his achievements written, also at the time, by the men best qualified by opportunity and judgment—by Berry or Miller at the Nile, by Stewart at Copenhagen, by Collingwood and in the logs of selected ships at Trafalgar.

It is not in tactics alone that Nelson's genius has been misunderstood and undervalued. In almost every point of his profession he has been described as really inferior, achieving success only by some accident. The man who had been first lieutenant of a smart frigate in the West Indies, and who, for three years, commanded the Agamemnon in the most treacherous of all seas, has been spoken of as 'no seaman,' unable even to put a ship about; and the man whose keen insight into the designs of the enemy repeatedly won for him the approval of his government, has been spoken of as ignorant of strategy. His forecast of the designs of the French on Italy (pp. 94-5) proved curiously accurate; and it is at least permitted us to believe that the mischief might have been prevented could Nelson have commanded the Genoese coast with such a squadron as he repeatedly asked for (pp. 89, 92), and had the main fleet effectively co-operated with him. This was his opinion, both at the time, in 1796, and four years later, when he wrote—'I say that the British fleet could have prevented the invasion of Italy, and at that time we had nothing to do; and if our friend Hotham had kept his fleet on that coast, I assert, and you will agree with me, no army from France could have been furnished with stores or provisions; even men could not have marched' (p. 242).

The constant pains he was at to acquire intelligence appear in many instances; amongst others, the mission of Captain Durban to Majorca (p. 370), or of Lieutenant Woodman to the Black Sea (p. 340); but his instinctive appreciation of the political state of the several countries with which he was brought in contact was no less remarkable, as was, perhaps, more especially shown in his letter of 28 June 1803 (p. 308), written within a few days of his arrival in the Mediterranean and warmly commended by the government. A further testimony to the same effect is given by Mr. Croker in his lately published ' Correspondence and Diaries ' (vol. ii. p. 233), which is curious as suggesting a reason for much of the existing misconception of Nelson's work. He is relating a conversation with the Duke of Wellington at Walmer, on 1 October 1834, and says:

'We were talking of Lord Nelson, and some instances were mentioned of the egotism and vanity that derogated from his character. "Why," said the Duke, "I am not surprised at such instances, for Lord Nelson was, in different circumstances, two quite different men, as I myself can vouch, though I only saw him once in my life, and for perhaps an hour. It was soon after I

---

[1] Sir Arthur Wellesley returned from India in the summer of 1805. The interview here described must therefore have taken place in the end of August or beginning of September of that year.

returned from India.[1] I went to the Colonial Office in Downing Street and there I was shown into the little waiting-room on the right hand, where I found, also waiting to see the Secretary of State, a gentleman whom, from his likeness to his pictures and the loss of an arm, I immediately recognised as Lord Nelson. He could not know who I was, but he entered at once into conversation with me, if I can call it conversation, for it was almost all on his side and all about himself; and in, really, a style so vain and silly as to surprise and almost disgust me. I suppose something that I happened to say may have made him guess that I was somebody, and he went out of the room for a moment, I have no doubt to ask the office-keeper who I was, for when he came back he was altogether a different man, both in manner and matter. All that I had thought a charlatan style had vanished, and he talked of the state of this country and of the aspect and probabilities of affairs on the Continent with a good sense and a knowledge of subjects both at home and abroad that surprised me equally and more agreeably than the first part of our interview had done: in fact he talked like an officer and a statesman. The Secretary of State kept us long waiting, and certainly for the last half or three-quarters of an hour, I don't know that I ever had a conversation that interested me more. Now if the Secretary of State had been punctual and admitted Lord Nelson in the first quarter of an hour, I should have had the same impression of a light and trivial character that other people have had; but luckily I saw enough to be satisfied that he was really a very superior man. But certainly, a more sudden and complete metamorphosis I never saw."'

That Nelson, on one side of his character, had the innocent and unblushing vanity of a child is confirmed by the independent testimony of dozens of credible witnesses [1] and by his own writing, as on pp. 3, 6, 8; and it is probably this which has given rise to the very general belief that his great, his peculiar merit was his transcendent courage, and that in his case, as in many others, Fortune favoured the brave. A careful examination of his correspondence and papers shows that this was not the case; and that his

---

[1] See, for instance, Mrs. St. George's [Mrs. Trench's] *Journal kept during a Visit to Germany in* 1799, 1800, pp. 76, 81.

successes were the result of ceaseless forethought and exact study, guided by genius of the highest order.

But of the many persistent misrepresentations which have clung to Nelson's history, the greater number are of importance only to the professional student. There is however one which strikes at his character as a man of probity and honour, and demands a closer investigation: it is that which relates to his doings in the Bay of Naples in June 1799. So far as Nelson was really concerned, the whole story is told in his correspondence (pp. 197-202, 239, 300); but this is not the story which, invented by Neapolitan traitors, published in English by Miss Williams,[1] and reproduced by Southey, by James, by Alison, by Brougham, by Mackintosh, and a host of other writers of more or less repute, has passed current as history and been very generally accepted as such.

It is perhaps from the pages of Southey that the greater number of English readers have received their impressions as to these events. What Southey says is that Nelson having declared ' that he would grant rebels no other terms than those of unconditional submission . . . the garrisons, taken out of the castles [Uovo and Nuovo] under pretence of carrying the treaty into effect, were delivered over as rebels to the vengeance of the Sicilian Court. A deplorable transaction! a stain upon the memory of Nelson and the honour of England! To palliate it would be in vain; to justify it would be wicked: there is no alternative . . . but to record the disgraceful story with sorrow and with shame.'

Southey is wrong. There is another alternative. We neither palliate, nor justify, nor record; we deny. The story is a base and venomous falsehood. The rebels surrendered and were taken out of the castles on 26 June, the day after they had received Nelson's declaration (p. 198) that he would not permit them to embark or to quit the castles; that they must surrender themselves to the king's mercy. They accordingly came out trusting to the judgment of their sovereign (p. 301), and with a full knowledge that the treaty was annulled. The charge of treachery made by the traitors and adopted by Southey is absolutely without a shadow of foundation.

---

[1] *Sketches of the State of Manners and Opinions in the French Republic towards the close of the Eighteenth Century*, vol. i. pp. 123-223.

The only question which can really be raised is as to Nelson's conduct in annulling the treaty. He called it an infamous treaty; and it is difficult to see how any impartial judge reading its clauses —how the rebels were to march out with the honours of war, were to have a free passage to France, were to have hostages for the due fulfilment of the conditions—can give it any other name. But Nelson's objection went beyond this and was pronounced before he knew the terms of the treaty. He pronounced it infamous because Ruffo was expressly forbidden by his instructions to treat at all (p. 300), and his doing so was in itself treason. It was to this that Nelson applied the term infamous, much to the disgust afterwards of Captain Foote, who, as the senior English officer present, had signed the treaty. It was not, however, till eight years later, on the publication of Harrison's 'Life of Nelson,' that Foote learned the way it had been spoken of, and published what he called his 'Vindication,' in which, by laying down as axiomatic certain very controvertible statements, he pretends to show that the term 'infamous' should be applied to Nelson's conduct rather than to his. The capitulation—he says—was 'actually signed in the name of his Sicilian Majesty and his allies by those officers who were undoubtedly authorised to enter into and sign such treaties:' but this is utterly false: neither he nor any of the other signatories had any authorisation whatever, and Ruffo had instructions to the contrary. Again, says Captain Foote, 'A treaty or capitulation cannot be infringed without a breach of faith: it is a sacred engagement, the obligation of which no sophistry can destroy.' But in point of fact a treaty or capitulation granted by parties not authorised, is not binding and can be set aside at the discretion of a higher competent authority, always provided that the party capitulating is not placed in a worse condition than it was; that the capitulation has not been partially carried out. This was the exact case in Naples Bay when Nelson arrived there on 24 June. Castellamare had capitulated on terms granted by unauthorised officers; but the capitulation had taken effect, and was therefore, sorely against his will, approved by Nelson. The castles of Uovo and Nuovo had also capitulated, but the capitulation had not taken effect, and Nelson unhesitatingly and righteously annulled it.

A similar attack has been made on Nelson's character for the sanctioning and ordering the execution of Caracciolo (pp. 201-2). When the lies are cleared away, it is difficult to understand the objection. That Caracciolo was a traitor under circumstances of peculiar flagrancy and had taken a leading part in the rebellion, there was not a shadow of a doubt. His treason was more than admitted, it was boasted of by his friends.[1] That he was a man of good family and high naval rank was, in reality, an aggravation of his guilt. That he was seventy years of age, is false : he was forty-seven.[2] That he was included in the capitulation of the castles, and was taken out of one or other of them on the faith of the capitulation, is false : he had fled to the mountains when he saw the capitulation imminent; a reward had been offered for his apprehension; he was accordingly apprehended and brought on board the Foudroyant on 29 June, three days after the surrender of the castles. That he was promptly tried, found guilty and hanged, is true enough. The statement that Count Thurn was his personal enemy is unsupported by evidence, and—true or false—has nothing to do with the matter; for no attempt has ever been made to show that the finding of the Court was wrong : his guilt has been held to be his glory. As to the sentence and the carrying it out, whatever people may think now, then, at least, death was held to be the natural and necessary reward of unsuccessful treason. Nelson was certainly not a cruel or bloodthirsty man; but he was at Naples to maintain the authority of the established government against the machinations of the French; and the summary punishment of the leaders of the rebellion was the truest kindness to the nation at large.

The statement that Nelson was influenced in this matter by Lady Hamilton is also unsupported by evidence, and is, in itself, extremely improbable : but the persistently repeated statements that Lady Hamilton was 'present at the execution,' that she took a boat and lay off under the very yard-arm of the Minerva, or that she said to Nelson, 'Come Bronte, let us have another look at poor Caracciolo,' are wicked lies, without any foundation but the

---

[1] Amongst many others, see *Rapporto al Cittadino Carnot, Ministro della Guerra, da Francesco Lomonaco*, p. 158.

[2] *Blackwood's Magazine*, May 1877, vol. cxxi. p. 580.

malice of traitors. The 'Bronte' story is so palpably false—for the title was not conferred on Nelson till two months after Caracciolo's execution—that its acceptance can only result from malignity, or ignorance, or both. I see no reason whatever for supposing that in this matter, as in every other point of his professional life, Nelson was not guided by his sense of prudence, of justice, and of honour; for believing that Caracciolo did not richly deserve the fate he met with; and it is worth noting that had Troubridge instead of Nelson been in command, he, so far as we can judge by his letters (pp. 193-4), would have acted in a precisely similar manner.

Southey has laid great stress on a supposed want of proper authority. He says—' Had [Nelson] the authority of his Sicilian Majesty for proceeding as he did? If so, why was not that authority produced? If not, why were the proceedings hurried on without it? Why was the trial precipitated, so that it was impossible for the prisoner, if he had been innocent, to provide the witnesses who might have proved him so?' The questions are absurd and childish. From first to last, in all the volumes that have been written on the subject, no suggestion has ever been made that the prisoner was innocent, or that any witnesses could have proved him so. By his own friends and accomplices, the facts are fully admitted: the defence is, not that Caracciolo did not wage war against the established government of his country, not that he did not aid the foreign invader to the utmost of his power, but that his doing so was a virtue. The government of Naples was a grinding tyranny; the king was an ignorant and weak-minded fool; the queen was a bloodthirsty harlot; the revolution was, therefore, righteous, and Caracciolo was not a traitor, but a patriot and a hero. With such allegations I am now in no way concerned. Nelson was sent to Naples, not to try the Neapolitan constitution, but to maintain it; not to judge the king and queen, but to uphold them. As matter of fact, however, I may point out that the insurrection was not, as the traitors have represented it, the passionate outburst of a people longing to be free, but the welcome given to the French invaders by a few men, mostly of the professional or professorial class, who conceived that the republic would open to them a political career which the monarchy denied. From the French alone it received its impulse; from their presence, it drew its strength; and with their departure it collapsed. The opinion of the masses was entirely in favour of the king and constitution.

As to Nelson's authority, the mere facts are sufficient. It is not usual for an admiral, when giving an order, to make a public display of his commission: it is known to exist, and his order is executed as a matter of course. If Thurn and the other Sicilian officers had not known the extent of Nelson's authority, they would have hesitated to obey; had Caracciolo not known it—and it will be remembered that he had been serving under Nelson's orders but a few months before—he would have raised an objection as to the competence of the court-martial. When those whom it concerned, —the king, Nelson, Thurn, and Caracciolo—were all satisfied, who is Southey, that he should raise this maudlin cry of sickly sentimentalism over the death of a perjured and convicted traitor?

It is no part of my plan to enter at any length into the discussion of Nelson's private life. That he separated from his wife is noted in a letter to Mr. Davison (p. 270), and it is generally understood that the cause of this separation was Nelson's attachment to Lady Hamilton. But concerning the nature of that attachment it is quite impossible to decide. Those will speak the most positively who have least examined it. That Nelson was passionately devoted to Lady Hamilton is certain; but whether the devotion took the form of adultery may be doubted; and whether Horatia was the child of Nelson and Lady Hamilton, or of either of them, is a question that cannot be categorically answered. It may however be pointed out that though Horatia was born in January 1801, a feminine critic, so keen and outspoken as Mrs. St. George, saw no trace of an approaching confinement in Lady Hamilton's figure, in October 1800; and that Lady Hamilton, during her stay in Dresden, not only gave repeated representations of her celebrated attitudes, but danced the Tarantola, and went through a great deal more exertion than a woman in her supposed condition would be likely to undertake. It may further be noted that Horatia's eyes are spoken of as 'sloes,'[1] whilst Nelson's were grey, and

---

[1] Egerton MS. 1623, f. 85.

Lady Hamilton's light blue; that Nelson never spoke of the child except as his 'adopted daughter,' and that Lady Hamilton positively denied being the mother. One letter indeed, given by Pettigrew (vol. ii. p. 652), would be conclusive, if its authenticity were established; but Pettigrew, in quoting it, has given no details of the letter itself; and its matter is too strange, too widely different from anything else either Nelson or Lady Hamilton ever wrote, to permit its acceptance without a close scrutiny. At present it rests merely on Pettigrew's statement; and Pettigrew was far from an exacting critic. He has thus accepted as Nelson's own composition some feeble verses (vol. ii. p. 17), which, if we may judge by the style and turn of expression, were the production of Lord William Gordon, the friend of the Duke of Queensberry, and the acknowledged author of the verses in the Egerton MS. just referred to. To suppose them Nelson's is to suppose that Nelson could write grammatical twaddle in verse, though in prose, grammar and twaddle were equally foreign to his style; and is further to suppose that the evening of a hard-fought day, 2 April 1801, after a sleepless night (p. 254), was the particular time that Nelson spent in writing this trash. I do not believe that he ever, in his whole life, wrote a line of verse, or could have written one even if he had wished. But the whole of the Nelson-Hamilton correspondence is in a very unsatisfactory state. Few of the originals are known, and the letters published by Harrison, or in 'Letters of Lord Nelson to Lady Hamilton' are certainly garbled, even when they are not altogether fictitious. Of this last nature is one which has been often quoted, but which I have not admitted here into the text, as being a palpable forgery. It is supposed to have been written from Syracuse on 22 July 1798, and runs:

'My dear Friends—Thanks to your exertions, we have victualled and watered: and surely watering at the fountain of Arethusa, we must have victory. We shall sail with the first breeze, and be assured I will return either crowned with laurels or covered with cypress.'

The laurel and cypress sentence may possibly be Nelson's; but assuredly he never meddled with the fountain of Arethusa; and the 'Thanks to your exertions, we have victualled and watered' is flatly contradicted by the letter to Sir William Hamilton of the same date (p. 144). But this fictitious letter is the only evidence on record of the action of Lady Hamilton in this matter. That she afterwards taught Nelson to believe in her action we know from the solemn expression of his last wishes (p. 428), but the reality of it seems very doubtful.

There are many other points connected with Nelson's career on which I am tempted to pause for a moment; but I recall to mind my intention to leave the narration of what he taught and what he did entirely to himself and to those immediately round him. Plain and direct statements so made need little comment or explanation; and the necessary deductions from them can be most profitably worked out by the thoughtful reader, each one for himself. If what I have said and done renders the task simpler and easier, if it tends to form a more exact appreciation of the genius of our great hero, then indeed I may say—'I have done the State some service.'

LETTERS AND JOURNALS

OF

HORATIO, VISCOUNT NELSON.

In October 1799, Lord Nelson wrote the following sketch for Mr. McArthur, then editing the 'Naval Chronicle,' in concert with the Rev. J. S. Clarke. It constituted the basis of the biographical notice published in the third volume of the 'Naval Chronicle;' and was afterwards printed in its original form, though with some verbal alterations, in Clarke and McArthur's 'Life of Nelson.'

My dear Sir,—I send you a sketch of my life, which I am sensible wants your pruning-knife before it is fit to meet the public eye, therefore I trust you and your friend will do that, and turn it into much better language. I have been, and am, very unwell, therefore you must excuse my short letter. I did not even know that such a book as yours was printed, therefore I beg you will send me the two volumes, and consider me as a sincere friend to the undertaking.

J. McArthur, 15 Oct. 1799. Port Mahon.

Horatio Nelson, son of the Reverend Edmund Nelson, Rector of Burnham Thorpe, in the county of Norfolk, and Catherine his wife, daughter of Doctor Suckling, Prebendary of Westminster, whose grandmother was sister to Sir Robert Walpole, Earl of Orford.

'Sketch of my Life.'

I was born 29 September, 1758, in the parsonage-house, was sent to the high school at Norwich, and afterwards removed to North Walsham; from whence, on the disturbance with Spain relative to the Falkland Islands [in 1770], I went to sea with my uncle, Captain Maurice Suckling, in the Raisonable of 64 guns. But the business with Spain being accommodated, I was sent in a West India ship belonging to the house of Hibbert, Purrier, and Horton, with Mr. John Rathbone, who had formerly been in the navy, in the Dreadnought with Captain Suckling. From this voyage I returned to the Triumph at Chatham in July 1772; and, if I did not improve in my education, I returned a practical seaman, with a horror of the Royal Navy, and with a saying, then constant with the seamen, 'Aft the most honour, forward the better man!'—It was many weeks before I got in the least reconciled to a man-of-war, so deep was the prejudice rooted; and what pains were taken to instil this erroneous principle in a young mind! However, as my ambition was to be a seaman, it was always held out as a reward, that if I attended well to my navigation, I should go in the cutter and decked long-boat, which was attached to the commanding officer's ship at Chatham. Thus by degrees I became a good pilot, for vessels of that description, from Chatham to the Tower of London, down the Swin, and to the North Foreland; and confident of myself amongst rocks and sands, which has many times since been of the very greatest comfort to me. In this way I was trained, till the expedition towards the North Pole was fitted out; when, although no boys were allowed to go in the ships (as of no use), yet nothing could prevent my using every interest to go with Captain Lutwidge in the Carcass; and, as I fancied I was to fill a man's place, I begged I might be his coxswain: which, finding my ardent desire for going with him, Captain Lutwidge complied with, and has continued the strictest friendship to this moment. Lord Mulgrave, who I then first knew, continued his kindest friendship and regard to the last moment of his life. When the boats were fitting out to quit the two ships blocked up in the ice, I exerted myself to have the command of a four-oared cutter raised upon, which was given me, with twelve men; and I prided myself in fancying I could navigate her better than any other boat in the ship.

On our arrival in England, and paid off, 15 October [1773], I found that a squadron was fitting out for the East Indies; and nothing less than such a distant voyage could in the least satisfy my desire of maritime knowledge: and I was placed in the Seahorse of 20 guns, with Captain Farmer, and watched in the foretop; from whence in time I was placed on the quarter-deck: having, in the time I was in this ship, visited almost every part of the East Indies, from Bengal to Bussorah. Ill health induced Sir Edward Hughes, who had always shown me the greatest kindness, to send me to England in the Dolphin of 20 guns, with Captain James Pigot, whose kindness at that time saved my life. This ship was paid off at Woolwich on 24 September, 1776. On the

26th I received an order from Sir James Douglas, who commanded at Portsmouth, to act as lieutenant of the Worcester, 64, Captain Mark Robinson, who was ordered to Gibraltar with a convoy. In this ship I was at sea with convoys till 2 April, 1777, and in very bad weather. But although my age might have been a sufficient cause for not entrusting me with the charge of a watch, yet Captain Robinson used to say, 'he felt as easy when I was upon deck, as any officer in the ship.'

On [9] April, 1777, I passed my examination as a lieutenant; and received my commission the next day, as second lieutenant of the Lowestoft frigate of 32 guns, Captain (now Lieutenant-Governor of Greenwich Hospital) William Locker. In this ship I went to Jamaica; but even a frigate was not sufficiently active for my mind, and I got into a schooner,[1] tender to the Lowestoft. In this vessel I made myself a complete pilot for all the passages through the (Keys) Islands situated on the north side [of] Hispaniola. Whilst in this frigate, an event happened which presaged my character; and, as it conveys no dishonour to the officer alluded to, I shall relate it.

Blowing a gale of wind, and very heavy sea, the frigate captured an American letter of marque. The first lieutenant was ordered to board her, which he did not do, owing to the very high sea. On his return on board, the captain said, 'Have I no officer in the ship who can board the prize?' On which the master ran to the gangway, to get into the boat; when I stopped him, saying, 'It is my turn now; and if I come back, it is yours.' This little incident has often occurred to my mind; and I know it is my disposition, that difficulties and dangers do but increase my desire of attempting them.

Sir Peter Parker, soon after his arrival at Jamaica, 1778, took me into his own flag-ship, the Bristol, as third lieutenant; from which I rose by succession to be first. Nothing particular happened whilst I was in this ship, which was actively employed off Cape François, being the commencement of the French war.

On 8 December, 1778, I was appointed commander of the Badger brig; and was first sent to protect the Mosquito shore, and the Bay of Honduras, from the depredations of the American privateers. Whilst on this service, I gained so much the affections of the settlers, that they unanimously voted me their thanks, and expressed their regret on my leaving them; entrusting to me to describe to Sir Peter Parker and Sir John Dalling their situation,

[1] The Little Lucy; so called after a daughter of Captain Locker.

should a war with Spain break out. Whilst I commanded this brig, H.M.S. Glasgow, Captain Thomas Lloyd, came into Montego Bay, Jamaica, where the Badger was laying: in two hours afterwards she took fire by a cask of rum; and Captain Lloyd will tell you, that it was owing to my exertions, joined to his, that her whole crew were rescued from the flames.

On 11 June, 1779, I was made post into the Hinchingbrook. When, being at sea, and Count d'Estaing arriving at Hispaniola with a very large fleet and army from Martinique, an attack on Jamaica was expected. In this critical state, I was by both admiral and general entrusted with the command of the batteries at Port Royal; and I need not say, as the defence of this place was the key to the port of the whole naval force, the town of Kingston, and Spanish Town, it was the most important post in the whole island.

In January 1780, an expedition being resolved on against St. Juan's, I was chosen to command the sea part of it. Major Polson, who commanded, will tell you of my exertions:[1] how I quitted my ship, carried troops in boats one hundred miles up a river, which none but Spaniards since the time of the buccaneers had ever ascended. It will then be told how I boarded, if I may be allowed the expression, an outpost of the enemy, situated on an island in the river; that I made batteries, and afterwards fought them, and was a principal cause of our success. From this scene I was appointed to the Janus, 44, at Jamaica, and went to Port Royal in the Victor sloop.

My state of health was now so bad, that I was obliged to go to England in the Lion, the Honourable William Cornwallis, captain; whose care and attention again saved my life. In August 1781, I was commissioned for the Albemarle; and, it would almost be supposed, to try my constitution, was kept the whole winter in the North Sea. In April 1782, I sailed with a convoy for Newfoundland and Quebec, under the orders of Captain Thomas Pringle. From Quebec, during a cruise off Boston, I was chased by three French ships of the line, and the Iris frigate: as they all beat me in sailing very much, I had no chance left, but running them amongst the shoals of St. George's Bank. This alarmed the line-of-battle ships, and they quitted the pursuit; but the frigate continued,

---

[1] Two narratives of that expedition have been published; one by Dr. Benjamin Moseley in his *Treatise on Tropical Diseases*, 8vo. London, 1803-4; and another by Dr. Thomas Dancer, entitled *A Brief History of the late Expedition against Fort St. Juan, so far as it relates to the Diseases of the Troops*, 4to. Kingston, 1792.

and at sunset was little more than gunshot distant : when, the line-of-battle ships being out of sight, I ordered the main-top-sail to be laid to the mast; on this the frigate tacked, and stood to rejoin her consorts.

In October I sailed from Quebec with a convoy to New York, where I joined the fleet under the command of Lord Hood ; and in November I sailed with him to the West Indies, where I remained till the peace ; when I came to England, being directed in my way to attend H.R.H. the Duke of Clarence on his visit to the Havana; and was paid off at Portsmouth on 3 July, 1783. In the autumn I went to France, and remained there till the spring of the year 1784; when I was appointed to the Boreas frigate, of 28 guns, and ordered to the Leeward Islands station.

This station opened a new scene to the officers of the British navy. The Americans, when colonists, possessed almost all the trade from America to our West India Islands; and on the return of peace, they forgot, on this occasion, that they became foreigners, and of course had no right to trade in the British colonies. Our governors and custom-house officers pretended, that by the Navigation Act they had a right to trade; and all the West Indians wished what was so much for their interest.

Having given governors, custom-house officers, and Americans, notice of what I would do, I seized many of their vessels, which brought all parties upon me; and I was persecuted from one island to another, so that I could not leave my ship. But conscious rectitude bore me through it ; and I was supported, when the business came to be understood, from home ; and I proved (and an Act of Parliament has since established it) that a captain of a man-of-war is in duty bound to support all the maritime laws, by his Admiralty commission alone, without becoming a custom-house officer.

In July 1786, I was left with the command till June 1787, when I sailed for England. During the winter H.R.H. the Duke of Clarence visited the Leeward Islands in the Pegasus frigate, of which he was captain. And in March, this year, I married Frances Herbert Nisbet, widow of Dr. Nisbet, of the island of Nevis ; by whom I have no children.

The Boreas being paid off at Sheerness, on 30 November, I lived at Burnham Thorpe, county of Norfolk, in the parsonage-house. In 1790, when the affair with Spain, relative to Nootka Sound, had near involved us in a war, I made use of every interest to get a ship, ay, even a boat, to serve my country, but in vain :

there was a prejudice at the Admiralty evidently against me, which I can neither guess at, or in the least account for.

On 30 January, 1793, I was commissioned in the very handsomest way for the Agamemnon, 64; and was put under the command of that great man and excellent officer, Lord Hood, appointed to the command in the Mediterranean. The unbounded confidence on all occasions placed in me by his lordship will show his opinion of my abilities; having served in the command of the seamen landed for the sieges of Bastia and Calvi. His lordship, in October 1794, left the Mediterranean to Admiral Hotham, who also honoured me with the same confidence. I was in the actions of 13 and 14 March, 1795, and 13 July in the same year. For the share I had in them, I refer to the admiral's letters. I was then appointed by Admiral Hotham to co-operate with the Austrian general, De Vins, which I did all the time Admiral Hotham retained the command, till November; when he was superseded by Sir John Jervis, now Earl St. Vincent.

In April 1796, the commander-in-chief so much approved of my conduct, that he directed me to wear a distinguishing pennant. In June I was removed from the Agamemnon to the Captain; and on 11 August appointed a captain under me. Between April and October, I was employed in the blockade of Leghorn, taking Porto Ferrajo, the island of Capraja, and finally in the evacuation of Bastia; when having seen the troops in safety to Porto Ferrajo, I joined the admiral in St. Fiorenzo, and proceeded with him to Gibraltar; from whence in December I was sent in La Minerve frigate, Captain George Cockburn, to Porto Ferrajo, to bring down our naval stores, &c. On the passage we captured a Spanish frigate, La Sabina, of 40 guns, 28 eighteen-pounders on her main deck, as will appear by my letter.

From sailing from Porto Ferrajo on 29 January, 1797, to the finish of the action, 14 February, I refer to the account published by Colonel Drinkwater. The king for my conduct gave me a gold medal, and the city of London a gold box.

In April I hoisted my flag as rear-admiral of the blue, and was sent to bring down the garrison of Porto Ferrajo: which service performed, I shifted my flag from the Captain to the Theseus on 27 May, and was employed in the command of the inner squadron in the blockade of Cadiz. It was during this period that perhaps my personal courage was more conspicuous than at any other period of my life. In an attack of the Spanish gunboats, I was boarded in my barge with its common crew of ten men, coxswain,

Captain Fremantle, and myself, by the commander of the gunboats. The Spanish barge rowed twenty-six oars, besides officers, thirty in the whole; this was a service hand to hand with swords, in which my coxswain, John Sykes (now no more), saved twice my life. Eighteen of the Spaniards being killed and several wounded, we succeeded in taking their commander.

On 15 July, I sailed for Teneriffe: the event, I refer to my letter of that expedition. Having lost my right arm, for this loss and my former services his Majesty was pleased to settle 800*l.* a year; and by some unlucky mismanagement of it, I was obliged to go to England; and it was 13 December, 1797, before the surgeons pronounced me fit for service. On 19 December, the Vanguard was commissioned for my flagship.

On 1 April, 1798, I sailed with a convoy from Spithead: at the back of the Wight, the wind coming to the westward, I was forced to return to St. Helen's, and finally sailed on the 9th, carrying a convoy to Oporto and Lisbon. I joined Earl St. Vincent off Cadiz, on 29 April; on the 30th I was ordered into the Mediterranean. I refer to the printed narrative of my proceedings to the close of the battle of the Nile.

On 22 September, 1798, I arrived at Naples, and was received as a deliverer by the king, queen, and the whole kingdom. [On] 12 October the blockade of Malta took place, which has continued without intermission to this day. On 21 December, 1798, his Sicilian Majesty and family embarked in the Vanguard, and were carried to Palermo in Sicily. In March [1799], I arranged a plan for taking the islands in the Bay of Naples, and for supporting the royalists who were making head in the kingdom. This plan succeeded in every part. In May I shifted my flag, being promoted to be rear-admiral of the red, to the Foudroyant, and was obliged to be on my guard against the French fleet. In June and July I went to Naples, and, as his Sicilian Majesty is pleased to say, I reconquered his kingdom, and placed him on his throne. On 9 August I brought his Sicilian Majesty back to Palermo, having been upwards of four weeks on board the Foudroyant.

On the 13th, his Sicilian Majesty presented me with a sword magnificently enriched with diamonds, the title of Duke of Bronte, and annexed to it the feud of Bronte, supposed to be worth 3,000*l.* per annum. On the arrival of the Russian squadron at Naples, I directed Commodore Troubridge to go with the squadron, and blockade closely Civita Vecchia, and to offer the French most favourable conditions, if they would evacuate Rome and Civita

Vecchia; which terms the French general Grenier complied with, and they were signed on board the Culloden; when a prophecy, made to me on my arrival at Naples, was fulfilled, viz. that I should take Rome with my ships.

Thus may be exemplified by my life, that perseverance in any profession will most probably meet its reward. Without having any inheritance, or having been fortunate in prize-money, I have received all the honours of my profession, been created a peer of Great Britain, &c. &c., as set forth in the annexed paper; and I may say to the reader, 'Go thou, and do likewise.'

'The annexed paper.'

Presents received for my services in the Mediterranean between 1 October, 1798, and 1 October, 1799:

From my own most gracious Sovereign, a Peerage of Great Britain, and a gold medal.

From the Parliament of Great Britain, for my life and two next heirs, 2,000*l.* per annum.

From the Parliament of Ireland not known, but supposed the same as given to St. Vincent and Duncan, 1,000*l.* per annum.

From the Honourable East India Company, 10,000*l.*

From the Turkey Company, a piece of plate.

From Alexander Davison, Esq., a gold medal.

City of London, a sword.

The captains who served under my orders in the battle of the Nile, a sword.

The Grand Signor, a diamond aigrette, or plume of triumph, valued at 2,000*l.* Ditto, a rich pelisse, valued at 1,000*l.* The Grand Signor's mother, a box set with diamonds, valued at 1,000*l.*

Emperor of Russia, a box set with diamonds, and a most elegant letter—2,500*l.*

King of the Sicilies, a sword, richly ornamented with diamonds, and a most elegant and kind letter, 5,000*l.*; and the Dukedom of Bronte, with an estate supposed worth 3,000*l.* per annum.

King of Sardinia, a box set with diamonds, and a most elegant letter, 1,200*l.*

The island of Zante, a gold-headed sword and cane, as an acknowledgment that had it not been for the battle of the Nile they could not have been liberated from French cruelty.

City of Palermo, a gold box and chain, brought on a silver waiter.

SELECT LETTERS AND PAPERS.

I passed my degree as Master of Arts on the 9th instant (that is, passed the lieutenant's examination), and received my commission on the following day for a fine frigate of 32 guns. So I am now left in the world to shift for myself, which I hope I shall do so as to bring credit to myself and friends.

Wm. Nelson, 14 April.

This 'fine frigate' was the Lowestoft, Captain William Locker, with whom Nelson contracted a firm friendship that was broken only by death. On joining the ship, his uncle, Captain Maurice Suckling, with whom he first came to sea in the Raisonable, and at this time Comptroller of the Navy, wrote him a long letter of advice, some fragments only of which have been preserved : such as they are, however, they throw an interesting light on the state of naval discipline and the condition of our ships of war in 1777.

To keep a ship of war in that state which is understood by the expressions commonly made use of, 'being in very high order,' or, 'being really a man-of-war,' the following rules are necessary to be strictly observed by the commanding officer.

Capt. Suckling to Lieut. Nelson, 1777.

1. He should observe always to keep the yards particularly square, and every rope fore and aft hauled tight, and never to suffer any rope to be hanging over the bows, or any other part of the ship whatever.

2. He should always be particular in having the hammocks well stowed in the nettings, and never suffer any to be hanging up below, after a certain hour, which hour should be eight in the morning.

3. He should always keep the hammocks and the clothes very clean, and likewise the ship, the decks of which and the outside, he should be very particular in; and which, unless some unforeseen accident occurs, he should never neglect washing every morning.

4. He ought to fix particular days in the week for the people to wash their clothes, and particular ones for washing between decks.

5. He should never allow anything to be hanging about in the rigging, or any ropes to be towing overboard with things to them when in harbour, but on the washing days, unless rainy weather; when, on the first fine day he may make an exception to the first part of the rule, and likewise to the other by washing between decks and seeing that every man has his things thoroughly dried; and in that case it would be proper to smoke the ship; it should likewise be done after a gale of wind at sea.

6. He should choose particular hours in the day for the purser's

steward to serve provisions &c. to the ship's company, which ought to be done twice a day ; and there should likewise be fixed certain hours for going to the holds, to get up water or other provisions, which time should be when the hands are turned out of a morning, or in the evening.

7. He should always see that the keys of the different store-rooms are not kept out of his cabin longer than while they are busy at the store-room ; and his constant order should be that a midshipman attend the store-room. That the steward may not serve out anything but at the fixed hours, he should see that the keys are returned when the time is expired. He should never suffer any keys to go from his cabin after gun-fire at night.

8. When they are employed about the powder, he should see that a midshipman attends the light-room ; nor should he suffer any person to go to the magazine, without the master-at-arms to attend, or ship's corporal.

9. He should, unless he means to oblige some particular friend, always hoist the boats in at sunset ; but his invariable rule should be, never to keep a boat out after gun-fire.

10. Unless some particular duty prevents, he should always pipe the hammocks down at sunset.

11. Every day at seven bells, before noon, and at the same time before four in the afternoon, he should make everybody leave off work, and have the decks swept fore and aft.

12. On the washing days, he should break those that are washing off at six bells, that the ship's sides may be washed before dinner.

13. He should, when washing the decks, always see that the gunner and his crew wash the guns well ; and if in a large ship, he should always take care that the gunner and his mate attend to squaring the ports when they are hauled up of a morning, which, if the weather will permit, should be done at the time the top-gallant yards are got up.

14. He should always be particular in working his sails together ; for nothing is so lubberly as to hoist one sail after another.[1]

On 8 December, 1778, Nelson was appointed commander of the Badger brig ; and on 11 June, 1779, was posted into the Hinchingbrook.

Capt. Locker, 7 June, 1779.

I suppose before this you have heard of the fate of the poor Glasgow ; indeed it was a most shocking sight ; and had it happened half an hour later, in all probability a great many people would have been lost. She anchored at half-past three [in Montego Bay], and at six she was in flames, owing to the steward attempting to steal rum out of the after-hold.

12 Aug.

Jamaica is turned upside down since you left it. The Count d'Estaing is at the Cape with twenty sail of the line ; and a flag-

---

[1] Clarke and McArthur: vol. i. pp. 366–67. With these instructions, which a smart old captain considered it necessary to give a capable lieutenant in 1777, compare the description of French men-of-war a few years later given by Sir Gilbert Blane in *Observations on the Diseases of Seamen*, p. 109 ; and by Admiral Jurien, the father of the present Admiral Jurien de la Gravière, in *Souvenirs d'un Amiral*, tom. i. p. 16.

ship, with eight or nine more, are at Port au Prince; the latter fleet fell in with the Charon and Pomona, in the night, but they got off by good sailing. They say that there are 20,000 men at the Cape ready to embark, and 5,000 at Port au Prince. He arrived at the Cape last Saturday fortnight, with 125 sail, men-of-war and transports. . . .

As I have told you what we may expect, I will tell you the measures taken to defend the island: 5,000 men are encamped between the Ferry and Kingston, 1,000 in Fort Augusta, 300 at the Apostles' Battery, and we expect to have 500 in Fort Charles, where I am to command. Lion, Salisbury, Charon, and Janus, in a line from the Point to the outer shoal; Ruby and Bristol in the narrows going to Kingston, to rake any ships that may attack Fort Augusta; Pomona and Speke Indiaman above Rock Fort, and Lowestoft at the end of the dock-wall. Expresses go to-morrow morning to all quarters. Resource and Penelope off the east end to cruise: four fire-ships are down here, two of them commissioned. I have very fairly stated our situation, and I leave you in England to judge what stand we shall make; I think you must not be surprised to hear of my learning to speak French.

23 Jan. 1780.

I arrived here from a cruise in the middle of December, and received your letter from London with great pleasure. . . . I sailed in the Hinchingbrook from Port Royal in the middle of September, to join the Niger and Penelope. We took four sail, for which I shall share about 800*l.* sterling. . . . The Salisbury has brought in a Spanish store-ship, mounting fifty-six guns, four hundred men, from Cadiz to Port Omoa, after a smart action of two hours and a half. The Salisbury lost nine men; the Don fifty men.

Our mess is broke up. Captain Cornwallis and myself live together. I hope I have made a friend of him, which I am sure from his character you will be glad to hear. . . . The Spanish ship is to be made a ship of 36 guns. The admiral offered her to me, which I declined. He says he will give me the first frigate. He has appointed me to go with an expedition which is now on foot against the city of Granada, upon the Lake of Nicaragua.

In 1803, Nelson wrote the following remarks on this expedition for the second edition of Dr. Moseley's 'Treatise on Tropical Diseases:'

Had the expedition arrived at San Juan's harbour in the month of January, the violent torrents would have subsided, and of course the whole army would not have had occasion, which was the case in April, to get wet three or four times a day in dragging the boats. They would then have arrived at the Castle by the middle of February, and had between two or three months of fair season to have established themselves, with all the stores, in the healthy country of Granada and Leon: and then, I think, a road for carriages might have been made from Bluefields harbour, a healthier place than San Juan's, to the Lake Nicaragua.

The fever which destroyed the army and navy attached to that expedition, was invariably from twenty to thirty days before it attacked the new-comers; and I cannot give a stronger instance than that in the Hinchingbrook, with a complement of two hundred men, eighty-seven took to their beds in one night; and of the two hundred, one hundred and forty-five were buried in mine and Captain Collingwood's time: and I believe very few, not more than ten, survived of that ship's crew; a proof how necessary expedition is in those climates.

Nelson himself, as has been already told,[1] left the expedition and returned to Jamaica, on appointment to the Janus, 44. His health, however, was completely shattered; and he was obliged (30 August, 1780) to apply to the commander-in-chief for permission to return to England. This was granted, as being, by the report of the medical survey, absolutely necessary; and he sailed a few days afterwards in the Lion.

Capt. Locker,
23 Jan. 1781.
Bath.

I have been so ill since I have been here, that I was obliged to be carried to and from bed, with the most excruciating tortures, but, thank God, I am now upon the mending hand. . . . I am sorry to hear the account of your friend, Captain Sutton;[2] but I well know the situation of a ship just from the river, and I have no doubt but the court-martial will consider it in that light.

15 Feb.

My health, thank God, is very near perfectly restored; and I have the perfect use of all my limbs, except my left arm, which I can hardly tell what is the matter with it. From the shoulder to my fingers' ends are as if half dead; but the surgeon and doctors give me hopes it will all go off. I most sincerely wish to be employed, and hope it will not be long.

Rev. W. Nelson,
24 Aug.

Yesterday I went down to Woolwich and hoisted my pennant

[1] See *ante*, p. 4.
[2] Captain Evelyn Sutton of the Isis, 50, reprimanded by court-martial, 22 January, for not doing his utmost to take or destroy the Dutch 50-gun ship Rotterdam, off Beachy Head, on 31 December, 1780. The Isis was newly commissioned, not fully manned, and what men she had not yet quartered. The court, taking this into consideration, was of opinion that Captain Sutton was highly reprehensible for the precipitate manner in which he carried his ship alongside the enemy.

[on board the Albemarle]: and I am perfectly satisfied with her, as a twenty-eight gun frigate. She is in dock, alongside the Enterprize, and in some respects, I think, excels her. She has a bold entrance, and clean run. The Enterprize, a lean bow, which does not answer so well with copper, as they always allow for sheathing, which is upwards of an inch more in thickness, therefore she wants that much. The Albemarle is not so wide, upon the gun-deck, by four inches, but the same beam; the gun-deck six feet high; between decks very low indeed, about five feet. She is now coppering, and will not be out of dock this fortnight, at least. The Admiralty have been very civil, having given me the choice of all my officers, which I am much pleased with.

I have talked with Mr. Suckling about your going chaplain in the navy, and he thinks, as I do, that fifty pounds where you are, is much more than equal to what you can get at sea; but in that I know you will please yourself, therefore shall not attempt to state any argument to dissuade you from it. As to my real opinion, whether or no you will like it, I say, as I always did, that it is five to one you will not. If you get with a good man, and with gentlemen, it will be tolerable; if not you will soon detest it. My quarter-deck is filled, much to my satisfaction, with very genteel young men and seamen.   9 Sept.

I am now full manned, and ready for any service. I have an exceeding good ship's company. Not a man or officer in her I would wish to change. She appears to sail also very well. Where I am going, I know not, but suppose I shall be gone from here in the next week, when I will write again.   18 Oct. Sheerness.

I have been very busy in getting my ship's company in order for service. They are, in my opinion, as good a set of men as I ever saw: indeed, I am perfectly satisfied with both officers and ship's company. All my marines are likewise old standers. . . .   Capt. Locker, 21 Oct.

What sad news from America: for my part, I cannot understand Mr. Graves' letter; the French are here and there, I supposed in sight, to windward of him; at last a frigate goes to look for them, and finds them very safe in the Chesapeake. I much fear for Lord Cornwallis: if something was not immediately done, America is quite lost.

I arrived here on the 4th instant with the Argo and Enterprize, and found about fifty sail in the Roads waiting for convoy; but   Phil. Stephens, 5 Nov.[1] Elsinore.

---

[1] Public Record Office: Captains' Letters. This letter is not given by Nicolas.

upon information from the consul here, I find that they are now upon their passage, and in ten days or a fortnight there will arrive here upwards of a hundred sail more, and afterwards there will be near forty sail that will not be down the Baltic till near Christmas; therefore it is impossible I can obey their lordships' order of taking the last ships from the Baltic this season; as waiting for those few would endanger an immense fleet at this late season of the year. In about three weeks from this day I think of sailing from hence, if the wind is fair.

<small>Phil. Stephens, 18 Dec.[1] Yarmouth Roads.</small>

I arrived here yesterday noon in my way to the Downs, with such ships of the Baltic fleet as are bound to Portsmouth and Plymouth. The wind being far southerly and blowing fresh obliged me to anchor here, and as it still continues in that quarter I cannot get from this place. The instant the wind gets to the westward, I shall make all despatch possible in getting to the Downs.

<small>Capt. Locker, 22 Dec.</small>

I have almost been froze on the other side the water: here we find it quite summer. We have not had any success; indeed, there is nothing you can meet, but what is in force: the Dutch have not a single merchantman at sea. One privateer was in our fleet, but it was not possible to lay hold of him. I chased him an hour, and came fast up with him, but was obliged to return to the fleet. I find since, it was the noted Fall, the pirate. . . . What fools the Dutch must have been not to have taken us into the Texel. Two hundred and sixty sail the convoy consisted of. They behaved, as all convoys that ever I saw did, shamefully ill; parting company every day.

<small>Rev. Wm. Nelson, 28 Jan. 1782. Downs.</small>

At eleven on Monday morning [1 January], we sailed with sixty-five sail, and next day, at noon, was at the back of the Goodwin Sands. The ships in the Downs took us for a Dutch fleet going down Channel; and many of the men-of-war were under sail to come after us, when a cutter went in, and told them who we were. We all got safe in that night, and next [day] I delivered my charge up to the admiral. Here I have been laying ever since without orders; and in such a long series of bad weather as is seldom met with. . . . At last I was ordered round to Portsmouth to take in eight months' provisions, and I have no doubt was meant to go to the East Indies with Sir Richard Bickerton, which I should have liked exceedingly, but alas, how short-sighted are the best of us. On 26 January, at eight in the morning, it blew a hard gale of wind at NNW., a large East India store ship drove from her anchors,

[1] Public Record Office: Captains' Letters. This letter is not given by Nicolas.

and came on board us. We have lost our foremast, and bowsprit, mainyard, larboard cathead, and quarter gallery, the ship's head, and stove in two places on the larboard side—all done in five minutes. What a change! but yet we ought to be thankful we did not founder. We have been employed since in getting jury-masts, yards, and bowsprit, and stopping the holes in our sides. What is to become of us now, I know not. She must go into dock, and I fear must be paid off, she has received so much damage.

I am now waiting at Spithead for a wind to bring me into the harbour to be docked and repaired; what will become of me afterwards I know not. . . . I wish I could congratulate you upon a rectory instead of a vicarage: it is rather awkward wishing the poor man dead, but we all rise by deaths. I got my rank by a shot killing a post-captain, and I most sincerely hope I shall, when I go, go out of [the] world the same way; then we go all in the line of our profession—a parson praying, a captain fighting. *8 Feb.*

I am ordered to Cork to join the Dædalus, Captain Pringle, and go with a convoy to Quebec; where, worse than all to tell, I understand I am to winter. I want much to [get] off from this damned voyage, and believe, if I had time to look a little about me, I could get another ship. Mr. Adair, who attends on Mr. Keppel, might tell him that in such a country I shall be laid up: for he has told me, that if I was sent to a cold damp climate, it would make me worse than ever. Many of my navy friends have advised me to represent my situation to Admiral Keppel, and they have no doubt but he would give me other orders, or remove me; but as I received my orders from Lord Sandwich, I can't help thinking it wrong to ask Mr. Keppel to alter them. *Capt. Locker, 2 April. Portsmouth.*

Admiral Barrington hoists his [flag] after the court-martial is assembled to-morrow, on board the Britannia. Lord Longford introduced me to him this morning, and told him who I was; it is from that quarter, could I stay long enough in port, that I expect a better ship. Admiral Barrington takes twelve sail of the line, as soon as ready; he is in very good spirits; he gets amongst all the youngsters here, and leaves out the old boys.

We arrived here with the convoy on 1 July, and I sailed upon a cruise the 4th, and returned to Quebec on 17 September, knocked up with the scurvy; having [for] eight weeks, myself and all the officers [lived] upon salt beef; nor had the ship's company had a fresh meal since 7 April. In the end, our cruise has been an unsuccessful one; we have taken, seen, and destroyed more enemies *19 Oct. R. St. Lawrence.*

than is seldom done in the same space of time, but not one arrived in port. But, however, I do not repine at our loss: we have in other things been very fortunate, for on 14 August we fell in with, in Boston Bay, four sail of the line, and the Iris, French man-of-war, part of M. Vaudreuil's squadron, who gave us a pretty dance for between nine or ten hours; but we beat all except the frigate, and though we brought to for her, after we were out of sight of the line-of-battle ships, she tacked and stood from us.¹ Our escape I think wonderful: they were, upon the clearing up of a fog, within shot of us, and chased us the whole time about one point from the wind: the frigate, I fancy, had not forgot the dressing Captain Salter had given the Amazon,² for daring to leave the line-of-battle ships.

Rev. Edm. Nelson, 19 Oct.

I expected to have sailed for England on 1 November, but our destination is now altered, for we sail with a fleet for New York to-morrow; and from there I think it very likely we shall go to the grand theatre of actions, the West Indies; but in our line of life we are sure of no one thing. When I reach New York, you shall hear what becomes of me; but whilst I have health it is indifferent to me (were it not for the pleasure of seeing you and my brothers and sisters) where I go.

Health, that greatest of blessings, is what I never truly enjoyed till I saw fair Canada. The change it has wrought, I am convinced, is truly wonderful.

Capt. Locker, 17 Nov. New York.

I found Lord Hood here upon my arrival, and I have requested him to take me with him to the West Indies: he has wrote to Admiral Digby for me, and I was to have sailed with [the] fleet as this day, but for some private reasons, when my ship was under sail from New York to join Lord Hood, at Sandy Hook, I was sent for on shore, and told I was to be kept forty-eight hours after the sailing of the fleet: it is much to my private advantage, but I had much rather have sailed with the fleet: if there is wind enough they sail this day. . . .

I am a candidate with Lord Hood for a line-of-battle ship: he has honoured me highly by a letter, for wishing to go off this station, to a station of service, and has promised me his friendship. Prince William is with him; I think it is a prelude to the Digby's going off this station; money is the great object here, nothing else is attended to.

---

¹ See *ante*, p. 5.
² 29 July, 1782. See Beatson's *Nav. and Mil. Memoirs*, vol. v. p. 545.

The fleet arrived [at Port Royal] the 4th instant, and I suppose will be ready for sea the last day of this month, although stores are as scarce at Jamaica as ever: sixteen topmasts were wanted for the line-of-battle ships, and there was not one in the island of Jamaica; and the fleet must have been sent to sea short of masts, had not providentially a French mast-ship, belonging to Monsieur Vaudreuil's fleet, come alongside the Albemarle, and was captured by her. She has nearly a hundred topmasts for large ships, with a number of lower masts and yards. She will clear upwards of 20,000*l*. What a good prize if the fleet had not been in sight. They do not deserve to share for her: we had chased to leeward, and she had passed every ship in the fleet without being noticed. . . . They had parted from Vaudreuil in a gale of wind, and could not fetch St. John's, Porto Rico, which was their *rendezvous*, and therefore very fortunately came in our way. The French fleet, finding we were off Monte Christi, went through the Mona Passage, and have been seen in sight of the island of Curaçoa, but where they are God knows. I am sent out by Lord Hood to find them if I can.

25 Feb. 1783. Off C. Tiburon

My situation in Lord Hood's fleet must be in the highest degree flattering to any young man. He treats me as if I was his son, and will, I am convinced, give me anything I can ask of him: nor is my situation with Prince William less flattering. Lord Hood was so kind as to tell him (indeed I cannot make use of expressions strong enough to describe what I felt), that if he wished to ask questions relative to naval tactics, I could give him as much information as any officer in the fleet. He will be, I am certain, an ornament to our service. He is a seaman, which you could hardly suppose. Every other qualification you may expect from him. But he will be a disciplinarian, and a strong one: he says he is determined every person shall serve his time before they shall be provided for, as he is obliged to serve his.

On Thursday, the 6th instant, a few leagues to windward of Monte Christi, I fell in with his Majesty's ship Resistance, Captain King. From him I received information that the French had taken the Turk's Island, on 13 February, with one hundred and fifty regulars, and three vessels of war.

Lord Hood 9 March.

As it would be very little loss in my getting to the eastward, making the Turk's Island, I determined to look what situation the French were in, and if possible to retake it. The Tartar, who joined company a few hours afterwards, I ordered to put herself under my command, which, with the Resistance and La Coquette,

c

a French ship of war, prize to the Resistance, made a tolerable outward show. On Friday evening, the Albemarle, Resistance, and Drake, anchored at the island. The Tartar, Captain Fairfax, I imagine, could not keep his anchorage upon the bank. He went to sea, nor have I heard or seen anything of him since. I can have no doubt but Captain Fairfax has good reasons why he did not join me again. This reduced our small force one-third (the Coquette, a larger ship, kept off and on the whole time of our stay). I sent Captain Dixon on shore with a flag of truce to demand a surrender of the islands. With much confidence of his superior situation, the commander of the French troops sent an answer that he should defend himself.

On Saturday morning, at daylight, one hundred and sixty-seven seamen and marines were landed from the ships under the command of Captain Charles Dixon, who very much obliged me by offering to command them. At eleven o'clock, Captain Dixon thought a division of the enemy's force might be made by sending the brigs off the town, to give him an opportunity of pushing on to the enemy's works. I ordered the Drake, under the command of Lieutenant Hinton, and the Admiral Barrington, Lieutenant Cunningham, who joined at this instant, to go off the town, and batter it. Upon their getting within shot, I was very much surprised to see a battery of three guns open upon them, but notwithstanding such an unexpected attack, they were both brought to an anchor opposite the battery in a masterly manner; and the steady constant fire they kept up for upwards of an hour, does great honour to the gentlemen who commanded them, and to their officers and men. The master of the Drake is wounded, and the boatswain and six men aboard the Admiral Barrington. Captain Dixon at this time observed that the guns were fought by seamen, and that the troops were waiting to receive him with several field-pieces; and that they had a post upon the side of the hill with two pieces of cannon. With such a force, and their strong situation, I did not think anything further could be attempted.

Capt. Locker, 26 June. Portsmouth.

After all my tossing about into various climates, here at last am I arrived, safe and sound. I found orders for the Albemarle to be paid off at this place. On Monday next I hope to be rid of her. My people I fancy will be pretty quiet, if they are not set on by some of the ships here.

The Albemarle was paid off on Thursday, 3 July.

My time, ever since I arrived in town, has been taken up in attempting to get the wages due to my good fellows, for various ships they have served in the war. The disgust of the seamen to the navy is all owing to the infernal plan of turning them over from ship to ship, so that men cannot be attached to their officers, or the officers care twopence about them.

Capt. Locker, 12 July. London.

My ship was paid off last week, and in such a manner that must flatter any officer, in particular in these turbulent times. The whole ship's company offered, if I could get a ship, to enter for her immediately; but I have no thought of going to sea, for I cannot afford to live on board ship in such a manner as is going on at present.

Yesterday, Lord Hood carried me to Saint James's, where the king was exceedingly attentive: on Monday or Tuesday I am to be at Windsor, to take leave of Prince William, previous to his embarkation for the Continent.

In October, Nelson obtained six months' leave to go to France, and left London on the 21st, in company with Captain Macnamara, an old messmate in the Bristol. On their way, they visited Captain Locker at Malling, slept at his house, and went on to Dover the next day.

We slept at Dover, and next morning at seven o'clock put to sea with a fine north-west wind, and at half-past ten we were safe at breakfast in Monsieur Grandsire's house at Calais. His mother kept it when Hogarth wrote his 'Gate of Calais.' Sterne's 'Sentimental Journey' is the best description I can give of our tour. Mac advised me to go first to St. Omer, as he had experienced the difficulty of attempting to fix in any place where there are no English; after dinner we set off, intended for Montreuil, sixty miles from Calais: they told us we travelled *en poste*, but I am sure we did not get on more than four miles an hour. I was highly diverted with looking what a curious figure the postilions in their jack boots, and their rats of horses, made together. Their chaises have no springs, and the roads generally paved like London streets; therefore you will naturally suppose we were pretty well shook together by the time we had travelled two posts and a half, which is fifteen miles, to Marquise. Here we [were] shown into an inn —they called it—I should have called it a pigstye: we were shown into a room with two straw beds, and, with great difficulty, they mustered up clean sheets; and gave us two pigeons for supper, upon a dirty cloth, and wooden-handled knives—O what a transition from happy England!

Capt. Locker, 2 Nov. St. Omer.

But we laughed at the repast, and went to bed with the determination that nothing should ruffle our tempers. Having slept very

c 2

well, we set off at daylight for Boulogne, where we breakfasted: this place was full of English, I suppose because wine is so very cheap. We went on after breakfast for Montreuil, and passed through the finest corn country that my eyes ever beheld, diversified with fine woods, sometimes for two miles together through noble forests. The roads mostly were planted with trees, which made as fine an avenue as to any gentleman's country seat. Montreuil is thirty miles from Boulogne, situated upon a small hill, in the middle of a fine plain, which reached as far as the eye could carry you, except towards the sea, which is about twelve miles from it. We put up at the same house, and with the same jolly landlord that recommended Le Fleur to Sterne. Here we wished much to have fixed, but neither good lodgings, or masters, could be had here; for there are no middling class of people: sixty noblemen's families lived in the town, who owned the vast plain round it, and the rest very poor indeed. This is the very finest country for game that ever was; partridges twopence halfpenny a couple, pheasants and woodcocks in proportion, and in short, every species of poultry. We dined, supped, lay, and breakfasted next day, Saturday: then we proceeded on our tour, leaving Montreuil you will suppose with great regret.

We reached Abbeville at eight o'clock: but unluckily for us, two Englishmen, one of whom called himself Lord Kingsland, I can hardly suppose it to be him, and a Mr. Bullock, decamped at three o'clock that afternoon in debt to every shopkeeper in the place. These gentlemen kept elegant houses, horses, &c.: we found the town in an uproar; and as no masters could be had at this place that could speak a word of English, and that all masters that could speak English grammatically attended at the places that are frequented by the English, which is, St. Omer, Lisle, Dunkirk, and Boulogne, to the northward of Paris, and as I had no intention of travelling to the South of France till the spring at any rate, I determined, with Mac's advice, to steer for St. Omer, where we arrived last Tuesday: and I own I was surprised to find that instead of a dirty, nasty town, which I had always heard it represented, [it is] a large city, well paved, good streets, and well lighted.

We lodge in a pleasant French family, and have our dinners sent from a *traiteur's*. There are two very agreeable young ladies, daughters, who honour us with their company pretty often: one always makes our breakfast, and the other our tea, and play a game at cards in an evening. Therefore I must learn French if 'tis only for the pleasure of talking to them, for they do not speak a word of English. Here are a great number of English in this place, but we visit only two families; for if I did I should never speak French. Two noble captains are here—Ball and Shepard;[1] you do not know, I believe, either of them; they wear fine epaulettes, for which I think them great coxcombs:[2] they have not visited me, and I shall not, be assured, court their acquaintance.

Since I wrote last I have been very near coming to England, occasioned by the melancholy account I have received of my dear sister's death.[3] My father, whose grief upon the occasion was intolerable, is, I hope, better; therefore I shall not come over. She died at Bath after a nine days' illness, in the 21st year of her age; it was occasioned by coming out of the ball-room immediately after dancing. *26 Nov*

The French goes on but slowly; but patience, of which you know I have not much, and perseverance, will, I hope, make me master of it. Here are two navy captains, Ball and Shepard, at this place, but we do not visit; they are very fine gentlemen with epaulettes: you may suppose I hold them a little cheap for putting on any part of a Frenchman's uniform.

Amongst the few friends Nelson made at St. Omer was Mr. Andrews, a clergyman, with two daughters, one of whom Nelson described as 'very beautiful,' 'the most accomplished woman my eyes ever beheld.' Her charms made havoc of his heart, and led him, immediately on his return to England, to write a letter to his uncle, in which, after some preamble, he went on:

There is a lady I have seen, of a good family and connections, but with a small fortune—1,000*l*. I understand. The whole of my income does not exceed 130*l*. per annum. Now I must come to the point: will you, if I should marry, allow me yearly 100*l*. until my income is increased to that sum, either by employment, or any other way? A very few years I hope would turn something up, if my friends will but exert themselves. If you will not give me the above sum, will you exert yourself with either Lord North or Mr. Jenkinson, to get me a guard-ship, or some employment in a public office where the attendance of the principal is not necessary, and of which they must have such numbers to dispose of? In the India Service I understand (if it remains under the Directors) their marine force is to be under the command of a captain in the Royal Navy: that is a station I should like. *Wm. Suckling, 14 Jan. 1784.*

---

[1] Alexander John Ball, afterwards one of Nelson's most valued friends, and James Keith Shepard.

[2] Epaulettes were first ordered to be worn as part of the English naval uniform on 1 June, 1795.

[3] Anne Nelson died 15 November 1783.

You must excuse the freedom with which this letter is dictated; not to have been plain and explicit in my distress had been cruel to myself. If nothing can be done for me, I know what I have to trust to. Life is not worth preserving without happiness; and I care not where I may linger out a miserable existence. I am prepared to hear your refusal, and have fixed my resolution if that should happen; but in every situation, I shall be a well-wisher to you and your family, and pray they or you may never know the pangs which at this instant tear my heart.

It is believed that Mr. Suckling generously acceded to this request; but for some reason, which does not appear, the marriage did not take place. There was, however, no breach of friendly relations; and George Andrews, a brother of the young lady, afterwards served with Nelson as midshipman or lieutenant both in the Boreas and Agamemnon.

Rev. W. Nelson, 20 Jan. London.

I arrived in town on Saturday week, but my time has been so much taken up by running at the ring of pleasure, that I have almost neglected all my friends;—for London has so many charms that a man's time is wholly taken up. . . .

The present Ministry will stay in, there is no doubt, in spite of Mr. Fox and all that party. If the Ministry had not a majority to-day, it is confidently asserted the Parliament will be dissolved. I hope it will, that the people may have an opportunity of sending men that will support their interests, and get rid of a turbulent faction who are striving to ruin their country.

Capt. Locker, 23 Jan.

I have paid my visit to Lord Howe,[1] who asked me if I wished to be employed, which I told him I did, therefore it is likely he will give me a ship. I shall not conclude my letter till late, as perhaps I may hear how matters are likely to go in the House of Commons. Lord Hood's friends are canvassing, although not openly, for his interest in case of a dissolution; and it is confidently asserted that Mr. Fox will never get Westminster again. I dined on Wednesday with his lordship, who expressed the greatest friendship for me, that his house was always open to me, and that the oftener I came the happier it would make him.

Rev. W. Nelson, 31 Jan. Bath.

I wish sincerely your business had been got through before the late Administration were turned out. If you are not to get it before they come into power again, I am afraid you will stay a long while. As to your having enlisted under the banners of the Walpoles, you might as well have enlisted under those of my grandmother. They are altogether the merest set of cyphers that ever existed—in public affairs I mean. Mr. Pitt, depend upon it, will stand against all

[1] Then First Lord of the Admiralty.

opposition: an honest man must always in time get the better of a villain; but I have done with politics; let who will get in, I shall be left out.

In about a week or fortnight I think of returning to the Continent, till autumn, when I shall bring a horse, and stay the winter at Burnham. I return to many charming women, but no charming woman will return with me. I want to be a proficient in the language, which is my only reason for returning. I hate their country and their manners.

Yesterday I was appointed to the command of the Boreas frigate. She is ready to sail from Woolwich, but to what part of the world I know not. My wish is to get the East India station. I have not taken possession yet, but I am told she is a very fine frigate, well manned, and ready to sail, so that probably my next will be from the Nore or the Downs. I can't say any more at present, being fully employed in spending my money to fit my ship out. 19 March, London.

I understand she is going to the Leeward Islands; and I am asked to carry out Lady Hughes[1] and her family—a very modest request, I think: but I cannot refuse, as I am to be under the command of this gentleman, so I must put up with the inconvenience and expense, two things not exactly to my wish. The ship is full of young midshipmen, and everybody is asking me to take some one or other. I am told she is well officered and manned; I wish I may find her so. Capt. Locker, 23 March.

You ask, by what interest did I get a ship? I answer, having served with credit was my recommendation to Lord Howe, First Lord of the Admiralty. Anything in reason that I can ask, I am sure of obtaining from his justice. Rev. W. Nelson, 29 March.

This morning, I received information that sixteen of his Majesty's subjects were detained by force on board of a Dutch Indiaman, upon which I demanded and received them on board. The master of the ship has refused, notwithstanding all arguments that I could make use of (by the lieutenant), to give up their chests, upon pretence they are in debt to the ship, although most of them have been four or five months in the Dutch India Company's service. Having repeatedly refused to give up their clothes, I have ordered that no boats shall be permitted to go on board, or to leave the ship; and have ordered the Nimble cutter Phil. Stephens, 14 April. Downs.

[1] Wife of Sir Richard Hughes, Commander-in-Chief on the Leeward Islands station.

to put the above orders into execution. I must desire as soon as possible to have their lordships' orders how to act upon this occasion.

I beg you will also assure their lordships that every politeness and attention has been shown to the Dutchman upon this occasion. I have sent to acquaint him that he will not be suffered to leave the Downs till this matter is settled.

7 P.M.

All disputes with the Dutch East Indiaman are amicably settled, the master having given up their clothes, bedding, &c.

Capt. Locker. 21 April. Portsmouth.

Since I parted from you, I have encountered many disagreeable adventures. The day after I left you, we sailed at daylight, just after high water. The damned pilot—it makes me swear to think of it—ran the ship aground, where she lay with so little water that the people could walk round her till next high water. That night and part of the next day, we lay below the Nore with a hard gale of wind and snow; Tuesday I got into the Downs; on Wednesday I got into a quarrel with a Dutch Indiaman who had Englishmen on board, which we settled, after some difficulty. The Dutchman has made a complaint against me; but the Admiralty fortunately have approved my conduct in the business, a thing they are not very guilty of where there is a likelihood of a scrape. And yesterday, to complete me, I was riding a blackguard horse that ran away with me [on the] Common, carried me round all the works into Portsmouth, by the London gates, through the town, out at the gate that leads to [the] Common, where there was a waggon in the road, which is so very narrow that a horse could barely pass. To save my legs, and perhaps my life, I was obliged to throw myself from the horse, which I did with great agility, but unluckily upon hard stones, which has hurt my back and my leg, but done no other mischief. It was a thousand to one that I had not been killed. To crown all, a young girl was riding with me; her horse ran away with mine; but most fortunately a gallant young man seized her horse's bridle a moment before I dismounted, and saved her from the destruction which she could not have avoided.

Rev. W Nelson, 23 April.

Come when you please, I shall be ready to receive you. Bring your canonicals and sermons. Do not bring any Burnham servants. In less than a fortnight my ship will not sail. I have a fine talkative lady for you to converse with.

Mr. Nelson accordingly joined the Boreas as chaplain, and went out in her to the West Indies; but after a few months was obliged to return to England on account of his health.

We arrived here on the 1st after a pleasant passage, the ladies quite well, and satisfied with the ship. To-morrow I sail, for I am tired of this place, and Lady Hughes wishes to see her husband: and I shall not be sorry to part with them, although they are very pleasant good people: but they are an incredible expense.

<small>Capt. Locker, 7 June. Madeira.</small>

Collingwood[1] is at Grenada, which is a great loss to me; for there is nobody that I can make a confidant of. The little man, Sandys,[2] is a good-natured laughing creature, but no more of an officer as a captain than he was as a lieutenant. Was it not for Mrs. Moutray,[3] who is very, very good to me, I should almost hang myself at this infernal hole. Our admiral[4] is tolerable, but I do not like him, he bows and scrapes too much for me; his wife has an eternal clack, so that I go near them as little as possible: in short, I detest this country, but as I am embarked upon this station I shall remain in my ship. Our ears here are full of wars in the East; is there any likelihood of a war? I am in a fine [condition] for the beginning of one; well officered and manned.

<small>24 Sept. Antigua.</small>

This station is far from a pleasant one. The admiral and all about him are great ninnies. . . . Coll. desires me to say he will write you soon such a letter that you will think it a history of the West Indies. What an amiable good man he is! all the rest are geese. . . . I am in my way to examine a harbour said to be situated in the island of St. John's, capable, it is supposed, to contain a fleet of men-of-war during the hurricane seasons. It is odd this fine harbour, if such a one there is, should not have been made use of long ago; but there is an order from the Admiralty to send a frigate to examine it: it is said here to belong to the Danes; if so, they will not let me survey it.[5]

<small>23 Nov.</small>

The longer I am upon this station the worse I like it. Our commander has not that opinion of his own sense that he ought to have. He is led by the advice of the islanders to admit the Yankees to a trade; at least to wink at it. He does not give himself that weight that I think an English admiral ought to do. I, for one, am determined not to suffer the Yankees to come where my ship is; for I am sure, if once the Americans are admitted to any kind of intercourse with these islands, the views of the

<small>15 Jan. 1785. St. Kitts.</small>

---

[1] Cuthbert (afterwards Lord) Collingwood, then commanding the Mediator.
[2] Charles Sandys, Captain of the Latona.
[3] Wife of Captain John Moutray, commissioner of the navy at Antigua.
[4] Sir Richard Hughes.
[5] The survey was, however, made: the original chart, signed 'Horatio Nelson,' is in the Public Record Office, Admirals' Despatches, Leeward Islands, No. 8.

loyalists in settling Nova Scotia are entirely done away. They will first become the carriers, and next have possession of our islands, are we ever again embroiled in a French war. The residents of these islands are Americans by connection and by interest, and are inimical to Great Britain. They are as great rebels as ever were in America, had they the power to show it.

After what I have said, you will believe I am not very popular with the people. They have never visited me, and I have not had a foot in any house since I have been on the station, and all for doing my duty by being true to the interests of Great Britain. A petition from the president and council has gone to the governor-general and admiral, to request the admission of Americans. I have given my answer to the admiral upon the subject; how he will like it I know not: but I am determined to suppress the admission of foreigners all in my power. I have told the customs that I will complain if they admit any foreigner to an entry:—an American arrives; sprung a leak, a mast, and what not, makes a protest, gets admittance, sells his cargo for ready money; goes to Martinique, buys molasses, and so round and round. But I hate them all. The loyalist cannot do it, consequently must sell a little dearer.

We have here the first mention of a difficult and intricate business which lasted during the whole time the Boreas was upon the station, and afterwards. The letters and papers on the subject, addressed to the admiral, the Admiralty, the secretary of state, and the king himself, are numerous and lengthy. In June 1786 Nelson drew up a very long and exhaustive narrative, several copies of which appear to have been circulated; but these exact details have now little interest, and the story is told with sufficient fullness in a letter to Captain Locker, dated off Martinique, 5 March, 1786.

Capt. Locker, 5 March, 1786.

It was near the hurricane months when I arrived in this country; consequently nothing could be done till they were over in November, when the squadron arrived at Barbadoes, and the ships were to be sent to the different islands, with orders only to examine the anchorages, and whether there was wood and water. This did not appear to me to be the intent of placing men-of-war in peaceable times; therefore I asked Collingwood to go with me (for his sentiments and mine were exactly similar) to the admiral. I then asked him if we were not to attend to the commerce of our country, and to take care that the British trade was kept in those channels that the navigation laws pointed out. He answered, he had no orders, nor had the Admiralty sent him any Acts of Parliament. I told him it was very odd, as every captain of a man-of-war was furnished with the statutes of the Admiralty, in which was the Navigation Act, which Act was directed to admirals, captains, &c., to see it carried into execution. He said he had never seen the book; but having produced and read the laws to him, he seemed convinced that men-of-war were sent abroad for some other purpose than to be made a show of. (The rebel Americans at this time filled our ports.) Sir Richard then gave orders to all the squadron to see the Navigation Act carried into execution. When I went to my station at St. Kitts, I turned away all the rebels, not choosing to seize them at that time, as it would have appeared a trap for them.

In December, to my astonishment, comes down an order from him, telling us he had received good advice, and requiring us not to hinder the Americans from coming in, and having free egress and regress, if the governors chose to allow them; and a copy of the order he sent to the governors and presidents of the islands. The General Shirley and others began by sending letters not far different from orders, that he should admit them in such and such situations; telling me the admiral had left it to them, but they thought it right to let me know it. Mr. Shirley I soon trimmed up and silenced. Sir Richard Hughes' was a more delicate business; I must either disobey my orders, or disobey Acts of Parliament, which the admiral was disobeying. I determined upon the former, trusting to the uprightness of my intention, and believed that my country would not allow me to be ruined by protecting her commerce. I first, to Sir Richard, expatiated upon the navigation laws to the best of my ability; told him I was certain some person had been giving him advice, which he would be sorry for having taken against the positive directions of an Act of Parliament; and that I was certain Sir Richard had too much regard for the commerce of Great Britain to suffer our worst enemies to take it from us; and that too at a time when Great Britain was straining every nerve to suppress illegal trade at home, which only affected the revenue; and that I hoped we should not be singular in allowing a much more ruinous traffic to be carried on under the king's flag; and in short, that I should decline obeying his orders, till I had an opportunity of seeing and talking to him, at the same time making him an apology.

At first, I hear, he was going to send a captain to supersede me; but having mentioned the matter to his captain, he was told that he believed all the squadron thought he had sent illegal orders, therefore did not know how far they were obliged to obey them. This being their sentiments, he could not try me here, and now he finds I am all right, and thanks me for having put him right. I told the custom-houses I should, after such a day, seize all foreigners in our islands, and keep them out to the utmost of my power till that time: the custom-houses fancied I could not seize without a deputation, therefore disregarded my threats. In May last I seized the first: I had the governor, the customs, all the planters upon me; subscriptions were soon filled to prosecute me; and my admiral stood neuter, although his flag was then in the roads. Before the first vessel was tried, I had seized four others; and having sent for the masters on board to examine them, and the marines on board the vessels, not allowing some of them to go on shore, I had writs taken out against me, and damages laid for the enormous sum of 4,000*l*. sterling.

When the trial came on, I was protected by the judge for the day; but the marshal was desired to arrest [me], and the merchants promised to indemnify them for the act; but the judge having declared he would send him to prison if he dared to do it, he desisted. I fortunately attached myself to an honest lawyer; and don't let me forget, the President of Nevis offered in court to become my bail for 10,000*l*. if I chose to suffer the arrest. He told them I had done only my duty; and although he suffered more in proportion than any of them, he could not blame me. At last, after a trial of two days, we carried our cause, and the vessels were condemned. I was a close prisoner on board for eight weeks, for had I been taken, I most assuredly should have been cast for the whole sum. I had nothing left but to send a memorial to the king, and he was good enough to order me to be defended at his expense, and sent orders to Mr. Shirley to afford me every assistance in the execution of my duty, and referring him to my letters, &c., as there was in them what concerned him not to have suffered.

The Treasury, by the last packet, has transmitted thanks to Sir Richard Hughes, and the officers under him, for their activity and zeal in protecting the commerce of Great Britain. Had they known what I have told you (and if my friends think I may, without impropriety, tell the story myself, I shall do it when I get home), I don't think they would have bestowed thanks in that quarter and have neglected me. I feel much hurt that after the loss of health and risk of fortune, another should be thanked for what I did against his orders. I either deserved to be sent out of the service, or at least have had some little notice taken of me. They have thought it worthy of notice, and have neglected me; if this is the reward for a faithful discharge of my duty, I shall be careful and never stand forward again; but I have done my duty, and have nothing to accuse myself of.

This intricate question had scarcely been raised before Nelson found himself entangled in another, of more peculiarly professional interest. It was, at that time, the custom of the Admiralty to appoint to every dockyard, at home or abroad, a captain of the navy, on half-pay, as a commissioner. These appointments were considered to be, and actually were, purely civil. It was established by numerous precedents that the officers holding them had no executive authority. It was therefore, by some extreme carelessness, or want of apprehension, that Sir Richard Hughes authorised Captain Moutray, the commissioner at Antigua, to hoist a broad pennant in the absence of the flag; and issued an order to the several captains 'to conform themselves to Captain Moutray's directions, to apply to him for all necessary orders relating to the duty and business of the port, so far as the ship under their several commands might be concerned, and to show him all the usual marks of respect due to an officer wearing a distinguishing pennant.' The correspondence tells the rest.

Some damages having happened to the Boreas, she was obliged to go into English Harbour to get them repaired. The Latona was laying there, with a broad pennant flying at the main top-gallant masthead. Upon inquiry, I found Commissioner Moutray had directed Captain Sandys to hoist it; but as Captain Sandys had no orders from you to receive it, I did not think proper to pay the least attention to it, well knowing that Mr. Moutray was not second officer in the command in English Harbour during the hurricane season. Whatever he had been before I know not, but I looked upon him as effectually superseded by my sitting as president of court-martials when he was upon the spot in his naval uniform, and acting in an official capacity as a commissioner of the navy. I feel it a misfortune that so young a captain should be the senior upon this station. Had it been otherwise, a man of more service must have been in the unpleasant situation in which I stand; but my best endeavours, however deficient they may be, shall always be exerted in supporting the dignity of my brother captains, and I trust we shall also have the support of such a character as Sir Richard Hughes.

Sir R. Hughes, 12 Feb. Carlisle Bay.

Having lately held a correspondence with Sir Richard Hughes, and Mr. Moutray, a commissioner of his Majesty's navy, resident at the island of Antigua, upon the subject of a distinguishing pennant which the said commissioner thinks he has not only a

Phil. Stephens, 17 Feb.

right to hoist on board any one of his Majesty's ships, but also to direct the operations of his Majesty's squadron upon this station in the absence of the admiral, the whole of the papers upon this subject Sir Richard Hughes has done me the honour to say he shall inclose to you for their lordships' information; therefore it is only necessary for me to elucidate and explain the motives that have actuated my conduct through the whole of this business.

The matter is grounded upon my idea (for I never saw any commission whatever) that Mr. Moutray is not commissioned in such a manner as will authorise him to take upon him the liberty of hoisting a broad pennant, or the directing the captains of his Majesty's ships; but let me first beg their lordships will be assured that I never have received official information that Commissioner Moutray is appointed a commodore upon this station, or put in any commission, but that of commissioner of the navy. I must beg their lordships' indulgence to hear reasons for my conduct, that it may never go abroad into the world, I ever had an idea to dispute the orders of my superior officer; neither admiral, commodore, or captain.

I arrived in English Harbour, 28 July, 1784, to lay up for the hurricane season. Till 1 November, 1784, numerous were the orders I received, and eventually with this direction, to 'Horatio Nelson, Esq., captain of his Majesty's ship Boreas, and second officer in the command of his Majesty's ships in English Harbour, Antigua.' At this time, I need not to say that Mr. Moutray was not a commodore: the whole of the squadron did, I am sure, look upon him as a half-pay captain, commissioner of the navy. Thus the matter stood for three times that I went into English Harbour. At St. Christopher's I heard, as their lordships will be informed, that Commissioner Moutray was authorised to hoist a distinguishing or broad pennant. I did not pretend to think upon the matter: it might probably be so, and my answer to the admiral was, that if Commissioner Moutray was put into commission, I should have great pleasure in serving under him. I have no doubt that Sir Richard Hughes believed that Mr. Moutray was commissioned as a commodore; but at the same time I trust that he thought that the officers under his command knew their duty too well, to obey any half-pay captain; and that he might safely trust the honour of the navy to those under him (that they would not act improperly upon this business), and that they would be well informed that the man who they received orders from, was empowered to give them.

On 5 February, 1785, upon my arrival in English Harbour, I found the Latona with a broad pennant flying. As her captain was junior to me, I sent to know the reason for her wearing it. Her captain came on board, who I asked the following questions:

Q. Have you any order from Sir Richard Hughes to wear a broad pennant? *A.* No.

Q. For what reason do you then wear it in the presence of a senior officer?

A. I hoisted it by order of Commissioner Moutray.

Q. Have you seen by what authority Commissioner Moutray was empowered to give you orders? *A.* No.

Q. Sir, you have acted wrong, to obey any man who you do not know is authorised to command you.

A. I feel I have acted wrong; but being a young captain, did not think proper to interfere in this matter, as there were you and other older officers upon this station.

I did not choose to order the commissioner's pennant to be struck, as Mr. Moutray is an old officer of high military character; and it might hurt his feelings to be supposed wrong by so young an officer. When Commissioner Moutray sent me orders, I answered him, that I could not obey him till he was in commission. As I never heard further upon the subject from him, I took for granted he saw I was perfectly right, or he would have produced his commission, which would instantly have cleared up the business, if it was dated since I had, by orders from Sir Richard Hughes, executed the office of second in command in English Harbour.

This is the whole and every circumstance that has arisen upon this business, and have from time to time confirmed me in the opinion, that I am second officer in the command of his Majesty's ships upon this station.

The Admiralty minute on this letter, May 4, 1785, is: 'However improper he might conceive Mr. Moutray's appointment to have been, he would have done well to have submitted his doubts to the commander-in-chief upon the station, instead of taking upon himself to control the exercise of the functions of his appointment.' The minute of the same date, on Sir Richard Hughes's letter on this subject, is: 'Answer this conformable to the minute just now sent out upon Captain Nelson's letter. But that as the appointment of a commissioner of the navy at Antigua has been discontinued, it is unnecessary for their lordships to send any particular instruction for preventing anything of the like kind happening in future.'[1]

---

[1] P.R.O. Admirals' Despatches, Leeward Islands, No. 8. The minute seems to have escaped the search of Nicolas, who says in a note to this correspondence that 'their lordships' decision had not been found.'

Through all this dispute, however, there was no ill-feeling towards the commissioner, to whom Nelson was warmly attached, and whose wife he adored. She it was of whom he wrote:

Rev. W. Nelson, 20 Feb.

My dear sweet friend is going home. I am really an April day; happy on her account, but truly grieved were I only to consider myself. Her equal I never saw in any country or in any situation. She always talks of you, and hopes, if she comes within your reach, you will not fail visiting her. If my dear Kate goes to Bath next winter, she will be known to her;. for my dear friend has promised to make herself known. What an acquisition to any female to be acquainted with: what an example to take pattern from. Moutray has been very ill: it would have been necessary he should have quitted this country, had he not been recalled. All my children are well except one, young Andrews. He came out in the Unicorn: do you remember him? On 11 November last, he was forced by Mr. Stainsbury to fight a duel, which terminated fatally for the poor lad: the ball is lodged in his back, and whether he will ever get the better of it God knows. He has kept his bed ever since. His antagonist, and Mr. Oliver, his second, are in irons since the duel. They will stand a good chance of hanging if the youth should unfortunately die.

Capt. Locker, 16 March. St. Kitts.

Moutray is gone home a few days ago, so that I lose my only valuable friend in these islands. ... All the navy are very unpopular, from the governor downwards, for hindering the American ships from trading to the islands. I seldom go on shore, hardly once a month. ... Our admiral with his family are just making the tour of the islands; they find, probably, more satisfaction in visiting them than I do, for they are a sad set. Yesterday being St. Patrick's Day, the Irish colours with thirteen stripes in them was hoisted all over the town. I was engaged to dine with the president, but sent an excuse, as he suffered those colours to fly. I mention it only to show the principle of these vagabonds.

! Deprived of the society of Mrs. Moutray, Nelson was not long in devoting himself to Mrs. Nisbet, a young widow, to whom, within a few months, he became engaged. And as before, when he had hoped to marry Miss Andrews, so now again he had recourse to his uncle.

Wm. Suckling, 14 Nov. Nevis.

When I open my business, you will perhaps smile in the first instance, and say, 'This Horatio is for ever in love.' My present attachment is of pretty long standing; but I was determined to be fixed before I broke this matter to any person. The

lady is a Mrs. Nisbet, widow of a Dr. Nisbet, who died eighteen
months after her marriage, and has left her with a son. From her
infancy (for her father and mother died when she was only two
years of age), she has been brought up by her mother's brother,
Mr. Herbert, President of Nevis, a gentleman whose fortune and
character must be well known to all the West Indian merchants,
therefore I shall say nothing upon that head. Her age is twenty-
two; and her personal accomplishments you will suppose *I think*
equal to any person's I ever saw : but, without vanity, her mental
accomplishments are superior to most people's of either sex; and
we shall come together as two persons most sincerely attached to
each other from friendship. Her son is under her guardianship,
but totally independent of her.

But I must describe Herbert to you, that you may know
exactly how I stand; for when we apply for advice, we must tell
all circumstances. Herbert is very rich and very proud : he has
an only daughter, and this niece, who he looks upon in the same
light, if not higher. I have lived at his house, when at Nevis,
since June last, and am a great favourite of his. I have told him
I am as poor as Job; but he tells me he likes me, and I am
descended from a good family, which his pride likes; but he also
says, ' Nelson, I am proud, and I must live like myself, therefore I
can't do much in my lifetime: when I die she shall have twenty
thousand pounds; and if my daughter dies before me, she shall
possess the major part of my property. I intend going to England
in 1787, and remaining there my life; therefore, if you two can
live happily together till that event takes place, you have my
consent.' This is exactly my situation with him; and I know the
way to get him to give me most, is not to appear to want it : thus
circumstanced, who can I apply to but you ? The regard you have
ever expressed for me leads me to hope you will do something.
My future happiness, I give you my honour, is now in your power;
if you cannot afford to give me anything for ever, you will, I am
sure, trust to me, that if I ever can afford it, I will return it to
some part of your family. I think Herbert will be brought to give
her two or three hundred a year during his life; and if you will
either give me, I will call it—I think you will do it—either one
hundred a year, for a few years, or a thousand pounds, how
happy you will make a couple who will pray for you for ever.
Don't disappoint me, or my heart will break: trust to my
honour to do a good turn for some other person if it is in
my power. I can say no more, but trust implicitly to your

D

goodness, and pray let me know of your generous action by the first packet.

Rev. W. Nelson, 1 Jan. 1786. Nevis.

The admiral lives in a boarding-house at Barbadoes, not much in the style of a British admiral. Lady H., with her daughter, Mrs. Browne, in St. John's, Antigua. They all pack off next May certainly, and I hope most devoutly they will take the admiral with them, but he wishes much to remain another station. He is too much of a fiddler for me.

Capt. Locker, 5 March. Off Martinique.

For this last year I have been plagued to death. This station has not been over pleasant: had it not been for Collingwood, it would have been the most disagreeable I ever saw. Little ——, poor fellow, between Bacchus and Venus, is scarcely ever thoroughly in his senses. I am very sorry for him, for his heart is good; but he is not fit to command a man-of-war: his ship is the merest privateer you ever saw. Such men hurt the service more than it is in the power of ten good ones to bring back. The rest of the captains I know nothing of; nor am I ambitious of the honour of their acquaintance. Sir Richard Hughes you know, probably better than myself, and that he is a fiddler; therefore, as his time is taken up tuning that instrument, you will consequently expect the squadron is cursedly out of tune. I don't like to say much against my commander-in-chief; there has been too much of that the late war; but as I only tell it to you as a friend, you will not let it go further than you think right.

Wm. Suckling, 5 July. Nevis.

I wish I could tell you I was well, but I am far from it. My activity of mind is too much for my puny constitution. I am worn to a skeleton, but I trust that the doctors and asses' milk will set me up again. Perhaps you will think it odd if I do not mention Mrs. Nisbet;—I can only asssure you, that her heart is equal to her head, which every person knows is filled with good sense. My affection for her is fixed upon that solid basis of esteem and regard that I trust can only increase by a longer knowledge of her.

You have been my best friend, and I trust will continue as long so as I shall prove myself, by my actions, worthy of supplying that place in the service of my country, which my dear uncle [Maurice] left for me. I feel myself, to my country, his heir; and it shall, I am bold to say, never lack the want of his counsel;—I feel he gave it to me as a legacy, and had I been near him when he was removed, he would have said, 'My boy, I leave you to my country. Serve her well, and she'll never desert, but will ultimately reward you.' You who know much of me, I believe and hope, think me not unworthy your regards.

<small>Rev. W. Nelson, 25 Sept. Antigua.</small>

You cannot have an idea of the plague and trouble I have had with these governors and people, and the number of letters I have been obliged to write upon those subjects. However, I have smoothed the way for those who may come after me. The captains of men-of-war are now invested with great additional powers, enough to carry on the business of doing good for the nation without interruption.

<small>Capt. Locker, 27 Sept.</small>

If you got my letter from Barbadoes in May last (I ought to be ashamed of the date) you will have some idea of my troubles; nor will they ever end, I plainly perceive, while I am in this country; for it will always be the case, where officers neglect their duty, there rogues thrive; and God knows there is not a custom-house officer, governor, &c. that I have met with, who have done their duty; therefore the latter party is kept up, and my hands full of business. It is not more strange than true, that I was not only obliged to support myself against the most violent prosecutions that could be laid against an officer; and instead of being supported by my admiral, I was obliged to keep him up, for he was frightened at this business, which, although, I hope, completed now, he appeared ready (I thought), when he got home, to receive any thanks which might be offered him for his alertness and attention to the navigation of Great Britain. God knows, I envy no man praises; but don't let him take what is due to others.

<small>Mrs. Nisbet, 13 Dec. Antigua</small>

We arrived here this morning at daylight. His Royal Highness [Prince William] dined with me, and of course the governor. I can tell you a piece of news, which is, that the prince is fully determined, and has made me promise him, that he shall be at our wedding; and he says he will give you to me. His Royal Highness has not yet been in a private house to visit, and is determined never to do it, except in this instance. You know I will ever strive to bear such a character as may render it no discredit to any man to take notice of me. There is no action in my whole life but what is honourable; and I am the more happy at this time on that account; for I would, if possible, or in my power, have no man near the prince, who can have the smallest impeachment as to character: for as an individual I love him, as a prince I honour and revere him. My telling you this history is as to myself: my thoughts on all subjects are open to you. We shall certainly go to Barbadoes from this island, and when I shall see you is not

D 2

possible for me to guess: so much for marrying a sailor. We are often separated, but I trust our affections are not by any means on that account diminished. Our country has the first demand for our services; and private convenience, or happiness, must ever give way to the public good.

Capt. Locker, 29 Dec.

You will know long before this reaches you, that Prince William is under my command: I shall endeavour to take care he is not a loser by that circumstance. He has his foibles as well as private men, but they are far overbalanced by his virtues. In his professional line, he is superior to near two-thirds, I am sure, of the list; and in attention to orders, and respect to his superior officers, I know hardly his equal: that is what I have found him. Some others, I have heard, will tell another story.

Phil. Stephens, 7 Jan. 1787. Antigua.

I was exceedingly sorry to find that the Pegasus [commanded by his Royal Highness Prince William Henry] was not only very leaky, but that there was every appearance her iron work was much corroded. After wooding and watering the squadron in Prince Rupert's, I proceeded to this harbour, where I arrived on 13 December. The Pegasus was immediately hauled to the wharf, and it was found that the leak was occasioned by her wooden ends forward being very open, nearly all her bolts about her bows were found very much corroded, and were so bad, that I have ordered her to be new bolted. The cheeks of her head have been taken off, and the seams were found so open, as plainly to show they had not been examined into at the port she fitted out at: some of the chain plates have also been found unfit for service, and the generality of the bolts which hold them were so loose in the ship, as to be drawn out by the hand. This has occasioned her to be so long in the harbour.

By way of enforcing discipline, and perhaps persuading himself that he really was captain of his own ship, Prince William had given or thought he had given, an order that no boat was to leave the ship without his knowledge; or, if he was absent, being reported to him on his return. Mr. Schomberg, the first lieutenant, was either ignorant of this order, or conceived that it did not apply to him: he was, therefore, very much nettled at finding himself publicly reprimanded for disobeying it, and wrote to Nelson, the senior officer present, applying for a court-martial. Nelson replied that he would order a court-martial as soon as possible, and at the same time placed him under arrest.

23 Jan.

General order, 28 Jan.

For the better maintaining discipline and good government in the king's squadron under my command,

I think it necessary to inform the officers, that if any one of them shall presume to write to the commander of the squadron (unless there shall be ships enough present to bring them to immediate trial) for a court-martial to investigate their conduct on a frivolous pretence, thereby depriving his Majesty of their services, by obliging the commander of the squadron to confine them, that I shall and do consider such conduct as a direct breach of the 14th and part of the 19th Articles of War; and shall order them to be tried for the same.

I am at this moment honoured with your letter of this day's date, requesting that I would be kind enough to furnish you with the charge or charges which you suppose I mean to exhibit against you, that you may, whenever a court-martial offers, give as little trouble as possible; as you have reason to believe that your long and close confinement must arise from some other cause than that of your own wishes expressed to me in your letter dated 23 January.

Lt. Schomberg, 18 April.

In answer, I beg leave to assure you that I never was more hurt, than that an officer whom I very much respected, should do such an improper act as to deprive his Majesty of his services at a time they were wanted. My orders to the squadron were to prevent other officers from falling into the same error. I have not, nor can any other person, have any charge against you, until the court-martial which you desired to be held to investigate your conduct is over; and then I can tell you I have no charge whatsoever against you. Your confinement is your own. Had you not wrote to me for a court-martial, I dare say you never would have given me occasion to put you under arrest. Had I not ordered you into arrest, you might then have accused me of having left you again to be unjustly accused, as set forth in your letter.

No opportunity for the court-martial occurred; and on 11 May the prince wrote to Nelson:

'It is highly requisite for his Majesty's service that Lieutenant Isaac Schomberg should be brought to trial, particularly after having been kept under suspension rather than confinement for one hundred and seven days. Justice calls loudly for a man so long in his situation to be as soon delivered from his captivity as possible. The only means to effect that must be a court-martial. You, sir, are thoroughly acquainted with all the proceedings, and know the uneasiness of mind I have suffered, and the vast desire I must have to see the affair of this unhappy and deluded man settled; and as you have mentioned to me in your letter that his Majesty's ship Maidstone has gone in search of that piratical vessel, and as no official accounts are yet come out concerning the approaching arrival of a commander-in-chief to his Majesty's ships on this station, and as the time is now almost come for his Majesty's ship under my command to return to the coast of North America, where it is likely that there will not be a sufficient number of his Majesty's ships and vessels to try the said Lieutenant Schomberg, I entirely coincide in opinion with you, sir, that it is not only for the advantage of his Majesty's service, but that justice requires that his Majesty's ship Pegasus should proceed, in her way to North America, to Jamaica. I am using the utmost despatch, and am confident I shall have the honour of paying my personal respects to you in a few days at furthest, my health being so much better that I am able to conduct the duty of the ship.'

And again on 13 May:

'My going to Jamaica is really necessary, not only for my own ease and peace of mind, but for the king's service, to deliver this miserable object from his long confinement. The sloop's going with me is a judicious arrangement of yours, to prevent delay. Gardner, being an officer of experience and judgment, will be able to give me good advice how to pursue the best mode through this difficult and disagreeable affair. I wish to God it had never happened, or that Schomberg had seen his error sooner.'

The Pegasus was accordingly sent to Jamaica, with an official statement of the case against Mr. Schomberg, and also a private letter from Nelson to the commodore.

Comdore. Gardner, 13 May. Nevis.

In a public letter, a commander would be wrong to set forth all the reasons which influence his conduct; but as I hope to have your approbation, I take the liberty of mentioning a few circumstances.

His Royal Highness will give you an account of Lieutenant Schomberg's conduct, and of his having put him into arrest for disobedience of orders, &c., and that on Mr. Schomberg's making proper apologies, he forgave him. Indeed, his Royal Highness's narrative is so explicit, that I cannot inform you so fully as that will. His Royal Highness, I can have no doubt, gave the orders alluded to, although Mr. Schomberg might have misunderstood them. I am sure, sir, you will consider his Royal Highness stands in a very different situation to any other captain; his conduct will be canvassed by the world, when ours would never be heard of.

Mr. Schomberg was our friend Cornwallis's first lieutenant in the Canada. I can only suppose that he thought the prince was determined to take the first opportunity of bringing him to a court-martial, that he wrote for this for such a trivial matter. Indeed, what leads me to consider that as his motive was, when his Royal Highness told him how wrong he was to write for a court-martial on himself, he told him that every officer who served under him must be broke, and the sooner he was from under his command the better; and that if a court-martial acquitted him, he would write to quit the ship. This matter has made the prince very uneasy, for he says no person can tell he gave Mr. Schomberg those orders but himself, and Schomberg denies them. The day the matter happened, his Royal Highness dined in the country, and I attended him. On the road he told me how unpleasant it was that Schomberg would act in that manner when he had only forgiven him a few days before; but he said, in future, if any person committed faults, he would insert it in the public order-book of the ship, which he did, on this occasion, the next day. On that evening when I returned from dining, I found Mr. Schomberg's letter. I immediately sent for his Royal Highness, and I told him that in his elevated situation in life the world looked more to him than any other person, that Mr. Schomberg had neither more nor less than accused him of putting his name to an untruth: therefore I thought it my duty, although the matter was so trivial, to take Lieutenant Schomberg from under his directions, by suspending him from duty, or it might be said I had left him in that disagreeable situation, merely because he served under the prince; and that it very much concerned his Royal Highness to show the world he had put his name to nothing but the truth.

In order to show my disapprobation of officers writing for courts-martial, to vindicate their conduct for trivial matters, I gave out the inclosed order,[1] that others might not fall into the same error. It might soon have risen to such a height, that if a topsail was not thought properly or briskly reefed, by a captain, or some other trivial matter, and he reprimanded the officer, the officer would say, 'Sir, I think it properly done, and I shall write for a court-martial to vindicate my conduct from your unjust accusation.' If this was to be allowed, farewell discipline: the service is ruined: his Majesty may be deprived of the services of his officers; and the best-laid schemes may be frustrated by the malignity of individuals, or pique against their commanders.

At Jamaica, the commodore succeeded in arranging this unpleasant matter without a court-martial; but Nelson, on his return to England, was called on to give his reasons for sending the Pegasus and Rattler to Jamaica. He thereupon, 10 July, 1787, forwarded a full statement of the case, which was not considered sufficient; and the Secretary of the Admiralty signified to him that—'My lords are not satisfied with the reasons you have given for altering the destination of the Pegasus, and for sending the Rattler sloop to Jamaica; and that for having taken upon you to send the latter away from the station to which their lordships had appointed her, you will be answerable for the consequence, if the Crown should be put to any needless expense upon that account.'

[1] See *ante*, p. 36.

On 12 March, 1787, Nelson was married to Mrs. Nisbet, the prince, according to his old promise, giving the bride away.

(?) Mr. Pitt, 4 May. Nevis.

On 13 April, Messrs. Higgins and Wilkinson, merchants in the town of St. John's, in the island of Antigua, gave his Royal Highness information that frauds had been committed upon Government. As his Royal Highness could not attend to this matter, he desired me to do what was right in the business; since which time I have endeavoured to make myself master of this subject, and have examined a variety of books and papers, particularly those of a Mr. Whitehead, who appears a principal agent. It is necessary to observe, that Higgins and Wilkinson were partners of Whitehead, under the firm of Whitehead and Co., but have now parted from him, and possessed themselves of all his books and papers, from which it appears that Government has been defrauded in a most scandalous and infamous manner. The only emulation I can perceive is, who could cheat most. . . . These gentlemen have been in various employments in the different islands, under those employed in the victualling &c., and they assure me that they are certain they can discover frauds in Antigua to near 500,000*l.*; St. Lucia, 300,000*l.*; Barbadoes, 250,000*l.*; and at Jamaica, 1,000,000*l.* The sum is immense. Whether they can make it out, time must determine. However, they only wish to be rewarded for what is actually recovered, and they are both shrewd sensible men; and must know they are for ever ruined in this country, if they do not make out what they have so boldly asserted.

Sir C. Middleton, 2 May.

Mr. Wilkinson was brought up under Muir and Atkinson, and is a very shrewd sensible man. Higgins is likewise a man of business. Wilkinson has been in various departments of Government, in St. Lucia, Barbadoes, &c., and assures me, he can discover all the frauds committed there, as easy as these, if Government think proper to reward them. Indeed they do not seem to be playing the fool; for if nothing is recovered, they desire nothing, and of what is actually recovered, only a certain percentage.

The Boreas arrived at Spithead on 4 July, 1787. A few days afterwards, the Earl of Cork wrote to Nelson, apparently asking for his advice as to what he ought to do with his son, the Hon. Courtenay Boyle, then a midshipman of the Boreas. In these days of education, instruction, and cram, Nelson's views on this important question have a peculiar interest.

E. of Cork, 22 July.

In the first place, it is necessary that he should be made complete in his navigation; and if the peace continues, French is absolutely necessary. Dancing is an accomplishment that probably a sea officer may require. You will see almost the necessity of it, when employed in foreign countries; indeed, the honour of the nation is so often entrusted to sea officers, that there is no accomplishment which will not shine with peculiar lustre in them. He must nearly have served his time, therefore he cannot be so well employed as in gaining knowledge.

After some weeks at Portsmouth, the Boreas, about the middle of August, went round to the Nore, where, much to her captain's disgust, she was made a receiving ship, and was not paid off till the beginning of December 1787. Nelson was then placed on half-pay; and notwithstanding repeated applications, remained unemployed, until he was appointed to the Agamemnon, in January 1793. During the greater part of these years, he and his wife resided, in idyllic retirement, with his father, at Burnham Thorpe; where he occupied himself in the garden or on the farm, often—it is said—digging with a violent industry, as though for the mere purpose of tiring himself out. But he is described as also giving much time to reading the current periodicals, to studying charts, to writing, or to drawing plans.[1] It would be interesting to know what these plans were; but unfortunately no trace of them remains. The correspondence during these years is very scanty.

I am at this moment under a prosecution by some Americans, for seizing their vessels in the West Indies; but I have wrote them word, that I will have nothing to do with them, and they may act as they think proper. Government, I suppose, will do what is right, and not leave me in the lurch. We have heard enough lately of the consequence of the Act of Navigation to this country. They may take my person; but if sixpence would save me from a prosecution, I would not give it. *Capt. Locker, 3 April, 1788. Bath.*

My brother having written me that you wished to have the letter of Messrs. Wilkinson and Higgins to me, I have sent it. These gentlemen desire I will do them justice with your board as to their ability to discover what they have pledged themselves to do. By the papers I saw, it conveyed to my idea most clearly the frauds (if they were not made for the purpose, which I cannot suppose), and that it would be no very difficult matter to find it out. Nothing, I thought, could prevent these gentlemen bringing it to light, but what I mentioned to you when I had the honour of seeing you on this subject. These people must be fools indeed to effectually ruin themselves for a momentary reflection on the characters of these people. All their hopes of advantage certainly now arise from proving what they have alleged; and as they have only asked for rewards for what can be actually recovered, I cannot suppose but *(?) Sir C. Middleton, 30 April. Exmouth.*

[1] Clarke and McArthur, vol. i. p. 109.

they are most serious in the progress of this discovery. In the West Indies they are most effectually ruined as merchants. It has been alleged they are bad men, and were partakers in these frauds. Admitting it to be so, much good often arises from bad motives; therefore to benefit the public I should never ask or care from what motives the good arises. Their letters to his Royal Highness Prince William are only repetitions, I take for granted, of their memorial and petition to Mr. Pitt, and some compliments to my assiduity while in that country. They are certainly men of strong natural parts, and appear wonderfully expert at the percentage.

Herc. Ross, 6 May.

My integrity cannot be mended, I hope; but my fortune, God knows, has grown worse for the service. So much for serving my country. But the devil, ever willing to tempt the virtuous (pardon this flattery of myself), has made me offer, if any ships should be sent to destroy his Majesty of Morocco's ports, to be there; and I have some reason to think, that should any more come of it, my humble services will be accepted. I have invariably laid down, and followed close, a plan of what ought to be uppermost in the breast of an officer: that it is much better to serve an ungrateful country, than to give up his own fame. Posterity will do him justice: a uniform conduct of honour and integrity seldom fails of bringing a man to the goal of fame at last.

Prince William, 2 June. London.

My Prince,—It was not until a very few days ago, that I heard your Royal Highness was going the cruise with the squadron now at Spithead. I am most sincerely glad to hear it, and am assured it is quite the thing you wish. Your Royal Highness knows everything relative to a single ship; and it can only be by commanding a fleet which will establish your fame, make you the darling of the nation, and hand down your name with honour and glory to posterity.

Indeed I have another very strong reason for being pleased at your serving near home, which is, that the actions of all officers, however brilliant, are wonderfully obscured by serving at a distance, for the capture of a privateer makes more noise, taken in the Channel, than a frigate, or even a ship of the line, afar off. Therefore, although the discipline and high order of your ship is known to many others as well as myself, yet it will now be much more talked of; and the king will be more acquainted with the exact state of the Andromeda than [by] any representations made from abroad. I am most totally ignorant whether to expect you back with the fleet, or if you proceed abroad; should the former be the case, if your Royal Highness comes within the reach of my purse I shall most certainly pay my humble duty. Should the latter take place, I shall, as soon as I know to what part of the world you are destined, trouble your Royal Highness with letters, an honour which you have most condescendingly permitted me.

I am most truly sensible of your kindness to me on all occasions, and although Mr. Herbert was hard enough to withstand your solicitations, yet my obligation is the same; there may be a thing, perhaps, within reach of your Royal Highness; therefore, trusting to your goodness, I shall mention it. The Princess Royal must very soon have a household appointed her. I believe a word from your Royal Highness would obtain a promise of a situation in her Royal Highness's establishment not unbecoming the wife of a captain in the navy; but I have only ventured to say thus much, and leave the issue to your better judgment; being, with the highest regard and attachment,

Your Royal Highness's most faithful   HORATIO NELSON.

On 23 January, 1789, Nelson received a letter from Mr. Wilkinson, dated in the previous October, in which he stated that he 'wrote that letter from the gaol of the island of Antigua, into which he had been placed by a quirk of the Solicitor-General's,' and he complained bitterly of the treatment he had received from that officer, attributing it to his discovery of Mr. Whitehead's frauds. That Whitehead had acted fraudulently, and that the Solicitor-General favoured that person, is shown by 'A Resolution of the Honourable House of Assembly in the Island of Antigua on the 4th day of June, 1788—That it be resolved that William Whitehead, surviving partner of Francis Colley, has been guilty of gross imposition on the Committee of both Houses of the Legislature appointed to examine the accounts of Francis Colley and Co., and of a flagrant attempt to defraud the public of this island. Ayes 15. Noes 2.' The two Noes being Mr. Solicitor-General and Archibald Gloster, Esq.

Wilkinson and Higgins, 24 Jan. 1789.

I am most sincerely sorry for your situation, and hope that Government will afford you every assistance, in bringing to maturity the good work begun under my auspices. But I would have you recollect that although Government business may be slow, yet it is sure. I am assured the business will never be dropped; and that all proper rewards and recompenses will be made you. His Grace of Richmond, after a long silence, has at last assured me that every proper measure shall be taken, and that you shall receive the reward you asked. All the other boards will do you ample justice. I cannot but lament that your discovery should not have been made to a man of more consequence than myself; for in this country I am not in office, and am so much retired from the busy scenes of power, that although I have every inclination,

I have not the ability of doing more than representing your situation.

28 Nov.

I received your letter of 11 September, the beginning of this month, and sent it to Sir Charles Middleton, without any comments of mine; as to me it seemed to require no explanation. When it was returned, it was wrote me that if I chose the letter should be made public, to send it to the Navy Board; reports having been circulated by high officers, that they feared all this business would end in smoke; and that you had shifted your ground, and were very wavering in your opinions: for that at first you had said, that nothing was to be done in the West Indies; and now, that nothing could be done at four thousand miles' distance. [As to] certain opinions which I had formed, although I am not a man who wishes to say much on anything without being asked, yet on this occasion, common justice would not allow me to be silent, when such (as appears to me) false reports were in circulation. I therefore wrote to the Navy Board, of which the following is an extract: viz. 'Having heard a report that these gentlemen had deviated from the first line of procedure they had adopted, it becomes (I hope the Board will think) a line of justice in me to give my reasons why I do not think so. When the information was given, and in all their subsequent communications with me, they have uniformly and constantly protested against placing their confidence in his Majesty's law officers in the West Indies. That a trial in England, although it might prove certain facts, yet was by no means the object they had in view when the information was given. Their object, I have constantly understood, was an inquiry and examination, on the large scale, of examining merchants, their books, &c., and tracing the frauds home to every delinquent; who being made to refund, was the source from whence these gentlemen expected their rewards to have arisen.'

On the 27th, yesterday, I received the following answer: 'We have sent the letters and inclosures to Mr. Dyson, our solicitor, and desired him to lay them before the Attorney-General for his opinion as to what steps are proper to be taken thereon, and to use every means in his power to investigate and bring forward the whole of the business so soon as possible.' Retired as I am, upwards of one hundred and twenty miles from London, I can render you little if any assistance in getting forward in this business; and good wishes, without something more powerful, are of no avail in this country. I can only sit down and think. Sir John Laforey is going out with the command, and will probably be the man to investigate the frauds committed in the naval yard &c. during the war.

In May 1790, on hearing of the dispute with Spain relative to Nootka Sound, and the consequent 'armament,' Nelson again applied for employment, but, as on previous occasions, without success.

My not being appointed to a ship is so very mortifying, that I cannot find words to express what I feel on the occasion; and when I reflect on your Royal Highness's condescension in mentioning me to Lord Chatham, I am the more hurt and surprised. Sure I am, that I have ever been a zealous and faithful servant, and never intentionally have committed any errors; especially as till very lately I have been honoured by the notice of the Admiralty. The attachment, which I trust has never been found to vary, since I first was introduced to you by Lord Hood, had invariably for its object one point—nothing else for myself did I ever presume to solicit—that I might have the distinguished honour of being one of your supporters in a line of battle; then it would be shown, that no person had your fame more at heart than myself. I dare not venture a wish that your Royal Highness should trouble yourself again in my behalf.

Duke of Clarence, 24 June, 1790.

Your Royal Highness will not, I trust, deem it improper (although I have no doubt it will be thought unnecessary) at this time to renew my expressions of invariable attachment not only to your Royal Highness, but to my king: for I think very soon every individual will be called forth to show himself, if I may judge from this county, where societies are formed, and forming, on principles certainly inimical to our present constitution both in Church and State, of which our dissenters are the head, and in this county they have great riches. Sorry am I to believe that others give a countenance to these societies, who ought to conduct themselves otherwise.

Duke of Clarence, 3 Nov. 1792.

In what way it might be in the power of such an humble individual as myself to best serve my king, has been matter of serious consideration, and no way appeared to me so proper as asking for a ship; and on Saturday last Lord Chatham received my letter asking for the command of one; but as I have hitherto been disappointed in all my applications to his lordship, I can hardly expect any answer to my letter, which has always been the way I have been treated: but neither at sea, nor on shore, through the caprice of a minister, can my attachment to my king be shaken; and which will never end but with my life.

In answering this letter, on 6 December, the prince, after expressing his indignation at Lord Chatham's treatment of Nelson, and remarking on the state of affairs, added : 'Should matters between the two countries grow serious, you must be employed. Never be alarmed : I will always stand your friend. I wish you would write me word how you and Lord Hood stand at present.'

Duke of Clarence, 10 Dec.

Respecting my present situation with Lord Hood, I can readily and truly answer. We have not for a long time had any communication with each other. Our familiar correspondence ceased on a difference of opinion. In the Spanish armament, when almost the whole service were called forth, I asked Lord Hood to interest himself with Lord Chatham, that I might be appointed to a ship. His lordship having declined doing it, has prevented my troubling him again for his interest or influence. However, in consideration of our former intimacy, whenever I have gone to London, I have hitherto thought it right to leave my name at his lordship's door. I certainly cannot look on Lord Hood as my friend; but I have the satisfaction of knowing, that I never gave his lordship just cause to be my enemy.

Our lord lieutenant has summoned a meeting of the Norfolk justices on Tuesday next, the 11th ; and I have no doubt but they will resolve to do collectively, what none of them chose to do individually—to take away the licences from those public-houses who allow of improper societies meeting at them, and to take up those incendiaries who go from alehouse to alehouse, advising the poor people to pay no taxes, &c. In this neighbourhood, a person of the name of Priestley, a clergyman, has held this language to a circle of ten miles round him ; and, a few days past, I asked a justice of the peace, 'why, as such a man's conduct was known, that he was not taken up?' His answer was, 'that no justice would render himself unpopular at this time, by being singular; for that his life and property were gone, if the mob arose: but that when the justices all agreed to act in a uniform manner, this man should certainly be taken hold of, if he went on with such conduct.'

That the poor labourer should have been seduced by promises and hopes of better times, your Royal Highness will not wonder at when I assure you, that they are really in want of everything to make life comfortable. Part of their wants, perhaps, were unavoidable, from the dearness of every article of life; but much has arose from the neglect of the country gentlemen, in not making their farmers raise their wages, in some small proportion, as the prices of necessaries increased. . . . Their wages have been raised within these three weeks, pretty generally, one shilling a week: had it been done some time past, they would not have been discontented, for a want of loyalty is not amongst their faults; and many of their superiors in many instances might have imitated their conduct with advantage. The wise precautions of Government have certainly given a vigour to the loyal of the nation, who are most undoubtedly by far the majority; and the disaffected join them at present, for fear of being suspected; therefore I have no doubt but our tranquillity will be restored.

After clouds comes sunshine. The Admiralty so smile upon me, that really I am as much surprised as when they frowned. Lord Chatham yesterday made many apologies for not having given me a ship before this time, and said, that if I chose to take a sixty-four to begin with, I should be appointed to one as soon as she was ready; and whenever it was in his power, I should be removed into a seventy-four. Everything indicates war. One of our ships, looking into Brest, has been fired into;[1] the shot is now at the Admiralty. Mrs. Nelson, 7 Jan. 1798. London.

Lord Hood tells me that I am now fixed for the Agamemnon at Chatham, and that whatever men are raised for her, will be taken care of on board the Sandwich. I have sent out a lieutenant and four midshipmen to get men at every seaport in Norfolk, and to forward them to Lynn and Yarmouth: my friends in Yorkshire and the north tell me they will send what men they can lay hands on to the regulating captains at Whitby and Newcastle. . . . Lord Hood has been very civil indeed. I think we may be good friends again. From what Lord Howe writes me, I think the ship will be commissioned within a fortnight, and I shall join her directly. Comdore. Locker, 26 Jan.

On 30 January, Nelson was appointed to the command of the Agamemnon, 64, and he joined her on 6 February.

I have the pleasure of telling you that my ship is, without exception, the finest sixty-four in the service, and has the character of sailing most remarkably well. I have only got a few men, and very hard indeed they are to be got, and without a press I have no idea our fleet can be manned. Rev. W. Nelson, 10 Feb. Chatham.

If the wind is to the northward of west, we go down the river to-morrow, and are ordered to proceed to Spithead with all Mrs. Nelson, 15 March.

[1] The Childers brig, on 2 January.

Rev. W. Nelson, 18 April. Nore.	possible despatch, as we are wanted, Lord Hood[1] writes me word, for immediate service; and hints, we are to go a cruise, and then to join his fleet at Gibraltar: therefore I am anxious to get to Spithead. I never was in better health.

I not only like the ship, but think I am well appointed in officers, and we are manned exceedingly well; therefore have no doubt but we shall acquit ourselves well, should the French give us a meeting. . . . To me it is perfectly indifferent to what quarter of the world we go: with a good ship and ship's company we can come to no harm. We appear to sail very fast: we went, coming out, nearly as fast, without any sail, as the Robust did under her topsails. |
Mrs. Nelson, 29 April. Spithead.	We arrived at Spithead last night, and this morning have got my orders to go to sea until the 4th of May, when I shall be at Portsmouth. Lord Hood will then be there, and it is now certain that I am going with him. We are all well: indeed, nobody can be ill with my ship's company, they are so fine a set.
6 May. Spithead.	I arrived here last night, and rather expected to have seen you here; but Mr. Matcham told you right, there is no certainty in winds and waves. We had some blowing weather, but nothing for Agamemnon to mind. We fell in with two French frigates, and two armed vessels, who got into La Hogue harbour, where we could not follow for want of a pilot. I was again ordered to sea this morning, but am now stopped, as my ship wants many things before she sails for the Mediterranean. Lord Hood is expected to-night.
Rev. W. Nelson, (?) 20 May. At sea.	What we have been sent out for is best known to the great folks in London: to us, it appears, only to hum the nation and make tools of us, for where we have been stationed, from ten to twenty leagues to the westward of Guernsey, no enemy was likely to be met with, or where we could protect our own trade. Thus five ships have been sported with. I don't like it, nor does our admiral. We are to be off Falmouth to-morrow, and expect fresh orders, or to be joined by Lord Hood. I think Torbay will finish this cruise. The French have eight sail of the line in different parts of the bay, and six frigates: three of each are always at sea, and England not able or willing to send a squadron to interrupt them. My ship sails well; very few will outsail her, and she is very tolerably manned.
Mrs. Nelson, 5 June. At sea.	I expected, when Lord Hood joined, that we should have gone to Gibraltar; but what his instructions or orders are I cannot guess.

[1] Appointed Commander-in-Chief in the Mediterranean.

I have not seen him since he joined us, a fortnight to-morrow; nor had even a boat hoisted out. Our weather, although not bad, has been very unpleasant—foggy with drizzling rain. Agamemnon sails admirably; we think better than any ship in the fleet. Our force is eleven sail of the line, frigates, &c. &c., and in very tolerable order. We have had some naval evolutions when the weather would permit.

After cruising off Scilly with Lord Hood for a fortnight, in very unpleasant weather, the arrival of the Mediterranean convoy relieved us from a station where we could hardly expect to see an enemy, and the last India convoy passing us in the evening, made Lord Hood quite satisfied. We are nine days from Scilly; a very good passage for a fleet: and during our run have taken nothing but a miserable National brig of eight guns. If we go on so, we shall soon make fortunes. Last night six sail of us parted from Lord Hood to water at Cadiz, in order that no time may be lost in watering so large a fleet at Gibraltar. Rev. W. Nelson, 15 June. Off Cadiz.

We came out [of Cadiz] this morning, having completed our ship with everything except wine, which is to be done at Gibraltar. The Spaniards have been very civil to us. We dined on board the Concepcion of one hundred and twelve guns, with the admiral; and all restraints of going into their arsenals and dockyards were removed. They have four first-rates in commission at Cadiz, and very fine ships, but shockingly manned. If those twenty-one sail of the line which we are to join in the Mediterranean are not better manned, they cannot be of much use. I am certain if our six barges' crews, who are picked men, had got on board one of their first-rates, they would have taken her. The dons may make fine ships—they cannot, however, make men. Mrs. Nelson, 23 June.

The fleet sailed from Gibraltar on 27 June, and a convoy of fifty sail of merchant ships, with a brisk wind at west, and soon got off Cape Gata, since which time we have had either Levanters or calms. . . . We saw a fleet off Alicant on the close of the 7th, and lay-to mid-channel between that place and Iviza. At daylight we formed our line, and soon perceived them to be the Spanish fleet, twenty-four sail of the line. The dons did not, after several hours' trial, form anything which could be called a line of battle ahead. However, after answering our private signals, the Spanish admiral sent down two frigates, with answers to Lord Hood's letters by L'Aigle, acquainting him that as his fleet was sickly 1,900 men, he was going to Cartagena. The captain of the frigate said, 'It was no wonder they were sickly, for they had been sixty days at sea.' Duke of Clarence, 14-25 July.

This speech to us appeared ridiculous; for from the circumstance of having been longer than that time at sea, do we attribute our getting healthy. It has stamped with me the extent of their nautical abilities: long may they remain in their present state. It appeared odd to me that no salutes whatever took place. Yesterday, the 13th, the frigates joined the fleet. Inglefield brings nothing new respecting the Toulon fleet, except that the French are preparing their ships with forges for shot. This information, I humbly think (if true), would have been as well kept secret; but as it is known, we must take care to get so close that their red shots can do no mischief. The fleet received orders yesterday to consider Marseilles and Toulon as invested, and to take all vessels of whatever nation bound into those ports. This has pleased us; and may possibly induce these red-hot gentlemen to come out.

Our fleet is healthy: we sail in three divisions, led by Victory, Colossus, and Agamemnon. We do not keep in so compact an order as we ought, and the lord does not spare signals. . . . On the 16th, the fleet stood close into Toulon, and sent in a flag of truce. . . . On 25 July the flag of truce joined from Toulon; the enemy did not give us a clear answer whether they would exchange prisoners with us. They have seventeen sail of the line ready for sea, and four fitting, the Commerce de Marseilles one of them; she carries 136 guns, having guns on her gangways; the prisoners believe her sides are so thick that our shot will not go through them; and that she can with ease take the Victory. We form various conjectures whether they will come out or not; in my opinion they will: when they have twenty-one sail ready and we under twenty, the people will force them out.

Mrs. Nelson, 4 August. Off Toulon.

Whether the French intend to come out seems uncertain; they have a force equal to us. Our Jacks would be very happy to see it; and, as our fleet is in the fullest health, I dare say we should give a good account of them. I hardly think the war can last; for what are we at war about? . . . Lord Hood has sent to offer me a seventy-four, but I have declined it; as the Admiralty chose to put me into a sixty-four, there I stay. I cannot give up my officers.

Capt. Locker, 20 August.

Lord Hood went with the fleet ten days past to speak to the Genoese about supplying the French with corn, and bringing back French property under neutral papers, for our being here is a farce if this trade is allowed. By all accounts we learn the district of Provence would gladly become a separate republic under the protection of England. The people of Marseilles have said they would destroy Toulon to accomplish this measure. In short, France will be dismembered, but in all their misery they have no thought of kingly government.

On 23 August, 1793, commissioners from Marseilles, expecting to meet commissioners from Toulon, came on board the Victory, to treat for peace on the basis of declaring a monarchical form of government in France. Lord Hood accordingly issued a proclamation to the inhabitants of the South of France; and General Carteaux's success at Marseilles so alarmed the Toulonese, that they placed the citadel and forts on the coast provisionally at his disposal.

As soon as the treaty was concluded, Agamemnon, a fast sailer, was sent off with letters to the Courts of Turin and Naples, for ten thousand troops, to secure our possession. I should have liked to have stayed one day longer with the fleet, when they entered the harbour; but service could not be neglected for any private gratification. . . . What an event this has been for Lord Hood: such a one as history cannot produce its equal; that the strongest place in Europe, and twenty-two sail of the line &c. should be given up without firing a shot. It is not to be credited.

Mrs. Nelson, 11 Sept. Naples.

On Sunday, 25 August, a party deposed Admiral Trogoff, and placed St. Julien at the head of the fleet, manned sixteen sail of the line, and were determined to come out and fight us, who were only twelve sail, Lord Hood having sent away the other part of his fleet, to give them the option: the fleet regret they did not: the issue we should doubtless have liked better than laying them up dismantled. The perseverance of our fleet has been great, and to that only can be attributed our unexampled success. Not even a boat could get into Marseilles or Toulon, or on the coast, with provisions; and the old saying, 'That hunger will tame a lion,' was never more strongly exemplified. The Spanish fleet arrived as ours was sailing into the harbour, and joined in the general joy which this event must give to all Europe. St. Julien, with about four thousand men, left the fleet as ours entered, and joined General Carteaux, who, I think it probable, by this time, has attacked Toulon with the Parisian army.

I believe the world is convinced that no conquests of importance can be made without us; and yet, as soon as we have accomplished the service we are ordered on, we are neglected. If Parliament does not grant something to this fleet, our Jacks will grumble; for here there is no prize-money to soften their hardships; all we get is honour and salt beef. My poor fellows have not had a morsel of fresh meat or vegetables for near nineteen weeks; and in that time I have only had my foot twice on shore at Cadiz. We are absolutely getting sick from fatigue. No fleet, I am certain, ever served their country with greater zeal than this has done, from the admiral to the lowest sailor.

Admiral Goodall is governor of Toulon; Elphinstone, commander of the grand battery, at the harbour's mouth. I may have lost an appointment by being sent off; not that I wish to be employed out of my ship. I have sent in a vessel from Smyrna bound to Marseilles, and I think it probable she will be condemned, worth about 10,000*l*. I hope she may, it will add something to our comforts.

14 Sept.

Our news was received here with the greatest satisfaction. The king has twice sent for me, and I dine with him to-morrow, after he has made me a visit, which he is to do on board the Agamemnon. We are called by him the saviours of Italy, and of his dominions in particular. I have acted for Lord Hood with a zeal which no one could exceed, and am to carry from the king the handsomest letter, in his own handwriting, which could possibly be. This I got through Sir William Hamilton, and the Prime Minister [Sir John Acton], who is an Englishman. Lady Hamilton has been wonderfully kind and good to Josiah.[1] She is a young woman of amiable manners, and who does honour to the station to which she is raised. I am to carry Lord Hood six thousand troops from hence.

27 Sept.
Leghorn.

I was hurried from Naples by information of a French ship of war, and three vessels under her convoy being off. I had nothing left but to get to sea, which I did in two hours: expedition, however, has not crowned my endeavours with success; for I have seen nothing of them. I am here plagued with a French 40-gun frigate, who was to have sailed the day I arrived, and will take the first dark moment to get out. I am determined in my mind to pursue him. I hope to sail to-morrow if this gentleman does not; and shall lie in his route to intercept him if he sails.

I have just heard, that last night the crew of my neighbour deposed their captain, made the lieutenant of marines captain of the ship, the sergeant of marines lieutenant of marines, and their former captain sergeant of marines. What a state! they are mad enough for any undertaking. They say, as they have five hundred men on board, they will go to sea this night in spite of me: I shall be surprised at nothing they may attempt.

28 Sept.

We have been looking out all night for our neighbour to cut his cables, as it has blown a gale of wind and rain; but he lay in

---

[1] Josiah Nisbet, Nelson's stepson, at this time a midshipman of the Agamemnon.

such a position that he could not cast his ship without getting on board us, which he did not choose to risk.

Our force now at Toulon, on shore, is 12,500 men, and before November is out will be 30,000, when the whole of this country will fall to us, for they hate the Convention. The white flag is flying in all the ships and forts, under which we fight on shore. . . . The Spaniards behave so infamously that I sincerely wish not one ship or soldier was in Toulon: they will do nothing but plunder and cut the throats of poor wretches who have surrendered to the British.

<small>Wm. Suckling, 11 Oct. Off Corsica.</small>

Lord Hood is now quite as he used to be: he is so good an officer, that everybody must respect him. All the foreigners at Toulon absolutely worship him; were any accident to happen to him, I am sure no person in our fleet could supply his place. Every day at Toulon has hitherto afforded some brilliant action on shore, in which the sea officers have made a conspicuous figure; Elphinstone in particular, who is a good officer and gallant man. I have only been a spectator; but had we remained, I should certainly have desired to be landed. Some of our ships have been pegged pretty handsomely; yet such is the force of habit, that we seem to feel no danger.

<small>Mrs. Nelson, 12 Oct.</small>

On 22 October, being then on her way to Cagliari, and some 40 or 50 miles ENE of her port, the Agamemnon fell in with and engaged a squadron of French frigates. In writing of the circumstance to Lord Hood, he transmitted the following extract from the log as the simplest account of what had taken place.

At 2 A.M. saw five sail standing across us to the NW by the wind. At 2.30 they tacked by signal of rockets, then about three miles on our weather bow: at 4 got within hail of a frigate, but was careful not to fire into her, thinking she might be a Neapolitan or Sardinian frigate with a convoy. On receiving no answer and the ship making sail, fired a shot ahead of her, when she set all her sails, and steering two points from the wind, we after her with every sail set, keeping her two points on the bow, to prevent her from getting before the wind. The other ships on our weather quarter steering after us. The chase made many signals till daylight, when she hoisted National colours, and began firing stern-chasers, and by yawing, which her superiority in sailing enabled her to do, gave us many broadsides. We could only at times bring any guns to bear upon her, and then only a few of the foremost ones. At 7, took the ships on our weather quarter to be one of the line, two frigates, and an armed brig, but whilst the breeze continued fresh, the chase and ourselves left them fast. At 9 we run into almost a calm, the ships on our quarter bearing NW by W, coming fast up with us; the chase hauled up to join them, being in a shattered condition, and making signals to her consorts, who steered to join her; when they brought to, hoisted out their boats, and sent to her. The enemy were four frigates, two of them carrying 28 eighteen-pounders on their main-decks. The enemy from this time till noon had the option of bringing us to action whenever they pleased; but we having our main top-mast shot to pieces, main-mast, mizen-mast, and fore-yard badly wounded, could not haul our wind till noon, repairing our rigging, masts, and yards, steering for Cagliari. Found we had one man killed, and six wounded. People employed knotting and splicing the rigging.

At noon, Cape Rosso, NW, distance 6 or 7 leagues. Latitude observed 39° 34′ N.

Wm. Suckling, 5 Dec. Off Corsica.

I am just returned from Tunis, where I have been under Commodore Linzee, to negotiate for a French convoy from the Levant. You will believe the English seldom get much by negotiation except the being laughed at, which we have been; and I don't like it. Had we taken, which in my opinion we ought to have done, the men-of-war and convoy, worth at least 300,000*l.*, how much better we could have negotiated—given the Bey 50,000*l.* he would have been glad to have put up with the insult offered to his dignity. The French sent him very great presents; and he bought, through fear of us, several rich cargoes, for one-third of their value. The ships of war so much believed we should have attacked them, that, at first, they hauled their ships almost aground, but latterly almost insulted us. Thank God, Lord Hood, whom Linzee sent to for orders how to act, after having negotiated, ordered me from under his command, and to command a squadron of frigates off Corsica and the coast of Italy, to protect our trade, and that of our new ally, the Grand Duke of Tuscany, and to prevent any ship or vessel, of whatever nation, from going into the port of Genoa. I consider this command as a very high compliment, there being five older captains in the fleet.

Phil. Stephens, 26 Dec.[1] Leghorn Roads.

Being now senior captain here, I think it my duty to acquaint their lordships of the reports which are here respecting Toulon; viz.: That on the 13th the heights were covered with a most numerous Convention army; that Lord Hood, seeing the place was untenable against such superior forces, had issued a proclamation for the inhabitants to be prepared for what would probably

---

[1] Public Record Office. Captains' Letters. This letter is not given by Nicolas.

happen, the evacuation of the place; that on the 17th, at night, a general attack was made on all our outposts, many of which were carried, and the troops were obliged to retire from the others, destroying the works as well as a short time would allow and spiking the guns; that on the 18th, Lord Hood had ordered all the Neapolitan troops to be embarked, together with as many Royalists as could find ships to carry them; that our fleet and that of Spain was moored under La Malgue, and that when he left the place, the white colours were still flying in the town and at Fort La Malgue; that soon after he left the harbour, an amazing fire broke out and a great explosion, which he supposed was the ships fitted with powder blowing up and the arsenal on fire; that it being calm, he returned to the harbour in his boat and saw the arsenal and the whole French fleet in flames, with part of the town, and that they were all destroyed, except the Commerce de Marseilles, 130 guns, Le Pompée, 74, and La Perle frigate; that the disaffected in the town had begun to plunder and to commit every excess of riot. The whole Neapolitan fleet are said to have been seen at sea, going to Port Spezia. This account is confirmed by the arrival of two other vessels with families from Toulon. I have the greatest pleasure in saying that Lord Hood was said to be perfectly well.

Nothing is received official from Lord Hood. Four sail are arrived with wounded soldiers and sailors from the hospital: all agree in the main point, but differ in the telling.

27 Dec. 6 P.M.

I left Leghorn on the 3rd, and very soon got off here, since which time we have had nothing but hard gales of wind, and the heaviest rains I almost ever met with. I am waiting anxiously for troops from Lord Hood, to take S. Fiorenzo and the frigates, which will fall into our hands a few hours after their arrival. I was most unfortunately driven a few miles to leeward two days ago, in the height of the gale; and a frigate took that opportunity of sailing from S. Fiorenzo to Calvi with provisions. One of my frigates exchanged a few shots with her, but at too great a distance to prevent her getting in. I had so closely blockaded Calvi, that they must have surrendered to me at discretion; not a vessel had before got in for the six weeks I have been stationed here. This supply will keep them a week or two longer. We now know from a deserter, that it was the Melpomene who engaged us on 22 October: she had twenty-four men killed, and fifty wounded, and was so much damaged as to be laid up dismantled in S. Fiorenzo.

Mrs. Nelson, (?) 16 Jan. Off Calvi.

Mrs. Nelson, 30 Jan. 1794. Leghorn.

I was blown off my station on the 28th, in the hardest gale almost ever remembered here. The Agamemnon did well, but lost every sail in her. Lord Hood had joined me off Corsica the day before; and would have landed the troops, but the gale has dispersed them over the face of the waters. The Victory was very near lost; however, we are safe. A number of transports are missing. I am fearful the enemy will get their troops from France before I can return to my station, which will be a vexing thing after my two months' hard fag. . . . On 21 January, the French having their storehouse of flour near a water-mill close to S. Fiorenzo, I seized a happy moment, and landed sixty soldiers and sixty seamen, in spite of opposition. At landing, the sailors threw all the flour into the sea, burned the mill—the only one they had, and returned on board without the loss of a man.

Lord Hood, 8 Feb Off Porto Nuovo.

Yesterday at Porto Nuovo they hoisted National colours as I passed, also the vessels as I passed, as also the vessels in the harbour. I went to La Vasina, but there was no ship there. Captain Fremantle tells me, a ship under Ragusan colours is in Bastia. This morning being very fine, I anchored off Rogliano, and sent on shore to say that I was come to deliver them from the Republicans, and wished to be received as a friend, but that if a musket was fired, I would burn the town. . . . [On receiving an insolent and defiant] answer, I landed, and struck the National colours with my own hand on the top of an old castle, and ordered the tree of liberty in the centre of the town to be cut down, not without great displeasure from the inhabitants. The military commandant retired to a hill about two miles distant, where he paraded the troops, and kept the National flag flying all day. We destroyed about five hundred tuns of wine ready to be shipped, and ten sail of vessels.

Mrs. Nelson, 13 Feb.

I am just going into Leghorn to get water. Corsica I hope will fall in due time: Commodore Linzee has the command of the sea business, Lord Hood is in the offing. . . . Corsica is a wonderfully fine island. We are anxious to hear how Parliament likes the war. I am still of opinion it cannot last much longer; not by the French having an absolute monarchy again, but by our leaving them alone; perhaps the wisest method we can follow.

Lord Hood, 19 Feb.

I had a good opportunity of looking at Bastia this morning; its means of defence are as follows: On the town wall next the sea, about twenty embrasures; to the southward of the town, two guns are mounted on a work newly thrown up, and an officer's guard encamped there; they are also throwing up a small work commanding a large road to the southward of the town, which leads towards the mountains. I observed at the back of the town four stone works, all with guns: two of them appeared strong, the others are stone guardhouses. In the mole is La Flêche, 20 guns, which came out from Tunis with the other frigates; she is dismantled, and her guns are put on the outworks. . . .

I carefully examined the landing-places near Bastia, and can take upon me to say, that troops and cannon may be landed with great ease to the southward of the town at any distance you please, on a level country. If I may be permitted to judge, it would require 1,000 troops, besides seamen, Corsicans, &c., to make any successful attempt against Bastia. The enemy, from all accounts I could learn, have about 400 regulars; and altogether 2,000 men carrying muskets.

S. Fiorenzo was taken possession of without opposition on 17 February.

I was honoured by your letter of the 19th, yesterday morning, and beg leave most sincerely to congratulate your lordship on the taking Fiorenzo. . . . I am now going to take another look at [Bastia], when I shall send this letter. To the northward of the town, at three miles distance, troops may be safely landed; and a good road for marching all the way to Bastia, but not for heavy artillery; but probably landing-places may be found to the northward of Bastia, much nearer than three miles. I see the little camp with two guns *en barbette* is intended to prevent landing to the southward, as I dare say the shot will reach to the opening of the lagoon; but then troops may land under cover of gunboats and other small vessels, although ships cannot get in. But every defence of Bastia is plainly to be seen from the sea, and in my opinion will soon fall. *Lord Hood, 22 Feb. Saturday.*

It is only just now I have been able to examine Bastia more closely. I find the enemy every hour are strengthening their works. The two guns mounted *en barbette* are now making a half-moon battery. As I passed close with Romulus and Tartar, the enemy opened their fire from the battery. We directly dislodged them, and they to a man quitted the works. The town opened on us with shot and shells, but without doing us any damage of consequence: our guns were so exceedingly well pointed, that not one shot was fired in vain; a parcel of powder for one battery blew up, and did apparently considerable damage. Indeed, my lord, I wish the troops were here: I am sure, in its present state it will *Sunday, noon.*

soon fall. I don't think the Corsicans have the strong post General Paoli mentions, or I must have known it. They tell me the garrison of Fiorenzo is got into Bastia.

<small>Mrs. Nelson, 28 Feb. Off Bastia.</small>

Our little brush last Sunday happened at the moment when part of our army made their appearance on the hills over Bastia, they having marched over land from S. Fiorenzo, which is only twelve miles distant. The general sent an express to Lord Hood at Fiorenzo to tell him of it. What a noble sight it must have been! indeed, on board it was the grandest thing I ever saw. If I had carried with me 500 troops, to a certainty I should have stormed the town, and I believe it might have been carried. Armies go so slow, that seamen think they never mean to get forward; but I dare say they act on a surer principle, although we seldom fail. . . .

<small>4 March.</small>

You will be surprised to hear that the English general, Dundas, has retired from before Bastia without making an attack. God knows what it all means. Lord Hood is gone to S. Fiorenzo to the army, to get them forward again. A thousand men would to a certainty take Bastia: with 500, and Agamemnon, I would attempt it. Lord Hood said publicly, that if he thought it proper to give me three sail of the line and 500 men, he was sure I should take the town, although probably not the heights; but he would not sacrifice his seamen and ships in doing what the finest army of its size that ever marched could, and wish to do. . . . We now know that I was very near getting possession on Sunday, the 23rd. If I had force to go again and cannonade it, I believe I should yet get it. My seamen are now what British seamen ought to be, to you I may say it, almost invincible: they really mind shot no more than peas.

<small>Lord Hood, 5 March. Off Bastia.</small>

By a Ragusa vessel come out since your lordship's departure, I learn that the enemy are in the greatest apprehension of our landing near the town, which, in my opinion, would fall on the first vigorous attack. That the works on the hills would annoy the town afterwards is certain, but the enemy being cut off from all supplies (the provisions in the town being of course in our possession) would think of nothing but making the best terms they could for themselves. They are now at work on the hill near Cardo, and are also beginning a work on a hill above it, and have made a road to the top of the mountains. . . . The enemy have just begun a battery in the town, just to the northward of the mole, at the place I conceived our troops might have landed.

The relations between Lord Hood and the general had meantime become exceedingly strained. Hood was anxious to push on at once and attack Bastia : Dundas refused to co-operate unless he had a reinforcement of 2,000 men from Gibraltar. Hood was urgent : Dundas was obstinate : and the bitterness of the letters which passed between them was but scantily veiled by the forms of official courtesy. On 5 March, Dundas wrote : 'I consider the siege of Bastia, with our present means and force, to be a most visionary and rash attempt, such as no officer could be justified in undertaking ;' and Hood replied on the 6th : 'I must take the liberty to observe that however visionary and rash an attempt to reduce Bastia may be in your opinion, to me it appears very much the reverse, and to be perfectly a right measure ; and I beg here to repeat my answer to you, upon your saying two days ago, that I should be of a different opinion to what I had expressed, were the responsibility upon my shoulders—"that nothing would be more gratifying to my feelings than to have the whole responsibility upon me ;" as I am now ready and willing to undertake the reduction of Bastia at my own risk, with the force and means at present here, being strongly impressed with the necessity of it.'

. . . Sent an officer overland to Lord Hood, with my opinion that it was yet possible to take Bastia with 500 regulars and two or three ships. Received a letter from Lord Hood, to say he would send me two gunboats, according to my desire. When I get them the inhabitants of Bastia sleep no more. Journal, 6 March.

You may be assured I shall undertake nothing but what I have moral certainty of succeeding in : had this day been fine it was my intention to have towed the Agamemnon in-shore, and to have destroyed the house which the enemy has fortified for musketry, and also the new battery which is nearly finished : I think we should have been out of the range of shot from the town. When the gunboats arrive, they may perhaps do it better; certainly with less risk than ourselves. It must be destroyed, or the Corsicans will be obliged to give up a post which the enemy would immediately possess; and of course throw us on that side at a greater distance from Bastia. I hope our troops will soon join. Lord Hood, 11 March.

I send this overland, and shall thank your lordship to signify your wishes by the bearer of my letter. We are really without firing, wine, beef, pork, flour, and almost without water : not a rope, canvas, twine, or nail in the ship. The ship is so light, she cannot hold her side to the wind; yet if your lordship thinks or wishes me to remain off Bastia, I can by going to Porto Ferrajo, get water and stores, and twenty-four hours at Leghorn will give us provisions ; and our refitting, which will take some time, can be put off a little. My wish is to be present at the attack of Bastia ; and if your lordship intends me to command the seamen who may 16 March. Off Bastia.

be landed, I assure you I shall have the greatest pleasure in doing it, or any other service where you may think I can do most good: even if my ship goes into port to refit, I am ready to remain. We are certainly in a bad plight at present, not a man has slept dry for many months.

Wm. Suckling, 18 March.

We are still blocking up Bastia, the attack of which has been given up in a most extraordinary manner; I will make what might, if it had not now met the sanction of men of science, have been deemed a most impertinent observation, viz. that Bastia, from a place I had found on a much closer examination than our general Dundas, could be attacked to great advantage. I wrote Lord Hood requesting an engineer and artillery officer might be sent to examine. To-day I have been with them, and their report is most favourable for an attack. Our weather is now but indifferent; but hitherto I have so close blocked up the place, that one pound of coarse bread sells for three livres. If the army will not take it, we must, by some way or other. General Dundas has quitted the command,[1] differing in opinion with Lord Hood. . . .

Rev. W. Nelson, 26 March. Off Bastia.

General d'Aubant, with 2,000 as fine troops as ever marched, has thought it improper to attack Bastia, which has only 800 Frenchmen to defend it, and that as to taking it, that is impossible. As I had examined the ground, perhaps more than the general, Sir James Erskine St. Clair,[2] Major Koehler, Colonel Moore, or any other, I ventured to give my opinion very freely to Lord Hood, that not to attack our enemy I should consider as a national disgrace. An artillery officer of great merit, Lieutenant Duncan, I requested his lordship would ask the general to permit to come to me. He came with Mr. de Butts, a young engineer. They agreed with me in opinion the place might be attacked, probably with success. Lord Hood sent for me to Fiorenzo to concert measures. The general has refused us a single soldier, and scarcely any stores. We have only about 700 men to land, troops who are embarked to serve as marines, whilst the general has 1,300 troops and artillery &c. to defend S. Fiorenzo. I am to command the seamen landed from the fleet. I feel for the honour of my country, and had rather be beat than not make the attack. If we do not try we never can be successful. I own I have no fears for the final issue; it will be conquest, certain we will deserve it.

[1] He was succeeded by Brigadier-General Abraham d'Aubant. Compare *Life and Letters of Sir Gilbert Elliot*, first Earl of Minto, vol. ii. p. 232.
[2] Adjutant-General to the Forces; afterwards Earl of Rosslyn.

The Romney, with Lieutenant Duncan on board, was therefore sent to Naples, to endeavour to procure there the necessary mortars, shells, and artillery stores; and Sir William Hamilton was requested to use his influence, so that they might be sent, and with the utmost expedition.

3 *April.*—Landed for the siege of Bastia. Journal.

4 *April.*—10 A.M. the troops—consisting of artillery and gunners 66; of the eleventh regiment 257; of the twenty-fifth 123; of the thirtieth 146; of the sixty-ninth 261; of the marines 218; and of chasseurs 112; total 1,183, and 250 seamen—landed at the tower of Miomo, three miles to the northward of Bastia, under the command of Lieutenant-Colonel Villettes, and Captain Horatio Nelson, who had under him Captains Hunt, Serocold, and Bullen.

What my situation is, is not to be described. I am everything, yet nothing ostensible; enjoying the confidence of Lord Hood and Colonel Villettes, and the captains landed with the seamen obeying my orders. We have been landed two days complete; are within 700 yards of the outworks, and 1,800 of the citadel. Our battery will open in about two days, of eight twenty-four pounders and eight mortars. I have little doubt of our success; and if we do, what a disgrace to the Fiorenzo wise-heads: if we do not, it can only be owing to their neglect in not attacking the place with us. Wm. Suckling, 6 April. Camp near Bastia.

We are here with a force not equal to our wishes or wants, and with only half of what is at present in this island. General d'Aubant will not attack our enemy, with two thousand as fine troops as ever marched, whilst we are here beating them from post to post with one thousand. . . . The island, however, is to belong to England; reinforcements are expected, and our generals will, I am sure, be ordered to act. My ship lies on the north side of the town, with some frigates, and Lord Hood is on the south side. It is very hard service for my poor seamen, dragging guns up such heights as are scarcely credible. Mrs. Nelson, 22 April.

Your lordship knows exactly the situation I am in here. With Colonel Villettes I have no reason but to suppose I am respected in the highest degree; nor have I occasion to complain of want of attention to my wishes for the good of the service from any parties; but yet I am considered as not commanding the seamen landed. My wishes may be, and are, complied with; my orders would possibly be disregarded: therefore, if we move from hence, I would wish your lordship to settle that point. Your lordship will not, I trust, take this request amiss: I have been struggling with it since the first day I landed. Lord Hood, 24 April.

I am happy that my ideas of the situation I am in here so per- 25 April.

fectly agree with your lordship's. . . . I don't complain of anyone, but an idea has entered into the heads of some under him, that Captain Hunt's command was absolutely distinct from me; and that I had no authority whatever over him, except as a request. It was even doubted whether I had a right to command the officers and seamen landed from the Agamemnon—that word, 'attached to the batteries,' was wrested to a meaning very different from your lordship's thoughts. . . . When your lordship may judge it proper, I will thank you for an order to command the seamen without any distinction as to any particular services.

The conduct of Brigadier-General d'Aubant is so extraordinary that anything he possesses[1] appears not sufficient to atone for such an expression as 'will not entangle himself in any co-operation.'

Mrs. Nelson, 1–4 May.

Recollect that a brave man dies but once, a coward all his life long. We cannot escape death; and should it happen to me in this place, remember, it is the will of Him, in whose hands are the issues of life and death. As to my health, it was never better, seldom so well. I have no fears about the final issue of the expedition—it will be victory, Bastia will be ours; and if so, it must prove an event to which the history of England can hardly boast an equal. Time will show the enemy's force; if it is small, the Fiorenzo commanders ought to be blamed; if it is large, they are highly culpable, for allowing a handful of brave men to be on service unsupported. My only fears are, that these soldiers will advance when Bastia is about to surrender, and deprive us of part of our glory.

Bastia is a beautiful place, and the environs delightful, with the most romantic views I ever beheld. . . . I will tell you as a secret, [it] will be ours between the 20th and 24th of this month, if succours do not get in. Our ships are moored across the harbour's mouth, and three boats from each ship row guard every night.

Negotiations were, in fact, opened on the 19th, and the garrison capitulated on the 21st. Lord Hood, in his official letter of 24 May, after relating the circumstances, wrote:

'I am unable to give due praise to the unremitting zeal, exertion, and judicious conduct of Lieutenant-Colonel Villettes, who had the honour of commanding his Majesty's troops: never was either more conspicuous. Major Brereton and every officer and soldier under the lieutenant-colonel's orders are justly entitled to my warmest acknowledgments; their persevering ardour and desire to distinguish themselves cannot be too highly spoken of, and which it will be my pride to remember to the latest period of my life.

'Captain Nelson, of his Majesty's ship Agamemnon, who had the

[1] Nelson wrote originally: 'that anything he possesses, even his life, appears not,' &c.

command and directions of the seamen in landing the guns, mortars, and stores, and Captain Hunt, who commanded at the batteries very ably assisted by Captain Buller and Captain Serocold, and the Lieutenants Gore, Hotham, Stiles, Andrews, and Brisbane, have an equal claim to my gratitude, as the seamen under their management worked the guns with great judgment and alacrity. Never was an higher spirit or greater perseverance exhibited, and I am happy to say that no other contention was at any time known than who should be most forward and indefatigable for promoting his Majesty's service; for although the difficulties they had to struggle with were many and various, the perfect harmony and good humour that universally prevailed throughout the siege overcame them all. Captain Hunt, who was on shore in the command of the batteries, from the hour the troops landed to the surrender of the town, will be the bearer of this despatch, and can give any further information you may wish to know respecting the siege.'

When the despatch came back to the fleet in the 'Gazette,' Nelson considered that his services were slightingly mentioned, and that Captain Hunt's were magnified at his expense. The last paragraph, especially, gave him great offence, and he expressed himself with a bitterness of which the next letter is a sample.

Lord Hood and myself were never better friends; nor, although his letter does, did he wish to put me where I never was—in the rear. Captain Hunt, who lost his ship, he wanted to push forward for another—a young man who never was on a battery, or ever rendered any service during the siege: if any person ever says he did, then I submit to the character of a story-teller. Poor Serocold, who fell here, was determined to publish an advertisement, as he commanded a battery under my orders. The whole operations of the siege were carried on through Lord Hood's letters to me. I was the mover of it—I was the cause of its success. Sir Gilbert Elliot will be my evidence, if any is required. I am not a little vexed, but shall not quarrel. We shall be successful here; and a stranger and a landsman will probably do me that credit which a friend and brother officer has not given me.

Wm. Suckling, 16 July. Camp, Calvi.

This was, however, long afterwards. At the time he was quite satisfied with Lord Hood's official thanks addressed to him and to the officers and seamen, through him. This form shows clearly enough that Nelson was, as he claimed to be, the commanding officer; though it suited Hood to push Hunt into prominent notice.

All has been done by seamen, and troops embarked to serve as marines, except a few artillery under the orders of Lord Hood, who has given in this instance a most astonishing proof of the vigour of his mind, and of his zeal and judgment. His thanks to the seamen probably will find its way into the newspapers: they are as handsome as can be penned. Four thousand five hundred men have laid down their arms to under 1,200 troops and seamen: it is such

Rev. W. Nelson, 30 May. Bastia.

an event as is hardly on record. Seventy-seven pieces of ordnance, with an incredible quantity of stores, are taken, with a man-of-war of 22 guns. The Fortunée was destroyed at Fiorenzo, the Minerva taken, La Flêche here; therefore three out of four of my antagonists are gone. The Melpomene is at Calvi, and will, I hope, fall into our hands with Mignonne, a small frigate. Thus I shall still have the satisfaction of seeing this squadron taken, which could not have happened had they not fallen in with me. They were bound to Nice, but Melpomene being so much damaged, they were obliged to put into Corsica. I have now on board two captains of the frigates, twenty officers, and 300 seamen. All join in our praise, but they accuse each other: the officers saying the crew would not fight; the people abuse their officers, and both parties join in abusing the commodore, captain of Fortunée, for not coming down to us, when we were crippled. I don't think they are the men who would have taken Agamemnon, but they behaved shamefully in not trying.

Sir Gil. Elliot,[1] 12 June. Bastia.

[At 9.30 A.M. on 9 June, the Dido] was seen to the westward, with the signal flying for the enemy's fleet to the westward. Lord Hood instantly made the signal for a general chase. When the frigate joined, Sir Charles Hamilton acquainted his lordship that he left the French fleet at eight o'clock at night on the 8th, twelve leagues off the island of Santa Margarita, laying to with their heads off shore. Lord Hood then made the signal for to chase NW, which we did, till dark, when the fleet was collected round the Victory, she carrying all her plain sails during the night, and having frigates in every direction. At noon, on the 10th, being nearly on the station where the enemy was seen, and in sight of the French coast, Lord Hood thought fit to order Agamemnon to Bastia, to convoy the troops to Mortella Bay, and to get everything in readiness to land them at Calvi at a moment's notice. . . . I lost sight of the Victory at half-past five o'clock on Tuesday afternoon, with thirteen sail of the line and several frigates standing with an easy sail in-shore . . . . The enemy are nine sail of the line and seven other vessels. If Lord Hood can get hold of these gentry, he will give a most glorious account of them I am certain.

Lord Hood, 19 June. Calvi.

On my arrival in Mortella Bay, on the 15th instant, General Stuart was anxious to proceed on our expedition against Calvi, in which I own I most heartily concurred with him, believing ourselves

---

[1] Sir Gilbert Elliot, afterwards Lord Minto; at this time Commissary Plenipotentiary in Corsica, and afterwards Viceroy.

safe under your lordship's wing. I sailed on the 16th, in the evening from Mortella Bay, and anchored here on the 17th, at night. Yesterday was taken up in looking at the enemy, and this morning at daylight, the troops, 1,450, were landed, together with seventy volunteers from the transports, thirty men which I took out of the Inflexible, and one hundred seamen from the Agamemnon.

Lord Hood, 21 June. Camp.

Our landing-place is very bad; the rocks break in this weather so far from the shore, and the mountain we have to drag the guns up so long and so steep, that the whole of yesterday we were only able to get one gun up, and then we have one mile and a half at least to drag them. I hope before long we shall be able to land some to the eastward of Cape Revellata; but it being within half gun-shot of the enemy, it cannot at present be done. Your lordship so well knows our want of seamen here, that I am sure I need not mention it: we shall have more than forty pieces of ordnance to drag over these mountains: my numbers are two hundred, barely sufficient to move a twenty-four pounder.

Journal, 27 June.

Got up two ten-inch howitzers, and were employed all the day in carrying the heavy guns and carriages about three-quarters of a mile forward, during a constant rain. Throughout the whole time a gale of wind cut off all intercourse with the ships. At one o'clock in the afternoon, the French came out, and made an attempt to turn both flanks of the Corsicans. A gunboat also came out to support their rear, and the enemy advanced under cover of a heavy cannonade. Our light corps were under arms to support the Corsicans if necessary, and the seamen got down two field-pieces and fired at the gunboat, which instantly rowed away. The enemy rather forced our Corsicans to fall back, on which I went with General Stuart to them: they kept up a smart firing of musketry, and regained their post. Colonel Sabbatini, their commandant, was killed, with two or three others, and five or six were wounded. The enemy retired to their works about four o'clock.

Lord Hood, 5 July. Camp.

It was the general's intention, as he told me yesterday, to make a feint of attacking Monachesco, which of course would draw off the attention of the enemy from our people making the battery. From some cause it was eleven o'clock before the battery could be begun; and before twelve, from the impossibility of completing it and getting the guns into it before daylight, every bag and cask was obliged to be carried back again. The failure of any plan must be distressing to him: I am sure I feel it. Wherever it lays, it does not rest with us. We were at our posts one hour before any creature made their appearance. I think, from what

F

the general told me last night, our battery will not be begun this night. A happy degree of irregularity, I can't help thinking, is sometimes better than all this regularity. . . .

Journal.

Throughout the whole of 8 July, both sides had kept up a constant and heavy fire. They totally destroyed two of our twenty-four-pounders, greatly damaged a twenty-six-pounder, and shook our works very much. One of their shells burst in the centre of our battery, amongst the general, myself, and at least one hundred persons, and blew up our battery magazine, but, wonderful to say, not a man was much hurt. We, on our part, did considerable damage to the Mozelle and Fountain battery; but when any of their guns were disabled, they had others to supply their place. At night we repaired our works, and got two of the Agamemnon's eighteen-pounders to replace the twenty-four-pounder.

By ten o'clock on the 9th, we had evidently the superiority of fire, and before night had dismounted every gun in the Fountain battery and Mozelle, which bore upon us; but the guns in Saint Francesco annoyed us considerably, being so much on our left flank, and at so great a distance, that we could not get our guns to bear on it with any effect. In the night we mounted the howitzer of ten inches, 150 yards in the rear, and a little to the left of our battery, both of which fired on the enemy every three minutes during the night to prevent their working. Hallowell and myself each take twenty-four hours at the advanced battery.

On the 10th at daylight, we opened our fire on the Mozelle, and occasionally a gun on the Fountain battery, and found that the enemy had not done any work in that battery during the night, everything being exactly in the same state. At the Mozelle they had placed great numbers of sand-bags, to prevent our shot from striking under the arches of the bomb-proof of the cavaliere, which we did yesterday by beating down the merlins of the lower work. By seven o'clock in the morning the sand-bags were mostly beat down, and our fire went on without any opposition. By the evening, the Mozelle was much shaken, and I am sure a breach may be made practicable whenever the general thinks it right to turn his attention to it.

At daylight on the 12th, the enemy opened a heavy fire from the town and San Francesco, which, in an extraordinary manner, seldom missed our battery; and at seven o'clock I was much bruised in the face and eyes, by sand from the works struck by shot. The Mozelle was by this time much breached. At night replaced the guns destroyed, and fired a gun and mortar every three minutes.

Lord Hood, 13 July. — My eye is better, and I hope not entirely to lose the sight. I shall be able to attend my duty this evening if a new battery is to be erected. Hallowell, who is a worthy good man, and myself, feel ourselves fully equal to whatever duty can be performed by our seamen landed: should we want assistance I will acquaint your lordship.

Lord Hood, 16 July. — I have the pleasure to say the breaches, for there are two, are much enlarged this day, and the general has told me, in confidence, his plan for to-morrow night, when success will attend us, I have little doubt. The enemy, by their mode of firing this day, are aware of our intentions, for they have tried the range of the different grounds we are to possess. I don't think it is always necessary to summons a place before an attack, nor that it precludes the besieged from honourable terms. I have served as commanding sea-officer on shore, when we attacked, and the besieged, when they thought proper, sent out a flag of truce. At this place, if they had been aware of our getting so near them in the first position we could not have done it, the ground is so very unfavourable.

To this Lord Hood replied on the next day, 17 July:

'I perfectly agree with you that a town not being summoned does not preclude the inhabitants from honourable terms, but according to the rules of war generally practised, a summons is sent, as it gives a fair opening to the besieged, if they are actuated by the same principles, that of sparing the effusion of blood, after security is offered to persons and property. At the same time, in critical situations there may be objections to it, and I was convinced they existed in the first instance, but I am doubtful whether they do so now. However, I shall say not another word upon the subject, although the rapidity with which the French are getting on at Toulon makes it indispensably necessary for me to put the whole of the fleet under my command in the best possible state for service; and I must soon apply to the general for those parts of the regiments now on shore, ordered by his Majesty to serve in lieu of marines, to be held in readiness to embark at the shortest notice. I shall delay the application as long as possible, and I am now sending L'Aigle to look into Toulon. I write this in confidence.'

Lord Hood 18 July. — When I wrote your lordship last I had no idea I could have wrote again until the Mozelle was carried; but such things are. I hope to God the general, who seems a good officer and an amiable man, is not led away; but Colonel Moore is his great friend.

Yesterday, at noon, I found all was given up as last night, that things might be got forward for the grand battery against the town. In the evening the general took me aside to say I had got him nearly into a scrape, for that I had wrote your lordship that the Mozelle was to be stormed as this night, for that a Corsican colonel (I think) had landed from the Victory, and been to him to offer his services, and that he was told on board the Victory what was to happen. I told the general that I certainly had wrote so to you, but I was sure it went no further; and that as to the storming, everybody these three days past had fixed each night for the storm. There seems a little jealousy of my communicating with you daily; and I rather think the question to me last evening was to know if I told you anything. We must go on, let Moore say what he pleases.

Lord Hood immediately replied:
'I thank you for your letter, and desire to have a daily account how things go on. I most earnestly entreat you will give no opinion unless asked, what is right or not right to be done; but whatever that may be, keep it to yourself, and be totally silent to everyone, except in forwarding all proposed operations. Have no jealousies, I beg of you, and avoid giving any most carefully. I have not seen a Corsican officer to have any conversation with respecting Calvi. Colunna was here three days ago with some gentlemen and ladies, from Algajola, and this morning Tartarelli came on board, just to make his bow, and was not with me five minutes, and I said not a word to either about the siege, and I do entreat you will not suggest the least hint to any person whatever about the summons to the garrison. The utmost caution is necessary in you to be silent: say so to Hallowell, or you will both get into a difficulty. You must, I am sure, see the force of what I say, as you cannot be insensible, from what you have said, that there is some of Saint Fiorenzo leaven existing. A word to the wise is sufficient. If you do not bring yourself into a scrape by talking, you may depend upon it, I shall not do it, as I shall know nothing to the general of what you have ever written to me; but beware of the colonel you mention.'

Lord Hood, 20 July.

What seems wanting is more seamen, a number sufficient to make the battery, and to drag the guns without any help, with all the supplies for those guns. The army are harassed to death, and the enemy have, it seems, 2,000 men in arms at Calvi, therefore the general wants from your lordship to make our number 500 working men. From various causes we are not more than 220 working men, and after 120 men are deducted for the present battery, we have not more than 100 working men.

The general is going to send to Bastia for 300 troops to assist the army in the land duty which they now have. Gunpowder is wanted, as also shot in such quantities as I fear it is out of your lordship's power to supply, for we have no chance of success but by battering a breach, which without more ammunition could not be done ; and it was come to the point either to go on or give it up. I told the general that I was sure that if you had the means of supplying his wants I was certain he would have them ; but I believed neither shot nor powder was to be got from the ships. The general then said, as San Francesco was destroyed, why could not ships be laid against the walls ? I took the liberty of observing that the business of laying wood before walls was much altered of late : and that even if they had no hot shot, which I believe they had, that the quantity of powder and shot which would be fired away on such an attack could be much better directed from a battery on shore. All our conversation was with the greatest politeness, and he thanked me for my assistance ; but it was necessary to come to the point whether the siege should be persevered in or given up. If the former, he must be supplied with the means, which were more troops, more seamen to work, and more ammunition.

We will fag ourselves to death, before any blame shall lie at our doors ; and I trust it will not be forgotten, that twenty-five pieces of heavy ordnance have been dragged to the different batteries and mounted, and all, but three at the Royal Louis battery, have been fought by seamen, except one artilleryman to point the guns, and, at first, an additional gunner to stop the vent ; but, as I did not choose to trust a seaman's arms to any but seamen, he was withdrawn : all the mortars have also been worked by seamen : every man landed is actually half barefooted. I am far from well ; but not so ill as to be confined. My eye is troublesome, and I don't think I shall ever have the perfect sight of it again. In one week at farthest after our batteries are open, I think Calvi will be ours. *22 July.*

You will probably have heard that flags of truce have been passing between us and the garrison. What the basis is I am not exactly in a situation to be made acquainted with ; but if I am not mistaken, it is for a suspension of hostilities for a certain time, when, if no succours arrived, then to enter into a capitulation. . . . We have much more to dread from the climate than from the fire of the enemy ; I would not give them one hour's truce. They know their climate, that it is an enemy we can never conquer ; for if the siege is prolonged one week more, half this army will be sick. *Sir G. Elliot, 30 July.*

All we have to guard against is unnecessary delay : the climate is the only enemy we have to fear ; that we can never conquer. The garrison knew it, and wished to make use of their knowledge *Lord Hood, 31 July.*

Our fire has had all the effect which could be hoped for. Except one general discharge, and a gun now and then still at us, we have had no opposition. Every creature (very few excepted) of the troops are in the lower town, which we are to respect, it being full of black flags. Far be it from me to cast a reflection on the general's humanity; I admire it; but there are times, and I think the present is one, when it would be more charitable to our troops to make the enemy suffer more, than for our brave fellows to die every hour, four or five of a day. Why might not the general send notice, that they must remove from the lower town all their sick to the upper town, for that it might be a necessary measure to destroy it? In that case, they would be so crowded, the casements being filled with sick, that a few hours must make them submit to any terms. We cannot fire at the small craft which lay under the walls, for the lower town, and these vessels I dare say are filled with people or troops.

The general is very unwell, not able to remain here last night. I have not heard of him this morning. This is my ague day, but I hope this active scene will keep off the fit. It has shook me a good deal; but I have been used to them, and don't mind them much. Lieutenant Byron, heir to the title of Lord Byron, was killed yesterday afternoon.

The men at this time suffered much from the heat; more especially those exposed to the sun in the batteries.

Lord Hood, 5 August.

I do not find the strong winds have lessened our sick. We now only keep half our seamen at the batteries, yet we have seventy sick on shore, and I sent thirty to the Agamemnon yesterday. The troops are worse than ourselves by far.

On 10 August, Calvi surrendered, and with the town the English obtained possession of the two frigates Melpomene and Mignonne.

Duke of Clarence, 10 Aug.

The climate here, from July to October, is most unfavourable for military operations. It is now what we call the dog-days, here it is termed the lion sun; no person can endure it: we have upwards of one thousand sick out of two thousand, and the others not much better than so many phantoms. We have lost many men from the season, very few from the enemy. I am here the reed amongst the oaks: all the prevailing disorders have attacked me, but I have not strength for them to fasten upon: I bow before the storm, whilst the sturdy oak is laid low. One plan I pursue, never to employ a doctor; nature does all for me, and Providence protects me. Always happy, if my humble but hearty endeavours can serve my king and country.

The French fleet are still in Golfe Jouan, and so securely moored, that it is said we cannot get at them with our ships. They are guarded as much as possible from fire-ships by a line of frigates outside the large ships, and a line of gunboats outside them, and at night a line of launches; the whole is protected by very formidable batteries. When they came out of Toulon, by some mistake, they were represented to Admiral Hotham as nine sail of the line, whereas time has shown they were only seven; which induced a most gallant officer to bear up for Calvi, and there he intended to fight them, sooner than they should throw in succours: had he known they were only an equal force, I am sure he would have given a good account of them.

I left Calvi on the 15th, and hope never to be in it again. I was yesterday in S. Fiorenzo, and to-day shall be safe moored, I expect, in Leghorn; since the ship has been commissioned, this will be the first resting-time we have had. As it is all past, I may now tell you, that on 10 July, a shot having hit our battery, the splinters and stones from it struck me with great violence in the face and breast. Although the blow was so severe as to occasion a great flow of blood from my head, yet I most fortunately escaped, having only my right eye nearly deprived of its sight; it was cut down, but is so far recovered as for me to be able to distinguish light from darkness. As to all the purposes of use, it is gone; however, the blemish is nothing, not to be perceived, unless told. The pupil is nearly the size of the blue part, I don't know the name. At Bastia, I got a sharp cut in the back. You must not think that my hurts confined me: no, nothing but the loss of a limb would have kept me from my duty, and I believe my exertions conduced to preserve me in this general mortality. *Mrs. Nelson, 18 August. Off Leghorn.*

When Lord Hood quits this station, I should be truly sorry to remain; he is the greatest sea-officer I ever knew; and what can be said against him, I cannot conceive; it must only be envy, and it is better to be envied than pitied. But this comes from the army, who have also poisoned some few of our minds. The taking of Bastia, contrary to all military judgment, is such an attack on them that it is never to be forgiven. *12 Sept.*

Lord Hood is inclined to take me home with him, and turn us into a good seventy-four; for although I have been offered every seventy-four which has fallen vacant in this country, yet I could not bring myself to part with a ship's company with whom I have *Wm. Suckling, 20 Sept. Genoa.*

gone through such a series of hard service as has never before, I believe, fallen to the lot of any one ship.

We are sent here to keep peace and harmony with Genoa; and I believe none has been injured by the blockade but ourselves; for I am assured here it never was felt; for all ships which did not escape the vigilance of our cruisers, went into the neighbouring ports, and small vessels carried their cargoes along shore, the underwriters paying the expenses.

<small>Mrs. Nelson, 3 Oct. Off Golfe Jouan.</small>

Lord Hood is gone to Leghorn to receive his despatches by a messenger, who is arrived from England, and most probably we shall only see him to take leave. Admiral Hotham will be commander-in-chief; and with new men, new measures are generally adopted, therefore I can at present say nothing about myself, except that I am in most perfect health. We have here eleven sail of the line, the enemy have fourteen; seven here and seven at Toulon. They will probably before the winter is over effect a junction, when our fleet will be kept together; but whenever they choose to give us a meeting, the event I have no doubt will be such as every Englishman has a right to expect.

<small>12 Oct.</small>

Lord Hood left us yesterday: therefore our hopes of my going home at present are at an end: however, we must not repine: at all events I shall cheat the winter, and, as I understand I am to have a cruise, it may possibly be advantageous. Lord Hood is very well inclined towards me; but the service must ever supersede all private consideration.

<small>Capt. Locker, 10 Oct. Off Golfe Jouan.</small>

The French ships in the bay are so fortified, that we cannot get at them without a certainty of the destruction of our own fleet. At Toulon, six sail of the line are ready for sea in the outer road, and two nearly so in the arsenal. When Victory is gone we shall be thirteen sail of the line, when the enemy will keep our new commanding officer in hot water (Hotham), who missed, unfortunately, the opportunity of fighting them, last June.

<small>Rev. W. Nelson, 26 Oct. Leghorn.</small>

The enemy have a fleet, in point of number, superior to ours, we having only fourteen sail of the line. The junction of the two squadrons off Golfe Jouan and Toulon may be made whenever they please, for in the winter we cannot blockade them. What object they may have in view no one can tell, but if it is Italy, no action will take place here before February, for before their army can risk being cut off, there must be a sea action to force us into port; when, if we are not completely victorious—I mean, able to remain at sea whilst the enemy must retire into port—if we only make a Lord Howe's victory, take a part, and retire into port, Italy is lost.

Matters are fast drawing to a crisis in this country. Our transports, which have been detained at Toulon, since they carried over the garrison of Calvi, were liberated on 20 November; their sails, which had been taken from them, being sent on board, and sixteen hours allowed them to depart. Not a man was allowed to go on shore during their stay, and the answers of Jean Bon St. André were insolent in the highest degree to modest and proper requests. He sent a message to Lord Hood, not knowing of his departure, that, if he sent any more flags to the port of the mountain, he would burn the vessels. They have fifteen sail of the line ready for sea, with which they say they will fight our fleet. Now, as Admiral Hotham is gone off Toulon with thirteen sail of the line, they may if they please. I am, as you will believe, uneasy enough, for fear they will fight, and Agamemnon not present—it will almost break my heart; but I hope the best—that they are only boasting at present, and will be quiet till I am ready.

Wm. Suckling, 28 Nov. Leghorn.

This letter is on the subject of our Bastia and Calvi prize-money. What I have got at present is nothing: what I have lost is, an eye, 300*l*., and my health; with the satisfaction of my ship's company being completely ruined: so much for debtor and creditor. It is absolutely necessary you should know how the prize-money is to be distributed. It may be necessary, and I think must be finally determined by the king in council. Shall those who were present at the commencement, those who only came time enough to see the enemy's flags struck, share equal to us who bore the burden of the day? It must be considered as very different to sharing prize-money at sea. There the object, if resistance was made, could be assisted: with us it was quite different. Far be it from me to be illiberal. Those ships who rowed guard the whole time, as Victory, Princess Royal, and Fortitude, and Agamemnon, are the only ships who remained the whole siege; Gorgon, great part: L'Imperieuse, certain; and Fox cutter. How the others are to be discriminated, I cannot say. I think you ought to get the opinion of two good counsel, and from their opinion you may form some judgment what may be necessary to be done.

J. McArthur, 28 Nov. Leghorn.

The fleet goes to sea on the 22nd or 23rd, thirteen sail of the line. The French have fifteen in the outer road of Toulon, and fifty sail of large transports ready at Marseilles; therefore it is certain they have some expedition just ready to take place, and I have no doubt but Spezia is their object. We expect soon to be joined by some Neapolitan ships and frigates: I have no

Duke of Clarence, 19 Jan. 1795. S. Fiorenzo.

idea we shall get much good from them: they are not seamen, and cannot keep the sea beyond a passage.

Wm. Suckling, 7 Feb. S. Fiorenzo.

This day twelvemonth saw the British troops land at this place, for the purpose of turning the French out of the island; and the more I see of its produce, and convenient ports for our fleets, the more I am satisfied of Lord Hood's great wisdom in getting possession of it; for had his lordship not come forward with a bold plan, all our trade and political consequence would have been lost in Italy: for, after the evacuation of Toulon, to what place were we to look for shelter for our fleet, and the numerous attendants of victuallers, store-ships, and transports? Genoa was inimical to us, and, by treaty, only five sail of the line could enter her ports at the same time. If we look at Tuscany, she was little better than forced to declare for us, and ever since wishing to get her neutrality again. . . . All our trade, and of our allies, to Italy, must pass close to Corsica: the enemy would have had the ports of this island full of row-galleys; and, from the great calms near the land, our ships of war could not have protected the trade—they can always be taken under your eye: the Spanish ports and Neapolitan are so distant from the scene of war that they could not have been used, even would the dons have made us welcome, which I doubt. The loss to the French has been great indeed; all the ships built at Toulon have their sides, beams, decks, and straight timbers from this island. The pine of this island is of the finest texture I ever saw; and the tar, pitch, and hemp, although I believe the former not equal to Norway, yet were very much used in the yard at Toulon. So much for the benefit of it to us during the war; and, in peace, I see no reason but it may be as beneficial to England as any other part of the king's dominions.

Mrs. Nelson. 25 Feb. Leghorn.

We arrived here last night after a very bad cruise. This country, I understand, will in a very few days declare its neutrality; therefore, as all powers give up the contest, for what has England to fight? I wish most heartily we had peace, or that all our troops were drawn from the continent, and only a naval war carried on, the war where England can alone make a figure.

TRANSACTIONS ON BOARD HIS MAJESTY'S SHIP AGAMEMNON, AND OF THE FLEET, AS SEEN AND KNOWN BY CAPTAIN NELSON.

Sunday, 8 *March.*—At 5 P.M. the Mozelle [frigate] made the signal for a fleet to the westward. The admiral made the signal to unmoor, and to prepare to weigh after dark.

9 *March.*—5 A.M. the signal to weigh, the wind blowing a fine

breeze from the eastward. At 8, every ship was without the Melora. . . . At 5.30 P.M. the Meleager made the signal for the enemy's fleet, eighteen sail. At 8, the admiral made the signal that the enemy's fleet were supposed to be near.

10 *March.*—10 A.M. the Mozelle made the signal for a fleet, twenty-five sail, in the NW: signal for a general chase in that quarter. At 5.30 P.M. the Mozelle made the signal that the enemy were upon a wind on the starboard tack. At 6, signal to form in two divisions. Stood to the northward till midnight, when the admiral made the signal to form in the order of battle.

11 *March.*—At daylight nothing in sight. . . . In the afternoon saw a French brig to the westward making signals.

12 *March.*—At daylight our fleet much scattered. At 6 A.M. Princess Royal made the signal for the enemy's fleet, south. We endeavoured to join the Princess Royal, which we accomplished at 9. Light airs, southerly: the enemy's fleet nearing us very fast, our fleet nearly becalmed. At 9.15, Admiral Goodall [in Princess Royal] made the signal for the ships near to form ahead and astern of him, as most convenient: Admiral Hotham [in Britannia] made the same signal. Our ships endeavouring to form a junction; the enemy pointing to separate us, but under a very easy sail. They did not appear to me to act like officers who knew anything of their profession. At noon, they began to form a line on the larboard tack, which they never accomplished. At 2 P.M. they bore down in a line ahead, nearly before the wind, but not more than nine sail formed. They then hauled the wind on the larboard tack; about three miles from us, the wind southerly, Genoa lighthouse NNE about five leagues; saw the town very plain. At 3.15 P.M. joined Admiral Hotham, who made the signal to prepare for battle; the body of the enemy's fleet about three or four miles distant. At 4.6, signal to form the order of battle on the larboard tack: 4.30, signal for each ship to carry a light during the night. At 5.16, signal for each ship to take suitable stations for their mutual support, and to engage the enemy as they came up. Our fleet at this time was tolerably well formed, and with a fine breeze, easterly; which, had it lasted half an hour, would certainly have led us through the enemy's fleet, about four ships from the van ship, which was separated from the centre about one mile. At 5.45, the fleet hoisted their colours. At dark, the wind came fresh from the westward. At 6.55, the signal to wear together. A fresh breeze all night: stood to the southward all night, as did the enemy.

13 *March.*—At daylight, the enemy's fleet in the SW, about

three or four leagues with fresh breezes. Signal for a general chase. At 8 A.M. a French ship of the line carried away her main and fore topmasts. At 9.15, the Inconstant frigate fired at the disabled ship, but receiving many shot, was obliged to leave her. At 10 A.M. tacked and stood towards the disabled ship, and two other ships of the line. The disabled ship proved to be the Ça Ira of 84 guns (36 ... 24 ... 12 prs. French weight), 1,300 men; [the others were the] Sans Culotte, 120 guns; and the Jean Bart, 74 guns. We could have fetched the Sans Culotte, by passing the Ça Ira to windward, but on looking round I saw no ship of the line within several miles to support me; the Captain was the nearest on our lee quarter. I then determined to direct my attention to the Ça Ira, who, at 10.15, was taken in tow by a frigate; the Sans Culotte and Jean Bart keeping about gunshot distance on her weather bow. At 10.20 the Ça Ira began firing her stern chasers. At 10.30 the Inconstant passed us to leeward, standing for the fleet. As we drew up with the enemy, so true did she fire her stern-guns that not a shot missed some part of the ship, and latterly the masts were struck every shot, which obliged me to open our fire a few minutes sooner than I intended, for it was my intention to have touched his stern before a shot was fired. But seeing plainly from the situation of the two fleets, the impossibility of being supported, and in case any accident happened to our masts, the certainty of being severely cut up, I resolved to fire so soon as I thought we had a certainty of hitting. At 11.15 A.M., being within one hundred yards of the Ça Ira's stern, I ordered the helm to be put a-starboard, and the driver and after-sails to be braced up and shivered, and as the ship fell off, gave her our whole broadside, each gun double-shotted. Scarcely a shot appeared to miss. The instant all were fired, braced up our after-yards, put the helm a-port, and stood after her again. This manœuvre we practised till 1 P.M., never allowing the Ça Ira to get a single gun from either side to fire on us. They attempted some of their after-guns, but all went far ahead of us. At this time the Ça Ira was a perfect wreck, her sails hanging in tatters, mizen top-mast, mizen topsail, and cross jack yards shot away. At 1 P.M. the frigate hove in stays, and got the Ça Ira round.

I observed the guns of the Ça Ira to be much elevated, doubtless laid for our rigging and distant shots, and when she opened her fire in passing, the elevation not being altered, almost every shot passed over us, very few striking our hull. The captain of the Ça Ira told Admiral Goodall and myself, that we had killed and wounded one hundred and ten men, and so cut his rigging to pieces that it was impossible for him to get up other topmasts.

As the frigate first, and then the Ça Ira, got their guns to bear, each opened her fire, and we passed within half pistol-shot. As soon as our after-guns ceased to bear, the ship was hove in stays, keeping, as she came round, a constant fire, and the ship was worked with as much exactness as if she had been turning into Spithead. On getting round, I saw the Sans Culotte, who had before wore with many of the enemy's ships, under our lee bow, and standing to pass to leeward of us, under top-gallant sails. At 1.30 P.M. the admiral made the signal for the van-ships to join him. I instantly bore away, and prepared to set all our sails, but the enemy having saved their ship, hauled close to the wind, and opened their fire, but so distant as to do us no harm; not a shot, I believe, hitting. Our sails and rigging were very much cut, and many shot in our hull and between wind and water, but, wonderful, only seven men were wounded. The enemy as they passed our nearest ships opened their fire, but not a shot, that I saw, reached any ship except the Captain, who had a few passed through her sails. Till evening, employed shifting our topsails and splicing our rigging. At dark, in our station: signal for each ship to carry a light. Little wind: south-westerly all night: stood to the westward, as did the enemy.

14 *March*.—At daylight, taken aback with a fine breeze at NW, which gave us the weather-gage, whilst the enemy's fleet kept the southerly gage. Saw the Ça Ira, and a line-of-battle ship, who had her in tow about three and a half miles from us, the body of the enemy's fleet about five miles. 6.15 A.M., signal for the line of battle, SE and NW; 6.40, for the Captain and Bedford to attack the enemy. At 7 A.M., signal for the Bedford to engage close; Bedford's signal repeated for close action. 7.5, for the Captain to engage close. Captain's and Bedford's signals repeated; at this time, the shot from the enemy reached us, but at a great distance. 7.15, signal for the fleet to come to the wind on the larboard tack. This signal threw us and the Princess Royal to the leeward of the Illustrious, Courageux, and Britannia. 7.20, the Britannia hailed, and ordered me to go to the assistance of the Captain and Bedford. Made all sail: Captain lying like a log on the water, all her sails and rigging shot away: Bedford on a wind on the larboard tack. 7.15, signal to annul coming to the wind on the larboard tack. 7.35, signal for the Illustrious and Courageux to make more sail. 7.42, Bedford to wear, Courageux to get in her station. At this time, passed the Captain; hailed Admiral Goodall, and told him Admiral Hotham's orders, and desired to know if I should go ahead of him. Admiral Goodall

desired me to keep close to his stern. The Illustrious and Courageux took their stations ahead of the Princess Royal, the Britannia placed herself astern of me, and Tancredi lay on the Britannia's lee quarter. At 8 A.M. the enemy's fleet began to pass our line to windward, and the Ça Ira and Le Censeur were on our lee side; therefore the Illustrious, Courageux, Princess Royal, and Agamemnon were obliged to fight on both sides of the ship. The enemy's fleet kept the southerly wind, which enabled them to keep their distance, which was very great. From 8 to 10, engaging on both sides. About 8.45, the Illustrious lost her main and mizen masts. 9.15, the Courageux lost her main and mizen masts. At 9.25, the Ça Ira lost all her masts, and fired very little. At 10 Le Censeur lost her main-mast. 10.5, they both struck. Sent Lieutenant George Andrews to board them. By computation the Ça Ira is supposed to have about 350 killed and wounded on both days, and Le Censeur about 250 killed and wounded. From the lightness of the air of wind, the enemy's fleet and our fleet were a very long time in passing, and it was past 1 P.M. before all firing ceased, at which time the enemy crowded all possible sail to the westward, our fleet laying with their heads to south-east and east.

[Official return of English loss: 75 killed, 280 wounded.]

Capt. Locker, 21 March. Spezia.

You will have heard of our brush with the French fleet, a battle it cannot be called, as the enemy would not give us an opportunity of closing with them. . . . Admiral Hotham has had much to contend with, a fleet half manned, and in every respect inferior to the enemy; Italy calling him to her defence; our newly acquired kingdom calling might and main, our reinforcements and convoy hourly expected; and all to be done without a force by any means adequate to it. The French were sent out as for certain conquest; their orders were positive to search out our fleet, and to destroy us. . . . I firmly believe they never would have fought us, had not the Ça Ira lost her topmasts, which enabled the Agamemnon and Inconstant to close in with her, and so cut her up that she could not get a topmast up during the night, which caused our little brush the next day. All the enemy's ships are fitted with forges, and fired from some guns constantly hot shot and shells, but they appear ashamed of their orders, which are positive from the Convention, and find nothing superior to the old mode of fighting. I only [wish] some of their own ships will suffer by having such a furnace in their cockpit, which will end such a diabolical practice.

Fortune in this late affair has favoured me in a most extraordinary manner, by giving me an opportunity which seldom offers of being the only line-of-battle ship who got singly into action on the 13th, when I had the honour of engaging the Ça Ira, absolutely large enough to take Agamemnon in her hold. I never saw such a ship before. [God's providence protected us] in a most wonderful manner; . . . whole broadsides within half-pistol shot missing my little ship, whilst ours was in the fullest effect. . . . Our sails were ribbons, and all our ropes were ends; [but, in the two days, we had only thirteen men slightly wounded]. Had our good admiral have followed the blow, we should probably have done more, but the risk was thought too great. Rev. W. Nelson, 25 March. Spezia.

I am absolutely at this moment in the horrors, fearing, from our idling here, that the active enemy may send out two or three sail of the line and some frigates to intercept our convoy, which is momentarily expected. In short, I wish to be an admiral, and in the command of the English fleet; I should very soon either do much, or be ruined. My disposition cannot bear tame and slow measures. Sure I am, had I commanded our fleet on the 14th, that either the whole French fleet would have graced my triumph, or I should have been in a confounded scrape. I went on board Admiral Hotham as soon as our firing grew slack in the van, and the Ça Ira and Censeur had struck, to propose to him leaving our two crippled ships, the two prizes, and four frigates, to themselves, and to pursue the enemy; but he, much cooler than myself, said, 'We must be contented, we have done very well.' Now, had we taken ten sail, and had allowed the eleventh to escape, when it had been possible to have got at her, I could never have called it well done. Goodall backed me; I got him to write to the admiral, but it would not do: we should have had such a day as, I believe, the annals of England never produced. Mrs. Nelson, 1 April. S. Fiorenzo.

The arrival of a reinforcement from Brest, at Toulon, of six sail of the line, two frigates, and two cutters, has, for the present moment, rather altered the complexion of affairs in this country; but I have no doubt administration has taken care to send us at least an equal number of ships, although unfortunately they are not yet arrived. The enemy have now actually ready to sail from Toulon twenty sail of the line, and two sail of the line are launched, and will be ready in fourteen days from this date. We have ready for sea, and in perfect good order, fourteen sail of the line, five three-deckers, six seventy-fours, and two sixty-fours, English, one seventy-four Neapolitan. The Courageux is sent for Duke of Clarence, 16 April. S. Fiorenzo.

from Leghorn, and will be ready in about three weeks, as will the Censeur, who is to be manned, if necessary, to fight the enemy, superior as they are, out of the frigates; so that we shall be sixteen sail of the line, a force by no means possible for the enemy to injure. [Rénaudin], the late captain of the Vengeur, commands the ships from Brest, and all our prisoners told us of this reinforcement; but it was not thought right to believe them. Should the attempts of the enemy be against this island, I have no doubt but they will fail. . . . I own myself to be rather of opinion that the attempt of the enemy will be against Italy; their fleet to anchor in Talamone Bay, and their troops to land at Orbetello.

24 April. Off Cape Corse.

We sailed a week past from Fiorenzo, and are to call off Minorca, to know what our allies, the Spaniards, intend to do with twenty-one sail of the line, which are lying in Mahon. Contrary winds have kept us here, and every moment we expect the enemy's fleet to heave in sight. We are thirteen English sail of the line, and two Neapolitan seventy-fours, one of which joined this morning, and, I am sorry to say, was matter of exultation to an English fleet: the Courageux is not yet ready to join us. I hope, and believe, if we only get three sail from England, that we shall prevent this fleet of the enemy from doing further service in the Mediterranean, notwithstanding the red-hot shot and combustibles, of which they have had a fair trial, and found them useless. They believed that we should give them no quarter; and it was with some difficulty we found the combustibles, which are fixed in a skeleton like a carcass; they turn into a liquid, and water will not extinguish it. They say the Convention sent them from Paris, but that they did not use any of them, only hot shot.

Rev. W. Nelson, 24 April.

What the new lords of the Admiralty are after, to allow such a reinforcement to get out here, surprises us all. Lord Chatham did better than this sleeping. Nothing this war has ever been half so badly managed as we find the new Admiralty.

Wm. Suckling, 24 April.

We are put to sea, not only as being more honourable, but also as much safer, than skulking in port: nor do I think that our small fleet would be a very easy conquest; but our zeal does not in the least justify the gross neglect of the new Admiralty Board. Lord Chatham was perhaps bad: in this fleet we find, from woeful experience, that this is ten times worse. Our merchants are ruined for want of convoy, which it has never been in our power to grant them. Had not our late action proved more distressing to the enemy than the Admiralty had any right to suppose, we should before this time have been driven out of the Mediterranean. Every moment I expect to see the enemy's fleet; for they must be as badly managed as ourselves, if they do not embrace the present favourable moment for any enterprise they may have in their heads.

Admiral Hotham is very well, but I believe heartily tired of his temporary command; nor do I think he is intended by nature for a commander-in-chief, which requires a man of more active turn of mind. Capt. Locker, 4 May. Leghorn.

Reports of this day say that the French are sailed from Toulon with eighteen or twenty sail of the line: if only the former, we shall be very happy to meet them, and I doubt not of obtaining a complete victory: if the latter we shall come to no harm, but cannot, in the common course of events, expect any success against such a great superiority: fourteen English, and two Neapolitans, is our force. Wm. Suckling, 4 May.

The French have not yet sailed from Toulon, but all ready— twenty-one sail of the line, thirteen frigates. Truly sorry am I that Lord Hood does not command us: he is a great officer; and were he here, we should not now be skulking. 7 June. Off Port Mahon.

We have been cruising off here for a long month, every moment in expectation of reinforcements from England. Our hopes are now entirely dwindled away, and I give up all expectation; then comes accounts of Lord Hood's resignation. Oh, miserable Board of Admiralty! They have forced the first officer in our service away from his command. The late board may have lost a few merchant vessels by their neglect: this board has risked a whole fleet of men-of-war. Great good fortune has hitherto saved us, what none in this fleet could have expected for so long a time. Near two months we have been skulking from them. Had they not got so much cut up on 14 March, Corsica, Rome, and Naples would at this moment have been in their possession, and may yet if these people do not make haste to help us. Rev.W Nelson, 8 June

The changes and politics of ministers and men are so various, that I am brought to believe all are alike; the loaves and fishes are all the look-out. The ins and outs are the same, let them change places. . . . Rev. D. Hoste, 22 June.

We have just got accounts that the French fleet is at sea, twenty-two sail of the line. Sir Sidney Smith did not burn them all—Lord Hood mistook the man: there is an old song, 'Great talkers do the least, we see.' Admiral Hotham is waiting here with twenty English and two Neapolitan ships of the line, for our invaluable convoy of stores, provisions, and troops from Gibraltar. I hope the enemy will not pass us to the westward, and take hold of them. This fleet must regret the loss of Lord Hood, the best officer, take him altogether, that England has to boast of. Lord Howe certainly is a great officer in the management of a fleet, but that is all. Lord Hood is equally great in all situations which an admiral can be placed in. Our present admiral is a worthy good man, but not by any means equal to either Lord Hood or Lord Howe.

<small>Rev. W. Nelson, 22 June.</small>

Admiral Man joined us on the 14th, with six sail of the line, so that we are now twenty sail of the line, English, and two Neapolitans. We have this day accounts of the French fleet's being at sea with twenty-two sail of the line, and innumerable frigates, &c. We are waiting for our valuable convoy from Gibraltar, expected every moment; are totally ignorant which way the enemy's fleet are gone; hope sincerely they will not fall in with our convoy, but our admiral takes things easy. Lord Hood's absence is a great national loss.

<small>Mrs. Nelson, 1 July. S. Fiorenzo.</small>

The French fleet of seventeen sail of the line are out, but only to exercise their men, at least our good admiral says so: however, they may make a dash, and pick up something. We have Zealous, seventy-four, and three ordnance ships expected daily from Gibraltar. I hope they will not look out for them. Two French frigates were for ten days very near us, as we are informed by neutral vessels. I requested the admiral to let me go after them; but he would not part with a ship of the line. When the fleet bore away for this place, he sent two small frigates, Dido and Lowestoft, to look into Toulon; and the day after they parted from us, they fell in with the two frigates.[1] It was a very handsome done thing in the captains, who are Towry and Middleton, and much credit must be due to these officers and their ships' company.

<small>Capt. Locker, 8 July. Off C. Corse.</small>

We are now at sea, looking for the French fleet, which chased myself and two frigates into Fiorenzo, yesterday afternoon. The admiral had sent me, and some frigates, to co-operate with the Austrian general in the Riviera of Genoa; when off Cape delle Mele, I fell in with the enemy, who, expecting to get hold of us, were induced to chase us over, not knowing, I am certain, from their movements, that our fleet was returned into port. The chase lasted twenty-four hours, and, owing to the fickleness of the winds in these seas, at times was hard pressed; but they being neither seamen nor officers, gave us many advantages. Our fleet had the mortification to see me seven hours almost in their possession; the

---

[1] Minerve and Artémise, when the Minerve was captured. A full and exact account of this very brilliant action is given by James.

shore was our great friend, but a calm and swell prevented our fleet from getting out till this morning. The enemy went off yesterday evening, and I fear we shall not overtake them; but in this country no person can say anything about winds. If we have that good fortune, I have no doubt but we shall give a very good account of them, seventeen sail of the line, six frigates; we twenty-three of the line, and as fine a fleet as ever graced the seas.

Yesterday we got sight of the French fleet; our flyers were able to get near them, but not nearer than half-gunshot: had the wind lasted ten minutes longer, the six ships would have each been alongside six of the enemy. Man[1] commanded us, and a good man he is in every sense of the word. I had every expectation of getting Agamemnon close alongside an 80-gun ship, with a flag, or broad pennant; but the west wind first died away, then came east, which gave them the wind, and enabled them to reach their own coast, from which they were not more than eight or nine miles distant. Rowley [in the Cumberland] and myself were just again getting into close action, when the admiral made our signals to call us off; [the wind being directly into the Gulf of Frejus, where the enemy anchored after dark]. The Alcide, 74, struck, but soon afterwards took fire, by a box of combustibles in her fore-top, and she blew up; about two hundred French were saved by our ships. In the morning I was certain of taking their whole fleet, latterly of six sail. I will say no ships could behave better than ours, none worse than the French; but few men are killed, but our sails and rigging are a good deal cut up.

<small>14 July.</small>

Thus has ended our second meeting with these gentry. In the forenoon we had every prospect of taking every ship in the fleet; and at noon, it was almost certain that we should have had the six near ships. The French admiral, I am sure, is not a wise man, nor an officer: he was undetermined whether to fight or to run away: however, I must do him the justice to say, he took the wisest step at last.

<small>Duke of Clarence, 15 July.</small>

On 15 July, 1795, Nelson received from Admiral Hotham the following order:

'You are hereby required, and directed to proceed forthwith, in the ship you command, with the [Meleager, Ariadne, Tarleton, Resolution cutter,] whose captains have my orders to follow your directions off Genoa, where, upon your arrival, you are to confer with Mr. Drake, his Majesty's minister at that place, on such points as may be deemed essential towards your co-operating with General de Vins, the commander-

---

[1] Rear-Admiral Robert Man, with his flag in the Victory.

in-chief of the allied armies in Italy, for the benefit of the common cause against the enemy, carrying the same into execution as expeditiously as possible.'

Fr. Drake,[1] 18 July. Genoa.

I beg to submit to your excellency whether it will not be proper for you to write to Admiral Hotham, stating the absolute necessity of stopping all the trade which may pass between Genoa, France, and places occupied by the armies, and that Ventimiglia must be considered as a place under that description. . . . However, so sensible am I of the necessity of vigorous measures, that if your excellency will tell me that it is for the benefit of his Majesty's service, that I should stop all trade between the neutral towns and France, and places occupied by the armies of France, considering Ventimiglia in that situation, I will give proper directions to the squadron under my command for that purpose.

Adml. Hotham, 22 July. Vado Bay.

I arrived at Genoa on the evening of the 17th, and found there two French frigates and two brigs. I sailed with Mr. Drake from Genoa at daylight on the 20th, and arrived here yesterday morning. I have had a conference with the Austrian general, De Vins, who seemed extremely glad to see us. At present I do not perceive any immediate prospect of their getting on to the westward, it appearing to be the general's opinion, that the enemy must be reduced in their provisions, before the Austrians can make advances; and that for the present, famine is to do more than the sword. . . . The Austrian general having fitted out many privateers, has taken several vessels laden with corn for France; and I trust, with the disposition of the ships under my command, I shall be able to stop all intercourse with France from the eastward. . . .

In respect to Vado Bay, had it not been called a bay, I should never have named it one: it is a bend in the land, and since I have been here, by no means good landing. The water is deep, good clay bottom, and plenty of fresh water; open from E to S. To the east the land is at a great distance; but I think a fleet may ride here for a short time in the summer months.

Mrs. Nelson, 24 July, Vado Bay.

The service I have to perform is important, and, as I informed you a few days ago from Genoa, I am acting, not only without the orders of my commander-in-chief, but in some measure contrary to them. However, I have not only the support of his Majesty's ministers, both at Turin and Genoa, but a consciousness that I am doing what is right and proper for the service of our king and country. Political courage in an officer abroad is as highly necessary as military courage.

[1] Minister at Genoa.

The advanced posts of the Austrian army are at Loano, 12,000 men; the other part is at Vado, 20,000; a finer body of men I never saw, and the general seems inclined to go forward, if England will perform her part, which I hope she will; but the co-operation expected of us is the putting a stop to all supplies going to France; a measure Admiral Hotham may possibly hesitate complying with. Mr. Trevor and Mr. Drake have both wrote to him on the absolute necessity of the measure; in the meantime, in consequence of similar representations, I have directed the squadron under my orders to detain all vessels, to whatever nation they may belong, bound to France, or to any place occupied by the armies of France. This good effect has already resulted from the measure, that the Genoese are alarmed, and will be careful how they send their vessels to an almost certain capture. Insurance is not at present to be had; the capture of a Tuscan vessel or two will stop the Leghorn trade. The only fears that seem to me to strike England, are of the Barbary States; but is England to give up the almost certainty of finishing this war with honour, to the fear of offence to such beings? Forbid it honour and every tie which can bind a great nation. If supplies are kept from France for six weeks, I am told, most probably the Austrian army will be at Nice, which will be a great event for us.

Sir G. Elliot, 27 July. Leghorn.

I have not, I believe, wrote you since our miserable action of the 13th. To say how much we wanted Lord Hood at that time, is to say, will you have all the French fleet or no action? for the scrambling distant fire was a farce; but if one fell by such a fire, what might not have been expected had our whole fleet engaged? Improperly as the part of the fleet which fired got into action, we took one ship: but the subject is unpleasant, and I shall have done with it. I am now co-operating with the Austrian army, under General de Vins, and hope we shall do better there. If the admiral will support the measures I have proposed, I expect, by the middle of September, we shall be in Nice, and of course have the harbour of Villafranca for our squadron. But Hotham has no head for enterprise, perfectly satisfied that each month passes without any losses on our side. I almost, I assure you, wish myself an admiral, with the command of a fleet. Probably, when I grow older, I shall not feel all that alacrity and anxiety for the service which I do at present. . . .

Rev. W. Nelson, 29 July. G. of Genoa.

From the vigorous measures I am taking with the Genoese, I am most unpopular here. I cannot perhaps, with safety, land at Genoa, but half measures will never do when I command. All war or all peace is my idea, and the old Austrian general is entirely of my way of thinking. Hotham is coming to look at us, with the fleet, but the command rests with me; and very probably I shall be ordered to hoist a distinguishing pennant. Do not be surprised if you hear that we are once more in possession of Toulon. Had Lord Hood been here, I have no doubt but we should have been there at this moment.

This stoppage of the French trade at once drew a vehement protest from the Genoese, acting under French influence. Their neutrality, they said, was violated: their ports were blockaded. A great deal of the correspondence at this time refers to these complaints, and the measures which had been adopted.

Fr. Drake, 6 August.

The disposition and acts of my cruisers will soon prove incontestably that Genoa is not blockaded, as all vessels will arrive in perfect security which are not French, or laden with French property. It ever has been customary to endeavour to intercept enemy's vessels coming from neutral ports, and . . . I have been most careful to give no offence to the Genoese territory or flag. Were I to follow the example which the Genoese allow the French, of having some small vessels in the port of Genoa, that I have seen towed out of the port, and board vessels coming in, and afterwards return into the mole, there might then certainly be some reason to say their neutral territory was insulted; but the conduct of the English is very different.

Sir G. Elliot, 13 August. Vado Bay.

I had letters from good Lord Hood: however wrong he might have been in writing so strongly (he allows he has) to the Admiralty, the nation has suffered much by his not coming to this country; for an abler head, or heart more devoted to the service of his country, is not readily to be met with. Admiral Hotham is daily expected here, and my humble plans may be put aside, or carried into execution by other officers, which I should not altogether like; however, I think the admiral will stay here as little while as possible. The strong orders which I judged it proper to give on my first arrival, have had an extraordinary good effect; the French army is now supplied with almost daily bread from Marseilles; not a single boat has passed with corn. The Genoese are angry, but that does not matter.

26 August. Alassio.

To the Commander of the National Corvette.—Sir,—The French having taken possession of the town and coast of Alassio. I cannot but consider it as an enemy's coast; therefore, to prevent destruction to the town, I desire the immediate surrender of your vessel. If you do not comply with my desire, the consequences must be with you and not with Your very humble Servant, HORATIO NELSON.

This corvette of 10 guns, together with a gunboat, two galleys, and eight store ships of small size, were taken possession of or destroyed, without resistance; but thinking that the Genoese might possibly complain of a violation of their neutrality, Nelson wrote privately :

Dear Sir,—As it is perfectly understood by the Genoese republic that the part of the Riviera in the possession of the French army will be considered, whilst they remain in it, as an enemy's country by the allied powers, I thought it much better not to say anything about it in my public letter, for I do not believe there will be any representation from the deed I did yesterday, for not a boat or message came from the town during my stay. On my approach, Genoese colours were hoisted on a small battery of two brass guns, which I laid the Agamemnon within pistol-shot of. The French lined the beach, with their colours at the head of their battalions, but humanity to the poor inhabitants would not allow me to fire on them. The same motives induced me to summons the corvette to surrender, as our fire must have greatly injured the town. My summons induced the crew to abandon her. Latterly the French cavalry fired so hot on our boats at the west end of the town that I was obliged to order the Meleager to fire a few shot to protect them, and I have reason to believe the enemy suffered some loss.

<small>Adml. Hotham, 27 August.</small>

The Ariadne by the great zeal of Captain Plampin to do much, having already taken the two small galleys, got on shore, but she was got off without any damage; but it retarded our operations a little, and gave the enemy an opportunity of landing more of their cargoes than I intended, by our boats being employed in assisting her. The corvette is the long black polacca ship which kept close alongside the Sans Culotte on 13 July, and outsails us all. The galleys and gunboat I shall sell to the Austrian general, or the King of Sardinia, if he will buy them.

I have only to conclude by saying that Mr. Drake, who I left at Vado, much approved of my expedition.

My dear Coll.—I cannot allow a ship to leave me without a line for my old friend, who I shall rejoice to see; but I am afraid the admiral will not give me that pleasure at present. . . . My command here is so far pleasant as it relieves me from the inactivity of our fleet, which is great indeed, as you will soon see. From the event of Spain making peace, much may be looked for—perhaps

<small>Capt. Collingwood, 31 August. Vado Bay.</small>

a war with that country: if so, their fleet (if no better than when our allies) will soon be done for. Reports here say they mean to protect Genoese and other vessels from search by our cruisers, in the Gulf of Genoa. If so, the matter will soon be brought to issue; for I have given positive directions to search such vessels, denying the right of the Spaniard to dictate to us what ships we shall or shall not search. The Genoese are going, it is said, to carry a convoy with provisions to their towns in the Riviera of Genoa, in possession of the French army. However cruel it may appear to deprive poor innocent people of provisions, yet policy will not allow it [not] to be done; for if the inhabitants have plenty, so will the enemy, and therefore I have directed them to be brought into Vado. So far have I gone; and trust I have acted, and shall act, so as to merit approbation. Our admiral, *entre nous*, has no political courage whatever, and is alarmed at the mention of any strong measure; but, in other respects, he is as good a man as can possibly be.

Mrs. Nelson, 1 Sept. Vado Bay

We have made a small expedition with the squadron, and taken a French corvette and some other vessels, in which affair I lost no men; but since, I have not been so successful. I detached Mr. Andrews to cut off a ship from Oneglia: on his passage, he fell in with three Turkish vessels, as it has since turned out, who killed and wounded seventeen of my poor fellows. Seven are already dead, and more must be lost by the badness of their wounds; and I am sorry to add, that the Turks got into Genoa, with six millions of hard cash: however, they who play at bowls must expect rubs; and the worse success now, the better, I hope, another time. Our fleet is still at Leghorn. Collingwood I hear is arrived in the Excellent, 74, with the convoy from England. I am almost afraid that the campaign in this country will end in a very different manner from what might have been expected; but I will do my best until it finishes.

Sir G. Elliot, 24 Sept. Leghorn.

The news I can tell you is very little. The general seemed to make excuses for his not going on, apparently to me very frivolous, and I am sure it was his intention to have laid part of the blame of the want of success in this campaign to the non-cooperation of the British fleet; and, as it was, he said, impossible to force the enemy's works at St. Esprit, he seemed very much inclined to rest for the winter at Vado. However, to leave him without an excuse on my part, I went down the coast to the westward, as far as Nice, and sounded and examined every port. On my return, I offered to carry five thousand men at one time, and to land them, bag and baggage, with their field-pieces, and to insure their safe convoys of provisions. This would have cut off all supplies for the enemy to the eastward, and they must, in my opinion, have abandoned their stupendous works at St. Esprit. To this paper the general gave me another plan, which he thought would be better; but as this requires a small degree of assistance from Admiral Hotham, it cannot be carried into execution till I hear from the admiral. I only want transports, and if he gave me one 74, I verily believe we shall yet possess Nice. Mr. Drake perhaps tells you how we are obliged to manœuvre about the general; but the politics of courts are so mean, that private people would be ashamed to act in the same way: all is trick and finesse, to which is sacrificed the common cause. The general wants a loophole, but I hope he will not have one; he shall not if I can help it, for I want Villafranca for a good anchorage this winter. From what motives I don't know—I hope, from a good one—the general sent orders to attack the enemy's strongest post at St. Esprit. After an attack of ten hours, it was carried. The general seems pleased, and says, if he can carry one other, the enemy must retire, which would give us the country as far as Oneglia.

As soon as [the French squadron at Genoa] knew of my absence, they made a push, and I fear are all got off. Two of our frigates were seen firing at them; but I have not much expectation of their success. It was a near touch, for I came back the next morning, after they had sailed on the preceding evening. . . . In the opinion of the Genoese, my squadron is constantly offending: so that it almost appears a trial between us, who shall first be tired, they of complaining, or me of answering them. However, my mind is fixed; and nothing they can say will make me alter my conduct towards them.

Mrs. Nelson, 5 Oct. Vado Bay.

My situation with this army has convinced me of the futility of continental alliances. The conduct of the court of Vienna, whatever may be said by the House of Commons to the contrary, is nothing but deception: I am certain, if it appears to that court to be their interest to make peace with France, it will be instantly done. What is Austria better than Prussia? In one respect, Prussia perhaps may be better than Austria: the moment he got our money he finished the farce: Austria, I fear, may induce us to give her more: for to a certainty she will not carry on another campaign without more money. But it appears to me that the continuance or cessation of the war depends entirely on the French nation themselves; it will now be seen whether they are willing to receive and

Wm. Suckling, 27 Oct. Off Marseilles.

join the Count d'Artois and have royalty; or if they oppose him, that they are determined to be a republic. If the first, at this moment of writing all must be nearly finished: if they destroy the emigrants landed at Charente, it is clear the French nation wish to be a republic; and the best thing we can do, is to make the best and quickest peace we can: the landing the emigrants is our last trial; and if that fail, we have done our utmost to place Louis upon the throne. To me, I own, all Frenchmen are alike: I despise them all. They are (even those who are fed by us) false and treacherous: even Louis XVIII. receives our money, and will not follow our advice, and keep up the dignity of the King of France at Verona.

Fr. Drake,
12 Nov.
Vado Bay.

Nothing will be wanting on the part of my squadron to cover the general's flank by sea. . . . Flora and a brig are now cruising off Noli and Pietra; but I fear they may be blown off the coast. The weather is so severe, that either the French or the Austrians must quit the hills; and as some Austrian soldiers have died with the cold on their posts, the enemy cannot be very comfortable. . . .

Reports say, and I believe it is true, that Admiral Hotham has struck his flag and given up the command, as also Admiral Goodall; and that Sir Hyde Parker commands the fleet until Sir John Jervis's arrival. Captain Frederick has hoisted a distinguishing pennant, and commands the third division of the fleet. This cannot, my dear Sir, but make me feel, that I am the first officer commanding a squadron, destined to co-operate with the Austrians and Sardinians, who has been without a distinguishing pennant: most have had a broad pennant, but that I neither expected nor wished for; yet I think, as I have had the pleasure to give satisfaction to our allies, that the ministry, if you thought proper to represent it, would order me a distinguishing pennant from my having this command, or some other mark of their favour.

Nelson was senior, on the post list, to Captain Frederick, and not unnaturally felt hurt at not having been already ordered a distinguishing pennant. He frequently reverts to the subject in his correspondence about this date.

Duke of
Clarence,
18 Nov.
Genoa.

E. Nepean,
13 Nov.

Almost every day produces such changes in the prospect of our affairs, that in relating events I hardly know where to begin. The two armies are both so strongly posted, that neither is willing to give the attack; each waits to see which can endure the cold longest; [at present it is intense, what could not have been expected in this country; without snow, but most intense frosts and northerly winds, blowing hard]. The French general has laid an embargo on all the vessels on the coast, near a hundred sail, and it would not surprise me if he is meditating a retreat, in case his plans do not succeed; which I hope they will not, as the prevention of them in a great measure depends on our naval force under my orders. This has called me here, where a circumstance has arisen, that has given us the alarm sooner than was intended.

<small>Duke of Clarence, 18 Nov.</small>

An Austrian commissary was travelling from Genoa towards Vado, with 10,000*l.* sterling, and it was known he was to sleep at a place called Voltri, about nine miles from Genoa. This temptation was too great for the French captain of the Brune, in concert with the French minister, to keep his word of honour; and the boats of that frigate, with some privateers, went out of the port, landed, and brought back the money. The next day, 11 November, recruiting was publicly carried on in the town of Genoa, and numbers enlisted; and on the 13th at night, as many men as could be collected were to sail under convoy of the Brune, and to land, and take a strong post of the Genoese, between Genoa and Savona. A hundred men were to have been sent from the French army at Borghetto, and an insurrection of the Genoese peasantry was to have been encouraged; which I believe would have succeeded for several miles up the country. General de Vins must have sent four or five thousand men, probably, from his army, which would have given the enemy a fairer prospect of success in their intended attack. The scheme was bold, but I do not think it would have succeeded in all points.

However, my arrival here on the 13th in the evening caused a total change. The frigate, knowing her deserts, and what had been done here before with the transports and privateers, hauled from the outer to the inner mole, and is got inside the merchant ships, with her powder out, for no ships can go into the inner mole with powder on board; and as I have long expected an embarkation from the French army from the westward, to harass General de Vins, there I was fully on my guard. Whilst I remain here, no harm can happen, unless, which private information says is likely to take place, that four sail of the line and some frigates are to come here, and take Agamemnon and her squadron. What steps the Austrian generals, and ministers, will adopt to get redress, for this (I fear allowed) breach of neutrality, on the part of the Genoese Government, I cannot yet tell. It is a very extraordinary circumstance, but a fact, that since my arrival, respect to the neutral port has not been demanded of me: if it had, my answer was ready, 'that it was useless and impossible for me to give it.' As the breach of the neutrality has not been noticed, I fancy they are aware of my answer, and therefore declined asking the question. A superior force to the French must now always be kept here; but, I own, I think the French will make a push from Toulon to drive us away, that they may do something, and they have no time to lose. Sir Hyde Parker is gone to the westward, and my force is very much reduced, at a time I humbly conceive it wants addition.

At last, on 23 November, the French made their grand attack on the Austrian position, and with complete success. It forms the subject of many letters at this period.

Sir G. Elliot, 4 Dec. At sea.

My campaign is closed by the defeat of the Austrian army, and the consequent loss of Vado and every place in the Riviera of Genoa, and I am on my way to refit poor Agamemnon and her miserable ship's company at Leghorn. We are, indeed, worn out; except six days I have never been one hour off the station. I have to regret, but mean not to complain, that my force was too small for the services which I wished to perform. If I had been favoured with the two 74-gun ships, which I have often asked for, I am fully persuaded that the last attack never would have been made. Instead of this increase of force, my frigates were withdrawn from me without my knowledge, and I had only Flora and Speedy, brig, left with me; these were, I fancy, blown off the coast, and only Agamemnon remained. The extraordinary events which have taken place near Genoa, and the plan which was laid by the French to take post between Voltri and Savona, perhaps you are acquainted with; if not, I will tell you.

Seven hundred men were enlisted and embarked ([together with] 7,000 stand of arms) on board the Brune, French frigate, in Genoa, and on board many small privateers and one brig; these were on a certain night to have landed in a strong post between Voltri and Savona, to be joined in small feluccas by one thousand men from Borghetta. An insurrection of the Genoese peasantry, we have every reason to believe, would have been made for forty miles up a valley towards Piedmont. The money going from Genoa tempted these people to make an attack before their time, which certainly caused the plan to miscarry. On the great preparation at Genoa, Agamemnon was called for, might and main, to prevent the plan, which I most effectually did; and so fearful was the imperial minister and general of my leaving Genoa, that I was told that if I quitted Genoa, the loss of 3,000 Austrians was the certain consequence; thus I was put in the cleft stick. If I left Genoa, the loss of 3,000 men would be laid to my charge; if I was not at Pietra, the gunboats would, unmolested, harass the left flank of the army; and the defeat may very probably be laid to the want of assistance of the Agamemnon. However, my being at Genoa, although contrary to my inclination, has been the means of saving from 8,000 to 10,000 men, and amongst others, General de Vins himself, who escaped by the road, which, but for me, the enemy would have occupied. I must regret not having more force.

My orders left at Vado, for the station of Southampton and Inconstant, taken from me, will show that not a gunboat, if my orders had been obeyed, could have annoyed the army. Mr. Drake, who has been on the spot, and Mr. Trevor, who has known all my proceedings, are pleased to highly approve my conduct; and I also have had, to 9 November, the full approbation of every general in the army. That the gunboats harassed them I am truly sorry for; it only becomes me to show I could not help it—not that I believe they would not have been beaten without the gunboats, for the right wing, twelve miles from the shore, was entirely defeated, and the left retreated but not in much order. I fancy, from what I hear, no defeat was ever more complete; on the other hand, I know all the generals wished for nothing more than orders to quit the coast. They say, and true, they were brought on it, at the express desire of the English, to co-operate with the fleet, which fleet nor admiral they never saw. There certainly are other and much better posts to prevent the invasion of Italy than Vado.

A few days later, Nelson learned that complaints of the non-cooperation of the English squadron actually had been made; and on 10 December, he wrote to Mr. Drake, enclosing a letter for the Austrian general, in defence of his conduct. Drake, however, did not forward it; submitting to Nelson, in a letter of 7 January, 1796, whether it would be proper to offer any justification of their conduct to a foreign general; and whether, in any case, they ought not to remain silent, till some specific charges were brought forward. He also said : ' It certainly was unfortunate that your squadron should have been so reduced as to have rendered it impossible for you to provide for every service which was required of you by the Austrian generals; but I am entirely persuaded, that on this, as well as on every other occasion, you employed the force which you had in the manner the most beneficial to the common cause; and it is with great satisfaction I assure you, that anxious as the Austrian generals are to transfer the blame of the misfortunes of 23 November from themselves to us, they have always done ample justice to your zealous and able conduct : their complaints turn upon the insufficiency of the force under your command, and not upon the mode in which that force was employed.'

I have had letters from my poor lieutenants and midshipmen [who were taken prisoners at Vado], telling me that few of the French

Mrs.
Nelson,
18 Dec.
Leghorn.

soldiers are more than twenty-three or twenty-four years old; a great many do not exceed fourteen years, all without clothes; and my officers add, they are sure my barge's crew would have beat a hundred of them, and that, had I seen them, I should not have thought, if the world had been covered with such people, that they could have beat the Austrian army. The oldest officers say, they never heard of so complete a defeat, and certainly without any reason.

Sir J.
Jervis,
21 Dec.
Leghorn
Roads.

We are getting on very fast with our caulking; our head is secured; our rigging nearly overhauled; and our other matters in as great a state of forwardness as I could expect at this season of the year. I hope, by the first week in January, the Agamemnon will be as fit for sea as a rotten ship can be.

Mrs.
Nelson,
6 Jan.
1796.
Leghorn.

The French, I am certain, will, this spring, make a great exertion to get into Italy, and I think Sir John Jervis must be active to keep them out. By 1 February, fifteen sail of the line will be ready at Toulon, with 140 transports, and 200 flat boats adapted for the coast of Italy. The prevention of the intentions of the enemy requires great foresight; for, if once landed, our fleet is of no use, and theirs would retire into Toulon or some secure port: had they done so last year, where would have been the advantage of our action? The French will improve on their last year's folly: I am convinced in my own mind, that I know their very landing-place. If they mean to carry on the war, they must penetrate into Italy. Holland and Flanders, with their own country, they have entirely stripped; Italy is the gold mine, and, if once entered, is without the means of resistance.

20 Jan.
S. Fiorenzo.

We were received, not only with the greatest attention, but with much apparent friendship. . . . I found the admiral anxious to know many things, which I was a good deal surprised to find had not been communicated to him from others in the fleet; and it would appear, that he was so well satisfied with my opinion of what is likely to happen, and the means of prevention to be taken, that he had no reserve with me respecting his information and ideas of what is likely to be done.

As the result of this conference, Nelson was ordered to resume his former station off Genoa, and sailed the same day.

27 Jan.
Gulf of
Genoa.

The fleet was not a little surprised at my leaving them so soon, and, I fancy, there was some degree of envy attached to the surprise, for one captain told me, 'You did just as you pleased in Lord Hood's time, the same in Admiral Hotham's, and now again with Sir John

Jervis; it makes no difference to you who is commander-in-chief.'
I returned a pretty strong answer to this speech. My command
here is to prevent any small number of men from making a descent
in Italy.

As yet, I appear to stand well with Sir John Jervis, and it shall 17 Feb.
Off the
Hières.
not be my fault if I do not continue to do so: my conduct has no
mystery. I freely communicate my knowledge and observations,
and only wish, that whatever admiral I serve under may make a
proper use of it. God forbid, I should have any other consideration
on service, than the good of my country. I am now sent to examine
the state of the ships in Toulon; their numbers we know full well,
but the accounts of the state they are in are so contradictory, as to
leave us uncertain. Sir John Jervis is at present inferior to the
French: they have built five sail of the line since we left Toulon.

I am now on my way to Genoa, having been joined by the 28 Feb.
admiral on the 23rd, off Toulon. The French have thirteen sail
of the line and five frigates ready for sea; and four or five, which
are in great forwardness, are fitting in the arsenal. Sir John Jervis,
from his manner, as I plainly perceive, does not wish me to leave
this station. He seems at present to consider me more as an
associate than a subordinate officer; for I am acting without any
orders. This may have its difficulties at a future day; but I make
none, knowing the uprightness of my intentions.

I think by the end of this month the enemy's fleet will be at Capt.
Locker,
4 March.
Genoa
Mole.
sea, and as they have a great number of transports ready at Mar-
seilles, I firmly believe the fleet from Cadiz, perhaps joined by some
from L'Orient or Brest, will join them, when one week's very
superior fleet will effect a landing between Spezia and Leghorn,
I mean on that coast of Italy, when they will of course possess
themselves of Leghorn, and there is nothing to stop their progress
to Rome and Naples: we may fight their fleet, but unless we can
destroy them, their transports will push on and effect their landing.
What will the French care for the loss of a few men-of-war? It is
nothing if they can get into Italy. This [is] the gold mine, and
what, depend on it, they will push for.

I arrived yesterday morning at Genoa, and held a conference Sir J.
Jervis,
16 March.
with Mr. Drake. He expressed himself pleased at your determina-
tion to give the Austrian general a meeting, whenever he pleased to
bring his army on the coast; but, at the same time, he said, he found
it extremely difficult to make them hear of the Riviera. . . . The
commander-in-chief of the army was not yet fixed on; but it was
understood that the archduke was to be the nominal, and General

Beaulieu the active commander-in-chief, that Beaulieu wished to meet the French in the plains of Lombardy, and then to follow up the blow, which he had no doubt would be decisive. I could not help observing, that the very reason why the general wished to meet them in a particular place would of course be the reason why the French would not penetrate by that route; [and] that [respecting] the information, which I had received, of the intention of the Directory to order the movement of their army in three columns, one by Ceva, another by the pass of the Bocchetta, and another to march through the Genoese territory, or be carried coastways to Spezia, which would give them an easy entry into the plains of Italy, I had no doubt the two first would be feints, and the last the real plan. I must here observe that before night Mr. Drake had this same information communicated to him; and also, that a body of troops would be embarked on board the fleet, the moment Richery arrived from Cadiz, and a push made for Spezia. This information induced me more strongly, if possible, than ever, to press the measure of taking Vado or Spezia with all possible expedition; and that without one or the other was done, it was impossible for you to answer for the safety of Italy coastways; and that it was now perfectly clear for what the two hundred flat boats were built, and the numerous gunboats fitted out. Mr. Drake told me that he had already pressed the measure of taking Vado, and would continue it, and also would press instantly the necessity of possessing Spezia if I would say the Austrians should be supported from attacks by sea by our naval force; which, I said, there could be no doubt of, for it would be the home of our squadron employed on this coast. He then desired me to give my opinion in writing, as the authority of a sea officer would have more weight than all he could urge to them; this is the cause of my writing the letter, on which I am so anxious to obtain your sentiments.

<small>18 March. Off the Ilières.</small>

I wish much to have the honour of seeing you, and the moment I hear of your arrival at S. Fiorenzo, I shall go there. When you did me the honour to offer me the Zealous, you was acquainted with my reasons for not accepting her. In any situation, if you approve of my conduct, I beg leave to assure you, I shall feel pleasure in serving under your command; and in case a promotion of flags should take place, I am confident that your mention of me to Lord Spencer would be sufficient to have my flag ordered to be hoisted in this country. The Zealous, most probably, is disposed of long before this: if not, and you approve of me for this command, either as captain or admiral, I am at your disposal.

I was favoured on the first of this month with your letter of 29 March, and on [the 2nd] I went to Fiorenzo to talk with Sir John Jervis. We may rely on every support and effectual assistance from him: we have only to propose, and, if possible, it will be done. I hope the galleys and gunboats will be sent in abundance, and I have a plan for forcing them to be useful; which is, to buy two tartans, fit them as heavy gunboats, and occasionally man them from the shipping of my squadron. This will enable me to go myself, or send a captain to command the whole, in which case I shall be sure that the service will be performed. . . . You may assure General Beaulieu, that on whatever part of the coast he comes, I shall never quit him. If he is able, and willing, and expeditious, I am sure we shall do much. The admiral has directed me to wear a broad pennant, and this was done in the handsomest manner.

Fr. Drake, 6 April. Genoa.

The battle of Montenotte was fought on 12 April.

Captain Cockburn will convey to you all the news, certainly none of it is pleasing; and I own I regret more the good fortune of the enemy in getting their convoy into Vado, than all which has happened on shore. By the time I sail, I will make myself master of the exact force of the enemy that has escaped us; report says, two frigates and sixteen transports. They may be alarmed for a night or two, and it may go off: if you therefore think that the attempt to take the frigates and transports is proper by boats, I beg leave to offer myself for that distinguished command. The barges and pinnaces will be more than thirty. I think it may be done; at least, if you approve of the measure, nothing shall be wanting on my part for its complete success. My idea is, for ten barges to attack each frigate, one boat to be especially appointed with a most confidential officer, to cut the cable of each frigate; if the wind is off the land, in ten minutes they must drive out of soundings, and ten boats would be left for the attack of the transports. I should wish you to consider the matter, and I am then certain what is proper will be done. To-morrow evening, at dark, I shall sail from hence, and will be with you on Wednesday morning. I grieve when the French have any good fortune by sea.

Sir J. Jervis, 18 April. Genoa Mole.

This morning, having received information that a convoy, laden with stores for the French army, had anchored at Loano, I lost no time in proceeding off that place with the [Meleager, Diadem, Peterel]. On my approach, I was sorry to observe, that instead of a convoy, only four vessels were lying under the batteries, which

25 April. Off Loano.

H

opened on our approach, and the fire was returned as our ships got up, under cover of which, our boats boarded the four vessels, and brought them off: the vessels lying very near the shore, a heavy fire of musketry was kept up on our boats; and it is with the greatest grief I have to mention that Lieutenant James Noble, of the Agamemnon, a most worthy and gallant officer, is, I fear, mortally wounded. From our ships keeping under the fire of their batteries, we sustained no damage; the Agamemnon was, I believe, the only ship struck by shot. The principal part of this service fell on our boats, whose conduct and gallantry could not on any occasion have been exceeded, and I wish fully to express the sense I entertain of the gallantry of every officer and man employed on this occasion.

J. Trevor, 28 April.

How I lament the prospect of affairs in Piedmont! and I hear from Genoa that the King of Sardinia is certainly negotiating a peace with the French. How sad all this is, when we know to what shifts the French army is put, absolutely for common necessaries; and should the whole force of the enemy be turned against General Beaulieu, I suppose he must retreat, and leave the enemy unmolested, to journey to all parts of Italy, unless, which I fear is not likely, that double the number of Beaulieu's army is sent from Germany. It would seem that a proper number of troops has not been sent to insure success, but very few more than last year, and the enemy have doubled their army. I still hope, from the conduct of the French, that the Piedmontese will rouse to a man, and [sic] the French. This they may do, if they are one-half as zealous to defend their country as the enemy is to plunder it. We English have to regret that we cannot always decide the fate of empires on the sea.

I am hunting for the French convoy, and if I find them in any place where there is a probability of attacking them, you may depend they shall be either taken or destroyed at the risk of my squadron; for at this moment I feel their convoy is of more consequence than my squadron, which is built to be risked on proper occasions.

F. Drake, 28 April.

I want to take or destroy the convoy expected, and you may depend it shall be done if there is the smallest possibility. You will, and I wish all the allies would, give me credit for my earnest endeavours to destroy the enemy. I have not a thought on any subject separated from the immediate object of my command, nor a wish to be employed on any other service. So far the allies, if I may be allowed the expression, are fortunate in having an officer of this character;

but I cannot command winds and weather. A sea officer cannot, like a land officer, form plans; his object is to embrace the happy moment which now and then offers—it may be this day, not for a month, and perhaps never.

Peace is concluded between the Sardinians and the French— most likely hostile to us. . . . I think, in case of a Spanish war, Naples is preparing to desert us also, and Spain is certainly going to war with somebody. Cornwallis's trial was to come on 5 April. How extraordinary! he was the last man I could have supposed would have done a wrong thing, and I cannot, with all my partiality for him, bring myself to think it right that he deserted his command. But I suspect some ill-treatment of the Admiralty after he sailed, which induced him to return.

Capt. Collingwood, 1 May.

It is said, that on the 1st instant the French took possession of Alessandria. I have still hopes from General Beaulieu; should these people follow him into the plain, his force is very respectable. The French are levying contributions of money, bread, &c. all over Piedmont, and it is said the Piedmontese have paid more already than they used to pay their king for several years.

Sir J. Jervis, 4 May. Off Cape Noli.

I am sorry to say, Mr. Brame sent me a letter published by Salicetti, saying that the French had defeated Beaulieu, on the 11th were at Lodi, and taken all the artillery and camp of the Austrians. The story is very ill told, and I should doubt much had I not unfortunately been in the habit of believing accounts of French victories.

Sir G. Elliot, 16 May.

The French have lost great numbers in passing the Po and another river, but they have enough left, for the Emperor has not reinforced his army. I very much believe that England, who commenced the war with all Europe for her allies, will finish it by having nearly all Europe for her enemies. Should all the powers in this country make peace, the French possess themselves of Leghorn and other places to cut off our supplies, Corsica will be the only tie to keep our great fleet in the Mediterranean; how far the conduct of those islanders, taken in a general scale, deserves that a fleet and army should be kept for their security, is well deserving of serious consideration.

We arrived here yesterday morning in a gale of wind, and I hope to have my ship ready for sea by the 20th or 21st. . . . As the French cannot want supplies to be brought into the Gulf of Genoa, for their grand army, I am still of opinion, that if our frigates are wanted for other services, they may very well be spared

Sir J. Jervis, 18 May. Leghorn.

from the Gulf. Money, provisions, and clothes the enemy have in abundance; and they command arsenals to supply their wants in arms and ammunition.

I have felt, and do feel, Sir, every degree of sensibility and gratitude for your kind and flattering attention, in directing me to hoist a distinguishing pennant; but as the service, for which it was intended to be useful, is nearly if not quite at an end, I assure you I shall have no regret in striking it; for it will afford me an opportunity of serving nearer your flag, and of endeavouring to show, by my attention in a subordinate station, that I was not unworthy of commanding.

31 May. Off Oneglia. At 2 P.M. yesterday, seeing some vessels running along shore which I believed to be French, and knowing the great consequence of intercepting the cannon and ordnance stores which I had information were expected from Toulon, to be landed at S. Pietro d'Arena for the siege of Mantua, I made the signal for a general chase, when the vessels got close under a battery and anchored. Three o'clock, the Meleager and Agamemnon anchored; as, soon afterwards, did the Peterel and Speedy. After a short resistance from the battery and vessels, we took possession of them. It is impossible I can do justice to the alacrity and gallantry ever conspicuous in my little squadron. Our boats boarded the National ketch in the fire of three eighteen-pounders, and of one eighteen-pounder in a gunboat. The Blanche and Diadem being to leeward, the former could not anchor until the vessels had struck; but the boats of all the ships were active in getting them off the shore, the enemy having cut their cables when they surrendered. The Agamemnon's masts, sails, and rigging are a little cut, but of no material consequence.

The vessels captured were the man-of-war ketch, the gunboat, and five transports; two of them laden with guns, mortars, and artillery stores; one with wheelbarrows and intrenching tools; one with brandy, and one with Austrian prisoners.

2 June. Off Nice. I have sent the Diadem, with all the prizes, except the armed ketch, first to San Fiorenzo, where the brig, and, if not too leaky, the ketch, loaded with ordnance stores, are to be left; and I have wrote the Viceroy, that if he wants any of them for the island, I will direct them to be landed. The mortars are wonderfully fine, thirteen and a half inch; but the number of either cannon or mortars we know not. . . . By papers found, sixteen sail of transports are destined for Vado, with ordnance stores for the siege, and cannoniers. I wish we may get any of the others, but the chance is much against us: I can only promise that I will not miss an opportunity. I have an account of the exact force of the enemy on 6 February, sent to General Bonaparte; it consists, including the garrison of Toulon and the whole coast, of 65,000 men. The army, when Bonaparte took the command, was effective 30,875. Probably many of the 65,000 are gone forward; but still, on the whole, the force is not so great as I believed. . . . I have got the charts of Italy sent by the Directory to Bonaparte; also Maillebois' wars in Italy, Vauban's attack and defence of places, and Prince Eugene's history; all sent for the general. If Bonaparte is ignorant, the Directory, it would appear, wish to instruct him: pray God he may remain ignorant.

Two days after we took the vessel with Austrian troops on board, 5 June. who had been made prisoners by the French, a boat came off to Captain Cockburn, with a Genoese master and the crew of the vessel, and papers, to say they were chartered by the Spanish consul at Savona, to carry these troops to Barcelona for the Swiss regiment. I have examined some of the Austrians, who say that they were marched by a guard to the vessel, and, when on board, a person gave them thirty sous each, and told them they were going to Spain, where they would find many of their comrades. The men say it was against their inclination, and that they wish to return to their own service, or to serve with the English till there is an opportunity. Knowing, as I do, that the French absolutely sell them to the Spaniards, I have no difficulty in keeping them, to be returned to their own sovereign. . . . They want a change of apparel, which, if we get no work for it, the German Government ought to pay, and a bed each; they are as fine healthy-looking men as I ever saw, the oldest of one hundred and fifty-two is thirty-four years of age. I think till we have an opportunity of sending them to General Beaulieu, they would add to the strength of our ships, five ships thirty each: this is submitted with deference to your better judgment.

A letter from Sir John Jervis to Mr. Jackson, Secretary of Legation at Turin, dated off Toulon, 15 August, 1796, puts this business in a still clearer light:

'From a Swiss dealer in human flesh, the demand made upon me to deliver up 152 Austrian grenadiers, serving on board his Majesty's fleet under my command, is natural enough; but that a Spaniard, who is a noble creature, should join in such a demand, I must confess astonishes me; and I can only account for it by the Chevalier Camano being ignorant that the persons in question were prisoners of war in the last affair with General Beaulieu, and are not deserters, and they were most basely sold by the French commissaries in the Western Riviera of Genoa, to the vile crimps who recruit for the foreign regiments in the service of Spain. It is high time a stop should be put to this abominable traffic, a million times more disgraceful than the African slave trade; and I trust the strong remonstrances about to be made by the Court of Vienna to the Court of Madrid will produce the desired effect.'

On 11 June, 1796, Commodore Nelson left the Agamemnon, and hoisted his distinguishing pennant in the Captain, of 74 guns.

Capt. Locker, 20 June.

For this last fortnight my destination has been so often changed, that I have been very uncertain whether I was to go home or stay.... Orders came out for a second-rate and the worst ship of the line to go home with the convoy: there could be no doubt but Agamemnon must be the ship; and had the corn ships, which were momentarily expected, arrived, I must have gone. However, when it was known in the fleet, many wished to go, and the captain of this ship [the Captain] had the preference, he being in a very bad state of health.

Rev. Wm. Nelson, 20 June.

If my flag comes out, I shall most probably hoist it in the Goliath, as she is new coppered. In other respects, she is not so desirable as this ship, for I hear she is wretchedly manned, and worse disciplined. The latter I don't mind, if I have but the stuff to work upon. I have selected a Captain Miller to be my captain, about thirty-five years of age: in my opinion a most exceeding good officer and worthy man. If we have a Spanish war, I shall yet hope to make something this war. At present, I believe I am worse than when I set out—I mean in point of riches, for if credit and honour in the service are desirable, I have my full share. Opportunities have been frequently offered me, and I have never lost one of distinguishing myself, not only as a gallant man, but as having a head; for, of the numerous plans I have laid, not one has failed, nor of opinions given, has one been in the event wrong.

Sir J. Jervis, 23 June. Genoa.

The complaints of the Genoese Government [about breaches of neutrality] are so ridiculous, that I hardly know what to say. If we are to allow the free passage of the enemy coastways, we are useless.... The best mode, in my opinion, is to speak openly— that so long as the French are in possession of batteries on the coast, which fire on our ships, so long we shall consider it as an enemy's coast. I have the pleasure to say that our conduct has so completely alarmed the French, that all their coasting trade is at an end; even the corvette, gunboats, &c. which were moored under the fortress of Vado, have not thought themselves in security, but are all gone into Savona Mole, and unbent their sails.

As I wrote you from Genoa was my intention, I made the best of my way to this place, but from calms and contrary winds, it was yesterday morning before I anchored in the northern road of Leghorn. . . . The French took possession of the town about one o'clock, and immediately fired on the Inconstant, and a prize of Captain Hood's, loaded with timber, but without doing them any damage. The exertions of Captain Fremantle must have been very great, for the consul and Mr. Fonnereau tell me, that except bad debts, and the loss of furniture, nothing of any great consequence is left in the town.[1]

28 June. Leghorn Roads.

I have received directions from the admiral to blockade the port of Leghorn, and to be aiding and assisting to your excellency in preventing any attempts of the French on the island of Corsica, and in such other matters as you may wish, and is in my power.

Sir G. Elliot, 2 July. S. Fiorenzo.

You will give me credit, I am sure, for my fullest exertion in the execution of this duty, and that if, on every occasion, I do not comply with all your wishes, it is the want of the means, and not the want of inclination.

In carrying out these instructions, Nelson, on 6 July, desired Mr. Brame, the English consul at Genoa, to give official notice of the blockade to the Government of Genoa and to all the foreign ministers and consuls ; on the 7th, he himself gave notice to the several consuls at Leghorn, and, on the 10th, in accordance with the wish of Sir Gilbert Elliot, he took possession of Porto Ferrajo and the island of Elba, the governor accepting the offered terms without resistance.

The blockade of Leghorn is complete ; not a vessel can go in or come out without my permission. Yesterday a Dane came out loaded with oil and wine for Genoa: I told him he must return, or I should send him to Corsica. His answer was, 'I am a neutral, and you may take me, but I will not return.' However, I took possession, and intended giving him to a Corsican privateer ; in

Sir J. Jervis, 18 July. Leghorn Roads.

---

[1] Captain Fremantle's official report of his proceedings was published in the *London Gazette* of 23 August, 1796. On transmitting it to the Admiralty, Sir John Jervis said that 'the retreat of the British factory with most of their property' was owing 'to the unparalleled exertions of Captain Fremantle.' It will be interesting to compare with this the account given by Lanfrey (*Histoire de Napoléon*, tom. i. p. 143): 'Les Anglais avaient déjà reçu l'éveil, et, lorsque nous entrâmes dans la ville, leurs bâtiments, au nombre de plus de quarante, prenaient le large sous les yeux de Murat et des deux commissaires, Garcau et Saliectti, accourus à la hâte pour se saisir de cette riche proie. Le coup était en partie manqué, à leur grand désappointement. Ils durent se contenter de s'emparer des marchandises anglaises pour une somme d'environ 12 millions.' From Nelson's information, it would appear that they must have made the convenient and profitable blunder of mistaking Tuscan property for English.

about two hours, he begged I would allow him to return. This, I am satisfied, was a trial of what I intended; for he said, all the neutrals were determined to come out. If we are firm, the Grand Duke will sorely repent his admission of the French. His repeated proclamations for the people to be quiet, have given time to the French to lay powder under all the works; and, in case of disturbance, they say, up shall go the works. Cannon are pointed from the wall to every street, and all the cannon and mortars are mounted.

Duke of Clarence, 20 July. Leghorn Roads.

You will hear of our taking possession of Porto Ferrajo: if we had not, to a certainty the French would, and then they would have been too near Corsica, where I fear we have an ungrateful set of people; and one party acknowledged friends to the French, which, although greatly outnumbered by our friends, constantly makes disturbances.

Mrs. Nelson, 2 August.

Had all my actions been gazetted, not one fortnight would have passed during the whole war without a letter from me: one day or other I will have a long gazette to myself; I feel that such an opportunity will be given me. I cannot, if I am in the field for glory, be kept out of sight. Probably my services may be forgotten by the great, by the time I get home; but my mind will not forget, nor cease to feel a degree of consolation and of applause superior to undeserved rewards. Wherever there is anything to be done, there Providence is sure to direct my steps. Credit must be given me in spite of envy.

Sir G. Elliot, 5 August.

It has ever pleased God to prosper all my undertakings, and I feel confident of His blessing on this occasion. I ever consider my motto, *Fides et Opera*.[1]

(?) 5 August.

From the total deprivation of trade in Leghorn, more than 50,000 people are thrown out of employment, and I believe it is within compass when we include the whole canal trade to every part of Italy. Hundreds have been on board in small boats, to beg bread. All agree they have repeatedly represented to the Grand Duke the miserable state to which they are reduced, and the answer they have repeatedly received, was to beg of them to remain quiet. All this, your lordship knows most probably from our minister; but the lower order in Leghorn assure me, that they can nor will any

---

[1] It does not appear that Nelson used any armorial bearings until after he was made a Knight of the Bath, in May 1797, when arms were assigned to him, and he then adopted this motto. Before that time he generally used a seal with the cipher 'A. N.,' which had probably belonged to his sister Anne; or a large seal with the head of Neptune engraved on it.

longer be put off by promises; that the French shall quit Leghorn, and that they are determined to rise on them if they are not out of the town on 15 August, and that they shall not celebrate their fête of 10 August. I do not fail to give every encouragement to these good dispositions, and assurances of my hearty assistance in case the French do not go off. The plans are laid, but it would be wrong to put them on paper in this uncertain state of the safety of posts. The French here are grown complaisant; the inhabitants, of course, very insolent; they tell them, 'You shall go by the 15th.' The soldiers every night desert by ten and twenty. The other night, an officer and twenty cavalry went off. We will not go to Mantua to be killed, is their common talk.

I am not sanguine without good reason, but I have at present not the smallest doubt but by the 16th Leghorn will be free.

A week later, Nelson was busy concerting, with Sir Gilbert Elliot, measures to drive the French out, for which purpose a detachment of troops was to be sent from Corsica: a regular siege, he wrote on 11 August, was out of the question; but though the French would say they would die in the works, a mortar battery would probably bring them to reason. On the 15th, he was at Bastia, superintending the shipment of the heavy stores for the little expedition: on the 18th he was back at Leghorn: it was not till the 19th that he received news of the defeat which the Austrians had sustained at Lonato and Castiglione; and though the loss was spoken of as a severe check rather than an overwhelming defeat, it was still sufficient to render the contemplated attack unseasonable.

I have still my doubts as to a Spanish war, and if it is, with your management I have no fears as to any fatal consequences; their fleet is ill-manned, and worse officered I fancy, and they are slow. *Sir J. Jervis, 16 Aug.*

Fame says we are to have a Spanish war in this country. The only consequence it can be to us may be the necessary evacuation of Corsica, and that our fleet will draw down the Mediterranean. The dons will suffer in every way for their folly, if they are really so foolhardy as to go to war to please the French. . . . As to our news here, the Austrians do not seem victorious anywhere, and the consequence is, the French force friends where they are superior. Corsica is threatened and will probably fall, for the French have a very strong party in the island. This is not strange. All their connections are with the French. Great numbers of Corsican officers are in high stations in their army, which cannot be the case with ours. *Rev. Edm. Nelson, 19 Aug.*

Our affairs in Corsica are gloomy; there is a very strong

Duke of Clarence, 19 August.

republican party in that island, and they are well supported from France; the first favourable moment, they will certainly act against us. The French are endeavouring to get over from the continent twenty and thirty men at a time, and they will accomplish it in spite of all we can do.

As to our fleet, under such a commander-in-chief as Sir John Jervis, nobody has any fears. . . . We are now twenty-two sail of the line, the combined fleet will not be above thirty-five sail of the line, supposing the dons detach to the West Indies. I will venture my life Sir John Jervis defeats them; I do not mean by a regular battle, but by the skill of our admiral, and the activity and spirit of our officers and seamen. This country is the most favourable possible for skill with an inferior fleet; for the winds are so variable, that some one time in twenty-four hours you must be able to attack a part of a large fleet, and the other will be becalmed, or have a contrary wind; therefore I hope Government will not be alarmed for our safety—I mean more than is proper. I take for granted they will send us reinforcements as soon as possible, but there is nothing we are not able to accomplish under Sir John Jervis.

Sir G. Elliot, 27 August.

I am on my way to the fleet; it is a great object that the ship should join, and as there is no captain joined her, I think it advisable to go in her myself. If the Spaniards go to war with us, which I own I cannot even yet bring myself to believe, I hope to be in time to assist our worthy admiral, and at all events I shall wish to talk a little with him.

Nelson arrived back on his station before Leghorn on 2 September: on the 4th he was at Genoa, where a number of bullocks bought for the fleet had been stopped by the Genoese Government, and were detained in spite of Nelson's vehement protests. This and other aggressions in support of the French formed the subject of a long correspondence, which has now little interest except as marking the ignominious end of the once glorious republic.

Fr. Drake, 9 Sept.

The French seem to dictate to this government what they shall do. . . . The Russian minister has just sent me word that, last night, the Doge put the question to the senate to give me thirty bullocks, but it was overruled, and I am not to have one. The principal argument was, we shall offend the French, and we had better offend the English than them, for they will not injure us so much.

Sir J. Jervis, 11 Sept.

This government is in terror of the French: many of its members are bought over, and all, I believe, think that the English would be a far more generous enemy than the French: therefore, they would rather offend us than them. In my conversation with the Doge, I hinted (on his rather insinuating that a great army close to their gates might cut off all supplies of meat for the city) that we had the power to cut off supplies of corn and wood which come by sea. His answer was, what was true, that a small country like Genoa was in a terrible situation between great powers at war. I urged our claim to justice, having conformed to the laws of Genoa. He admitted we had justice and right on our side. . . . Every day French vessels come to Genoa laden with powder, shot, &c., and land them at San Pietro d'Arena, where the French have large magazines of powder, and other stores. They have four guns mounted on the beach, for their protection, and are going to erect a large battery and have one thousand men to defend it. They have demanded one of the large palaces for an hospital, and taken it. If the war continues, it must end in the French taking possession of Genoa (supposing their success continues).

The practical and continued hostility of Genoa, thus a slave to French influence, was at length held by the Viceroy of Corsica, to deprive it of its privileges as a neutral; and on 15 September he requested Nelson to co-operate with a body of troops ordered to take possession of Capraja, where an agent of France had been for some time openly established, and where French privateers had been openly received. The island was quite unable to resist the force sent against it, and surrendered at the first summons, on 18 September. On the 20th, standing over to Leghorn, Nelson fell in with a Spanish frigate, to whose captain he wrote:

Having heard that several English ships have been detained in the ports of Spain, and also that the court of Spain has made an alliance offensive and defensive,[1] I desire to know of you, on your honour, if you know that there is war between England and Spain? 20 Sept.

The Spaniard answered that he had no knowledge of any declaration of war, or of any such offensive or defensive alliance with France; that, on the contrary, his instructions were to maintain the good understanding which existed between the two countries, Spain and England. To this Nelson replied:

It is not possible for me to desire a Spanish officer to do what would be considered in the smallest degree dishonourable. 20 Sept.

I am in doubt whether it is war or peace between the two courts. You say you are sure that all is peace, and that the most perfect good understanding subsists between the two courts. Thus

[1] A treaty offensive and defensive between France and Spain had, in fact, been signed on 19 August, 1796: and on 11 October, war was declared by Spain against Great Britain.

circumstanced, I have to request, as a mark of your desire to cement that harmony, that you will attend me to Bastia, to speak with the Viceroy of Corsica on this very delicate question. Should you refuse to comply with this most reasonable request, the fatal consequences must rest with you, and I must do my duty in using force.

The Spaniard positively refused to go to Bastia, but consented to return to Spain; a compromise which, after a further interchange of letters, Nelson accepted, and so the frigates parted company.

Sir G. Elliot, 24 Sept.

I send you my letter to the admiral about a Spanish frigate. I longed to take her, but dare not. You will see that the don fancies the business hangs in my refusing him leave to enter Leghorn, and not daring he should return to Spain to make his complaints, without speaking to your excellency; whereas, in truth, I wished to have brought him to Bastia, to ask your advice whether I should not take him. However, I have acted on the safe side: if we are not to have a war, this act of violence will easily be got over; and if we are, I hope my not taking this fine frigate will redound to the honour of some of our active frigate commanders.

Sir J. Jervis, 28 Sept.

During the course of yesterday, I received repeated information of the movements of the privateers with the Corsicans on board; the whole number of Corsicans is nine hundred, including all the officers; six brass twelve-pounders are embarked, thirty-five cases of small arms, and various other articles, in from fifteen to twenty privateers, and I am certain they mean to sail the first favourable moment. The Corsicans behave so ill at Leghorn, that the French are determined to send them off, upon the general principle of action of the French—'If you succeed, so much the better for us; if you do not, we get rid of a set of scoundrels.'

The point for me to consider is, where will the French land in Corsica? The twelve-pounders can only be to possess a port (that they meant to have gone by Capraja, at least to possess it, is certain). I am on my way to concert with his excellency how I can best use my small force to his advantage, considering the other services I have to look to.

He then proceeded to state the different possibilities as they appeared to him, and the measures which he proposed to adopt. These, however, fell through, in consequence of the determination, which had been come to in England, to leave Corsica to itself. Sir John Jervis had, indeed, already written to Nelson on 25 September: 'Having received orders to co-operate with the viceroy in the evacuation of the island of Corsica, and afterwards to retreat down the Mediterranean with his Majesty's fleet under my command, I desire you will lose no time in going over to Bastia, and consulting with the viceroy upon the best means of performing the operation, and to give every assistance in your power towards the completion of it ; leaving the blockade of Leghorn under the direction of Captain Cockburn.'

To which, on the 30th, Nelson replied :

Last night, on my arrival, I received your most secret orders ; but I believe many people in this island have an idea that something like your orders is going forward. I shall not fail to arrange what transports may be necessary for each port, which is all that I can do until matters are brought to greater maturity. The viceroy thinks there will not be more than about 600 émigrés, Corsicans and French, and the stores I do not believe are very many ; for the ordnance which we found in the different fortifications, the viceroy will not, I fancy, think it right to take away. His excellency is very much distressed by this measure, and fancies the island is at this moment in a most perfect state of loyalty to the king, and affection for the British nation : but what strikes me as a greater sacrifice than Corsica, is the King of Naples. If he has been induced to keep off the peace, and has perhaps engaged in the war again by the expectation of the continuance of the fleet in the Mediterranean, hard indeed is his fate : his kingdom must inevitably be ruined.

Sir J. Jervis, 30 Sept. Bastia.

We are all preparing to leave the Mediterranean, a measure which I cannot approve. They at home do not know what this fleet is capable of performing; anything, and everything. Much as I shall rejoice to see England, I lament our present orders in sackcloth and ashes, so dishonourable to the dignity of England, whose fleets are equal to meet the world in arms ; and of all the fleets I ever saw, I never beheld one in point of officers and men equal to Sir John Jervis's, who is a commander-in-chief able to lead them to glory.

Mrs. Nelson, (?) 17 Oct.

I have the honour to acquaint you that I arrived at Bastia on the 14th, and was joined between that time and the 19th by the Egmont, Captain, Excellent, and Southampton. The ships of the line were moored opposite the town, the embarkation of provisions and stores commenced on the 15th, and was continued without intermission till the 19th at sunset. In that night every soldier and other person were brought off with perfect good order from the north end of the town.

Sir J. Jervis, 21 Oct. Porto Ferrajo.

The Corsicans sent to Leghorn for the French, as was natural for them, in order to make their peace ; and the enemy was in one

Duke of Clarence, 25 Oct.

end of Bastia, before we had quitted the other. . . . Our troops are ordered to Porto Ferrajo, which can be defended against any number of the enemy for a length of time; and the port, although small, will hold with management our whole fleet and transports.

As soon as all our transports are arrived at Elba, we are to go out to look for Man, who is ordered to come up: we shall then be twenty-two sail of such ships as England hardly ever produced, and commanded by an admiral who will not fail to look the enemy in the face, be their force what it may: I suppose it will not be more than thirty-four sail of the line. We may reasonably expect reinforcements from England; for whilst we can keep the combined fleet in the Mediterranean, so much more advantageous to us; and the moment we retire, the whole of Italy is given to the French. Be the successes of the Austrians what they may, their whole supply of stores and provisions comes from Trieste, across the Adriatic to the Po, and when this is cut off, they must retire. If the dons detach their fleet out of the Mediterranean, we can do the same—however, that is distant. I calculate on the certainty of Admiral Man's joining us, and that in fourteen days from this day we shall have the honour of fighting these gentlemen: there is not a seaman in the fleet who does not feel confident of success.

Towards the end of September, Admiral Don Juan de Langara with the Spanish fleet, consisting of nineteen sail of the line, ten frigates, and some corvettes, put to sea from Cadiz and proceeded to Cartagena, where they were joined by seven line-of-battle ships, thus making twenty-six sail of the line. With this force, Langara appeared off Cape Corse on 15 October, at which time the English fleet, amounting to only fourteen sail of the line, was at anchor in Mortella Bay. Instead, however, of attacking it, the Spanish admiral went to Toulon, where he arrived on the 26th. The combined fleet then consisted of thirty-eight sail of the line and nearly twenty frigates.

Capt. Locker, 5 Nov.

We left S. Fiorenzo on the 2nd, at night, and are now seeing our Smyrna convoy part of the way down the Straits, and hope to meet Admiral Man, who has, more than a month past, known the situation of our gallant admiral.

Capt. Collingwood, 1 Dec.

Man is certainly gone to England, and the consequences, after Cornwallis, may be guessed at.

The fleet arrived at Gibraltar on 1 December. On the 10th, the admiral received instructions to complete the evacuation of the Mediterranean by withdrawing the garrison from Porto Ferrajo. This duty was entrusted to Nelson, who for the special service was ordered to hoist his broad pennant on board the Minerve frigate and to take the Blanche under his command. The two ships sailed from Gibraltar on the 15th. The following extract from the Minerve's log appears to have been written by Nelson himself.

Tuesday, 20 December,[1] off Cartagena, P.M. Fresh gales and cloudy weather. At 5, spoke H.M. ship Blanche, and ordered her to steer 20 miles NE by E. Shortened sail, 6.30, brought to on the starboard tack. At 10, the Blanche made signal to speak us: bore down to her. The captain told me he saw two Spanish frigates to leeward: cleared for action and bore down. At 10.40, I passed under the stern of one of them, which I hailed. Knowing it to be a Spaniard, and not being answered, I commenced action with her by firing a broadside into her. At 11, saw the Blanche engage the other. At 11.30, saw the mizen mast of the ship I was engaged with, fall. Wore ship occasionally, to prevent her going to leeward, which I saw she endeavoured to effect. At 1.20 A.M. she hailed us, and struck her colours. I sent the lieutenant to take possession of her. He sent the Spanish captain on board, who surrendered himself, and gave up his sword: told me his name was Don Jacobo Stuart, and that the frigate was the Santa Sabina, mounting 40 guns, 20 18-pounders on the main-deck, 280 men. Took her in tow, and made sail to the SE. Sent the second lieutenant and 24 men on board her to clear her decks, &c. The people on board La Minerve employed repairing damages, &c. At 3.30, saw another frigate standing towards us, which supposed to be H.M. ship Blanche: 4.15, she hailed our prize in Spanish, and fired a broadside into her; in consequence of which we cast off the prize, which stood to the eastward. At 4.30, commenced action with her. At 5, she wore ship and stood from us. Saw three other ships astern, which, as daylight cleared away, proved to be two line-of-battle ships and a frigate, which the ship we had last engaged joined, and then all made sail in chase of us. Light airs and baffling weather: made all sail possible; our prize in sight, bearing about ENE, Blanche bearing west. 7, do. weather: the people employed repairing damages, fishing lower masts which were badly wounded. Sabina hoisted English colours over the Spanish, and stood to the NE, which induced the largest line-of-battle ship to give up the pursuit of us and follow her. At 9.30, she brought the Santa Sabina to, when her mizen masts went over the side, and she was retaken. The other line-of-battle ship and two frigates continued in chase of us. Saw a fleet bearing E, supposed them to be the Spanish fleet. Made signal for the Blanche to join us, which she did not answer.

[1] 19 December by the civil calendar.

In the first action, had 7 seamen and marines killed, and 34 wounded : second action, 10 wounded. At noon, fresh breezes and hazy weather : one line-of-battle ship and two Spanish frigates in chase of us.

Whilst the Minerve was engaged with the Sabina, the Blanche had also compelled the other frigate to haul down her colours, but was prevented taking possession of her by the approach of the Spanish squadron. On 24 December, Don Jacobo Stuart, captain of the Sabina, was sent to Cartagena to be exchanged against Lieutenants Culverhouse and Hardy, who had been taken prisoners when the Sabina was recaptured.

<small>Rev. Edm. Nelson, 1 Jan. 1797.</small>

My late action will be in the 'Gazette,' and I may venture to say it was what I know the English like. My late prisoner, a descendant from the Duke of Berwick, son of James II., was my brave opponent; for which I have returned him his sword, and sent him in a flag of truce to Spain. I felt it consonant to the dignity of my country, and I always act as I feel right, without regard to custom : he was reputed the best officer in Spain, and his men were worthy of such a commander; he was the only surviving officer.

On 26 December, Nelson arrived at Porto Ferrajo, but found that General de Burgh, in command of the troops, did not think himself authorised to abandon the place without positive orders; though he wrote to Nelson on the 28th : 'My only motive for urging delay arises from a wish to have my proceedings in some measure sanctioned by orders we ought to expect, and by no means from an idea that we assist the service by staying here; for I have always held the opinion that the signing of a Neapolitan peace with France ought to be our signal for departure.'

<small>Lt.-Gen. de Burgh, 29 Dec.</small>

My answer will be full to the point, that my instructions, written and verbal, are clear, that this place is not to be kept on the consideration of its being any longer useful to his Majesty's fleet, that the fleet has no longer any inducement to come on the coast of Italy. I shall withdraw nearly all the supplies from this place whether the troops quit it or not, and reduce the naval force here as much as possible. The object of our fleet in future is the defence of Portugal, and keeping in the Mediterranean the combined fleets. To these points my orders go, and I have no power of deviating from them.

<small>(?) 20 Jan.</small>

The whole of the ships of war which Sir John Jervis has appropriated for the service of the evacuation of this place being now either in the port, or near approaching it, I have therefore to request that you will be pleased to inform me, with as little delay as possible, whether it is your intention to embark the troops and stores now here, or any of them.

Should your answer be in the affirmative, every measure shall be taken by me for the speedy arrival of the troops in Gibraltar and Portugal; and should it be a negative, in that case I shall, according to my instructions, withdraw all our naval stores and establishment, and as many ships of war as I think can possibly be spared from the service which may be required of them here, our fleet being now particularly instructed to attend to the preservation of Portugal.

The general having declined to evacuate Porto Ferrajo, as you will observe by the copy of the letter transmitted herewith, I have, notwithstanding, withdrawn all our naval establishment from this place, having first completed every ship to as much stores as her captain pleased to take. Every transport is completely victualled, and arranged, that every soldier can be embarked in three days. I mean to look into Toulon, Mahon, and Cartagena, that I may be able to tell you the apparent state of the combined fleet.

Sir J. Jervis, 25 Jan. Porto Ferrajo.

With Sir Gilbert Elliot and his staff as passengers, the Minerve and the frigate squadron left Porto Ferrajo on 29 January. After looking into Toulon, and seeing that the Spanish fleet had left Cartagena, Nelson was in feverish haste to rejoin the admiral. On 9 February he arrived at Gibraltar, where he learnt that the Spaniards had passed to the westward four days before, though three of their ships had been sent into Gibraltar Bay with supplies for their troops. From these Nelson received his missing lieutenants, Culverhouse and Hardy, and sailed in the forenoon of 11 February. On the 13th the Minerve rejoined the admiral, having, on her way from Gibraltar, passed through the Spanish fleet. Nelson at once returned to his own ship, the Captain; and Sir Gilbert Elliot and his staff were ordered a passage to England in the Lively frigate, which, at Sir Gilbert's special request, was detained to carry home the news of the expected engagement. It was thus that Colonel Drinkwater, at that time Sir Gilbert Elliot's aide-de-camp, was a spectator of the battle, and was afterwards led to publish that detailed narrative[1] which, as we have seen,[2] Nelson accepted as a standard reference, and which, notwithstanding some exaggerations, and some mistakes of detail, is still the best and fullest account of the battle that has been written. The commander-in-chief in his official letter, dated in Lagos Bay, 15 February, described it only in the most general terms. After speaking of his certain intelligence on the night of the 13th, of the near approach of the Spanish fleet, he continued: 'I anxiously awaited the dawn of day, when, being on the starboard tack, Cape St. Vincent bearing E by N, 8 leagues, I had the satisfaction

---

[1] *Narrative of the Battle of St. Vincent*, by Colonel Drinkwater Bethune; 2nd edit. 1840. The first edition, which was published anonymously in the spring of 1797, is very scarce, having been mostly pulped, as unsaleable.
[2] See *ante*, p. 6.

of seeing a number of ships extending from SW to S, the wind then at W by S. At 10.49, the weather being extremely hazy, La Bonne Citoyenne made the signal that the ships seen were of the line, twenty-five in number; his Majesty's squadron under my command, consisting of fifteen ships of the line, happily formed in the most compact order of sailing, in two lines. By carrying a press of sail, I was fortunate in getting in with the enemy's fleet at 11.30, before it had time to connect and form a regular order of battle. Such a moment was not to be lost; and confident in the skill, valour, and discipline of the officers and men I had the happiness to command, and judging that the honour of his Majesty's arms, and the circumstances of the war in these seas, required a considerable degree of enterprise, I felt myself justified in departing from the regular system; and, passing through their fleet, in a line formed with the utmost celerity, tacked and thereby separated one-third from the main body after a partial cannonade, which prevented their re-junction till the evening; and by the very great exertions of the ships, which had the good fortune to arrive up with the enemy on the larboard tack, the ships [Salvador del Mundo, 112; San Josef, 112; San Nicolas, 80; San Ysidro, 74] were captured, and the action ceased about five o'clock in the evening.'

A FEW REMARKS RELATIVE TO MYSELF IN THE CAPTAIN, IN WHICH MY PENNANT WAS FLYING ON THE MOST GLORIOUS VALENTINE'S DAY, 1797.[1]

[On 13 February, at 6 P.M. shifted my pennant from La Minerve frigate to the Captain.

Valentine's Day, at daylight, signal to prepare for battle. At 10, saw some strange ships standing across the van of our fleet, on the larboard tack, which was sailing in two divisions, eight in the weather, seven in the lee, on the starboard tack. About 11, signal to form the line as most convenient. At 11.25, the action commenced in the van, then passing through the enemy's line.]

At one P.M., the Captain having passed the sternmost of the enemy's ships which formed their van and part of their centre, consisting of seventeen sail of the line, they on the larboard, we on the starboard tack, the admiral made the signal to 'tack in succession;' but I, perceiving the Spanish ships all to bear up before the wind, or nearly so, evidently with an intention of forming their line going large, joining their separated division, at that time engaged with some of our centre ships, or flying from us—to prevent either of their schemes from taking effect, I ordered the ship to be wore, and passing between the Diadem and Excellent, at a quarter past one o'clock was engaged with the headmost and of course leeward-

[1] There are two copies of this paper; the one an autograph draught, the other a copy prepared for publication, signed and witnessed by Captains Miller and Berry, but with some passages omitted. It is this version which is here given, with the omitted passages inserted in brackets. See *post*, p. 118.

most of the Spanish division. The ships which I know were, the Santissima Trinidad, 126; San Josef, 112; Salvador del Mundo, 112; San Nicolas, 80; another first-rate, and seventy-four, names not known. I was immediately joined and most nobly supported by the Culloden, Captain Tronbridge. The Spanish fleet, from not wishing (I suppose) to have a decisive battle, hauled to the wind on the larboard tack, which brought the ships afore-mentioned to be the leewardmost and sternmost ships in their fleet. For near an hour, I believe (but do not pretend to be correct as to time), did the Culloden and Captain support this apparently, but not really, unequal contest; when the Blenheim, passing between us and the enemy, gave us a respite, and sickened the dons. At this time, the Salvador del Mundo and San Ysidro dropped astern, and were fired into in a masterly style by the Excellent, Captain Collingwood, who compelled the San Ysidro to hoist English colours, and I thought the large ship Salvador del Mundo had also struck; but Captain Collingwood, disdaining the parade of taking possession of beaten enemies, most gallantly pushed up, with every sail set, to save his old friend and messmate, who was to appearance in a critical state. The Blenheim being ahead, and the Culloden crippled and astern, the Excellent ranged up within ten feet of the San Nicolas, giving a most tremendous fire. The San Nicolas luffing up, the San Josef fell on board her, and the Excellent passing on for the Santissima Trinidad, the Captain resumed her situation abreast of them, and close alongside. At this time the Captain having lost her foretop-mast, not a sail, shroud, or rope left, her wheel shot away, and incapable of further service in the line, or in chase, I directed Captain Miller to put the helm a-starboard, and calling for the boarders, ordered them to board.

The soldiers of the 69th Regiment, with an alacrity which will ever do them credit, and Lieutenant Pierson of the same regiment, were amongst the foremost on this service. The first man who jumped into the enemy's mizen-chains was Captain Berry,[1] late my first lieutenant; (Captain Miller was in the very act of going also, but I directed him to remain;) he was supported from our spritsail-yard, which hooked in the mizen-rigging. A soldier of the 69th Regiment having broke the upper quarter-gallery window, jumped in, followed by myself and others as fast as possible. I found the cabin-doors fastened, and some Spanish officers fired their

---

[1] Captain Berry was then a passenger in the Captain, having lately been promoted to the rank of commander. He was posted on 6 March following, for his gallantry at St. Vincent.

pistols [at us through the window]; but having broke open the doors, the soldiers fired, and the Spanish brigadier (commodore with a distinguishing pennant) fell, as retreating to the quarter deck, on the larboard side, near the wheel. Having pushed on the quarter-deck, I found Captain Berry in possession of the poop, and the Spanish ensign hauling down. I passed with my people and Lieutenant Pierson on the larboard gangway to the forecastle, where I met two or three Spanish officers prisoners to my seamen, and they delivered me their swords.

At this moment, a fire of pistols or muskets opened from the admiral's stern gallery of the San Josef [by which about seven of my men were killed and some few wounded, and about twenty Spaniards]. I directed the soldiers to fire into her stern; and, calling to Captain Miller, ordered him to send more men into the San Nicolas, and directed my people to board the first-rate, which was done in an instant, Captain Berry assisting me into the main chains. At this moment a Spanish officer looked over the quarter-deck rail, and said—'they surrendered;' from this most welcome intelligence it was not long before I was on the quarter-deck, when the Spanish captain, with a bow, presented me his sword, and said the admiral was dying of his wounds below. I asked him, on his honour, if the ship were surrendered? he declared she was; on which I gave him my hand, and desired him to call to his officers and ship's company, and tell them of it—which he did; and on the quarter-deck of a Spanish first-rate, extravagant as the story may seem, did I receive the swords of vanquished Spaniards; which, as I received, I gave to William Fearney, one of my bargemen, who put them with the greatest sangfroid under his arm. I was surrounded by Captain Berry, Lieutenant Pierson, 69th Regiment, John Sykes, John Thomson, Francis Cook, all old Agamemnons, and several other brave men, seamen and soldiers: thus fell these ships.

[The Victory passing saluted us with three cheers, as did every ship in the fleet. The Minerve sent a boat for me, and I hoisted my pennant on board her, directing Captain Cockburn to put me on board the first uninjured ship of the line, which was done; and I hoisted my pennant in the Irresistible, but the day was too far advanced to venture on taking possession of the Santa Trinidad, although she had long ceased to resist, as it must have brought on a night action with a still very superior fleet. At dusk, I went on board the Victory, when the admiral received me on the quarter-deck, and having embraced me, said he could not sufficiently thank me, and used every kind expression which could not fail to make me happy. On my return on board the Irresistible, my bruises were looked at, and found but trifling, and a few days found me as well as ever.]

HORATIO NELSON.
RALPH WILLETT MILLER.
E. BERRY.

[Don Francisco Xavier Winthuysen, Rear-Admiral, died of his wounds on board the San Josef. Don Tomas Geraldino, killed on board the San Nicolas when boarded by the Captain.]

My dearest Friend,—' A friend in need is a friend indeed,' was never more truly verified than by your most noble and gallant conduct yesterday in sparing the Captain from further loss; and I beg, both as a public officer and a friend, you will accept my most sincere thanks. I have not failed, by letter to the admiral, to represent the eminent services of the Excellent. *Capt. Collingwood, 15 Feb.*

This letter ought not to be separated from Collingwood's reply of the same date :

'My dear good Friend,—First let me congratulate you on the success of yesterday, on the brilliancy it attached to the British navy, and the humility it must cause to its enemies; and then let me congratulate my dear commodore on the distinguished part which he ever takes when the honour and interests of his country are at stake. It added very much to the satisfaction which I felt in thumping the Spaniards, that I released you a little. The highest rewards are due to you and Culloden : you formed the plan of attack—we were only accessories to the dons' ruin; for had they got on the other tack, they would have been sooner joined, and the business would have been less complete. We have come off pretty well, considering : eleven killed, and fourteen wounded. You saw the four-decker going off this morning to Cadiz— she should have come to Lagos, to make the thing better, but we could not brace our yards up to get nearer.'

The Captain is a wreck in hull and masts. We know not, exactly, but suppose near sixty killed : amongst the slightly wounded is myself, but it is only a contusion and of no consequence, unless an inflammation takes place in my bowels, which is the part injured. But they who play at balls must expect rubbers. *Sir G. Elliot, 15 Feb.*

I hope you will agree with me in opinion, and if you can be instrumental in keeping back what I expect will happen, it will be an additional obligation, for very far is it from my disposition to hold light the honours of the Crown; but I conceive to take hereditary honours without a fortune to support the dignity, is to lower that honour it would be my pride to support in proper splendour. On 1 June, 12 April, and other glorious days, baronetage has *16 Feb.*

been bestowed on the junior flag officers: this honour is what I dread, for the reasons before given, and which I wish a friend to urge for me to Lord Spencer, or such other of his Majesty's ministers as are supposed to advise the Crown. There are other honours, which die with the possessor, and I should be proud to accept, if my efforts are thought worthy of the favour of my king.

On 20 February, and long before the news of the battle of St. Vincent arrived in England, Nelson was promoted to the rank of Rear-Admiral of the Blue.

Capt. Locker, 21 Feb.

I send you a short detail of the transactions of the Captain; and if you approve of it, are at perfect liberty to insert it in the newspapers, inserting the name of Commodore instead of 'I.' Captains Miller and Berry &c. have authenticated the truth, till my quitting the San Josef to go on board the Minerve, and farther than this the detail should not be printed. As I do not write for the press, there may be parts of it which require the pruning-knife, which I desire you will use without fear. I pretend not to say that these ships might not have fell, had I not boarded them; but truly it was far from impossible but they might have forged into the Spanish fleet as the other two ships did. I hope for a good account of the Santissima Trinidad; she has been seen without masts, and some of our frigates near her.

Mrs. Nelson, 28 Feb. Lisbon.

We got up here with our prizes this afternoon: the more I think of our late action, the more I am astonished; it absolutely appears a dream. The Santissima Trinidad, of four decks, lost five hundred killed and wounded; had not my ship been so cut up, I would have had her; but it is well, thank God for it! As to myself, I assure you I never was better, and rich in the praises of every man from the highest to the lowest in the fleet. The Spanish war will give us a cottage and a piece of ground, which is all I want. I shall come one day or other laughing back, when we will retire from the busy scenes of life: I do not, however, mean to be a hermit; the dons will give us a little money.

I go to sea the day after to-morrow in this ship [Irresistible], with a squadron to be off Cadiz, consisting of the Irresistible, Orion, &c. Sir John Jervis has already spread the frigates; and I shall return by the time his fleet is ready for sea.

This squadron was under orders to cruise about 25 leagues SSW of Cape St. Vincent, and from that towards the African coast, in hopes of intercepting the Viceroy of Mexico, who, with three ships of the line and a large treasure, was expected at Cadiz.

I am looking out with an anxious eye for the Viceroy of Mexico, but I fear he will go to Teneriffe. The Spanish fleet is, fit and unfit, thirty sail of the line in Cadiz, and I suppose twenty will be ready for sea by the first week in April. I am assured fifteen sail of the line are ordered to Ferrol, and both squadrons are destined for Brest, making thirty sail from the two ports of Cadiz and Ferrol. I trust Sir John Jervis will be reinforced; at present his situation is not very pleasant. Eighteen two-decked ships are to perform two services; at least this is what strikes me as necessary, viz. to see our army safe from Elba, and to prevent the Spanish fleet sailing with impunity from Cadiz. If Sir John stays off Cadiz, the French will push out two or three sail of the line, and most probably take our army; if he goes into the Straits, the detachment from Cadiz gets unmolested to Ferrol: here is a choice of difficulties. I have ventured to propose to the admiral, letting me go with two or three sail of the line, off Toulon, or to Elba, as may be necessary, and for the fleet to stay outside. I beg your Royal Highness will not think I am in the habit of advising my commander-in-chief; but Sir John Jervis has spoiled me by encouraging me to give my opinion freely. *Duke of Clarence, 22 March. Off C. St. Vincent.*

On 1 April, Nelson received a letter from Lord Spencer, acquainting him, in the most flattering language, that his Majesty had signified his intention of conferring on him the Most Honourable Order of the Bath. This was the honour which Nelson had specially desired: and it appears certain that the recognition of his services took that particular form in consequence of the representation of Sir Gilbert Elliot, to whom Nelson had confided his wish.[1] The appointment was dated 17 March, but was not gazetted till 27 May.

I beg you will thank all our friends for their kind congratulations; and I must be delighted, when, from the king to the peasant, all are willing to do me honour. But I will partake of nothing but what shall include Collingwood and Troubridge. We are the only three ships who made great exertions on that glorious day: the others did their duty, and some not exactly to my satisfaction. We ought to have had the Santissima Trinidad and the Soberano, seventy-four. They belonged to us by conquest, and only wanted some good fellow to get alongside them, and they were ours. But it is well; and for that reason only we do not like to say much. *Rev. Wm. Nelson, 6 April. Off C. St. Vincent.*

Sir John Jervis is not quite contented, but says nothing publicly. An anecdote in the action is honourable to the admiral, and to

[1] See *ante*, p. 118.

Troubridge and myself. Calder [the first captain of the Victory] said, 'Sir, the Captain and Culloden are separated from the fleet, and unsupported: shall we recall them?'—'I will not have them recalled. I put my faith in those ships: it is a disgrace that they are not supported and separated.'

Sir J. Jervis, 11 April.

I shall endeavour by fair means to accomplish your wishes in the blockade. I have myself no idea that the Spanish fleet will be ready for sea for some months; and I own that my feelings are alive for the safety of our army from Elba. If the French get out two sail of the line, which I am confident they may do, our troops are lost, and what a triumph would that be to them! I know you have many difficulties to contend with, but I am anxious that nothing should miscarry under your orders. If you think a detachment can be spared, I am ready to go and do my best for their protection.

Consequent on this letter, the admiral sent Nelson orders to go up to Elba in the Captain, with the Colossus and Leander, and bring away the garrison, if, indeed, it was not already on its way down the Mediterranean. Before receiving these orders, however, Nelson had again written:

12 April.

Troubridge talked to me last night about the Viceroy at Teneriffe. Since I first believed it was possible that his Excellency might have gone there, I have endeavoured to make myself master of the situation and means of approach by sea and land. I shall begin by sea.

The Spanish ships generally moor with two cables to the sea, and four cables from their sterns to the shore; therefore, although we might get to be masters of them, should the wind not come off the shore, it does not appear certain we should succeed so completely as we might wish. As to any opposition, except from natural impediments, I should not think it would avail. I do not reckon myself equal to Blake; but if I recollect right, he was more obliged to the wind coming off the land, than to any exertions of his own:[1] fortune favoured the gallant attempt, and may do so again. But it becomes my duty to state all the difficulties, as you have done me the honour to desire me to enter on the subject.

[1] Nelson refers here to an erroneous statement in Campbell's *Lives of the Admirals*, vol. ii. p. 108; according to which, Blake succeeded in the attack, and burnt the whole Spanish fleet down to the water's edge, except two ships which sank: 'and the wind then veering to the south-west, he passed with the fleet safe out of the port again.' But according to Blake's despatch, printed by order of Parliament, the wind did not veer to the south-west till two days afterwards.

The approach by sea to the anchoring place is under very high land, passing three valleys; therefore the wind is either in from the sea, or squally with calms from the mountains. Sometimes in a night a ship may get in with the land-wind and moderate weather. So much for the sea attack, which, if you approve, I am ready and willing to look at, or to carry into execution. But now comes my plan, which could not fail of success, would immortalise the undertakers, ruin Spain, and has every prospect of raising our country to a higher pitch of wealth than she ever yet attained: but here soldiers must be consulted, and I know from experience, excepting General O'Hara, they have not the same boldness in undertaking a political measure that we have; we look to the benefit of our country, and risk our own fame every day to save her: a soldier obeys his orders, and no more. By saying soldiers should be consulted, you will guess I mean the army of 3,700 men from Elba, with cannon, mortars, and every implement now embarked; they would do the business in three days, probably much less. I will undertake with a very small squadron to do the naval part. The shore, although not very easy of access, yet is so steep, that the transports may run in and land the army in one day. The water is conveyed to the town in wooden troughs: this supply cut off, would probably induce a very speedy surrender: good terms for the town, private property secured to the islanders, and only the delivery of public stores and foreign merchandise demanded, with threats of utter destruction if one gun is fired. In short, the business could not miscarry.

Now it comes for me to discover what might induce General de Burgh to act in this business. All the risk and responsibility must rest with you. A fair representation should also be made by you of the great national advantages that would arise to our country, and of the ruin that our success would occasion to Spain. Your opinion besides should be stated, of the superior advantages a fortnight thus employed would be of to the army, to what they could do in Portugal; and that of the six or seven millions sterling, the army should have one half. If this sum were thrown into circulation in England, what might not be done? It would insure an honourable peace, with innumerable other blessings. It has long occupied my thoughts.

Should General de Burgh not choose to act, after having all these blessings for our country stated to him, which are almost put into our hands, we must look to General O'Hara. The Royals, about 600, are in the fleet, with artillery sufficient for the purpose.

You have the power of stopping the store-ships; 1,000 more men would still insure the business, for Teneriffe never was besieged, therefore the hills that cover the town are not fortified to resist any attempt of taking them by storm; the rest must follow—a fleet of ships, and money to reward the victors. But I know with you, and I can lay my hand on my heart and say the same—It is the honour and prosperity of our country that we wish to extend.

The same day, 12 April, having received the admiral's orders, he turned over the command of the blockade of Cadiz to Sir James Saumarez, then captain of the Orion, and, with the ships appointed, sailed for Elba. On the 21st, he met the garrison off the south end of Corsica, and at once turned back, desiring to rejoin the commander-in-chief without loss of time, as it was rumoured that the Spanish fleet was on the point of putting to sea. The getting back, however, took him more than a month: and he did not join the admiral off Cadiz till 24 May, when he was ordered to hoist his flag in the Theseus, and to take command of the inshore squadron.

J. M'Arthur, 1 June.

We are off Cadiz with a greater inferiority than before. I am barely out of shot of a Spanish rear-admiral. We have every day flags of truce; the dons hope for peace, but must soon fight us, if the war goes on. I wish it was all over, for I cannot fag much longer; and, to please our fleet, I hear that a squadron is looking out, in the limits of this station, for the galleons daily expected: what a special mark of favour to us, who are enabling them to cruise so much at their ease!

Sir J. Jervis, 13 June, 9 P.M.

What the intentions of the dons are, I know not; but their movements would assure me, if English, that they are on the eve of coming out. We see that thirteen sail of the line are unmoored and hove short. I saw Gravina cat his anchor, and they did it briskly; but the accommodation ladder of his ship was not in at sunset. The signals which they have been making this day are not their usual harbour signals. I will give them credit for their alertness, if they come out in the morning. This squadron have their bulkheads down, and in perfect readiness for battle, and to weigh, cut, or slip, as the occasion may require. I have given out a line of battle—myself to lead; and you may rest assured that I will make a vigorous attack upon them, the moment their noses are outside the Diamond. Pray do not send me another ship, for they may have an idea of attacking the squadron; and if you send any more, they may believe we are prepared, and know of their intention.

A few nights ago a paper was dropped on the quarter deck, of which this is a copy: 'Success attend Admiral Nelson! God bless Captain Miller! We thank them for the officers they have placed over us. We are happy and comfortable, and will shed every drop of blood in our veins to support them, and the name of the Theseus shall be immortalised as high as the Captain's. SHIP'S COMPANY.'

<small>Mrs. Nelson, 15 June.</small>

We are looking at the ladies walking the walls and mall of Cadiz, and know of the ridicule they make of their sea officers. Thirty sail are now perfectly ready, and, the first east wind, I expect the ships from the Mediterranean, which will make them forty sail of the line. We are now twenty; some of our ships being always obliged to be absent for water, provisions, &c. However equal we may be to do the business, yet I cannot bring myself to believe that it is good policy to leave us so inferior, whatever honour there may be in it. The merchants of Cadiz have repeatedly petitioned Government to force out the fleet; and say truly that ten sail of the line had better be sacrificed than the loss of their three ships from Lima, and their homeward convoy, which must fall into the hands of the English, if they are not forced from before the harbour. I am of opinion that some morning, when least expected, I shall see them tumbling out of Cadiz. We in the advance are, night and day, prepared for battle: our friends in England need not fear the event. At present we are all quiet in our fleet; and, if Government hang some of the Nore delegates, we shall remain so. I am entirely with the seamen in their first complaint. We are a neglected set, and, when peace comes, are shamefully treated; but, for the Nore scoundrels, I should be happy to command a ship against them.

<small>Rev. D. Hoste, 30 June.</small>

We will begin this night by ten o'clock; and I beg that all the launches of the fleet may be with me by eight, or half-past at farthest, with their carronades and plenty of ammunition; also all the barges or pinnaces to come to me. I wish to make it a warm night at Cadiz. The town and their fleet are prepared, and their gunboats are advanced; so much the better. If they venture from their walls, I shall give Johnny his full scope for fighting.

<small>Sir J. Jervis, 3 July.</small>

In obedience to your orders, the Thunderer bomb was placed . . . within 2,500 yards of the walls of Cadiz; and the shells were thrown from her with much precision . . . but, unfortunately, it was soon found that the large mortar was materially injured, from its former services; I therefore judged it proper to order her to return. . . . The Spaniards having sent out a great number of

<small>4 July.</small>

mortar gunboats and armed launches, I directed a vigorous attack to be made on them, which was done with such gallantry, that they were drove and pursued close to the walls of Cadiz, and must have suffered considerable loss : and I have the pleasure to inform you, that two mortar boats and an armed launch remained in our possession.

I feel myself particularly indebted, for the successful termination of this contest, to the gallantry of Captains Fremantle and Miller, the former of whom accompanied me in my barge; and to my coxswain, John Sykes, who, in defending my person, is most severely wounded; as was Captain Fremantle, slightly, in the attack. And my praises are generally due to every officer and man, some of whom I saw behave in the most noble manner; and I regret it is not in my power to particularise them. I must also beg to be permitted to express my admiration of Don Miguel Tyrason, the commander of the gunboats. In his barge, he laid my boat alongside, and his resistance was such as did honour to a brave officer; eighteen of the twenty-six men being killed, and himself and all the rest wounded.

Symptoms of mutiny had shown themselves on board some of the ships of the fleet off Cadiz. On Friday, 7, and Saturday, 8 July, four mutineers of the St. George were tried by a court-martial; and on the latter day, Sir John Jervis wrote two notes respecting them to Nelson. In the first he said, 'If these four unfortunate men receive sentence of death, as there is every reason to believe they will, from the strong and direct evidence which came home to the bosoms of all yesterday, and the court-martial ends this day, they will suffer at 6 o'clock in the evening.' As the trial did not terminate until after sunset, the sentence was not carried into execution the same evening; and Sir John Jervis consequently wrote to Rear-Admiral Nelson : 'The sentence must be carried into execution to-morrow morning, although it is Sunday, and you will take care to have the boats of the detached squadron up in time.' In another letter to Nelson, dated Sunday evening, 9 July, Sir John Jervis said : ' Vice-Admiral Thompson has presumed to censure the execution on the Sabbath, in a public letter; and I have insisted on his being removed from this fleet immediately, or that I shall be called home; and I have stipulated for no more admirals.' Writing to Earl Spencer on that day, the commander-in-chief observed : 'The court-martial on the mutineers of the St. George did not finish before sunset yesterday, or they would have been executed last night. The most daring and profligate of them confessed to the clergyman who attended him, that the plan had been in contemplation six months, in concert with the Britannia, Captain, Diadem, and Egmont. I hope I shall not be censured by the bench of bishops, as I have been by Vice-Admiral [Thompson,] for profaning the Sabbath : the criminals asked five days to prepare, in which they would have hatched five hundred treasons : besides that, we are provoking the Spanish fleet to come out by every means in our power; and seven-and-twenty gun and mortar boats did actually advance, dastardly enough, it must be confessed, and cannonaded the advanced squadron, now composed of ten sail of the line, on seeing twenty barges and pinnaces go to attend the execution of the sentence.' On 22 September, the Admiralty acknowledged the receipt of Lord St. Vincent's letter announcing the execution of the mutineers on the Sunday, and expressed 'their very high approbation' of his 'conduct on that unpleasant and urgent occasion.'

In the first place I congratulate you on the finish, as it ought, of the St. George's business, and I (if I may be permitted to say so) very much approve of its being so speedily carried into execution, even although it is Sunday. The particular situation of the service requires extraordinary measures. I hope this will end all the disorders in our fleet: had there been the same determined spirit at home, I do not believe it would have been half so bad; not but that I think Lord Howe's keeping back the first petition was wrong. *Sir J. Jervis, 9 July.*

I am sorry that you should have to differ with Vice-Admiral Thompson, but had it been Christmas Day instead of Sunday, I would have executed them. We know not what might have been hatched by a Sunday's grog. *Sir R. Calder, 9 July.*

Had my orders been well executed, not a Spanish gun or mortar boat would have been left at Cadiz. Our loss of men is most trifling; but, however that might have been, I had rather see fifty shot by the enemy, than one hanged by us. It is good at these times to keep the devil out of their heads. *Capt. J. N. Inglefield, 11 July.*

Mazaredo is alarmed; has drawn all his ships between St. Mary's and Cadiz; and if you make haste with the sea-mortar, I will bomb him out of Cadiz Bay. Three fires were seen in the town, but they were got under without much difficulty. I laid myself with the bomb on the strong face of Cadiz, seventy guns and eight mortars. They expected me on the weak side. The next night I took them on the soft side, and eighty shells fell in the town, and some over it amongst their shipping. Yesterday, in the Theseus, I had the honour of every gun from the southern part of Cadiz, and of every gun and mortar boat. I could not get them out so far as I wished, or some of them should have paid me a visit. I sent ninety-one prisoners into Cadiz, whom I took on the night of the 3rd; and, as to killed, I know nothing about them: eighteen were killed in the commanding officer's boat, that had the presumption to lay my barge aboard, manned with some of the Agamemnon's people. My squadron is now ten sail of the line. If they come out, there will be no fighting beyond my squadron.

Sir John Jervis having received intelligence that a richly laden Spanish ship, from Manilla to Cadiz, was at Santa Cruz, determined to carry out Nelson's suggestion of attacking that place; but without any such force of soldiers as Nelson had considered necessary. On 14 July, after a personal conference with the commander-in-chief, Nelson received the following instructions : ' You are hereby required and directed to take the ships [Theseus, Culloden, Zealous, Leander, Seahorse, Emerald, Terpsichore, Fox cutter] under your command, their captains being instructed to obey your orders, and to proceed with the utmost expedition off the island of Teneriffe, and there make your dispositions for taking possession of the town of Santa Cruz, by a sudden and vigorous assault. In case of success, you are authorised to lay a heavy contribution on the inhabitants of the town and adjacent district, if they do not put you in possession of the whole cargo of El Principe d'Asturias, from Manilla, bound to Cadiz, belonging to the Philippine Company, and all the treasure belonging to the Crown of Spain ; and you are to endeavour to take, sink, burn, or otherwise destroy, all vessels of every description, even those employed in the fishery, on the coast of Africa, unless a just contribution is made for their preservation by the inhabitants of the Canary Islands ; and having performed your mission, you are to make the best of your way back, to join me off this port.'

Sir J. Jervis, 24 July, 8 P.M. Off Santa Cruz.

I shall not enter on the subject while we are not in possession of Santa Cruz; your partiality will give credit, that all has hitherto been done which was possible, but without effect : this night I, humble as I am, command the whole, destined to land under the batteries of the town, and to-morrow my head will probably be crowned with either laurel or cypress.

27 July. Off Santa Cruz.

In obedience to your orders to make a vigorous attack on Santa Cruz, in the island of Teneriffe, I directed from the ships under my command, 1,000 men, including marines, to be prepared for landing, under the direction of Captain Troubridge, of his Majesty's ship Culloden, and Captains Hood, Thompson, Fremantle, Bowen, Miller and Waller, who very handsomely volunteered their services ; and although I am under the painful necessity of acquainting you that we have not been able to succeed in our attack, yet it is my duty to state that I believe more daring intrepidity was never shown than by the captains, officers, and men you did me the honour to place under my command.

Inclosed I transmit to you a list of the killed and wounded, and amongst the former, it is with the deepest sorrow I have to place the name of Captain Richard Bowen, of his Majesty's ship Terpsichore, than whom a more enterprising, able, and gallant officer does not grace his Majesty's naval service; and with great regret I have to mention the loss of Lieutenant John Gibson, commander of the Fox cutter, and a great number of gallant officers and men.

Abstract List of Killed, Wounded, Drowned, and Missing.

	Killed	Wounded	Drowned	Missing
Officers	6	5	1	—
Seamen	28	90 }	97	5
Marines	16	15 }		
Total	50	110	98	5

A DETAIL OF THE PROCEEDINGS OF THE EXPEDITION AGAINST THE TOWN OF SANTA CRUZ, IN THE ISLAND OF TENERIFFE [TRANSMITTED TO SIR JOHN JERVIS].

On Friday, the 21st instant (July), I directed to be embarked on board the Seahorse, Terpsichore, and Emerald frigates, one thousand men (including 250 marines, under the command of Captain Thomas Oldfield), the whole commanded by Captain Troubridge, attended by all the boats of the squadron, scaling ladders, and every implement which I thought necessary for the success of the enterprise. I directed that the boats should land in the night, between the fort on the north-east side of the Bay of Santa Cruz and the town, and endeavour to make themselves masters of that fort, which when done, to send in my summons, the liberal terms of which I am confident you will approve.

Although the frigates approached within three miles of the place of debarkation by twelve o'clock, yet from the unforeseen circumstance of a strong gale of wind in the offing, and a strong current against them in-shore, they did not approach within a mile of the landing-place when the day dawned, which discovered to the Spaniards our force and intentions. On my approach with the line-of-battle ships, Captains Troubridge and Bowen, with Captain Oldfield, of the marines, came on board, to consult with me what was best to be done, and were of opinion, if they could possess themselves of the heights over the fort above mentioned, that it could be stormed, to which I gave my assent, and directed the line-of-battle ships to batter the fort, in order to create a diversion; but this was found impracticable, not being able to get nearer the shore than three miles, from a calm and contrary currents, nor could our men possess themselves of the heights, as the enemy had taken possession of them, and seemed as anxious to retain them, as we were to get them. Thus foiled in my original plan, I considered it for the honour of our king and country not to give over the attempt to possess ourselves of the town, that our enemies might be convinced there is nothing which Englishmen are not equal to; and confident in the bravery of those who would be employed in the service, I embarked every person from the shore on the 22nd at night.

On the 24th, I got the ships to an anchor about two miles to the northward of the town, and made every show for a disposition of attacking the heights, which appeared to answer the end, from the great number of people they had placed on them. The Leander, Captain Thompson, joined this afternoon, and her marines were added to the force before appointed, and Captain Thompson also volunteered his services.

At 11 o'clock at night the boats of the squadron, containing between six and seven hundred men, one hundred and eighty men on board the Fox cutter, and about seventy or eighty men in a boat we had taken the day before, proceeded towards the town. The divisions of the boats, conducted by all the captains, except Fremantle and Bowen, who attended with me to regulate and lead the way to the attack; every captain being acquainted that the landing was to be made on the mole, and from whence they were to proceed, as fast as possible, into the great square, where they were to form, and proceed on such services as might be found necessary. We were not discovered till within half gunshot of the landing-place, when I directed the boats to cast off from each other, give an hurrah and push for the shore. A fire of thirty or forty pieces of cannon, with musketry, from one end of the town to the other, opened upon us, but nothing could stop the intrepidity of the captains leading the divisions. Unfortunately, the greatest part of the boats did not see the mole, but went on shore through a raging surf, which stove all the boats to the left of it.

For the detail of their proceedings, I send you a copy of Captain Troubridge's account to me, and I cannot but express my admiration of the firmness with which he and his brave associates supported the honour of the British flag.

Captains Fremantle, Bowen, and myself, with four or five boats, stormed the mole, although opposed apparently by 400 or 500 men, took possession of it, and spiked the guns; but such a heavy fire of musketry and grape-shot was kept up from the citadel and houses at the head of the mole, that we could not advance, and we were all nearly killed or wounded.

The Fox cutter, in rowing towards the town, received a shot under water, from one of the enemy's distant batteries, immediately sunk, and Lieutenant Gibson, her commander, with ninety-seven men, were drowned.

Captain Troubridge's letter, dated 25 July, forms a necessary supplement to this.

'From the darkness of the night, I did not immediately hit the mole, the spot appointed to land at, but pushed on shore under the enemy's battery, close to the southward of the citadel. Captain Waller landed at the same instant, and two or three other boats. The surf was so high, many put back: the boats were full of water in an instant, and stove against the rocks, and most of the ammunition in the men's pouches wet. As soon as I had collected a few men, I immediately pushed, with Captain Waller, for the square, the place of rendezvous, in hopes of there meeting you and the remainder of the people, and waited about an hour, during which time I sent a sergeant with two gentlemen of the town to summons the citadel. I fear the sergeant was shot on his way, as I heard nothing of him afterwards.

'The ladders being all lost in the surf, or not to be found, no immediate attempt could be made on the citadel. I therefore marched to join Captains Hood and Miller, who, I had intelligence, had made good their landing to the SW of the place I did, with a body of men. I endeavoured then to procure some intelligence of you and the rest of the officers, without success. By daybreak we had collected about eighty marines, eighty pikemen, and one hundred and eighty small-arm seamen. These, I found, were all that were alive that had made good their landing. With this force, having procured some ammunition from the Spanish prisoners we had made, we were marching to try what could be done with the citadel without ladders, but found the whole of the streets commanded by field-pieces, and upwards of eight thousand Spaniards and one hundred French under arms, approaching by every avenue. As the boats were all stove, and I saw no possibility of getting more men on shore—the ammunition wet, and no provisions—I sent Captain Hood with a flag of truce to the governor, to say I was prepared to burn the town, which I should immediately put in force if he approached one inch further: and, at the same time, I desired Captain Hood to say it would be done with regret, as I had no wish to injure the inhabitants: that if he would come to my terms, I was ready to treat, which he readily agreed to: a copy of which I had the honour to send you by Captain Waller, which, I hope, will meet your approbation, and appear highly honourable.

'From the small body of men, and the greater part being pike and small-arm seamen, which can be only called irregulars, with very little ammunition in the pouches but what was wet in the surf at landing, I could not expect to succeed in any attempt upon the enemy, whose superior strength I have before mentioned. The Spanish officers assure me they expected us, and were perfectly prepared with all the batteries, and the number of men I have before mentioned under arms; with the great disadvantage of a rocky coast, high surf, and in the face of forty pieces of cannon, though we were not successful, will show what an Englishman is equal to.

K

'TERMS AGREED UPON WITH THE GOVERNOR OF THE CANARY ISLANDS.—
That the troops &c. belonging to his Britannic Majesty shall embark
with all their arms of every kind, and take their boats off, if saved, and
be provided with such other as may be wanting ; in consideration of
which it is engaged on their part they shall not molest the town in any
manner by the ships of the British squadron now before it, or any of
the islands in the Canaries ; and prisoners shall be given up on both
sides.'

Sir J. Jervis, 16 August. I rejoice at being once more in sight of your flag, and with your permission will come on board the Ville de Paris, and pay you my respects. A left-handed admiral will never again be considered as useful, therefore the sooner I get to a very humble cottage the better, and make room for a better man to serve the State.

E. Nepean, 1 Sept. Seahorse, Spithead. I have the honour to acquaint you of my arrival here. And I have to request their lordships' permission to go on shore for the recovery of my wounds.

Sir A. S. Hamond, 8 Sept. Bath. Success covers a multitude of blunders, and the want of it hides the greatest gallantry and good conduct. You will see by my journal the first attack on the 21st, under Troubridge, completely failed; and it was the 25th before it could be again attacked, which gave four days for collecting a force to oppose us. Had I been with the first party, I have reason to believe complete success would have crowned our endeavours. My pride suffered; and although I felt the second attack a forlorn hope, yet the honour of our country called for the attack, and that I should command it. I never expected to return, and am thankful. I shall not go to town till the 20th, or my arm is well : I suffer a good deal of pain, owing to a cold falling on it.

Lord Spencer, 27 Sept. I take the liberty of transmitting to your Lordship certificates of the loss of my right eye at the siege of Calvi ; and I beg also to acquaint you that I was slightly wounded during the siege of Bastia, and most severely bruised on 14 February last; and I likewise send herewith a general statement of my services this war, all which I have to request you will have the goodness to lay before the king, when you shall judge proper.

Memorial to the king. To the King's most excellent Majesty, the memorial of Sir Horatio Nelson, K.B., and Rear-Admiral in your Majesty's fleet, humbly sheweth,—that, during the present war, your memorialist has been in four actions with the fleets of the enemy—viz. on 13 and 14 March, 1795, on 13 July, 1795, and on 14 February, 1797 ; in three actions with frigates ; in six engagements against batteries; in ten actions in boats employed in cutting out of harbours, in destroying vessels, and in taking three towns. Your memorialist has also served on shore with the army four months, and commanded the batteries at the sieges of Bastia and Calvi.

That during the war he has assisted at the capture of seven sail of the line, six frigates, four corvettes, and eleven privateers of different sizes, and taken and destroyed near fifty sail of merchant vessels; and your memorialist has actually been engaged against the enemy upwards of one hundred and twenty times. In which service your memorialist has lost his right eye and arm, and been severely wounded and bruised in his body. All of which services and wounds your memorialist most humbly submits to your Majesty's most gracious consideration.

Lord Spencer says, my pension will be the same as those for 1 June, 712*l.* with the deductions. My poor arm continues quite as it was, the ligature still fast to the nerve, and very painful at times. The moment I am cured I shall offer myself for service; and if you continue to hold your opinion of me, shall press to return with all the zeal, although not with the personal ability, I had formerly. *Lord St. Vincent. 6 Oct. London.*

Any event [1] which has the prospect of adding to your felicity cannot but afford me pleasure; and I most heartily congratulate you on becoming one of *us,* and we shall have great pleasure in being known to Mrs. Berry. I am confident nothing will alter you for the worse, and I wish you to be no better; therefore we will leave off further complimenting. *Capt. Berry, 28 Nov*

The Foudroyant will be launched in January, and in commission early in February.

If you mean to marry, I would recommend your doing it speedily, or the to be Mrs. Berry will have very little of your company; for I am well, and you may expect to be called for every hour. We shall probably be at sea before the Foudroyant is launched. Our ship is at Chatham, a seventy-four, and she will be choicely manned. This may not happen, but it stands so to-day. *8 Dec,*

My dear Bertie,—I thank you very much for your early notice of the event of Captain Williamson's long trial.[2] The court has been a most patient, and certainly a most lenient one. As to myself, upon the general question, that if a man does not do his utmost in time of action, I think but one punishment ought to be inflicted. *Capt. Thos. Bertie, 4 Jan. 1798. Bath.*

[1] Captain Berry's marriage, which took place on 12 December, 1797.
[2] Dismissed his ship and placed at the bottom of the list of post-captains for misconduct in command of the Agincourt at Camperdown.

Not that I take a man's merit from his list of killed and wounded, for but little may be in his power; and if he does his utmost in the station he is placed, he has equal merit to the man who may have his ship beat to pieces, but not his good fortune. I dare say there were some favourable circumstances on W.'s trial, and it is a virtue to lean on the side of mercy; and I have only to hope it will have its effect upon officers going into action. I would have every man believe, I shall only take my chance of being shot by the enemy, but if I do not take that chance, I am certain of being shot by my friends.

On 29 March, Nelson hoisted his flag, as Rear-Admiral of the Blue, on board the Vanguard, at Spithead; and sailed from St. Helens on 10 April.

Lady Nelson, 1 May. Lisbon.

I joined the fleet yesterday, and found Lord St. Vincent everything I wished him; and his friends in England have done me justice for my zeal and affection towards him. I have my fears that he will not be much longer in this command, for I believe he has written to be superseded, which I am sincerely sorry for. It will considerably take from my pleasure in serving here; but I will hope for the best. The dons have, I find, long expected my return with bomb-vessels, gunboats, and every proper implement for the destruction of Cadiz and their fleet. They have prepared three floating batteries to lie outside their walls, to prevent the fancied attack; and, lo, the mountain has brought forth a mouse:—I am arrived with a single ship, and without the means of annoying them. The admiral probably is going to detach me with a small squadron; not on any fighting expedition, therefore do not be surprised if it should be some little time before you hear from me again.

On the same 1 May, Lord St. Vincent wrote to Lord Spencer: 'The arrival of Admiral Nelson has given me new life: you could not have gratified me more than in sending him; his presence in the Mediterranean is so very essential, that I mean to put the Orion and Alexander under his command, with the addition of three or four frigates, and to send him away the moment the Vanguard has delivered her water to the inshore squadron, to endeavour to ascertain the real object of the preparations making by the French.' And on the following day he sent Nelson a 'most secret' order, which, after reciting intelligence that a considerable armament was preparing at Toulon, and a number of transports collecting at Marseilles and Genoa, for an embarkation of troops, directed him to proceed with such of the squadron as might be at Gibraltar, up the Mediterranean, and to endeavour to ascertain, either on the coast of Provence or Genoa, the destination of that expedition, which, according to some reports, was Sicily and Corfu, and according to others, Portugal or Ireland. If he found that the enemy intended to join a squadron of Spanish ships said to be equipping at Carthagena, to which he was also to give his attention, he was to despatch the Bonne Citoyenne or Terpsichore with the information to Lord St. Vincent, and to continue, with the rest of the squadron, on that service as long as he might think it necessary. If the enemy's armament was coming down the Mediterranean, he was to take special care not to suffer it to pass the Straits before him, so as to impede his joining Lord St. Vincent in time to prevent a union between it and the Spanish fleet in Cadiz Bay.'

The Vanguard arrived at Gibraltar on 4 May, and sailed on the 8th, with the Orion and Alexander, the frigates Flora, Emerald, Terpsichore, and the Bonne Citoyenne in company.

This morning, the Terpsichore captured a small French corvette, of six guns and sixty-five men, which came out of Toulon at 11 o'clock last night. From the general report of vessels spoke, you will observe the uniformity of the reports—viz. that an expedition is preparing to sail from Toulon. We have separately examined the crew of this corvette, and, from the whole, I believe the following may be depended on as near the truth—that Bonaparte arrived at Toulon last Friday, and has examined the troops which are daily embarking in the numerous transports; that vessels with troops frequently arrive from Marseilles; it is not generally believed that Bonaparte is to embark, but no one knows to what place the armament is destined. Fifteen sail of the line are apparently ready for sea, but nineteen are in the harbour, and yet it is said only six sail of the line are to sail with the transports now ready; that about 12,000 men are embarked; their cavalry arrived at Toulon, but I cannot learn that any are yet embarked. Reports say they are to sail in a few days, and others that they will not sail for a fortnight.

Lord St. Vincent, 18 May. Off Cape Sicie.

I have no further particulars to tell you than are in my public letter. 'They order their matters so well in France that all is secret.

18 May.

I am sorry to be obliged to inform you of the accidents which have happened to the Vanguard. On Saturday, 19 May, it blew strong from the NW. On Sunday it moderated so much as to enable us to get our top-gallant masts and yards aloft. After dark it began to blow strong; but as the ship was prepared for a gale, my mind was easy. At half-past one A.M. on Monday, the main-top-mast went over the side, as did soon afterwards the mizen-mast. As it was impossible for any night signal to be seen, I had hopes we should be quiet till daylight, when I determined to wear, and scud before the gale; but about half-past three the foremast went in three pieces, and the bowsprit was found to be sprung in three

24 May. S. Pietro.

places. When the day broke, we were fortunately enabled to wear the ship with a remnant of the sprit-sail. The Orion, Alexander, and Emerald wore with us; but the Terpsichore, Bonne Citoyenne, and a French Smyrna ship, continued to lay to under bare poles. Our situation was twenty-five leagues south of the islands of Hieres; and as we were laying with our head to the NE, had we not wore, which was hardly to be expected, the ship must have drifted to Corsica. The gale blew very hard all the day, and the ship laboured most exceedingly. In the evening, being in latitude 40° 50′ N, I determined to steer for Oristano Bay, in the island of Sardinia: during the night, the Emerald parted company, for what reason I am at present unacquainted with. Being unable to get into Oristan, the Alexander took us in tow, and by Captain Ball's unremitting attention to our distress, and by Sir James Saumarez's exertions and ability in finding out the island of S. Pietro and the proper anchorage, the Vanguard was, on 23 May, at noon, brought safely to an anchor into the harbour of S. Pietro.

Lady Nelson, 24 May.

Figure to yourself a vain man, on Sunday evening at sunset, walking in his cabin with a squadron about him, who looked up to their chief to lead them to glory, and in whom this chief placed the firmest reliance, that the proudest ships, in equal numbers, belonging to France, would have bowed their flags, and with a very rich prize lying by him. Figure to yourself this proud, conceited man, when the sun rose on Monday morning, his ship dismasted, his fleet dispersed, and himself in such distress that the meanest frigate out of France would have been a very unwelcome guest.

A few days later, 29 May, Captain Berry wrote to his father-in-law a more detailed account of the dismasting of the Vanguard, and continued: 'For want of masts we rolled dreadfully. The storm did not abate till Tuesday afternoon, which enabled the Alexander to take us in tow. Our situation on Tuesday night was the most alarming I ever experienced: we stood in for the island of Sardinia, and approached the SW side of the island, intending to go into Oristano Bay, which we were not acquainted with, but it was absolutely necessary to go somewhere. Finding we could not fetch Oristano, the admiral determined to try for S. Pietro, which we could have fetched had the breeze continued, but unfortunately it fell light airs, and at times almost calm; so much so, that we had determined to order the Alexander to cast off the hawser, and desire her to shift for herself—trust to our own fate, but not involve any other ship in our difficulties. All this time there was a heavy western swell driving in towards the shore, so that at midnight we were completely embayed. You may easily figure to yourself our situation, and the feelings of those who knew the danger, when I tell you I could easily distinguish the surf breaking on the rocky shore; still there was hope anchorage might be found, though we knew of none. We therefore bent our cables and prepared for the worst, anxiously wishing for daybreak, which at length arrived, and we found ourselves about five miles from the shore, the western swell still continuing to drive us in, and no wind to enable us to get off. Indeed, the Vanguard was a perfect wreck, but the Alexander still had us in tow. Fortunately, at about six o'clock on Wednesday, 23 May, a breeze sprang up, the Alexander's sails filled, we weathered the rocks to windward of the island of S. Pietro, and before twelve we anchored in six fathoms, and fine smooth water—a luxury to us scarcely to be equalled, and if ever there was a satisfaction at being in distress, we felt it. The ready assistance of our friends Sir James Saumarez, captain of the Orion, 74, and Captain Alexander John Ball, of the Alexander, 74, by their united efforts, and the greatest exertion we all used, the Vanguard was equipped in four days, and actually at sea, not bound (I would have you observe) to Gibraltar or any English port to be refitted, but again cruising after the enemy on their own coasts! with a main top-mast for a fore-mast, and a topgallant-mast for a top-mast, consequently everything else reduced in proportion. By our superiority of sailing with other ships, we find the loss trifling to what it would have been to the generality of ships.'

On 24 May, Lord St. Vincent was joined by Sir Roger Curtis, bringing with him a strong reinforcement. He had already, on the 19th, received orders, referring to the French armament at Toulon, 'to lose no time in detaching from your fleet a squadron, consisting of twelve sail of the line, and a competent number of frigates, under the command of some discreet flag officer, into the Mediterranean, with instructions to him to proceed in quest of the said armament; and on falling in with it, or any other force belonging to the enemy, to take or destroy it.' At the same time, in a private letter, dated 29 April, Lord Spencer, after dwelling on the extreme importance of carrying out these orders, even though considerable hazard should be thereby incurred, continued: 'If you determine to send a detachment, I think it almost unnecessary to suggest to you the propriety of putting it under the command of Sir H. Nelson, whose acquaintance with that part of the world, as well as his activity and disposition, seem to qualify him in a peculiar manner for that service.'

That Lord Spencer was confirmed in his selection of Nelson for this command by Sir Gilbert Elliot, then Lord Minto, appears by a letter from Lord Minto to Nelson, dated 25 April, in which, however, he adds that Lord Spencer said, 'His opinion was already exactly the same with mine; he might venture to assure me there was no chance of any other person being thought of for the command, and that your name would certainly have been the first that would have occurred to himself;'[1] and Sir Edward Berry, in a letter to Nelson, dated 30 December, 1798, says: 'The Duke of Clarence desired I would tell you from him that it was the king that sent you with the squadron up the Mediterranean and formed the whole plan.' But as the king knew little and understood nothing about naval matters, the Duke of Clarence no doubt meant to imply that the selection and plan were made by himself. In point of fact, then, the propriety of the selection of Nelson for this

[1] Tucker's *Memoirs of the Earl of St. Vincent*, vol. I. p. 348.

command would seem to have occurred independently to everyone in a position to judge and not biassed by personal interests; but St. Vincent, writing to Nelson on 22 June, had to say: 'Sir William Parker and Sir John Orde have written strong remonstrances against your commanding the detached squadron, instead of them. I did all I could to prevent it, consistently with my situation; but there is a faction fraught with all manner of ill-will to you, that, unfortunately for the two baronets, domined over any argument or influence I could use. They will both be ordered home the moment their letters arrive.'

The reinforcements sent to Nelson brought him also the following instructions from the commander-in-chief, dated 21 May:

'In pursuance of instructions I have received from the Lords Commissioners of the Admiralty, to employ a squadron of his Majesty's ships within the Mediterranean, under the command of a discreet officer (copies of which are inclosed and of other papers necessary for your guidance), in conformity thereto, I do hereby authorise and require you, on being joined by the [Culloden, Goliath, Minotaur, Defence, Bellerophon, Majestic, Audacious, Zealous, Swiftsure, Theseus,] to take them and their captains under your command, in addition to those already with you, and to proceed with them in quest of the armament preparing by the enemy at Toulon and Genoa, the object whereof appears to be either an attack upon Naples and Sicily, the conveyance of an army to some part of the coast of Spain, for the purpose of marching towards Portugal, or to pass through the Straits, with the view of proceeding to Ireland. On falling in with the said armament, or any part thereof, you are to use your utmost endeavours to take, sink, burn, or destroy it. Should it appear to you, from good authority, on your arrival up the Mediterranean, that the enemy's force capable of being sent to sea should be inferior to what is reported by the intelligence herewith transmitted, you are in this case to direct such ships to rejoin me as may not absolutely be required to insure your superiority the moment you shall find yourself in a situation so to do. You are to remain upon this service so long as the provisions of your squadron will last, or as long as you may be enabled to obtain supplies from any of the ports in the Mediterranean, and when, from the want of provisions or any other circumstance, you shall be no longer able to remain within the Straits, or that the enemy's armament should escape to the westward of you, which you will take especial care to prevent, you are to lose no time in rejoining me, wherever I may be. On the subject of supplies, I inclose also a copy of their lordships' order to me, and do require you strictly to comply with the spirit of it, by considering and treating as hostile any ports within the Mediterranean (those of Sardinia excepted), where provisions or other articles you may be in want of, and which they are enabled to furnish, shall be refused; and you are to treat in like manner, and capture the ships and vessels of powers or states adhering to his Majesty's enemies, or under other circumstances enumerated in the said order, determining to the best of your judgment upon the several cases under this head, that may occur during your command.'

To these was added: 'It appears that their Lordships expect favourable neutrality from Tuscany and the Two Sicilies. In any event, you are to exact supplies of whatever you may be in want of from the territories of the Grand Duke of Tuscany, the King of the Two Sicilies, the Ottoman territory, Malta, and ci-devant Venetian dominions now belonging to the Emperor of Germany. The Dey [of Algiers is reported to be] extremely well disposed towards us. The Bey of Tunis, by the report of Captain Thompson of his Majesty's ship the Leander, is also perfectly neutral and good-humoured. From the Bashaw of Tripoli, I have every reason to believe, any ships of your squadron having occasion to touch there will be received in the most friendly manner. In a private letter from Lord Spencer, I am led to believe that you are perfectly justifiable in pursuing the French squadron to any part of the Mediterranean, Adriatic, Morea, Archipelago, or even into the Black Sea, should its destination be to any of those parts ; and thoroughly sensible of your zeal, enterprise, and capacity, at the head of a squadron of ships so well appointed, manned, and commanded, I have the utmost confidence in the success of your operations.'

With the same northerly wind that dismasted the Vanguard, the French had put to sea on 20 May.

The Mutine, Captain Hardy, joined me on the 5th, at daylight, with the flattering account of the honour you intended me of commanding such a fleet. Mutine fell in with Alcmène, off Barcelona, on the 2nd. Hope had taken all my frigates off the rendezvous, on the presumption that a ship which had lost her foremast must return to an arsenal. I thought Hope would have known me better. I joined dear Troubridge [with the reinforcement of ten sail of the line, and the Leander] on the 7th, but it has been nearly calm ever since, which grieves me sorely. . . . The French have a long start, but I hope they will rendezvous in Talamone Bay ; for the 12,000 men from Genoa in 100 sail of vessels, escorted by a frigate, had not sailed on the 2nd. *Lord St. Vincent, 11 June.*

As I am not quite clear, from General Acton's letters to you of 3 and 9 April, what co-operation is intended by the court of Naples, I wish to know perfectly what is to be expected, that I may regulate my movements accordingly, and beg clear answers to the following questions and requisitions: Are the ports of Naples and Sicily open to his Majesty's fleet ? Have the governors orders for our free admission, and for us to be supplied with whatever we may want ? *Sir Wm. Hamilton 12 June. Off Elba.*

If it is convenient, I much wish for some frigates and other fast-sailing vessels, for, by a fatality, all mine have left me. I want information of the French fleet ; for I hope they have passed Naples. I want good pilots—say six or eight, for the coast of Sicily, the Adriatic, or for whatever place the enemy's fleet may be at; for I mean to follow them if they go to the Black Sea.

I have heard by a vessel just spoke with, that the French fleet

14 June.
Off Civita Vecchia.
were seen off the north end of Sicily, steering to the eastward, on 4 June. If they mean an attack on Sicily, I hope by this time they have barely made a landing, for if their fleet is not moored in as strong a port as Toulon, nothing shall hinder me from attacking them; and, with the blessing of Almighty God, I hope for a most glorious victory. I send Captain Troubridge to communicate with your excellency, and, as Captain Troubridge is in full possession of my confidence, I beg that whatever he says may be considered as coming from me. Captain Troubridge is my honoured acquaintance of twenty-five years, and the very best sea-officer in his Majesty's service. I hope, pilots will be with us in a few hours; for I will not lose one moment after the brig's return, to wait for anything.

Lord Spencer,
15 June.
Off Ponza.
The last account I had of the French fleet was from a Tunisian cruiser, who saw them on the 4th, off Trapani, in Sicily, steering to the eastward. If they pass Sicily, I shall believe they are going on their scheme of possessing Alexandria, and getting troops to India—a plan concerted with Tippoo Saib, by no means so difficult as might at first view be imagined; but be they bound to the antipodes, your Lordship may rely that I will not lose a moment in bringing them to action, and endeavour to destroy their transports. I shall send Captain Troubridge on shore to talk with General Acton, and I hope the King of Naples will send me some frigates; for mine parted company on 20 May, and have not joined me since. The whole squadron is remarkably healthy, and perfectly equal to meet the French fleet.

Sir W. Hamilton,
17 June.
Naples Bay.
In my present state, if I meet the enemy at sea, the convoy will get off, for want of frigates. I submit this to you, to urge General Acton upon. If the enemy have Malta, it is only as a safe harbour for their fleet, and Sicily will fall the moment the king's fleet withdraws from the coast of Sicily.

18 June.
I send you an extract of the Admiralty orders to Earl St. Vincent, by which it would appear as determined by the Cabinet to keep a superior fleet to the enemy in the Mediterranean; for the Admiralty, you know, can give no such orders, but by an order from the Secretary of State. As for what depends on me, I beg, if you think it proper, to tell their Sicilian Majesties, and General Acton, that they may rest assured that I shall not withdraw the king's fleet but by positive orders or the impossibility of procuring supplies. I wish them to depend upon me, and they shall not be disappointed.

I have thought so much, and heard so much, of the French,

since I left Naples, that I should feel culpable, was I for a moment to delay expressing my sentiments on the present situation of the kingdom of the Two Sicilies. ...

20 June.
Off Messina.

I shall begin by supposing myself commanding a fleet attending an army which is to invade Sicily. If the general asked if Malta would not be a most useful place for the depôt of stores &c. &c., my answer would be, if you can take Malta, it secures the safety of the fleet, transports, stores, &c., and insures your safe retreat should that be necessary; for if even a superior fleet of the enemy should arrive, before one week passes, they will be blown to leeward, and you may pass with safety. This would be my opinion.
... I find plenty of goodwill towards us, with every hatred towards the French; but no assistance for us—no hostility to the French. On the contrary, the French minister is allowed to send off vessels to inform the fleet of my arrival, force, and destination, that instead of my surprising them, they may be prepared for resistance. But this being past, I shall endeavour briefly to state what in my opinion is now best to be done, and what Naples ought to do, if it is earnestly wished to save Sicily. I shall suppose the French not advanced since the last accounts, but still on Gozo and Comino, the fleet anchored between them. By the communication from Naples, they will be formed in the strongest position, with batteries and gunboats to flank them. We shall doubtless injure them, but our loss must be great; and I do not expect to force them from the anchorage, without fire-ships, bomb-vessels, and gunboats, when one hour would either destroy or drive them out. If our fleet is crippled, the blockade ends. ... It has been and may yet be in the King of Naples' power, by giving me help of every kind, directly to destroy this armament, and force the army to unconditional submission. ... But not a moment must be lost—it can never be regained.

The French having possessed themselves of Malta, on Friday, the 15th of this month, the next day the whole fleet, consisting of sixteen sail of the line, frigates, bomb-vessels, &c., and near three hundred transports, left the island. I only heard this unpleasant news on the 22nd, off Cape Passaro. As Sicily was not their object, and the wind blew fresh from the westward, from the time they sailed, it was clear that their destination was to the eastward; and I think their object is, to possess themselves of some port in Egypt, and to fix themselves at the head of the Red Sea, in order to get a formidable army into India; and, in concert with Tippoo

G. Baldwin,[1]
26 June.

[1] Consul at Alexandria.

Saib, to drive us, if possible, from India. But I have reason to believe, from not seeing a vessel, that they have heard of my coming up the Mediterranean, and are got safe into Corfu. But still I am most exceedingly anxious to know from you if any reports or preparations have been made in Egypt for them; or any vessels prepared in the Red Sea, to carry them to India, where, from the prevailing winds at this season, they would soon arrive; or any other information you would be good enough to give me, I shall hold myself much obliged.

The Mutine, which had been sent to Alexandria with the foregoing letter to Mr. Baldwin, rejoined the squadron on the 29th, but without having obtained any intelligence of the French fleet.

Lord St. Vincent, 29 June. Off Alexandria.

Although I rest confident that my intentions will always with you have the most favourable interpretations, yet where success does not crown an officer's plan, it is absolutely necessary that he should explain the motives which actuate his conduct, and therefore I shall state them as briefly as possible.

Captain Troubridge joined me on 7 June. From calms it was the 12th before I got round Cape Corse (I must here state, that I had nothing in the shape of a frigate except the Mutine brig). I then sent the Mutine to look into Talamone Bay, which, as all the French troops had not left Genoa on the 6th, I thought a probable place for the rendezvous of a large fleet; for, completely ignorant as I was of the destination of the enemy, I felt it my duty to take every precaution not to pass them. On the 13th, the Mutine looked into Talamone Bay, but found nothing there. I ran the fleet between Planosa, Elba, and Monte Christo, and on the 14th at noon was off Civita Vecchia, when we spoke a Tunisian cruiser, who reported that he had spoken a Greek on the 10th, who told him that on the 4th he had passed through the French fleet off the NW end of Sicily, steering to the eastward. From this moment I was in anxious expectation of meeting with despatch boats, Neapolitan cruisers &c. with letters for me from Naples, giving me every information I could desire (but my hopes were vain). On the 15th, I made the Ponza Islands, where not finding a cruiser, I sent Captain Troubridge in the Mutine to talk with Sir William Hamilton and General Acton, and to state my distress for frigates.

On the 17th, in the Bay of Naples, I received my first letter from Sir William Hamilton, and in two hours Captain Troubridge returned with information, that the French fleet were off Malta on the 8th, going to attack it, that Naples was at peace with the French republic, therefore could afford us no assistance in ships, but that, under the rose, they would give us the use of their ports, and sincerely wished us well, but did not give me the smallest information of what was, or likely to be, the future destination of the French armament. With this comfortable account, I pushed for the Faro [of] Messina. On my way I heard of the French landing in Malta, and that on Tuesday the 12th they had taken the old city : that the fleet was anchored between Gozo and Malta. On the 20th, off Messina, the English consul came on board to tell me that Malta had surrendered on the 15th, the Russian minister having arrived the day before from Malta, when the intelligence came over, but I received not the smallest information or notice from the Sicilian Government. Keeping the Sicilian shore on board, on the 21st, I was close off Syracuse and hoisted our colours. A boat in the evening rowed out about a mile, but although I brought to and sent the Mutine in shore, she rowed back again. On the 22nd, in the morning, being off Cape Passaro, the Mutine spoke a brig which sailed from Malta the day before. The master reported that Malta surrendered on Friday, 15 June, and that on Saturday, the 16th, the whole French fleet left it, as was supposed, for Sicily : that a French garrison was left in the town, and French colours flying. The wind at this time was blowing strong from the WNW. The vessel had been spoken three hours before, and was gone out of my reach. I could not get to Malta till it moderated, and then I might get no better information. Thus situated I had to make use of my judgment. With information from Naples, that they were at peace with the French republic, that General Bonaparte had sent on shore to Sicily, that the King of Naples need not be alarmed at the French armament, for it had not Sicily for its object. It was also certain the Sicilian Government were not alarmed, or they would have sent off to me. I recalled all the circumstances of this armament before me, 40,000 troops in 280 transports, many hundred pieces of artillery, waggons, draught-horses, cavalry, artificers, naturalists, astronomers, mathematicians, &c. The first rendezvous in case of separation was Bastia, the second Malta—this armament could not be necessary for taking possession of Malta. The Neapolitan ministers considered Naples and Sicily as safe ; Spain, after Malta, or indeed any place to the westward, I could not think their destination, for at this season the westerly winds so strongly prevail between Sicily and the coast of Barbary, that I conceive it almost impossible to get a fleet of transports to the westward. It then became the serious question, where are they gone? Here I had deeply to regret my want of frigates, and I desire it may be understood, that if one-half the frigates your lordship had ordered under my command had been with me, that I could not have wanted information of the French fleet. If to Corfu, in consequence of my approach (which they knew from Naples on the 12th or 13th), they were arrived by this time, the 22nd.

Upon their whole proceedings, together with such information as I have been able to collect, it appeared clear to me, that either they were destined to assist the rebel Pacha and to overthrow the present Government of Turkey, or to settle a colony in Egypt, and to open a trade to India by way of the Red Sea; for, strange as it may appear at first sight, an enterprising enemy, if they have the force or consent of the Pacha of Egypt, may with great ease get an army to the Red Sea, and if they have concerted a plan with Tippoo Saib, to have vessels at Suez, three weeks at this season is a common passage to the Malabar coast, when our India possessions would be in great danger.

I therefore determined, with the opinion of those captains in whom I place great confidence,[1] to go to Alexandria; and if that place or any other part of Egypt was their destination, I hoped to arrive time enough to frustrate their plans. The only objection I can fancy to be started is, 'You should not have gone such a long voyage without more certain information of the enemy's destination:' my answer is ready—who was I to get it from? The Governments of Naples and Sicily either knew not, or chose to keep me in ignorance. Was I to wait patiently till I heard certain accounts? If Egypt was their object, before I could hear of them they would have been in India. To do nothing, I felt was disgraceful: therefore I made use of my understanding, and by it I ought to stand or fall. I am before your Lordship's judgment, which in the present case I feel is the tribunal of my country, and if, under all circumstances, it is decided that I am wrong, I ought, for the sake of our country, to be superseded; for at this moment, when I know the French are not in Alexandria, I hold the same opinion as off Cape Passaro—viz. that under all circumstances I was right in steering for Alexandria, and by that opinion I must stand or fall. However erroneous my judgment may be, I feel conscious of my honest intentions, which I hope will bear me up under the greatest

---

[1] Sir James Saumarez, Troubridge, Ball, and Darby, who were signalled to come on board the Vanguard, immediately after the Mutine had spoken the vessel on 22 June.

misfortune that could happen to me as an officer—that of your Lordship's thinking me wrong.

It may be doubted whether this letter was actually sent. It stands indeed in the Letter Book; but Captain Ball, to whom the draft was shown, gave a strong opinion against it: feeling, he wrote, 'a regret, that your too anxious zeal should make you start an idea, that your judgment was impeachable, because you have not yet fallen in with the French fleet, as it implies a doubt, and may induce a suspicion, that you are not perfectly satisfied with your own conduct. I should recommend a friend, never to begin a defence of his conduct before he is accused of error.'

I arrived off Alexandria on the 28th ultimo, and found lying there one Turkish ship of the line, four frigates, about twelve other Turkish vessels in the old port, and about fifty sail of different nations' vessels in the Franks' port. I directed Captain Hardy, of the Mutine, to run close in, and to send an officer on shore with my letter to Mr. Baldwin, and to get all the information in his power. Herewith I send you the officer's report. Mr. Baldwin had left Alexandria near three months. We observed the line-of-battle ship to be landing her guns, and that the place was filling with armed people. After receiving this information, I stretched the fleet over the coast of Asia, and have passed close to the southern side of Candia, but without seeing one vessel in our route; therefore to this day I am without the smallest information of the French fleet since their leaving Malta. I own I fully expected to have found despatches off this end of Candia; for both Sir William Hamilton and General Acton, I now know, said they believed Egypt was their object; for that when the French minister at Naples was pressed, on the armament appearing off Sicily, he declared that Egypt was their object. I have again to deeply regret my want of frigates, to which I shall ever attribute my ignorance of the situation of the French fleet.

<small>Lord St. Vincent, 12 July. 12 lgs. W of Candia.</small>

It is an old saying, 'The devil's children have the devil's luck.' I cannot find, or to this moment learn, beyond vague conjecture where the French fleet are gone to. All my ill-fortune, hitherto, has proceeded from want of frigates. Off Cape Passaro, on 22 June, at daylight, I saw two frigates, which were supposed to be French, and it has been said since that a line-of-battle ship was to leeward of them, with the riches of Malta on board, but it was the destruction of the enemy, not riches for myself, that I was seeking. These would have fallen to me if I had had frigates, but except the ship of the line, I regard not all the riches in this world. From every

<small>Sir W. Hamilton, 20 July. Syracuse.</small>

information off Malta I believed they were gone to Egypt. Therefore, on the 28th, I was communicating with Alexandria in Egypt, where I found the Turks preparing to resist them, but know nothing beyond report. From thence I stretched over to the coast of Caramania, where not meeting a vessel that could give me information, I became distressed for the kingdom of the Two Sicilies, and having gone a round of 600 leagues at this season of the year (with a crippled ship) with an expedition incredible, here I am as ignorant of the situation of the enemy as I was twenty-seven days ago. I sincerely hope that the despatches which I understand are at Cape Passaro will give me full information. I shall be able for nine or ten weeks longer to keep the fleet on active service, when we shall want provisions and stores.

Lady Nelson, 20 July.

I have not been able to find the French fleet, to my great mortification, or the event I can scarcely doubt. We have been off Malta, to Alexandria in Egypt, Syria, and are returned here without success: however, no person will say that it has been for want of activity. I yet live in hopes of meeting these fellows; but it would have been my delight to have tried Bonaparte on a wind, for he commands the fleet, as well as the army.

Lord St. Vincent, 20 July. Syracuse.

Yesterday I arrived here, where I can learn no more than vague conjecture that the French are gone to the eastward. Every moment I have to regret the frigates having left me, to which must be attributed my ignorance of the movements of the enemy. Your Lordship deprived yourself of frigates to make mine certainly the first squadron in the world, and I feel that I have zeal and activity to do credit to your appointment, and yet to be unsuccessful hurts me most sensibly. But if they are above water, I will find them out, and if possible bring them to battle. You have done your part in giving me so fine a fleet, and I hope to do mine in making use of them. We are watering, and getting such refreshments as the place affords, and shall get to sea by the 25th. It is my intention to get into the mouth of the Archipelago, where, if the enemy are gone towards Constantinople, we shall hear of them directly: if I get no information there, to go to Cyprus, when, if they are in Syria or Egypt, I must hear of them.

Sir W. Hamilton, 22 July. Syracuse.

I have had so much said about the King of Naples' orders only to admit three or four of the ships of our fleet into his ports, that I am astonished. I understood that private orders, at least, would have been given for our free admission. If we are to be refused supplies, pray send me by many vessels an account, that I may in good time take the king's fleet to Gibraltar. Our treatment is scandalous for a great nation to put up with, and the king's flag is insulted at every friendly port we look at.

The fleet is unmoored, and the moment the wind comes off the land, shall go out of this delightful harbour, where our present wants have been most amply supplied, and where every attention has been paid to us; but I have been tormented by no private orders being given to the governor for our admission. I have only to hope that I shall still find the French fleet, and be able to get at them: the event then will be in the hands of Providence, of whose goodness none can doubt. 23 July.

Whereas I think it requisite that an officer of your rank should have charge of my despatches to the Earl of St. Vincent, commander-in-chief, you are hereby required and directed to take charge of them, and go on board the Leander, Captain Thompson, who is ordered to carry you, without loss of time, to the commander-in-chief. After having delivered my despatches, you are to give him all further information relative to the late victory over the French fleet off the mouth of the Nile. Capt. Berry, 2 August.

Almighty God has blessed his Majesty's arms in the late battle, by a great victory over the fleet of the enemy, who I attacked at sunset on 1 August, off the mouth of the Nile. The enemy were moored in a strong line of battle for defending the entrance of the bay (of Shoals), flanked by numerous gunboats, four frigates, and a battery of guns and mortars on an island in their van; but nothing could withstand the squadron your Lordship did me the honour to place under my command. Their high state of discipline is well known to you, and with the judgment of the captains, together with their valour, and that of the officers and men of every description, it was absolutely irresistible. Could anything from my pen add to the character of the captains, I would write it with pleasure, but that is impossible. Lord St. Vincent, 3 Aug. Vanguard off the mouth of the Nile.

I have to regret the loss of Captain Westcott of the Majestic, who was killed early in the action; but the ship was continued to be so well fought by her first lieutenant, Mr. Cuthbert, that I have given him an order to command her till your Lordship's pleasure is known.

The ships of the enemy, all but their two rear ships, are nearly dismasted; and those two, with two frigates, I am sorry to say, made their escape; nor was it, I assure you, in my power to prevent them. Captain Hood most handsomely endeavoured to do it, but I had no ship in a condition to support the Zealous, and I was obliged to call her in.

L

The support and assistance I have received from Captain Berry cannot be sufficiently expressed. I was wounded in the head, and obliged to be carried off the deck; but the service suffered no loss by that event: Captain Berry was fully equal to the important service then going on, and to him I must beg leave to refer you for every information relative to this victory. He will present you with the flag of the second in command, that of the commander-in-chief being burnt in L'Orient.

Herewith I transmit you lists of the killed and wounded, and the lines of battle of ourselves and the French.

Of these lists the following is an abstract:

English	Number of				French	Number of		How disposed of
	Guns	Men	Killed	Wounded		Guns	Men	
Vanguard	74	595	30	75	L'Orient	120	1,010	Burnt
Orion	74	590	13	29	Le Franklin	80	800	Taken
Culloden	74	590	0	0	Le Tonnant	80	800	Do.
Bellerophon	74	590	49	148	Le Guerrier	74	700	Do.
Defence	74	590	4	11	Le Conquérant	74	700	Do.
Minotaur	74	640	23	64	Le Spartiate	74	700	Do.
Alexander	74	590	14	58	Le Timoléon	74	700	Burnt
Audacious	74	590	1	35	Le Souverain Peuple	74	700	Taken
Zealous	74	590	1	7	L'Heureux	74	700	Do.
Swiftsure	74	590	7	22	Le Mercure	74	700	Do.
Majestic	74	590	50	143	L'Artémise	36	300	Burnt
Goliath	74	590	21	41	L'Aquilon	74	700	Taken
Theseus	74	590	5	30	La Sérieuse	36	300	Sunk
Leander	50	343	0	14	L'Hercule (bomb)	—	50	Burnt
					La Fortune	18	70	Taken
					Le Guillaume Tell	80	800	Escaped
					Le Généreux	74	700	Do.
					La Justice	40	400	Do.
					La Diane	40	400	Do.
Total	1,012	8,068	218	677	Total	1,196	11,230	

Nelson's official reference to Captain Berry for 'every information relative to the victory,' gives a stamp of authenticity to the account which Berry published shortly after his arrival in England, and which, in the following year, Nelson personally approved.[1]

Capt. Berry's narrative.

Sir Horatio Nelson had been detached by Earl St. Vincent into the Mediterranean with the Vanguard, of 74 guns, the rear-admiral's flagship; the Orion and Alexander, of 74 guns each; the Emerald and Terpsichore, frigates; and La Bonne Citoyenne, sloop of war.

Nothing material occurred to the squadron from the day it sailed from Gibraltar, which was on 9 May, till the 22nd, when, being in the Gulf of Lion, at 2 A.M. a most violent squall of wind took the Vanguard, which carried away her topmasts, and at last her foremast.

---

[1] See *ante*, p. 7. The account was first published in *The True Briton* and *The Sun* newspapers, and afterwards in pamphlet form, under the title 'Authentic Narrative of the proceedings of his Majesty's squadron under the command of Rear-Admiral Sir Horatio Nelson, from its sailing from Gibraltar to the conclusion of the battle of the Nile; drawn up from the minutes of an officer of rank in the squadron.' The edition here quoted from is the 3rd; its date of 1798 marks its rapid sale.

The other ships experienced the fury of the gale, but not in the same degree as the Vanguard, a stronger vein of the tempest having taken that ship. The three line-of-battle ships lost sight of the frigates on the same day; and at the moment of the misfortune which fell upon the Vanguard, the British squadron was not many leagues distant from the French fleet under Bonaparte, which had on that very day set sail from Toulon.

The squadron bore up for Sardinia, the Alexander taking the Vanguard in tow, and the Orion looking out ahead to endeavour to get a pilot, for the purpose of gaining San Pietro Road. On the 24th, with very great difficulty we reached that anchorage, where we were in hopes of meeting with a friendly reception, which our distresses seemed to demand from a neutral power; the governor of S. Pietro, however, had orders from the French not to admit any British ship; but their utmost hostility could not prevent us from anchoring in the road. . . . Captain Berry, with the very able assistance he received from Sir James Saumarez and Captain Ball, was enabled with great expedition to equip the Vanguard with a jury fore-mast, jury main and mizen topmasts, and to fish the bowsprit, which was sprung in many places; and on the fourth day from our anchoring in S. Pietro Road, we again put to sea with top-gallant yards across.

The admiral, eager to execute the orders which he had received, did not think of sailing to Naples, or any other port where he could have received the most open and friendly assistance, in getting the ship properly refitted, which her condition evidently required, but immediately steered for his appointed rendezvous; nor did he ever express the smallest intention of shifting his flag to either of the other ships, which to many officers the peculiar circumstances of his own ship might have seemed to render desirable. . . . The admiral and officers of the Vanguard indeed had the happiness to find that the ship sailed and worked as well as the other ships, notwithstanding her apparently crippled condition.

The squadron reached the rendezvous on 4 June, and on the following day was joined by La Mutine, Captain Hardy, who was charged with orders to the admiral, and who brought the highly acceptable intelligence that Captain Troubridge had been detached with ten sail of the line, and a 50-gun ship, to reinforce us. . . .

On the 8th, at noon, we had the happiness to discover from the mast-head ten sail, and it was not long before we recognised them to be British ships of war, standing upon a wind in close line of battle with all sails set. Private signals were exchanged, and before sunset the so much wished for junction was formed. . . .

The admiral had received no instructions what course he was now to steer, and no certain information respecting the destination of the enemy's fleet; he was left, therefore, entirely to his own judgment. He had the happiness, however, to find that to the captains of his squadron he had no necessity to give directions for being in readiness for battle. On this point their zeal anticipated his utmost wishes, for the decks of all the ships were kept perfectly clear night and day, and every man was ready to start to his post at a moment's notice. It was a great satisfaction to him, likewise, to perceive that the men of all the ships were daily exercised at the great guns and small arms, and that everything was in the best state of preparation for actual service.

The admiral knew that the enemy had sailed with a NW wind, which naturally led him to conclude that their course was up the Mediterranean. He sent La Mutine to Civita Vecchia, and along the Roman coast to gain intelligence, and steered with the fleet for Corsica, which he reached on 12 June. Several vessels had been spoken with on the passage thither, but no intelligence whatever had been obtained from them. He continued his course on the 13th between Corsica and Elba, and between Planosa and Elba, through the latter of which passages large ships or fleets had not been accustomed to pass. We made the Roman coast, and were rejoined by La Mutine, without gaining any intelligence, notwithstanding the active exertions of Captain Hardy. The admiral now determined to steer towards Naples, in the hope of some satisfactory information. It had been reported that the plundering Algiers was the object of the French armament; but this account was too vague to warrant the admiral's implicitly adopting it. We saw Mount Vesuvius on the 16th, and detached Captain Troubridge, in La Mutine, to obtain what information he could from Sir William Hamilton. He returned with a report only that the enemy had gone to Malta. The admiral now lamented that even a day had been lost in visiting the Bay of Naples, and determined, by the shortest cut, to make the Faro di Messina, which the fleet passed through on the 20th, with a fair wind. The joy with which the Sicilians hailed our squadron, when it was discovered by them to be British, gave the most sincere satisfaction to everyone on board of it. A vast number of boats came off, and rowed round it with the loudest congratulations, and the sincerest exultation, as the Sicilians had been apprehensive that the French fleet was destined to act against them, after the capture of Malta. Here we gained intelligence from the British consul that Malta had actually surrendered. We had now hopes of being able to attack the enemy's fleet at Gozo, where it was reported they were anchored, and the admiral immediately formed a plan for that purpose.

We were now steering with a press of sail for Malta, with a fresh breeze at NW. On 22 June, La Mutine, at daylight in the morning, spoke a Genoese brig from Malta, which gave intelligence that the French had sailed from thence on the 18th, with a fresh gale at NW. The admiral was not long in determining what course he should take, and made the signal to bear up and steer to the SE with all possible sail. At this time we had no certain means of ascertaining that the enemy were not bound up the Adriatic.

From the day we bore up, till 29 June, only three vessels were spoken with, two of which had come from Alexandria and had not seen anything of the enemy's fleet; the other had come from the Archipelago, and had likewise seen nothing of them. This day we saw the Pharos Tower of Alexandria, and continued nearing the land with a press of sail, till we had a distinct view of both harbours; and to our general surprise and disappointment we saw not a French ship in either of them. La Mutine communicated with the governor of Alexandria, who was as much surprised at seeing a British squadron there as he was at the intelligence that a French fleet was probably on its passage thither.

It now became a subject of deep and anxious deliberation with the admiral what could possibly have been the course of the enemy, and what their ultimate destination. His anxious and active mind, however, would not permit him to rest a moment in the same place; he therefore shaped his course to the northward, for the coast of Karamania, to reach as quickly as possible some quarter where information could most probably be obtained, as well as to supply his ships with water, of which they began to run short.

On 4 July we made the coast of Karamania. Steering along the south side of Candia, carrying a press of sail both night and day with a contrary wind, on the 18th we saw the island of Sicily, when the admiral determined to enter the port of Syracuse. With this harbour no person in the fleet was acquainted; but by the skill and judgment of the officers, every ship got safely in, and immediately proceeded to get in water &c. with all possible expedition. This was the first opportunity that the Vanguard had of receiving water on board from 6 May, so that not only the stock of that ship, but of several others of the squadron, was very nearly exhausted. Although there was no proper or regular watering place, yet the exertions of the officers and men enabled us to put to sea again in five days, and on the 25th the squadron again put to sea.

We received vague accounts while at Syracuse, that the enemy's fleet had not been seen, in the Archipelago nor the Adriatic, nor had they gone down the Mediterranean; the conclusion then seemed to be, that the coast of Egypt was still the object of their destination; and neither our former disappointment, nor the hardships we had endured from the heat of the climate, though we were still to follow an uncertain pursuit, could deter the admiral from steering to that point where there was a chance of finding the enemy.

Now that it is ascertained by events, that Alexandria was the object of the enemy, it may seem strange that they should have been missed by us, both in our passage thither, and our return to Syracuse; but it appeared that the French steered a direct course for Candia, by which they made an angular passage towards Alexandria, whilst we steered a straight course for that place, without making Candia at all, by which we of course very considerably shortened the distance. The smallness of our squadron made it necessary to sail in close order, and therefore the space which it covered was very limited; and as the admiral had no frigates that he could detach upon the look-out, added to the constant haze of the atmosphere in that climate, our chance of descrying the enemy was very much circumscribed. The distance likewise between Candia and the Barbary coast, about 35 leagues, leaves very sufficient space for more than two of the largest fleets to pass without mutual observation, particularly under the circumstances described.

On our return to Syracuse, the circumstance of our steering to the northward, while the enemy kept a southern course for Alexandria, makes it obvious that our chance of falling in with them was even less than before.

On 25 July we left Syracuse, still without any positive information respecting the enemy, but it occurred to the admiral that some authentic intelligence might be obtained in the Morea. We steered for that coast, and made the Gulf of Coron on the 28th. Captain Troubridge was again employed on that important service of obtaining intelligence, and was despatched in the Culloden into Coron, off which place, by the great exertions of that able officer, the fleet was not detained above three hours. He returned with intelligence from the Turkish governor, that the fleet had been seen steering to the SE from Candia about four weeks before. . . .

Upon the information obtained by Captain Troubridge, the admiral determined again to visit Alexandria, and carried all sail, steering for that place, which he had the pleasure to descry on 1 August at noon; but not as before, it now appearing full of vessels of various kinds; and we soon had the satisfaction of seeing the French flag flying on board some of the ships. The utmost joy seemed to animate every breast on board the squadron, at sight of the enemy; and the pleasure which the admiral himself felt was perhaps more heightened than that of any other man, as he had now a certainty by which he could regulate his future operations.

The admiral had, and it appeared most justly, the highest opinion of, and placed the firmest reliance on, the valour and conduct of every captain in his squadron. It had been his practice during the whole of the cruise, whenever the weather and circumstances would permit, to have his captains on board the Vanguard, where he would fully develop to them his own ideas of the different and best modes of attack, and such plans as he proposed to execute upon falling in with the enemy, whatever their position or situation might be, by day or by night. There was no possible position in which they could be found, that he did not take into his calculation, and for the most advantageous attack of which he had not digested and arranged the best possible disposition of the force which he commanded. With the masterly ideas of their admiral, therefore, on the subject of naval tactics, every one of the captains of his squadron was most thoroughly acquainted; and upon surveying the situation of the enemy, they could ascertain with precision what were the ideas and intentions of their commander, without the aid of any further instructions; by which means signals became almost unnecessary, much time was saved, and the attention of every captain could almost undistractedly be paid to the conduct of his own particular ship, a circumstance from which, upon this occasion, the advantages to the general service were almost incalculable.

It cannot here be thought irrelevant to give some idea of what were the plans which Admiral Nelson had formed, and which he explained to his captains with such perspicuity as to render his ideas completely their own. To the naval service, at least, they must prove not only interesting, but useful.

Had he fallen in with the French fleet at sea, that he might make the best impression upon any part of it that should appear the most vulnerable, or the most eligible for attack, he divided his force into three sub-squadrons, viz.:

Vanguard,	Orion,	Culloden,
Minotaur,	Goliath,	Theseus,
Leander,	Majestic,	Alexander,
Audacious,	Bellerophon,	Swiftsure.
Defence,		
Zealous,		

Two of these sub-squadrons were to attack the ships of war, while the third was to pursue the transports, and to sink and destroy as many as it could.

The destination of the French armament was involved in doubt and uncertainty; but it forcibly struck the admiral, that, as it was commanded by the man whom the French had dignified with the title of the conqueror of Italy, and as he had with him a very large body of troops, an expedition had been planned which the land force might execute without the aid of their fleet, should the transports be permitted to make their escape, and reach in safety their place of rendezvous; it therefore became a material consideration with the admiral so to arrange his force as at once to engage the whole attention of their ships of war and at the same time materially to annoy and injure their convoy. It will be fully admitted, from the subsequent information which has been received upon the subject, that the ideas of the admiral upon this occasion were perfectly just, and that the plan which he had arranged was the most likely to frustrate the design of the enemy.

It is almost unnecessary to explain his projected mode of attack at anchor, as that was minutely and precisely executed in the action which we now come to describe. These plans, however, were formed two months before an opportunity presented itself of executing any of them, and the advantage now was, that they were familiar to the understanding of every captain in the fleet.

It has been already mentioned that we saw the Pharos of Alexandria at noon on 1 August. The Alexander and Swiftsure had been detached ahead on the preceding evening, to reconnoitre the ports of Alexandria, while the main body of the squadron kept in the offing. The enemy's fleet was first discovered by the Zealous, Captain Hood, who immediately communicated, by signal, the number of ships, sixteen, lying at anchor in line of battle, in a bay upon the larboard bow, which we afterwards found to be Aboukir Bay. The admiral hauled his wind that instant, a movement which was immediately observed and followed by the whole squadron; and at the same time he recalled the Alexander and Swiftsure. The wind was at this time NNW, and blew what seamen call a top-gallant breeze. It was necessary to take in the royals when we hauled upon a wind. The admiral made the signal to prepare for battle and that it was his intention to attack the enemy's van and centre, as they lay at anchor, and according to the plan before developed. His idea in this disposition of his force was, first to secure the victory, and then to make the most of it according to future circumstances. A bower cable of each ship was immediately got out abaft, and bent forward. We continued carrying sail, and standing in for the enemy's fleet in a close line of battle. As all the officers of our squadron were totally unacquainted with Aboukir Bay, each ship kept sounding as she stood in. The enemy appeared to be moored in a strong and compact line of battle close in with the shore, their line describing an obtuse angle in its form, flanked by numerous gunboats, four frigates, and a battery of guns and mortars, on an island in their van. This situation of the enemy seemed to secure to them the most decided advantages, as they had nothing to attend to but their artillery, in their superior skill in the use of which the French so much pride themselves, and to which indeed their splendid series of land victories are in a great measure to be imputed.

The position of the enemy presented the most formidable obstacles;

but the admiral viewed these with the eye of a seaman determined on attack, and it instantly struck his eager and penetrating mind, that where there was room for an enemy's ship to swing, there was room for one of ours to anchor. No further signal was necessary than those which had already been made. The admiral's designs were as fully known to his whole squadron, as was his determination to conquer, or perish in the attempt. The Goliath and Zealous had the honour to lead inside, and to receive the first fire from the van ships of the enemy, as well as from the batteries and gunboats with which their van was strengthened. These two ships, with the Orion, Audacious, and Theseus, took their stations inside of the enemy's line, and were immediately in close action. The Vanguard anchored the first on the outer side of the enemy, and was opposed within half pistol-shot to Le Spartiate, the third in the enemy's line. In standing in, our leading ships were unavoidably obliged to receive into their bows the whole fire of the broadsides of the French line, until they could take their respective stations; and it is but justice to observe, that the enemy received us with great firmness and deliberation, no colours having been hoisted on either side, nor a gun fired, till our van ships were within half gunshot. At this time the necessary number of our men were employed aloft in furling sails, and on deck, in hauling the braces, &c. preparatory to our casting anchor. As soon as this took place, a most animated fire was opened from the Vanguard, which ship covered the approach of those in the rear, which were following in a close line. The Minotaur, Defence, Bellerophon, Majestic, Swiftsure, and Alexander, came up in succession, and passing within hail of the Vanguard, took their respective stations opposed to the enemy's line. All our ships anchored by the stern, by which means the British line became inverted from van to rear. Captain Thompson, of the Leander, of fifty guns, with a degree of skill and intrepidity highly honourable to his professional character, advanced towards the enemy's line on the outside, and most judiciously dropped his anchor athwart hawse of Le Franklin, raking her with great success, the shot from the Leander's broadside which passed that ship all striking L'Orient, the flag-ship of the French commander-in-chief.

The action commenced at sunset, which was at 6.31 P.M., with an ardour and vigour which it is impossible to describe. At about seven o'clock total darkness had come on, but the whole hemisphere was, with intervals, illuminated by the fire of the hostile fleets. Our ships, when darkness came on, had all hoisted their distinguishing lights, by a signal from the admiral. The van ship of the enemy, Le Guerrier, was dismasted in less than twelve minutes, and, in ten minutes after, the second ship, Le Conquérant, and the third, Le Spartiate, very nearly at the same moment were also dismasted. L'Aquilon and Le Peuple Souverain, the fourth and fifth ships of the enemy's line, were taken possession of by the British at half-past eight in the evening. Captain Berry, at that hour, sent Lieutenant Galway, of the Vanguard, with a party of marines, to take possession of Le Spartiate, and that officer returned by the boat the French captain's sword, which Captain Berry immediately delivered to the admiral, who was then below, in consequence of the severe wound which he had received in the head during the heat of the attack. At this time it appeared that victory had already declared itself in our favour, for although L'Orient, L'Heureux, and Le Tonnant were not taken possession of, they were considered as completely in our power, which pleasing intelligence Captain Berry had likewise the satisfaction of communicating in person to the admiral.

At ten minutes after nine, a fire was observed on board L'Orient, the French admiral's ship, which seemed to proceed from the after part of the cabin, and which increased with great rapidity, presently involving the whole of the after part of the ship in flames. This circumstance Captain Berry immediately communicated to the admiral, who, though suffering severely from his wound, came up upon deck, where the first consideration that struck his mind was concern for the danger of so many lives, to save as many as possible of whom he ordered Captain Berry to make every practicable exertion. A boat, the only one that could swim, was instantly despatched from the Vanguard, and other ships that were in a condition to do so, immediately followed the example; by which means, from the best possible information, the lives of about seventy Frenchmen were saved. The light thrown by the fire of L'Orient upon the surrounding objects, enabled us to perceive with more certainty the situation of the two fleets, the colours[1] of both being clearly distinguishable. The cannonading was partially kept up to leeward of the centre till about ten o'clock, when L'Orient blew up with a most tremendous explosion. An awful pause and death-like silence for about three minutes ensued, when the wreck of the masts, yards, &c., which had been carried to a vast height, fell down into the water, and on board the surrounding ships. A port fire from L'Orient fell into the main royal of the Alexander, the fire occasioned by which was, however, extinguished in about two minutes, by the active exertions of Captain Ball.

After this awful scene, the firing was recommenced with the ships to leeward of the centre, till twenty minutes past ten, when there was a total cessation of firing for about ten minutes; after which it was revived till about three in the morning, when it again ceased.

After the victory had been secured in the van, such British ships as were in a condition to move, had gone down upon the fresh ships of the enemy, which occasioned these renewals of the fight, all of which terminated with the same happy success in favour of our flag. At five minutes past five in the morning, the two rear ships of the enemy, Le Guillaume Tell and Le Généreux, were the only French ships of the line that had their colours flying. At fifty-four minutes past five, a French frigate, L'Artémise, fired a broadside and struck her colours; but such was the unwarrantable and infamous conduct of the French captain, that after having thus surrendered, he set fire to his ship, and with part of his crew made his escape on shore. Another of the French frigates, La Sérieuse, had been sunk by the fire from some of our ships; but as her poop remained above water, her men were saved upon it, and were taken off by our boats in the morning.

The Bellerophon, whose masts and cables had been entirely shot away, could not retain her situation abreast of L'Orient, but had drifted out of the line to the lee side of the bay, a little before that ship blew up. The Audacious was in the morning detached to her assistance.

At eleven o'clock, Le Généreux and Guillaume Tell, with the two

---

[1] In accordance with an order from Lord St. Vincent, the English ships, on this occasion, wore the white ensign, notwithstanding Nelson's being at the time Rear-Admiral of the Blue.

frigates, La Justice and La Diane, cut their cables and stood out to sea, pursued by the Zealous, Captain Hood, who, as the admiral himself has stated, handsomely endeavoured to prevent their escape; but as there was no other ship in a condition to support the Zealous, she was recalled.

The whole day of the 2nd was employed in securing the French ships that had struck, and which were now all completely in our possession, Le Tonnant and Timoléon excepted; as these were both dismasted, and consequently could not escape, they were naturally the last of which we thought of taking possession. On the morning of the 3rd, the Timoléon was set fire to, and Le Tonnant had cut her cable and drifted on shore, but that active officer, Captain Miller, of the Theseus, soon got her off again, and secured her in the British line.

The British force engaged consisted of twelve ships of 74 guns, and the Leander of 50. From the over anxiety and zeal of Captain Troubridge to get into action, his ship, the Culloden, in standing in for the van of the enemy's line, unfortunately grounded upon the tail of a shoal running off from the island, on which were the mortar and gun batteries of the enemy; and notwithstanding all the exertions of that able officer and his ship's company, she could not be got off. This unfortunate circumstance was severely felt at the moment by the admiral and all the officers of the squadron; but their feelings were nothing compared to the anxiety and even anguish of mind which the captain of the Culloden himself experienced, for so many eventful hours. There was but one consolation that could offer itself to him in the midst of the distresses of his situation, a feeble one it is true—that his ship served as a beacon for three other ships, viz. the Alexander, Theseus, and Leander, which were advancing with all possible sail set close in his rear, and which otherwise might have experienced a similar misfortune, and thus in a greater proportion still have weakened our force. It was not till the morning of the 2nd that the Culloden could be got off, and it was found she had suffered very considerable damage in her bottom, that her rudder was beat off, and the crew could scarcely keep her afloat with all pumps going. The resources of Captain Troubridge's mind availed him much, and were admirably exerted upon this trying occasion. In four days he had a new rudder made upon his own deck, which was immediately shipped; and the Culloden was again in a state for actual service, though still very leaky.

The admiral, knowing that the wounded of his own ships had been well taken care of, bent his first attention to those of the enemy. He established a truce with the commandant of Aboukir, and through him made a communication to the commandant of Alexandria, that it was his intention to allow all the wounded Frenchmen to be taken ashore to proper hospitals, with their own surgeons to attend them; a proposal which was assented to by the French, and which was carried into effect on the following day. The activity and generous consideration of Captain Troubridge were again exerted at this time for the general good. He communicated with the shore, and had the address to procure a supply of fresh provisions, onions &c. which were served out to the sick and wounded, and which proved of essential utility. On the 2nd [of August], the Arabs and Mamelukes, who during the battle had lined the shores of the bay, saw with transport that the victory was decisively ours, an event in which they participated with an exultation almost equal to our own; and on that and the two following nights, the whole coast and country were illuminated as far as we could see, in celebration of our victory. This had a great effect upon the minds of our prisoners, as they conceived that this illumination was the consequence, not entirely of our success, but of some signal advantage obtained by the Arabs and Mamelukes over Bonaparte. . . .

Immediately after the action, some Maltese, Genoese, and Spaniards, who had been serving on board the French fleet, offered their services in ours, which were accepted; and they expressed the greatest happiness at thus being freed, as they themselves said, from the tyranny and cruelty of the French.

On the fourth day after the action, Captain Berry, of the Vanguard, sailed in the Leander[1] of 50 guns, with the admiral's despatches to the commander-in-chief, Earl St. Vincent, off Cadiz, containing intelligence of the glorious victory which he had obtained.

The account of the battle, written to his wife, by Captain Miller of the Theseus is of almost equal authority to that by Sir Edward Berry, and supplies some additional and most interesting details.

On 28 July, being off the Gulf of Coron in the Morea, the Culloden stood into it, and learnt from the Turkish governor that the enemy were at Alexandria, and brought out with her a French brig loaded with wine. Soon after she joined the admiral, he bore up for Alexandria with the signal flying, that he had intelligence of the enemy, and, constantly keeping the worst sailing ship under all sail, we arrived off that port 1 August, at noon, and, seeing nothing of the French there, stood alongshore to the eastward, when, about three-quarters past 2, the Zealous made the signal for 16 sail of the line at an anchor, and soon after we discovered them from this ship. Here let me pause, till I can make you perfectly understand the state of the fleet at that moment. We had a fine breeze of north wind, smooth water, and fair weather, the body extending about three miles easterly and westerly without being in any order of sailing, and going about five miles an hour under topsails generally. The Culloden under all sail about seven miles astern, with the wine brig in tow; the Alexander and Swiftsure being far ahead on the look-out, and chasing when we were steering SE by E, were thrown considerably to leeward by our change of course after making Alexandria; and at the time of the enemy being discovered, I should think were full nine miles to the southward of us. The Zealous and Goliath were the most advanced ships next the admiral, and a posse of us near him; the Majestic and Leander, I believe, the sternmost, exclusive of the Culloden: the general signal of recall having been made about 2 o'clock, the Swiftsure and Alexander standing towards us with all sail on a wind, and the Mutine within hail of the admiral.

At 3 the admiral made the signal to prepare for battle. At 3.30 for the Culloden to quit the prize. At 4.25 to prepare for battle, with the sheet cable out of the stern port, and springs on the bower

Capt. Miller's narrative.

[1] On 18 August, the Leander was met near Candia by the Généreux, and captured after a gallant resistance, in the course of which Berry was severely wounded. He was afterwards released on parole, but did not arrive in England till the beginning of December.

anchor, &c. &c. At 4.54 that it was the admiral's intention to attack the van and centre of the enemy. At 5.40 to form the line of battle as most convenient ahead and astern of the admiral ; and immediately after, for the leading ship to steer one point more to starboard. The Goliath was leading, the Zealous next, then the Vanguard ; the Theseus followed close to her stern, having the Bellerophon close on the weather quarter, and Minotaur equally so on the lee quarter : I do not recollect the order of the other ships. We wore gradually round, preserving our order till we brought the wind on the starboard beam, when the admiral hove to, to speak the Mutine about three miles from the enemy, who were making signals and heaving on their springs. I took this opportunity to pass the admiral to leeward, and endeavour to obtain the honour of leading the fleet into battle, as the Culloden, the only ship ahead of us in the regular line, was still considerably distant : but Captain Berry hailed as we passed, and gave me the admiral's order to become his second ahead, in consequence of which I hove to close ahead of him, and the Orion and Audacious passed us. We had before got springs on both our bower anchors, the stream-cable passed out of the stern-port, and bent to its anchor ; and were now doing the same by the sheet, being in all other respects in the most perfect order for battle. The enemy had 13 large ships anchored in close order of battle, in the form of a bow, with the convex part to us, L'Orient, of 120 guns, making the centre of it, the string of the bow being NW & SE, and four frigates a little within them, with a gun and mortar battery on a small island about three-quarters of a mile from their van ship, and three mortar boats placed near the frigates. In about five minutes after bringing to, the admiral made the signal to make sail again, the leading ship first, when the Goliath, in a very gallant and masterly manner, led along the enemy's line, gradually closing with their van, which, as well as the battery on the island, opened its fire.

At 6.40 the admiral made the signal to engage the enemy close, the Goliath passing round, and raking the enemy's van ship (the Guerrier), brought up with her stern anchor inside of and abreast their second ship, the Conquérant. Zealous following likewise raked the Guerrier, brought down her foremast, and came-to with her stern anchor on her inner bow. The Orion, from her previous situation, described a little wider circle, passed the off side of the Zealous, and made a wider sweep in order to come-to with one of her bowers ; in doing which she completely knocked up the Sérieuse frigate, which lay in her way, having made such a wreck of her, that on her driving, presently after, on a shoal, all her masts fell, and she filled with water. I think the Orion must have touched the ground from the time between her passing the Zealous and her coming-to nearly abreast the inner side of the fifth ship (the Peuple Souverain) ; for, though she passed the Zealous before us, we had completely brought up abreast the inner beam of the Spartiate, the third ship, and had been in action with her four or five minutes before the Orion came-to. In running along the enemy's line in the wake of the Zealous and Goliath, I observed their shot sweep just over us, and knowing well that at such a moment Frenchmen would not have coolness enough to change their elevation, I closed them suddenly, and, running under the arch of their shot, reserved my fire, every gun being loaded with two and some with three round shot, until I had the

Guerrier's masts in a line, and her jib-boom about six feet clear of our rigging; we then opened with such effect, that a second breath could not be drawn before her main and mizen mast were also gone. This was precisely at sunset, or 44 minutes past 6; then passing between her and the Zealous, and as close as possible round the off side of the Goliath, we anchored exactly in a line with her, and, as I have before said, abreast the Spartiate; the Audacious having passed between the Guerrier and the Conquérant, came-to with her bower close upon the inner bow of the latter. We had not been many minutes in action with the Spartiate when we observed one of our ships (and soon after knew her to be the Vanguard) place herself so directly opposite to us on the outside of her, that I desisted firing on her, that I might not do mischief to our friends, and directed every gun before the mainmast on the Aquilon, and all abaft it on the Conquérant, giving up my proper bird to the admiral: the Minotaur, following the admiral, placed herself on the outer side of the fourth ship (Aquilon), and the Defence on the fifth, or Peuple Souverain. The Bellerophon, I believe, dropped her stern anchor well on the outer bow of L'Orient (seventh ship), but it not bringing her up, she became singly opposed to the fire of that enormous ship before her own broadside completely bore, and then sustained the greater part of her loss; she then either drifted or sailed along the French line, and came to anchor about six miles eastward of us, where we discovered her next morning (without a mast standing), with her ensign on the stump of the main-mast. Captain Darby was wounded at the beginning, and poor Daniel, 1st lieutenant, as well as the 2nd and 4th, killed. As well as I can learn, the Majestic, whether owing to the thickness of the smoke at the shutting in of the evening, or that her stern cable did not bring her up in time, ran her jib-boom into the main rigging of L'Heureux, ninth ship, and remained a long time in that unfortunate position, suffering greatly: poor Westcott was almost the first that fell, being killed by a musket-ball in the neck. She got disentangled, and brought her broadside to bear on the starboard bow of the Mercure, the tenth ship, on whom she took a severe revenge; having laid that bow almost open, she also had only a foremast standing at daylight. My noble and glorious neighbour, on 14 February, the gallant Captain Troubridge, of the Culloden, had the misfortune to strike and stick fast, spite of all his efforts, on a shoal but little out of gunshot of the battle, to his inconceivable mortification, though individually it could not have happened better than to him, or publicly worse, as no naval character for indefatigable zeal, courage, and ability stands higher than his, or is built on a broader basis; while, on the other hand, it was to us the loss of force of a ship that is without a superior. I think it very likely she saved the three following ships from the same mischance. My worthy friends Hallowell and Ball got among us a few minutes after 8 o'clock, the Swiftsure coming-to with her stern anchor, upon the outer quarter of the Franklin (the sixth ship) and bow of L'Orient, so as to fire into both, and the Alexander bringing up with her stern anchor close upon the inner quarter of L'Orient. When the five headmost ships of the enemy were completely subdued, which might have been about nine or half-past, the Leander came-to with her stern anchor upon the inner bow of the Franklin, being thus late by preferring assistance to the Culloden.

Having now brought all our ships into battle, which you are to suppose raging in all magnificent, awful, and horrific grandeur, I proceed to relate the general events of it as I saw them. The Guerrier and Conquérant made a very inefficient resistance, the latter being soon stripped of her main and mizen masts; they continued for a considerable time to fire, every now and then, a gun or two, and about 8 o'clock, I think, were totally silent. The Spartiate resisted much longer, and with serious effect, as the Vanguard's killed and wounded announces, who received her principal fire; her larboard guns were fired upon us in the beginning with great quickness, but after the admiral anchored on his starboard side, it was slow and irregular, and before or about 9 o'clock she was silenced, and had also lost her main and mizen masts: the Aquilon was silenced a little earlier, with the loss of all her masts, having the whole fire of the Minotaur on her starboard side, and, for some time, near half ours on her larboard bow. Le Peuple Souverain was, about the same time, entirely dismasted and silenced, and drifted between the Franklin and Orion, when the Leander came into the battle, and took her place immediately on the Franklin's larboard bow, the Swiftsure having been long on her starboard quarter, and Defence, after Le Peuple Souverain drifted away, firing upon her starboard bow. While she was thus situated, scarcely returning any fire, L'Orient caught fire on the poop, when the heavy cannonade from all the Alexander's and part of the Swiftsure's guns became so furious, that she was soon in a blaze, displaying a most grand and awful spectacle, such as formerly would have drawn tears down the victor's cheeks; but now pity was stifled as it rose, by the remembrance of the numerous and horrid atrocities their unprincipled and bloodthirsty nation had and were committing; and when she blew up, about 11 o'clock, though I endeavoured to stop the momentary cheer of the ship's company, my heart scarce felt a single pang for their fate. Indeed, all its anxiety was in a moment called forth to a degree of terror for her, at seeing the Alexander on fire in several places; and a boat that was taking in a hawser, in order to warp the Orion further from L'Orient, I filled with fire-buckets, and sent instantly to her, and was putting the engine in another just returned from sounding, when I had the unspeakable happiness of seeing her get before the wind, and extinguish the flames: there was now no firing, except towards the French rear, and that quite a broken, disconnected one.

Just after L'Orient blew up, I discovered by the moonlight a dismasted frigate on our inner beam, and sent Lieutenant Brodie to take possession of her if, on hailing, she surrendered, and, if not, to burn false fires, that we might compel her to it; the first took place, and he sent me the captain and three officers of the Sérieuse frigate, which, having been severely handled by the Orion, had got aground, and filled with water in trying to escape, and all her masts gone: her crew, except thirty, had abandoned her. I, at this time, also perceived a group of the enemy's ships about a mile and a half within us, which must have moved there after the attack; and sent one of the mates to sound between us and them (the master being employed sounding within us, and examining the state of the Sérieuse); and being, as well as the officers and people, greatly fatigued, I was happy to snatch half an hour's sleep, from which, in a little time, I was roused by Captain Hood of the Zealous, who came to propose that our ships and the Goliath should go down to the group of ships; when, finding that my boat was sounding between us and them, it was agreed to wait the report of the officer on that service: meanwhile we prepared for it, and were lifting our bower anchor, when an officer from the Swiftsure came to say, the admiral wished us all to go to the assistance of the Alexander and Majestic, then exchanging an irregular fire with the enemy's rear; and while we were lifting our stern anchor for that purpose, a lieutenant of the Alexander came from the admiral to us, and any other ships that could renew the action, to desire us to go down to these ships, and slip our cable if necessary. All firing had now ceased about ten minutes, I therefore hove up the stern anchor, and ran down under stay-sails till I passed the Majestic, when we dropped our sheet anchor, and having run out a cable, let go our bower, so as to present our broadside to the enemy in a line with the Alexander, and leave a clear opening for the Majestic (who appeared to have suffered much) to fire through. We were some time before we had our broadside to bear, our bower not at first holding; but happily the enemy made no use of the opportunity, though three of their broadsides bore on our bow from the different distances of about two and a half to five cables; besides these, which were two 80s and two 74s, one of which appeared not to have suffered anything, there were two 74s on our starboard quarter that did not appear to have been at all in action, about half gunshot from us; a 36-gun frigate, about the same distance, whose broadside bore immediately on our stern, and two others of 40 guns, at the longest range of shot, being the group I have before mentioned. Finding myself thus situated, a principal object to all the French ships, and the sole one to the group, I was resolved to remain quiet as long as they, and the Alexander and Majestic chose to be so, to give time to the Goliath, Zealous, and Leander, to join us, neither of which were yet moving; and I sent an officer to tell Hood I waited for them. My people were also so extremely jaded, that as soon as they had hove our sheet anchor up, they dropped under the capstan-bars, and were asleep in a moment in every sort of posture, having been then working at their fullest exertion or fighting, for near twelve hours, without being able to benefit by the respite that occurred; because, while L'Orient was on fire, I had the ship completely sluiced, as one of our precautionary measures against fire or combustibles falling on board us, when she blew up.

It was some time before daylight that we reached our new position: observing the Guillaume Tell moving, and having the Généreux and her exactly in one, as she passed under our stern, I could no longer wait, particularly as none of the other English ships were yet in motion, but, precisely at sunrise, opened my fire on these two ships, as the Alexander and Majestic did immediately after; this was directly returned, principally by the Guillaume Tell and Tonnant. After a little time, perceiving they all increased their distance, we veered to two cables on each anchor, and soon after the Leander came down, and having anchored without the Alexander, commenced a very distant fire. These four ships having at length by imperceptible degrees got almost to the utmost range of shot, we turned our whole fire upon the two line-of-battle ships that were on our quarter, and whom we had now long known to be on shore; the Majestic and Alexander firing a few shots over us at them, as the Leander may perhaps have done. In a short time we compelled L'Heureux, 74, to strike her colours, and I sent Lieutenant Brodie to take possession of her, and from her to hail the other ship to strike immediately, or she would else soon be involved in so much smoke and fire, that we, not being able to see her colours come down, might unintentionally destroy all on board her. Just as the boat got there, the Goliath anchored on our outer quarter and began to fire, but desisted on my hailing her; and, presently after, Mercure, of 74 guns, hauled her colours down; as L'Artémise, 36, after firing her guns shotted, had also done just before. I sent Lieutenant Hawkins to take possession of Mercure, and Lieutenant Hoste of L'Artémise; the former, on a lieutenant of the Alexander afterwards coming, delivered her into his charge, and returned on board; and when the latter got within about a cable's length of L'Artémise, perceiving she was set on fire by a train, and that her people had abandoned her on the opposite side, he also returned on board: after burning about half an hour, she blew up. This dishonourable action was not out of character for a modern Frenchman: the devil is beyond blackening.

We were now thus situated in the Theseus: our mizen-mast so badly wounded that it could bear no sail; our fore and main yard so badly wounded that I almost expected them to come down about our ears, without sail; the fore-topmast and bowsprit wounded; the fore and main sail cut to pieces, and most of the other sails much torn; nine of our main, and several fore and mizen shrouds, and much of our other standing and running rigging shot away; eight guns disabled, either from the deck being ploughed up under themselves, or carriages struck by shot, or the axle-trees breaking from the heat of the fire; and four of them lower deckers. In men we were fortunate beyond anything I ever saw or heard of; for though near 80 large shot struck our hull, and some of them through both sides, we had only six men killed and thirty-one wounded: Providence, in its goodness, seemed willing to make up to us for our heavy loss at Santa Cruz. Hawkins and myself were the only officers from whom blood was drawn, and that in a very trifling way.

The enemy were anchored again at the long range of shot, and many large boats from the shore were passing to and fro among them; and the Justice frigate was playing about under sail, and at length stood out of the bay, as if to make her escape. The Zealous, after being some time under way without the fleet, was at this time standing down towards us, but stood out again as the admiral made her signal to chase the frigate, who stood back into the bay, the Zealous remaining outside. Hearing it was the enemy's intention to take their men out of their line-of-battle ships and set them on fire (for, from what information we had, we supposed them on shore, being ourselves in four and a half fathoms), I caused a cool and steady fire to be opened on them from our lower deckers only, all of which being admirably pointed by Lieutenant England, who commanded that deck, they soon drove the boats entirely away from all their ships, and doubtless hulled them frequently, particularly the Timoléon. The boats having abandoned them, the Guillaume Tell, the Généreux, the Timoléon, with the Justice and Diane frigates, got under way, and stood out of the bay in line of battle; the Timoléon, being under our fire all the time, cast in shore, and, after appearing to make another attempt to wear, stood directly for the shore, and as she struck, her foremast went over the bows; the Tonnant being dismasted, remained where she was. The admiral made the Zealous, Goliath, Audacious, and Leander signals to chase the others; the Zealous very gallantly pushed at them alone, and exchanged broadsides as she past close on the different tacks; but they had so much the start of the other ships, and now of the Zealous, who had suffered much in her rigging, and knowing also they were remarkably fast sailors, the admiral made the general signal of recall, and these four ships were soon out of sight. The ships under way being readier, having suffered less damage in the action, been not half the time engaged, or done half as much as ourselves, I gave up all further thoughts of the Tonnant, except sending a boat to see if she had surrendered, which, being menaced by her guns, returned. In the evening I went on board the admiral, who I before knew was wounded. I found him in his cot, weak but in good spirits, and, as I believe every captain did, received his warmest thanks, which I could return from my heart, for the promptness and gallantry of the attack. I found him naturally anxious to secure the Tonnant and Timoléon, and that the Leander was ordered to go down for that purpose in the morning; I told him if there was any difficulty I would also go down in the morning, notwithstanding the state of the ship. Seeing the Leander get under way we hove up to our best bower; sent our prisoners and their baggage, which lumbered our guns, on board the Goliath, and got a slip buoy on the end of the sheet cable. The Swiftsure's boat returning from having been with a flag of truce to summons the Tonnant, informed us that the answer of the captain was, that he had 1,600 men on board, and unless the admiral would give him a ship to convey them to Toulon, he would fight to the last man—a true French gasconade; we immediately slipped the sheet cable, and hoisted our topsails, and seeing the admiral make the Leander's signal to engage the enemy, which must have been the moment of his receiving this French reply, we hove up our best bower and ran down directly for the Tonnant, with the master sounding in a boat ahead; as we cast so as to open the view of our broadside to her, she hoisted truce colours; when we got within a cable and a half of her, having only 25½ feet water, we let go our anchor, veered to within half a cable of her and hauled upon our spring, which was parted. It was now, however, of no consequence, as just after we came to, she allowed the Leander's boat to come on board, and was soon after under English colours; the Leander had brought-to about two or three cables without us while we were going down. The Timoléon being abandoned by her crew, was set on fire with her colours flying, and soon blew up. There being no longer an enemy to contend with, we beat the retreat and solemnly returned thanks to Almighty God, through whose mercy we had been instrumental in obtaining so great and glorious a victory to his Majesty's arms. . . .

I have omitted to say the Franklin did not submit till after L'Orient had been some time on fire. I do not vouch for what I have said of the Bellerophon and Majestic, as among several disagreeing I have been unable to collect, what I could say is certainly exact history; but speaking generally, there appears to be a glorious emulation among all, to do service to their king and country, and honour to themselves. On more particular inquiries respecting the Majestic and Bellerophon, it appears to me that the Majestic, as I have mentioned before, did not bring up on letting go her anchor, till she got her bowsprit foul of the bowsprit of L'Heureux, in which position she lay one hour, able to make use of but few guns, and the Tonnant firing into her quarter with her stern chase in addition to such guns as L'Heureux could bring to bear : on getting disentangled, she lay athwart the Mercure's bow, and raked her with great effect. On L'Orient taking fire, the Tonnant, Heureux, and Mercure cut their cables ; the former dropped a little way past the Guillaume Tell and anchored again; the other two, each with a stay sail or two set, ran aground. The Timoléon, Guillaume Tell, and Généreux veered, I fancy, to two cables, by which several means, and L'Orient blowing up, a vacancy of about a mile was left in the French line. The Bellerophon remained alongside L'Orient till near 8 o'clock, when Captain Darby, who had been severely wounded in the head, came on deck again, and seeing L'Orient on fire between decks, ordered the cable to be cut, and drifted away as before described, without main or mizen mast, and his foremast fell soon after this fire was extinguished on board L'Orient. There cannot be much error in time for these reasons—a prisoner now on board this ship who was a lieutenant of the Tonnant, and speaks very good English, describes an English ship dismasted by L'Orient and the Tonnant ; and says that after she cut her cable and dropped away from L'Orient, two other ships came, one on her bow and one under her stern : these ships were the Alexander and Swiftsure, who came in about 8 o'clock.

Evan Nepean, 7 August.

In an event of this importance, I have thought it right to send Captain Capel with a copy of my letter (to the commander-in-chief) overland, which I hope their Lordships will approve ; and beg leave to refer them to Captain Capel, who is a most excellent officer, and fully able to give every information.

Sir W. Hamilton, 9 Aug.

I have intercepted all Bonaparte's despatches, going to France. This army is in a scrape, and will not get out of it.

The Governor of Bombay, 9 Aug. Mouth of the Nile.

As I know Mr. Baldwin has some months left Alexandria, it is possible you may not be regularly informed of the situation of affairs here. I shall, therefore, relate to you, briefly, that a French army of 40,000 men in 300 transports, with thirteen sail of the line, eleven frigates, bomb vessels, gunboats, &c., arrived at Alexandria on 1 July: on the 7th, they left it for Cairo, where they arrived on the 22nd. During their march they had some actions with the Mamelukes, which the French call great victories. As I have Bonaparte's despatches before me (which I took yesterday), I speak positively: he says, 'I am now going to send off to take Suez and Damietta;' he does not speak very favourably of either the country or people: but there is so much bombast in his letters, that it is difficult to get near the truth ; but he does not mention India in these despatches. He is what is called organising the country, but you may be assured is master only of what his army covers.

From all the inquiries which I have been able to make, I cannot learn that any French vessels are at Suez, to carry any part of this army to India. Bombay, if they can get there, I know is their first object; but, I trust, Almighty God will in Egypt overthrow these pests of the human race. It has been in my power to prevent 12,000 men from leaving Genoa, and also to take eleven sail of the line and two frigates; in short, only two sail of the line and two frigates have escaped me. This glorious battle was fought at the mouth of the Nile, at anchor: it began at sunset, 1 August, and was not finished at three the next morning; it has been severe, but God blessed our endeavours with a great victory. I am now at anchor between Alexandria and Rosetta, to prevent their communication by water, and nothing under a regiment can pass by land. The French have 4,000 men posted at Rosetta to keep open the mouth of the Nile. Alexandria, both town and shipping, are so distressed for provisions, which they can only get from the Nile by water, that I cannot guess the good success which may attend my holding our present position, for Bonaparte writes his distress for stores, artillery, things for their hospital, &c. All useful communication is at an end between Alexandria and Cairo: you may be assured I shall remain here as long as possible. Bonaparte had never yet to contend with an English officer; and I shall endeavour to make him respect us.

Was I to die this moment, 'Want of frigates' would be found stamped on my heart. No words of mine can express what I have and am suffering for want of them. *Lord Spencer, 9 August.*

I send you a packet of intercepted letters, some of them of great importance; in particular, one from Bonaparte to his brother. He writes such a scrawl, no one not used to it can read; but luckily, we have got a man who has wrote in his office, to decipher it.

I send Sir James Saumarez with [seven of] the ships and [six of the] prizes, the others not being yet ready. Although I keep on, yet I feel that I must soon leave my situation up the Mediterranean to Troubridge; than whom, we both know no person is more equal to the task. I should have sunk under the fatigue of refitting the squadron, but for him, Ball, Hood, and Hallowell: not but that all have done well, but those are my supporters. My head is ready to split, and I am always so sick: in short, if there be no fracture, my head is severely shaken. *Lord St. Vincent, 10 August.*

A. Davison,
11 August.

The French army is in a scrape. They are up the Nile without supplies. The inhabitants will allow nothing to pass by land, nor H. N. by water. Their army is wasting with the flux, and not a thousand men will ever return to Europe.

Capt.
Hood,
Zealous,
15 August.

You are hereby required and directed to take under your command the [Swiftsure, Goliath, Alcmène, Seahorse, Emerald] (they having my instructions to follow your orders), and to cruise off Alexandria, or remain at anchor, as you may judge most proper for the more effectually preventing any supplies being thrown into that port for the French fleet, and to endeavour to intercept the French convoy with provisions, which is expected to arrive there soon; as also to prevent, as much as possible, all communication between the French army at Rosetta, and their fleet at Alexandria: and you are to continue on this service until 30 September next. But should you receive any intelligence, or anything happen which may make it necessary for you to remain longer on this service, you are in that case to remain so long as you may think it proper. And on your return you are to send a boat on shore at Syracuse for instructions; not finding any there, you are to proceed with all despatch to Naples.

E. Nepean,
16 August.

Six of the prizes sailed yesterday under Sir James Saumarez. Three others, viz. Guerrier, Heureux, and Mercure, are in the act of repairing. In this state I received last evening Earl St. Vincent's most secret orders, and most secret and confidential letters relative to the important operations intended to be pursued in the Mediterranean. Thus situated, it became an important part of my duty to do justice between my king and country, and the brave officers and men who captured those ships at the battle of the Nile. It would have taken one month, at least, to have fitted those ships for a passage to Gibraltar, and not only at a great expense to Government, but with the loss of the services of at least two sail of the line. I therefore, confiding that the Lords Commissioners will, under the present circumstances, direct that a fair value shall be paid for those ships, ordered them to be burnt, after saving such stores as would not take too much time, out of them; and I have further thought it my duty to tell the squadron the necessity I am under, for the benefit of the king's service, of directing their property to be destroyed; but that I had no doubt but Government would make them a liberal allowance, all which I hope their Lordships will approve of.

Lord St.
Vincent,
19 August.

If I could have assured myself that Government would have paid a reasonable value for Conquérant and Souverain, I would have ordered them to be burnt; for they will cost more in refitting, and by the loss of line-of-battle ships attending them, than they are worth; but the other four are a treasure to our navy. You will see what I have written to Mr. Nepean, on my ordering Guerrier, Heureux, and Mercure to be destroyed, and it will, I hope, meet your approbation and support. The case is hard upon poor fellows at a distance, if they do not pay us liberally. . . .

Whether I shall be able to stay in the Mediterranean is yet a matter of doubt; but if nothing very particular demands my half head, it is my present intention to go to you, and for England. . . . My head is so wrong, that I cannot write what I wish in such a manner as to please myself; but I have reason to be thankful.

To this subject of burning the prizes Nelson repeatedly referred, and stated the case, at length, in a letter (7 Sept.) to Lord Spencer, who replied (24 Dec.):

'Your letter of 7 September, which relates to the prizes which you burnt off Aboukir, has been under consideration of Government; and though the case is one for which there has never yet been any precedent, and by the strict rules of the service could not be admitted as a claim, yet, I believe, I can take upon me to assure you, that the singular merits of your situation will have such weight as to induce us to deviate from the usual practice, and an arrangement is making to allow a sum equivalent to the value of the least valuable of the other prizes, as it is reasonable to suppose, that those which you were under the necessity of burning were the worst conditioned ships among those which were captured.'

I have more than once thought that the Mediterranean fleet has been put in our power to annihilate, therefore I had the advantage of my predecessors. I regret that one escaped, and I think, if it had pleased God that I had not been wounded, not a boat would have escaped to have told the tale; but do not believe that any individual in the fleet is to blame. In my conscience, I believe greater exertions could not have been, and I only mean to say, that if my experience could (in person) have directed those exertions of individuals, there was every appearance that Almighty God would have continued to bless my endeavours for the honour of our king, the advantage of our country, and for the peace and happiness (I hope) of all Europe. It is no small regret that L'Orient is not in being to grace our victory. She was completely beat, and I am sure had struck her colours before she took fire; for as she had lost her main and mizen masts, and on her flagstaff, which Hood cut from her wreck, was no flag, it must be true

Lord Minto, 29 August. Off Rhodes.

that the flag was hauled down, or it would have been entangled with the rigging, or some remnant remained at the mast-head.

W. Wyndham, 21 Aug.

She had on board near six hundred thousand pounds sterling; so says the adjutant-general of the fleet, who was saved out of her, and although he does not say she struck her colours, yet he allows that all resistance on her part was in vain. Admiral Brueys was killed early in the battle, and from the commencement of the fight, declared all was lost. They were moored in a strong position in a line of battle, with gunboats, bomb vessels, frigates, and a gun and mortar battery on an island in their van, but my band of friends was irresistible.

Marquis de Niza, 8 Sept. At sea.

It is a matter of regret to me, and, I am sure, it must be to your Excellency, that your squadron did not join me before 1 August, when not a single French ship could have escaped us; but as that is past remedy, it is necessary to look forward to the next important service we can render the common cause, which, in my opinion, is to prevent the French army from getting any supplies of stores by water from Alexandria. Captain Hood will explain, I am confident, the whole of my ideas on that point: Captain Hood was directed not to leave Alexandria before 30 September, longer than which his provisions will not last. I therefore beg leave to represent to your Excellency what advantage it will be, if you will take Captain Hood's station and remain on it till 20 October, by which time I shall hope to have the ships now with Captain H. returned to Alexandria. This I state as the longest period: I hope to have ships there much sooner.

18 Sept.

Being informed by Captain Hood of your return from Alexandria, I beg to represent to your Excellency the great benefit it would be to the common cause should you proceed off Malta, and attempt to intercept a French ship of the line and two frigates that made their escape from Alexandria, and which are cruising there, having been driven out of the ports of Malta by the Maltese, who are in arms against the French, and have retaken several of their towns and the castle of St. Angelo. . . . By your Excellency's cruising there for a short time, it might be the means of driving the French from the island, as well as protecting the Colossus, and some victuallers and storeships sent up by Earl St. Vincent for the use of the squadron under my command.

Capt. Hood, 13 Sept.

I was in hopes the Marquis de Niza would have stayed off Alexandria till the end of October, but as he is returning, we have only to trust to ourselves. I am sensible of the great importance of keeping up the blockade, for we must destroy that army. I have ordered Minotaur and Audacious to Naples. I therefore wish you to remain as much longer after 30 September as you with propriety can. I will send three ships as quickly as possible, but I fear it will be late in October.

On the day Hoste left me, I was taken with a fever, which has very near done my business: for eighteen hours, my life was thought to be past hope; I am now up, but very weak both in body and mind, from my cough and this fever. I never expect, my dear Lord, to see your face again: it may please God, that this will be the finish to that fever of anxiety which I have endured from the middle of June; but be that as it pleases His goodness—I am resigned to His will. . . . *[Lord St. Vincent, 20 Sept.]*

. . . Your arrangements, my dear Lord, shall be, and ever are, as punctually attended to by me, as if you were present; for I hold it to be the highest contempt, to alter the mode of discipline and regulations established by the commander-in-chief. My first order was, to pay the strictest attention to all the orders and regulations of the commander-in-chief; and I can truly say, that I have endeavoured to support your orders with all my might.

The Vanguard arrived in the Bay of Naples on the 22nd. Culloden I found at Castel-à-Mare, preparing to heave down. His first side will be hove out on the 28th. The whole ship is very rotten, and nothing but the exertion of a Troubridge could have kept her afloat. Alexander has a new main and mizen mast (those which were purchased for Vanguard), but I hope that the Vanguard's two masts, by good fishing, will hold fast until I can send her to Gibraltar, some months hence. . . . *[27 Sept. Naples.]*

Dear Troubridge, whom we went to visit yesterday, is better than I expected; the active business, and the scolding he is obliged to be continually at, does him good. I am not surprised that you wish him near you; but I trust you will not take him from me. I well know he is my superior; and I so often want his advice and assistance.

I trust in a week we shall all be at sea. I am very unwell, and the miserable conduct of this Court is not likely to cool my irritable temper. It is a country of fiddlers and poets, whores and scoundrels. *[30 Sept.]*

My dear Madam,—I cannot be an indifferent spectator to what has [been] and is passing in the Two Sicilies, nor to the misery which (without being a politician) I cannot but see plainly is *[Lady Hamilton, 3 Oct.]*

ready to fall on those kingdoms, now so loyal, by the worst of all policy—that of procrastination. Since my arrival in these seas in June last, I have seen in the Sicilians the most loyal people to their sovereign, with the utmost detestation of the French and their principles. Since my arrival at Naples I have found all ranks, from the very highest to the lowest, eager for war with the French, who, all know, are preparing an army of robbers to plunder these kingdoms and destroy the monarchy. I have seen the minister of the insolent French pass over in silence the manifest breach of the third article of the treaty between his Sicilian Majesty and the French Republic. Ought not this extraordinary conduct to be seriously noticed? Has not the uniform conduct of the French been to lull governments into a false security, and then to destroy them? As I have before stated, is it not known to every person that Naples is the next marked object for plunder? With this knowledge, and that his Sicilian Majesty has an army ready (I am told) to march into a country anxious to receive them, with the advantage of carrying the war from, instead of waiting for it at home, I am all astonished that the army has not marched a month ago.

I trust that the arrival of General Mack will induce the Government not to lose any more of the favourable time which Providence has put in their hands; for if they do, and wait for an attack in this country, instead of carrying the war out of it, it requires no gift of prophecy to pronounce that these kingdoms will be ruined, and the monarchy destroyed. But should, unfortunately, this miserable ruinous system of procrastination be persisted in, I would recommend that all your property and persons are ready to embark at a very short notice. It will be my duty to look and provide for your safety, and with it (I am sorry to think it will be necessary) that of the amiable queen of these kingdoms and her family.

Capt. Ball, 4 Oct.

You are hereby required and directed to proceed in his Majesty's ship Alexander, under your command, off the island of Malta, taking with you the ships [Terpsichore, Bonne Citoyenne, Incendiary], whose captains have my orders to follow your directions, and to use your endeavour to blockade the ports of that island, so as to prevent any supplies getting in them for the French troops, as well as to prevent the escape of the French ships now in that place.

The duties assigned to the Mediterranean fleet at this time are thus stated in a letter from the Secretary to the Admiralty to Lord St. Vincent, dated 3 October:

'In the present state of affairs in the Mediterranean their Lordships conceive that the objects principally to be attended to by the squadron employed there, are :

'1st. The protection of the coasts of Sicily, Naples, and the Adriatic, and in the event of war being renewed in Italy, an active co-operation with the Austrian and Neapolitan armies.

'2ndly. The cutting off all communication between France and Egypt, that neither supplies nor reinforcements may be sent to the army at Alexandria.

'3rdly. The blocking-up of Malta, so as to prevent provisions from being sent into it.

'4thly. The co-operating with the Turkish and Russian squadrons which are to be sent into the Archipelago.'

By the Neapolitan courier, I am informed of the declaration of war of the Porte against the French. . . . I have directed the squadron blockading the transports in Alexandria, to remain on that service as long as possible, or till they are relieved by the Turkish fleet. Part of my squadron sailed yesterday to blockade Malta; myself and three sail of the line will also sail in three days. You may assure the Grand Signior that I shall be happy in co-operating to destroy the common enemy, who are the pest of the human race. . . . Malta, Corfu, and those islands are my object after Egypt, and therefore I hope that the Russian fleet will be kept in the East; for if they establish themselves in the Mediterranean, it will be a bad thorn in the side of the Porte. [J. Spencer Smith,[1] 7 Oct.]

Vanguard, Minotaur, Audacious, and Goliath, sail on Saturday next; Culloden will get away the week following. I admit three weeks is a long time to refit a fleet after a battle, but when it is considered that nearly every mast in the fleet has taken much more time than if they had been new, that Naples Bay is subject to a heavy swell, of which we have felt the inconvenience; and that we go to sea victualled for six months, and in the highest health and discipline, I trust some allowance will be made for me. Every transport goes with me to Syracuse. Naples sees this squadron no more, except the king calls for our help, and if they go on, and lose the glorious moments, we may be called for to save the persons of their majesties. [Lord Spencer, 9 Oct.]

[I wrote to you by the Leander] authorising you to add a paragraph to my public letter, if you thought it more to the advantage of Troubridge, but I thought it better to make no mention of his disaster; for I consider Captain Troubridge's conduct as fully entitled to praise as any one officer in the squadron, and as highly [Lord St. Vincent, 19 Oct.]

[1] Minister at Constantinople.

deserving reward. He commanded a division equally with Sir James Saumarez, by my order of June; and I should feel distressed if any honour is granted to one, that is not granted to the other. ... I know the knight has wrote to the first lord, but the eminent services of our friend deserve the very highest rewards. I have experienced the ability and activity of his mind and body: it was Troubridge that equipped the squadron so soon at Syracuse —it was he that exerted himself for me after the action—it was Troubridge who saved the Culloden, when none that I know in the service would have attempted it—it was Troubridge whom I left as myself at Naples to watch movements—he is, as a friend and an officer, a *nonpareil!*

On 15 October, Nelson in the Vanguard, with Minotaur, Audacious, Goliath, and Mutine brig in company, left Naples.

24 Oct. This day, at noon, I arrived off Malta, and joined the Marquis de Niza, who very handsomely had shifted his flag from the Principe to the Sebastian, in order to continue the blockade, and to permit Colossus to proceed in the execution of your orders. The Principe and Rainha being under the necessity of going to Naples to refit, the marquis I have ordered to Naples, as now he is not wanted here, to refit, and be ready to act as the times may require, and the King of Naples may wish him.

On 22 October, the Marquis de Niza had written to Lord Nelson, representing that, as he was under Nelson's orders, he ought to be considered as an admiral commanding an English squadron, and that the officers of a rank inferior to his ought to be under his orders, when they were not under Nelson's eye, adding: 'I do not desire to have the power to direct them in the smallest degree contrary to any commands they may receive from you, or from any officer who is my senior; I merely wish that they should have the same deference for me that they would show to any officer of my rank who has the honour of serving under you. It is not any personal consideration which has urged me to make this representation; but it is my duty to preserve the honour of my nation, as well as my military rank and especially the good of the service and the support of discipline.'

This letter Nelson received on arriving off Malta, and at once replied:

Marquis de Niza, 24 Oct. I am honoured with your Excellency's letter of this evening; and in my public situation I have the honour to acquaint you, that I consider your Excellency as an officer serving under my command, and standing precisely in the same situation as an English rear-admiral, junior to me; which is, having no power or authority to give the smallest order to any ship or vessel, but those who I may think right to place, by order, under your command.

To which, in a private note he added:

If your Excellency had recollected, I am confident your knowledge of service would not have occasioned you the trouble of writing me a letter. On service with us it is necessary for the commander-in-chief, or the officer commanding by order from the commander-in-chief, to give the superior officer, when thought right to detach, orders to take such ships and captains under his command, and also an order for the captains of such ships to obey their superior officer serving under the commander-in-chief or detached commander. In the present orders to your Excellency, no ships are placed under your orders but those of her most faithful Majesty. 24 Oct.

Nelson now learned with astonishment that not the smallest supply of arms or ammunition had been sent from Sicily, although he had been distinctly told by the Neapolitan ministers, 'that the governor of Syracuse had orders to supply secretly the inhabitants of Malta with arms and ammunition, and that the officers were gone to Malta to encourage the Maltese in their resistance against the French;' and General Acton had declined his offer of transport, assuring him that supplies had been already sent.

When I come to Naples I can have nothing pleasant to say of the conduct of his Sicilian Majesty's ministers towards the inhabitants of Malta, who wish to be under the dominion of their legitimate sovereign. The total neglect and indifference with which they have been treated, appears to me cruel in the extreme. Had not the English supplied fifteen hundred stand of arms, with bayonets, cartouch boxes, and ammunition, &c., and the marquis supplied some few, and kept the spirit of these brave islanders from falling off, they must long ago have bowed to the French yoke. Could you, my dear Sir William, have believed, after what General Acton and the Marquis de Gallo had said in our various conversations relative to this island, that nothing had been sent by the Governor of Syracuse secretly—was the word used to us—or openly, to this island? And I am further assured that the Governor of Syracuse never had any orders sent him to supply the smallest article. I beg your Excellency will state this in confidence to General Acton. I shall most assuredly tell it to the king. Sir W. Hamilton, 27 Oct. Off Malta.

And so, having given Captain Ball of the Alexander orders to take the Audacious, Goliath, Terpsichore, and Incendiary under his command, and to 'undertake a strict blockade of the island of Malta,' 'consulting with the Maltese delegates upon the best methods of distressing the enemy,' and 'using every effort to cause them to quit the island, or oblige them to capitulate;' and particular instructions, in the event of a capitulation, to insist on the delivery of 'the French ships Guillaume Tell, Diane, and Justice,' Nelson left Malta on the night of 30 October, and arrived at Naples on 5 November. On the 13th he commenced a long letter to Lord Spencer, which he continued on different days, till the 18th, and in which he described the political situation in full detail; bewailing the impossibility of stirring up the Neapolitans to active measures: they would only say that they wished the French to be aggressors; as if the openly and notoriously collecting an army to overrun Naples were not an aggression of the most serious nature. They were also destitute of money.

Lord Spencer, 18 Nov.

I see the finest country in the world full of resources, yet not enough to supply the public wants: all are plundering who can get at public money or stores. In my own line I can speak. A Neapolitan ship of the line would cost more than ten English ships fitting out. Five sail of the line must ruin the country. Everything else is, I have no doubt, going on in the same system of thieving. I could give your Lordship so many instances of the greatest mal-conduct of persons in office, and of those very people being rewarded. If money could be placed in the public chest at this moment, I believe it would be well used; for the sad thing in this country is, that although much is raised, yet very little reaches the public chest.

Having taken 5,000 troops on board the ships of the English and Portuguese squadrons, Nelson left Naples on 22 November, and arrived at Leghorn on the 28th. The place yielded to the first summons, and was at once taken possession of. On the 30th, Nelson sailed again for Naples, leaving Niselli, the Neapolitan general, and Troubridge in command, not without some demur on the part of the captains of the Portuguese ships, who had the rank of commodore.

Lord Spencer, 29 Nov. Leghorn.

I am so much in the habit of writing my mind freely, that I cannot say what I wish in a stiff, formal letter. I am confident your Lordship will not expose me, should I occasionally write too freely of what I see and know. Under this impression, I say that the Portuguese squadron are totally useless. The Marquis de Niza has certainly every good disposition to act well; but he is completely ignorant of sea affairs. I expect to hear they have all had disasters, and that they are returned to Naples. All their commanders are commodores, and it is ridiculous to hear them talk of their rank, and of the impossibility of serving under any of my brave and good captains. Yet these men are English.[1] I say Niza is by far the best amongst them, and I shall keep up a good harmony with him.

---

[1] Their names were Stone, Mitchell, and Campbell.

I expect dear Hood every moment from Egypt; his provisions must be very short; he deserves great credit for his perseverance. I hope the good Turk will have relieved him, but the Russians seem to me to be more intent on taking ports in the Mediterranean than destroying Bonaparte in Egypt.

Lord St. Vincent, 6 Dec. Naples.

I most heartily congratulate you on the conquest of Minorca—an acquisition invaluable to Great Britain, and completely in future prevents any movements from Toulon to the westward. My situation in this country has had doubtless one rose, but it has been plucked from a bed of thorns. Nor is my present state that of ease; and my health, at best but indifferent, has not mended lately. Naples is just embarked in a new war: the event, God only knows; but, without the assistance of the Emperor, which is not yet given, this country cannot resist the power of France.

Comre. Duckworth, 6 Dec. Naples.

It is reported, and, indeed, is certain, that the Neapolitan officers, and many of their men, are run away even at the sight of the enemy. As must ever be the case, several brave officers have fallen. I know not the extent of the disaster, but I believe it is very bad. Keep something very often at Leghorn, for I think it very probable that I may be forced to send for you in a hurry. Everything you may send here, let them anchor cautiously if my flag is not here.

Capt. Troubridge, 9 Dec. Naples.

I perfectly agree with you that a delayed war on the part of the Emperor will be the destruction of this monarchy, and of course to the new-acquired dominions of the Emperor in Italy. Had the war commenced in September or October, all Italy would at this moment have been liberated. This month is worse than the last; the next will render the contest doubtful, and in six months, when the Neapolitan republic will be organised, armed, and with its numerous resources called forth, I will suffer to have my head cut off, if the Emperor is not only defeated in Italy, but that he totters on his throne at Vienna.

Sir Morton Eden,[1] 10 Dec.

The Neapolitan officers have not lost much honour, for God knows they have but little to lose; but they lost all they had. Mack has supplicated the king to sabre every man who ran from Civitá Castellana to Rome. He has, we hear, torn off the epaulettes of some of these scoundrels, and placed them on good serjeants. I will, as briefly as I can, state the position of the army, and its lost honour, for defeat they have had none. The right wing, of

Lord Spencer, 11 Dec.

---

[1] Minister at Vienna.

nineteen thousand men, under General St. Philip and Michaux (who ran away at Toulon), were to take post between Ancona and Rome, to cut off all supplies and communication. Near Fermo they fell in with the enemy, about three thousand. After a little distant firing, St. Philip advanced to the French general, and returning to his men, said, 'I no longer command you,' and was going off to the enemy. A serjeant said, 'You are a traitor! What! have you been talking to the enemy?' St. Philip replied, 'I no longer command you.' 'Then you are an enemy?' and levelling his musket, shot St. Philip through the right arm. However, the enemy advanced; he was amongst them. Michaux ran away, as did all the infantry, and had it not been for the good conduct of two regiments of cavalry, would have been destroyed. So great was their panic, that cannon, tents, baggage, and military chest—all were left to the French. Could you credit, but it is true, that this loss has been sustained with the death of only forty men?

Sir W. Hamilton, 14 Dec.

As I have been informed that this kingdom is invaded by a formidable French army, I think it my duty to acquaint your Excellency, for the information of the English merchants and others residing at Naples, that the three English transports in this bay have my directions to receive such effects of the English as they can stow, and that the whole squadron is ready to receive their persons, should such an event be found necessary as for them to embark.

N.B.—I need not say that I mean valuable effects, and not household furniture. I also beg leave to recommend that anything sent on board ship should be done with as little bustle and as much secrecy as possible.

Capt. Troubridge, 15 Dec. Naples.

Things are in such a critical state here, that I desire you will join me without one moment's loss of time, leaving the Terpsichore in Leghorn roads to bring off the Great Duke, should such a measure be necessary. . . . The king is returned here, and everything is as bad as possible. For God's sake make haste! Approach the place with caution. Messina, probably, I shall be found at; but you can inquire at the Lipari Islands if we are at Palermo.

Comre. Duckworth, 22 Dec.

Their Sicilian Majesties with their august family arrived in safety on board the Vanguard last night at nine o'clock, feeling it a necessary measure in the present moment. You will therefore acquaint all ships, that may be with you, of this circumstance, that they may approach Naples with caution; and if you have an opportunity, pray tell Lord St. Vincent of this event when you write, for I have no English vessel with me.

On the 22nd, I wrote a line to Commodore Duckworth, telling him that the royal family of the Two Sicilies were safely embarked on board the Vanguard, and requested him to take the first opportunity of acquainting your Lordship of this event. For many days previous to the embarkation it was not difficult to foresee that such a thing might happen; I therefore sent for the Goliath from off Malta, and for Captain Troubridge in the Culloden, and his squadron from the north and west coast of Italy, the Vanguard being the only ship in Naples Bay. On the 14th, the Marquis de Niza, with three of the Portuguese squadron, arrived from Leghorn, as did Captain Hope in the Alcmène from Egypt: from this time, the danger for the personal safety of their Sicilian Majesties was daily increasing, and new treasons were found out, even to the Minister of War. The whole correspondence relative to this important business was carried on with the greatest address by Lady Hamilton and the queen, who being constantly in the habits of correspondence, no one could suspect. It would have been highly imprudent in either Sir William Hamilton or myself to have gone to court, as we knew that all our movements were watched, and even an idea by the Jacobins of arresting our persons as a hostage (as they foolishly imagined) against the attack of Naples, should the French get possession of it. Lady Hamilton, from this time to the 21st, every night received the jewels of the royal family, &c. &c., and such clothes as might be necessary for the very large party to embark, to the amount, I am confident, of full two millions five hundred thousand pounds sterling. On the 18th, General Mack wrote that he had no prospect of stopping the progress of the French, and entreated their Majesties to think of retiring from Naples with their august family as expeditiously as possible. All the Neapolitan navy were now taken out of the mole, consisting of three sail of the line and three frigates: the seamen from the two sail of the line in the bay left their ships and went on shore: a party of English seamen with officers were sent from the Vanguard to assist in navigating them to a place of safety. From the 18th, various plans were formed for the removal of the royal family from the palace to the water-side; on the 19th, I received a note from General Acton, saying, that the king approved of my plan for their embarkation; this day, the 20th and 21st, very large assemblies of people were in commotion, and several people were killed, and one dragged by the legs to the palace. The mob by the 20th

Lord St. Vincent, 28 Dec. Palermo.

were very unruly, and insisted the royal family should not leave Naples; however, they were pacified by the king and queen speaking to them. . . .

On the 21st, at 8.30 P.M. three barges with myself and Captain Hope, landed at a corner of the arsenal. I went into the palace and brought out the whole royal family, put them into the boats, and at 9.30 they were all safely on board the Vanguard, when I gave immediate notice to all British merchants that their persons would be received on board every and any ship in the squadron, their effects of value being before embarked in the three English transports who were partly unloaded, and I had directed that all the condemned provisions should be thrown overboard, in order to make room for their effects. Sir William Hamilton had also directed two vessels to be hired for the accommodation of the French emigrants, and provisions were supplied from our victuallers; in short, everything had been done for the comfort of all persons embarked.

I did not forget in these important moments that it was my duty not to leave the chance of any ships of war falling into the hands of the French, therefore every preparation was made for burning them before I sailed; but the reasons given me by their Sicilian Majesties induced me not to burn them till the last moment. I, therefore, directed the Marquis de Niza to remove all the Neapolitan ships outside the squadron under his command, and if it was possible, to equip some of them with jury masts and send them to Messina; and whenever the French advanced near Naples, or the people revolted against their legitimate Government, immediately to destroy the ships of war, and to join me at Palermo, leaving one or two ships to cruise between Capri and Ischia in order to prevent the entrance of any English ship into the Bay of Naples. On the 23rd, at 7 P.M., the Vanguard, Sannite, and Archimedes, with about twenty sail of vessels left the Bay of Naples; the next day it blew harder than I ever experienced since I have been at sea. Your Lordship will believe that my anxiety was not lessened by the great charge that was with me, but not a word of uneasiness escaped the lips of any of the royal family. On the 25th, at 9 A.M., Prince Albert, their Majesties' youngest child, having eat a hearty breakfast, was taken ill, and at 7 P.M. died in the arms of Lady Hamilton; and here it is my duty to tell your Lordship the obligations which the whole royal family as well as myself are under on this trying occasion to her Ladyship. They necessarily came on board without a bed, nor could the least preparation be made for their reception. Lady Hamilton provided her own beds, linen, &c., and became their slave; for except one man, no person belonging to royalty assisted the royal family, nor did her Ladyship enter a bed the whole time they were on board. Good Sir William also made every sacrifice for the comfort of the august family embarked with him. I must not omit to state the kindness of Captain Hardy and every officer in the Vanguard, all of whom readily gave their beds for the convenience of the numerous persons attending the royal family.

At 3 P.M., being in sight of Palermo, his Sicilian Majesty's royal standard was hoisted at the main-top-gallant-mast head of the Vanguard, which was kept flying there till his Majesty got into the Vanguard's barge, when it was struck in the ship and hoisted in the barge, and every proper honour paid to it from the ship. As soon as his Majesty set his foot on shore, it was struck from the barge. The Vanguard anchored at 2 A.M. of the 26th; at 5, I attended her Majesty and all the princesses on shore; her Majesty being so much affected by the death of Prince Albert that she could not bear to go on shore in a public manner. At 9 A.M. his Majesty went on shore, and was received with the loudest acclamations and apparent joy.

Sir Sidney Smith, 31 Dec. Palermo.

I have been honoured with your letter, from off Malta, with its several inclosures: viz. An extract of a letter from Lord Grenville to John Spencer Smith, Esq. &c., 'And his Majesty has been graciously pleased to direct that your brother, Sir Sidney Smith, shall proceed to Constantinople, with the 80-gun ship, Le Tigre. His instructions will enable him to take the command of such of his Majesty's ships as he may find in those seas, unless, by any unforeseen accident, it should happen that there should be among them any of his Majesty's officers of superior rank; and he will be directed to act with such force, in conjunction with the Russian and Ottoman squadrons, for the defence of the Ottoman Empire, and for the annoyance of the enemy in that quarter.' Also an extract of another letter from Lord Grenville to yourself and brother. And Earl St. Vincent having sent me an extract of a letter from Earl Spencer to him, saying that, for certain circumstances, you should be the officer selected for the command of a small squadron in the Levant seas; and his Lordship having also informed me that Captain Miller was the officer of your choice, and desiring me to give you a frigate, or a sloop of war, till Captain Miller's arrival, you may rest assured that I shall most strictly comply with the instructions sent by Lord Grenville to your brother: also those of Earl Spencer and Earl St. Vincent. For this purpose I must desire that you will lose no time in proceeding to Alexandria, to take upon you the command of the blockade, &c., which I shall direct to be delivered up to you; and, from my heart, I wish you every success. The united squadrons of Turks and Russians, and of two sail of the line under your command, must be sufficient for the two ships *armés en flûte*, and three frigates, which, thank God, are all the enemy have left in those seas. I have the honour to be, Sir, your most obedient servant, NELSON.

Lord St. Vincent, 31 Dec.

My dear Lord,—I do feel, for I am a man, that it is impossible for me to serve in these seas, with the squadron under a junior officer. Could I have thought it!—and from Earl Spencer! Never, never was I so astonished as your letter made me. As soon as I can get hold of Troubridge, I shall send him to Egypt, to endeavour to destroy the ships in Alexandria. If it can be done, Troubridge will do it. The Swedish knight[1] writes Sir William Hamilton, that he shall go to Egypt, and take Captain Hood and his squadron under his command. The knight forgets the respect due to his superior officer: he has no orders from you to take my ships away from my command; but it is all of a piece. Is it to be borne? Pray grant me your permission to retire, and I hope the Vanguard will be allowed to convey me and my friends, Sir William and Lady Hamilton, to England. God bless you, my dear Lord, and believe me your most affectionate friend, NELSON.

Lord Spencer, 1 Jan. 1799.

Having left the command of the two sail of the line in the Levant seas to Sir Sidney Smith, than whom, I dare say, no one could be so proper—Commodore Duckworth will ably, I am sure, watch Toulon, for I shall very soon, I hope, be able to send him one or two sail of the line; and Captain Troubridge, or some other of my brave and excellent commanders, being left to guard Sicily and the coast of Italy, I trust I shall not be thought hasty in asking permission to return to England for a few months, to gather a little of that ease and quiet I have so long been a stranger to.

Captain Troubridge goes directly to Egypt, to deliver up to Sir Sidney Smith the blockade of Alexandria, and the defence of the Ottoman Empire by sea; for I should hope that Sir Sidney Smith will not take any ship from under my command, without my orders; although Sir Sidney, rather hastily in my opinion, writes Sir William Hamilton, that Captain Hood naturally falls under his orders. I am probably considered as having a great force; but I

[1] Sir Sidney Smith, Knight Grand Cross of the Order of the Sword of Sweden.

always desire it to be understood, that I count the Portuguese as nothing but trouble.

Although, from the custom of our service, you would of course fall under the orders of every captain senior to yourself, yet as I cannot yet comprehend your rank, and this not being a time to enter on that subject, I direct you therefore, if you cannot by the rules of your service put yourself under the command of a very old and respectable officer, Captain Louis, that you will co-operate with Captain Louis in the service he is ordered upon on the coast of Italy towards Leghorn, and you will remain on this service until further orders from me, or Captain Louis's consent for your leaving it.

<small>Commdre. Mitchell, Portuguese ship Saint Sebastian, 6 Jan.</small>

Although I could not think the Neapolitans to be a nation of warriors, yet it was not possible to believe that a kingdom with 50,000 troops, and good-looking young men, could have been overrun by 12,000 men, without anything which could be called a battle. Certainly not 100 Neapolitans have been killed; but such things are, if I am not dreaming. Poor Mack came on board the Vanguard on the 23rd. My heart bled for him: he is worn to a shadow. On the 3rd, at night, 8,000 French attempted to force Mack's lines at Capua, in which were 25,000 men. They did not succeed; this is all we know. I do not flatter myself that all that remains are good men and true. I pray they may be. The nobles of Naples—I speak as the queen tells me—are endeavouring to negotiate a truce or peace with the French, and [have] offered to exclude the present king from the throne, and to form a republic under French protection. There is another party who wish the Duke of Parma's son, who is married to a Spanish princess, should be king under French and Spanish protection. How it will end, God only knows!

<small>Lieut.-Gen. Stuart, Minorca, 7 Jan. Palermo.</small>

Amongst the many letters of congratulation which were showered on Nelson at this period, the following from Lord Howe, dated Grafton Street, 3 October, 1798, has a peculiar interest, the more so from its being written so short a time before Howe's death on 5 August, 1799.

'Sir,—Tho' conscious how many letters of congratulation you are likely to receive by the same conveyance, on the subject of your despatches by Captain Capel, I trust you will forgive the additional trouble of my compliments on this singular occasion, not less remarkable for the skill, than cool judgment testified under the considerable disadvantages in the superior force and situation of the enemy, which you had to surmount. I am, with great esteem, Sir, your most obedient servant, Howe.'

On this letter Nelson with his own hand noted, on 4 June, 1799:

Sir Edward Berry informed Lord Nelson that on meeting Lord Howe soon after the battle of the Nile, his Lordship said, 'It stood unparalleled, and singular in this instance, that every captain distinguished himself.' He spoke very handsomely, in every respect, about it.

His immediate answer was:

Lord Howe, 8 Jan. Palermo.

My Lord,—It was only this moment that I had the invaluable approbation of the great, the immortal Earl Howe—an honour the most flattering a sea-officer could receive, as it comes from the first and greatest sea-officer the world has ever produced. I had the happiness to command a band of brothers; therefore, night was to my advantage. Each knew his duty, and I was sure each would feel for a French ship. By attacking the enemy's van and centre, the wind blowing directly along their line, I was enabled to throw what force I pleased on a few ships. This plan my friends readily conceived by the signals (for which we are principally, if not entirely, indebted to your Lordship), and we always kept a superior force to the enemy. At twenty-eight minutes past six, the sun in the horizon, the firing commenced. At five minutes past ten, when L'Orient blew up, having burnt seventy minutes, the six van ships had surrendered. I then pressed further towards the rear; and had it pleased God that I had not been wounded and stone blind, there cannot be a doubt but that every ship would have been in our possession. But here let it not be supposed, that any officer is to blame. No; on my honour, I am satisfied each did his very best. I have never before, my Lord, detailed the action to anyone; but I should have thought it wrong to have kept it from one who is our great master in naval tactics and bravery. May I presume to present my very best respects to Lady Howe, and to Lady Mary; and to beg that your Lordship will believe me ever your most obliged,

NELSON.

Lord S Vincent, (?) 15 Jan.

General Acton has just sent me notice, that General Pignatelli has signed an armistice with the French, in which the name of the king is not mentioned, and that his Majesty has entirely disapproved of this proceeding; and also that the Ligurian Republic had declared war against his Sicilian Majesty. What may arise from day to day is perhaps difficult to say, but unless some great change of measures, in my opinion, Sicily will soon be in great danger.

Commodore Campbell is just arrived from Naples. He has burned the Neapolitan ships before the time specified in my orders to the Marquis de Niza, of which the king has complained to me, and I have entirely disapproved of Commodore Campbell in this matter. The French are in full possession of Capua, and come to Naples as a friendly place. If I get a copy of the articles before Captain Hope sails, I shall send them. In this new case, I have offered to go to the Bay of Naples myself, but both the king and queen have so seriously pressed me not to move, that I cannot do it; they have fears; and have confidence in me, for their safety. Sicily is in this state—free from Jacobins, hate the French, love the English, and discontented with their present situation.

When Malta is finished, you shall go down when you please. We have a report here that a Russian ship has paid you a visit, with proclamations for the island. I hate the Russians, and if she came from their admiral at Corfu, he is a blackguard. Respecting the situation of Malta with the King of Naples, it is this—he is the legitimate sovereign of the island : therefore, I am of opinion his flag should fly. At the same time, a Neapolitan garrison would betray it to the first man who would bribe him. I am sure the king would have no difficulty in giving his sovereignty to England; and I have lately, with Sir William Hamilton, got a note that Malta should never be given to any power without the consent of England. *Capt. Ball, 21 Jan.*

Naples was perfectly quiet on the 18th. The provisional government is placed by the people in the hands of three very gallant, and, fame says, loyal officers. All are turned out and obliged to fly who made the infamous armistice with the French. But, alas! here is no energy in the government to profit of favourable moments. The mob to-day loyal, may to-morrow turn the contrary. The Portuguese have, contrary to my orders, destroyed the Neapolitan navy. This caused much anger, both with the king and people of all descriptions.

Sir Sidney Smith, from a letter he wrote Earl St. Vincent, off Malta, has given great offence, having said that he presumed all the ships in the Levant being junior to him, he had a right to take them under his command. His Lordship has in consequence given him a broad hint, and has taken him down very handsomely; and, to prevent any further mistakes of this kind, has ordered Sir Sidney to put himself immediately under my command, which I suppose *31 Jan.*

the great plenipo will not like. However, he has brought this upon himself.

Lady Parker, 1 Feb.

My health is such that without a great alteration, I will venture to say a very short space of time will send me to that bourne from whence none return; but God's will be done. After the action I had nearly fell into a decline, but at Naples my invaluable friends Sir William and Lady Hamilton nursed and set me up again. I am worse than ever: my spirits have received such a shock that I think they cannot recover it.

Lord St. Vincent, 3 Feb.

The Incendiary is just come from Ball, off Malta, and has brought me information that the attempt of the storming the city of Valetta had failed, from (I am afraid I must call it) cowardice. They were over the first ditch and retired—damn them! But I trust the zeal, judgment, and bravery of my friend Ball and his gallant party will overcome all difficulty.

Capt. Ball, 4 Feb.

Although I regret that the malconduct of the Maltese has caused the enterprise to fail, yet I trust that at a future day it will succeed. I am satisfied, my dear friend, that you and your brave companions have done all which was possible to do. Respecting the corn wanted for Malta, I wrote yesterday to General Acton, and received the answer, of which I inclose you a copy. This evening I saw the king, and he is exceedingly angry to think that his faithful Maltese subjects should want for any comforts or necessaries which it is in his power to bestow. I would wish you to send over to Girgenti or Alicata, in order to secure the safe arrival of the corn in Malta.

Commdre. Duckworth, 8 Feb.

As the Vesuvian Republic is formed under the protection of the French, there can be no doubt that it is at war with Great Britain: therefore, the property of all those who have not left this new state, ought to be good and lawful prize. Gaeta, and the coast to Naples, and Castellamare, with the islands of Ischia, Procida, and Capri, have flying the new flag

Yellow		Yellow
Red	or	Red
Blue		Blue

Salerno has not yet joined, nor any of the coast of Calabria. I have given orders here to seize all vessels belonging to the above-mentioned places. . . .

Everything is wanting for the defence of this country and Calabria; and a messenger goes off this day for Vienna to point out their deplorable situation; but if the emperor will not act, both Sicily and Sardinia must belong to the French.

I well know your own goodness of heart will make all due allowances for my present situation, and that truly I have not the time or power to answer all the letters I receive at the moment; but you, my old friend, after twenty-seven years' acquaintance know that nothing can alter my attachment and gratitude to you: I have been your scholar; it is you who taught me to board a Frenchman, by your conduct when in the Experiment;[1] it is you who always told me, 'Lay a Frenchman close, and you will beat him,' and my only merit in my profession is being a good scholar.

Capt. Locker, 9 Feb.

Whatever has been the result of your expedition to Egypt, I am confident it is such as will do you credit; and if you, and my other brave friends, are well in health, all is well. You will find that I have ordered all our transports from Syracuse to Palermo; for, in truth, I do not think this country safe from the infection which has spread itself over Calabria, and yet I am certain the Sicilians hate the French. I am anxious for the safety of Messina; for until the tri-coloured flag fly there, I am in [no] fear for the rest of the island: therefore, I wish you to go to Messina, approaching it with caution. Look at its state, and if you think that 300 good marines can be raised from the ships with you, and that they may be of great use in defence of the citadel, I would have you land them for the use of the citadel, under the command of Major Oldfield, or the senior marine officer with you, if he is equally good. I would have you remain at Messina till you can hear from me, keeping three ships with you. . . . I wish the great Sir Sidney Smith may return with you; for I hope he will not be wanted in the Levant, and we want him here. It had been my intention, provided the citadel could have been defended by 1,200 men, to have put you and some of my brave friends into it with seamen and marines; but as 3,000 are necessary for its defence, it is beyond my power. We can only do our best to serve the good cause, and hope the great powers will not suffer this fine island to fall to the French. The Russians, we know, are in the Tyrol, and I hope the Germans will join them on their entering Italy, when the French yet may be drove out of the kingdom of Naples.

Capt. Troubridge, 18 Feb.

The appointment of Sir Sidney Smith to a semi-independent command had been, all along, a source of much annoyance to Nelson; the

---

[1] Captain Locker was first lieutenant of the Experiment of 20 guns, commanded by Captain Sir John Strachan, on 19 June, 1757, when she fell in with Le Télémaque, a French ship of 26 guns, which was boarded and carried by the Experiment's men led by Mr. Locker.

more so, by reason of the vanity and assumption which were marked features of Sir Sidney's character. This annoyance is expressed in many letters, especially to Lord St. Vincent, who was scarcely less displeased than Nelson himself, not only at the manner of Sir Sidney's appointment, which was a ministerial blunder, but at Sir Sidney's arrogance and singular want of tact.

Lord St. Vincent, 8 March.

The arrival of the Bonne Citoyenne enables me to send the ministers' letters from Constantinople; but, in truth, I am at a loss to guess when Sir Sidney Smith writes to me as minister or captain in the navy; as the latter, they are highly indecent to write to an officer of my rank. You will agree with me, that the manner of saying the same thing makes it proper or otherwise; but Sir Sidney's dictatorial way of writing is what I never before met with. I shall, my Lord, keep a sufficient force in the Levant for the service required of us, but not a ship for Captain Smith's parade and nonsense—Commodore Smith—I beg his pardon, for he wears a broad pennant—has he any orders for this presumption over the heads of so many good and gallant officers with me?[1] Whenever Sir Sidney Smith went on board the Tigre in state, as he calls it, the royal standard was hoisted at the masthead, and twenty-one guns fired. The Turks, however, who love solid sense and not frippery, see into the knight, and wonder that some of Sir Sidney's superiors were not sent to Constantinople: but I have done with the knight.

God bless you, and ever believe me your affectionate NELSON.

Sir W. S. Smith, 8 March.

Sir,—I have received your letters of 23 January, and of 6, 10, 23 February. Your situation as joint-minister at the Porte makes it absolutely necessary that I should know who writes to me—therefore, I must direct you, whenever you have ministerial affairs to communicate, that it is done jointly with your respectable brother, and not mix naval business with the other, for what may be very proper language for a representative of majesty, may be very subversive of that discipline of respect from the different ranks in our service. A representative may dictate to an admiral—a captain of a man-of-war would be censured for the same thing; therefore you will see the propriety of my steering clear between the two situations. I have sent you my orders, which your abilities as a sea-officer will lead you to punctually execute. Not a ship more than the service requires shall be kept on any particular

---

[1] Lord St. Vincent wrote in reply, on 28 April, that Sir Sidney Smith had no authority to wear a distinguishing pennant, unless Nelson had given it; and he expressed in strong terms his disapprobation of Sir Sidney's letters to Lord Nelson, and of the 'bombast' in those to Earl Spencer.

station; and that number must be left to my judgment, as an admiral commanding the squadron detached by the commander-in-chief to the extent of the Black Sea. I shall of course keep up a proper communication with the Turkish and Russian admirals, which no captain of a man-of-war under my orders must interfere in. I am, Sir, your very humble servant, NELSON.

So far as Nelson was concerned, the difficulty was settled by the following letter from Lord Spencer, dated 12 March :
'On the subject of Sir Sidney Smith, there must certainly have been some very great misunderstanding, as it never was our intention here that he should consider himself as a commander-in-chief, or that he should be authorised to take a single gunboat even from under your command without your orders. He was sent to serve in the Mediterranean fleet, and, of course, under your command, as well as that of every other officer senior to him under Lord St. Vincent ; but from the circumstance of his connection with the king's minister at the Ottoman Porte, and his own acquaintance with several of the principal persons at Constantinople, it was judged advisable by government to join his name in the full powers which had been granted to his brother, to conclude a treaty with that court, and Lord St. Vincent was accordingly directed to send him up in the first instance to Constantinople, as the very uncertain state of the Continent, at the time he received his orders for sailing, made it not improbable that he might arrive there before the courier overland. He was, however, most specifically and pointedly told by me, before his departure, that he would most probably find senior officers to him in the Levant, and I had not the most distant idea of his being any otherwise considered than under your Lordship's orders, which I understand from Lord St. Vincent he has since been more regularly informed of, by an order from him.'

At nine o'clock I was most agreeably surprised with the appearance of General Stuart, who has brought with him 1,000 English troops. This conduct of the general most assuredly demands the warmest gratitude from his Sicilian Majesty, and I have no doubt but Sir Charles will experience it. This goodness reflects on him the highest honour. He has probably, by his quick decision, not only saved this kingdom, but may be the instrument of driving the French out of Naples. Lord St. Vincent, 10 March. Palermo.

Captain Troubridge arrived here last evening, and has delivered to me all the papers he received from you, amongst which I see a form of a passport; and Captain Troubridge tells me it was your intention to send into Alexandria, that all French ships might pass to France. Now, as this is in direct opposition to my opinion, which is, never to suffer any one individual Frenchman to quit Egypt, I must therefore strictly charge and command you, never Sir W. S. Smith, 18 March.

to give any French ship or man leave to quit Egypt. And I must also desire that you will oppose by every means in your power any permission which may be attempted to be given by any foreigner, admiral, general, or other person: and you will acquaint those persons, that I shall not pay the smallest attention to any such passport after your notification; and you are to put my orders in force, not on any pretence to permit a single Frenchman to leave Egypt. Of course, you will give these orders to all the ships under your command.

The following is the form of passport referred to:
'De par le Chevalier SIDNEY SMITH, Grand Croix de l'Ordre Royal et Militaire de l'Epée de Suède, Ministre Plénipotentiaire de Sa MAJESTÉ BRITANNIQUE près la PORTE OTTOMANE et Chef de son Escadre dans les Mers du Levant.

'Tous Amiraux, Généraux et Officiers, tant Militaires que Civils de Sa MAJESTÉ BRITANNIQUE, ceux de ses Alliés et des Puissances amies, sont priés de laisser librement et sûrement passer le nommé . . . . . âgé de . . . . ans, taille de . . . . cheveux et sourcils . . . . yeux . . . . nez . . . . bouche . . . . visage . . . . allant à . . . . . . et de lui prêter aide et assistance en cas de besoin, pour poursuivre sa destination. Bon pour . . . . mois.

'Donné à bord du Vaisseau de Sa MAJESTÉ le . . . .
'No. . . . .   ce . . . . .
'Signature du porteur.   'W. SIDNEY SMITH.
. . . .
          'Par ordre,
          'John Keith, Secretary.'

Lord St. Vincent, 20 March. Palermo.

Troubridge arrived from Egypt the 16th. I am endeavouring to do little matters for his squadron, but we have not a store to give him, and I also know your wants. A squadron, under Troubridge, goes directly into the Bay of Naples. I wish first to take the island of Procida, which will secure tolerable anchorage, and effectually blockade Naples. It must, also, have the effect of preventing the French from detaching any troops from Naples to the Provinces, who are all loyal. The Court tells me that twelve thousand Russians and fifteen thousand Turks are ready to cross the Adriatic, to land in the kingdom of Naples; if so, our squadron will create a powerful diversion. Sir William Sidney Smith has the blockade of Alexandria entrusted to him. I send you copies of my letters to him: for the victory of the Nile would in my opinion be useless if any ship or Frenchman is suffered to return to Europe. I hope you will approve of my conduct; for as a captain to an admiral, either Sir Sidney Smith or myself must give way. Troubridge could not destroy the transports by shells, as all the mortars burst and six fire-ships were lost in a gale of wind. Besides, Alexandria is now so well fortified, that it will be a very difficult matter to take it, unless the plague thin their ranks. Bonaparte is at Cairo, not more than sixteen thousand strong. He must and will fall sooner or later, if Sir Sidney does not allow him to retreat by sea. As to myself, I am at times ill at my ease, but it is my duty to submit, and you may be sure I shall not quit my post without absolute necessity. If the emperor moves, I hope yet to return the royal family to Naples.

The ambassador of Bonaparte [has been] intercepted by my friend Troubridge, on his way to Constantinople, and amongst other articles of his instructions is a very important one—viz. an offer to enter on terms for his quitting Egypt with his army. This offer is what I have long expected the glorious battle of the Nile would produce; but it was my determination from that moment never, if I could help it, to permit a single Frenchman to quit Egypt.

W. Wyndham.
22 March.

Captain Sir William Sidney Smith, who has the present command of the squadron off Alexandria, I have reason to believe, thinks differently from me, and will grant passports for the return of that part of the French army which God Almighty permits to remain. I have, therefore, thought it highly proper to send Captain Sir Sidney Smith the order of which I transmit a copy; for I consider it nothing short of madness to permit that band of thieves to return to Europe. No; to Egypt they went with their own consent, and there they shall remain whilst Nelson commands the detached squadron; for never, never, will he consent to the return of one ship or Frenchman.

Whereas it is of the utmost importance that the city and towns in the Bay of Naples should be immediately blockaded to prevent the French forces in those places from getting any supplies of corn or other articles by sea, and it being expedient that an officer of your distinguished merit and abilities should command the blockade, in order to render it the more effectual, you are hereby required and directed to take under your command the [Minotaur, Zealous, Swiftsure, Seahorse, Perseus bomb, and El Corso sloop,] embarking on board them the governor of Procida and two hundred troops, as also such officers as are ordered by his Sicilian Majesty to embark with them, and proceed to the Bay of Naples. And it being necessary that the squadron employed on this service should have some safe anchorage, the more effectually to carry on the said blockade, and the island of Procida affording the anchorage desired, you will use your endeavours to seize and get possession of the said island of

Capt. Troubridge, Culloden, 28 March. Palermo.

Procida, if possible, and reinstate the governor in the command thereof, and using every means in your power to conciliate the affections of the loyal part of the inhabitants; and also those of the islands of Ischia and Capri, and, if possible, bring them to their former allegiance; and also to communicate with the loyal inhabitants of Naples, as much as is in your power and by every opportunity; but by no means to fire upon the city without further orders from me, or circumstances render it necessary to fire on some parts of it, in case of the loyal taking arms against the French. And you will use every effort to prevent all supplies of corn, or other articles, from entering the city and ports in the Bay of Naples; and also of Gaeta and its vicinity, and along the Roman coast to Cività Vecchia. And as it is said the Ponza Islands continue in their allegiance to his Sicilian Majesty, you will direct that all protection and assistance may be given to them, should they stand in need. And you will consider that every means is to be used not only by yourself, but by all those under your command, to communicate with the inhabitants on all the northern coast of the kingdom of Naples and the islands before mentioned, and as much as in your power to cultivate a good understanding with them and conciliate their affections, in order to induce them to return to their allegiance to his Sicilian Majesty, and to take arms to liberate their country from French tyranny and oppressive contributions.

Lord Spencer, 6 April.

The possession of Malta by England would be a useless and enormous expense; yet any expense should be incurred, rather than let it remain in the hands of the French. Therefore, as I did not trouble myself about the establishing again the Order of St. John at Malta, Sir William Hamilton has the assurance from his Sicilian Majesty that he will never cede the sovereignty of the island to any power, without the consent of his Britannic Majesty. The poor islanders have been so grievously oppressed by the order, that many times have we been pressed to accept of the island for Great Britain; and I know if we had, his Sicilian Majesty would have been contented. But, as I said before, I attach no value to it for us.[1]

The Bashaw of Tripoli, having made a treaty with Bonaparte, on 24 February, and received a present of a diamond, I wrote him

---

[1] Nicolas considers this opinion extraordinary. But all the later operations of the war showed clearly enough that, as against France or Spain, Minorca or Sardinia was infinitely preferable as a *place d'armes*, in the days when the overland route or Suez Canal, steam and coaling stations, were unknown and undreamt of.

a letter on the subject, and sent it by the Vanguard; Captain Hardy brought me back a letter of promise of future good conduct. . . .

Being sensible that a close blockade of Naples with the largest force I could collect, must prevent any French troops from being sent against the Italian armies (as they are called) in the Provinces, I sent my friend Troubridge, with five sail of the line, on this service, and directed him to use every means in his power to take Procida, in order to secure the anchorage: he sailed on the 31st ultimo. Yesterday I had the most satisfactory letters from him, of his complete possession of all the islands in the Bay of Naples, and of his getting possession of all Jacobin municipality, officers, &c. Some well-timed and speedy punishments will have the happiest effects. The French are not more than 2,000 troops in Naples, and about 2,000 civic troops; the last are weathercocks, and will always be on the side of the conqueror. We are anxious for the promised succours of Russian troops; 10,000 would possess Naples in twenty-four hours.

As leading to a correct estimate of after events in the Bay of Naples, in which Nelson's conduct has been much criticised, Troubridge's letters at this time have an extreme importance, independent of their great historical interest. On 3 April he wrote:

'If the nobility were men of principle and of respectability, it would be easy to get the Neapolitan soldiers and militia to declare for their king. I wish we had a few thousand good English troops: I would have the King of Naples on his throne in forty-eight hours. I beg your Lordship will particularly recommend Captain Chianchi; he is a fine hardy seaman, a good and loyal subject, desirous of doing everything for the welfare of his country. If the navy of the King of Naples had been composed of such men, the people would never have revolted. I have a villain, by name Francesco, on board, who commanded the castle at Ischia, formerly a Neapolitan officer, and of property in that island. The moment we took possession of the castle, the mob tore this vagabond's coat with the tricoloured cape and cap of liberty button to pieces, and he had then the impudence to put on his Sicilian Majesty's regimentals again: upon which I tore his epaulette off, took his cockade out, and obliged him to throw them overboard; I then honoured him with double irons. The mob entirely destroyed the tree of liberty, and tore the tricoloured flag into ten thousand pieces, so that I have not been able to procure even a small remnant to lay at the king's feet. I, however, send two pieces of the tree of liberty for his Majesty's fire.'

On 4 April he added: 'The whole of the chief Jacobins are quarrelling about their honesty. I have just received an account that a priest, named Albavena, is preaching up revolt in Ischia; I have sent 60 Swiss and 300 loyal subjects to hunt him, and shall have him, I expect, dead or alive to-day. I pray your Lordship to send an honest judge here, to try these miscreants on the spot, that some proper examples may be made. — 2 P.M. Pray press the court to send the judge by the return of the Perseus, as it will be impossible to go on, else ; the villains increase so fast on my hands, and the people are calling for justice : eight or ten of them must be hung.'

And on the 9th : 'I just learn that Caracciolo has the honour to mount guard as a common soldier, and was yesterday a sentinel at the palace : he has refused service. I believe, they force everyone to do duty as militia.'

Duke of Clarence, 10 May.

In addition to my want of power to detail events, I am at this moment seriously unwell ; and nothing but the very peculiar circumstances of the times, with the confidence reposed in me, not only by your royal father and my commander-in-chief, but also by their Sicilian Majesties and the whole nation, could induce me to remain. They all know that I have no desire but of approving myself a most faithful servant to my gracious king ; therefore, there is nothing which I propose that is not, as far as orders go, implicitly complied with. But the execution is dreadful, and almost makes me mad. However, as his Sicilian Majesty has now ordered two generals to be tried for cowardice and treachery, and, if found guilty, that they shall be shot or hanged ; should this be effected, I shall have some hopes that I have done good. I ever preach that rewards and punishments are the foundation of all good government : unfortunately, neither the one nor the other have been practised here.

Difficulties had been continually arising out of the claim made by the captains of the Portuguese ships of the line, having the nominal rank of commodore, to command the captains of English ships. Nelson had all along refused to entertain the claim. He now wrote privately to Commodore Mitchell, the senior of the Portuguese officers :

Commdre. Sampson Mitchell, 13 April.

I have Lord St. Vincent's opinion, which perfectly agrees with mine, that every captain under my command, in a line-of-battle ship, must command the chef-de-division in the Portuguese service. . . . There is only one circumstance : if you cannot remain, your ship must, and the next senior officer must necessarily command her. The Marquis de Niza, I apprehend, cannot alter my destination of your ship ; nor will he, I am sure, encourage disobedience to my orders for the public good.

Lord Spencer, 29 April. Palermo.

Since I wrote you last, things have been every day improving in the kingdom of Naples ; and from appearances, I think it very probable that in ten days their Sicilian Majesties may be again in Naples. . . .

The communication with Naples is so open, that a general took a boat from the city, and came on board Troubridge, to consult about surprising St. Elmo. The civic guard have individually declared that they assemble to keep peace in the city, and not to fight. Many of the principal Jacobins have fled, and Caracciolo has resigned his situation as head of the marine. This man was fool enough to quit his master when he thought his case desperate; yet, in his heart, I believe he is no Jacobin. The fishermen, a few days ago, told him publicly, 'We believe you are loyal, and sent by the king; but much as we love you, if we find you disloyal, you shall be amongst the first to fall.' I am not in person in these busy scenes, more calculated for me than remaining here giving advice; but their Majesties think the advice of my incompetent judgment valuable at this moment, therefore I submit, and I can only say that I give it as an honest man, one without hopes or fears; therefore they get at the truth, which their Majesties have seldom heard.

Our friend Troubridge had a present made him the other day, of the head of a Jacobin; and makes an apology to me, the weather being very hot, for not sending it here! *Lord St. Vincent, 6 May.*

It was sent to Troubridge with a letter, stating that it was the head of one Giffoni, who had been employed in the administration of Ruggi, and begging Troubridge to accept it as a proof of the writer's attachment to the king's cause—'A jolly fellow!' noted Troubridge on the copy which he forwarded to Nelson.

Three or four frigates and as many corvettes have made their escape from Alexandria. Sir William Sidney Smith having left it on 7 March, these ships escaped between 5 and 18 April. I think they are gone to Tripoli; if so, as I have sent Commodore Campbell, I hope to hear a good account of them. *R.-Adml. Duckworth, 9 May.*

The conduct of the king's officer sent to Orbetello and Longone has been so infamous, that Troubridge is almost mad with rage, and I am in a fever. *Lord St. Vincent, 9 May.*

I have wrote strongly to General Acton of the infamous conduct of Yauch.[1] *Capt. Troubridge, 9 May.*

General Acton, in fact, wrote to Nelson, on the same 9 May, 'The conduct of Yauch deserves inquiry, and punishment if found guilty, as I believe his conduct shows it evidently. Orders are given for a courtmartial. The king begs and hopes that Captain Troubridge will direct some of his officers to attend to it, with the officers of this service, and order accordingly what shall be thought proper at the conclusion of it.'

[1] See *post*, p. 194.

Capt. Ball,
12 May,
Palermo.

The French fleet, of nineteen sail of the line, have before this joined the Spanish fleet, of twenty-five sail of the line, at Cadiz. What the event of the action has been off Cadiz, time only can discover. When the junction is effected, Lord St. Vincent comes up the Mediterranean to join his detached squadrons. You will, therefore, if the Russian squadron is before Malta, proceed with all the line-of-battle ships and the Thalia frigate, off Port Mahon, and deliver my letter to Rear-Admiral Duckworth, and follow his orders for your further proceedings. Should, unfortunately, the Russian squadron not be with you, you must send the Audacious and Goliath to Mahon, and the cutter direct with my letter to Earl St. Vincent at Gibraltar. If Vice-Admiral Ouschakoff is with you, you will lay my letter before him, and the Ottoman admiral if with him, and submit it to their consideration, to send as many ships as possible to Minorca, in order to reinforce Earl St. Vincent.

No time must be lost. If any of your ships meet Commodore Campbell, tell him to go to Mahon.

Lord St. Vincent,
12 May.

Eight, nine, or ten sail of the line shall, in a few days, be off Mahon, ready to obey your orders (not in the port). I hope the Russians are off Malta. If so, I have wrote to the admiral to send some of his ships to Minorca. In short, you may depend upon my exertion, and I am only sorry that I cannot move to your help: but this island appears to hang on my stay. Nothing could console the queen this night, but my promise not to leave them unless the battle was to be fought off Sardinia.

Capt. Troubridge,
13 May.
Palermo.

As the French fleets have passed the Straits of Gibraltar, and have been seen near Minorca, you are immediately, on the receipt hereof, to join me, with all the ships of the line under your orders, at this place, and if you could spare a frigate, so much the better —disposing of the small vessels to the best advantage, and leaving whom you think proper in the command.

Lord St. Vincent,
14 May.

In consequence of the very important intelligence brought me last night, of the French fleet having passed the Straits' mouth, I shall alter my plan of sending such ships as I can collect, which I hope will be ten sail of the line, off Mahon, and rendezvous with the whole of them off the island of Maritimo, hoping that Rear-Admiral Duckworth will send his squadron to reinforce me, which will enable me to look the enemy in the face; but should any of the Russians and Turks be off Malta, I hope to get a force of different nations equal to the enemy, when not a moment shall be lost in bringing them to battle.

If the line-of-battle ships have not all sailed, I desire you will bring them all with you immediately, and make the utmost despatch in joining me at this place. The Vanguard is under way, and I only wait for you to join. I am all impatience until you join me.

Capt. Troubridge, 17 May. Palermo.

It is well here to record Troubridge's opinion of men and things, up to the time of his turning over the command in the Bay of Naples to Captain Foote of the Seahorse frigate. The following extracts from Troubridge's letters to Nelson are therefore given:

18 *April.*—' The judge made an offer, two days since, if I wished it, to pass sentence; but hinted that it would not be regular on some. I declined having anything to do with it. The trials are curious; frequently the culprit is not present. The odium I find is intended to be thrown on us. I will out-manœuvre him there, and push him hard too.'

25 *April.*—' Oh, how I long to have a dash at the thieves! A person, just from Naples, tells me the Jacobins are pressing hard the French to remain; they begin to shake in their shoes. Those of the lower order now speak freely. The rascally nobles, tired of standing as common sentinels, and going the rounds, say, if they had known as much as they do now, they would have acted differently.'

27 *April.*—' I have had a long talk with the judge about the villainous priests. I am completely stupid. I have been all day since four o'clock this morning examining vagabonds of different descriptions; and as no one ever gives a direct answer, and not being possessed of much patience, I am quite fagged out. . . . The work we have to do is nothing; but the villainy we must combat is great indeed, and wears us all out. I shall weather all yet, I trust. I have just flogged a rascal for loading his bread with sand; the loaf hung round his neck all the time, and when he was taken on shore afterwards, to be shown to the people.'

1 *May.*—' Caracciolo, I am now satisfied, is a Jacobin. I inclose you one of his letters. He came in the gunboats to Castellamare himself, and spirited up the Jacobins.'

7 *May.*—' I have just had a long conversation with the judge. He tells me he shall finish his business next week; and that the custom with his profession is, to return home the moment they have condemned. He says he must be embarked immediately, and hinted at a man-of-war. I found also from his conversation, that the priests must be sent to Palermo, to be disgraced by the king's order, and then to be returned for execution to this place. An English man-of-war to perform all this! at the same time making application to me for a hangman, which I positively refused. If none could be found here, I desired he would send for one from Palermo. I see their drift: they want to make us the principals, and to throw all the odium upon us. I cannot form the least idea of their law process, as carried on against the prisoners, for the culprits are seldom present while the trial is proceeding. . . . The examples of villains and cowards which the archduke has made, has driven away my melancholy fever. I send the general from Longone and Orbetello, for the King of Naples to follow such an example.

o

He has desired to speak to me, but I have declined having anything to do with him until he clears up his dastardly conduct to his king.'

(?) 8 *May.*—' I am in such a rage at the cowardly and treacherous conduct of the general who was sent to Longone and Orbetello, that I am really unable to tell the story, and therefore send Captain Oswald to relate all. Orbetello is sold, and I fear Longone will be the same. I desired the general, and all his cowardly gang, to get out of a British man-of-war. We want people to fight; he does not come under that description. I told him plainly that his king would never do well until he hanged half his officers. I hope the king will order this general to give an account of himself, and not leave him here as a nuisance. . . . Pray, my dear Lord, hear Oswald, and urge the king to make an example of this general. I am really very ill. I must go to bed. This treachery fairly does me up.'

11 *May.*—' Much matter will come out to prove he would not land. When the court-martial is ordered, which, by General Acton's letter, we may expect immediately—as he is in the service of another sovereign, I submit to your Lordship if we had not better leave them to themselves. Oswald and the Russian will give evidence to his refusing to land. If this colonel, who at present commands here, is president, he will be shot. If that should be the case, shall I confirm the sentence? My hand will not shake signing my name. Without some examples, nothing can go well. . . . His Majesty will, I hope, the moment he regains Naples, make some great examples of his villainous nobles. Pignatelli has loaded my man with irons for carrying the letter sent by her Majesty for him, through Lady Hamilton: I trust, before long, I shall have a pull at his nose for it. I have two or three to settle with, if we get in.'

14 *May.*—' You will see, my Lord, by the inclosed translation of Prince Trabia's letter, that his Majesty has ordered a court-martial to try Marshal Yauch; but as there are only four officers here of the rank qualified to sit, according to the Neapolitan laws, I think he cannot legally be tried, until his Majesty sends over three more officers. I should have been happy to have sat on it, and to have directed some of our captains to have accompanied me; but as we are not in his Sicilian Majesty's service, it would have caused some noise at home, and certainly would not have been legal.'

Lord St. Vincent, 23 May. Off Maritimo.

On the 17th, the Culloden, Minotaur, Swiftsure, and St. Sebastian, arrived off Palermo, but it blew so hard from the ESE that the ships were obliged to strike yards and top-masts: this gale continued to the 20th, when I put to sea. . . . Zealous joined at daylight of the 21st, as did the Swallow, Portuguese corvette, with a letter from Rear-Admiral Duckworth, saying he was waiting your Lordship's arrival.

This morning I arrived off Maritimo, and was sorry to find neither Captain Ball's squadron or any account from him; I can only have two queries about him—either that he has gone round to Messina, imagining that the French fleet were close to him, or he is taken. Thus situated, I have only to remain on the north side of Maritimo, to keep covering Palermo, which shall be protected to the last, and to wait intelligence or orders for regulating my further proceedings. Your Lordship may depend that the squadron under my command shall never fall into the hands of the enemy; and before we are destroyed, I have little doubt but the enemy will have their wings so completely clipped that they may be easily overtaken.

Your Lordship is acquainted with my intentions of raising the blockade of Malta and of uniting my whole force off Maritimo. I have not yet heard from Captain Ball, what he has done, in consequence of my orders. He was apprised, by the Cameleon, of the French fleet being in the Straits, and she passed on for St. Jean d'Acre on the 17th; therefore we are completely on our guard. Your Lordship having informed me of your intentions, also with what was, at that time, the situation of the two fleets, French and Spaniards, leaving me to act as I thought best from the situation of affairs, I have determined to carry the ships to the Bay of Palermo, to complete their provisions to six months, and as much wine as they stow, and to hold them in momentary readiness to act as you may order or the circumstances call for. My reason for remaining in Sicily is the covering the blockade of Naples, and the certainty of preserving Sicily in case of an attack. . . . But from the favourable aspect of affairs in Italy, I am sure no attack will be made here, whilst the French know we have such a force to act against them. If Captain Ball has not entirely given up the blockade of Malta, and the poor islanders have not given up to the French, I intend to continue the blockade with two ships of the line, a frigate, two sloops and a cutter; for as the danger, from your happy arrival, is not so great, I will run the risk of the ships for a short time. The Russians will, I am told, be off there in a week or fortnight.

28 May. Off Trapani.

I have our dear Troubridge for my assistant; in everything we are brothers. Hood and Hallowell are as active and good as ever: not that I mean to say any are otherwise; but you know these are men of resources. Hardy was bred in the old school, and I can assure you, that I never have been better satisfied with the real good discipline of a ship than the Vanguard's. I hope from my heart that you will meet the dons alone: if the two fleets join, I am ready, and with some of my ships in as high order as ever went to sea. The Russian ships are blocking up Ancona; but again the Généreux has escaped them. As to politics, they are my abomina-

30 May. Palermo.

tion: the ministers of kings and princes are as great scoundrels as ever lived.

Capt. Foote, 6 June. Your news of the hanging of thirteen Jacobins gave us great pleasure; and the three priests, I hope, return in the Aurora, to dangle on the tree best adapted to their weight of sins. The news from all parts of the Continent is excellent. Turin was taken on 7 May, and the king's government re-established. We know nothing of the fleet, and are, as you will believe, all anxiety.

On 8 June, Lord Nelson shifted his flag from the Vanguard to the Foudroyant, taking with him from the Vanguard Captain Hardy, five lieutenants, the surgeon, chaplain, and several mates and midshipmen.

Lord St. Vincent, 10 June. We have a report that you are going home. This distresses us most exceedingly, and myself in particular; so much so, that I have serious thoughts of returning, if that event should take place. But for the sake of our country, do not quit us at this serious moment. I wish not to detract from the merit of whoever may be your successor; but it must take a length of time, which I hope the war will not give, to be in any manner a St. Vincent. . . .

In consequence of the ill state of his health, Lord St. Vincent left the command with Vice-Admiral Lord Keith, and sailed from Mahon for Gibraltar on June 23. But even previously to this, during Lord St. Vincent's illness, Lord Keith had commanded the squadron on a cruise, with orders to look into Toulon and search along the coast, in the endeavour to get some exact news of the allied fleet. From off Monaco, he had written to Nelson on 6 June, that not being able to learn where the enemy was, he felt obliged to return to Minorca, which was left defenceless, but that he sent the Bellerophon and Powerful to reinforce him.

Lord Keith, 16 June. At sea. I was honoured with your letter of 6 June, by the Bellerophon and Powerful, on the 13th, being then on my way to Naples with troops, &c., in order to finish all matters in that kingdom, and again place his Majesty on his throne. But considering the force of the French fleet on the coast of Italy, twenty-two sail of the line, four of which are first-rates, and that probably the ships left at Toulon would have joined them by the time I was reading the letters (the force with me being only sixteen sail of the line, not one of which was of three decks, three being Portuguese, and one of the English a sixty-four, very short of men), I had no choice left, but to return to Palermo, and land the troops, ammunition, &c.; which having done, I am now at sea proceeding off Maritimo, where I hope to be joined by the Alexander and Goliath. . . . My force will then be eighteen sail of the line, with the notations as above mentioned. I shall wait off Maritimo, anxiously expecting such a reinforcement as may enable me to go in search of the enemy's fleet, when not one moment shall be lost in bringing them to battle ; for I consider the best defence for his Sicilian Majesty's dominions, is to place myself alongside the French.

On the return of our squadron, which the Jacobins gave out was for fear of the French fleet, all is undone again, although they had in some measure agreed to terms: therefore his Majesty has requested my immediate presence in the Bay of Naples. R.-Adml. Duckworth, 21 June.

The squadron entered the Bay of Naples on 24 June. Having, on his passage, learned that Captain Foote had signed a treaty with the garrisons of the castles of Uovo and Nuovo, in which the principal Neapolitan rebels had taken refuge, Nelson, considering any such treaty 'infamous,' and finding a flag of truce still flying on the castles, as well as on board the Seahorse, instantly annulled the truce, by signal.

Opinion delivered before I saw the treaty of armistice, &c., only from reports met at sea. Opinion on the armistice, 24 June.

The armistice I take for granted is, that if the French and rebels are not relieved by their friends in twenty-one days from the signing the armistice, then that they shall evacuate Naples, in this infamous manner to his Sicilian Majesty, and triumphant to them, as stated in the article.

All armistices signify that either party may renew hostilities, giving a certain notice fixed upon by the contracting parties. In the present instance, I suppose the cardinal thought that in twenty-one days he had not the power of driving the French from the castle of St. Elmo, or the rebels from the lower castles of Uovo and Nuovo. The French and rebels thought that if they could not be relieved in twenty-one days, they could, when unable to remain any longer, covenant to be removed to a place where they may be in a situation to renew their diabolical schemes against his Sicilian Majesty and the peace and happiness of his faithful subjects, and their removal to be at the expense of his Majesty ; and those enemies and rebels to be protected by the fleet of his Sicilian Majesty's faithful ally, the King of Great Britain. Therefore evidently this agreement implies that both parties are supposed to remain *in statu quo* ; but if either party receive relief from their situation, then the compact of course falls to the ground, and is of no effect ; for if one party can be liberated from the agreement, it naturally implies the other is in the same state. And I fancy the question need not be asked whether, if the French fleet arrived this day in the Bay of Naples, whether the French and rebels would adhere one moment to the armistice? 'No!' the French admiral would say, 'I am not come here to look on, but to act.' And so says the British admiral; and declares on his honour that the arrival of either fleet, British or French, destroys the compact, for neither can lie idle.

Therefore, the British admiral proposes to the cardinal to send, in their joint names, to the French and rebels, that the arrival of the British fleet has completely destroyed the compact, as would that of the French if they had had the power (which, thank God, they have not) to come to Naples.

Therefore, that it shall be fixed that in two hours the French shall give possession of the castle of St. Elmo to his Sicilian Majesty's faithful subjects, and the troops of his allies; on which condition alone, they shall be sent to France without the stipulation of their being prisoners of war.

That as to rebels and traitors, no power on earth has a right to stand between their gracious king and them: they must instantly throw themselves on the clemency of their sovereign, for no other terms will be allowed them; nor will the French be allowed even to name them in any capitulation. If these terms are not complied with, in the time above mentioned—viz. two hours for the French, and instant submission on the part of the rebels— such very favourable conditions will never be again offered.

NELSON.

Read and explained, and rejected by the cardinal.

In writing this opinion, Nelson was mistaken as to the nature of the treaty, which was not for an armistice, but a definite capitulation. The rectification of this mistake did not, however, alter his views, and he equally annulled the treaty.

Notification, 25 June.

Declaration sent to the Neapolitan Jacobins in the castles of Uovo and Nuovo.

Rear-Admiral Lord Nelson, K.B., commander of his Britannic Majesty's fleet in the Bay of Naples, acquaints the rebellious subjects of his Sicilian Majesty in the castles of Uovo and Nuovo, that he will not permit them to embark or quit those places. They must surrender themselves to his Majesty's royal mercy.

The governor of St. Elmo, 25 June.

His eminence the Cardinal de Ruffo and the commanding officer of the Russian army having sent you a summons to surrender, I acquaint you, that unless the terms are acceded to within two hours, you must take the consequences. I shall not agree to any other.

As you will believe, the cardinal and myself have begun our career by a complete difference of opinion. He will send the rebels to Toulon: I say they shall not go. He thinks one house in Naples more to be prized than his sovereign's honour. Troubridge and Ball are gone to the cardinal, for him to read my declaration to the French and rebels, whom he persists in calling patriots— what a prostitution of the word! I shall send Foote to get the gunboats from Procida. I wish the fleet not to be more than two-thirds of a cable from each other. I shall send you a sketch of the anchorage, in forty fathom water. The Foudroyant to be the van ship. If the French fleet should favour us with a visit, I can easily take my station in the centre.

<small>R.-Adml. Duck-worth, 25 June.</small>

On 26 June, Cardinal Ruffo came on board the Foudroyant, where a discussion of several hours' duration took place between him and Lord Nelson, in the presence of Sir William and Lady Hamilton, who acted as interpreters; but all Nelson's arguments failed to convince the cardinal that the treaty was, *ipso facto*, terminated by the arrival of the English fleet, and that as its conditions had not been executed, it required the ratification of his Sicilian Majesty. Nelson, therefore, expressed his own opinion to that effect in the annexed memorandum, and proceeded to act according to his own views, by taking possession of the castles, and making prisoners of all the Neapolitans in them: after which, he invested St. Elmo, with the seamen and marines of his ships, under the command of Captain Troubridge.

Rear-Admiral Lord Nelson arrived with the British fleet on 24 June in the Bay of Naples, and found a treaty entered into with the rebels, which, in his opinion, cannot be carried into execution, without the approbation of his Sicilian Majesty.

<small>Memo. 26 June.</small>

I am happy in being able to congratulate their lordships on the possession of the city of Naples. St. Elmo is yet in the hands of the French, but the castles of Uovo and Nuovo I took possession of last evening, and his Sicilian Majesty's colours are now flying on them. . . . The moment I can find the city a little quieted, guns shall be got against St. Elmo, when, I am sure, the French will be glad to surrender. . . . In my present position, I have not the smallest alarm should the enemy favour us with a visit, inferior as my force is to oppose them.

<small>Evan Nepean, 27 June.</small>

On the 17th the Alexander and Goliath joined me from off Malta; leaving to look out in that quarter, three sloops of war;—the force with me was now fifteen sail of two-decked ships, English, and three Portuguese, with a fire-ship and cutter. On the 20th, the Swallow, Portuguese corvette, brought me your Lordship's

<small>Lord Keith, 27 June, Bay of Naples.</small>

despatch of the 17th, acquainting me of the near approach of the squadron under Sir Alan Gardner, and that Lord Keith was going in search of the French fleet.[1] As I had now no prospect of being in a situation to go in search of the enemy's fleet, which at least is twenty-five sail of the line, and might be reinforced with two Venetian ships, although I was firmly resolved they should not pass me without a battle, which would so cripple them that they might be unable to proceed on any distant service, I determined to offer myself for the service of Naples, where I knew the French fleet intended going. With this determination I pushed for Palermo, and on the 21st I went on shore for two hours, saw their Majesties and General Acton, who repeated to me what the general had wrote (but which I had not received), to request that I would instantly go into the Bay of Naples to endeavour to bring his Sicilian Majesty's affairs in that city to a happy conclusion.

I lost not one moment in complying with the request, and arrived in the Bay of Naples on the 24th, when I saw a flag of truce flying on board his Majesty's ship Seahorse, Captain Foote, and also on the castles of Uovo and Nuovo. Having on the passage received letters informing [me] that an infamous armistice was entered into with the rebels in those castles, to which Captain Foote had put his name, I instantly made the signal to annul the truce, being determined never to give my approbation to any terms with rebels, but that of unconditional submission. The fleet was anchored in a close line of battle, NW by N and SE by S, from the mole head one and a half mile distant, flanked by twenty-two gun and mortar boats, which I recalled from Procida. I sent Captains Troubridge and Báll instantly to the cardinal vicar-general, to represent to his eminence my opinion of the infamous terms entered into with the rebels, and also two papers which I inclose. His eminence said he would send no papers, that if I pleased I might break the armistice, for that he was tired of his situation. Captain Troubridge then asked his eminence this plain question : ' If Lord Nelson breaks the armistice, will your eminence assist him in his attack on the castles ? ' His answer was clear, ' I will neither assist him with men or guns.' After much communication, his eminence desired to come on board to speak with me on his situation. I used every argument in my power to convince him that the treaty and armistice was at an end by the arrival of the fleet ; but an admiral is no match in talking

---

[1] It would appear from this sentence that the letter was written to Lord St. Vincent, though addressed to Lord Keith.

with a cardinal. I therefore gave him my opinion in writing—viz. 'Rear-Admiral Lord Nelson, who arrived in the Bay of Naples on 24 June with the British fleet, found a treaty entered into with the rebels, which he is of opinion ought not to be carried into execution without the approbation of his Sicilian Majesty, Earl St. Vincent, Lord Keith.'[1]

Under this opinion the rebels came out of the castles, which were instantly occupied by the marines of the squadron. On the 27th Captains Troubridge and Ball, with 1,300 men, landed from the ships, united with 500 Russians and a body of royalists, half of whose officers are, I have every reason to believe, rebels—cowards they have already proved themselves. Our batteries are open on St. Elmo, and a few days will, I hope, reduce it. The Alexander and another are just going to resume their station off Malta, which I am confident will very soon surrender, now all hopes of relief are cut off. I shall not fail to keep up a constant communication with your Lordship, and have the honour to be with greatest respect, your most obedient faithful servant, NELSON.

Caracciolo was executed on board his Sicilian Majesty's ship Minerva, on 29 June.

PROCLAMATION.

Horatio Lord Nelson, admiral of the British fleet in the Bay of Naples, gives notice to all those who have served as officers, civil or military, in the service of the infamous Neapolitan Republic, that, if in the space of twenty-four hours for those who are in the city of Naples, and forty-eight hours for those who are within five miles of it, they do not give themselves up to the clemency of the king, to the officer commanding the castles Uovo and Nuovo, Lord Nelson will consider them still as in rebellion, and enemies of his Sicilian Majesty.

29 June

To Count Thurn, commodore and commander of his Sicilian Majesty's frigate La Minerva.

By Horatio Lord Nelson, &c. &c. &c.

Whereas Francisco Caracciolo, a commodore in the service of his Sicilian Majesty, has been taken, and stands accused of rebellion against his lawful sovereign, and for firing at his colours hoisted on board his frigate the Minerva, under your command,

You are, therefore, hereby required and directed to assemble

---

[1] In the original, which is autograph, 'Lord Keith' is written in above the line; an evident afterthought, probably when the postscript was added and the intended address changed.

five of the senior officers under your command, yourself presiding, and proceed to inquire whether the crime with which the said Francisco Caracciolo stands charged, can be proved against him; and if the charge is proved, you are to report to me what punishment he ought to suffer.

Given on board the Foudroyant, Naples Bay, 29 June, 1799.
NELSON.

To Commodore Count Thurn, commander of his Sicilian Majesty's frigate La Minerva.
By Horatio Lord Nelson, &c. &c. &c.

Whereas a board of naval officers of his Sicilian Majesty hath been assembled to try Francisco Caracciolo for rebellion against his lawful sovereign, and for firing at his Sicilian Majesty's frigate La Minerva;

And whereas the said board of naval officers have found the charge of rebellion fully proved against him, and have sentenced the said Caracciolo to suffer death;

You are hereby required and directed to cause the said sentence of death to be carried into execution upon the said Francisco Caracciolo accordingly, by hanging him at the fore yard-arm of his Sicilian Majesty's frigate La Minerva, under your command, at five o'clock this evening; and to cause him to hang there until sunset, when you will have his body cut down, and thrown into the sea.

Given on board the Foudroyant, Naples Bay, 29 June, 1799.
NELSON.

Lord Spencer, 13 July.

On my fortunate arrival here I found a most infamous treaty entered into with the rebels, in direct disobedience of his Sicilian Majesty's orders. I had the happiness of saving his Majesty's honour, rejecting with disdain any terms but unconditional submission, to rebels. Your Lordship will observe my note, and opinion to the cardinal.[1] The rebels came out of the castles with this knowledge, without any honours, and the principal rebels were seized and conducted on board the ships of the squadron. The others, embarked in fourteen polacres, were anchored under the care of our ships. His Majesty has entirely approved of my conduct in this matter. I presume to recommend Captain Troubridge for some mark of his Majesty's favour; it would be supposing you, my dear Lord, was ignorant of his merit, was I to say more than that he is a first-rate general.

[1] See *ante*, pp. 198, 201.

Lord Keith writes me, if certain events take place, it may be necessary to draw down this squadron for the protection of Minorca. Should such an order come at this moment, it would be a cause for some consideration whether Minorca is to be risked, or the two kingdoms of Naples and Sicily. I rather think my decision would be to risk the former.

The expected orders reached him the same day in a letter from Lord Keith, dated 27 June.

'Events which have recently occurred render it necessary that as great a force as can be collected should be assembled near the island of Minorca; therefore, if your Lordship has no detachment of the French squadron in the neighbourhood of Sicily, nor information of their having sent any force towards Egypt or Syria, you are hereby required and directed to send such ships as you can possibly spare off the island of Minorca to wait my orders; and I will take care, so soon as the enemy's intentions shall be frustrated in that quarter, to strengthen your Lordship as soon as possible.'

To this he immediately replied:

I have to acknowledge the receipt of your Lordship's orders of 27 June, and as soon as the safety of his Sicilian Majesty's kingdoms is secured, I shall not lose one moment in making the detachment you are pleased to order. At present, under God's providence, the safety of his Sicilian Majesty and his speedy restoration to his kingdom depends on this fleet: and the confidence inspired even by the appearance of our ships before the city is beyond all belief; and I have no scruple in declaring my opinion that should any event draw us from the kingdom, that if the French remain in any part of it, disturbances will again arise, for all order having been completely overturned, it must take a thorough cleansing, and some little time, to restore tranquillity. [Ld. Keith, 13 July.]

I rejoice that you gave Mr. Bolton the money, and I wish it made up 500*l*. I never regarded money, nor wanted it for my own use; therefore, as the East India Company have made me so magnificent a present, I beg that 2,000*l*. of it may be disposed of in the following manner: five hundred pounds to my father; five hundred to be made up to Mr. Bolton, and let it be a God-send, without any restriction; five hundred to Maurice, and five hundred to William. And if you think my sister Matcham would be gratified by it, do the same for her. If I were rich I would do more; but it will very soon be known how poor I am, except my yearly income. I am not surprised at my brother's death;[1] three are now dead, younger than myself, having grown to man's age. [Lady Nelson, 14 July.]

[1] The Reverend Suckling Nelson: died in April 1799.

Evan Nepean,
14 July.

Herewith I have the honour of sending you copies of my letters to the commander-in-chief, and the capitulation granted to the French in St. Elmo. All the chief rebels are now on board his Majesty's fleet; Capua and Gaeta will very soon be in our possession, when the kingdom will be liberated from anarchy and misery.

Capt. Troubridge,
17 July.

When you send in a summons to the commander of the French troops in Capua, his Sicilian Majesty approves that, on condition the commander immediately gives up Capua and Gaeta, that after laying down their arms, colours, &c., the French garrison shall be permitted to go to France without any restrictions. If this is not complied with, prisoners of war, and as degrading terms as it is in your power to give them—no covered waggons, no protection to rebels—in short, the allies must dictate the terms.

On 19 July, Nelson received the following from Lord Keith, dated at Port Mahon, 9 July:

'Having reason to believe, from the repeated information I have received (the latest of which is herewith inclosed), that the enemy have no intention of attempting an impression on the island of Sicily, or of reinforcing their army in Egypt and Syria, but, on the contrary, being inclined to think that their efforts are likely to be directed against Ireland, and that they are bent towards the ocean, I judge it necessary that all, or the greatest part of the force under your Lordship's orders, should quit the island of Sicily, and repair to Minorca, for the purpose of protecting that island during the necessary absence of his Majesty's squadron under my command, or for the purpose of co-operating with me against the combined force of the enemy, wherever it may be requisite. Your Lordship is therefore hereby required and directed to quit the island of Sicily with the whole of your force, or to detach the next senior officer for the time being, with the greatest part thereof, should you deem it absolutely necessary, for the good of his Majesty's service, and the interest of his allies, that some part of it should continue there, under your Lordship's or any other officer's direction. Your Lordship, with the whole force, or such part of it as you may bring with you, or such senior officer, with that part to be detached under his direction, in the event of your Lordship's judging it absolutely necessary to leave some part of it at Sicily, as above mentioned—is to proceed to join me at this place, and in case of my absence, to follow the orders and directions which will be left in charge of the commanding officer of his Majesty's ships and vessels at this port.'

This order was accompanied by a private letter:

'Dear Nelson,—I came in here yesterday to get some water, and had not anchored an hour, when I heard the combined fleets had left Cartagena, and steered to the west. I am now unmooring, with very little water in the ships; for this island does not afford much more than we drink. If this island is left without ships, it will fall. The Spaniards will send their armament, with two ships of the line, frigates, and gunboats—a great many of which are at the different ports opposite, to convoy and cover the landing. You must, therefore, either come, or send Duckworth, to govern himself as circumstances offer, until I can determine to a certainty the intentions of the enemy.'

My Lord,—I am this moment honoured with your order of the 9th, directing me to detach from the island of Sicily, the whole, or such part of the force, as might not be necessary in that island. Your Lordship, at the time of sending me the order, was not informed of the change of affairs in the kingdom of Naples, and that all our marines and a body of seamen are landed, in order to drive the French scoundrels out of the kingdom, which with God's blessing will very soon be effected, when a part of this squadron shall be immediately sent to Minorca; but unless the French are at least drove from Capua, I think it right not to obey your Lordship's order for sending down any part of the squadron under my orders. I am perfectly aware of the consequences of disobeying the orders of my commander-in-chief; but, as I believe the safety of the kingdom of Naples depends at the present moment on my detaining the squadron, I have no scruple in deciding that it is better to save the kingdom of Naples and risk Minorca, than to risk the kingdom of Naples to save Minorca. Your Lordship will, I hope, approve of my decision, and believe me, with the greatest respect,

Your Lordship's faithful and obedient servant, NELSON.

Ld. Keith, 19 July.

With the official letter, he also sent a private note :

My dear Lord,—I grieve most exceedingly that you had not the good fortune to fall in with the French fleet before they formed their junction with the dons, although I am sure, when you are united with the Channel fleet, that you will send them to the devil. My answer to your order is of such a nature that I deem it improper in a private letter to give a reason, therefore I decline touching on the subject.

19 July.

You will easily conceive my feelings at the order this day received from Lord Keith ; but my mind was fully prepared for this order; and more than ever is my mind made up, that, at this moment, I will not part with a single ship, as I cannot do that without drawing a hundred and twenty men from each ship now at the siege of Capua, where our army is gone this day. I am fully aware of the act I have committed ; but, sensible of my loyal intentions, I am prepared for any fate which may await my disobedience. Capua and Gaeta will soon fall ; and the moment the scoundrels of

Lord Spencer, 19 July.

French are out of the kingdom, I shall send eight or nine ships of the line to Minorca.

Evan Nepean, 19 July.

I send you copy of Lord Keith's order to me, my answer, and a copy of a letter I have received since my determination was made (not at this moment to send a single man from this squadron). I feel the importance of the decision I have taken, and know I subject myself to a trial for my conduct; but I am so confident of the uprightness of my intentions for his Majesty's service, and for that of his Sicilian Majesty, which I consider as the same, that, with all respect, I submit myself to the judgment of my superiors.

The following extract from Nepean's reply, dated 20 August, is a necessary supplement to this remarkable correspondence:

'With respect to that part of your Lordship's letter to the commander-in-chief, in which you mention that one thousand of the best men were landed from the squadron, to march, under the command of Captains Troubridge and Hallowell, against Capua, their lordships have desired me to observe to you, that although in operations on the sea coast it may frequently be highly expedient to land a part of the seamen of the squadron, to co-operate with and to assist the army, when the situation will admit of their being immediately re-embarked, if the squadron should be called away to act elsewhere, or if information of the approach of an enemy's fleet should be received—yet their lordships by no means approve of the seamen being landed to form a part of an army to be employed in operations at a distance from the coast, where, if they should have the misfortune to be defeated, they might be prevented from returning to the ships, and the squadron be thereby rendered so defective as to be no longer capable of performing the services required of it; and I have their lordships' commands to signify their directions to your Lordship not to employ the seamen in like manner in future.

'I have also to acknowledge the receipt of your Lordship's letter of 19 July, inclosing the copy of an order you had received from Vice-Admiral Lord Keith, directing you to proceed with the whole, or to detach a part of the squadron under your command to Minorca, and also the copy of your letter to his lordship in answer thereto, and I have their lordships' commands to acquaint you, that although the co-operation of a British naval force with the army of his Sicilian Majesty might be, and it appears to have been necessary, yet, as from the information your Lordship had received from Lord Keith, you must have been satisfied that nothing was to be apprehended from the enemy's fleet, it does not appear to their lordships to have been necessary that the whole of the squadron under your command should have been kept for such co-operation, but that a part of it would have been sufficient, not only to have inspired that confidence, which your Lordship states to have been the result of its appearance, but also to have afforded effectual assistance to his Sicilian Majesty; and that their lordships do not, therefore, from any information now before them, see sufficient reason to justify your having disobeyed the orders you had received from your commanding officer, or having left Minorca exposed to the risk of being attacked, without having any naval force to protect it.'

I earnestly trust that your exertions will be crowned with success, and that Bonaparte is gone to the devil. As Lord Keith writes to you, I shall not say much of what is passing to the west, except that the French fleet, united to the Spanish (43 sail of the line) sailed from Cartagena on 29 June, and Lord Keith was in Mahon on 9 July. My belief is, that the whole force will push into the Tagus, and carry Lisbon, and of course Portugal, by a *coup*. Others think Ireland will be their object; time, and a short time, must discover their plans to us. In the meantime, we can only sincerely lament that the scoundrels have escaped the vigilance of Lord Keith. Minorca is menaced; but I think will not be attacked.

Sir W. S. Smith. 20 July.

Yesterday brought us letters from your worthy brother; and we had the great pleasure of hearing that your truly meritorious and wonderful exertions were in a fair train for the extirpation of that horde of thieves who went to Egypt with that arch-thief, Bonaparte. I beg you will express to good Captain Miller,[1] and to all the brave officers and men who have fought so nobly under your orders, the sense I entertain of your and their great merit. I am sorry at present it is not in my power to send you even a sloop of war; for Lord Keith has ordered every ship, not absolutely necessary for Sicily, to repair to Minorca, which is menaced with an attack. I think Lord Keith will follow to the Channel; if so, and when I see what is left me (for at present everything from Sicily to Gibraltar has passed the Straits), I shall have pleasure in giving you a small but active squadron; for, while the French remain in any part of Egypt, I see Great Britain must do everything.

24 July.

On 22 July, Nelson received a more positive order dated off Formentera, 14 July:

'Your Lordship is hereby required and directed to repair to Minorca, with the whole, or the greater part, of the force under your Lordship's command, for the protection of that island, as I shall, in all probability, have left the Mediterranean before your Lordship will receive this.'

To disobey this was too much, even for Nelson.

You are hereby required and directed to take under your command the [Powerful, Majestic, Vanguard, and Swallow corvette] whose captains have my directions to follow your orders, and proceed with them to Mahon, in the island of Minorca, and on your arrival there to take also under your orders such of his Majesty's ships as you may find in that port, leaving it entirely to your well-

R.-Adml. Duckworth. 22 July.

[1] Captain Miller was unfortunately killed on 14 May; see *post*, p. 211.

known abilities and judgment to act with them in the best manner for the protection of that island and the good of his Majesty's service.

<small>Private Memorandum.</small>

Mr. Lock [consul-general at Naples] having for several days been soliciting me for the exclusive privilege of supplying the squadron with fresh beef, upon a due consideration I wrote the following note, and left it with my secretary. Mr. Lock came to me and said that he could point out to me that Government had been grossly imposed upon in the purchase of fresh beef—that he knew, or had seen, one account, which was only 700*l.* [for] which bills had been drawn upon Government [for] 850*l.* The exact sums may not be correct, but I am sure that 150*l.* was the difference mentioned by the consul. On my saying that if it was so I was obliged to him for the information, but that I doubted it, as all vouchers, before they were brought to the captains for signature, were testified as to the price by two respectable merchants—his answer was, that the signature of merchants was nothing, they could be got to sign anything. I then asked Mr. Lock who this notorious fraud had been committed by, which he refused to tell me; on which I called Captain Hardy, and told him as he, with all the captains and pursers of the fleet, were accused by Mr. Lock of being thieves, I should leave him to settle the business, and that I should give out an order for inquiry in the morning. This order Mr. Lock begged me not to give out, and, through Sir William Hamilton, saying it was only a private communication. My answer to this application was, that the consul having on his Majesty's quarter-deck, under my flag, made such an accusation, nothing could be more public; and that if I attempted to conceal it, the next thing he would do would be to accuse me of being the cheat—therefore, nothing should prevent my giving out a public order. Mr. Lock's next request was, that I would not mention his name, which I complied with; but, as the conversation was heard by hundreds, it could not be kept a secret. The manner and language of Mr. Lock was highly insulting to my rank and situation, under my flag, and in the presence of his Sicilian Majesty, his court, and his Majesty's representative.

<small>Ch. Lock, 23 July.</small>

In my situation I never have or ever will interfere in the victualling his Majesty's ships under my command. Each captain is at liberty to purchase the provisions and wine, when it can be had of the best quality, and at the cheapest rate.

<small>Memo. 24 July.</small>

Whereas I have received information that most gross abuses

have been practised in the purchase of fresh beef for the use of the squadron under my command, to the great detriment of Government, it is my positive direction that in future the vouchers are strictly examined, and the prices of every article purchased be properly ascertained by the signing officers, and attested by two respectable merchants on shore, before the vouchers are signed.

In consequence of this order, Captains Martin of the Northumberland, Hood of the Zealous, Darby of the Bellerophon, Foley of the Goliath, and Hardy of the Foudroyant, wrote to Lord Nelson a few days afterwards, stating that the fresh beef and wine supplied to their ships had been of the best quality, and, as they believed, had been purchased at the market prices.

I thank you truly for your letter of 9 June, containing an extract of one from your brother, who has done so much at Acre. It is like his former conduct; and I can assure you, no one admires his gallantry and judgment more than myself. But if I know myself, as I never have encroached on the command of others, so I will not suffer even my friend Sir Sidney to encroach upon mine. I dare say he thought he was to have a separate command in the Levant. I find upon inquiry it never was intended to have any one in the Levant separate from me. *J. S. Smith, 25 July.*

The French fleet passed the Straits out of the Mediterranean on 8 or 9 July. Capua surrendered on the 27th. The capitulation of Gaeta was sent to Naples, and was ratified on the 31st. Nelson's letters are merely inclosing copies of Troubridge's, with which he wrote:

I most sincerely congratulate their Lordships on the entire liberation of the kingdom of Naples from the French robbers; for by no other name can they be called for their conduct in this kingdom. This happy event will not, I am sure, be the less acceptable from being principally brought about by part of the crews of his Majesty's ships under my orders, under the command of Captain Troubridge. His merits speak for themselves. His own modesty makes it my duty to state, that to him alone is the chief merit due. *Evan Nepean, 1 Aug.*

On the capitulation going back to Gaeta, the French commandant demanded some further concessions; and Captain Louis, of the Minotaur, who had been charged to see the embarkation properly conducted, forwarded the Frenchman's objections to Nelson. This brought down on him a vehement, though not unfriendly reproof.

You carried with you the treaty, and, in two hours after your arrival, and the capitulation was presented, you was to take possession of the gates, and in twenty-four hours the garrison were to be *Capt. Louis, 3 August.*

embarked. I am hurt and surprised that the capitulation has not been complied with. It shall be, and the commander has agreed to it. I have not read your paper inclosed. You will execute my orders, or attack it. The fellow ought to be kicked for his impudence. You will instantly take possession of the gates and the fortress. I had reason to expect it had been done long ago. I am very much hurt that it has not.

4 August.

I have received your letter of yesterday, and am happy to find that all matters are settled. I was sorry that you had entered into any altercation with the scoundrel. The capitulation once signed, there could be no room for dispute. There is no way of dealing with a Frenchman but to knock him down. To be civil to them is only to be laughed at, when they are enemies.

Capt. Troubridge,
5 August.

Whereas it is necessary for the good of his Majesty's Service, that an officer above the rank of post-captain should command the squadron in Naples Bay, and along the coast, especially as a number of foreign ships of war are expected; you are, therefore, hereby required and directed to hoist a broad red pennant at the main-topgallant-mast-head of the ship you command, and to wear the same during the continuance of your services on this coast, or until further orders.

On 5 August, the Foudroyant sailed from Naples with the king on board, and arrived at Palermo on the 8th.

R.-Adml. Duckworth,
20 August.

Whereas the commander-in-chief hath informed me, that he was proceeding with the fleet into the Western Ocean, and perhaps, off Brest,—you are therefore hereby required and directed to proceed, or send two ships of the line to Gibraltar, and render every assistance in your power to General O'Hara and the garrison there, and by keeping the ports of the Barbary States and the Gut of Gibraltar open, to protect the trade until the arrival of three sail of the line more, which will be sent you with frigates, sloops, &c. When they have joined, you will then proceed off Cadiz and watch that port, keeping the Straits open, and also, as far as you are able, watch over and protect the trade of Lisbon and Oporto to the utmost of your power, acquainting the Lords Commissioners of the Admiralty and me, with any events that may happen, necessary for them or me to know. And in the event of the return of the Spanish fleet to Cadiz, or such a number of them as you may not be able to cope with, you will be particularly careful to guard against surprise, and prevent them getting up the Mediterranean before you, so as to surprise the squadron off Minorca; and send a frigate or other vessel off Cape St. Vincent or to Lisbon, with the news, to prevent any of our trade falling into their hands, and make the best of your way up to join the squadron off Minorca, sending also some vessel to apprise me of such event, that all the force may be collected as soon as possible.

And this order was accompanied by a long private letter, to the same effect, but in greater detail.

My dear Sir,—I have received with the truest satisfaction all your very interesting letters to 16 July. The immense fatigue you have had in defending Acre against such a chosen army of French villains, headed by that arch-villain Bonaparte, has never been exceeded, and the bravery shown by you and your brave companions is such as to merit every encomium which all the civilised world can bestow. As an individual, and as an admiral, will you accept of my feeble tribute of praise and admiration, and make them acceptable to all those under your command. . . . I hope Alexandria is long before this in your possession, and the final blow given to Bonaparte; but I hope no terms will ever be granted for his individual return to Europe.

Be assured, my dear Sir Sidney, of my perfect esteem and regard, and do not let any one persuade you to the contrary. But my character is, that I will not suffer the smallest tittle of my command to be taken from me; but with pleasure I give way to my friends, among whom I beg you will allow me to consider you, and that I am, with the truest esteem and affection, your faithful humble servant, NELSON.

Sir W. S. S. Smith, 20 August.

It is with extreme concern I have to mention the death of Captain Miller of his Majesty's ship Theseus, who was killed on board that ship on 14 May last, by the explosion of some shells on the quarter-deck, which killed twenty-six men, wounded forty-five, and nine were drowned by jumping overboard. The ship is much damaged, but has been in part repaired.

E. Nepean, 23 August.

The Russians are anxious to get to Malta, and care for nothing else—therefore I hope you will get it before their arrival. The Stromboli carries a mortar, and I think from the number of men which can be landed from the squadron, that we shall very soon call it ours.

Capt. Ball, 5 Sept.

Having secured the free access of the Straits by the force detached to Gibraltar, and, from your account and Hood's, being

Com. Troubridge, 7 Sept.

P 2

perfectly at my ease about Minorca, you have my full permission to either immediately send Louis to Cività Vecchia, with what vessels you can give him, or to keep under sail when you think the Russians and Turks are approaching, and go direct to Cività Vecchia, and try what can be done; and if you can get possession, then to land not only your marines, but such other force as you can spare, and not to move till further orders from me; for, as I have before said, I am perfectly easy about Minorca. Now you know my sentiments, you will act and arrange accordingly; but this must be kept secret, or we shall give jealousy to the Russians. As for the Turks, we can do anything with them. They are good people, but perfectly useless.

R.-Adml. Duckworth, 12 Sept.

When winter gets a little more advanced, all the present ships off Malta must go down the Mediterranean, and some part to England; therefore, keep no more ships below Minorca than you think the service requires: for I had plenty of reasons lately to write to the Admiralty, that if a naval force should be wanted for the coast of Italy, that England must find it; for the Russian admiral has told me, his ships cannot keep the sea in the winter; and I see no desire to go to sea in the summer. The Turks are returned to Constantinople, having had a fray with the Sicilians, in which many lives were lost.

If I am left in the command even for a few months, I shall send those French frigates[1] which cannot be manned to England, and for that purpose fifty good men shall be left by those ships going to England. The Alceste may serve for a convoy for Leghorn or Sardinia, for provisions; but Junon and Courageux cannot be made useful, at least I am told so; and to keep them lying at Mahon appears to me a waste of public money. My mind is fixed that I will not keep one ship in the Mediterranean which is not fit for *any* service. During the winter, those half-fit drain us of all the stores, and render us all useless.

Marquis de Niza, 13 Sept.

If Mr. Vaubois puts his garrison afloat, I have no doubt but some of your ships will catch him. If such an event should happen, push immediately part of your ships on the west side of Sardinia, and part on the east side. The latter, in my opinion, will be his route, and he will be taken; but no time must be lost in the pursuit.

[1] Junon (afterwards called Princess Charlotte), Alceste, Courageux, and two brigs, Salamine and Alerte (afterwards called Minorca), taken off Cape Sicie, by a detachment of Lord Keith's squadron, on 18 June, 1799.

I approve very much of your directing guns to be landed from the Alexander. I would have every exertion used, and every nerve strained, to finish this tedious blockade.

They have more troops in Minorca than they know what to do with. I wished Sir James St. Clair Erskine to let me have 1,200 for either the Roman State or for Malta; but I have not been able to succeed at this moment—under pretence that General Fox is hourly expected, and it would not be proper to lessen the garrison under these circumstances; and then Sir James enters upon the difficulty of the undertaking in a true soldier way. *Com. Troubridge, 16 Sept.*

I was sorry to find [by your letter of 5 September] that, under your present circumstances, it was not in your power to make such a detachment as I so earnestly requested, and which I am convinced would have so much assisted the King of Naples in restoring peace and quietness to his kingdoms, by first driving the French out of the Roman State. Whenever you can with propriety send these troops, it will be my business to take care they be properly conveyed; and nothing you will believe will be wanting on my part to afford them every support, either in the attack of Civitâ Vecchia, in landing them in the city of Naples, or in sending them to finish this very tedious business of Malta. Certainly some small articles necessary for a siege would be desirable to be brought. If on the continent, particularly entrenching tools; gunpowder, &c., we can get from Gaeta. If Malta may be judged more eligible, mortars and shells are the principal things wanted. Guns can be landed from our ships, but shot of 32 pounds and downwards may be wanted. I know if we could get an outwork, Vaubois would be forced to give up. *Sir J. St. C. Erskine, 17 Sept.*

I am sure you will make every arrangement in your power should Sir James Erskine wish to embark any troops. I am ignorant of what transports are at Mahon, but the Princess Charlotte, if a hundred men from four different ships could be lent to her, would carry a great number of troops. . . . Totally ignorant as I am of the frigates and sloops left me by Lord Keith, I cannot fix what shall be in my power to give to Minorca. But take care of it I will, but not a ship more than is necessary. The object is to prevent troops passing from the Continent to the Island. *Capt. Darby, 18 Sept.*

I have received your letter of 20 August[1] conveying their Lordships' disapprobation of my conduct in having sent a part of the crews of the squadron against Capua, and their direction not *E. Nepean, 20 Sept.*

[1] See *ante*, p. 206.

to employ them in like manner in future. And I also observe, and with great pain, that their Lordships see no cause which could justify my disobeying the orders of my commanding officer, Lord Keith, or for leaving Minorca exposed to the risk of being attacked.

I have to request that you will have the goodness to assure their Lordships that I knew when I decided on those important points, that perhaps my life, certainly my commission, was at stake by my decision; but, being firmly of opinion that the honour of my king and country, the dearest object of my heart [was involved], and that to have deserted the cause and person of his Majesty's faithful ally, his Sicilian Majesty, would have been unworthy my name and their Lordships' former opinion of me, I determined at all risks to support the honour of my gracious sovereign and country, and not to shelter myself under the letter of the law, which I shall never do when put in competition with the public service.

I only wish to appeal to his Sicilian Majesty, Sir John Acton, and his Excellency Sir William Hamilton, whether they are not clearly of opinion, that if I had drawn any part of the force landed from the squadron from the shore, that Capua and Gaeta would at this moment have been in the hands of the French: and who can say what evil consequences might not have ensued from it?

A. Davison, 23 Sept.

In my state, of what consequence is all the wealth of this world? I took for granted the East India Company would pay their noble gift to Lady Nelson, and whether she lays it out in house or land is, I assure you, a matter of perfect indifference. I have given away 2,000*l.* of it to my family, in expectation it had been paid. Ah, my dear friend, if I have a morsel of bread and cheese in comfort, it is all I ask of kind Heaven, until I reach the estate of six feet by two, which I am fast approaching. I had the full tide of honour, but little real comfort. If the war goes on, I shall be knocked off by a ball, or killed with chagrin. My conduct is measured by the Admiralty, by the narrow rule of law, when I think it should have been done by that of common sense. I restored a faithful ally by breach of orders; Lord Keith lost a fleet by obedience, against his own sense. Yet as one is censured the other must be approved. Such things are.

Lord Spencer, 25 Sept.

I have certain information from Toulon, of 15 September, that five vessels are loading salt provisions for Malta; also that the two old Venetian ships were loading stores for the above destination. One frigate and two corvettes are also ready for sea. A ship of the line which I suppose to be the Généreux, is heaving down, and another old ship is repairing. I shall keep an eye to that quarter

—not by blocking Toulon; for, the first NW wind, they would get out in spite of us. I shall place ships in the track from Toulon to Ajaccio, for on that coast I think they will go, and also off the Island of Lampedusa, stretching to Cape Bon, in Africa. I may be wrong, but I feel confident I am right; for if I cannot get troops, starving is our only hopes. . . . I know I am a bad hand at describing my operations; I only beg your indulgence, that my works may speak for themselves.

I have desired Commodore Troubridge to send you, for the information of their Lordships, extracts of all his letters to me, with the terms entered into with the French for the evacuation of the city of Rome and Cività Vecchia, on which event I sincerely congratulate their Lordships. E. Nepean, 1 Oct.

I send you General Naselli, your old Leghorn friend, who is going governor to Rome. The court has nobody better—you may think they can have nobody worse. The Portuguese squadron, by letter received this day, are ordered to Lisbon. I am more than ever anxious for your arrival, that, at least, we may lay wait for the ships from Toulon. I have wrote again and again to Mahon for troops, but without effect. I have this day given my opinion in writing, that his Sicilian Majesty should desire the garrison of Messina to go to Malta, and also to Admiral Ouschakoff to be wrote to, for ships and troops from Naples. Nothing shall be wanting on my part, but I am almost mad with the manner of going on here. Com. Troubridge, 2 Oct.

As the reduction of the Island of Malta is of the greatest consequence to the interests of the Allied Powers at war with France, and the withdrawing the squadron of his Most Faithful Majesty under your command, at this time, from the blockade of that island, will be of the most ruinous consequences to their interests, particularly when an enemy's fleet of thirteen sail of the line are daily expected in those seas, and two sail of the line and several other ships with provisions and stores, for the relief of Malta, are now lading at Toulon; you are hereby required and directed, in consideration of the above circumstances, and notwithstanding the orders you may have received from your court to return to Lisbon, not on any consideration whatsoever to withdraw one man from that island, which may have been landed from the squadron from under your Excellency's command, or detach one ship down the Mediterranean, until further orders from me for that purpose. Marquis de Niza, 3 Oct.

And this order was accompanied by a private letter to the same effect.

5 Oct.

Having this day received information that the French ships from Toulon are at sea, with transports, bound to Malta, I am anxious in the extreme to know the result of their approach. I pray God it may have been glorious to you, by the destruction of all the scoundrels; therefore I beg your Excellency will send me the account by the Salamine, who is ordered to join me at Mahon.

Sir J. St. C. Erskine, 11 Oct. At sea.

I have with great difficulty induced his Sicilian Majesty to permit Sir John Acton to write to Colonel Graham, that he might take 500 men from the citadel of Messina, for the important service of Malta; and Sir John has wrote in the same strong manner to the Russian admiral at Naples, for 700 troops. I have 500 English and Portuguese marines on shore on the island; and if I am so happy as for you and General Fox to agree to the sending 1,000 or 1,200 men, I am sure we shall have it; and without their assistance I fear we shall miscarry in spite of all our exertions.

Duke of Clarence, 17 Oct. Port Mahon.

Having on 1 October received the terms on which the French were to evacuate the city of Rome and Cività Vecchia on the 2nd, the Phaëton arrived bringing me an account, that, on 8 and 9 September, thirteen large ships, supposed to be of the line, had been seen off Cape Ortegal. On this information, in case they should be bound into the Mediterranean, I directed the Culloden and Minotaur, with some small vessels that were off Cività Vecchia, to proceed immediately, and join me off Mahon harbour; the Foudroyant arriving the same day, I sailed from Palermo on the morning of the 5th. I had hardly got clear of the gulf when I met the Salamine with information from Mahon, that on 28 September, a vessel from Tunis to Minorca had fallen in with two strange sail of the line, frigates and other vessels, to the amount of twenty, steering towards Malta. As I have seven sail of the line, one frigate, and three sloops on the service there, I had to send the brig to ascertain the event. This news which I still hope is false, did not tend to make me easy, as in truth I required, being very unwell; however, the more difficulty, the more exertion is called for.

On the 12th, I got off Mahon, and, having given all necessary directions for the ships on that station, I made sail for Gibraltar. In the evening, between this island and Majorca, I fell in with the Bulldog, having on board Sir Edward Berry, who brought me letters from Rear-Admiral Duckworth, discrediting the account of the enemy's ships being off the coast of Portugal; with this knowledge I instantly returned to Mahon, where so much has required doing, that, except to pay my visit to the General, and to the naval yard, I have not been out of the ship. General Fox being hourly expected, it has not been in my power to arrange a plan of operations for the immediate reduction of Malta, should it not be effectually relieved by these ships; which is an object of very great importance to us and his Majesty's allies: but as neither the brig nor any vessel is arrived, I am in total darkness; nor are the ships from Cività Vecchia come in. However, I sail to-morrow for Palermo, to see what is going on, and prepare all the force I can spare for Malta.

Lord Nelson sailed from Mahon in the Foudroyant on the 18th, and arrived at Palermo on 22 October.

I earnestly desire that your Excellency will not think of quitting Malta till I have a proper force to relieve you. We shall soon have an army against it, and I am yet in hopes that you will be there, with the ships of her Most Faithful Majesty, when it surrenders. You was the first at the blockade, and I hope will be at its surrender. *Marquis de Niza, 24 Oct. Palermo.*

The details you have given me, although unsuccessful at Aboukir, will, by all military men, ever reflect upon you and your brave companions the highest honour; and I beg you will tell all those whose conduct you have so highly approved, that their merits (even of the lowest) will be duly appreciated by us, and for which reason I have given all the promotion, and shall continue to do it, if they deserve it, amongst them. All the arrangements for your young men are filled up as you desired, and, you shall ever find, that although I am jealous of having a particle of my honour abridged, yet that no commanding officer will be so ready to do everything you can wish. We have but little here of stores; but I have stripped the Foudroyant of everything. At Mahon there is nothing; but your demands, with a bare proportion for the Theseus, go to-morrow for Gibraltar; and although I am pretty sure you will not receive half what your ships want, I shall urge Inglefield to send you everything he can. *Sir W. S. Smith, 24 Oct.*

You will have heard, probably, that Lord St. Vincent still retains the Mediterranean command, and that I am, by order, acting till his return—therefore, I have not the power of giving commissions, or anything more than acting orders. As to getting Neapolitan gunboats to you, there are many reasons against it. In the first, they have none for such a voyage: this is enough;

but, was not this sufficient, it would be a thing impossible. I believe we are as bad a set to deal with, for real service, as your Turks.

I have just got a report that appears to have some foundation, that Bonaparte has passed Corsica in a bombard, steering for France. No crusader ever returned with more humility—contrast his going in L'Orient.

Chev. Italinsky, 24 Oct.

Malta is in my thoughts, sleeping and waking. I have talked fully to Sir John Acton on the subject, and his Excellency will write to you fully upon it. . . . Could I order British troops from Minorca, they should have been at Malta, ready to co-operate most cordially with the Russian troops; but, alas, they are under the orders of General Fox, who is not yet arrived from England. General Sir James St. Clair Erskine, the present commanding officer, has prepared 1,500 excellent troops, besides the garrison of Messina, with stores of every description, should General Fox approve of the plan we have made; but they will not move without knowing when, and how many Russian troops will be there to co-operate with them. No time should be lost. The Portuguese squadron is ordered home, and I have no ships to relieve them at present. I wish I could be with you and the admiral for a few minutes to fix all matters. Believe me, there is not a thing that the admiral could propose, that I would not meet him half-way. The honour and glory of the Emperor Paul is as dear to me, both from my duty and inclination, as that of my own sovereign; and I am sure that we shall disoblige our royal masters, if we do not as cordially unite together for the destruction of the French villains, as they are happily doing in the North Seas, both at sea and on shore. I beg the admiral will consider this letter as jointly wrote to him and you, as it is more pleasant to me for your upright and honourable heart to interpret for me than a stranger.

Sir J. St. C. Erskine, 26 Oct.

I am in desperation about Malta. We shall lose it, I am afraid past redemption. . . . If Ball can hardly keep the inhabitants in hope of relief by the 500 men landed from our ships, what must be expected when 400 of them, and four sail of the line, will be withdrawn? and if the islanders are forced again to join the French, we may not find even landing a very easy task, much less to get again our present advantageous position. I therefore entreat for the honour of our king, and for the advantage of the common cause, that, whether General Fox is arrived or not, at least the garrison of Messina may be ordered to hold post in Malta until a sufficient force can be collected to attack it, which I flatter myself will in time be got together; but while that is effecting, I fear our being obliged to quit the island; therefore, I am forced to make this representation. I know well enough of what officers in your situation can do; the delicacy of your feelings on the near approach of General Fox I can readily conceive; but the time you know nothing about; this is a great and important moment, and the only thing to be considered, Is his Majesty's service to stand still for an instant? . . . If we lose this opportunity it will be impossible to recall it. If possible, I wish to take all the responsibility.

I know, my dear Sir James, your zeal and ability, and that delicacy to General Fox has been your sole motive for not altering the disposition of the troops; but I hope General Fox is with you, and I am sure, from his character, he will approve of my feelings on the subject. If he is not, I must again earnestly entreat that, at least, you will give directions for Colonel Graham to hold Malta till we can get troops to attack La Valetta. May God direct your counsels for the honour of our king and his allies, and to the destruction of the French.

Erskine could not, however, be induced to see the matter in this light; and writing to Lord Nelson on 31 October, said: 'The probability of General Fox being able to form and detach such a corps as may be adequate to undertake the siege of Malta, becomes now much more doubtful: a few days, however, must clear up all these points. I find that the Marquis de Niza, Captain Ball, and General Acton, have all written, to try to induce General Graham to embark with a part of his corps for Malta: in answer to which he has acted in strict obedience to his instructions, and in my opinion with the most perfect propriety; for no officer would have been justified, even if left to his discretion, in forming a project for besieging 5,000 men, and proceeding on active operations, with a corps of 500 men only. I mention this, because I collect from Graham's letter that the last application was pressed, even after his answer that he could not take any step without orders from Minorca.'

I received your letters relative to your going down the Mediterranean. By every tie of honour to your court, the ally of my gracious Sovereign, do not quit the blockade of Malta, or withdraw a man from the island, until I can get troops and ships to relieve them, for which purpose I have sent an express both to Naples and Minorca, pressing for orders for the garrison of Messina to go directly to Malta. If you quit your most important station till I can get these things, depend upon it, your illustrious Prince will disapprove of (in this instance) your punctilious execution of orders. Ever believe me your obliged and affectionate friend,

BRONTE NELSON.

Marquis de Niza, 27 Oct.

Emperor of Russia, 31 Oct.

Sire,—As Grand Master of the Order of Malta, I presume to detail to your Majesty what has been done to prevent the French from re-possessing themselves of the island, blockading them closely in La Valetta, and what means are now pursuing to force them to surrender.

On 2 September, 1798, the inhabitants of Malta rose against the French robbers, who, having taken all the money in the island, levied contributions; and Vaubois, as a last act of villainy, said, as baptism was of no use, he had sent for all the church plate. On the 9th, I received a letter from the deputies of the island, praying assistance to drive the French from La Valetta. I immediately directed the Marquis de Niza, with four sail of the line, to support the islanders. At this time, the crippled ships from Egypt were passing near it, and 2,000 stand of arms, complete, with all the musket-ball cartridges, were landed from them, and 200 barrels of powder. On 24 October, I relieved the marquis from the station, and took the island of Gozo—a measure absolutely necessary, in order to form the complete blockade of La Valetta, the garrison of which, at this time, was composed of 7,000 French, including the seamen, and some few Maltese; the inhabitants in the town, about 30,000; the Maltese in arms, volunteers, never exceeded 3,000. I entrusted the blockade to Captain Alexander John Ball, of the Alexander, 74, an officer not only of the greatest merit, but of the most conciliating manners. From that period to this time, it has fell to my lot to arrange for the feeding of 60,000 people, the population of Malta and Gozo, the arming the peasantry, and, the most difficult task, that of keeping up harmony between the deputies of the island. Hunger, fatigue, and corruption appeared several times in the island, and amongst the deputies. The situation of Italy, in particular this kingdom, oftentimes reduced me to the greatest difficulties where to find food. Their Sicilian Majesties, at different times, have given more, I believe, than 40,000*l.* in money and corn. The blockade has, in the expense of keeping the ships destined alone for this service, [cost] full 180,000*l.* sterling. It has pleased God hitherto to bless our endeavours to prevent supplies getting to the French except one frigate and two small vessels, with a small portion of salt provisions.

Your Majesty will have the goodness to observe, that, until it was known that you were elected Grand Master, and that the Order was to be restored in Malta, I never allowed an idea to go abroad that Great Britain had any wish to keep it. I therefore directed his Sicilian Majesty's flag to be hoisted, as, I am told, had the Order not been restored, that he is the legitimate sovereign of the island. Never less than 500 men have been landed from the squadron, which, although, with the volunteers, not sufficient to commence a siege, have yet kept posts and battery not more than 400 yards from the works. The quarrels of the nobles, and misconduct of the chiefs, rendered it absolutely necessary that some proper person should be placed at the head of the island. His Sicilian Majesty, therefore, by the united request of the whole island, named Captain Ball for their chief director, and he will hold it till your Majesty, as Grand Master, appoints a person to the office. Now the French are nearly expelled from Italy by the valour and skill of your generals and army, all my thoughts are turned towards the placing the Grand Master and the Order of Malta in security in La Valetta, for which purpose, I have just been at Minorca, and arranged with the English general a force of 2,500 British troops, cannon, bombs, &c. &c., for the siege. I have wrote to your Majesty's admiral, and his Sicilian Majesty joins cordially in the good work of endeavouring to drive the French from Malta.

I deferred writing in expectation of receiving the plan of the arms you sent to Lord Grenville, but which has never reached me. I should be much obliged to you for them, but now I suppose the ducal arms of Bronte must have a place. If his Majesty approves of my taking the title of Bronte, I must have your opinion how I am to sign my name. At present I describe myself 'Lord Nelson, Duke of Bronte in Sicily.' As the pelisses given to me and Sir Sidney Smith are novel, I must beg you will turn in your mind how I am to wear it when I first go to the king; and, as the aigrette is directed to be worn, where am I to put it? In my hat, having only one arm, is impossible, as I must have my hand at liberty; therefore, I think, on my outward garment. Sir I. Heard, Garter King of Arms, 1 Nov.

I have just received the Imperial Order of the Crescent from the Grand Signior, a diamond star; in the centre, the crescent and a small star.

[My hope of obtaining troops from Minorca is much diminished by a letter from General Sir James Erskine writing me word] that the 28th Regiment was ordered for England, and that he expected General Fox every moment, and that [till] he was here, the General would not on any consideration break his orders for any object.

Much as I approve of strict obedience to orders—even to a Lord Spencer, 6 Nov.

court-martial to inquire whether the object justified the measure —yet to say that an officer is never, for any object, to alter his orders, is what I cannot comprehend. The circumstances of this war so often vary, that an officer has almost every moment to consider—What would my superiors direct, did they know what is passing under my nose? The great object of the war is—Down, down with the French! To accomplish this, every nerve, and by both services, ought to be strained.

The services of Captain Ball will not, I am confident, be forgot by you, but I feel sensible that my pen is far unequal to do justice to the merit of my friends; for could I have described the wonderful merit of Sir Thomas Troubridge and his gallant party in the kingdom of Naples—how he placed his battery, as he would his ship, close alongside the enemy—how the French commander said, 'This man fancies he is on board ship—this is not the mode a general would adopt;' in what a few days this band went to the siege of Capua, where, whatever was done, was done by the English and Portuguese, for the Russians would fight, but not work. The Neapolitan corps were in air, and 600 Swiss were all who Troubridge could depend upon. If I had, as their chief, a looker-on, a pen to describe their extraordinary merits, they would not be diminished by the comparison of our success in Holland, or by the gallant exertions of my friend, Sidney Smith—of whose zeal, judgment, and gallantry, no man is more sensible than myself—and be equally entitled to the thanks of their country, by its representatives in Parliament.

Duke of Clarence, 9 Nov.

General Koehler does not approve of such irregular[1] proceedings as naval officers attacking and defending fortifications. We have but one idea—to get close alongside. None but a sailor would have placed a battery only a hundred and eighty yards from the Castle of St. Elmo; a soldier must have gone according to art, and the ZZ way; my brave Sir Thomas Troubridge went straight, for we have had no time to spare.

E. Nepean, 10 Nov.

Yesterday the Vincejo brig, who I had sent to look into Toulon on the 16th, joined me with an account that the two Venetian ships *armés en flûte*, two frigates and two corvettes, sailed from Toulon on the 16th, in the evening, loaded with provisions; and that the Généreux and three frigates were ready for sea. As Captain Long judged Malta their object, he made sail for that island and

[1] See *ante*, p. 60.

gave the Marquis de Niza that information. As I have placed for the moment nine sail of the line, one frigate, and three corvettes in the track to that island, I hope they cannot relieve it: for if they do, we shall all have to begin again, and I believe worse, for we shall be drove off the island; but it has been no fault of the navy that it has not been attacked by land, but we had neither the means ourselves, or the influence with others who had the power.

I have received by post your answer to my letter from the Bay of Naples, in which you beg me to accept your acknowledgments for the trouble I had taken in investigating the report made by Mr. Lock, on the subject of the purchase of fresh beef. I must own, that I conceived your letter couched in terms of such coldness, as a little surprised me; but it was not till this moment of the departure of Captain Hardy, that I have heard a report, circulated by Mr. Lock, that you had received a letter from him on this subject, and that you had thanked him for having saved Government 40 per cent. If it is true, which I cannot believe, that you had wrote Mr. Lock any letters on this subject, I desire to say, and not to be misunderstood, that the conduct of the Board is very reprehensible, and scandalous in its treatment to me, the commanding officer of his Majesty's fleet in the Mediterranean. I hope you will send these expressions to our superiors, the Board of Admiralty; for if it is true, which I cannot believe, it would make it more scandalous not to have sent me copies of these letters. I will never, for any power on earth, retract a syllable of what I have wrote in this letter. I defy any insinuations against my honour. Nelson is as far from doing a scandalous or mean action as the heavens are above the earth. I will now tell you the result of the inquiry of an honest man, a faithful servant of his king and country, was (from the papers I sent to your Board), that the accusation of Mr. Lock was malicious and scandalous; and if any board or individual apply any softer terms to the papers sent you by me, I desire to apply the same terms to them.

I have ever treated all boards, and every individual with the greatest respect and consideration; but when my honour, or that of my brave friends is concerned, I will never stop till the examination is made; for Mr. Lock would not, or could not (which I believe), but both are equally criminal, bring forward any single point of accusation. I therefore demand that you will direct (subject to my inspection) a strict and impartial inquiry to be made into this saving of 40 per cent. I have only to observe, that Mr. Lock

Commissioners of the Victualling Board, 14 Nov.

never made any complaint of the price, until I wrote a note to say that I should not interfere in the purchase—that he that sold the best and cheapest, would, of course, be the seller.[1] I have desired Captain Hardy to call on your Board on this subject, as he was captain of the Foudroyant at this time, and knows perfectly my opinion of Mr. Lock.

In replying to this letter, on 20 December, the Commissioner of the Victualling Board said, 'After declaring to your Lordship that we never had any correspondence with Mr. Lock on the subject to which it relates, we submit to your Lordship's own reflection the manner in which you have thought proper to arraign the conduct of this Board merely upon a rumour, the authenticity of which you twice profess yourself to disbelieve.'
It was nevertheless true, and the commissioner's denial of the correspondence was as gross an equivocation as any member of even a public board ever perpetrated. Their message to Mr. Lock had been transmitted verbally through his father and sister; the former of whom wrote to him that Mr. Marsh, one of the commissioners of the Victualling Board, had said that the Board 'felt very much obliged to Mr. Lock's interference, being persuaded that it has occasioned the fleet's being victualled forty per cent. lower than it would otherwise have been;' and his sister wrote on 8 September, that Sir William Bellingham (the Chairman of the Board), who had dined with them on the preceding day, had repeated the same statement, and said that 'they are greatly obliged to you, and feel themselves so,' with more to the same purport.

General Graham[1]
25 Nov.

Commodore Sir Thomas Troubridge is the officer destined by me to co-operate with you for the reduction of Malta. One more able and active could not be selected from our service; and as the commodore is in full possession of my sentiments on every point, there can no doubt arise on any subject, which he cannot immediately clear up. Ball has been, by his Sicilian Majesty, the legitimate sovereign of the island, placed at the head of the Maltese, in both a civil, and, as I understand, military capacity. His conciliating manners will overcome all difficulty with the inhabitants. They adore him; therefore, I think, in any capitulation, he should sign. I will not state the necessity of a most cordial co-operation with the Russian general. It is the desire of our government to gratify the Emperor in every wish about the order of Malta.

The orders to Sir Thomas Troubridge to proceed on this service are dated the same day.

W. Wyndham,
26 Nov.

Yesterday, an order came from General Fox for the garrison of

[1] See *ante*, p. 208.

Messina to proceed to Malta, and as the Russians are destined for the same object, I hope we shall very soon be in possession of it.

The situation of our affairs with the Barbary States calls for serious attention; for, from the circumstances of the war, it has been impossible to make them fear us as they ought, particularly Algiers; and that state is now getting to such a pitch of insolence that cannot much longer go unchastised. But I well know in England how an officer would be reprobated, was he to permit this, and in the contest, which could not be long, any English vessels be taken. These states have taken many Maltese vessels and Neapolitans, having a pass, as they call it, from me. As no vessel, either at Malta or Naples, on our first going there, would go to sea, without a paper signed by me, his Sicilian Majesty desired me many times under his own hand, to sign the passport, which was a recommendation to the allies of Great Britain to the vessel described, she being employed to carry provisions for the use of those fighting the common enemy. I never signed one of those papers that I did not declare that it could be of no use for protection, and that I thought it was consigning seamen, poor creatures, to slavery. The answer always was, we are not worse for your signing, may be better, and our seamen will not go to sea without it. Many of these passes were respected by Tripoli and Tunis; but the Algerine cruisers paid not the smallest attention, and several vessels loaded with salt, for the supply of the capital, have been taken, and their crews, sixty-five in number, are now in slavery.

Lord Spencer, 29 Nov.

As the greatest number of their papers were signed on board the Foudroyant at Naples, by desire of General Acton, and the government of the city, at whose head was Cardinal Ruffo, it was not known under what circumstances the papers were signed—therefore, Prince Luzzi, Secretary of State, addressed a despatch to Sir William Hamilton, a copy of which, and his excellency's answer, I send you. I also send some papers, sent me by Major Magra, also an account of an Algerine firing, in the Bay of Tunis, at an English vessel. I do not say, or think, that the papers signed by me, ought, by the laws of nations, to protect traders, but under all circumstances the Barbary States ought to be made sensible of the attention which is due to the signature of an English admiral, and that, at least, the poor people ought to be liberated.

The Dey of Algiers has been several times very impertinent about giving supplies for Minorca, and is getting from one insolence to another, which, if not checked by vigorous measures, will end in

Q

a quarrel. My idea is for me to go to him, and settle the business, and if I find that he will be insolent, to show him in the moment that he cannot go robbing in the Mediterranean without the consent of Britain. I think the greatest part of his cruisers would be seized in a month, and then bring him to reason. Terror is the only weapon to wield against these people. To talk kindly to them is only to encourage them. Demand nothing that is not just, and never recede, and settle the whole in half an hour. I should say to him that 'I expected that, being embarked in the same cause, you would not have taken vessels only carrying provisions for people fighting against the French, but you had not humanity enough to do this. However, I insist that you shall not keep the poor people in slavery. It was by my having too good an opinion of you that they fell into your hands. With respect to the presuming to fire at any vessel in a neutral port bearing the English flag, the most ample satisfaction must be made.' I hope we shall soon be rid of Malta, and then our ships for a little time cannot be so well employed. If this letter ought to be addressed to the board, I beg of you to lay it before them; but I consider it, and its inclosure, as a letter for the Cabinet Minister.

Commissioners for Victualling, 5 Dec.

Letters which had passed between Mr. Lock and myself, brought forward yesterday, in the presence of Sir William Hamilton, a meeting between us; and as it turns out that false friends in this country, and nonsensical ones in England, have been the cause of Mr. Lock's highly improper conduct, and as any inquiry can only end in the ruin of Mr. Lock's character, I consent not to desire the inquiry demanded in my letter of 14 November, by Captain Hardy. It was justice to the public and a vindication of my own honour, that I sought, and not ruin to a young man setting off in life with a family of children. This lesson will, I trust, and believe, be of more use to Mr. Lock than the approbation of ignorant people. I do not mean to withdraw a syllable of my last letter to the board, for they will see that I did not believe them capable of such conduct; only to that part which gives up the demand for inquiry. If there are those residing in Somerset Place who merit the full force of some of my words, let them have it. One of my greatest boasts is, that no man can ever say I have told a lie.

Sir W. S. Smith, 8 Dec.

All our Mediterranean operations are pretty nearly at a standstill; for the enemy have no fleet at this moment to make us keep a good look-out, although I should not be surprised if the whole combined fleet should again pay us a visit this winter. They were perfectly ready for sea the latter end of October, forty-eight sail of the line. Admiral Duckworth, with all the ships, frigates, &c., is ordered by the Admiralty from Gibraltar, to go off Ferrol; and I think from thence will be called to the Channel; therefore, at this moment I have only two sail of the line, and not more than two frigates, in a condition to go to sea. Our Government naturally look to the Russians for aid here, but they will find their mistake: the Russian ships are not able to keep the sea. I am now trying to bring our long blockade of Malta to a close; the garrison of Messina has been permitted to embark for that service, and 2,500 Russians are, I hope, at this moment at Malta. The French ships destined for the relief of Malta went to Villafranca, and landed their provisions and stores for the army, which has since been defeated by General Melas.

The Austrians are calling out for a naval co-operation on the coast of Genoa. They complain that the Russian ships never come near them. Our Government think, naturally, that eleven sail of the line, frigates, &c. should do something: I find they do nothing. *Gen. Fox, 14 Dec.*

I cannot allow you to pass from under my command without assuring you of my sincere and cordial thanks for your constant and ready obedience to every order and wish I have directed to your Lordship for the public service. . . . I have, in particular, to express to your Lordship my approbation of your judgment in continuing to obey my orders for the public service in remaining at Malta till I could get ships to relieve you, instead of an immediate obedience to your orders from the Court of Portugal, which, had you obeyed, the French would, most probably, [have] been in possession of the whole island, and the allies might not have been able to even effect a landing. Your orders, which it would be no longer proper to disobey, force me with regret to part from you. *Marquis de Niza, 18 Dec.*

Lord Elgin presses me, if it can be done, to send a larger squadron into the Levant seas. But your Lordship knows that is not possible, [nor], indeed, except to gratify the Turks is there any service for a large squadron, Malta having kept everything not wanted for other particular services. If I could have [had] any cruisers, as was my plan, off Cape Bon in Africa, and between Corsica and Toulon, Mr. Bonaparte could not probably have got to France; but if it bring on a confusion at Paris, I hope it will be for the best. *Lord Spencer, 18 Dec.*

Not knowing whether Rear-Admiral Duckworth hath left any ship to cruise between Cape Spartel and Cape St. Vincent, I have *E. Nepean, 18 Dec.*

put the Penelope¹ under Captain Morris's² orders, and directed him to cruise in such a position between those capes as he may think most eligible for annoying the enemy, as well as to keep a good look-out for the approach of the combined fleets, whom I have reason to suppose, from the information I have received, are destined for the Mediterranean; and, in case of their approach, to run for Minorca and Malta, to put them on their guard.

Lord Elgin, 21 Dec.

I have regretted sincerely the escape of Bonaparte; but those ships which were destined by me for the two places where he would certainly have been intercepted, were, from the Admiralty thinking, doubtless, that the Russians would do something at sea, obliged to be at Malta, and other services which I thought the Russian admiral would have assisted me in—therefore, no blame lays at my door. The Vincejo, a few days ago, took a vessel from Egypt with General Voix and seventy-five officers, mostly of Bonaparte's staff; and also Captain Long was happy enough to save the despatches, which were thrown overboard, but with an insufficient weight to instantly sink them. I send you copies of all those which you have not got. . . . I own my hope yet is, that the Sublime Porte will never permit a single Frenchman to quit Egypt; and I own myself wicked enough to wish them all to die in that country they chose to invade. We have scoundrels of French enough in Europe without them.

J. S. Smith, 22 Dec.

I have read with pleasure all that has passed in Egypt between Bonaparte, Kleber, and the Grand Vizir; and I send Lord Elgin some very important papers, which will show their very deplorable situation. But I cannot bring myself to believe they would entirely quit Egypt; and, if they would, I never would consent to one of them returning to the continent of Europe during the war. I wish them to perish in Egypt, and give a great lesson to the world of the justice of the Almighty. . . . Admiral Ouschakoff cannot be got to move; and by his carelessness, the fall of Malta is not only retarded, but the island may be lost. The ships in the harbour are ready for sea, and will try to escape. Four days ago three shells fell into the Guillaume Tell, and her poop is blown up.

E. Nepean, 23 Dec.

The Culloden, on going into the Bay of Marsa Scirocco, in the island of Malta, to land the cannon, ammunition, &c., taken on board that ship at Messina for the siege, struck on a rock, and Commodore Sir Thomas Troubridge has informed me that the rudder and greatest part of the false keel are carried away, and the

---

¹ Captain Blackwood. ² Of the Phaeton.

rudder would have been lost but for the timely exertion in getting a hawser secured through it; the pintles are all broke, and the ship was steered to the anchorage with her sails, where she is now in safety, but very leaky. If I can get her, the Alexander, and Lion, to England a few months hence, it is all that I can expect from them, as they are not fit to keep the sea.

You will see with some sorrow the accident which has befell the Culloden, and now it only remains for you to decide whether the services of Troubridge are to be lost in the Mediterranean: he must evidently have another ship, or be an established commodore. . . . I wish to have a squadron of two or three vessels off Cape Bon, in Africa, and another to assist the Austrians in the Riviera of Genoa; but I absolutely want more than I have for the blockade of Malta. The ships are ready to sail, and will probably try to escape as a last effort. The Russians, even if at sea, of which I see no prospect, cannot sail, or be of the least service. I have wrote very plainly to the Russian minister, that in my opinion the Emperor will not be well pleased with Admiral Ouschakoff. Culloden, Alexander, and Lion, cannot go to sea, and all I hope for is to get them to England a few months hence. *(Lord Spencer, 23 Dec.)*

[Five vessels laden with corn or flour for Malta are actually on their way.] General Acton assures me that there is a great scarcity of corn in this island, and that the granaries at Girgenti are not full of corn, and I must believe the want, when so large a bounty is given for the importation. . . . A general order for supplying our troops and ships will be repeated, but not for the supply of Malta, for General Acton declares they have it not to give; but that everything shall be done to give us content. *(Sir T. Troubridge, 29 Dec.)*

I send you orders for the different governors. You will see they are for the supply of the army and navy—therefore, whatever Graham and you send for, will, if possible, be granted. *(2 Jan. 1800.)*

Sir William is just come from General Acton, and has the promise that the corn bought by the Senate of Palermo at Girgenti shall go to Malta, and the corn here be landed for Palermo; and that an express shall be sent this day to Girgenti. I cannot do more than get these orders. . . . You had better send a vessel to Girgenti; and as it is very possible, after all, that no orders sent may be obeyed, I wish you would, if that should be the case, direct an express to be sent to me. *(7 Jan.)*

Whilst the Neapolitans were promising, the Maltese were dying. The following are some extracts from Sir Thomas Troubridge's letters to Lord Nelson:

1 *Jan.*—' We are dying off fast for want. I learn, by letters from Messina, that Sir William Hamilton says, Prince Luzzi refused corn some time ago, and Sir William does not think it worth while making another application. If that be the case, I wish he commanded at this distressing scene instead of me. Puglia had an immense harvest, near thirty sail left Messina before I did, to load corn ;—will they let us have any ? If not, a short time will decide the business. The German interest prevails. I wish I was at your Lordship's elbow for an hour—*all, all* will be thrown on you, rely on it.

5 *Jan.*—' I have this day saved 30,000 people from dying; but with this day my ability ceases. As the King of Naples, or rather the Queen and her party, are bent on starving us, I see no alternative, but to leave these poor unhappy people to starve, without our being witnesses to their distress. I curse the day I ever served the King of Naples. . . . If the Neapolitan government will not supply corn, I pray your Lordship to recall us. We are of no use. The Maltese soldiers must call on the French in Valetta, who have the ability to relieve them. The consequence will be, General Graham and his troops will be cut up to a man, if I do not withdraw them. I hourly expect him to apply to me for that purpose. All we brought, I shall leave—I mean the guns, &c. belonging to his Sicilian Majesty. I never expected to be treated in this manner by General Acton, who certainly influences the king's council : he complains he cannot get his orders put in force : how can he expect it, when he never punishes any of the traitors ? On the contrary, is he not daily promoting the traitors we exposed to him ? We have characters, my Lord, to lose ; these people have none. Do not suffer their infamous conduct to fall on us. Our country is just, but severe. I foresee we shall forfeit the little we have gained. Before supplies can possibly come, many thousands must perish, even if these supplies arrive in two days. The situation is worse than ever ; there are not even locusts. Such is the fever of my brain this minute, that I assure you, on my honour, if the Palermo traitors were here, I would shoot them first, and then myself. Girgenti, I beg to inform you, is full of corn—the money is ready to pay for it—we do not ask it as a gift.'

On 6 January Nelson received Lord Keith's order, dated off Vigo, 30 November, announcing his commission as commander-in-chief in the Mediterranean.

Lord Keith, 7 Jan.

To get to Malta—which has kept for sixteen months every ship I could lay my hands on fully employed, and has, in truth, almost broke my spirits for ever—I have been begging of his Sicilian Majesty small supplies of money and corn to keep the Maltese in arms, and barely to keep from starving the poor inhabitants. Sicily has this year a very bad crop, and the exportation of corn is prohibited. Both Graham and Troubridge are in desperation at the prospect of a famine. Vessels are here loading with corn for Malta ; but I can neither get the Neapolitan men-of-war or merchant-vessels to move. You will see by the report of the disposition of the ships, what a wretched state we are in. In truth, only the Foudroyant and Northumberland are fit to keep the sea. The Russians are on the 4th arrived at Messina; six sail of the line, frigates, &c., with two thousand five hundred troops. It is not to be expected that any one Russian man-of-war can or will keep the sea: therefore, the blockade by sea can only be kept up by our ships; and it is my intention, if the Foudroyant, or even a frigate, comes soon, to go for two days to Malta, to give the Russian admiral and general, Graham, Troubridge, and Governor Ball, a meeting—not only on the most probable means of getting the French out, but also of arranging various matters, if it should fall to our exertions. The Maltese have, Graham says, two thousand excellent troops; we have, soldiers and sailors, fifteen hundred; the Russians will land full three thousand. I hope the Ricasoli may be carried; and if it is, I think the French general will no longer hold out. What a relief this would be to us.

This moment has brought me your and Ball's letters of the 4th and 5th. I have sent to General Acton for an order for an immediate supply, and I hope to send it by the express. The frigate was to sail last night alone for Girgenti for some vessels loaded with corn, and to carry them to Malta; but she is not yet out of the mole. Nothing has been neglected on my part to get supplies for Malta, and by the greatest exertions, for this country is in absolute want. Mr. Noble, two days ago, went to Termini, twenty-four miles from Palermo, the greatest corn country in this Island. The granaries here are really empty, and what was in them of a very bad quality. The kingdom of Naples is full of corn, but, as we know, the Neapolitan seamen will not go to sea in the winter. . . . I send you Acton's letter to Sir William. If such lies can be told under my nose, what must be expected at a distance ? . . . You must in the last extremity seize vessels loaded with corn: the inhabitants cannot starve. If, unfortunately, you are forced to this measure, I am confident it will be exercised with great discretion.

Sir T. Troubridge, 8 Jan.

Troubridge had in fact anticipated this permission, and had sent the Stromboli, Captain Broughton, to Girgenti, where she had seized two vessels laden with corn. Of this summary proceeding, formal complaint was made through Acton and Hamilton, to which last Nelson replied:

I beg leave to express to your Excellency my real concern that even the appearance of the slightest disrespect should be offered, by any officers under my command, to the flag of his Sicilian Majesty; and I must request your Excellency to state fully to General Acton, that the act ought not to be considered as any intended disrespect to his Sicilian Majesty, but as an act of the most absolute and

Sir W. Hamilton, 10 Jan.

imperious necessity, either that the island of Malta should have been delivered up to the French, or that the king's orders should be anticipated for these vessels carrying their cargoes of corn to Malta. I trust, that the government of this country will never again force any of our royal Master's servants to so unpleasant an alternative.

<small>Sir T. Troubridge, 14 Jan.</small>

I have been this morning with General Acton, and I have spoke fully to him—plainer than I have always done is impossible. He has prepared a paper to lay before the king, respecting sending 2,600 troops from Sicily to Malta. This will, we know, be a work of some time; but if Graham thinks it will ease his soldiers, he might get 500 at a time. I told him fairly whatever troops were sent, they must only look to this [Government] for supplies, for that we should never ask what they had to eat. . . . I am sensible of the necessity you were under of getting provisions, but you will now know that no blame attaches itself to the King of Naples, or to Acton. The measure of sending into a port was strong; but at sea there could be no difficulty. I hope the urgency of the case will not happen again.

The French army in Egypt is not to be allowed to return to Europe, but to a prison in some of the States at war with France; therefore, if such an event should have happened, the French troops are to be seized and conducted to either Mahon, some of the States of the Allies, or even to England; and you will, therefore, if they should fall in your way, cause them to be seized, even if they are embarked in any Turkish, or any other nation's ships of war, or escorted by them.

<small>Sir W. S. Smith, 15 Jan.</small>

Lord Keith is anxious to know your state and condition, with an account of what is going on in Egypt. I have wrote to Lord Keith, and home, that I did not give credit that it was possible for you to give any passport for a single Frenchman, much less the army, after my positive order of 18 March, 1799.

<small>Lord Spencer, 23 Jan. Leghorn.</small>

I came here in order to meet Lord Keith, and we are going together to Palermo and Malta. If Sir James St. Clair Erskine or General Fox had felt themselves authorised to have given us two thousand troops, I think Malta by this time would have fallen, and our poor ships released from the hardest service I have ever seen. The going away of the Russians has almost done me up, but the King of Naples has ordered two thousand six hundred troops from Sicily to assist Graham, and they are to be under our command. It is true they are not good soldiers, but they will ease ours in the fatigues of duty. The feeding the inhabitants of Malta and paying two thousand of the people who bear arms, has been a continued source of uneasiness to my mind. His Sicilian Majesty has done more than it was possible to expect he had the ability of performing; for the revenues of his kingdom are hardly yet come round, and his demands are excessive from all quarters of his dominions.

My heart rejoices to hear you are so well recovered, and that there are hopes of your being employed in the home fleet, when our gentlemen will not find it so necessary, as it has been, to go into harbour to be refitted. But you will have an herculean labour to make them what you had brought the Mediterranean fleet to. Peers and Members of Parliament must attend their duty in London; but the nation will be better taken care of by their being off Brest. You taught us to keep the seamen healthy without going into port, and to stay at sea for years without a refit. We know not the meaning of the word. The Audacious, Alexander, and others, have never seen an arsenal since they have been under my command. Louis, to his great comfort, has had a treat of shifting his masts, and stayed six weeks in harbour; but he sees not a port again, if I had the command, for the next year. Our friend Troubridge is as full of resources as his Culloden is full of accidents; but I am now satisfied, that if his ship's bottom were entirely out, he would find means to make her swim. He must go home this summer, for he never can now go to sea, except for a fine passage, without being hove down.

Lord St. Vincent, 1 Feb. Off Monte Christo.

Young men will be young men, and we must make allowances. If you expect to find anything like perfection in this world you will be mistaken: therefore do not think of little nonsenses too much. Such strictness as you show to your duty falls to the lot of few, and no person in this world is more sensible of your worth and goodness in every way than myself. Let all pass over, and come and dine here. As you are ready to execute my orders, take this of coming to this house as a positive and lawful one. When I see a ship better ordered than the Foudroyant, I will allow you to confine yourself on board.

Sir Edward Berry, 7 Feb. Palermo.

On 20 January Nelson had joined Lord Keith at Leghorn. On 3 February the two arrived together at Palermo, and on the 11th proceeded off Malta, where, on the 15th, Lord Keith received intelligence of the approach of an enemy's squadron, intending, it might be supposed, to break the blockade. He accordingly, as he wrote to the Admiralty on the 20th, spread his squadron round Malta, with the success related by Nelson in a letter dated, 'Foudroyant, at sea off Cape di Corvo, eight leagues west of Cape Passaro, off shore four miles.'

Lord Keith, 18 Feb.

This morning at daylight, being in company with the [Northumberland, Audacious, and El Corso brig], I saw the Alexander in chase of a line-of-battle ship, three frigates, and a corvette. At about eight o'clock she fired several shot at one of the enemy's frigates, which struck her colours, and leaving her to be secured by the ships astern, continued the chase. I directed Captain Gould of the Audacious, and the El Corso brig, to take charge of this prize. At half-past one P.M. the frigates and corvette tacked to the westward; but the line-of-battle ship not being able to tack without coming to action with the Alexander, bore up. The Success being to leeward, Captain Peard, with great judgment and gallantry, lay across his hawse, and raked him with several broadsides. In passing the French ship's broadside, several shot struck the Success, by which one man was killed, and the master and seven men wounded. At half-past four, the Foudroyant and Northumberland coming up, the former fired two shot, when the French ship fired her broadside, and struck her colours. She proved to be the Généreux, of seventy-four guns, bearing the flag of Rear-Admiral Perrée, Commander-in-Chief of the French naval force in the Mediterranean, having a number of troops on board from Toulon, bound for the relief of Malta.

By inference, Lord Keith claimed so much of the credit of this capture as was due to the disposal of the ships by which it was effected. This Nelson did not allow, and wrote to his brother Maurice:

Maurice Nelson, (?) 20 Feb.

I have written to Lord Spencer, and sent him my journal, to prove that the Généreux was taken by me, and owing to my plan; that my quitting Lord Keith was at my own risk, and for which, if I had not succeeded, I might have been broke. If I had not, the Généreux would never have been taken.

On 24 February, Lord Keith directed Nelson to take on himself the immediate command of the squadron off Malta, with Syracuse, Agosta, or Messina as a rendezvous. On receipt of the order, Nelson wrote:

Lord Keith, 24 Feb.

My state of health is such, that it is impossible I can much longer remain here. Without some rest, I am gone. I must therefore, whenever I find the service will admit of it, request your permission to go to my friends, at Palermo, for a few weeks, and leave the command here to Commodore Troubridge. Nothing but absolute necessity obliges me to write this letter.

And in a private note of the same date he added:

I could no more stay fourteen days longer here, than fourteen years. I am absolutely exhausted, therefore I have been obliged to write you a public letter.

It has been my extraordinary good fortune to capture the Généreux, 74, bearing the flag of Rear-Admiral Perrée, and a very large storeship, with 2,000 troops and provisions and stores for the relief of La Valette. I came off Malta with my commander-in-chief, Lord Keith; we parted company in bad weather the same day. Having information that such a squadron had sailed from Toulon, Lord K. remained off Malta; but my knowledge of their track (rather my knowledge of this country from seven years' experience), I went towards the coast of Barbary, where three days afterwards I fell in with the gentlemen; those ships which fell in with me after our separation from the commander-in-chief attached themselves to my fortune. We took them after a long chase, four miles only from Sicily, and a few leagues from Cape Passaro. Perrée was killed by a shot from the Success frigate, Captain Peard. His ship struck when the Foudroyant fired only two shot; this makes nineteen sail of the line and four admirals I have been present at the capture of, this war. Ought I to trust Dame Fortune any more? her daughter may wish to step in and tear the mother from me. I have in truth serious thoughts of giving up active service—Greenwich Hospital seems a fit retreat for me after being evidently thought unfit to command in the Mediterranean. The Emperor of Russia has just granted my request for a cross of Malta to our dear and invaluable Lady Hamilton, also, of an honorary commandery to Captain Ball of the Alexander, who has with so much ability governed Malta for these last sixteen months. This fortunate capture I consider so much for the interest of the Grand Master, that I have presumed to send Admiral Perrée's sword to be laid at his feet. . . . We have been, and are, trying everything to induce the king to go to Naples, but hitherto in vain. I almost doubt Acton's sincerity as to wishing him, yet he appears as anxious as any of us: the Junto of State are as bad as the cardinal—all are open to the foulest corruption, and the presence of a monarch was never more necessary to heal the disorders of a kingdom. For some cause, which I do not understand, the pardon and act of oblivion is not yet issued, although I know it has been signed near three months; the heads of a whole kingdom cannot be cut off, be they ever such rascals.

Lord Minto, 26 Feb.

The French ships are perfectly ready to put to sea: six hundred Maltese have been raised to complete their complements, and Ball

Lord Keith, 28 Feb.

thinks they will assuredly attempt it the first fair wind. With the Alexander, who is just arrived, I shall anchor off La Valetta, and prevent their escape, if possible. The intended movements of their ships is a convincing proof to me that the garrison has lost all hopes of a successful resistance, and I wish that General Graham would make false attacks; but I am no soldier, therefore ought not to hazard an opinion. But if I commanded, I would torment the scoundrels night and day.

My state of health is very precarious. Two days ago I dropped with a pain in my heart, and I am always in a fever; but the hopes of these gentry coming out shall support me for a few days longer. I ardently desire to see this Malta business finished.

Gen. Graham, 3 March.

I beg leave, with all due deference to your superior judgment, to submit whether it would not be possible, by false attacks at night, and by a constant firing of guns and mortars, so to harass a half-starved garrison, as to induce them to give in, before some one of the vessels may arrive; for if the French Government persevere in their endeavours, at all risk of capture, to relieve by small vessels the distresses of the garrison, they must in time succeed.

Lord Keith, 8 March.

The fever still increases in the Northumberland, although every man is sent on shore the moment he is seized. The French prisoners are put into the Fame transport, and I shall soon try and remove them to the Island of Comino. I dread to hear of the ships with you; the disorder is, as you said, a jail fever, and of the worst kind.

I am sorry to tell you that my health continues to be so very indifferent, that I am obliged, in justice to myself, to retire to Palermo for a few weeks, and to direct Troubridge to carry on the service during my necessary absence.

Sir T. Troubridge, 20 March. Palermo.

We arrived here on the 16th, having had a very tedious passage. As yet it is too soon to form an opinion whether I can be cured of my complaint, which appears to me growing something like Oakes's. At present, I see but glimmering hopes, and probably my career of service is at an end, unless the French fleet shall come into the Mediterranean, when nothing shall prevent my dying at my post.

By my patent of creation, I find that my family name of Nelson has been lengthened by the words, 'of the Nile.' Therefore, in future my signature will be,

'Bronte Nelson of the Nile.'

Memo, 21 March.

I have this moment a courier from Constantinople stating, that the French treaty for quitting Egypt is ratified by the Porte, and that the ministers of England and Russia have acquainted the Porte of the determination of the allies not to suffer the French army to return to Europe, which the Turks have notified by a courier to General Kleber. The Russian squadron is on its way to cruise off Cape Bon for that purpose, and I again direct you to repeat the orders already given, for making the French from Egypt, under whatever protection they may be, of passports, or ships of war, come into some of the ports of the allies; for on no consideration must they be allowed to return to France, either in mass, or in separate ships.

Sir T. Troubridge, 28 March.

I have received no official reports; but I have letters from Commodore Troubridge, Captain Dixon, and Sir Edward Berry, telling me of the capture of the William Tell on the morn of 30 March, after a gallant defence of three hours. The Lion and Foudroyant lost each about forty killed and wounded; the French ship is dismasted; the French Admiral Decrès wounded; the Foudroyant much shattered. I send Sir Edward Berry's hasty note.

E. Nepean, 4 April.

Thus, owing to my brave friends, is the entire capture and destruction of the French Mediterranean fleet to be attributed, and my orders from the great Earl of St. Vincent fulfilled. Captain Blackwood of the Penelope, and Captain Long of the Vincejo, have the greatest merit. My task is done, my health is finished, and probably my retreat for ever fixed, unless another French fleet should be placed for me to look after.

The following is Sir Edward Berry's note, dated 'In great haste. Foudroyant, 30 March, 1800:

'My dear Lord,—I had but one wish this morning—it was for you. After a most gallant defence, Le Guillaume Tell surrendered. She is completely dismasted. The Foudroyant's lower masts and main topmast are standing, but every roll I expect them to go over the side, they are so much shattered. I was slightly hurt in the foot, and I fear about forty men are badly wounded, besides the killed, which you shall know hereafter.

'All hands behaved as you could have wished. How we prayed for you, God knows, and your sincere and faithful friend, E. BERRY.

'Love to all. Pray send this to my wife, or write Admiralty.
'Within hail before I fired.'

Capt. Blackwood, 5 April.

My dear Blackwood,—Is there a sympathy which ties men together in the bonds of friendship without having a personal knowledge of each other? If so (and, I believe, it was so to you), I was your friend and acquaintance before I saw you. Your conduct and character on the late glorious occasion stamps your fame beyond the reach of envy: it was like yourself—it was like the Penelope. Thanks; and say everything kind for me to your brave officers and men. When I receive any official letter on the subject, I shall notice your and their gallant services in the way they merit.

Lord Keith, 8 April.

I have the happiness to send you a copy of Captain Dixon's letter to Commodore Sir Thomas Troubridge, informing him of the capture of the William Tell; the circumstances attending this glorious finish to the whole French Mediterranean Fleet, are such as must ever reflect the highest honour to all concerned in it. The attention of the Commodore in placing officers and men to attend the movements of the French ships, and the exactness with which his orders were executed, are a proof that the same vigour of mind remains, although the body, I am truly sorry to say, is almost worn away. Then came the alacrity of the Vincejo, Captain Long, and other sloops of war; the gallantry and excellent management of Captain Blackwood of the Penelope frigate, who, by carrying away the enemy's main and mizen topmasts, enabled the Lion to get up, when Captain Dixon showed the greatest courage and officer-like conduct in placing his ship on the enemy's bow, as she had only 300 men on board, and the enemy 1,220. The conduct of these excellent officers enabled Sir Edward Berry to place the Foudroyant where she ought, and is the fittest ship in the world to be, close alongside the William Tell—one of the largest and finest two-decked ships in the world—where he showed that matchless intrepidity and able conduct, as a seaman and officer, which I have often had the happiness to experience in many trying situations. I thank God I was not present, for it would finish me could I have taken a sprig of these brave men's laurels: they are, and I glory in them, my darling children, served in my school, and all of us caught our professional zeal and fire from the great and good Earl of St. Vincent.

Sir W. Hamilton, 10 April. Palermo

Reports are brought to me, that the Spanish ships of war in this port are preparing to put to sea—a circumstance which must be productive of very unpleasant consequences, to both England and this country. It is fully known, with what exactness I have adhered to the neutrality of this port; for, upon our arrival here, from Naples, in December 1798, from the conduct of his Catholic Majesty's minister, I should have been fully justified in seizing these ships. . . . Profiting by my forbearance, they are fitting for sea. It is not possible, if they persist in their preparations, that I can avoid attacking them, even in the port of Palermo; for they never can or shall be suffered to go to sea, and placed in a situation of assisting the French, against not only Great Britain, but also the Two Sicilies. I have, therefore, to request, that your Excellency will convey my sentiments on this very delicate subject, to his Sicilian Majesty's ministers, that they may take measures to prevent such a truly unpleasant event happening, which would be as much against my wish as it can be against theirs.

Mr. Fox having, in the House of Commons, in February, made an accusation against somebody, for what he calls a breach of a treaty with rebels, which had been entered into with a British officer; and having used language unbecoming either the wisdom of a senator, or the politeness of a gentleman, or an Englishman, who ought ever to suppose that his Majesty's officers would always act with honour and openness in all their transactions; and as the whole affairs of the kingdom of Naples were, at the time alluded to, absolutely placed in my hands, it is I who am called upon to explain my conduct, and therefore send you my observations on the infamous armistice entered into by the cardinal; and on his refusal to send in a joint declaration to the French and rebels, I sent in my note, and on which the rebels came out of the castles, as they ought, and as I hope all those who are false to their king and country will, to be hanged, or otherwise disposed of, as their sovereign thought proper. The terms granted by Captain Foote of the Seahorse, at Castellamare, were all strictly complied with, the rebels having surrendered before my arrival. There has been nothing promised by a British officer, that his Sicilian Majesty has not complied with, even in disobedience to his orders to the cardinal. Show these papers to Mr. Rose, or some other; and, if thought right, you will put them in the papers.

A.Davison,
9 May.
Malta.

When I laid claim to my right of prize-money, as commanding admiral of the Mediterranean fleet, I had not an idea of Lord St. Vincent attempting to lay in any claim, for I have ever considered him as far from attempting, notwithstanding any law opinion, to take away my undoubted property. I am confident it will be given up, the moment you show his lordship my manner of thinking respecting the Nile prize money. No lawyer in Europe can, I am confident, make either the earl or myself do a dishonourable act, which this claim, if persisted in, would be; let my earl lay his hand on his heart, and say, whether his Nelson, subject to all the responsibility of this command, is not entitled to the pittance of prize-money—be it 5*l*. or 50,000*l*. it makes no difference. No admiral ever yet received prize-money, going for the benefit of his health from a foreign station, and Lord St. Vincent was certainly not eligible to have given me any order till his return to this station; and so think the Board of Admiralty, by their directions to me of 20 August, and many subsequent ones, which would have passed through Lord St. Vincent, had they considered him eligible to give orders; but whether they did or not I could not have obeyed. I trust I shall hear no more of this business, which I blush to think should have been brought forward.

The question, which was ultimately decided in Nelson's favour, was as to Lord St. Vincent's claim to share, as commander-in-chief, in all Mediterranean prize-money up to the time of Lord Keith assuming the command on 30 November, 1799; although, in point of fact, he had left the station some months before. Nelson, on the other hand, maintained that he, on the departure of Lord St. Vincent and also of Lord Keith, was left senior officer, and was *de facto* commander-in-chief, and ought to share as such. His statement of the case, apparently for Mr. Davison's guidance in the legal proceedings, is:

Lord Nelson received a letter from Mr. Nepean, dated 20 August, 1799, stating, that as the Earl of St. Vincent had returned to England, and Lord Keith, with the other flag-officers, having quitted the Mediterranean station, in pursuit of the enemy, Lord Nelson had become the senior officer of his Majesty's ships there, and that he had all the important duties of the station to attend [to]; and proceeds to direct his lordship's attention to the different points of the war, and of the operations to be carried on by the squadron under his command. Lord Nelson considers this order alone to be sufficient to entitle him to share for all captures, as the commander-in-chief for the time being, as he had all the responsibility; and in no instance before, have admirals claimed to share when they left the station where they commanded, on account of ill-health, or otherwise; and, as an instance, Lord Hood's going home for his health, as well as Lord Hotham, who were both retained in pay, but were not allowed to share any prize-money; and in the case of Lord Hood and Admiral Hotham, there was no claim whatever made by Lord Hood, because neither he nor any sea-officer thought he could have a shadow of claim for such. . . . If the Earl of St. Vincent was considered as commander-in-chief, as Mr. Tucker states him to be, why were not all the Admiralty orders sent to Lord Nelson addressed to the Earl of St. Vincent, as is usual, and by him transmitted to Lord Nelson? On the contrary, all orders from the Admiralty were addressed to Lord Nelson, as the commanding officer in the Mediterranean; and in no instance whatsoever did Lord Nelson receive any orders from the Earl of St. Vincent from the time he left the Mediterranean; and it is presumed that the Earl of St. Vincent did not interfere in the command, or give any orders or directions for the carrying on any service on the station. . . . Lord Nelson had it in his power to give directions to any of his Majesty's ships on the station, in contradiction to any orders given by the Earl of St. Vincent: on the contrary, the Earl of St. Vincent had it not in his power to give any orders in contradiction of those given by Lord Nelson, until his return within the limits of the Mediterranean station.

On 9 May the Admiralty sent orders to Lord Keith, that if Lord Nelson's health rendered him incapable of doing his duty, and he should be desirous of returning to England, he was to be permitted to do so, and to take his passage in the first ship Lord Keith might have occasion to send home, unless he should prefer returning by land, in which case he was to be at liberty to strike his flag in the Mediterranean, and come on shore. On the same day, Lord Spencer wrote to Nelson the following private letter:

'My dear Lord,—I have only time to write you a line by the messenger, who is just going, which I am desirous of doing, in order that the eventual permission, which we now send out for you to come home, in case your health should make it necessary, may not be misunderstood. It is by no means my wish or intention to call you away from service; but having observed that you have been under the necessity of quitting your station off Malta, on account of the state of your health, which I am persuaded you could not have thought of doing without such necessity, it appeared to me much more advisable for you to come home at once, than to be obliged to remain inactive at Palermo, while active service was going on in other parts of the station. I should still much prefer your remaining to complete the reduction of Malta, which I flatter myself cannot be very far distant, and I still look with anxious expectation to the Guillaume Tell striking to your flag. But if, unfortunately, these agreeable events are to be prevented by your having too much exhausted yourself in the service to be equal to follow them up, I am quite clear, and I believe I am joined in opinion by all your friends here, that you will be more likely to recover your health and strength in England than in an inactive situation at a foreign court, however pleasing the respect and gratitude shown to you for your services may be, and no testimonies of respect and gratitude from that court to you can be, I am convinced, too great for the very essential services you have rendered it.

'I trust that you will take in good part what I have taken the liberty to write to you as a friend, and believe me, when I assure you that you have none who is more sincerely and faithfully so than your obedient humble servant, SPENCER.'

<small>Lord Keith, (?) 6 June.</small>

I feel sensibly your kind intentions of accommodating us to England. The state of the Foudroyant renders it, I believe you will think it, right for her to go to England, when she has had some refit; for in her present state she would not be trusted at sea except for a passage of a few leagues. Where she put into port, if it blew fresh, I should have cut down her main and foremasts; but we have neither spars or cordage for to fit her. . . . I have not been able to man the William Tell to Minorca, nor, till 300 or 250 men are found for her, do I see how it can be effected. Troubridge says the Culloden is able to go to England. I say she ought not to be trusted. Fourteen days would heave her down at Mahon, and stop her leaks: 100 men from her, for she is full-manned, and good men, would greatly assist in navigating the William Tell to England; for she is well fitted with jury-masts.

Most sincerely do we congratulate you on the success of the navy, I may say, in the Riviera of Genoa; and you will now bear me out in my assertion, when I say that the British fleet could have prevented the invasion of Italy, and at that time we had nothing to do; and if our friend Hotham had kept his fleet on that coast, I assert, and you will agree with me, no army from France could have been furnished with stores or provisions; even men could not have marched. I hope our next account from you will be the surrender of Genoa.

On 10 June the Foudroyant, in company with the Alexander, Princess Charlotte, and a Neapolitan packet, sailed for Leghorn; having on board the Queen of Naples and her family, Sir William and Lady Hamilton, and Miss Knight.

<small>Lord Spencer, 17 June. Leghorn.</small>

Arrived here on the 14th, after a passage of five days; but it was the 16th before the weather would permit her Majesty to land. All the honours which his Majesty's ships could show to the queen have, I trust, been shown her—and too much to so great and good a monarch could not be done. The situation of the two armies renders the queen a little anxious; but her great mind is superior to all difficulties. I am waiting the orders of Lord Keith, and expect he will order the Foudroyant to carry me to England: for in this country she cannot be refitted. Four days out of seven I am confined to my bed, but I hope for better times.

In this wish as to the Foudroyant, Nelson was disappointed. On 19 June, Lord Keith sent him a positive order not to employ the line-of-battle ships in conveying back the Queen of Naples to Palermo (in case her Majesty did not proceed to Vienna); and authorising him to strike his flag, and proceed to England by land, or in the Princess Charlotte, or in any troop ship at Mahon, or in the Seahorse; but if, on his arrival at Mahon, he determined to remain on the station, he was to take upon him the duties of senior officer there.

This was accompanied by a private note:

'My dear Lord,—It is not matter of caprice, but of actual duty and necessity, which has obliged me to send the order, which I must desire to be final. Her Majesty is too just, and too well-informed, to place anything like neglect to me. With her good understanding I am sure to stand acquitted. So, my dear friend, let me insist that the ships instantly follow my public orders. The wretched situation to which we are reduced distracts me. I am told from England there is not a ship to be sent out. I am directed to undertake many and distant important services, which renders it impossible to let the Foudroyant go to England: her masts are made at Mahon.'

The idea of removing the Foudroyant has created an alarm at the Palace, and I send you a letter from thence. If Sir William and Lady Hamilton go home by land, it is my intention to go with them; if by water, we shall be happy in taking the best ship we can get; but we are all pledged not to quit the royal family till they are in perfect security. <small>Lord Keith, 24 June. Leghorn.</small>

On quitting the Foudroyant, Lord Nelson received this letter from his barge's crew, dated 26 June:

'My Lord,—It is with extreme grief that we find that you are about to leave us. We have been along with you (although not in the same ship) in every engagement your Lordship has been in, both by sea and land; and most humbly beg of your Lordship to permit us to go to England as your boat's crew in any ship or vessel, or in any way that may seem most pleasing to your Lordship. My Lord, pardon the rude style of seamen, who are but little acquainted with writing, and believe us to be, my Lord, your ever humble and obedient servants,
BARGE'S CREW OF THE FOUDROYANT.'

In company with the queen and her party, including Sir William and Lady Hamilton, Nelson left Leghorn on 17 July, and travelling by easy stages through Ancona, and thence in a Russian frigate to Trieste, reached Vienna towards the end of August. He left Vienna on 26 September, and passing through Prague, Dresden, and Hamburg, arrived at Yarmouth on 6 November.

I beg you will acquaint their Lordships of my arrival here this day, and that my health being perfectly re-established, it is my wish to serve immediately; and I trust that my necessary journey by land from the Mediterranean will not be considered as a wish to be a moment out of active service. <small>Evan Nepean, 6 Nov. Yarmouth.</small>

On 17 January, 1801, Nelson, now Vice-Admiral of the Blue, hoisted his flag on board the San Josef at Plymouth.

Lord Spencer, 17 Jan.

My dear Lord,—I was with Lord St. Vincent yesterday, when Sir Hyde Parker's letter arrived, announcing his appointment to the North Sea command. This naturally led to a confidential communication as to my views and present situation, and he gave me leave to tell you our conversation. Next to getting a command which I was a candidate for, whenever Lord Keith gave up his, of course my pleasure would have been to serve under him, but that circumstances had so altered since my arrival, that it was almost certain I should go to the Baltic; and I related our communication on this subject. The Earl was very handsome to me, and hoped that, by a temporary absence of a few months, I should not lose my San Josef, the finest ship in the world; and only one voice points out the Formidable as the ship fittest for me, for real and active service. . . . He mentioned several other ships, degrees below the Formidable, but entreated I would not go in the Windsor Castle; that she was such a leewardly ship that he knew she would break my heart; for that I should often be forced to anchor on a lee shore, and never could lead a division in a narrow sea like the Baltic. Having related this conversation, I shall leave the subject as far as relates to myself. It naturally enlarged on the best means of destroying the Danes, &c. &c., and I found him clearly of opinion that 10,000 troops ought to be embarked, to get at the Danish arsenal. I told him this matter had been canvassed with your Lordship, but the difficulty was, where to find such a general as was fit for the service. . . .

The San Josef, as far as relates to Captain Hardy, is ready for sea, but the dockyard have not done with her. My cabin is not yet finished, of course, nor even painted; but that I do not care about: I shall live in Captain Hardy's.

Lord St. Vincent, 20 Jan.

May this day, my dear Lord, which I am told is your birthday, come round as often as life is comfortable, and may your days be comfortable for many, many years. Almost my only ungratified wish is, to see you alongside the French admiral, and myself supporting you in the San Josef. We may be beat, but I am confident the world will believe we could not help it.

Sir E. Berry, 26 Jan.

I yesterday received your kind letter of the 20th, and I beg, if you think the 200*l.* is enough for poor dear Miller's monument, that you will direct Flaxman to instantly proceed about it, and as far as that sum, if no one subscribes, I will be answerable. If those of 14 February are to be allowed the honour of subscribing, I then think we ought to subscribe 500*l.*—a less sum would not be proper for such a body. Pray let me know the intended inscription, for we must take care not to say too much or too little. The language must be plain, as if flowing from the heart of one of us sailors who have fought with him.

I should hope our Baltic trip could not last eight weeks, for we must either get at some of the fleets before that time, or we shall be crippled, and not fit to seek new enemies. If we succeed, and succeed we must, or show strong reasons why we could not, the other powers will think seriously of their situation. I find Lord Spencer will not hear of any troops even for a sudden debarkation to storm a battery, and as I am only an underling I have only to obey, and do my utmost to fulfil the wishes and expectations of my superiors. Lord Spencer will get my letter where I again strongly request that the San Josef may be held for me till my return to you, and I shall feel grateful for your seconding me, for I have not the smallest interest. As far as relates to Captain Hardy the ship is ready, the Namur's all paid the advance and the marines, and every woman out of the ship; we can do no more, and I hope this post will produce orders to man us and to proceed to Torbay. The marines, I believe, will want a very serious inspection; they have no strength, and half of them cannot look over the poop hammocks; but more of this when we meet. I did not wish to begin a scene here; I should perhaps have been thought impertinent and troublesome, for, except in two or three captains, I see such slackness that in the Mediterranean I have not been used to; and it requires a man of our friend Collingwood's firmness to keep some of them to their duty. *Lord St. Vincent, 28 Jan.*

Pray tell Sir Isaac Heard that I cannot afford to pay for any honours conferred upon me. They are intended to do honour to this country, and to mark the gratitude of his Sicilian Majesty to his faithful ally, our gracious King, in my person, his faithful servant. As far as relates to the personal trouble of Sir Isaac, or any other friend, I am not backward in payment of thanks or money as the case requires; and for personal trouble I have already paid 41*l*., and have had no answer relative to the Imperial Order of the Crescent. Sir Isaac is bound in honour to follow up this application; for my wish is to have all my honours gazetted together; but paying those fees to Secretaries of State, Earl Marshals, &c. &c., without which I am told the king's orders will not be obeyed, it would in my opinion be very wrong to do it. I could say more on this subject, but I think it better not at present. *A. Davison, 28 Jan.*

17 Feb.

The Earl being at the head of the Admiralty, will, I hope, give a new spur to our just cause.

The higher the earl, the more we must attempt to wrest justice from him; and I hope your courage will not flag in the cause of an oppressed friend, even against much higher men than a First Lord of the Admiralty. I would sooner be turned on shore than give up an inch. But the earl has wrote me the moment he came from the king a very flattering letter, asking for my support: so I will support him as a great sea-officer; but was he forty times as great, I will not suffer him to rob me with impunity.

Lord St. Vincent, 20 Feb.

I have the order to put myself under Sir Hyde's command, but none from him yet to go to Portsmouth; but I take for granted I shall have them to-morrow, and we shall be ready to start at the moment.

1 March. Portsmouth.

The wind was yesterday at SSW, which has prevented Warrior, Defence, and Agincourt from sailing. Time[1] is our best ally, and I hope we shall not give her up, as all our allies have given us up. Our friend here is a little nervous about dark nights and fields of ice, but we must brace up; these are not times for nervous systems. I want peace, which is only to be had through, I trust, our still invincible navy.

Sir E. Berry, 9 March. Yarmouth.

As to the plan for pointing a gun truer than we do at present, if the person comes I shall of course look at it, and be happy, if necessary, to use it; but I hope we shall be able as usual to get so close to our enemies that our shot cannot miss their object, and that we shall again give our northern enemies that hail-storm of bullets which is so emphatically described in the Naval Chronicle, and which gives our dear country the dominion of the seas. We have it, and all the devils in hell cannot take it from us, if our wooden walls have fair play.

A. Davison, 16 March. Lat. 57° N.

I have not yet seen my commander-in-chief, and have had no official communication whatever. All I have gathered of our first plans I disapprove most exceedingly; honour may arise from them, good cannot. I hear we are likely to anchor outside Kronborg Castle, instead of Copenhagen, which would give weight to our negotiation: a Danish Minister would think twice before he would put his name to war with England, when the next moment he would probably see his master's fleet in flames, and his capital in ruins; but 'out of sight out of mind,' is an old saying. The Dane should see our flag waving every moment he lifted up his head.

[1] On another occasion, in conversation with General Twiss, Lord Nelson is said to have observed: 'Time, Twiss—time is everything; five minutes makes the difference between a victory and a defeat.'

The Admiralty orders to Sir Hyde Parker to enter the Baltic seem to have reached him about 22 March, though dated on the 15th. They were as follows :

'The Right Honourable Henry Dundas, one of his Majesty's Principal Secretaries of State, having, in his letter of yesterday's date, signified to us his Majesty's pleasure that whether the discussion supposed to be now pending with the Court of Denmark should be terminated by an amicable arrangement, or by actual hostilities, the officer commanding the fleet in the Baltic should, in either case (as soon as the fleet can be withdrawn from before Copenhagen consistently with the attainment of one or the other of the objects for which he is now instructed to take that station), proceed to Reval ; and if he should find the division of the Russian navy usually stationed at that port still there, to make an immediate and vigorous attack upon it, provided the measure should appear to him practicable, and such as in his judgment would afford a reasonable prospect of success in destroying the arsenal, or in capturing or destroying the ships, without exposing to too great a risk the fleet under his command.

'And Mr. Dundas having further signified to us his Majesty's pleasure that, consistently with this precaution, the said officer should be authorised and directed to proceed successively, and as the season and other operations will permit, against Cronstadt, and in general by every means in his power to attack and endeavour to capture or destroy any ships of war or others belonging to Russia, wherever he can meet with them, and to annoy that power as far as his means will admit, in every manner not incompatible with the fair and acknowledged usages of war ; and that with respect to Sweden, should the Court of Stockholm persist in her hostile engagements with that of Petersburg against this country, the same general line of conduct as hath been stated with respect to the ships and ports of the latter, should govern the said officer commanding the fleet in his proceedings against those of Sweden ; but that, in the contrary supposition (conceived not to be impossible) of this power relinquishing her present hostile plans against the rights and interests of this country, and of her renewing, either singly or in concert with Denmark, her ancient engagements with his Majesty, it will in such case be the duty of the said officer to afford to Sweden every protection in his power against the resentment and attacks of Russia. And Mr. Dundas having also signified that his Majesty being no less desirous of bringing the existing dispute with Sweden to this latter issue than he has shown himself so disposed with respect to Denmark, and upon the same principles, it will therefore be requisite that the said officer commanding in the Baltic should make such a disposition of his force as may appear best adapted to facilitate and give weight to the arrangement in question, provided it should be concluded with the Court of Denmark within the forty-eight hours allowed for this purpose, and the proposal of acceding to it which will be made to that of Sweden should be entertained by the latter, you are, in pursuance of his Majesty's pleasure, signified as above mentioned, hereby required and directed to proceed without a moment's loss of time into the Baltic, and to govern yourself under the different circumstances before stated to the best of your judgment and discretion, in the manner therein pointed out, transmitting from time to time to our secretary, for our information, an account of your proceedings, and such information as you may conceive to be proper for our knowledge. Given under our hands and seals, the 15th March, 1801. St. Vincent, T. Troubridge, J. Markham.'

Sir Hyde Parker, 24 March.

My dear Sir Hyde,—The conversation we had yesterday has naturally, from its importance, been the subject of my thoughts; and the more I have reflected, the more I am confirmed in opinion, that not a moment should be lost in attacking the enemy : they will every day and hour be stronger; we never shall be so good a match for them as at this moment. The only consideration in my mind is, how to get at them with the least risk to our ships. By Mr. Vansittart's[1] account, the Danes have taken every means in their power to prevent our getting to attack Copenhagen by the passage of the Sound. Kronborg has been strengthened, the Crown Islands fortified, on the outermost of which are twenty guns pointing mostly downwards, and only eight hundred yards from very formidable batteries placed under the citadel, supported by five sail of the line, seven floating batteries of fifty guns each, besides small craft, gunboats, &c. &c. ; and that the Reval squadron of twelve or fourteen sail of the line are soon expected, as also five sail of Swedes. It would appear by what you have told me of your instructions, that Government took for granted you would find no difficulty in getting off Copenhagen, and in the event of a failure of negotiation, you might instantly attack ; and that there would be scarcely a doubt but the Danish fleet would be destroyed, and the capital made so hot that Denmark would listen to reason and its true interest. By Mr. Vansittart's account, their state of preparation exceeds what he conceives our Government thought possible, and that the Danish Government is hostile to us in the greatest possible degree. Therefore here you are, with almost the safety, certainly with the honour of England more entrusted to you, than ever yet fell to the lot of any British officer. On your decision depends whether our country shall be degraded in the eyes of Europe, or whether she shall rear her head higher than ever : again do I repeat, never did our country depend so much on the success of any fleet as on this. How best to honour our country and abate the pride of her enemies by defeating their schemes must be the subject of your deepest consideration as commander-in-chief; and if what I have to offer can be the least useful in forming your decision, you are most heartily welcome.

[1] Mr. Nicholas Vansittart (afterwards Lord Bexley) had been sent on a special embassy to Copenhagen in the hope of preventing hostilities.

I shall begin with supposing you are determined to enter by the passage of the Sound, as there are those who think, if you leave that passage open, that the Danish fleet may sail from Copenhagen and join the Dutch or French. I own I have no fears on that subject; for it is not likely that whilst their capital is menaced with an attack, 9,000 of her best men should be sent out of the kingdom. I suppose that some damage may arise amongst our masts and yards; yet perhaps there will not be one of them but could be made serviceable again. You are now about Kronborg: if the wind be fair, and you determine to attack the ships and Crown Islands, you must expect the natural issue of such a battle—ships crippled, and perhaps one or two lost; for the wind which carries you in will most probably not bring out a crippled ship. This mode I call taking the bull by the horns. It, however, will not prevent the Reval ships, or Swedes, from joining the Danes: and to prevent this from taking effect, is, in my humble opinion, a measure absolutely necessary—and still to attack Copenhagen. Two modes are in my view; one to pass Kronborg, taking the risk of damage, and to pass up the deepest and straightest channel above the Middle Grounds; and coming down the Garbar or King's Channel, to attack their floating batteries, &c. &c., as we find it convenient. It must have the effect of preventing a junction between the Russians, Swedes, and Danes, and may give us an opportunity of bombarding Copenhagen. I am also pretty certain that a passage could be found to the northward of Saltholm for all our ships; perhaps it might be necessary to warp a short distance in the very narrow part. Should this mode of attack be ineligible, the passage of the Belt, I have no doubt, would be accomplished in four or five days, and then the attack by Dragör could be carried into effect, and the junction of the Russians prevented, with every probability of success against the Danish floating batteries. What effect a bombardment might have I am not called upon to give an opinion; but think the way would be cleared for the trial. Supposing us through the Belt with the wind first westerly, would it not be possible to either go with the fleet, or detach ten ships of three and two decks, with one bomb and two fire-ships, to Reval, to destroy the Russian squadron at that place? I do not see the great risk of such a detachment, and with the remainder to attempt the business at Copenhagen. The measure may be thought bold, but I am of opinion the boldest measures are the safest; and our country demands a most vigorous exertion of her force, directed with judgment. In supporting you, my dear Sir Hyde, through the arduous and important task you have undertaken, no exertion of head or heart shall be wanting from your most obedient and faithful servant, NELSON AND BRONTE.

Lord Nelson's official letter to Sir Hyde Parker, dated 3 April, describes the action of the 2nd only in general terms, the details referring to the conduct of different officers whom he wished to commend. A more detailed account of the battle is that written by Colonel Stewart, the commandant of the soldiers embarked in the fleet, and during the action actually on board the Elephant. The narrative begins with the embarkation at Portsmouth, and having described the voyage round to Yarmouth Roads, goes on :

Col. Stewart's narrative.

'Lord Nelson's plan would have been to have proceeded with the utmost despatch, and with such ships as were in readiness, to the mouth of Copenhagen Harbour ; then and there to have insisted on amity or war, and have brought the objects of Messrs. Drummond and Vansittart's negotiation to a speedy decision. He would have left orders for the remainder of the fleet to have followed in succession, as they were ready, and by the rapidity of his proceedings have anticipated the formidable preparations for defence which the Danes had scarcely thought of at that early season. The delay in Yarmouth Roads did not accord with his views. An order from the Admiralty arrived on 11 March, in consequence of which the fleet put to sea on the succeeding day. . . . Our fleet consisted of about fifty sail ; of these forty were pennants, sixteen being of the line. On the 15th we encountered a heavy gale of wind, which in some measure scattered the fleet and prevented our reaching the Naze until the 18th. On the next day, when off the Scaw, the whole were nearly collected ; a north-west wind blew, and an opportunity appeared to have been lost of proceeding through the Cattegat. Every delay, however trifling, gave cause for regret, and favoured the views of the Northern Coalition. . . . The commander-in-chief had probably, however, instructions by which he acted ; and if so, this, in addition to numerous instances of a similar nature, proves the propriety of discretionary powers whenever success is to depend on energy and activity. Lord Nelson was, as I understood, greatly vexed at the delay.

'On the 21st it blew hard ; we anchored for twenty-four hours, and did not arrive off the point of Elsinore until the 24th. The Blanche frigate, with Mr. Vansittart on board, preceded the fleet from the Scaw, and, landing him at Elsinore on the 20th, he joined Mr. Drummond at Copenhagen. The terms demanded by these gentlemen having been rejected, they returned to our fleet on the 24th, and left us for England on the succeeding day. The wind was again strong and favourable, and expectation was alive that we should have sailed through the Sound on the 25th ; it was, however, generally understood, that the formidable reports which had been made by Mr. Vansittart, and by the pilots whom we had brought with us, as to the state of the batteries at Elsinore, and of the defensive situation of Copenhagen, induced the commander-in-chief to prefer the circuitous passage by the Great Belt. Lord Nelson, who was impatient for action, was not much deterred by these alarming representations ; his object was to go to Copenhagen, and he said, " Let it be by the Sound, by the Belt, or anyhow, only lose not an hour." On the 26th the whole fleet accordingly sailed for the Great Belt; but after proceeding for a few leagues along the coast of Zealand, the plan was suddenly changed . . . . [and] the fleet returned to its former anchorage before sunset. As if a more than sufficient time had not been given for the Danes to prepare their defence, another message was sent, on 27 March, to the Governor of Elsinore, to discover his intentions relative to opposing our fleet, if it were to pass the Sound. He replied, "As a soldier I cannot intermeddle with politics; but I am not at liberty to suffer a fleet, whose intention is not yet known, to approach the guns of the Castle of Kronborg, which I have the honour to command. In case your Excellency should think proper to make any proposals to the King of Denmark, I wish to be informed thereof before the fleet approaches nearer to the Castle." Sir Hyde Parker replied, that "finding the intentions of the Court of Denmark to be hostile against his Britannic Majesty, he regarded his Excellency's answer as a declaration of war; and, therefore, agreeably to his instructions, could no longer refrain from hostilities, however reluctant it might be to his feelings."

'On the 29th Lord Nelson shifted his flag from the St. George to the Elephant, commanded by his intimate friend, Captain Foley, in order to carry on operations in a lighter ship. Both 28 and 29 March were unfortunately calm: orders had, however, been given to the fleet to pass through the Sound as soon as the wind should permit. At daylight, on the morning of the 30th, it blew a topsail breeze from NW. The signal was made, and the fleet proceeded in the order of battle previously arranged; Lord Nelson's division in the van, the commander-in-chief's in the centre, and Admiral Graves's in the rear: Captain Murray in the Edgar, with the fleet of bomb and gun vessels, took their station off Kronborg Castle on the preceding morning; and, upon the first Danish shot, opened their fire upon the castle. . . . It had been our intention to have kept in mid-channel; the forbearance of the Swedes not having been counted upon, the lighter vessels were on the larboard side of our line of battle, and were to have engaged the Helsingborg shore: not a shot, however, was fired, nor any batteries apparent, and our fleet inclined accordingly to that side, so as completely to avoid the Danish shot which fell in showers, but at least a cable's length from our ships. The Danish batteries opened a fire, as we understood, of nearly one hundred pieces of cannon and mortars, as soon as our leading ship, the Monarch, came abreast of them; and they continued in one uninterrupted blaze during the passage of the fleet, to the no small amusement of our crews; none of whom received injury, except from the bursting of one of our own guns. Some of our leading ships at first returned a few rounds, but, perceiving the inutility, desisted. The whole came to anchor about mid-day, between the island of Hveen and Copenhagen; the division under Captain Murray following as soon as the main body had passed. . . .

'Our fleet was no sooner at anchor than the commander-in-chief, accompanied by Lord Nelson, two or three senior captains, the commanding officer of the artillery and of the troops, proceeded in a schooner to reconnoitre the harbour and channels. We soon perceived that our delay had been of important advantage to the enemy, who had lined the northern edge of the shoals near the Crown batteries, and the front of the harbour and arsenal, with a formidable flotilla. The Trekroner battery appeared, in particular, to have been strengthened, and all the buoys of the Northern and the King's Channels had been removed. Having examined these points with some attention, the party returned to the London.

'The night of 30 March was employed by some of the intelligent masters and pilots, under the direction of Captain Brisbane, in ascertaining the channels round the great shoal called the Middle Ground, and in laying down fresh buoys, the Danes having either removed or misplaced the former ones. On the next day, the commander-in-chief and Lord Nelson, attended as before, with the addition of all the artillery officers, proceeded in the Amazon frigate, Captain Riou, to the examination of the northern channel, and of the flotilla from the eastward. Captain Riou became on this occasion first known to Lord Nelson, who was struck with admiration at the superior discipline and seamanship that were observable on board the Amazon during the proceedings of this day. The Danish line of defence was formed in a direct line eastward from the Trekroner battery, and extended at least two miles along the coast of Amager: it was ascertained to consist of the hulls of seven line-of-battle ships with jury masts, two only being fully rigged, ten pontoons or floating batteries, one bomb-ship rigged, and two or three smaller craft. On the Trekroner appeared to be nearly seventy guns; on the smaller battery, in-shore, six or seven guns; and on the coast of Amager several batteries which were within a long range of the King's Channel. Off the harbour's mouth, which was to the westward of the Trekroner, were moored four line-of-battle ships and a frigate; two of the former and the latter were fully rigged. Their whole line of defence, from one extreme point to the other, might embrace an extent of nearly four miles. The dockyard and arsenal were in line nearly south, within the Trekroner, about half a mile distant. A few shot were fired at the Amazon whenever we approached the leading ship of their line. The officers of artillery were desired to ascertain whether, in the event of the line of defence being in part or wholly removed, they could place their bomb-ships, of which there were seven, so as to play with effect on the dockyards and arsenal. After some hours' survey, the Amazon returned to the fleet, when the opinions of the artillery officers were given in the affirmative, if the flotilla to the eastward of the Crown batteries were removed. A council of war was held in the afternoon, and the mode which might be advisable for the attack was considered: that from the eastward appeared to be preferred. Lord Nelson offered his services, requiring ten line-of-battle ships, and the whole of the smaller craft. The commander-in-chief, with sound discretion, and in a handsome manner, not only left everything to Lord Nelson for this detached service, but gave two more line-of-battle ships than he demanded. During this council of war, the energy of Lord Nelson's character was remarked: certain difficulties had been started by some of the members, relative to each of the three Powers we should either have to engage, in succession or united, in those seas. The number of the Russians was, in particular, represented as formidable. Lord Nelson kept pacing the cabin, mortified at everything which savoured either of alarm or irresolution. When the above remark was applied to the Swedes, he sharply observed, "The more numerous the better;" and when to the Russians, he repeatedly said, "So much the better, I wish they were twice as many, the easier the victory, depend on it." He alluded, as he afterwards explained in private, to the total want of tactique among the northern fleets, and to his intention, whenever he should bring either the Swedes or Russians to action, of attacking the head of their line, and confusing their movements as much as possible. He used to say, "Close with a Frenchman, but out-manœuvre a Russian." The night of 31 March was employed, as the preceding, in ascertaining the course of the upper channel. Captain Brisbane was particularly active on this service, conducted under Lord Nelson's immediate directions.

'On the forenoon of 1 April the whole fleet removed to an anchorage within two leagues of the town, off the NW end of the Middle Ground. It was intended that the division under Lord Nelson should proceed from this point through the northern channel. His lordship, accompanied by a few chosen friends, made his last observations during that morning on board the Amazon, and about one o'clock, returning to the Elephant, he threw out the signal to weigh. The ships then weighed, and followed the Amazon in succession through the narrow channel. The wind was light, but favourable, and not one accident occurred. The buoys were accurately laid down, and the smaller craft distinctly pointed out the course. About dark, the whole fleet was at its anchorage off Dragör point; the headmost of the enemy's line not more than two miles distant. The small extent of the anchoring-ground, as the fleet did not consist of less than thirty-three pennants, caused the ships to be so much crowded, which the calmness of the evening increased, that had the enemy but taken due advantage of it by shells from mortar-boats, or from Amager Island, the greatest mischief might have ensued. They threw two or three about eight P.M., which served to show that we were within range. The Danes were, however, too much occupied during this night in manning their ships and strengthening their line; not from immediate expectation, as we afterwards learned, of our attack—conceiving the channel impracticable to so large a fleet, but as a precaution against our nearer approach. Our guard-boats were actively employed between us and the enemy, and Captain Hardy even rowed to their leading ship; sounding round her, and using a pole when he was apprehensive of being heard. His chief object was to ascertain the bearing of the eastern end of the Middle Ground—the greatest obstacle, as it proved, that we had to contend with.

'On board the Elephant, the night of 1 April was an important one. As soon as the fleet was at anchor, the gallant Nelson sat down to table with a large party of his comrades in arms. He was in the highest spirits, and drank to a leading wind, and to the success of the ensuing day. Captains Foley, Hardy, Fremantle, Riou, Inman, Admiral Graves, and a few others to whom he was particularly attached, were of this interesting party; from which every man separated with feelings of admiration for their great leader, and with anxious impatience to follow him to the approaching battle. The signal to prepare for action had been made early in the evening. All the captains retired to their respective ships, Riou excepted, who with Lord Nelson and Foley arranged the order of battle, and those instructions that were to be issued to each ship on the succeeding day. These three officers retired between nine and ten to the after-cabin, and drew up those orders. From the previous fatigue of this day, and of the two preceding, Lord Nelson was so much exhausted while dictating his instructions, that it was recommended to him by us all, and, indeed, insisted upon by his old servant, Allen, who assumed much command on these occasions, that he should go to his cot. It was placed on the floor, but from it he still continued to dictate. Captain Hardy returned about eleven, and reported the practicability of the channel, and the depth of water up to the ships of the enemy's line. Had we abided by this report, in lieu of confiding in our masters and pilots, we should have acted better The orders were completed about one o'clock, when half a dozen clerks in the foremost cabin proceeded to transcribe them. Lord Nelson's impatience again showed itself; for instead of sleeping undisturbedly, as he might have done, he was every half hour calling from his cot to these clerks to hasten their work, for that the wind was becoming fair; he was constantly receiving a report of this during the night. Their work being finished about six in the morning, his lordship, who was previously up and dressed, breakfasted, and about seven made the usual signal for all captains. The instructions were delivered to each by eight o'clock; and a special command was given to Captain Riou to act as circumstances might require. The land forces and a body of 500 seamen were to have been united under the command of Captain Fremantle and Colonel Stewart, and as soon as the fire of the Crown battery should be silenced, they were to storm the work and destroy it. The division under the commander-in-chief was to menace the ships at the entrance of the harbour; the intricacy of the channel would, however, have prevented their entering. Captain Murray in the Edgar was to lead.

'With the returning light, the wind had been announced as becoming perfectly fair. The pilots, who were in general mates of trading vessels from the ports of Scotland and north of England to the Baltic, and several of the masters in the navy were ordered on board the Elephant between eight and nine o'clock. A most unpleasant degree of hesitation prevailed amongst them all, when they came to the point about the bearing of the east end of the Middle Ground, and about the exact line of deep water in the King's Channel. Not a moment was to be lost; the wind was fair, and the signal made for action. Lord Nelson urged them to be steady, to be resolute, and to decide. At length Mr. Brierly, the master of the Bellona, declared himself prepared to lead the fleet; his example was quickly followed by the rest, they repaired on board of their respective ships, and at half-past nine the signal was given to weigh in succession. This was quickly obeyed by the Edgar, who proceeded in a noble manner for the channel. The Agamemnon was to follow, but happened to take a course in a direct line for the end of the shoal. The Polyphemus' signal, Captain Lawford, was then made, and this change in the order of sailing was most promptly executed. The Edgar was, however, unsupported for a considerable time; when within range of the Prövesteen, she was fired at, but returned not a shot until she was nearly opposite to the number which was destined for her by the instructions; she then poured in her broadsides with great effect. The Polyphemus was followed by the Isis, Bellona, and Russell; the former, commanded by Captain Walker, took her station most gallantly, and had the severest berth this day of any ship, the Monarch perhaps not excepted. The Bellona and Russell, in going down the channel, kept too close on the starboard shoal, and ran aground; they were, however, within range of shot, and continued to fire with much spirit upon such of the enemy's ships as they could reach. ... In going down the channel the water was supposed to shoal on the larboard shore; each ship had been ordered to pass her leader on the starboard side. When it came to the turn of the Elephant, his lordship, thinking that the two above-mentioned ships had kept too far in that direction, made the signal to close with the enemy. Perceiving that this was not done, which their being aground unknown to him was the cause of, he ordered the Elephant's helm to starboard, quitted the intended order of sailing, and went within those ships. The same course was consequently followed by the succeeding ships; as each ship arrived nearly opposite to her number in the Danish line, she let her anchor go by the stern, the wind nearly aft, and presented her broadside to the enemy.

'The action began at five minutes past ten. In about half an hour afterwards the first half of our fleet was engaged, and before half-past eleven the battle became general. The Elephant's station was in the centre, opposite to the Danish commodore, who commanded in the Dannebrog, 62, Commodore Fischer, Captain F. A. Braun. Our distance was nearly a cable's length, and this was the average distance at which the action was fought; its being so great caused the long duration of it. Lord Nelson was most anxious to get nearer; but the same error which had led the two ships on the shoal, induced our master and pilots to dread shoaling their water on the larboard shore: they, therefore, when the lead was a quarter less five, refused to approach nearer, and insisted on the anchor being let go. We afterwards found that had we but approached the enemy's line we should have deepened our water up to their very side, and closed with them: as it was, the Elephant engaged in little more than four fathom. The Glatton had her station immediately astern of us; the Ganges, Monarch, and Defiance ahead; the distance between each not exceeding a half cable. The judgment with which each ship calculated her station in that intricate channel was admirable throughout. The failure of the three ships that were aground, and whose force was to have been opposed to the Trekroner battery, left this day, as glorious for seamanship as for courage, incomplete. The lead was in many ships confided to the master alone; and the contest that arose on board the Elephant, which of the two officers who attended the heaving of it should stand in the larboard chains, was a noble competition, and greatly pleased the heart of Nelson as he paced the quarter-deck. The gallant Riou, perceiving the blank in the original plan for the attack of the Crown battery, proceeded down the line with his squadron of frigates, and attempted, but in vain, to fulfil the duty of the absent ships of the line. His force was unequal to it; and the general signal of recall, which was made about mid-action by the commander-in-chief, had the good effect of, at least, saving Riou's squadron from destruction.

'About 1 P.M. few if any of the enemy's heavy ships and praams had ceased to fire. The Isis had greatly suffered by the superior weight of the Prövesteen's fire; and if it had not been for the judicious diversion of it by the Désirée, Captain Inman, who raked her, and for other assistance from the Polyphemus, the Isis would have been destroyed. Both the Isis and Bellona had received serious injury by the bursting of some of their guns. The Monarch was also suffering severely under the united fire of the Holsteen and Sjelland ; and only two of our bomb-vessels could get to their station on the Middle Ground, and open their mortars on the arsenal, directing their shells over both fleets. Our squadron of gun-brigs, impeded by currents, could not, with the exception of one, although commanded by Captain Rose in the Jamaica, weather the eastern end of the Middle Ground, or come into action. The division of the commander-in-chief acted according to the preconcerted plan, but could only menace the entrance of the harbour. The Elephant was warmly engaged by the Dannebrog, and by two heavy praams on her bow and quarter. Signals of distress were on board the Bellona and Russell, and of inability from the Agamemnon. The contest, in general, although from the relaxed state of the enemy's fire it might not have given much room for apprehension as to the result, had certainly, at one P.M., not declared itself in favour of either side. About this juncture, and in this posture of affairs, the signal was thrown out on board the London for the action to cease.

'Lord Nelson was at this time, as he had been during the whole action, walking the starboard side of the quarter-deck ; sometimes much animated, and at others heroically fine in his observations. A shot through the mainmast knocked a few splinters about us. He observed to me, with a smile, "It is warm work, and this day may be the last to any of us at a moment;" and then stopping short at the gangway, he used an expression never to be erased from my memory, and said with emotion, "but mark you, I would not be elsewhere for thousands." When the signal, No. 39 [to discontinue the engagement], was made, the signal lieutenant reported it to him. He continued his walk, and did not appear to take notice of it. The lieutenant meeting his lordship at the next turn asked " whether he should repeat it ?" Lord Nelson answered, "No, acknowledge it." On the officer returning to the poop, his lordship called after him, "Is No. 16 [for close action] still hoisted ?" The lieutenant answering in the affirmative, Lord Nelson said, "Mind you keep it so." He now walked the deck considerably agitated, which was always known by his moving the stump of his right arm. After a turn or two, he said to me, in a quick manner, "Do you know what's shown on board of the commander-in-chief ? No. 39." On asking him what that meant, he answered, "Why, to leave off action." "Leave off action!" he repeated, and then added, with a shrug, "Now, damn me if I do." He also observed, I believe to Captain Foley, "You know, Foley, I have only one eye—I have a right to be blind sometimes ;" and then with an archness peculiar to his character, putting the glass to his blind eye, he exclaimed, "I really do not see the signal."[1] This remarkable

[1] It seems quite possible that the importance of this incident is commonly exaggerated. There is reason to believe that the signal was hoisted by Sir Hyde Parker, in accordance with a private understanding with Lord Nelson that it was to be considered optional; that Foley was in the secret; and that Nelson's pantomime was merely a little joke, or playing to the gallery, which, it must be

signal was, therefore, only acknowledged on board the Elephant, not repeated. Admiral Graves did the latter, not being able to distinguish the Elephant's conduct : either by a fortunate accident, or intentionally, No. 16 was not displaced. The squadron of frigates obeyed the signal, and hauled off. That brave officer, Captain Riou, was killed by a raking shot when the Amazon showed her stern to the Trekroner. . . .

'The action now continued with unabated vigour. About 2 P.M. the greater part of the Danish line had ceased to fire : some of the lighter ships were adrift, and the carnage on board of the enemy, who reinforced their crews from the shore, was dreadful. The taking possession of such ships as had struck was, however, attended with difficulty ; partly by reason of the batteries on Amager Island protecting them, and partly because an irregular fire was made on our boats as they approached, from the ships themselves. The Dannebrog acted in this manner, and fired at our boat, although that ship was not only on fire and had struck, but the commodore, Fischer, had removed his pennant, and had deserted her. A renewed attack on her by the Elephant and Glatton, for a quarter of an hour, not only completely silenced and disabled the Dannebrog, but by the use of grape, nearly killed every man who was in the praams ahead and astern of that unfortunate ship. On our smoke clearing away, the Dannebrog was found to be drifting in flames before the wind, spreading terror throughout the enemy's line. The usual lamentable scene then ensued ; and our boats rowed in every direction to save the crew, who were throwing themselves from her at every porthole ; few, however, were left unwounded in her after our last broadsides, or could be saved. She drifted to leeward, and about half-past three blew up.

'The time of half-past two brings me to a most important part of Lord Nelson's conduct on this day, and about which so much discussion has arisen ; his sending a flag of truce on shore. To the best of my recollection, the facts were as follow. After the Dannebrog was adrift, and had ceased to fire, the action was found to be over along the whole of the line astern of us, but not so with the ships ahead and with the Crown batteries. Whether from ignorance of the custom of war, or from confusion on board the prizes, our boats were, as before mentioned, repulsed from the ships themselves, or fired at from Amager Island. Lord Nelson naturally lost temper at this, and observed, "that he must either send on shore, and stop this irregular proceeding, or send in our fire-ships and burn them." He accordingly retired into the stern gallery, and wrote, with great despatch, that well-known letter to the Crown Prince, with the address, " To the brothers of Englishmen, the Danes."'

Lord Nelson has directions to spare Denmark, when no longer resisting ; but if the firing is continued on the part of Denmark, Lord Nelson will be obliged to set on fire all the floating batteries he has taken, without having the power of saving the brave Danes

---

admitted, he was sometimes guilty of. See *Recollections of the Life of the Rev. A. J. Scott* (1812), p. 70 ; and Ralfe's *Naval Biography*, vol. iv. p. 12.

who have defended them. Dated on board his Britannic Majesty's ship Elephant, Copenhagen Roads, 2 April, 1801.

NELSON AND BRONTE, Vice-Admiral,
under the Command of Admiral Sir Hyde Parker.

Col. Stewart's narrative.
'This letter was conveyed on shore through the contending fleets by Captain Sir Frederick Thesiger, who acted as his Lordship's aide-de-camp; and found the Prince near the sally-port, animating his people in a spirited manner. Whether we were actually firing at that time in the Elephant or not, I am unable to recollect; it could only have been partially, at such of the farthest ships as had not struck. The three ships ahead of us were, however, engaged; and from the superiority of the force opposed to them, it was by no means improbable that Lord Nelson's observing eye pointed out to him the expediency of a prudent conduct. Whether this suggested to him the policy of a flag of truce or not, two solid reasons were apparent, and were such as to justify the measure; viz., the necessity of stopping the irregular fire from the ships which had surrendered—and the singular opportunity that was thus given of sounding the feelings of an enemy who had reluctantly entered into the war, and who must feel the generosity of the first offer of amity coming from a conquering foe. If there were a third reason for the conduct of the noble admiral, and some of his own officers assert this, it was unnecessary that it should have been expressed; it was certainly not avowed, and will for ever remain a matter of conjecture. While the boat was absent, the animated fire of the ships ahead of us, and the approach of two of the commander-in-chief's division, the Ramillies and Defence, caused the remainder of the enemy's line to the eastward of the Trekroner to strike; that formidable work continued its fire, but fortunately at too long a range to do serious damage to anyone except the Monarch, whose loss in men, this day, exceeded that of any line-of-battle ship during the war. From the uninjured state of this outwork, which had been manned at the close of the action with nearly 1,500 men, it was deemed impracticable to carry into execution the projected plan for storming it; the boats for this service had been on the starboard side of each ship during the action. The firing from the Crown battery and from our leading ships did not cease until past three o'clock, when the Danish adjutant-general, Lindholm, returning with a flag of truce, directed the fire of the battery to be suspended. The signal for doing the same on our part was then made from our ship to those engaged. The action closed after five hours' duration, four of which were warmly contested.

'The answer from the Prince Regent was to inquire more minutely into the purport of the message. I should here observe, that previous to the boat's getting on board, Lord Nelson had taken the opinion of his valuable friends, Fremantle and Foley, the former of whom had been sent for from the Ganges, as to the practicability of advancing with the ships which were least damaged upon that part of the Danish line of defence yet uninjured. Their opinions were averse from it; and, on the other hand, decided in favour of removing our fleet, whilst the wind yet held fair, from their present intricate channel. Lord Nelson was now prepared how to act when Mr. Lindholm came on board, and the following answer was returned to the Crown Prince by Captain Sir Frederick Thesiger : '

Lord Nelson's object in sending on shore a flag of truce is humanity; he, therefore, consents that hostilities shall cease till Lord Nelson can take his prisoners out of the prizes, and he consents to land all the wounded Danes, and to burn or remove his prizes. Lord Nelson, with humble duty to his Royal Highness, begs leave to say, that he will ever esteem it the greatest victory he ever gained, if this flag of truce may be the happy forerunner of a lasting and happy union between my most gracious Sovereign and his Majesty the King of Denmark.

'His Lordship, having finished this letter, referred the adjutant-general to the commander-in-chief, who was at anchor at least four miles off, for a conference on the important points which the latter part of the message had alluded to; and to this General Lindholm did not object, but proceeded to the London. (Col. Stewart's narrative.)

'Lindholm returned to Copenhagen the same evening, when it was agreed that all prizes should be surrendered, and the suspension of hostilities continue for twenty-four hours; the whole of the Danish wounded were to be received on shore. Lord Nelson then repaired on board the St. George, and the night was actively passed by the boats of the division which had not been engaged, in getting afloat the ships that were ashore and in bringing out the prizes.'

ABSTRACT OF ENGLISH LOSS.

Killed.—Officers	20	
Seamen, marines, and soldiers	234	
		254
Wounded.—Officers	48	
Seamen, marines, and soldiers	641	
		689
Total killed and wounded		943

The official account of the battle, transmitted to his Royal Highness the Crown Prince by the Danish commander-in-chief, Olfert Fischer, is interesting not only in itself, but by reason of the correspondence between Lord Nelson and the Danish adjutant-general Lindholm, to which it gave rise.

'On 1 April, at 3.30 P.M., two divisions of the English fleet, under the command of Vice-Admiral Lord Nelson and a rear-admiral, weighed anchor, and stood eastwards and by south of the Middle Passage of the Road, where they anchored. This force consisted of twelve ships of the line, and several large frigates, gunboats, and other smaller vessels, in all thirty-one sail. (Commodore Fischer's Despatch.[1])

'On 2 April, at 9.45 A.M., the wind SE, both the vessels to the south and the vessels to the north of the Middle Road weighed anchor. The ships of the line and heavy frigates under Lord Nelson steered for

[1] The original is in 'Danske og Norske Sö-Heltes Bedrivter fra Aar 1797 til 1813,' ved J. P. With.

the King's Deep, to take their station in order along the line of defence confided to me. The gunboats and smaller vessels took their station nearer to the town; and the division of Admiral Parker, consisting of eight ships of the line and some small vessels, steered with a press of sail southwards to the right wing of defence. At 10.30 the foremost ships of Admiral Nelson's division passed the southernmost ships of the line of defence. I gave those ships that were within shot the signal for battle. The block ships Prövesteen and Vagrien, and immediately after these the Jylland, between which and the block ship Dannebrog the leading English ship (of 74 guns) fixed her station by throwing out one of her rear anchors, obeyed the signal by a well-directed and well-supported fire. By degrees the rest of the ships came up, and as they sailed past on both sides of the ships already at anchor, they formed a thick line, which, as it stretched northwards to the ship of the line, the Sjelland, engaged not more than two-thirds of the line of defence committed to me; while the Three Crowns battery, and the block ships Elephanten and Mars, with the frigate Hjelperen, did not come at all into the action. In half an hour the battle was general. Ten ships of the line, among which was one of 80 guns, the rest chiefly 74's, and from six to eight frigates, on the one side. On the other, seven block ships, of which only one of 74 guns; the rest of 64 and under, two frigates, and six small vessels. This was the respective strength of the two parties. The enemy had on the whole two ships to one, and the block ship Prövesteen had, besides a ship of the line and the rear-admiral, two frigates against her, by which she was raked the whole time, without being able to return a shot.

'If I only recapitulate historically what your Highness, and along with you a great portion of the citizens of Denmark and Europe, have seen, I may venture to call that an unequal combat, which was maintained and supported for four hours and a half with unexampled courage and effect, in which the fire of the superior force was so much weakened for an hour before the end of the battle, that several English ships, and particularly Lord Nelson's, were obliged to fire only single shots; that this hero himself, in the middle and very heat of the battle, sent a flag of truce on shore to propose a cessation of hostilities; if I add, that it was announced to me that two English ships of the line had struck, but being supported by the assistance of fresh ships, again hoisted their flags, I may, in such circumstances, be permitted to say, and I believe I may appeal to the enemy's own confession, that in this engagement Denmark's ancient naval reputation blazed forth with such incredible splendour, that I thank heaven all Europe are the witnesses of it. Yet the scale, if not equal, did not decline far to the disadvantage of Denmark. The ships that were first and most obstinately attacked, even surrounded by the enemy, the incomparable Prövesteen fought till almost all her guns were dismounted. But these vessels were obliged to give way to superior force, and the Danish fire ceased along the whole line from north to south.

'At 11.30 the Dannebrog, which lay alongside Admiral Nelson, was set on fire. I repaired with my flag on board the Holsteen, of the line belonging to the north wing. But the Dannebrog long kept her flag flying in spite of this disaster. At the end of the battle she had 270 men killed and wounded. At half-past two, the Holsteen was so shattered, and had so many killed and wounded, and so many guns dismounted, that I then caused the pennant to be hoisted, instead of my flag, and went on shore to the battery of the Three Crowns, from which I commanded the north wing, which was slightly engaged with the division of Admiral Parker, till about four o'clock, when I received orders from your Royal Highness to put an end to the engagement. Thus the quarter of the line of defence from the Three Crowns to the frigate Hjelperen was in the power of the enemy; and the Hjelperen thus finding herself alone, slipped her cables and steered to Stubben. The ship Elven, after she had received many shots in the hull, and had her masts and rigging shot away, and a great number killed and wounded, retreated within the Crowns. The gunboats Nyborg and Aggershuus, which last towed the former away when near sinking, ran ashore; and the Gerner floating battery, which had suffered much, together with the block ship Dannebrog, shortly after the battle blew up. Besides the visible loss the enemy have suffered, I am convinced their loss in killed and wounded is considerable. The advantage the enemy have gained by their victory, too, consists merely in ships which are not fit for use, in spiked cannon, and gunpowder damaged by sea water. The number of killed and wounded cannot yet be exactly ascertained, but I calculate it from sixteen to eighteen hundred men.'

It was by your own desire that I trouble you with a letter, after having tried the contest afloat with Denmark. I shall not trouble you with a history of battles. Suffice it to say, as far as we could, we have, by the blessing of God, been completely victorious. Circumstances threw me in the way of communicating with the Prince Royal of Denmark, and it has led to some messages passing between the shore and Sir Hyde Parker. I own I did not build much hopes on the success of negotiation, as it appears clearly to me that Denmark would at this moment renounce all her alliances to be friends with us, if fear was not the preponderating consideration. Sir Hyde Parker thought that probably some good might arise if I went on shore to converse with his Royal Highness; I therefore went yesterday noon, dined in the Palace, and, after dinner, had a conversation of two hours alone with the Prince (that is, no minister was present), only his adjutant-general, Lindholm, was in the room.

H. Addington, 4 April.

His Royal Highness began the conversation by saying how happy he was to see me, and thanked me for my humanity to the wounded Danes. I then said it was to me, and would be the greatest affliction to every man in England, from the king to the lowest person, to think that Denmark had fired on the British flag, and became leagued with her enemies. His Royal Highness stopped me by saying, that Admiral Parker had declared war against Denmark. This I denied, and requested his Royal Highness to send for the papers, and he would find the direct contrary, and that it was the furthest from the thoughts of the British admiral. I then asked if his Royal Highness would permit me to speak my mind freely on the present situation of Denmark, to which he having acquiesced, I stated to him the sensation which was caused in England by such an unnatural alliance with, at the present moment, the furious enemy of England. His answer was, that when he made the alliance, it was for the protection of their trade, and that Denmark would never be the enemy of England, and that the Emperor of Russia was not the enemy of England when this treaty was formed; that he never would join Russia against England, and his declaration to that effect was the cause of the emperor (I think he said) sending away his minister; that Denmark was a trading nation, and had only to look to the protection of its lawful commerce. His Royal Highness then enlarged on the impossibility of Danish ships under convoy having on board any contraband trade; but to be subjected to be stopped—even a Danish fleet by a pitiful privateer, and that she should search all the ships, and take out of the fleet any vessels she might please—was what Denmark would not permit. To this my answer was simply, 'What occasion for convoy to fair trade?' To which he answered, 'Did you find anything in the convoy of the Freya?' [I said] 'That no commander could tell what contraband goods might be in his convoy, &c. &c.; and as to merchants, they would always sell what was most saleable; that as to swearing to property, I would get anything sworn to which I pleased.' I then said, 'Suppose that England, which she never will, was to consent to this freedom and nonsense of navigation, I will tell your Royal Highness what the result would be—ruination to Denmark; for the present commerce of Denmark with the warring powers was half the neutral carrying trade, and any merchant in Copenhagen would tell you the same. If all this freedom was allowed, Denmark would not have more than the sixth part; for the State of Hamburg was as good as the State of Denmark in that case; and it would soon be said, we will not be stopped in the Sound—our flag is our protection; and Denmark would lose a great source of her present revenue, and the Baltic would soon change its name to the Russian Sea.' He said this was a delicate subject; to which I replied that his Royal Highness had permitted me to speak out. He then said, 'Pray answer me a question; for what is the British fleet come into the Baltic?' My answer—'To crush a most formidable and unprovoked coalition against Great Britain.' He then went on to say that his uncle [King George] had been deceived;

that it was a misunderstanding, and that nothing should ever make him take a part against Great Britain; for that it could not be his interest to see us crushed, nor, he trusted, ours to see him: to which I acquiesced. I then said there could not be a doubt of the hostility of Denmark; for if her fleet had been joined with Russia and Sweden, they would assuredly have gone into the North Sea, menaced the coast of England, and probably have joined the French, if they had been able. His Royal Highness said his ships never should join any Power against England; but it required not much argument to satisfy him that he could not help it.

In speaking of the pretended union of the northern Powers, I could not help saying that his Royal Highness must be sensible that it was nonsense to talk of a mutual protection of trade, with a Power who had none, and that he must be sensible that the Emperor of Russia would never have thought of offering to protect the trade of Denmark, if he had not had hostility against Great Britain. He said repeatedly, "I have offered to-day, and do offer my mediation between Great Britain and Russia.' My answer was, ' A mediator must be at peace with both parties. You must settle your matter with Great Britain. At present you are leagued with our enemies, and are considered naturally as a part of the effective force to fight us.'

Talking much on this subject, his Royal Highness said, ' What must I do to make myself equal?' Answer—' Sign an alliance with Great Britain, and join your fleet to ours.' His Royal Highness—' Then Russia will go to war with us; and my desire, as a commercial nation, is to be at peace with all the world.' I told him he knew the offer of Great Britain, either to join us, or disarm. ' I pray, Lord Nelson, what do you call disarming?' My answer was, ' That I was not authorised to give an opinion on the subject, but I considered it as not having on foot any force beyond the customary establishment.' Question—' Do you consider the guardships in the Sound as beyond that common establishment?' Answer—' I do not.' Question—' We have always had five sail of the line in the Cattegat and coast of Norway.' Answer—' I am not authorised to define what is exactly disarming, but I do not think such a force will be allowed.' His Royal Highness—' When all Europe is in such a dreadful state of confusion it is absolutely necessary that States should be on their guard.' Answer—' Your Royal Highness knows the offers of England to keep twenty sail of the line in the Baltic.' He then said, ' I am sure my intentions are very much misunderstood;' to which I replied, that Sir Hyde Parker had authorised me to say, that upon certain conditions his

Royal Highness might have an opportunity of explaining his sentiments at the Court of London—'I am not authorised to say on what conditions exactly.' Question—'But what do you think?' Answer—'First, a free entry of the British fleet into Copenhagen, and the free use of everything we may want from it.' Before I could get on, he replied quick, 'That you shall have with pleasure.' 'The next is, whilst this explanation is going on, a total suspension of your treaties with Russia. These, I believe, are the foundation on which Sir Hyde Parker only can build other articles for his justification in suspending his orders, which are plain and positive.' His Royal Highness then desired me to repeat what I had said, which having done, he thanked me for my open conversation; and I having made an apology if I had said anything which he might think too strong, his Royal Highness very handsomely did the same, and we parted; he saying that he hoped we would cease from hostilities to-morrow, as on such an important occasion he must call a Council. My reception was such as I have always found it—far beyond my deserts.

I saw Count Bernstoff[1] for a moment, and could not help saying he had acted a very wrong part in my opinion, in involving the two countries in their present melancholy situation, for that our countries ought never to quarrel. I had not time to say more, as the prince sent for me, and Count Bernstoff was called the moment I came out of the room. The king's brother and his son desired I might be presented to them, which I was, and then returned on board. Yesterday evening I received from General Adjutant Lindholm the English papers to 24 March, with a hope that what I had said to the prince would make peace. I find all the country hate both the Russians and Swedes.

Lord St. Vincent, (?) 5 April. Whether Sir Hyde Parker may mention the subject to you I know not, for he is rich, and does not want it. Nor is it, you will believe me, from any desire I possess to get a few hundred pounds, that actuates me to address this letter to you; but, my dear Lord, justice to the brave officers and men who fought on that day. It is true, our opponents were in hulks and floats only adapted for the position they were placed in; but that made our battle so much the harder, and victory so much the more difficult to obtain. Believe me, I have weighed all circumstances, and in my conscience I think that the king should send a gracious message to the House of Commons, for a gift to this fleet: for what must be the natural feelings of the officers and men belonging to it, to see their rich commander-

[1] Danish Minister for Foreign Affairs.

in-chief burn all the fruits of their victory, which, if fitted up and sent to England, as many of them might have been by dismantling part of our fleet, would have sold for a good round sum? Having mentioned the subject, I shall leave it to the better judgment of your Lordship and Mr. Addington.

On 9 April an armistice was agreed on, the stipulations of which were:
1. The immediate cessation of hostilities.
2. The Danish ships to 'remain in their present actual situation as to armament, equipment, and hostile position.' The 'Armed Neutrality,' so far as relates to Denmark, to be suspended. Sir Hyde Parker not to permit his ships to molest Danish territory or ships, or to approach in such a way as to cause uneasiness or jealousy.
3. This last clause to apply equally to any other English fleet.
4. Sir Hyde Parker's fleet to be permitted to provide itself at Copenhagen and elsewhere in Danish territory 'with everything which it may require for the health and comfort of the crews.'
5. The Danish prisoners to be landed, and a receipt to be given for them and the wounded which were landed after the action of the 2nd.
6. The Danish coasting trade not to be molested.
7. The armistice to continue for fourteen weeks.

A negotiator is certainly out of my line, but being thrown into it, I have endeavoured to acquit myself as well as I was able, and in such a manner as I hope will not entirely merit your disapprobation. If it unfortunately does, I have only to request that I may now be permitted to retire, which my state of health, and inconvenience from the loss of my limb has long rendered necessary. I trust you will take into consideration all the circumstances which have presented themselves to my view. 1st. We had beat the Danes. 2nd. We wish to make them feel that we are their real friends, therefore have spared their town, which we can always set on fire; and I do not think, if we burnt Copenhagen it would have the effect of attaching them to us; on the contrary, they would hate us. 3rd. They understand perfectly that we are at war with them for their treaty of armed neutrality made last year. 4th. We have made them suspend the operations of that treaty. 5th. It has given our fleet free scope to act against Russia and Sweden; 6th, which we never should have done, although Copenhagen would have been burnt, for Sir Hyde Parker was determined not to have Denmark hostile in his rear. Our passage over the Grounds might have been very seriously interrupted by the batteries near Dragör. 7th. Every reinforcement, even a cutter, can join us without molestation, and also provisions, stores, &c. 8th. Great Britain is left with the stake of all the Danish property in her hands, her colonies,

H. Addington, 9 April.

&c., if she refuses peace. 9th. The hands of Denmark are tied up; ours are free to act against her confederate allies. 10th. Although we might have burnt the city, I have my doubts whether we could their ships, [which lie moored in a single line in rear of a range of empty store-houses, and at a distance of at least 2,800 yards from our bombs]; therefore our shells have only the width of a line-of-battle ship, and every ship must be separately burnt, for they have plenty of room to haul any ship on fire clear of the others. All these considerations weighed deeply in my mind; added to which, having shown them that it was not because we feared fighting them that we negotiated, but for the cause of humanity towards Denmark, and the wish to conciliate their affections; all these matters have affected my mind, nor shall I have a moment's rest, till I know, at least, that I am not thought to have done mischief. After we had forced the expression of the suspension of the treaty of armed neutrality, a point very difficult for fear of Russia, I said to the prince, 'Now, Sir, this is settled, suppose we write peace instead of armistice?' to which he replied, that he should be happy to have a peace, but he must bring it about slowly, so as not to make new wars. We talked whether some method could not be thought of, to prevent the mortifications to which ships of war with convoys were liable, by being stopped; to which I answered, I thought there might very easily. I did not enter further on the subject with him, although I did to his adjutant-general of the fleet, Lindholm, who seems much in his confidence. My idea is, that no convoys shall be granted to any vessels bound to ports at war with us; and that if any such convoy is granted, that it shall be considered as an act of hostility; and that if any vessel under convoy proceeds to an enemy of England's port, that the owner shall lose the value of his ship and cargo, and the master be severely punished. On those foundations I would build a prevention against future disputes; but all these matters I leave to wiser heads. . . .

I have the pleasure to tell you that Count Bernstoff was too ill to make me a visit yesterday. I had sent him a message to leave off his ministerial duplicity, and to recollect he had now British admirals to deal with, who came with their hearts in their hands. I hate the fellow.

Colonel Stewart, a very fine gallant man, will give you every information.

General Lindholm, 22 April.

My dear Sir,—Commodore Fischer having, in a public letter, given an account to the world of the battle of the 2nd, and called upon his Royal Highness as a witness to the truth of it, I therefore think it right to address myself to you, for the information of his Royal Highness, as, I assure you, had this officer confined himself to his own veracity, I should have treated his official letter with the contempt it deserved, and allowed the world to appreciate the merits of the two contending officers. I shall make a few, and very few, observations on his letter. He asserts the superiority of numbers on the part of the British; it will turn out, if that is of any consequence, that the Danish line of defence, to the southward of the Crown Islands, was much stronger, and more numerous, than the British. We had only five sail of 74's, two 64's, two 50's, and one frigate engaged; a bomb-vessel towards the latter end threw some shells into the arsenal. Two 74's and one 64, by an accident, grounded; or the Crown Islands and the Elephant and Mars would have had full employment, and, by the assistance of the frigates, who went to try alone what I had directed the three sail of the line that grounded to assist them in, I have reason to hope they would have been equally successful as that part of the British line engaged.

I am ready to admit that many of the Danish officers and men behaved as well as men could do, and deserved not to be abandoned by their commander. I am justified in saying this, from Commodore Fischer's own declaration. In his letter he states that, after he quitted the Dannebrog, she long contested the battle. If so, more shame for him to quit so many brave fellows. Here was no manœuvring: it was downright fighting, and it was his duty to have shown an example of firmness becoming the high trust reposed in him. He went in such a hurry, if he went before she struck, which but for his own declaration I can hardly believe, that he forgot to take his broad pennant with him; for both pennant and ensign were struck together, and it is from this circumstance that I claimed the commodore as a prisoner of war. He then went, as he said, on board the Holsteen, the brave captain of which did not want him, where he did not hoist his pennant. From this ship he went on shore, either before or after she struck, or he would have been again a prisoner. As to his nonsense about victory, his Royal Highness will not much credit him. I sunk, burnt, captured, or drove into the harbour the whole line of defence to the southward of the Crown Islands.

He says he is told that two British ships struck. Why did he not take possession of them? I took possession of his as fast as they struck. The reason is clear—that he did not believe it. He must have known the falsity of the report, and that no fresh British ships did come near the ships engaged. He states, that the ship in which I had the honour to hoist my flag fired latterly only single guns. It is true; for steady and cool were my brave fellows, and did not wish to throw away a single shot. He seems to exult that I sent on shore a flag of truce. Men of his description, if they ever are victorious, know not the feeling of humanity. You know, and his Royal Highness knows, that the guns fired from the shore could only fire through the Danish ships, which had surrendered, and that if I fired at the shore it could only be in the same manner. God forbid I should destroy a non-resisting Dane! When they became my prisoners, I became their protector. Humanity alone could have been my object, but Mr. Fischer's carcase was safe, and he regarded not the sacred call of humanity. His Royal Highness thought as I did. It has brought about an armistice, which, I pray the Almighty, may bring about a happy reconciliation between the two kingdoms. As I have not the names of all the ships correct, only of the thirteen, including the seven sail of the line which struck, remained at anchor, and fell into my possession after the battle, I shall therefore be very much obliged to you for a correct list of their names, and the number of men, if possible to be obtained, on board each, and the numbers sent from the shore during the action; my earnest wish is to be correct; and believe me, dear Sir, with great esteem, your most obedient servant,

NELSON AND BRONTE.

To this letter, Adjutant-General Lindholm replied on 2 May:

'My Lord,—Your Lordship has imposed upon me a very painful task, by desiring me to communicate to his Royal Highness the Crown Prince the contents of that letter with which your Lordship has favoured me on 22 April, and in which you have treated Commodore Fischer with a severity which, as a brother officer, I cannot but think too great indeed. I conceive that your Lordship has felt a certain degree of displeasure at that incorrectness which you have thought to find in Commodore Fischer's official report, but your Lordship did not fully consider at that moment, that he himself might have received [an] incorrect report, a fatality to which every commander-in-chief is exposed. I flatter myself, from your Lordship's well-known candour and indulgence, that you will not think it presuming in me, or contrary to the respect I feel for your Lordship, if I take the opportunity of offering you some few observations, in vindication of the conduct of Commodore Fischer. But, first, let me have the honour to assure your Lordship, that I have not communicated to that officer your letter of 22 April, and that what I take the liberty of offering your Lordship is absolutely my private and individual opinion.

'Your Lordship thinks that Commodore Fischer has overrated the forces by which he was attacked, and underrated his own ; or that he wrongly asserts the superiority of numbers on the part of the British. I must confess that I am now, as I have always been, of opinion, that the squadron with which your Lordship attacked our southern line of defence, say all those ships and vessels lying to the southward of the Crown battery, was stronger than that line. I will say nothing about our not having had time sufficient to man our ships in the manner it was intended, they being badly manned, both as to number and as to quality of their crews, the greatest part of which were landsmen, people that had been pressed, and who never before had been on board a ship, or used to the exercise of guns. I will not mention our ships being old and rotten, and not having one-third of their usual complement of officers. I will confine myself to the number of guns, and from the ships named in your Lordship's official report, and there I find that your squadron carried 1,058 guns, of much greater calibre than ours, exclusive of carronades (which did our ships so much injury), also exclusive of your gun-brigs and bomb-vessels.

'Now, I can assure your Lordship, upon my honour, that to my certain knowledge the number of guns on board of those eighteen ships and vessels of ours which were engaged (including the small ship, the Elbe, which came into the harbour towards the end of the action), amount to 634. I have not included our eleven gunboats, carrying each two guns, as a couple of them had only an opportunity of firing a few shot. Nor need I to mention the Crown battery, on which sixty-six guns were mounted, as that battery did not fairly get into action, and only fired a few random shot. When Commodore Fischer left the Dannebrog, that ship was on fire, had many killed, several of its officers wounded, and others suffered much. It was, I conceive, the duty of the commander to remove his broad pennant to another ship, and he went on board the Holsteen, from whence he commanded the line of defence, and where he remained two hours, his broad pennant flying on board the said ship. When this ship was mostly disabled, the commodore went to the Crown battery, which also was under his command. He would, in my humble opinion, have been justified, from the wound he received on his head, to quit the command altogether when he left the Dannebrog, and no blame could ever have attached for it to his character as a soldier. I have given myself every possible pains to be informed whether Commodore Fischer's pennant had been removed before or after the ship struck, and the officers all agree in declaring, that the broad pennant had been replaced by a captain's pennant, both on board the Dannebrog and the Holsteen, previous to those ships hauling down their ensign. It is even remarkable that on board the Dannebrog, the man who had taken down the broad pennant, and hoisted the captain's pennant, was killed when coming down the shrouds, and fell upon deck with the commodore's pennant in his hand.

'I do not conceive that Commodore Fischer had the least idea of claiming as a victory, what, to every intent and purpose, was a defeat. He has only thought that this defeat was not an inglorious one, and that our officers and men displayed much bravery and firmness, against force so superior in every respect. Your Lordship's report, and your letter to me, prove it. I confess that your Lordship took all the vessels opposed to you, except five, carrying together eighty-six guns. I am of opinion, with your Lordship, that three ships of seventy-four guns each would have been a hard match for the Three Crowns battery, but they certainly would have been forced to go away. As to your Lordship's motives for sending a flag of truce to our Government, it can never be misconstrued, and your subsequent conduct has sufficiently shown that humanity is always the companion of true valour. You have done more; you have shown yourself a friend of the re-establishment of peace and good harmony between this country and Great Britain. It is therefore with the sincerest esteem I shall always feel myself attached to your Lordship, and it is with the greatest respect I have the honour to subscribe myself, my Lord, your Lordship's most obedient and most humble servant, H. LINDHOLM.'

General Lindholm, 3 May.

My dear Sir,—I was yesterday evening favoured with your reply to my letter of 22 April, and I have no scruple in assuring you, that if Commodore Fischer's letter had been couched in the same manly and honourable manner, that I should have been the last man to have noticed any little inaccuracies which might get into a commander-in-chief's public letter; and if the commodore had not called upon his Royal Highness for the truth of his assertions, I never should have noticed his letter. You have stated truly the force which would have been brought into action, but for the accidents of their getting aground, and, except the Désirée frigate, no other frigate or sloop fired a gun to the southward of the Crown Islands. I have done ample justice to the bravery of nearly all your officers and men; and as it is not my intention to hurt your feelings or those of his Royal Highness, but on the contrary, to try and merit your esteem, I will only say, that I am confident you would not have wrote such a letter. Nothing, I flatter myself, in my conduct ought to have drawn ridicule on my character from the commodore's pen; and you have borne the handsomest testimony of it, in contradiction to his. I thought then, as I did before the action and do now, that it is not the interest of our countries to injure each other. I am sorry that I was forced to write you so unpleasant a letter; but for the future I trust that none but pleasant ones will pass between us, for I assure you that I hope to merit the continuation of your esteem, and of having frequent opportunities of assuring you how I feel interested in being your sincere and faithful friend, NELSON AND BRONTE.

A. Davison, 23 April.

You will, at a proper time, and before my arrival in England, signify to Lady N. that I expect, and for which I have made such a very liberal allowance to her, to be left to myself, and without any inquiries from her; for sooner than live the unhappy life I did when last I came to England, I would stay abroad for ever. My mind is fixed as fate: therefore you will send my determination in any way you may judge proper.

On 5 May despatches arrived, dated 21 April, appointing Lord Nelson successor to Sir Hyde Parker, as commander-in-chief. According to Colonel Stewart's narrative: 'The first signal which Lord Nelson made, as commander-in-chief, was to hoist in all launches and prepare to weigh. This at once showed how different a system was about to be pursued; it having been intended that the fleet should await at anchor fresh instructions from England relative to the state of the northern affairs, an account of which had but lately been despatched. Lord Nelson, who foresaw every bad consequence from this inactive mode of proceeding, owed his bad health more to chagrin than to any other cause. The joy with which the signal was received not only manifested what are the customary feelings on those occasions, but was intended as peculiarly complimentary to the admiral. On 7 May, 1801, the fleet left Kjöge Bay, and, proceeding towards Bornholm, anchored, in blowing weather, off that island. The greater part was here left to watch the motions of the Swedes; and with a chosen squadron, consisting of his ten best sailing seventy-fours, two frigates, a brig, and a schooner, Lord Nelson sailed for the port of Revel.

A command never was, I believe, more unwelcomely received by any person than by myself. It may be at the expense of my life; and therefore, for God's sake, at least for mine, try if I cannot be relieved. The time was, a few months ago, that I should have felt the honour, and I really believe that I should have seen more of the Baltic, the consequence of which I can guess. But nothing, I believe, but change of climate can cure me, and having my mind tranquil. *A. Davison, 5 May.*

I am sorry that the armistice is only approved under *all* considerations. Now I own myself of opinion that every part of the *all* was to the advantage of our king and country. I stated many of my reasons for thinking it advantageous. We knew not of the death of Paul,[1] or a change of sentiments in the Court of Prussia, if her sentiments are changed. My object was to get at Revel before the frost broke up at Cronstadt, that the twelve sail of the line might be destroyed. I shall now go there as a friend, but the two fleets shall not form a junction, if not already accomplished, unless my orders permit it. My health is gone, and although I should be happy to try and hold out a month or six weeks longer, yet death is no respecter of persons. I own, at present, I should not wish to die a natural death. *H. Addington, 5 May.*

I have thought it right to address a letter to the Swedish

[1] On 24 March, 1801.

E. Nepean,
7 May. Off
Falsterholm.

admiral in respectful terms, signifying my wish, that the Swedish fleet would not come to sea, as I should be sorry, out of respect to the Emperor of Russia, to see hostilities committed, which must be the case if they put to sea. . . . With eleven sail of the line, a frigate, and two sloops, it is my intention to show myself in the Gulf of Finland; but in such a manner as I trust will be taken as a compliment by the Emperor of Russia, and at the same time with the precaution, that if the whole empire of Russia was hostile to us, their Lordships may be perfectly at ease for the safety of the squadron, in spite of all the power of Russia.

H. Addington, 8 May.

So much having been said, both by friends and enemies, why I sent on shore a flag of truce on 2 April, and but few seemed pleased with the armistice, I take the liberty of sending the reasons why I sent the flag of truce, and also my reasons why I think the armistice was a proper measure.

As both my friends and enemies seem not to know why I sent on shore a flag of truce—the former, many of them, thought it was a *ruse de guerre*, and not quite justifiable; the latter, I believe, attributed it to a desire to have no more fighting, and few, very few, to the cause that I felt, and which I trust in God I shall retain to the last moment, *humanity*. I know it must to the world be proved, and therefore I will suppose you all the world to me. First, no ship was on shore near the Crown batteries, or anywhere else, within reach of any shore, when my flag of truce went on shore. The Crown batteries, and the batteries on Amager and in the dockyard, were firing at us, one-half their shot necessarily striking the ships who had surrendered, and our fire did the same, and worse, for the surrendered ships had four of them got close together, and it was a massacre. This caused my note. It was a sight which no real man could have enjoyed. I felt when the Danes became my prisoners, I became their protector; and if that had not been a sufficient reason, the moment of a complete victory was surely the proper time to make an opening with the nation we had been fighting with.

When the truce was settled, and full possession taken of our prizes, the ships were ordered, except two, to proceed and join Sir Hyde Parker, and in performing this service, the Elephant and Defiance grounded on the Middle Ground. I give you, verbatim, an answer to a part of a letter from a person high in rank [1] about the Prince Royal, which will bear testimony to the truth of my

[1] Adjutant-General Lindholm. See *ante*, p. 270.

assertions: 'As to your Lordship's motives for sending a flag of truce to our government, it never can be misconstrued; and your subsequent conduct has sufficiently shown that humanity is always the companion of true valour. You have done more. You have shown yourself a friend of the re-establishment of peace and good harmony between this country and Great Britain.'

On the Armistice.—Much having been said relative to the bad terms of the armistice made with Denmark, I wish to observe, first, that the armistice was only intended [to be] a military one, and that all political subjects were left for the discussion of the ministers of the two powers. Peace, Denmark could not in the moment make with you, as the moment she made it with you, she would lose all her possessions except the Island of Zealand, and that also, the moment the frost set in; therefore there was no damage we could do her equal to the loss of everything. Our destruction would have been Copenhagen and her fleet; then we had done our worst, and not much nearer being friends. By the armistice we tied the arms of Denmark for four months from assisting our enemies and her allies, whilst we had every part of Denmark and its provinces open to give us everything we wanted. Great Britain was left the power of taking Danish possessions and ships in all parts of the world, whilst we had locked up the Danish navy, and put the key in our pocket; time was afforded the two countries to arrange matters on an amicable footing; besides, to say the truth, I look upon the Northern League to be like a tree, of which Paul was the trunk, and Sweden and Denmark the branches. If I can get at the trunk, and hew it down, the branches fall of course; but I may lop the branches, and yet not be able to fell the tree, and my power must be weaker when its greatest strength is required. If we could have cut up the Russian fleet, that was my object. Denmark and Sweden deserved whipping, but Paul deserved punishment. I own I consider it as a wise measure, and I wish my reputation to stand upon its merits.

It is my intention to send into Carlscrona a letter to the Swedish admiral; for, under present circumstances, it would be unpleasant to have a battle with the Swedes; therefore, if anything happens after the receipt of my letter, the blame will rest with them. *(Lord Carysfort,[1] 8 May.)*

The late commander-in-chief of the British fleet in the Baltic having, by request of the Emperor of Russia, allowed the Swedish trade in the Baltic to pass unmolested, I should be sorry that any *(The Swedish Admiral, 8 May.)*

[1] Envoy Extraordinary to the King of Prussia.

event could happen which might disturb for a moment the returning amity (I hope) between Sweden and Great Britain. I beg leave, therefore, to apprise your Excellency, that I have no orders to abstain from hostilities, should I meet the Swedish fleet at sea, which, as it lies in your power to prevent, I am sure you must take this communication as the most friendly proceeding on my part, and communicate it to your august Sovereign.

Count Pahlen, 9 May.

I am happy in this opportunity of assuring your Excellency, that my orders towards Russia from England are of the most pacific and friendly nature; and I have to request, that you will assure his Imperial Majesty, that my inclination so perfectly accords with my orders, that I had determined to show myself with a squadron in the Bay of Reval (or at Cronstadt, if the Emperor would rather wish me to go there), to mark the friendship which, I trust in God, will ever subsist between our two gracious Sovereigns; and it will likewise be of great service in assisting to navigate to England many of the English merchant-vessels who have remained all the winter in Russia. I have taken care in the squadron which I bring up with me, that there shall be neither bomb-ship, fire-ship, nor any of the flotilla, in order to mark the more strongly, that I wish it to be considered as a mark of the greatest personal respect to his Imperial Majesty.

N. Vansittart, 12 May. Gulf of Finland.

I feel, I assure you, most infinitely obliged by your truly kind and satisfactory letter of 8 April, for I know from experience how difficult it is for an officer to have his feelings properly represented at home. You did me full justice that I wanted to get at an enemy as soon as possible to strike a home stroke, and that Paul was the enemy most vulnerable, and of the greatest consequence for us to humble. On 2 April we could have been at Reval, and I know nothing at present which could have prevented our destroying the whole Russian force at that port. It would have brought, if not Paul to his senses, yet most probably both Sweden and Denmark; but mankind form opinions on what has happened, and seldom do that justice which both you and Mr. Addington did to my opinion, formed on the information and circumstances before me. The difficulty was to get our commander-in-chief to either go past Kronborg or through the Belt; because, what Sir Hyde thought best, and what I believe was settled before I came on board the London, was to stay in the Cattegat, and there wait the time when the whole naval force of the Baltic might choose to come out and fight—a measure, in my opinion, disgraceful to our country. I can only again repeat how much I feel your goodness in explaining the motives which actuated my conduct.

I hope another admiral is on his way to supersede me; for why am I to be kept here to die a natural death? I did not bargain for that when I came to the Baltic. It is now sixteen days that I have not been able to get out of my cabin; and Admiral Graves has been as many in bed. The country may do very well to fight a battle, but no man of common sense would remain; but, fight or not fight, as they please, I stay no longer than I get down, which I hope will be by 1 June, if I live so long. In forty-eight hours I shall have formed my opinion of the future plans of Alexander towards us; and I hope our ministry, from the papers I shall send them of my reception and treatment, will be fully equal to decide every [thing] which the Russian ministry intend doing in the present state of affairs.

<small>A. Davison, 12 May.</small>

I shall confine myself to what we clearly could have done with our Baltic fleet, such as it was after the conclusion of the armistice with Denmark. I shall not say more of the Swedes, than as we saw their force at Carlscrona, where they had wisely retired when they saw our frigates in the Baltic. On 19 April we had eighteen sail of the line and a fair wind. . . . The Russian fleet here was, I decidedly say, at our mercy. Nothing, if it had been right to make the attack, could have saved one ship of them in two hours after our entering the bay. . . . On Wednesday, 29 April, the Bay of Reval was clear of firm ice; and, on that day, the ice in the mole, about six feet thick, was cut, and three sail of the line got out, and moored on the eastern side of the bay, absolutely unprotected except by a battery of six guns. By the Sunday they were all out, fourteen sail of ships; but I am not certain yet whether the fleet was ten, eleven, or twelve ships of the line—two were three-decked ships; they sailed for Cronstadt the same day. I hope you will approve of our coming here; we now know the navigation, should circumstances call us here again.

<small>Lord St. Vincent, 16 May. Reval Bay.</small>

On 16 May Lord Nelson received a letter from Count Pahlen, dated 2-14 May, which, referring to Nelson's supposed intention of coming off Reval or Cronstadt with his whole fleet, went on to say : 'The Emperor, my master, does not consider such a step consistent with the desire professed by his Britannic Majesty of re-establishing the good feeling which has so long existed between the two monarchies. His Imperial Majesty thinks it, on the contrary, utterly opposed to the spirit of the instructions of the Court of London, as represented to him by Lord Hawkesbury. His Majesty has consequently ordered me to

acquaint you that the only guarantee of the loyalty of your intentions which he can accept, is the immediate withdrawal of your fleet; and that all negotiation with your court is impossible as long as a naval force is in sight of his ports. . . . His Majesty will have pleasure in yielding to such just demands as your king shall put forward in friendly negotiation; but anything which would give to these demands the appearance of conditions can only lead to the failure of the proposed result.' And much more to the same purport.

It was to this letter that Nelson answered:

Count Pahlen, 16 May.

I am this moment honoured with your Excellency's letter; and I only beg leave to refer you again to my letter of 9 May. You will there see, that not one seventh part of the fleet in point of numbers were coming into the Gulf of Finland; and that, as my intention was to pay a very particular respect to his Imperial Majesty, I submitted it to his pleasure which port he would wish me to come to, Reval or Cronstadt. Your Excellency will have the goodness to observe to the Emperor, that I did not even enter into the outer Bay of Reval without the consent of their excellencies the governor and admiral. My conduct, I feel, is so entirely different to what your Excellency has expressed in your letter, that I have only to regret that my desire to pay a marked attention to his Imperial Majesty has been so entirely misunderstood. That being the case, I shall sail immediately into the Baltic.

Lord St. Vincent, 17 May.

The answer from Count Pahlen, with all my correspondence, is under cover to Mr. Nepean; after such an answer, I had no further business here. Has the Count any meaning in his gross falsehoods, or has it been an entire misunderstanding of my letter? Time will show; but I do not believe he would have written such a letter if the Russian fleet had been in Reval. A word for myself: since 27 April I have not been out of my cabin, except in being obliged to do the civil thing at Reval; nor do I expect to go out until I land in England, or am carried out of the ship. I therefore most earnestly hope that some worthy admiral will be arrived to command this fleet, which I can truly say is deserving of any officer; for more zeal and desire to distinguish themselves I never saw.

Col. Stewart's narrative.

'The keeping his fleet continually on the alert, and the amply furnishing it with fresh water and provisions, were the objects of Lord Nelson's unremitted care; and to this may in a great measure be ascribed the uniform good health and discipline which prevailed. Another point to which he gave nearly equal attention was his economy of the resources of his fleet in regard to stores; their consumption was as remarkable for its smallness in the Baltic as it was in the fleet that was afterwards under his command in the Mediterranean.

His hour of rising was four or five o'clock, and of going to rest about ten; breakfast was never later than six, and generally nearer to five o'clock. A midshipman or two were always of the party; and I have known him send during the middle watch to invite the little fellows to breakfast with him when relieved. At table with them he would enter into their boyish jokes, and be the most youthful of the party. At dinner he invariably had every officer of his ship in their turn, and was both a polite and hospitable host. The whole ordinary business of the fleet was invariably despatched, as it had been by Earl St. Vincent, before eight o'clock. The great command of time which Lord Nelson thus gave himself, and the alertness which this example imparted throughout the fleet, can only be understood by those who witnessed it or who know the value of early hours. The Russian frigate Venus, with Admiral Tchitchagoff on board, met us on our return to Bornholm; she had been in search of us, with the answer to some pacific overtures that had passed between Sir Hyde Parker and the Russian Government, and which was of the most friendly description. Lord St. Helens also met us in the Latona, on his way to Petersburg on a special mission. At Rostock not an hour was lost in procuring fresh provisions for the fleet. The greatest veneration was here shown to the name of Nelson; and some distant inland towns of Mecklenburg sent even deputations, with their public books of record, to have his name written in them by himself. Boats were constantly rowing round his flag-ship, the St. George, with persons of respectability in them, anxious to catch a sight of this illustrious man. He did not again land whilst in the Baltic; his health was not good, and his mind was not at ease: with him, mind and health invariably sympathised.'

I hope Lord St. Helens will arrange amicably our affairs with the northern powers; and as to France, if she dares to stir off her shores, I only wish our seamen to meet them half seas over. As to myself, I am knocked up, and only want to enjoy, during this negotiation, a little repose, to enable me, if better men will not come forth, to meet these northern blades. They do not want for courage, that is certain; but in the management of their fleet they would, I am [sure,] miserably fail; and two-thirds of their numbers must beat them, if we make use of the skill God Almighty has blessed us with.

William Beckford, 24 May. Rostock.

On the evening of 26 May, Nelson received a letter from Count Pahlen, dated 6-18 May:

'Mylord,—Je ne saurais donner à votre Excellence un témoignage plus éclatant de la confiance que l'Empereur, mon maître, lui accorde qu'en lui annonçant l'effet qu'a produit sa lettre du 16 de ce mois. Sa Majesté Impériale a ordonné sur le champ la levée de l'embargo mis sur les navires anglais. Cette mesure aurait été remplie depuis longtemps si des circonstances antérieures à son règne n'eussent pas donné lieu à une démonstration hostile de votre gouvernement dans le nord, et mon auguste maître se livre avec plaisir à l'impulsion de son amour pour la justice dès l'instant où l'Europe ne peut plus être abusée par les apparences sur les motifs qui le font agir.

'Je regrette vivement, Mylord, que votre lettre précédente ait produit un mésentendu, mais celui qui connaît comme vous les loix de l'honneur et de la vraie dignité ne peut en être surpris. Sa Majesté Impériale me charge de mander à votre Excellence, qu'elle sera charmée de faire la connaissance personnelle du héros du Nil, et de vous voir à sa cour, si vos instructions vous permettent de quitter la flotte et d'aborder avec un seul vaisseau dans un de nos ports. J'ai l'honneur d'être, avec la plus haute considération, Mylord, de votre Excellence, le très humble et très obéissant serviteur, LE COMTE DE PAHLEN.'

To this he replied immediately, dating his letter ten o'clock at night :

Count Pahlen, 26 May.

I am this moment honoured with your Excellency's flattering letter of 6 May, O.S., and I assure you that his Imperial Majesty's justice has filled the idea I had formed of his excellent heart and head ; and I am sure the handsome manner in which the embargo has been taken off the British shipping will give the greatest pleasure to my good and gracious sovereign. I am truly sensible of the great honour done me by the invitation of his Imperial Majesty, and at a future time I hope to have the pleasure of presenting my humble duty. I have now only to pray, that a permanent (which must be honourable) peace may be established between our gracious sovereigns, and that our august masters' reigns may be blessed with every happiness which this world can afford.

H. Addington, 27 May.

I do not trouble you often with letters, as your time must be much more essentially employed than in reading any opinions of mine. As I send the facts themselves to the Admiralty, ministers can draw much better conclusions from them than a mere sea-officer ; but as it was the wish of Lord St. Helens for me to give my opinion, from what I had seen in Russia and my communication with them, I readily gave it—viz. The Emperor of Russia and his ministers wish for peace with us, but at the same time it is wished to hold up his character, therefore it is wished that he should have the appearance of arranging the peace of the North, and I am confident more would be given up by paying the Emperor that compliment than if we attempted to lay down the law ; and his Lordship was pleased to say that he should let the negotiation take that turn. Respecting privateers, I own I am decidedly of opinion that with very few exceptions they are a disgrace to our country; and it would be truly honourable never to permit one after this war. Such horrid robberies have been committed by them in all parts of the world, that it is really a disgrace to the country which tolerates them ; and the conduct of too many of our vice-admiralty courts has no wonder made neutral nations think of preventing such iniquitous proceedings. . . .

My complaint, I flatter myself, is better within these last two days; but we have lost so many of our finest young men by the disorder, and I know it is so deceitful, and no one will tell me anything of my disorder, that I only rely on Providence; I own I have no inclination to die a natural death at present.

My dear invaluable Friend,—Believe me, my heart entertains the very warmest affection for you, and it has been no fault of mine, and not a little mortification, that you have not the red ribbon and other rewards that would have kept you afloat, and not to have made you a commissioner; but as, I trust, the war is at a close, you must, like Lord Hood, take your flag when it comes to you, for who is to command our fleets in a future war? for whatever peace we may make under the present government of France cannot be lasting. I pity the poor Maltese; they have sustained an irreparable loss in your friendly counsel and an able director in their public concerns: you was truly their father, and, I agree with you, they may not like step-fathers; however, I hope that you will find as much pleasure in your new office as it is possible for it to afford, although I am sure it will not be equal to your merit. . . . *Capt. Ball, 4 June.*

I am just returned from the Gulf of Finland, Reval; and met Lord St. Helens at the entrance; by this, I am sure peace must be signed with Russia, and Denmark and Sweden have so completely lost their consequence by joining against us, that they must submit to what we settle with Russia. The northern fleets are only formidable in point of numbers; in every other respect they are insignificant; and if our fleet is active in the spring of the year may be got at separately; late in the summer they have their numerous flotilla, who can join in spite of all our efforts to prevent them, for there is a complete navigation inside, and amongst 10,000 islands. . . . Believe me at all times and places, for ever your sincere, affectionate, and faithful friend, NELSON AND BRONTE.

Having received information that a ship is bound from Copenhagen to Norway, loaded with cannon, and also that some other vessels are about sailing from Copenhagen, loaded with naval stores, contrary to the terms and spirit of not only the armistice, but also to the kindness of Sir Hyde Parker and the British Govern- *Capt. S. Sutton, Amazon, 11 June.*

---

[1] At this time Commissioner of the Navy at Gibraltar.

ment, who allowed provisions to pass from Denmark into Norway, I therefore desire that you will proceed through the Belt, and cruise between the Koll and the Island of Zealand, and endeavour to intercept the ships and vessels above described, as also all other vessels which may be bound from Copenhagen, or other parts of the Danish dominions, to Norway, Iceland, Faroe, or Greenland, loaded with warlike stores or naval stores; and you will send such ships as you may seize of the above description to England. And, as there is a squadron of Danish ships of war in Norway who may wish to get to Copenhagen, it is my directions that you do your utmost in endeavouring to prevent their coming to Copenhagen; but you are to acquaint the commander of your orders; and if he consents to remain with you till you receive directions from me or any other your superior officer for your conduct, in that case you are to allow him or them to keep their colours flying. But if they refuse your reasonable request, it is my directions that you use your utmost endeavours to take possession of him or them, and acquaint me, or the Secretary of the Admiralty, as the case may require, of your proceedings.

Gen. Lindholm, 12 June.

Respecting my permitting a Danish frigate to pass from Norway to Copenhagen, I beg leave to inform his Royal Highness, that I have no power whatever to grant such permission. On the contrary, the Government of Denmark having refused to allow of Norway being included in the armistice, I believe that there would be no impropriety in any English man-of-war attacking them in the ports of Norway, much less if they put to sea, as Denmark has refused the temporary neutrality for that kingdom; but I have no doubt the British Government will do everything of that nature which his Royal Highness may think proper to ask.

Being on the subject of Norway, I think it my duty to ask that it may be given in the name and by the authority of the Prince, an assurance that during the time which Sir Hyde Parker, and since the British Government, have given permission for provisions to be sent to Norway, that no warlike stores have been or will be sent into Norway, and that no gun-vessels have or will be sent from Norway to Copenhagen during the time the kindness of the British Government is continued to be received by the Danish Government.

E. Nepean, 12 June.

I am to acquaint you, for the information of the Lords Commissioners of the Admiralty, that the general conduct of Denmark has been so entirely different from what the armistice points out, that I do not think myself at liberty to proceed as I should think right, until I get their Lordships' instructions, which I trust will be soon. The armistice, except their ships being absolutely hauled out, has been totally disregarded. Ships have been masted, guns taken on board, floating batteries prepared; in short, everything is doing, as my reporters say, in defiance of the treaty, except hauling out and completing their rigging.

The moment I receive information that peace is made with Russia, I shall go over the Grounds, and anchor in Copenhagen Roads, ready to act as circumstances may require and their Lordships may direct, leaving eight sail of the line to watch the Swedes.

I hope the reply of the Admiralty to my letter of this day will be clear and explicit, whether the commander-in-chief is at liberty to hold the language becoming a British admiral? which very probably, if I am here, will break the armistice, and set Copenhagen in a blaze. I see everything which is dirty and mean going on, and the Prince Royal at the head of it; but your astonishment will cease when I assure [you] that a French republican officer, in his uniform, feathers, &c., is always with his Royal Highness. The measure is so indelicate towards England, that you will not be surprised if everything which is sacred amongst nations of honour should be broken. *Lord St. Vincent, 12 June.*

Lord Nelson cannot allow himself to leave the fleet without expressing to the admirals, captains, officers, and men, how sensibly he has felt, and does feel, all their kindness to him, and also how nobly and honourably they have supported him in the hour of battle, and the readiness which they have shown to maintain the honour of their king and country on many occasions which have offered. *Memorandum, 18 June. Kjöge Bay.*

In the summer of 1801, Bonaparte collected a flotilla and large army at Boulogne, with the avowed design of invading England. It was therefore determined to place a large force consisting of frigates, brigs, and smaller vessels, under the command of Lord Nelson, between Orfordness and Beachy Head. Lord St. Vincent's views on the subject were thus stated in a letter to Admiral Lutwidge, the commander-in-chief in the Downs, dated Admiralty, 24 July, 1801. 'The enemy's preparations on different parts of the coast, in the Channel, particularly opposite to you, beginning to wear a very serious appearance, and all our intelligence agreeing that a descent on some part of the coast is actually intended, it has naturally been matter of consideration, what measures would be most advisable to be taken for our defence; and after viewing the subject in every shape in which it could present itself, no plan appears to me to be so effectual for frustrating the enemy's designs as that of placing the whole of the force applicable to that particular service under the command of a flag officer who will have no other duty to perform than that of attending to this important object. I am aware that the measure I have mentioned will materially interfere with your command in the Downs; and I can assure you, with great truth, that I have so much respect both for your public and private character, that I should not have taken this, or any other measure that might be in any respect unpleasant to you, if I had thought it could have been avoided without detriment to the public service. The officer I have fixed upon is Viscount Nelson, who will, I think, hoist his flag in one of the frigates, and proceed immediately to the coast of France, to settle the necessary arrangements with the officers now employed there. The command in the Downs will of course be left in your hands, with the superintendence of what is generally understood to be the port-duty, while it may be requisite to continue Lord Nelson in this situation.'

Lord Nelson hoisted his flag in L'Unité frigate, at Sheerness, on 27 July.

Memorandum, submitted to the Admiralty, 25 July.

Besides the stationed ships at the different posts between the North Foreland and Orfordness, as many gun-vessels as can be spared from the very necessary protection of the coast of Sussex and of Kent to the westward of Dover should be collected, for this part of the coast must be seriously attended to; for supposing London the object of surprise, I am of opinion that the enemy's object *ought* to be the getting on shore as speedily as possible, for the dangers of a navigation of forty-eight hours appear to me to be an insurmountable objection to the rowing from Boulogne to the coast of Essex. It is therefore most probable (for it is certainly proper to believe the French are coming to attack London, and therefore to be prepared) that from Boulogne, Calais, and even Havre, the enemy will try and land in Sussex or the lower part of Kent; and from Dunkirk, Ostend, and the other ports of Flanders, to land on the coast of Essex or Suffolk; for I own myself of opinion that, the object being to get on shore somewhere within 100 miles of London as speedily as possible, the flats in the mouth of the Thames will not be the only place necessary to attend to; added to this, the enemy will create a powerful diversion by the sailing of the combined fleet, and the either sailing, or creating such an appearance of sailing, of the Dutch fleet, as will prevent Admiral Dickson from sending anything from off the great Dutch ports, whilst the smaller ports will spew forth its flotilla—viz. Flushing, &c. &c. It must be pretty well ascertained what number of small vessels are in each port.

I will suppose that 40,000 men are destined for this attack, or rather surprise, of London: 20,000 will land on the west side of Dover, sixty or seventy miles from London, and the same number on the east side: they are too knowing to let us have but one point of alarm for London. Supposing 200 craft, or 250, collected at Boulogne, &c., they are supposed equal to carry 20,000 men. In very calm weather they might row over, supposing no impediment, in twelve hours; at the same instant, by telegraph, the same number of troops would be rowed out of Dunkirk, Ostend, &c. &c. These are the two great objects to attend to from Dover and the Downs, and perhaps one of the small ports to the westward. Boulogne (which I call the central point of the western attack) must be attended to. If it is calm when the enemy row out, all our vessels and boats appointed to watch them must get into the Channel, and meet them as soon as possible: if not strong enough for the attack, they must watch, and keep them company till a favourable opportunity offers. If a breeze springs up, our ships are to deal *destruction*; no delicacy can be observed on this great occasion. But should it remain calm, and our flotilla not fancy itself strong enough to attack the enemy on their passage, the moment that they begin to touch our shore, strong or weak, our flotilla of boats must attack as much of the enemy's flotilla as they are able—say only one-half or two-thirds it will create a most powerful diversion, for the bows of our flotilla will be opposed to their unarmed sterns, and the courage of Britons will never, I believe, allow one Frenchman to leave the beach. A great number of Deal and Dover boats to be on board our vessels off the port of Boulogne, to give notice of the direction taken by the enemy. If it is calm, vessels in the Channel can make signals of intelligence to our shores from the North Foreland to Orfordness, and even as far as Solebay, not an improbable place, about seventy or eighty miles from London.

A flotilla to be kept near Margate and Ramsgate, to consist of gunboats and flat-boats; another squadron to be stationed near the centre, between Orfordness and North Foreland, and the third in Hollesley Bay. The floating batteries are stationed in all proper positions for defending the different channels, and the smaller vessels will always have a resort in the support of the stationed ships. The moment of the enemy's movement from Boulogne is to be considered as the movement of the enemy from Dunkirk. Supposing it calm, the flotillas are to be rowed, and the heavy ones towed (except the stationed ships); those near Margate, three or four leagues to the north of the North Foreland; those from Hollesley Bay, a little approaching the centre division, but always keeping an eye towards Solebay; the centre division to advance halfway between the two. The more fast rowing boats, called Thames galleys, which can be procured the better, to carry orders, information, &c. &c.

Whenever the enemy's flotilla can be seen, our divisions are to unite, but not intermix, and to be ready to execute such orders as may be deemed necessary, or as the indispensable circumstances may require. For this purpose, men of such confidence in each other should be looked for, that (as far as human foresight can go) no little jealousy may creep into any man's mind, but to be all animated with the same desire of preventing the descent of the enemy on our coasts. Stationary floating batteries are not, from any apparent advantage, to be moved, for the tide may prevent their resuming the very important stations assigned them: they are on no account to be supposed neglected, even should the enemy surround them, for they may rely on support, and reflect that perhaps their gallant conduct may prevent the mischievous designs of the enemy. Whatever plans may be adopted, the moment the enemy touch our coast, be it where it may, they are to be attacked by every man afloat and on shore: this must be perfectly understood. Never fear the event. The flat-boats can probably be manned (partly, at least) with the sea fencibles (the numbers or fixed places of whom I am entirely ignorant of), but the flat-boats they may man to be in grand and sub-divisions, commanded by their own captains and lieutenants as far as is possible. The number of flat-boats is unknown to me, as also the other means of defence in small craft; but I am clearly of opinion that a proportion of the small force should be kept to watch the flat-boats from Boulogne, and the others in the way I have presumed to suggest. These are offered as merely the rude ideas of the moment, and are only meant as a sea plan of defence for the city of London; but I believe other parts may likewise be menaced, if the Brest fleet, and those from Rochefort and Holland put to sea; although I feel confident that the fleets of the enemy will meet the same fate which has always attended them, yet their sailing will facilitate the coming over of their flotilla, as they will naturally suppose our attention will be called only to the fleets.

Lord St. Vincent, 28 July.

Everything must have a beginning, and we are literally at the foundation of our fabric of defence. I agree perfectly with you, that we must keep the enemy as far from our own coasts as possible, and be able to attack them the moment they come out of their ports. . . . Should the enemy approach our coasts near the Thames, our dockyards can man flat-boats if they are kept in readiness; and this yard has 100 men who can man two flats which are ordered to be fitted out. If the Unité arrives at the Nore this day, I shall go on board her, in order to show that we must all get to our posts as speedily as possible.

I had sent Captain Shepard to desire that a Mr. Salisbury would meet me; as he was a person of respectability, rich (got it by the fair trade), and of great influence amongst the seafaring men on that part of the coast, particularly about Whitstable. I made him sensible of the necessity of our ships which were to be stationed off the Sandheads being manned. He thought if the Admiralty, through me, gave the men assurances that they should be returned to their homes when the danger of the invasion was passed, that the seafolk would go; but that they were always afraid of some trick. *30 July. Deal.*

To-morrow I am going to the coast of France, and shall take an artillery officer with me, who will be able to form a judgment as to the possibility of the effect of shells on the enemy's vessels at Boulogne. Our means of defence so rapidly increase, that it will soon be almost improbable that the enemy should attempt to come out of their ports on the coasts near us. *H. Addington, 31 July.*

I have been looking at Boulogne this morning, and see their line of vessels, all armed, which lie outside the port. Captain Fyers, of the artillery, thinks that they are stationed to add strength to the place. The French are erecting batteries both for guns and mortars on each side of the town, as if fearful of an attack. All accounts agree, that fifty or sixty is the full number of boats, large and small, at Boulogne, and that these can be moved out of the reach of shells; however, I have sent for the bombs, and will try what can be done. *Lord St. Vincent, 2 August.*

The enemy have twenty-four armed vessels anchored outside the port of Boulogne. These appear to be incapable in the smoothest water of being rowed more than one and a half per hour. *E. Nepean, 3 August.*

The enemy's vessels, brigs, and flats (lugger-rigged), and a schooner, twenty-four in number, were this morning, at daylight, anchored in a line, in front of the town of Boulogne. The wind being favourable for the bombs to act, I made the signal for them to weigh, and to throw shells at the vessels: but as little as possible to annoy the town. The captains placed their ships in the best possible position, and in a few hours three of the flats and a brig were sunk; and in the course of the morning six were on *4 August.*

shore, evidently much damaged. At six this evening, being high water, five of the vessels which had been aground hauled with difficulty into the mole; the others remained under water. I believe the whole of the vessels would have gone inside the pier, but for want of water. What damage the enemy may have sustained beyond what we see is impossible to tell. The whole of this affair is of no further consequence than to show the enemy that they cannot with impunity come outside their ports. The officers of the artillery threw the shells with great skill.

Lord St. Vincent, 7 August. Margate Roads.

As Margate will probably serve as a model for the situation of all the sea-fencibles, I shall confine myself to it; and submit with deference, what in my humble opinion is best to be done. But as they are only the thoughts of the moment, you must make due allowances, and much must require arranging. Of the 2,600 sea-fencibles enrolled between Orfordness and Beachy Head, only 385 have offered themselves to go on board a ship and serve at the Sandheads, &c. The sea-fencibles of Margate, for instance, consist of 118 men, their occupation is piermen belonging to the Margate hoys, and some few who assist ships up and down the river. These men say, 'Our employment will not allow us to go from our homes beyond a day or two, and for actual service;' but they profess their readiness to fly on board, or on any other duty ordered, when the enemy are announced as actually coming on the sea. This we must take for granted is the situation of all other sea-fencibles. When we cannot do all we wish, we must do as well as we can. Our ships fitted for the service, on both shores, between Orfordness and the North Foreland, want 1,900 men, the river barges two or three hundred. Shall I try and arrange that, when the invasion is coming, these ships shall be manned from particular places? In that case we must get as many volunteers as we can at present to take care of our ships, and trust to their being manned at the last moment by the (almost) scrambling manner I have pointed out; in which case the unmanned ships must be brought from the end of Margate Sand into the Roads, and kept as safe as possible with a few men. Respecting the river barges, out of the twelve ordered to the Nore, I propose placing four on Whitstable Flat, and the others on the Essex side, about Mersea Island : these must be considered as belonging to the sea-fencibles, and in a certain degree under the orders of those captains, and the men exercised on board them. It is my intention to get over, if possible, to-morrow to Hollesley Bay or Harwich, and to have a meeting with Captains

Schomberg and Edge. My flotilla, I hope, will be finished by Wednesday, and I am vain enough to expect a great deal of mischief to the enemy from it. I am sure that the French are trying to get from Boulogne; yet the least wind at WNW, and they are lost. I pronounce that no embarkation can take place at Boulogne; whenever it comes forth, it will be from Flanders, and what a forlorn undertaking! consider cross tides, &c. &c. As for rowing, that is impossible. It is perfectly right to be prepared against a mad Government; but with the active force your Lordship has given me, I may pronounce it almost impracticable.

I shall be at the Nore by sunset. Mr. Spence, the maritime surveyor of this coast, is going to carry the Medusa out by a new channel. It is necessary I should know all that is to be known of the navigation; and I have been a tolerable pilot for the mouth of the Thames in my younger days. *10 August. Harwich.*

Great preparations at Ostend: Augereau commands that part of the army. I hope to let him feel the bottom of the Goodwin Sand. *Sir E. Berry, 10 August.*

[The several captains of the sea-fencibles] unanimously agree in one thing, of the loyalty of the men and of their readiness to fight in defence of their king and country; but as they represent that the sea-fencibles are composed of a description of men not generally liable to be impressed, and that they have all an occupation in the several places where they are enrolled; that to the majority of them it would be little short of ruin were they to give up their business; [that] many of them are merchants and masters of ships, who have come forward very handsomely in order to encourage their men; therefore, with deference to their Lordships' better judgment, I beg leave to state that I have directed cutters to go to such places and receive such volunteers as are to be got, and to remove our ships now at the Nore into the Bay of Hollesley, Wallet, and Margate Roads, that they may be ready to receive the sea-fencibles whenever the time arrives that every man must come forth, as when it comes to that point the business cannot last three days. I am led to believe that all our seafaring men would come forward with the greatest cheerfulness. *E. Nepean, 10 August.*

With respect to the river barges, it seems by all the captains' account to be a species of defence which the sea-fencibles will attend to with pleasure; therefore supposing that there are only twelve of these vessels now at the Nore, I propose that four should be stationed on Whitstable Flats, under the direction (as to the manning and exercising them) of Captain Hamilton and the captains under his directions; that six should instantly be sent to the mouth of Colchester and Malden river, under the direction of Captain Schomberg, and one in Woodbridge, and one in Orford river, under Captain Edge. Except from the necessity of placing large ships in the channels, the defence of our numerous landing-places is better adapted to our river barges than any other which we could adopt, for they require few men to take care of them, and would always be manned in a few minutes from the fencible corps. I am led to hope that 300 volunteers may be obtained from Essex and Suffolk. From Sussex and Kent, not a man has offered. The fencibles of Ramsgate said to Captain Rudsdell, 'If two gun-brigs are assigned to us, we will man them on the spur of the moment;' but our first defence is close to the enemy's ports, and when that is broke, others will come forth on our own coasts; but the Board have taken such precautions by having assigned such a respectable force under my orders, that I venture to express a well-grounded hope, that the enemy would be annihilated before they get ten miles from their own shores.

II. Addington, 12 August.

In my command I can tell you with truth, that I find much zeal and good humour; and should Mr. Bonaparte put himself in our way, I believe he will wish himself even in Corsica. I only hope, if he means to come, that it will be before 14 September, for my stamina is but ill-suited for equinoctial gales and cold weather.

Lord St. Vincent, 13 August. Downs.

I send you the reports of the sea-fencible captains in Sussex and lower Kent, that you may give them, if you please, to Nepean, but I thought it as well not to lay them before the Board; for the clerks in all the public offices chatter so much, that nothing is a secret. I have reports from our ships off Boulogne by a neutral just arrived: the account of troops given by the French scoundrels in our pay is as false as they are. I am certain that in the towns of Boulogne and the surrounding hills, the total number could not exceed 2,000 men. The Galgo arrived in the night from off Ostend. Captain Hawkins assures me that the boats collected at Ostend and Blankenberg may amount to sixty or seventy, that he is sure they could not carry more than fifty or sixty men each; he understood that the poor devils of fishermen are sent off for Brest. Where is our invasion to come from? The time is gone; owing to the precautions of Government, it cannot happen at this moment, and I hope that we shall always be as much on the alert as our enemies. We must constantly guard our coasts and the flats; for Malden River and the Flats of Whitstable should always be ready for service.

I now come to consider of an attack. Flushing is my grand object; but so many obstacles are in the way, and the risk is so great of the loss of some vessels, that, under all circumstances, I could hardly venture without a consultation with you, and an arranged plan, with the Board's orders. Might not a grand consultation be held for getting at the Dutch ships at Hellevoet, or to take possession of Flushing? But this must be a week's expedition for 4,000 or 5,000 troops. To crush the enemy at home was the favourite plan of Lord Chatham, and I am sure you think it the wisest measure to carry the war from our own doors. I purpose, if to be done, to take all the gun-vessels outside the pier of Boulogne—I should like your approbation. I own that this boat warfare is not exactly congenial to my feelings, and I find I get laughed at for my puny mode of attack. I shall be happy to lead the way into Hellevoet or Flushing, if Government will turn their thoughts to it: whilst I serve, I will do it actively, and to the very best of my abilities.

I have all night had a fever, which is very little abated this morning; my mind carries me beyond my strength, and will do me up; but such is my nature. I have serious doubts whether I shall be able, from my present feelings, to go to the Mediterranean; but I will do what I can—I require nursing like a child.

Having judged it proper to attempt bringing off the enemy's flotilla moored in the front of Boulogne, I directed the attack to be made by four divisions of boats for boarders, under the command of Captains Somerville, Cotgrave, Jones, and Parker, and a division of howitzer boats under Captain Conn. The boats put off from the Medusa at half-past eleven o'clock last night, in the best possible order, and before one o'clock this morning the firing began, and I had, from the judgment of the officers and the zeal and gallantry of every man, the most perfect confidence of complete success; but the darkness of the night, with the tide and half-tide, separated the divisions; and from all not arriving at the same happy moment with Captain Parker, is to be attributed the failure of success. But I beg to be perfectly understood that not the smallest blame attaches itself to any person; for although the divisions did not arrive together, yet each (except the fourth division, which could not be got up before day) made a successful

E. Nepean 16 August.

U

attack on that part of the enemy they fell in with, and actually took possession of many brigs and flats, and cut their cables; but many of them being aground, and the moment of the battle's ceasing on board them the vessels were filled with volleys upon volleys of musketry, the enemy being perfectly regardless of their own men, who must have suffered equally with us. It was therefore impossible to remain on board, even to burn them; but allow me to say, who have seen much service this war, that more determined, persevering courage, I never witnessed, and that nothing but the impossibility of being successful, from the causes I have mentioned, could have prevented me from having to congratulate their Lordships. But although, in value, the loss of such gallant and good men is incalculable, yet in point of numbers it has fallen short of my expectations. I must also beg leave to state that greater zeal and ardent desire to distinguish themselves by an attack on the enemy was never shown than by all the captains, officers, and crews of all the different descriptions of vessels under my command.

Lord St. Vincent, 16 August. I am sorry to tell you that I have not succeeded in bringing out or destroying the enemy's flotilla moored in the mouth of the harbour of Boulogne. The most astonishing bravery was evinced by many of our officers and men, and Captains Somerville, Cotgrave, and Parker exerted themselves to the utmost. We have lost many brave officers and men: upwards of one hundred killed and wounded. Dear little Parker, his thigh very much shattered; I have fears for his life. Langford shot through the leg. The loss has been heavy, and the object was great. The flotilla, brigs and flats, were moored by the bottom to the shore and to each other with chains; therefore, although several of them were carried, yet the heavy fire of musketry from the shore which overlooked them forced our people to leave them, without being able, as I am told, to set them on fire. No person can be blamed for sending them to the attack but myself; I knew the difficulty of the undertaking, therefore I ventured to ask your opinion.

Your kind letter I received half an hour before the attack; but, although I disapprove of unnecessary consultations as much as any man, yet [being] close to the Admiralty, I should not feel myself justified in risking our ships through the channels of Flushing without buoys and pilots, without a consultation of such men as your Lordship, and also I believe you would think an order absolutely necessary; but that must stand fast, for both Leyden and Medusa have lost all their best men—none else, of course, being sent.

Captain Somerville, who I never saw till a few days ago, showed all the courage and good conduct which was possible, and succeeded completely in the fighting part of the business. Conn, in the command of the howitzer-boats, did everything which was possible; indeed all behaved well, and it was their misfortune to be sent on a service which the precautions of the enemy rendered impossible to succeed in.

I have real thoughts of attacking the enemy at Flushing, if it be possible to be done, the moment Leyden and Medusa are manned. In that event I must run great risk, and only beg to be supported in case of failure. P.M. I find by Captain Owen's letters off Flushing, three days ago, that all the Dutch vessels have moved lower down the Doerlog Channel, evidently to defend it: I will go and look at them; but attack I cannot, without pilots, nor without sanction. I own I shall never bring myself again to allow any attack to go forward, where I am not personally concerned; my mind suffers much more than if I had a leg shot off in this late business. Had our force arrived, as I intended, 'twas not all the chains in France that could have prevented our folks from bringing off the whole of the vessels. . . . *17 August.*

I am fixed to look at Flushing, and prepared to attack it, if the pilots can be persuaded to take Leyden up; if it be within the pale of possibility, it shall be attempted. . . . *18 August.*

I believe Calais could be bombarded, but do you think it is an object? I should not like the bombs to go without me. Heavy sea, sick to death—this sea-sickness I shall never get over. *19 August.*

I purpose looking at Flushing, and if it is possible, I will go up and attack the ships in that road; but I fear no pilots will take charge of our ships, and it is a melancholy thing when the honour of our country is obliged to be submitted to a man of that class. Lord St. Vincent tells me he hates councils; so do I, between military men; for if a man consults whether he is to fight, when he has the power in his own hands, it is certain that his opinion is against fighting; but that is not the case at present, and I own I do want good counsel. Lord St. Vincent is for keeping the enemy closely blockaded; but I see that they get along shore inside their sandbanks, and under their guns, which line the coast of France. Lord Hood is for keeping our squadrons of defence stationary on our own shore (except light cutters, to give information of every movement of the enemy); for the time is approaching when a gale of westerly wind will disperse our light squadrons. . . . *H. Addington, 21 August.*

When men of such good sense, such great sea-officers, differ so widely, is it not natural that I should wish the mode of defence to be well arranged by the mature consideration of men of judgment? I mean not to detract from my judgment; even as it is, it is well known: but I boast of nothing but my zeal; in that I will give way to no man upon earth.

Admiral Lutwidge, 24 August.

Six pilots say that it is impossible, without buoys or beacons, for our ships to go to Flushing; and that if all the buoys and beacons were as usual, that we could not return without a fair wind and flowing water. Had I known as much before I sailed from the Downs, I would not have come such a wild-goose chase; but Captain Owen is close to us, and I shall know all Captain Owen's ideas. His zeal, I am afraid, has made him overleap sandbanks and tides, and laid him aboard the enemy; but I must clear away these little obstacles before I can give him scope for intentions. I admire his desire, and could join most heartily in it; but we cannot do impossibilities, and I am as little used to find out the impossibles as most folks; and I think I can discriminate between the impracticable and the fair prospect of success.

E. Nepean, 5 August.

I sailed from the Downs on Sunday, and off the North Foreland was joined by the squadron from Margate, making in the whole, when united off Westkapelle, thirty sail, from 64 guns to 14, including three bombs and three fire-vessels. From my consultation with the pilots on Sunday afternoon, I had not much hopes of being able to get at the enemy, supposing they lay even below Flushing; and yesterday afternoon, upon a further consultation with the pilots, I found that the attempt would be improper, for there were so many *ifs* necessary to bring us out again, that I gave the matter up. But further to satisfy my own mind, I this morning went on board the King George hired cutter, Mr. Yawkins, master, who carried me up the Welling Channel, four or five leagues from our ships, and near three from the enemy; the tide running strong up, and the wind falling, it was necessary to get out again. From this distant observation of Captain Gore and myself, with the local knowledge of Mr. Yawkins, I believe that the enemy's whole force consisted of a ship of the line (Dutch), French frigate, another small ship, and two or three brigs lying close to the town of Flushing, and abreast of it; which position being likewise abreast of the Dog Sand, would render a successful attack almost impossible; for even supposing ourselves able to get alongside the enemy, they could, whenever they pleased, with the flood tide, cut their cables and retreat towards the Rammekens, and leave us with the impossibility of anything else than silencing the fire from Flushing.

Under these circumstances, I hesitated not one moment to direct the ships and vessels with me to proceed to the several stations assigned them. . . . I cannot but admire Captain Owen's zeal in his anxious desire to get at the enemy, but under all the circumstances which I have stated, I could not think myself justifiable in acting against my own judgment.

Not one sea-fencible has come forth from either Kent or Sussex. The establishment of them was originally bad: for no man liable to be impressed should have been enrolled, unless they had large families. The threat of invasion is still kept up, and the French are trying to make their grand collection of boats at Boulogne; but I find it difficult to believe that they can ever get half-way over. Sir E. Berry, 2 Sept.

On or about 6 September, Lord Nelson received a paper entitled, 'Remarks by a Seaman on the Attack at Boulogne,' containing severe strictures on Lord Nelson's Official Despatch; to which was added, 'Should Lord Nelson wish the inclosed not to be inserted in the newspapers, he will please to inclose by return of post a bank note of 100*l*., to Mr. Hill, to be left at the Post Office till called for, London.'

Mr. Hill,—Very likely I am unfit for my present command, and whenever Government change me, I hope they will find no difficulty in selecting an officer of greater abilities; but you will, I trust, be punished for threatening my character. But I have not been brought up in the school of fear, and, therefore, care not what you do. I defy you and your malice.   NELSON AND BRONTE. Mr. Hill.

I send you a paper, and a note at the bottom. I have answered Mr. Hill's note, and it will be in London on Tuesday morning. If their Lordships think it proper to save me from such letters, they will be pleased to send proper people to take up whoever comes for Mr. Hill's letter. I have franked it with the following direction: E. Nepean, 6 Sept.

'Mr. Hill,
'To be left at the Post Office till called for.'

A man, a few days ago, sent me a letter demanding a bank note of 100*l*., or he would abuse me in the papers: I sent it of course to Nepean; the porter who went to the Post Office for my answer has been taken up, but he knew not his employer, [who] probably never will be caught. A. Davison, 14 Sept.

The people at the watering-places have been very free in their conversations, and I believe the Mayor of Deal either put a vaga-

Lord St. Vincent, 23 Sept.

bond in prison, or sent him out of town, for arraigning my conduct in being careless of poor seamen's lives; but I trouble not my head on these matters; my conscience tells me that I do my best. You will easily believe that I should have liked to have tried the business at Goree, but the objections to it were innumerable. You would have had Dickson and all of us, *the service*. If success attended it, it would be said, ' Ay, the Admiralty gave from partiality this to their favourite ' (for I do flatter myself I am a favourite). If it miscarried, then it would be said, ' That vain man, Nelson, thought he could do what no one else could, and his friends at the Admiralty had folly enough to believe his impossible schemes.'

I feel myself, my dear Lord, as anxious to get a medal or a step in the peerage as if I never had got either,—for ' if it be a sin to covet glory, I am the most offending soul alive '—I could lose only a few boats. If I succeeded and burnt the Dutch fleet, probably medals and an earldom. I must have had every desire to try the matter, regardless of the feelings of others; but I should not have been your Nelson, that wants not to take honours or rewards from any man; and if ever I feel great, it is, my dear Lord, in never having, in thought, word, or deed, robbed any man of his fair fame.

That wardrooms will prate, I believe none of us can doubt, and it has its bad effects. The boat service I believe is got very unpopular. G—— flogged some of his chaps severely for some very improper expressions. They belonged to the Unité, who was, I fancy, in very bad order. I assure you, my dear Lord, that I do not believe any admiral could be better supported than I am by all the captains under me.

(?) 29 Sept.

I have experienced in the Sound the misery of having the honour of our country intrusted to pilots, who have no other thought than to keep the ship clear of danger, and their own silly heads clear of shot. At eight in the morning of 2 April, not one pilot would take charge of a ship. Brierly, who was Davidge Gould's master in the Audacious, placed boats for me, and fixed my order. Everybody knows what I must have suffered; and if any merit attaches itself to me, it was in combating the dangers of the shallows in defiance of the pilots. . . .

I have answered Hawkins about the pilots exactly as you see it, that he was to go where he was ordered, without consulting pilots, and that when the ship was standing into danger, they were to point it out; but that it was not allowable for them to dictate where it was proper for a ship to be stationed in the Channel. . . .

This boat business must be over: it may be a part of a great plan of invasion, but can never be the only one; therefore, as our ships cannot act any more in lying off the French coast, I own I do not think it is now a command for a vice-admiral. Turn it in your mind. It is not that I want to get a more lucrative situation —far from it: I do not know, if the Mediterranean were vacant to-morrow, that I am equal to undertake it.

I am prepared to run a fire-brig into Boulogne harbour the first fresh wind at from WNW to N. But I shall stop until the assent or dissent comes by telegraph to-morrow. I intended not to have mentioned this matter to anyone, even to you, until the trial had been made. However, if we are on the eve of peace, which is Dungeness news, it would be a bad reconciliation. If I fail in this plan, I purpose to make an infernal of one of the bombs, and to have fire-boats, &c. &c., to keep them for ever in hot water. *Lord St. Vincent, 3 October.*

I am trying to get rid of my command, but I am to be forced to hold it, to keep the merchants easy till hostilities cease in the Channel. I must submit; for I do not wish to quarrel with the very great folks at the Admiralty the last moment. I have had hitherto one happiness under my command, that not one English boat has been captured by the enemy during the time of my command, within the limits of my station; this is a comfort, and I hope none will be captured during the short time we have to stay. I see you did not know of the peace when you wrote; England called loudly for it, and now I see it is to be abused; but Englishmen never are satisfied, full nor fasting. *A. Davison, 9 October.*

Can you cure madness? for I am mad to read that our damned scoundrels dragged a Frenchman's carriages. I am ashamed for my country. *Dr. Baird, 11 October.*

About this time, and at intervals during the next twelve months, Nelson wrote a very great many letters complaining that the victory at Copenhagen had not been duly recognised; there had been neither medals, nor thanks of the City of London: even the thanks of Parliament were given rather to Sir Hyde Parker for permitting the action, than to him and his comrades for fighting it. He was very angry, and he did not scruple to say so. The question continued to be mooted long after Nelson's death, and was not, indeed, finally settled till after the accession of William IV., when, on 6 October, 1830, the Secretary of the Admiralty wrote, by the King's orders, to Sir Thomas Foley and the other memorialists, that 'sensible as his Majesty is of your and their distinguished merit, there are general considerations connected with the subject which prevent his Majesty from complying with the request contained in the memorial.'

The Lord Mayor, 21 June, 1802. Merton.

My Lord,—A few days past, I saw in the newspapers that a motion had been made in a Court of Common Council, to thank me for my conduct in taking the command of a force destined to prevent any designs our enemies might have of approaching the City of London, but which motion stands over for some future Court. I have therefore to entreat that your Lordship will use your influence that no such motion may be brought forward.

There is not, my Lord, one individual in the world who appreciates the honour of having their conduct approved by the City of London higher than myself. I was desired to take the command in question in a very indifferent state of health, as I was flattered with the opinion that it would keep quiet the minds of all in London, and the coast between Beachy Head and Orfordness. This would have been a sufficient reason for me to have laid down my life, much less to suffer a little from ill-health; and, my Lord, his Majesty's Government gave me such a powerful force that the gallant officers and men I had the honour to command almost regretted that the enemy did not make the attempt of invasion. Therefore, you see, my Lord, I have no merit—I only did my duty with alacrity, which I shall always be ready to do when directed.

But, my Lord, if any other reason was wanting to prevent the City of London from thanking me for only showing an alacrity in stepping forth in time of danger, it is this—not four months before I was appointed to this command, I had the happiness of witnessing, under all its circumstances, the most hard-fought battle, and the most complete victory (as far as my reading goes), that ever was fought and obtained by the navy of this country. This battle, my Lord, had not the honour of being approved in the way which the City of London has usually marked their approbation: therefore I entreat that you will use your influence that no vote of approbation may ever be given to me for any services since 2 April, 1801; for I should feel much mortified when I reflected on the noble support I that day received, at any honour which could separate me from them, for I am bold to say, that they deserve every honour and favour which a grateful country can bestow.

I entreat your Lordship's indulgence for thus expressing my feelings, and again request that the intended motion of thanks may be withdrawn. I trust your Lordship will give [me] full credit for the high estimation in which I hold the City of London, and with what respect I am your Lordship's most obedient humble servant,

NELSON AND BRONTE.

If the victory of the 2nd [April] was real, the admirals, officers, and men, who fought and obtained the victory, are from custom entitled to the thanks of the City of London. Custom has never gone back to the first causers of victories, but simply to the victors. Lord St. Vincent had no thanks given him for the victory of the Nile, and Sir Hyde Parker, except being nearer the scene of action, had no more to do with that of Copenhagen than Lord St. Vincent. I cannot object to any thanks or rewards being bestowed on any man; but I have a fair claim from custom to be alone considered, through the whole of the battle, as the commander of the ships fighting. The thanks of Parliament went only to Sir Hyde's conduct in planning, not for the fighting; therefore I look forward with confidence to a sword from the City of London, and their thanks, and the freedom in a gold box to Admiral Graves. The City of London has never yet failed noticing sea victories, and I trust, as the first commercial city in the world, never will. I remember, a few years back, on my noticing to a Lord Mayor, that if the City continued its generosity, we should ruin them by their gifts, his Lordship put his hand on my shoulder and said—ay, the Lord Mayor of London said—' Do you find victories, and we will find rewards.' I have since that time found two complete victories. I have kept my word, and shall I have the power of saying that the City of London, which exists by victories at sea, has not kept its promise—a promise made by a Lord Mayor in his robes, and almost in the royal presence? I have a fair and honourable claim: my part of the honourable contract has been now doubly fulfilled.

A. Davison, 9 July.

In the months of July and August, 1802, Lord Nelson, accompanied by Sir William and Lady Hamilton, made a tour into Wales, consequent on which he submitted the following ' Memoranda respecting the Forest of Dean ' to Mr. Addington :

The Forest of Dean contains about 23,000 acres of the finest land in the kingdom, which, I am informed, if in a high state of cultivation of oak, would produce about 9,200 loads of timber, fit for building ships of the line, every year—that is, the forest would grow in full vigour 920,000 oak trees. The state of the forest at this moment is deplorable; for, if my information is true, there is not 3,500 load of timber in the whole forest fit for building, and none coming forward. It is useless, I admit, to state the causes of such a want of timber where so much could be produced, except that, by knowing the faults, we may be better enabled to amend ourselves.

First, the generality of trees, for these last fifty years, have been allowed to stand too long. They are passed by instead of removed, and thus occupy a space which ought to have been replanted with young trees.

Secondly, that where good timber is felled, nothing is planted, and nothing can grow self-sown; for the deer (of which now only a few remain) bark all the young trees. Vast droves of hogs are allowed to go into the woods in the autumn; and if any fortunate acorn escapes their search and takes root, then flocks of sheep are allowed to go into the forest, and they bite off the tender shoot. These are sufficient reasons why timber does not grow in the Forest of Dean.

Of the waste of timber in former times I can say nothing, but of late years it has been, I am told, shameful. Trees cut down in swampy places, as the carriage is done by contract, are left to rot, and are cut up by people in the neighbourhood. Another abuse is, the contractors, as they can carry more measurement, are allowed to cut the trees to their advantage of carriage, by which means the invaluable crooked timber is lost for the service of the navy. There are also—another cause of the failure of timber—a set of people called forest free miners, who consider themselves as having a right to dig for coal in any part they please. These people, in many places, inclose pieces of ground, which is daily increasing by the inattention, to call it by no worse name, of the surveyors, verderers, &c., who have the charge of the forest.

Of late years some apparently vigorous measures were taken for preserving and encouraging the growth of timber in the King's forests, and part of the Forest of Dean has been inclosed: but it is so very ill attended to, that it is little, if anything, better than the other part.

There is another abuse which I omitted to mention. Trees which die of themselves are considered as of no value. A gentleman told me, that in shooting on foot, for on horseback it cannot be seen, hid by the fern, which grows a great height, the trees of fifty years' growth, fit for buildings, fencing, &c., are cut just above ground entirely through the bark: in two years the tree dies, and it becomes either a perquisite, or is allowed to be taken away by favoured people. These shameful abuses are probably [not] known to those high in power; but I have gathered the information of them from people of all descriptions, and perfectly disinterested in telling me, or knowing that I had any view in a transient inquiry. But knowing the abuses, it is for the serious consideration of every lover of his country, how they can either be done away, or, at least, lessened—perhaps a very difficult or impossible task.

If the Forest of Dean is to be preserved as a useful forest for the country, strong measures must be pursued. First, the guardian of this support of our navy must be an intelligent, honest man, who will give up his time to his employment; therefore he must live in the forest, have a house, a small farm, and an adequate salary. I omitted to mention that the expense of a surveyor of woods, as far as relates to this forest, [ought] to be done away: verderer, as at present, also. The guardian to have proper verderers under him who understand the planting, thinning, and management of timber trees. These places should be so comfortable, that the fear of being turned out should be a great object of terror, and, of course, an inducement for them to exert themselves in their different stations. The first thing necessary in the Forest of Dean is to plant some acres of acorns; and I saw plenty of clear fields with cattle grazing in my voyage down the Wye. In two years these will be fit for transplanting.

N.B.—I am aware that objections have been made to the transplanting of oak. I am not knowing enough in this matter to say how far this is true when so young as two to five or six years. The next thing is to be careful to thin the trees; for more timber is lost by being too fearful of cutting down, than by badly thinning. A tree from ten years of age ought by a scale given to me by a very able man, to be as follows, viz.:

Number of trees that such land as the Forest of Dean may contain at different periods from their being first set:

Trees distant from each other. Feet.	Years after been set. Number.	Number of Trees in an acre.	Number of Trees to be thinned.
6	10	1,200	—
10	20	430	770
15	40	190	240
20	60	100	90
25	80	60	40
30	100	45	15

In forty years these forests will produce a great value of timber fit for many uses in the navy—indeed all, except for ships of the line.

If, on a due consideration, it is found not to be practicable for Government to arrange a plan for growing their own timber, then I would recommend at once selling the forests, and encourage the growth of oak timber. I calculate, that taking away the 3,500 load of timber at present fit for cutting, (or be it more or less), that the Forest of Dean will sell for 460,000*l*. I am sensible that what I have thrown together upon paper is so loose, that no plan can be drawn from it; but if these facts, which I have learnt from my late tour, may be in the least degree instrumental in benefiting our country, I shall be truly happy.

8 Nov.

Lord Nelson returns his most respectful compliments to the Lord Mayor elect, and the sheriffs, and is most exceedingly sorry that it is not in his power to do himself the honour and pleasure of dining with them at Guildhall on Lord Mayor's Day, for the following reasons:

Lord Nelson having waited with the greatest patience until every individual who had rendered the smallest service to the country had been marked by the City of London, wrote a letter to the Lord Mayor (Sir John Eamer), stating his sorrow that those under his command, who fought the most bloody battle, and obtained the most complete victory of any naval battle in this, or, Lord Nelson believes, in any war, had not had the honour to receive from the great City of London the same mark of approbation as had been bestowed on others; but Lord Nelson, being advised of the impropriety of pointing out what the City of London ought to have done, wrote another letter to the Lord Mayor, desiring to withdraw his letter.

But Lord Nelson's sentiments being precisely the same, and feeling for the situation of those brave captains, officers, and men, who so bravely fought, profusely bled, and obtained such a glorious, complete, and most important victory for their King and country, cannot do himself the honour and happiness of meeting his fellow-citizens on 9 November.

Lord Nelson flatters himself that the Lord Mayor elect, and the sheriffs, will approve of his feelings on this occasion, and consider that if Lord Nelson could forget the services of those who have fought under his command, that he would ill deserve to be so supported as he always has been.

Alex. Stephens,[1]
10 Feb.

By your letter, I believe that you wish to be correct in your history, and therefore wish to be informed of a transaction relative to Naples. I cannot enter at large into the subject to which you allude. I shall briefly say, that neither Cardinal Ruffo, or Captain Foote, or any other person, had any power to enter into any treaty with the rebels—that even the paper which they signed was not acted upon, as I very happily arrived at Naples, and prevented

[1] Author of *History of the Wars of the French Revolution*, 2 vols., 1803.

such an infamous transaction from taking place; therefore, when the rebels surrendered, they came out of the castles as they ought, without any honours of war, and trusting to the judgment of their sovereign. I put aside, and sent them notice of it, the infamous treaty, and the rebels surrendered, as I have before said. If you attend to that Mrs. Williams' book, I can assure you that nearly all relative to Naples is either destitute of foundation or falsely represented.

The following memorandum of a plan for manning the navy was submitted to Lord St. Vincent and Mr. Addington:

At a time when, I have been repeatedly told, the seamen, notwithstanding their good pay, and abundance of the very best provisions, manifest a reluctance to enter into the naval service, it becomes, in my humble opinion, a duty for people conversant with the manners and disposition of seamen, to turn their thoughts on the mode of inducing the seamen to be fond, and even desirous of serving in the navy, in preference to the merchant service. Their pay and provisions cannot possibly be improved from what they are at present; but I think a plan could be brought forward to register the certificates given to seamen; and a form of certificate to be general, and filled according to regulations issued by the Admiralty under the authority of an Act of Parliament. The greatest good would result from such a regulation to the seamen, who are by hundreds in distress in London, for want of certificates authenticating their persons; for want of which so many wrong seamen have been paid, that neither the Pay Office, nor any prize-agent, will venture to pay the seaman his just due: and the benefit to the seamen producing good characters, &c., never been concerned in mutinies, or deserted, &c., would much benefit them in getting good berths in the merchant service. 28 Feb.

When we calculate by figures on the expense of raising seamen, I think it is said, 20*l*. per man, that 42,000 seamen deserted during the late war, the loss in money, in that point alone, amounts to 840,000*l*.; without taking into consideration the greater expense of raising more men—and certainly not so good as those who have been used to the king's naval service. I shall therefore propose, that every seaman who has served faithfully five years in war, and by his certificates never been concerned in mutinies, nor deserted, shall receive every New Year's Day, or on the king's birthday, the sum of two guineas; and if he serves eight years, shall have four guineas, exclusive of any pension for wounds. It may appear at first sight, for the State to pay, an enormous sum; but when it is considered that the average life of a seaman is, from old age, finished at forty-five years, he cannot many years enjoy the annuity; to assist the paying which, the interest of the money saved by their not deserting would go very far, and perhaps as the merchants give large wages in war, a tax might be imposed when wages are above such a sum. It would answer one of these two purposes, either making the increase of wages in the merchants' service beneficial to those who serve their king and country in the navy; or, by keeping down the merchants' wages, render desertion the less desirable. Much, very much, can be said, and is necessary to be considered on this subject; but the more I think of it, the easier it appears to me to be put in practice. Prize-money to be as regularly paid in London, Portsmouth, Plymouth, &c., as seamen's wages: this is so easy and simple, that a very few days would, in my opinion, complete such a plan.

But the great thing necessary to guard against is desertion; for notwithstanding all that I have proposed to induce seamen to serve faithfully, yet a sum of money, and liquor, held out to a seaman, are too much for him: he allows himself to be seduced and hid, he first becomes fearful of apprehension, and then wishes and exerts himself to get out of the country in the merchants' employ. It will be found (if necessary to be inquired into at the Navy Office), and I know it, that whenever a large convoy is assembled at Portsmouth, and our fleet in port, not less than 1,000 men desert from the navy; and I am sure that one-third of this number, from loss of clothes, drinking, and other debaucheries, are lost by death to the kingdom. I shall only relate one fact of a thousand which could be brought forward. A ship from London clears at Gravesend for her voyage to India. Amongst other papers, the names of her crew and number are necessary; the names, qualities, &c., are properly filled up; the ship, to a common observer, is fully manned; but the fact is this, the ship is navigated to Portsmouth by ticket-men (men who are protected from the impress for some cause or other). The owner or captain sends to Portsmouth (to crimps) I have been told in one instance as far as fifty men—twenty-five able seamen, fifteen ordinary, and ten landsmen—the bounty being, of course, different according to their qualifications; the ticket-men leave the ship, the deserters to take up the names, and away they go.

Knowing the case, an Act of Parliament would, if not entirely, very nearly prevent this infamous conduct; the regulation, I think, would be very plain and easy. I am sensible that no plan for these very important purposes can be matured by any one head, much less by mine; but as the ideas flow from a pure source, and a sincere desire to benefit our king and country, I submit them, with deference, to much wiser and abler men than

NELSON AND BRONTE.

I have only a moment to answer your questions—war or peace? Every person has a different opinion. I fear perhaps the former, as I hope so much the latter. If war, I go to the Mediterranean in Hardy's frigate: the Victory is to be my ship—Sam Sutton to fit her out. You know how happy I should be to have you in any fleet I command, particularly on the day of battle: I should be sure of being well supported. You must judge for yourself about applying for employment; but I should think you will have no fears for a ship being forced upon you. In peace, mids may be difficult to get on board ship; but our establishment, even if blessed peace continues, will be large. Sir E. Berry, 26 March.

I agree with your Royal Highness most entirely, that the son of a Rodney[1] ought to be a protégé of every person in the kingdom, and particularly of the sea-officers; had I known that there had been this claimant, some of my own lieutenants must have given way to such a name, and he should have been placed in the Victory. She is full, and I have twenty on my list; but whatever numbers I have, the name of Rodney must cut many of them out. Duke of Clarence, 17 April.

You was so kind as to put in your pocket my crude ideas on the situation of our navy respecting the seamen.[2] The importance of the subject everyone must admit, and woeful experience tells us that something must be done on the occasion. I am sensible that my abilities are unequal to the task; but I should do injustice to my own feelings, and, I think, betray the confidence which has so often been reposed in me, was I not to bring them forward. One good effect must result from it, that in proving them bad, better will be brought forward. The mainspring of all my plan is that of certificates fully descriptive of the persons; the very greatest good must result from it. Names cannot be changed, as the gratuity will be looked forward to, therefore desertion will be less frequent, and easier detected. Pay, prize-money, &c. &c., could Sir W. Scott, 2 May.

---

[1] Lieutenant the Honourable Edward Rodney, youngest son of Admiral Lord Rodney: he was made a Commander in April 1805; posted in January 1806; and died in November 1828.

[2] See *ante*, p. 301.

rarely be paid to wrong persons; the seaman would have his money without the very great difficulty he meets with at present, and many executions would be avoided by the almost impossibility of the fraud of personification being committed (two, alas! suffered last week for this crime). If, my dear Sir William, you think, as I do, that something should be attempted at these times to make our seamen, at the din of war, fly to our navy, instead of flying from it, I am sure it could not be brought forward by anyone so ably as yourself; and if my feeble endeavours in so great a cause can be of the least use, I shall be too happy in offering my assistance.

Long before this armament, the paper was delivered to Mr. Addington and Lord St. Vincent: but I suppose they have not time to attend so much to this subject as, in my opinion, it merits.

Lord St. Vincent, 12 May.

Your mention of the Victory remaining some time in England, so much according with what I am told of Lord Keith's saying that he was to have her for the present—induces me to hope that if the Victory is ready, or as soon as she is, that I may have her; for all my things, servants, wines, &c. &c., are ordered to be sent to her, be where she will—even my sheep, poultry, hay, corn, and every comfort are ordered to her. But if Lord Keith, or any other man, is to have her for a given time, I must un-order all these things. I trust, my dear Lord, that I can take a French admiral as well as any of them, and have as much chance of falling in with one. I will call this morning for one moment on this subject.

Sir E. Nepean, 18 May. Portsmouth.

I arrived here about one o'clock this afternoon, and have hoisted my flag on board his Majesty's ship Victory. Captain Sutton informs me that she will be in every respect ready for sea on Friday morning.

The following orders were sent to Lord Nelson on 18 May:
' Whereas by our commission, bearing date the 16th instant, we have appointed your Lordship commander-in-chief of his Majesty's ships and vessels employed and to be employed in the Mediterranean; you are hereby required and directed to proceed forthwith to Portsmouth, and, hoisting your flag on board his Majesty's ship Amphion, make the best of your way to the island of Malta, where you may expect to find Rear-Admiral Sir Richard Bickerton; and on meeting the rear-admiral, take him and the ships and vessels there, as well as in the Mediterranean, under your command.

' On your Lordship's arrival at Malta, you are to lose no time in concerting with Sir Alexander Ball, his Majesty's commissioner at that island, such arrangements as may be necessary with a view to the protection and security of that island; you are then to proceed off Toulon, with such part of the squadron under your command as you may judge to be adequate to the service, and take such a position as may, in your Lordship's opinion, be most proper for enabling you to take, sink, burn, or otherwise destroy, any ships or vessels belonging to France, or the citizens of that Republic, and also for detaining and sending into port any ships or vessels belonging to the Batavian Republic, or the citizens thereof, that you may happen to fall in with. Your Lordship is to be very attentive to the proceedings of the French at Genoa, Leghorn, and other ports on that side of Italy, for the purpose of gaining the most early information of any armaments that may be forming there, either with a view to an attack upon Egypt or any other part of the Turkish dominions, or against the kingdoms of Naples and Sicily, or the islands of Corfu; and in the event of your having reason to believe that any such plan shall be in contemplation, your Lordship is to exert your best endeavours to counteract it, and to take, sink, burn, or destroy any ships or vessels which may be so employed; as well as to afford to the Sublime Porte and his Sicilian Majesty and their subjects, any protection or assistance which may be in your power, consistently with a due attention to the other important objects entrusted to your care.

'As it is highly important that your Lordship should be watchful of the conduct of the Court of Spain in the present moment, you are to direct your attention to the naval preparations that may be making in the several ports of that kingdom in the Mediterranean, as also at Cadiz, and to take every practicable means of obtaining, from time to time, all the intelligence you may be able to collect on that subject. Your Lordship is to take care that no interruption be offered by any of the ships or vessels under your command to any Spanish ships of war or trade, while they conduct themselves in a manner becoming a neutral nation; but, at the same time, your Lordship is to understand, that however desirable it may be to avoid any measure of hostility against that country, you are not to suffer any squadron of Spanish ships of war to enter a French port, or to form a junction with any squadron or ships or vessels of that, or the Batavian Republic. Your Lordship is also to be careful not to infringe the neutrality of other powers, so long as their conduct towards his Majesty and the commerce of his subjects shall be actuated by a similar principle. And whereas there is reason to believe that some of the French line-of-battle ships which have recently been employed in conveying troops to the French West India Islands may, on their return to Europe, attempt to proceed to the ports in the Mediterranean, your Lordship is to detach such part of the squadron under your command as you can spare from other more important services, as soon as possible, to Gibraltar, with orders to the senior officer of such detachment, after obtaining the best information he may be able to collect at that place, to take such a position as he may conceive to be most convenient, with a view to the intercepting the said ships, and any others belonging to the French or Batavian Republics, which may attempt to pass or repass the Straits ; and your Lordship is to apprise the senior officer, from time to time, of your movements, to the end that no delay that can be prevented may take place in the furnishing your Lordship with any orders or instructions which we may have occasion to send you, for the further regulation of your conduct ; and, finally, you are to transmit to our secretary, for our

x

information, frequent accounts of your proceedings, and every intelligence you may have obtained, proper for our knowledge. Given under our hands, the 18th May, 1803.

St. Vincent, Ph. Stephens, T. Troubridge.'

With further instructions to join Admiral Cornwallis off Brest, and to leave the Victory there should Cornwallis think it necessary, Nelson put to sea on the afternoon of the 20th.

Lord St. Vincent, 22 May, noon.

Close to Ushant—I am looking out for Cornwallis. I think we must see him before one, if he is this side the Saints, and I hope that he will not want the Victory.

3 p.m.

We are inside Ushant, but where is Cornwallis? However, I shall block up Brest till he comes to liberate me.

5.30 p.m.

In sight of Saint Matthew's. Murray says, if the fleet was off Brest, that they must be seen. Blows strong at north. What a wind for carrying us to Portugal!

6 p.m.

Just got hold of the Sirius. Captain Prowse tells me that the admiral is cruising WNW from the Saints' Bridge twenty leagues. I have demonstrated the Victory off Brest, and am now going to seek the admiral in the ocean.

23 May.

If I do not find him by six o'clock, if the weather will allow me [I shall] shift myself into the Amphion, and leave the Victory to look for Cornwallis. I am clear, by his conduct, that there can be nothing in Brest to demand his attention. It blows very strong, and a heavy sea.

6 p.m.

Captain Neve [of the Hazard] is on board. He supposes the admiral ten leagues off Ushant: therefore there is no looking for him, and I am embarking in the Amphion.

Admiral Cornwallis, 23 May, 6.30 p.m.

I have the honour to transmit you the directions of the Admiralty for my joining you off Brest; but as I have not been so fortunate as to meet you, and the whole business of the Mediterranean waiting my arrival, I have judged it proper to shift my flag to the Amphion, and to proceed in her. If you have no commands for the Victory, I trust you will order her to join me without a moment's loss of time.

Sir J. Acton, 10 June.

Mr. Elliot and myself both concur on the advantages which must accrue, could the kingdoms of Naples and Sicily be kept perfectly neutral, but we doubt of the French allowing the advantage of such a neutrality; and therefore, although it may not be in the power of Great Britain to keep the French troops out of the kingdom of Naples, yet that [it] is perfectly easy for us to keep them out of Sicily, which if they were once to get a footing in, it would be totally lost for ever. Therefore we must naturally look on this object, and never allow the possibility of such an event happening, so ruinous to their Majesties, and disadvantageous to Great Britain.

Mr. Falcon, our Consul at Algiers, having been sent away in a very improper manner from Algiers, I have not, as I have done to the States of Tunis and Tripoli, sent any civil message or notification of my arrival in these seas; it must depend on the wisdom of administration what line of conduct they mean to pursue, for, as is known to many Lords of your Board, our conduct must be decisive, whether it is under all circumstances to force the present consul on the Dey, or to submit to the Dey's having another consul named. . . . All I wish and submit to their Lordships, with great respect, is, that if the business is left to me, my orders may be decisive. The insolence of the Dey's cruisers is beyond whatever I have known, and if we give up one tittle of what we originally demand, we shall always be troubled with his insolence. The striking a sudden blow on his numerous cruisers is the only way we have of bringing him to terms. Should the business be left to me, I shall go to Algiers, and if the Dey refuses a complete acquiescence in our demands, instantly take all his cruisers.

<small>Sir E. Nepean, 2 June.</small>

It is a most important point to decide (the French having invaded the kingdom, although with a pretence not just or honourable,) when Sicily ought to be placed in a state of security. For the present, I am content to say that Messina need not be taken possession of; but the strictest watch must be kept by Sir John Acton, that we are not lulled into a fatal security, and thus lose both the kingdoms. If the French assemble a greater number of troops than usual at Brindisi, Otranto, and Tarento, or assemble any number of large boats at those places, particularly Tarento, then I think that not a moment should be lost to secure Sicily. In a small degree we risk it every day, in hopes of preserving the kingdom of Naples; but for the present moment I am, if Sir John Acton coincides with me, induced to participate in the risk. I shall instantly send two ships of war to cruise off Cape Spartivento, and towards the Gulf of Tarento, to give a check to the movements of troops by sea. By land I cannot judge of the time, but a few boats would very soon bring over from Reggio some thousands of troops; nor could all the navy of Europe prevent the passage, the current running seven miles an hour. Therefore I shall only observe again, that to save for the moment Naples, we

<small>H. Elliot, 25 June. Off Capri.</small>

risk the two kingdoms, and General Acton must join me in this heavy responsibility.

Capt. Richardson, June 26 June.

Whereas the French have taken possession of Pescara, Brindisi, Otranto, and Tarento, and it being apprehended that they will convoy their troops along shore either into Sicily or the coast of Calabria opposite to it, you are therefore hereby required and directed (notwithstanding former orders) to proceed with his Majesty's ship under your command, and cruise very diligently off Cape Spartivento and on the coast towards Tarento, for the purpose of intercepting any French troops, which I have reason to believe will be attempted to be convoyed along shore; and in the event of your falling in with them, to take, sink, burn, and destroy them, without regard to their being in any ship or vessel bearing a neutral flag. You are to continue on this service until you are relieved, or receive my further orders.

H. Addington, 28 June.

Knowing how very much you are pressed for time, I shall [write] as briefly as possible, consistent with telling you my sentiments on all the topics which I shall necessarily touch upon, with that sincerity which becomes me to you, be my opinion right or wrong.

I shall only say one word of Gibraltar, on which I had a serious conversation with Sir Thomas Trigge, on the impropriety of placing Dillon's regiment [1] as part of the garrison of Gibraltar. When we reflect how that regiment is composed, and that fifty men, the usual guard at Land Port Gate, by being corrupted might lose the place, who shall say Gibraltar is secure with those troops? If it is said, do not trust them with the guard, then you show your distrust, and naturally they become your enemies. The regiment of Rolle is a fine corps, and will serve faithfully, but I would not trust them at Gibraltar.

The next point I come to is Algiers. Mr. Falcon the consul having sent home his own account of the transaction, it rests with Government to determine what steps are to be taken. All that I entreat, if the matters are left to me to settle, [is] that our demands for satisfaction be fixed; for if we give way in the smallest thing, the insolence of the Dey will but increase. Whatever the wisdom of Government directs shall be attended to. The alternative must be instantaneous war on a refusal to our demands, or an entire acquiescence. Mr. F. thinks that the Dey never will receive him. He knows best the reasons why he thinks so. . . .

---

[1] That regiment, as also De Rolle's, was formed entirely of foreigners.

The Maltese are in the highest spirits, and sincerely hope that they will now be never separated from England. My opinion of Malta, as a naval station for watching the French in Toulon, is well known; and my present experience of what will be a three weeks' passage, most fully confirms me in it. The fleet can never go there if I can find any other corner to put them in: but having said this, I now declare, that I consider Malta as a most important outwork to India, that it will ever give us great influence in the Levant, and indeed all the southern parts of Italy. In this view, I hope we shall never give it up. I carried out orders from Lord Hobart that General Villettes was to hold 2,000 men at my requisition, if they could be spared from the defence of Malta, for the service of Sicily. The language of General Villettes was natural: 'The garrison appointed for Malta is not more than on the most economical number of men was judged sufficient: and, looking to the assistance of the Maltese in case of a siege, that these numbers of British troops were only sufficient for the ordinary duties, and that, when the Neapolitan troops went away (and he was ordered to send them away), the duty would be very severe; that the addition of Maltese troops, when trained and formed, would be little better than a well-formed militia; and, however much they undoubtedly would assist, yet they could not be counted as British troops; however, that he should not hesitate in providing 1,200 men and a corps of artillery for the service of Messina, whenever I might call for them:' and the general wished that I should mention this conversation when I had any opportunity of communicating with ministers. . . . Sir Alexander Ball thinks, that if half the troops were gone on other services, particularly to Sicily, that the Maltese would defend the island against any force the French could send, supported by our fleet. Truth probably lies between; but these sort of orders should never be left discretionary. You make an officer responsible for the safety of the place, yet tell him in the same breath, 'Send away so many men, if you can spare them without evident risk.' The conduct of the officer must be naturally to secure himself from the very great responsibility thrown upon him by such an order.

The state of Sicily is almost as bad as a civilised country can be. There are no troops fit to be called such, with a scarcity of corn never known, and of course bread so dear that the lower class of people are discontented. The nobles are oppressors, and the middle rank wish for a change; and although they would prefer us to the French, yet I believe they would receive the French rather than not change from the oppression of the nobles. The citadel of Messina is strong and in good order, but with a few miserable troops badly paid, if paid at all; therefore what could be expected from them? A French frigate has been there lately, a French aide-de-camp to the Grand Master, and, lastly, General Vial: they have good eyes, and many at Messina are seduced by them; and if the Neapolitan troops at Malta were removed there, I fear we should find more enemies and the French more friends. . . . I send you copies of my letters to Sir John Acton, the king and queen, with their answers, Mr. Elliot's, and likewise those I have sent to Lord St. Vincent, for him to lay them before the Cabinet. Here it is necessary to observe to you, that a sea-officer cannot hold any official correspondence but with the secretary of the Admiralty, without an order for that purpose, which is often given; therefore I have certainly irregularly sent them to Lord St. Vincent, as a cabinet minister—conceiving they are on subjects which the Board of Admiralty can have nothing to do with, much less the clerks of that office, through whose hands they must pass. . . .

Sardinia is declared neutral, but that no foreign troops would be allowed to land. I wish they may keep off the French. We have no troops to assist them, if they wanted our assistance.

Rome.—A letter from Mr. Jackson, his Majesty's minister to the King of Sardinia, of 17 June, says: 'I have seen the Secretary of State of this Government, and his Eminence told me there was no doubt that this State would be suffered to remain neuter, and consequently, that the ships of the belligerent powers will be received in the ports of the Pope's States.' This may be the case for the moment, but if we were to receive the least advantage by it, I am sure we should be turned out as heretofore.

Tuscany.—It is difficult to know how to consider this State; they are not our friends, and it would, perhaps, be hard to consider them as enemies. Yet why should France use them against us, and we suffer Leghorn to enjoy its commerce for the advantage, ultimately, of the French? for it is they who receive the fruits of the Tuscan labour and commerce. And as the French have declared Leghorn in a state of siege, I can see no impropriety of considering it so likewise, and for our Government to place it in a state of blockade whilst the French remain in it.

Genoa or Liguria.—The same as the Italian Republic; it is France as much as Toulon; it has not even a name of independence. Therefore I shall, as far as I see at this present moment, have no hesitation in considering all Genoese vessels as French. Everything at Genoa is French; therefore I hope that not a moment will be lost in declaring Genoa so considered. The blockade of Genoa ought to be declared instantly; if not, it will be what it always has been, the granary of the south of France and the north part of Italy. . . . I do not think that we ought to allow the French armies and friends to be maintained and enriched by our not blockading all the Genoese ports. I therefore hope that this will instantly be done. The Imperial and Greek flag are filling it and Leghorn with corn.

Morea.—It is perfectly clear that the French are at work in that country, either to prepare for their own reception, or to induce the Greeks to revolt against the Porte, and either way, it is a chain for their getting again to Egypt. If the French or their friends conquer the Morea, Egypt would be the price of returning it, unless by an alliance with the Mamelukes they can possess both.

To this long letter, I shall only beg to call your attention for what purpose the French are collecting such an army in Italy, where at present there can be no prospect of an army able to face them: 13,000 are in the kingdom of Naples, 8,000 are at this moment in Leghorn, 6,000 marched in on 28 June, the other parts of Italy are filling with troops, even drawing them from Switzerland. The objects must be the conquest of Naples (perhaps Sicily), and certainly getting over to the Morea; therefore I regret the removal of our Egyptian army, which in any of these enterprises have kept the French in check. *2 July.*

I joined our fleet yesterday. With the casual absence of one or two ships, we shall be always seven sail of the line; and as the French have at least seven—I believe nine—nearly ready, we are in hopes that Bonaparte may be angry, and order them out, which, I have no doubt, will put our ships in high feather; for I never knew any wants after a victory, although we are always full of them before. *9 July.*

Another great plan of Bonaparte's is now perfectly clear; he will attempt the Morea, either by assisting the Greeks in an insurrection against the Porte, or this may be done in concert with Russia. On this important subject we are both agreed, that it is very probable those two powers may have in view, by concert, the downfall of the Turkish Empire in Europe. Candia and Egypt would, of course, if this plan is followed, be given to the French, when, sooner or later, farewell India! But even supposing Russia has nothing to do with this plan, it would equally answer Bona- *Lord Moira, 2 July.*

parte's purpose of alarming the Porte, to do it by the Greeks or by assisting Ali Vizir in throwing off his dependence on the Porte; he would be equally ready to suppress or support even rebellion, provided the reward, Egypt, were the same. That is his great object at present, and for it he would sacrifice either Greeks, Russians, or Turks. We know he is not very scrupulous in the honourable means of accomplishing his darling object. . . . My firm opinion is, that the Mediterranean will again be an active scene; and if Ministers do not look out, I shall have the Brest fleet to pay me a visit; for as the army can only be moved by the protection of a superior fleet, that fleet they will try to have, and a month's start of us would do all the mischief.

Duke of Clarence, 5 July. Off Monaco. Owing to the frequent calms at this season in the Mediterranean, we have not yet joined Sir Richard, but I hope to see them to-morrow. Reports say that the fleet is in very good order as to discipline, but miserably off in respect to numbers; we have only to hope that the French will soon give us an opportunity of trying our strength with them. It is perhaps very difficult for anyone to say what are the plans of Bonaparte: he is assembling a very large army in Italy, and has already placed 13,000 men in the kingdom of Naples. I think it can only be with a view to conquer it, when it may, on some pretence or other, suit his convenience. The Morea, and ultimately Egypt, are in his view: therefore his assembling so many troops in Italy—they say full 80,000—can only be for the purpose of removing them across the Adriatic. With this idea, I fully expect that the French fleet from Brest will assuredly come into the Mediterranean, to protect this army across the water, and alongshore from Genoa, Leghorn, &c., which are full of troops. We must keep a good look out, both here and off Brest; and if I have the means, I shall try and fight one party or the other before they form a junction.

Lord St. Vincent, 8 July. Off Toulon. I joined the fleet this morning, and as far as outside show goes, they look very well; but they complain of their bottoms, and, as you will see, are very short of men. By the Toulon report, your Lordship will see that we are not very superior, if anything, in point of numbers; for it seems uncertain whether there are not more than the seven clearly in a state of forwardness. My reports from Italy say nine, five frigates and some corvettes. Seven of the line and five frigates are clearly to be seen, with two admirals and a commodore, and a commodore in the frigate. However, your Lordship may rely that I shall make the best of what I have; but you will see that I cannot detach any ships of the line for the

Straits' mouth. The Monmouth and Agincourt sail very ill, and in these times are hardly to be reckoned. I cannot send them to watch either Genoa or Leghorn; and if these gentry should come forth, I shall want all the 74's.

The French in Toulon are equal to me at this moment, but I do not think they will come out till they have a greater superiority. If they do, I shall be agreeably disappointed. The event, I trust, although we are miserably short of men, would be glorious, and hasten a peace. . . . A. Davison, 8 July.

I will not say more about securing Sicily than I have done. I send the Superb, 74, Captain Keats, one of the very best officers in his Majesty's navy. I have directed him to remain fourteen days at Naples, and if you represent by letter that it is, from extraordinary circumstances, necessary that he should remain longer, Captain Keats has directions to acquiesce. But I trust your Excellency will not do this unless such necessity does exist; for you will recollect that I am left with six sail of the line opposed to seven or nine—in which number are two 64-gun ships. But I take every responsibility to show my attention to the safety of the royal family of Naples. H. Elliot, 11 July.

Give me leave to introduce Captain Keats to your particular notice. His health has not been very good, but I hope he will soon recover; for his loss would, I assure you, be a serious one to our navy, and particularly to me; for I esteem his person alone as equal to one French 74, and the Superb and her captain equal to two 74-gun ships: therefore, if it is not necessary, you will not keep him, for another ship will be on her way to Naples at the time I guess she will be near her departure; and although I should be glad to see the French out, even six to nine, yet these are odds which, although I should not avoid, yet ought not to be seeking. 11 July.

The ships having come out on the expectation of a three weeks' cruise, I am, in turn, sending them into port, to prepare for a war cruise. Many of the ships have much scurvy in them, but onions and lemons I hope will eradicate that complaint, and a sight of the French squadron twenty leagues at sea will cure all our complaints. Lord St. Vincent, 12 July.

The Monmouth and Agincourt are certainly, for the men they have, most extraordinarily well-manned ships; but in point of sailing, the Britannia was, in her last days, a flyer compared to them. I verily believe that a French seventy-four, main-topsail to the mast, would beat them in turning to windward, but their men would be a sufficient number, filled up with landsmen, to man 13 July.

a three-decker: therefore if the Admiralty direct particular ships to be sent home when others are sent out, I hope these two will be amongst the first. When a winter's cruise comes, they never can keep company with the squadron.

Capt. Gore, Medusa, 21 July.

Whereas there is reason to believe that a squadron of the enemy's ships of war are coming from the West Indies or from Brest, to join the fleet in Toulon; you are therefore hereby required and directed to take your route from Cape Spartel towards Madeira, from thence to Cape St. Vincent, and to Cape Spartel, and to use every possible endeavour to gain such intelligence of the enemy's movements and intentions as you may judge necessary for my information, which you are to forward to me by a sloop of war from Gibraltar; but should you fall in with an enemy's squadron steering for the Mediterranean, you are in that case to join me on my rendezvous off Toulon without a moment's loss of time, sending a boat into Gibraltar to acquaint any of the squadron which may be there with such information, that if of the line they may join me immediately.

H. Elliot, 26 July.

I sincerely hope that the Superb has not been detained at Naples, for I can very ill spare the services of such a ship. The French squadron—seven sail of the line, five or six frigates, and six or seven corvettes—in the whole eighteen sail, are in appearance ready for sea, every sail bent. At this moment I am here with five sail of the line, and, when Monmouth goes to Naples, only four, to oppose this force. However, nothing shall induce me to neglect the personal safety of the royal family, and Monmouth shall go. Your Excellency is aware that I can send no ship to Naples which wants refitting, and, therefore, that parting with a perfect ship of the line is a serious thing. The Kent and Agincourt are gone to Malta, the Triumph to Gibraltar, and the Gibraltar wants to go into port to refit, having sprung her mizen-mast and main-yard. I wished to have sent her to Naples, but I am obliged to keep her and send a sound ship. However, this state of suspense will very soon be over. I only hope that Sicily will be guarded; that the French will demand it I am sure.

I have heard no rumours of a war with Algiers, nor do I believe a word of it; therefore I cannot begin with them. The French fleet from St. Domingo, I think, will come to the Mediterranean—perhaps, first to Cadiz, to get the Spaniards to escort them. If so, I may have two fleets to fight; but if I have the ships, the more the better.

We have a report through Italy of negotiations for peace and changes of administration. As for peace, we cannot have one but on degrading and dishonourable terms—sooner than which, we had better spend the last shilling in resisting like men. The Italian papers mention Mr. Yorke as First Lord of the Admiralty. If so, what becomes of the virtuous Sir T. T. and Tucker? But I care not who is in or out—I shall endeavour to do my duty to the country.

<small>A. Davison, 27 July.</small>

On 30 July the Victory joined the fleet, and Nelson at once hoisted his flag on board her, taking with him Captain Hardy, who superseded Sutton.

Whereas I have received information that there is a French seventy-four and some frigates at Cadiz, that may attempt the blocking up our trade entering the Straits, you are therefore hereby required and directed to proceed immediately with his Majesty's ship Donegal under your command, and take your station outside the Straits in such situation as you may judge most likely to fall in with the enemy's force above mentioned or any of their privateers or cruisers, as well as for the protection of the trade of his Majesty's subjects.

<small>Sir R. J. Strachan, 10 August.</small>

And on the 11th, a similar order was sent to Captain Cracraft of the Anson, to keep the Adriatic open to the trade, and prevent the enemy conveying troops across to the Morea from the heel of Italy.

I shall be truly thankful if you will have the goodness to put my Bronte estate in a train, that if I cannot receive the value of it, and have done with it, that, at least, I may receive the full rental regularly: for I never will lay out another sixpence on it, but am content to pay a certain sum for the attention of some respectable person to receive the rents and to remit them to London. As you are so good as to offer to attend to this serious concern to me, I will enter at large into the subject. I told Græfer, on first setting out, that I would give up two years' rent for fitting up a house and improving. I paid more attention to another sovereign than my own; therefore the king of Naples' gift of Bronte to me, if it is not now settled to my advantage, and to be permanent, has cost me a fortune, and a great deal of favour which I might have enjoyed, and [much] jealousy which I should have avoided. I repine not on those accounts. I did my duty, to the Sicilifying my own conscience, and I am easy. It will be necessary, before you can take any steps beyond inquiry, to know from Sir John Acton what has been done, and what is intended.

<small>A. Gibbs, Palermo, 11 August.</small>

All that I beg is, that the just thing may be done immediately, and that I may have it permanent. I shall never again write an order about the estate. If the estate cannot be returned, [on] my receiving the whole value, the income nett ought to be paid me, which the hospital received; [and this] as delivered to me, was 6,700 ounces on the average for seven years preceding.

Dr. Baird, August.

The fleet is healthy; but the last ships out, although they came to sea wretches, are, generally speaking, in the most healthy condition: they are in the best humour, which is a great conducer to health. I am obliged to turn myself to every corner which is open to us for supplies—from Malta the passage is so very long, that everything we have sent for has spoiled. I am now at work in Spain, and have procured some bullocks and a good supply of onions—the latter we have found the greatest advantage from. It has appeared odd to me, but all the ships' companies who have served here under the war (I mean that have not been paid off) are full of the scurvy. I am sure, from the high opinion which I entertain of your judgment, that whatever regulations you have recommended will be of great use; the health of our seamen is invaluable; and to purchase that, no expense ought to be spared.

Lord Radstock, 22 August.

I have had the pleasure of making acquaintance with your son. He sent me a drawing of the Esquerques as a present. Whenever the Medusa joins I will consult with Gore as to his coming directly into the Victory; but you may rely that he shall be made as soon after he has served his time as is in my power. The sons of brother-officers have an undoubted claim to our protection, and when to that is added the son of a very old friend, nothing can, my dear Lord, weigh stronger with me. Your conduct to me on 14 February[1] has proved you a noble man; and I am sorry to say that I fear we have some peers who do not answer that description. We are watching the coming of the French squadron: they are ready, and I do not think Bonaparte will allow them to remain longer in port.

II. Addington, 24 August.

I am looking out for the French squadron—perhaps you may think impatiently; but I have made up my mind never to go into port till after the battle, if they make me wait a year, provided the Admiralty change the ships, who cannot keep the sea in the winter, except Victory, Canopus, Donegal, and Belleisle. The Admiralty knows the state of the others, and will relieve them as soon as they can. The Triumph, Superb, Monmouth, Agincourt, Kent, Gibral-

[1] When Lord Radstock was third in command.

tar, and Renown, are certainly amongst the very finest ships in our service—the best commanded, and the very best manned, yet I wish them safe in England, where they would man, filled up with landsmen, fourteen sail of the line, and that I had ships not half so well manned in their room; for it is not a store-ship a week which could keep them in repair. This day, only six men are confined to their beds in the whole squadron.

At Marseilles are now ready to sail—the troops on board—a frigate, a corvette, and two armed transports, with 1,000 or 1,500 men under a General Ceroni, or Veroni. I believe they are bound to Corsica, to go over with the 5,000 Corsicans—if they get to Sardinia, it is gone. I am sending two frigates, the only ones I have with me, to cruise off Ajaccio, in Corsica, to try and intercept them; but what I mention these circumstances for is, that it may be necessary to mention it to the Russian Minister, for we may be accused of a breach of neutrality in Sardinia; for, being satisfied of the intention of the French invading Sardinia, I have directed the frigates to pursue them, even should they chase into Sardinia, and to take or destroy them, and also the Corsican troops; for if I wait till the island is taken I should feel deserving of reprobation. Of course they will say that we have broken the neutrality if we attack them in the ports of Sardinia before their conquest, and if we do not I shall be laughed at for a fool. Prevention is better than cure. . . . My station to the westward of Toulon, an unusual one, has been taken upon an idea that the French fleet is bound out of the Straits, and probably to Ireland. It is said 10,000 men are collecting at Toulon. . I shall follow them to the Antipodes. *(25 August.)*

The French fleet being perfectly ready for sea, seven of the line, six frigates, and some corvettes—two sail of the line are now rigging in the arsenal—I think it more than probable that they are bound to the westward, out of the Mediterranean. Therefore, as I am determined to follow them, go where they may, I wish you, in case they escape me, to send a frigate or sloop after them to find out their route, giving her a station where I may find her, and keep yourself either at the mouth of the Straits or off Europa Point, for I certainly shall not anchor at Gibraltar. You will, of course, keep this to yourself. *(Sir R. Strachan, 26 August.)*

Having received information that there is an embarkation of troops at Toulon (or Marseilles), intended to join the Corsicans, with a view to invade the island of Sardinia, and as I think Ajaccio is the most likely place in Corsica for their forming such junction, *(Capt. Donnelly, Narcissus, 26 August.)*

you are hereby required and directed to take his Majesty's ship Active under your command (whose captain has received my orders for that purpose), and proceed with all possible despatch, and take such station as you may judge most likely to intercept them, and prevent their landing or forming a junction with the Corsicans at Ajaccio or elsewhere; but should you fall in with them at sea, you are to use your utmost endeavours to take, sink, burn, or destroy the whole of them. If, however, the enemy should escape into any port of the Island of Sardinia, you are to proceed and attack them wherever you may fall in with them, without paying regard to any pretended flag of neutrality (except under the guns of Cagliari), or considering such port or place entitled to the respect of neutrality, but as an invaded country by the enemy. In the event of your finding them at Cagliari, that fort being sufficient to prevent the enemy's landing, you are to afford the viceroy every assistance in your power to enable him to destroy the enemy, and frustrate their designs against the dominions of his Most Sacred Majesty the King of Sardinia.

J. B. Gilbert,[1] 13 Sept.

You will have the goodness to present my respectful compliments to the captain-general, and assure him that the return of deserters shall be reciprocal on my part, and that I have forgiven them at his request. You will also inform his excellency that I have read with no small surprise a paper purporting to have been given in during the year 1771, and now ordered to be put in force. I am ready to admit that the king of Spain may order us to be refused admittance into his ports, may refuse us, even when there, the rights of hospitality, as his excellency has done those of civility, in not even asking Captain Whitby to sit down, although there were others in his presence seated. His sovereign may certainly, if he pleases, go to war with us—I deny none of these rights; but I claim every indulgence which is shown to the ships of our enemies. The French squadron at Corunna are acting almost as they please; the Aigle French ship of war is not turned out of Cadiz, the French frigate Revenge is permitted to go out of that port, cruise, and return with prizes, and sell them. I will not state that every Spanish port is a home for French privateers, for this is well known; and I am informed that even at Barcelona English vessels captured by the French have been sold there. You will acquaint his excellency that I claim for every British ship, or squadron, the right of lying as long as I please in the

---

[1] Consul at Barcelona.

ports of Spain, whilst it is allowed to other powers; that I claim the rights of hospitality and civility, and every other right which the harmony subsisting between our sovereigns entitles us to. You will acquaint his excellency that I can mean no disrespect personally to himself; but that it is a British admiral returning an answer to a Spanish captain-general, through the same channel which conveyed the message.

When British seamen and marines so far degrade themselves in time of war as to desert from the service of their own country and enter into that of Spain; when they leave one shilling per day, and plenty of the very best provisions, with every comfort that can be thought of for them—for twopence a day, black bread, horse-beans, and stinking oil for their food;—when British seamen or marines turn Spanish soldiers, I blush for them: they forfeit in their own opinion, I am sure, that character of love of their own country which foreigners are taught to admire. A Briton to put himself under the lash of a Frenchman or Spaniard must be more degrading to any man of spirit than any punishment I could inflict on their bodies. I shall leave the punishment to their own feelings, which, if they have any, and are still Englishmen, must be very great. But as they thought proper to abandon, voluntarily, their wives, fathers, mothers, and every endearing tie, and also all prospect of returning to their native country, I shall make them remain out of that country which they do not wish to see, and allow others, who love their country, and are attached to their families, to return in their stead. And, as they have also thought proper to resign all their pay, I shall take care that it is not returned to them, nor their 'R.' taken off; but it shall be noted against their names, 'Deserted to the Spaniards,' or 'Entered as a Spanish soldier,' as the case was. *General memo, 13 Sept.*

The above memorandum respecting the desertion of British seamen or marines is to be read to the respective companies of his Majesty's ships and vessels under my command, and copies thereof to be stuck up in the most public places of the ships, in order that the magnitude of the crime may be properly impressed on their minds.

I am much obliged to you for your goodness about the shells. I shall be very glad of a hundred for 12-pounders. I do not mean to use them at sea, for that I hope to consider burning our own ships; but in case they run ashore, then a few put into their sides will do their business. *General Villettes, 16 Sept.*

Sir A. J. Ball, 16 Sept.

I bear up for every gale. I must not in our present state quarrel with the north-westers—with crazy masts and no port or spars near us. Indeed, in the whole station, there is not a topmast for a seventy-four. On the 11th, a ship of the line and some frigates were outside Sepet; a rear-admiral, chef d'escadre, and another ship of the line, four in the whole, &c. Eight were under sail; but seeing Canopus stand under Sicie, they hauled their wind and worked in again. On the 12th and 13th they were at anchor. That night I sent Belleisle to work off the port, wind blowing strong out ESE and SE, which has drove us to twenty leagues west of Sicie. I am a little anxious at her not joining, but they must have more than common luck to get hold of her. The squadron has health beyond what I have almost ever seen, except our going to the Nile; and I hope, if the French will give us the opportunity, that our beef and pudding will be as well applied.

Sir E. Nepean, 24 Sept.

As it is more than probable that the fleet under my command will be obliged to keep the seas during the whole of the winter season, for the purpose of watching the enemy's ships at Toulon, and as there is in the Gulf of Lion, and its vicinity, upon an average, three days' gale of severe blowing weather out of the seven, which frequently comes on suddenly, and thereby exposes the topmasts, topsail-yards, and sails, to great hazard, under every care and attention; I am therefore to desire you will be pleased to communicate this circumstance to the Lords Commissioners of the Admiralty, and suggest to their Lordships the propriety of sending out a sufficient number of topmasts, topsail-yards, and spare sails for the ships they may judge necessary for the service before-mentioned as early as possible, there being none of the two former in store, either at Gibraltar or Malta.

Sir R. Strachan, 26 Sept.

The occurrences which pass every day in Spain forebode, I fancy, a speedy war with England; therefore it becomes proper for me to put you upon your guard, and advise you how to act under particular circumstances. By looking at the former line of conduct on the part of Spain, which she followed just before the commencement of the last war, we may naturally expect the same events to happen. The French Admiral Richery was in Cadiz, blocked up by Admiral Man: on 22 August they came to sea, attended by the Spanish fleet, which saw the French safe beyond St. Vincent, and returned into Cadiz. Admiral Man very properly did not choose to attack Admiral Richery under such an escort.[1] This is a prelude to what I must request your strict attention to; at the same time, I am fully aware that you must be guided, in some measure, by actual circumstances.

I think it very probable, even before Spain breaks with us, that they may send a ship or two of the line to see L'Aigle round Cape St. Vincent; and that if you attack her in their presence, they may attack you; and giving them possession of the Donegal would be more than either you or I should wish, therefore I am certain it must be very comfortable for you to know my sentiments. From what you hear in Cadiz, you will judge how far you may venture yourself in company with a Spanish squadron; but if you are of opinion that you may trust yourself near them, keeping certainly out of gun-shot, send your boat with a letter to the Spanish commodore, and desire to know whether he means to defend the French ships; and get his answer in writing, and have it as plain as possible. If it be 'yes, that he will fire at you if you attack the French under his protection,' then, if you have force enough, make your attack on the whole body, and take them all if you can, for I should consider such an answer as a perfect declaration of war. If you are too weak for such an attack, you must desist; but you certainly are fully authorised to take the ships of Spain whenever you meet them. Should the answer be ambiguous, you must then act as your judgment may direct you, and I am sure that will be very proper. Only recollect, that it would be much better to let the French ships escape, than to run too great a risk of losing the Donegal, yourself, and ship's company.

It is now near three months since my last letters were dated from England; and but for a French newspaper, which hitherto we have procured through Spain from Paris, we should not have known how the world went on; and reports have so often changed the First Lord of the Admiralty, that I know not if I am now writing to him; but that does not matter; I trust I am writing to an old friend, who sincerely wishes me as well as I do him.

Lord St. Vincent, 27 Sept.

I have said all my say long ago on the subject of the ships here; therefore I shall not bore you on that subject again. The fact is this—all the ships have expected every day before the war to go to England; therefore, when the war came, they wanted for everything—more especially to go to England. However, a good

---

[1] Another case in point had occurred in 1741, when, on 7 December, the French squadron, under De Court, protected the Spaniards from the attack of Haddock off Cape Gata.

deal of that fever is wore off, and we are really got to a state of health which is rarely witnessed. I have exerted myself to get all the good things we could from Spain, and latterly our cattle and onions have been procured from France; but from the apparent incivilities of the Spaniards, I suppose we are on the eve of being shut out. Our length of passage from Malta is terrible. We have not procured one single article of refreshment from thence since the fleet sailed, 18 May; therefore, if a fleet here had only Malta to trust to, the fleet must go to Malta, for the good things of Malta could never come to us; and in that case the French might do as they pleased between here and Gibraltar, for two months together. At this moment I think the squadron, as far as relates to me, are fit to go to Madras. Their hulls want docking. I hope to be able to keep the sea all the winter—in short, to stay at sea till the French choose to come to sea; and then I hope to send many of our ships who want what I cannot give them, to England, towing a line-of-battle ship. I believe we are uncommonly well disposed to give the French a thrashing, and we are keen; for I have not seen a French flag on the sea since I joined the squadron. A fortnight ago, three or four sail of the line were under sail, and some had got a few miles from Sepet, but I believe it was only for an exercise. Reports say they are hard at work, fitting out two new 80-gun ships. Their lower rigging is over the mast-heads. I wish they would make haste, for our gales of wind, Admiral Campbell says, are harder and more frequent than ever. I believe them much the same—always very violent, and a heavy sea.

H. Addington, 27 Sept. We are at this moment the healthiest squadron I ever served in, for the fact is we have no sick, and are all in good humour. The Spaniards are now so very uncivil to our ships, that I suppose we shall not be much longer friends. . . . I sent a few days ago to Minorca, but the Spaniards would not give our ship *pratique*; but Captain Donnelly learnt that there are three Frenchmen taking an account of the revenue and how it is raised, and making every minute inquiry. Does this portend a cession of that island? I fear it does, and the Minorquins think so. I should be very sorry to see that happen; for, however valuable and important Malta may be in other respects, and no man rates its value more than I do, yet as a place to get refreshments from, for a fleet off Toulon, it is useless; I always thought it, and now I know it. . . . Minorca may have its inconveniences, but its conveniences are so great that I trust at the moment a Spanish war is certain, that we shall be able to secure it.

We are healthy beyond example, and in great good humour with ourselves; and so sharp-set, that I would not be a French admiral in the way of any of our ships for something. I believe we are in the right fighting trim, let them come as soon as they please. I never saw a fleet altogether so well officered and manned. Would to God the ships were half as good, but they are what we call crazy.

A.Davison, 27 Sept.

On 4 October orders were issued for the blockade of Genoa and Spezia, on the receipt of the following letter from Lord Hobart, dated 23 August.

'In consequence of the information contained in your Lordship's letter to Mr. Addington of the 28 June—9 July,[1] and confirmed by various circumstances, it has been judged indispensably necessary for his Majesty's service, to give immediate orders that the ports of Genoa and Spezia should be placed in a state of blockade; and the regular notification thereof having been made to the ministers of the different neutral powers residing at this Court, your Lordship will receive the necessary instructions for your guidance by this opportunity from the Lords Commissioners of the Admiralty.

'The hostile conduct of the Government of Algiers towards the Maltese, since they have been under the protection of his Majesty, renders it necessary that your Lordship should immediately take measures for demanding that all Maltese captured by the Algerine cruisers during that period should be forthwith released, and delivered up to whomsoever you may depute to receive them; and in the event of the Regency of Algiers refusing to comply with your demand, I am commanded by his Majesty to direct that your Lordship do adopt the most vigorous and effectual measures for taking or destroying all ships and vessels belonging to the said Regency, or to the subjects thereof; and that you do pursue every mode of distressing that State, until the Dey shall manifest a disposition to comply with the just demand which your Lordship is hereby directed to make, in his Majesty's name, on behalf of the Maltese people living under the protection of his Majesty's Government.

'The very judicious observations contained in your Lordship's letter to Mr. Addington upon the political state of the South of Italy, and the opinions which you have detailed in your correspondence with his Majesty's minister at the Court of Naples, have been fully considered by his Majesty's confidential servants; and I have much satisfaction in acquainting your Lordship that the line of conduct which you have suggested for the Court of Naples to pursue, under the critical circumstances of its present situation, has been highly approved; and Mr. Elliot will be instructed by Lord Hawkesbury to continue to communicate with your Lordship upon every occasion relative to that subject.

'I am likewise to desire that your Lordship's correspondence upon these, and all other political subjects, should be addressed to me, that I may be enabled to lay them before the king, and to convey to you his Majesty's commands thereon.'

[1] See *ante*, p. 308.

H. Addington, 6 October.

The French admiral mounted yesterday morning his sea-vane, a thing which a landsman would not notice; but it gives a certainty to my mind that they wish to put to sea, and never was a squadron of British ships more anxious to meet them. I can have no excuse, nor do I want my country to make any for me: if I see the enemy, my exertions shall be used to lay the squadron well in, and the event, with the blessing of Providence on a just cause, we have no reason to fear.

Sir A. J. Ball, 6 October.

I had intended sending Sir Richard Bickerton to Malta, but I believe, from appearances, that the French fleet are so near putting to sea, that it would be cruel in me to send so excellent an officer and friend away, at a moment we may expect so glorious a harvest. I would give a good deal for a copy of the French admiral's orders. Report says it is Decrès, as he fought the Guillaume Tell so well. If he is a fighting man so much the better. I hope he will not run away; we may want heels to catch [him]— that is the only fear I have.

Capt. Schomberg, Madras, 7 October.

At this distance it is impossible for me to regulate everything with exactness. We must all in our several stations exert ourselves to the utmost, and not be nonsensical in saying, 'I have an order for this, that, or the other,' if the king's service clearly marks what ought to be done.

H. Elliot, 8 October.

I feel truly sensible of your kindness, and the trouble you have taken in detailing to me all the means of precaution which his Excellency Sir John Acton has taken respecting Sicily, and I fully rely that those measures will be continued, and that neither Sicily nor Naples will want our assistance. God knows, we have occasion enough for our troops without begging them to be received, and nothing but the strong order I brought out would have induced General Villettes to part with a man from Malta. General Villettes writes me the same good accounts from Messina as you have done. . . .

I assure your Excellency that I would not, upon any consideration, have a Frenchman in the fleet, except as a prisoner. I put no confidence in them. You think yours good, the queen thinks hers the same: I believe they are all alike. Whatever information you can get me, I shall be very thankful for, but not a Frenchman comes here. Forgive me: but my mother hated the French. . . .

Two French frigates have had a narrow escape. They have been chased twice—once into Corsica with the troops, by the Agincourt, 64: and on Sunday last, by two frigates, Active and Phœbe, into St. Tropez; but these fellows will not fight if they can help it. Never was health equal to this squadron. It has been within ten days of five months at sea, and we have not a man confined to his bed: therefore if these fellows wait till we are forced into port, they must wait some time.

May I presume to request of your Excellency to present my humble duty to the king and queen, and assure them of my eternal attachment to their royal persons and to all their family, and any other civil speeches you may be so good as to say for me. To be a courtier is your trade, and I know myself to be a cobbler at that work.

I send you my correspondence with the Bashaw of Tripoli, and your Lordship will observe that he is, as usual, most friendly disposed towards us. During the time of Bonaparte's greatest success in Egypt, he gave up to me as prisoners, the French consul and every Frenchman in his dominions, amounting to fifty-seven, and his arsenal was always open for the supply of our ships. I have not thought it, however, proper to notice the indirect application for gunpowder and grape-shot, on account of his war with the Americans, without the approbation of Government. Although the bashaw is fully entitled to every act of kindness from us, yet it will strike your Lordship, as it has me, that it might give cause for a discontent on the part of the Americans, which it must be our wish to avoid. . . . {Lord Hobart, 16 Oct.}

By letters from Mr. Elliot and Sir John Acton, I am glad to find that some active measures are taking for the security of Sicily, and putting Messina in such a state of defence that it cannot be taken by surprise. . . . I have always kept a ship at Naples for the personal security of the royal family; and I have strengthened the squadron which watches the French army in the heel of Italy, in case they should wish to cross to the Morea, which many think is their intention. What the real destination of the French fleet may be is very difficult for me to guess. Mr. Elliot thinks they will try to have Sicily previous to their going to Egypt; others think they may go direct to cover the army across to the Morea; others, that in the present unsettled state of Egypt, they may push with ten thousand men to Alexandria; and they may be bound outside the Mediterranean. Plausible reasons may certainly be given for every one of these plans, but I think one of the two last is their great object; and to those two points my whole attention is turned. If they put to sea, I hope to fall in with them, and then I have every reason to believe that all their plans will be frustrated.

Rev. W. Nelson, 18 Oct.

I sincerely hope that Canterbury will prove as profitable to you as to your predecessor last year; perhaps, if I take another French fleet, they may make you a bishop : therefore I shall try hard whenever they give me the opportunity. They are our superiors in numbers—they being eight to six, which is the force I can count upon being off Toulon; for one must be in turn in harbour watering, and I have Cadiz to watch with another, and one always at Naples, in case of accidents, for the security of the royal family; therefore, although the Admiralty may say I have ten at my orders, the fact is I can never count upon more than six. If I am so fortunate on the day of battle to have the seventh, I shall be very fortunate. For two days last week I was in a fever. A frigate spoke a Spanish vessel in the night, who said that he had seen a fleet of twelve sail of men-of-war off Minorca, steering to the westward. It was thick for two days, and our frigates could not look into Toulon; however, I was relieved, for the first time in my life, by being informed the French were still in port. They have a number of troops ready for embarkation; but as to their destination, that is a secret I am not entrusted with. The fleet has been five months at sea this day, and in two days I [shall] have been as long, but we are remarkably healthy, and in fine order to give the French a dressing. I shall try and do a little better with the Victory than Admiral Keppel. We are not remarkably well manned, but very well-disposed people.

Count Woronzow, 12 Oct.

The Count Mocenigo has sent me a complaint that three vessels, one under Russian colours and two under those of the Republic of the Seven Islands, have been taken by some English ships, and carried into Malta, and that the only answer the consul at Malta has obtained was, 'The Judge of the Vice-Admiralty Court is not yet arrived.' Without entering into the merits of the case, of which I can know nothing but from the reports sent me of ships detained or captured, whereof I send you a copy, your Excellency may rely there was great cause of suspicion that the vessels or cargoes, or both, were belonging to enemies, and were merely covered with neutral papers; and it even strikes me as odd in the complaint, they are stated as only bound to Messina, and that the other optional destination, Genoa, should be omitted. What occasion was there for concealing anything in an upright transaction? And there is another curious circumstance lately come to light, which is,

I believe, that on board the ship carrying Russian colours, a whole set of French papers have been found; however, your Excellency knows, that under such suspicious circumstances none but a judge can decide. My orders are positive for the respect due to the neutral flag; and with regard to Russia, I have repeated the orders for the strict observance of the seventh article of the treaty signed at St. Petersburg, the 5–17 June, 1801. I shall only lastly observe, that one hundred and seventy French vessels were in the Black Sea at the commencement of hostilities, and that by a magic touch of merchants, they became in a moment Russians, Imperials, Ionians, Ragusans, and not one French vessel remained!—Bravo!

I have sent to Sicily for the arms of Bronte, and the Heralds' College there has sent for my English arms, in order that they may be enrolled amongst those of the Sicilian nobility; therefore you will be so good as to send me out the same sort of thing which I sent to Germany. I very much doubt that I ever paid for that and several other things which you have done for me; therefore I desire (for in a man's trade there are no compliments) that you will send me out your regular bill, for I suppose you cannot live upon air, and if you are never paid, how is the pot to boil? When I take the French fleet, which I hope to do before Christmas, I suppose there will be more alterations.

G. Nayler,
York
Herald,
19 Oct.

The fleet being very much in want of water, I have taken the opportunity of the moonlight nights to come here in order to obtain it, and some refreshments for our crews, who have now been upwards of five months at sea. But our health and good humour is perfection, and we only want the French fleet out. This day week they had eight sail of the line ready, and a ninth fitting; so that we shall surely meet them some happy day, and I have no doubt but that we shall be amply repaid for all our cares and watchings. I have left frigates to watch them.

H. Elliot,
1 Nov.
Madalena
Islands.

We anchored in Agincourt Sound yesterday evening, and I assure you that I individually feel all the obligation due to you for your most correct chart and directions for these islands. We worked the Victory every foot of the way from Asinara to this anchorage, the wind blowing from Longo Sardo, under double-reefed topsails. I shall write to the Admiralty, stating how much they ought to feel obliged to your very great skill and attention in making this survey. This is absolutely one of the finest harbours I have ever seen.

Capt.
Ryves,
Gibraltar,
2 Nov.

Sir A. J. Ball, 7 Nov.

I do not think a Spanish war so near. We are more likely to go to war with Spain for her complaisance to the French; but the French can gain nothing, but be great losers, by forcing Spain to go to war with us; therefore I never expect that the Spaniards will begin, unless Bonaparte is absolutely mad, as many say he is. What! he begins to find excuses! I thought he would invade England in the face of the sun! Now he wants a three-days' fog, that never yet happened! and if it did, how are his craft to be kept together? He will soon find more excuses or there will be an end of Bonaparte, and may the devil take him!

Our two last reconnoitrings: Toulon has eight sail of the line, apparently ready for sea, five or six frigates, and as many corvettes—they count twenty-two sail of ships of war; a 74 is repairing. Whether they intend waiting for her I can't tell, but I expect them every hour to put to sea, and with troops; but their destination?—is it Ireland or the Levant? That is what I want to know. However, out they will come, and I trust we shall meet them. The event, with God's blessing on our exertions, we ought not to doubt; I really believe that we are the 'strong pull and pull together.' With this force opposed to me, I cannot with prudence leave myself with less than six sail of the line, and from various circumstances, ships going to water, &c., I am too often with only five frigates, and smaller vessels I am most distressed for. However, I send the Raven to be under Captain Schomberg's particular orders, for upon every occasion I had rather leave myself bare than have my friends complain. Lord St. Vincent's words are, ' We can send you neither ships or men, and with the resources of your mind, you will do without them very well.' Bravo, my Lord! I have all the inclination in the world to send Sir Richard Bickerton to Malta, but I dare not do it at this moment—not so much for the want of the ship, but from my sincere esteem for the admiral, and in charity to them both; for if the battle took place and Sir Richard absent, they would have reason to curse me for ever. But you may assure her ladyship that I know what attachment is, and that the admiral shall be the first detached after the battle; and if I can, on any belief that the enemy are not coming immediately to sea, he shall go before the battle.

General Memo, 7 Nov.

Lord Nelson is very sorry to find that notwithstanding his forgiveness of the men who deserted in Spain, it has failed to have its proper effect, and that there are still men who so far forget their duty to their king and country as to desert the service at a time when every man in England is in arms to defend it against the French. Therefore Lord Nelson desires that it may be perfectly understood, that if any man be so infamous as to desert from the service in future, he will not only be brought to a court-martial, but that if the sentence should be death, it will be most assuredly carried into execution.

If a pennant be shown over Signal No. 36, 'Engage the enemy on their starboard or weather side,' it signifies that ships are to engage on the enemy's starboard side, whether going large or upon the wind. Memo,
22 Nov

If a pennant be shown in the like manner over Signal No. 37, 'Engage the enemy on their larboard or lee side,' it signifies that ships are to engage on the enemy's larboard side, whether going large or upon a wind. These additions to be noted in the signal book in pencil only.

Saint George's ensigns are to be worn by every ship in action.

The French force, yesterday, at two o'clock, was correctly ascertained—eight sail of the line, eight frigates, and five or six corvettes, perfectly ready, and as fine as paint can make them. A ninth ship is visibly getting forward. I only hope in God we shall meet them. Our weather-beaten ships, I have no fears, will make their sides like a plum-pudding. H. Elliot,
24 Nov.
Off Toulon.

I have the honour to inclose, for your Excellency's information, two letters which will mark the conduct of the Spaniards towards us, and of which I doubt not but you will seriously complain. I trust that we shall be received in the Spanish ports in the same manner as the French. I am ready to make large allowances for the miserable situation Spain has placed herself in, but there is a certain line beyond which I cannot submit to be treated with disrespect. We have given up French vessels taken within gun-shot of the Spanish shore, and yet French vessels are permitted to attack our ships from the Spanish shore. Your Excellency may assure the Spanish Government, that in whatever place the Spaniards allow the French to attack us, in that place I shall order the French to be attacked. The old order of 1771, now put in force against us, is infamous; and I trust your Excellency will take proper steps that the present mode of enforcing it be done away. It is gross partiality, and not neutrality. J. H.
Frere,
28 Nov.

I herewith transmit you a report of survey on the main and

Sir E. Nepean, 4 Dec.

mizen rigging belonging to his Majesty's ship Excellent, together with a memorandum from Captain Sotheron, attached to the said report, which you will please to lay before the Lords Commissioners of the Admiralty for their information. It is much to be lamented that a ship so recently from England, and coming direct abroad from a king's yard, should have sailed in such a state; the master-attendant at Portsmouth must either have been blind to the situation of the rigging, or not have given himself trouble to discover its miserable state.

Duke of Clarence, 7 Dec.

The French fleet keep us waiting for them during a long and severe winter's cruise; and such a place as all the Gulf of Lion, for gales of wind from the NW to NE, I never saw, but by always going away large, we generally lose much of their force and the heavy sea of the gulf. However, by the great care and attention of every captain, we have suffered much less than could have been expected.

A. Davison, 12 Dec. Gulf of Palma.

My crazy fleet are getting in a very indifferent state, and others will soon follow. The finest ships in the service will soon be destroyed. I know well enough that if I was to go into Malta, I should save the ships during this bad season. But if I am to watch the French, I must be at sea, and if at sea, must have bad weather; and if the ships are not fit to stand bad weather, they are useless. I do not say much, but I do not believe that Lord St. Vincent would have kept the sea with such ships. But my time of service is nearly over. A natural anxiety, of course, must attend my station; but, my dear friend, my eyesight fails me most dreadfully. I firmly believe that, in a very few years, I shall be stone-blind. It is this only, of all my maladies, that makes me unhappy; but God's will be done.

Lord St. Vincent, 12 Dec.

The station I chose to the westward of Sicie, was to answer two important purposes: one to prevent the junction of a Spanish fleet from the westward, and the other to be to windward, so as to enable me, if the northerly gale came on to the NNW or NNE, to take shelter in a few hours either under the Hières Islands or Cape St. Sebastian; and I have hitherto found the advantage of the position. Now Spain, having settled her neutrality, I am taking my winter's station under St. Sebastian, to avoid the heavy seas in the gulf, and keep frigates off Toulon. From September we have experienced such a series of bad weather that is rarely met with, and I am sorry to say that all the ships which have been from England in the late war severely feel it.

The Kent has suffered so severely that she is going to Malta, and I much doubt our getting her to sea again under six weeks or two months, and the passage from Malta is hardly to be made with any ship. The Amazon, who I have not seen, but heard of, was three weeks from Malta as far as Minorca. In short, my dear Lord, if I was to allow this fleet to get into such a port as Malta, they had better be at Spithead. I know no way of watching the enemy but to be at sea, and therefore good ships are necessary. The Superb is in a very weak state, but her captain is so superior to any difficulties, that I hear but little from her. Triumph and Renown complain a good deal.

At Toulon the enemy are perfectly ready to put to sea, and they must soon come out, but who shall [say] where they are bound? My opinion is, certainly out of the Mediterranean. Malta is useless to me, and when I am forced to send a ship there, I never see her under two months. I am sure Toulon would be better watched from St. Helens than from Malta. Our ships are not in very good plight, and we want sails and spars for topmasts for 74s. There is not, I believe, one in this country. J. Tyson, 12 Dec.

As you from this day start in the world as a man, I trust that your future conduct in life will prove you both an officer and a gentleman. Recollect that you must be a seaman to be an officer, and also that you cannot be a good officer without being a gentleman. C. Connor, (?) Dec.

Were I to begin describing all the complaints and wants of this fleet, it would be exactly the same, I dare say, as you receive from all other stations; but as it can be attended with no good effect, I shall save myself the trouble of writing, and you of reading them. The storekeeper has sent two ships to the Adriatic [for] hemp, and therefore I hope that we shall in time get rope to supply our wants. Every bit of twice-laid stuff belonging to the Canopus is condemned, and all the running-rigging in the fleet, except the Victory's. We have fitted the Excellent with new main and mizen rigging; it was shameful for the dockyard to send a ship to sea with such rigging. The Kent is gone to Malta, fit only for a summer's passage. They are still under such alarm at Naples, that I cannot withdraw the Gibraltar. I have submitted to Sir Richard Strachan, whether the state of the French ships at Cadiz would allow of his coming to me for six weeks; for although I have no fears of the event of a battle with six to their eight, yet if I can have eight to their eight, I shall not despise the equality. We are not stoutly, or in any Sir T. Troubridge, 21 Dec.

manner well-manned in the Victory, but she is in very excellent order, thanks to Hardy; and I think, woe be to the Frenchman she gets alongside of.

You will see the reports respecting a naval hospital at Malta. It is curious that in a place taken by the close blockade of the navy, and when the only reason for keeping it was to have a naval station, that no spot has been allotted for a naval hospital; and we are upon sufferance from day to day. Bighi is certainly the only proper place, as it stands insulated with grounds, and has every means of comfort; but to complete it for 150 men would cost, besides the purchase of house and grounds, 1,000*l.*, and 2,000*l.* more to put it in order. Ball says 5,000*l.* would do the whole, but I say for 5, read 10,000*l.*

Lord
Hobart,
22 Dec.

If we could possess Sardinia, we should want neither Malta nor any other. This, which is the finest island in the Mediterranean, possesses harbours fit for arsenals, and of a capacity to hold our navy, within twenty-four hours' sail of Toulon; bays to ride our fleets in, and to watch both Italy and Toulon. No fleet could pass to the eastward between Sicily and the coast of Barbary, nor through the Faro of Messina. Malta, in point of position, is not to be named the same year with Sardinia. All the fine ports of Sicily are situated on the eastern side of the island, consequently of no use to watch anything but the Faro of Messina. And I venture to predict, that if we do not, the French will, get possession of that island. Sardinia is very little known. It was the policy of Piedmont to keep it in the background, and whoever it has belonged to, it seems to have been their maxim to rule the inhabitants with severity, in loading its produce with such duties as prevented the growth. I will only mention one circumstance as a proof: half a cheese was seized, because the poor man was selling it to our boats, and it had not paid the duty. Fowls, eggs, beef, and every article, are most heavily taxed. The [Court] of Sardinia certainly wants every penny to maintain itself; and yet I am told, after the wretched establishment of the island is paid, that the king does not receive 5,000*l.* sterling a year. The country is fruitful beyond idea, and abounds in cattle and sheep—and would in corn, wine, and oil. It has no manufactories. In the hands of a liberal Government, and freed from the dread of the Barbary States, there is no telling what its produce would not amount to. It is worth any money to obtain, and I pledge my existence it could be held for as little as Malta in its establishment, and produce a large revenue.

I have wrote to General Acton respecting the Gibraltar's joining me, yet your Majesty and family are the great objects of my care and attention; and although she would be acceptable on the day of battle, yet I trust, with the blessing of God on our just cause, that we shall give a very good account of the enemy without her. Therefore, whether the ship comes or not, entirely depends upon your Majesty's pleasure. *The King of Naples, 26 Dec.*

I leave it to the king's pleasure to send the Gibraltar for the battle or not. The safety of your royal family is one of the objects nearest my heart, and the destruction of the French fleet, in my opinion, more certainly assures that safety which is so dear to me. *The Queen of Naples, 26 Dec.*

The Kent being done up, and gone to Malta, has reduced me from seven sail of the line to six, therefore I have left it to the king's pleasure to send me the Gibraltar or not; and so entirely do I wish it to be left to the king, that I request your Excellency will not urge it, as you might naturally be supposed to do when the superiority is looked at; but the safety of the royal family shall not be risked one moment by me. *H. Elliot, 27 Dec. Madalena.*

We have had a most terrible winter: it has almost knocked me up. I have been very ill, and am now far from recovered, but I hope to hold out till the battle is over, when I must recruit myself for some future exertion.

An invasion of Sardinia is intended, immediately on our departure, by the French from Corsica. It is therefore my direction that you remain at your present anchorage, and use your utmost endeavours in preventing the invasion of the French, and give every aid and assistance in your power to the inhabitants, should it be attempted. *Capt. Parker, Amazon, Madalena, 4 Jan. 1804.*

This order was given at the request of the local authorities, and consequent on the capture of the mail from Antibes to Corsica, which betrayed the design of the French.

However [great] my distress is, and greater it cannot well be, for frigates and sloops, yet I could not allow the most important island and naval station in the Mediterranean to fall, whilst I have any means of preventing it. *Lord Hobart, 6 Jan.*

The ships in general, at present under my command, are very much in want of cordage, sails, and other stores, and the temporary supplies which have hitherto arrived from England are by no means adequate to their indispensable necessities. Commissioner Otway informs me, that they are so bare of stores at Gib- *Navy Board, 10 Jan.*

raltar as to be unable to supply the ships cruising in that vicinity; and Malta, from the storekeeper's account, is equally bare. I must here desire to mention, in justice to the storekeepers, that blame is not imputable to them on that account, as the ships that were in this country previous to and during the short interval of peace, being now obliged to keep the sea, have entirely eat up the stores, and their real wants not half complied with. I have applications from the different line-of-battle ships for surveys on most of their sails and running rigging, which cannot be complied with, as there is neither cordage nor sails to replace the unserviceable stores, and therefore the evil must be combated in the best manner possible. I have some time ago directed the naval storekeeper at Malta to purchase a quantity of hemp in the Adriatic for the purpose of making cordage, which shall be done as far as is practicable.

Lord St. Vincent, 11 Jan.

I had not forgot to notice the son of Lord Duncan. I consider the near relations of brother officers as legacies to the service. On the subject of promotions, I beg leave to say a few words, because I feel now exactly as you have felt in a similar situation to mine; and I rejoice that you are not only alive, but in office to bear witness to the truth of my words, which I should have quoted, even if you had not been in office, ' that it was absolutely necessary merit should be rewarded on the moment, and that the officers of the fleet should look up to the commander-in-chief for their reward: for that otherwise the good or bad opinion of the commander-in-chief would be of no consequence.' You always promoted meritorious officers out of the Victory and Ville de Paris and many private ships, for their merit. The good effect was, that whatever was undertaken, succeeded. I trust you will be so good as to state what you thought proper for the benefit of the service to the Admiralty, and be my friend at the Board. I have said enough for any friend to act upon, and I rely on your kind support. I shall certainly endeavour to imitate you, when you commanded here with so much advantage to your country. I shall not trouble you with complaints of ships, the Board shall be answered. Thank God, the health of the fleet has been wonderful, and I wish I could add my own; however, I hope to hold out to meet the French fleet, and after that I believe my career will finish.

In addition to my other cares, Sardinia must be guarded. The French most assuredly mean to invade it, first, I suppose, under a pretext for keeping us out of it, and then they will have it ceded to them. I have written to Lord Hobart on the importance of Sardinia. It is worth a hundred Maltas in position, and has the finest man-of-war harbour in Europe; they tell me it is superior to Beerhaven. In short, it has nothing but advantages. The mode of getting it is to be considered by ministers, but money will do anything in these days.

Sardinia, if we do not take it very soon, the French will have it, and then we lose the most important island, as a naval and military station, in the Mediterranean. It possesses, at the northern end, the finest harbour in the world; it equals Trincomalee. It is twenty-four hours' sail from Toulon; it covers Italy; it is a position that the wind which carries the French to the westward is fair for you to follow. In passing to the southward they go close to you. In short, it covers Egypt, Italy, and Turkey. Malta must not be mentioned in the same century. I delivered my opinion on the inutility of Malta as a naval station for watching Toulon. A fleet would sooner pass from St. Helens to Toulon than from Malta. If I lose Sardinia, I lose the French fleet.

Lord Minto, 11 Jan.

As I thought the appearance of the squadron might add weight to the mission (and the French fleet being in Toulon on the 6th), I stood over to Algiers, and made my appearance on the 17th. By Captain Keats' letters your Lordship will observe that the Dey was immovable, both as to receiving Mr. Falcon or giving up those persons the Government of Malta claimed as Maltese. . . . The insolence of the Dey is only to be checked (with due submission to whatever his Majesty may please to direct) by blockading Algiers, and his other ports of Bona and Oran, and to capture his cruisers, for the more that is given up to him the more he will demand with insolence in future. Therefore I should propose that, on 28 April next, when, if he means to send his cruisers to sea they will be out, that on that day every ship under my command should have strict orders (to open on that day) to take, sink, burn, and destroy every Algerine, and that on that day the ports of Algiers should be declared in a state of blockade. Thus the Dey could get neither commerce, presents, or plunder; and although the other powers may rejoice at the war with us, yet I am firmly persuaded that it will be most advantageous to us (and humiliating to the other powers whom he will squeeze) for the next one hundred years. If I should find his cruisers at sea before that time, in consequence of what has passed, I shall of course take them, but my wish is to make a grand *coup*.

Lord Hobart, 19 Jan. Off Algiers.

T. Jackson,[1]
10 Feb.

The storm is brewing, and there can be little doubt but that Sardinia is one of the first objects of its violence. Apropos—we have a report that the visit of Lucien Bonaparte is to effect an amicable exchange of Sardinia for Parma and Piacenza. This must not take place, or Sicily, Malta, Egypt, &c. &c., is lost, sooner or later. What I can do to ward off the blow shall be done, as I have already assured his Royal Highness the Viceroy. From Marseilles and Nice there are not less than 30,000 men ready for embarkation. Should Russia go to war with France, from that moment I consider the mask as being thrown off with respect to any neutrality of his Sardinian Majesty: therefore, if that should be the case, would the king consent to two or three hundred British troops taking post upon the Madalena? It would be a momentary check against an invasion from Corsica, and enable us to assist the northern part of Sardinia. You will touch upon this matter in the way you think most prudent, or entirely omit it. But there is only this choice—to lose the whole of Sardinia, or to allow a small body of friendly troops to hold a post at the northern end of the island. We may prevent: we cannot retake. Sardinia is the most important post in the Mediterranean. It covers Naples, Sicily, Malta, Egypt, and all the Turkish dominions; it blockades Toulon; the wind which would carry a French fleet to the westward is fair from Sardinia; and Madalena is the most important station in this most important island. I am told that the revenues, after paying the expenses of the island, do not give the king 5,000*l.* sterling a year. If it is so, I would give him 500,000*l.* to cede it, which would give him 25,000*l.* a year for ever. This is only my conversation, and not to be noticed—but the king cannot long hold Sardinia.

With respect to the history about the French privateers from Ancona, and the conduct of the English privateers at Fiumicino, I believe you are correct, but our enemies never adhere to it. They go in and out of the Spanish and Sicilian ports at all times, night and day—in short, to examine all vessels passing. But all privateers are very incorrect, and I sincerely wish there was no such vessels allowed. They are only one degree removed from pirates; but I believe an English armed vessel never yet trusted his cause to any Court but an English Court of Admiralty. However, I have no power over them. But certainly, if the custom of the port of Fiumicino has invariably been not to allow any corsair to sail out of the port until the twenty-four hours after the sailing of a neutral,

---

[1] Minister Plenipotentiary at the Court of Sardinia.

then our privateer ought to have been forced to conform. But I dare say the French go in and out of Ancona as they please, and if so the Court of Rome has no great cause of complaint. I can only again repeat, that over privateers I have no control.

All my force, except Gibraltar, is united, and for our numbers none better can be. If the Ferrol squadron joins the Toulon, they will much outnumber us, but in that case I shall never lose sight of them, and Sir Edward Pellew will soon be after them. The loss of the Raven is very great, and the Admiralty seem determined not to increase my force. I, at this moment, want ten frigates or sloops, when I believe neither the Ferrol or Toulon squadron could escape me. The Diana is ordered home from Gibraltar. It is shameful—Lord St. Vincent was not treated so. The moment I can possibly part with a vessel, you shall have another in the room of the Raven. We are, my dear friend, on the eve of great events; the sooner they come the better; 12,000 men are ready for embarkation at Toulon, and 16,000 at Nice, and as they have not transports, they must naturally expect more ships of war. The Admiralty tells me nothing, they know nothing; but my private letters say that the Brest squadron, as well as Ferrol, is bound here. If so, we shall have work enough upon our hands. But I am sure of my present force as far as it will go; we shall come to no harm.

Sir A. J. Ball, 11 Feb.

If the French unite their fleets outside of the Mediterranean with that at Toulon, it is not the Sublime Porte's being at peace with Bonaparte that will prevent an invasion of both the Morea and Egypt.[1] Your Highness knows them too well to put any confidence in what they say. Bonaparte's tongue is that of a serpent oiled. Nothing shall be wanting on my part to frustrate the designs of this common disturber of the human race.

The Grand Vizir, 11 Feb.

Most cordially do I hail and congratulate you on the return of St. Valentine; and may you, my dear Lord, live in health to receive them for many many years. This morning also, your nephew, Captain Parker, has very much pleased [me], (as indeed he always does). On Sunday, the 12th, I sent him to look into Toulon. As he was reconnoitring under Sepet, he saw a frigate rounding Porquerolle; the wind was right out of the harbour at north. At first the frigate seemed desirous to bring him to action, but the determined approach of the Amazon made him fly with every rag of sail: he ran through the Grand Pass, and got under Bregançon;

Lord St. Vincent, 14 Feb.

[1] Compare *Revue Maritime et Coloniale*, Nov. 1884; tom. lxxxiii. p. 261.

Z

some of the ships hoisted their yards up. I am rather glad that Parker did not bring her to action, for I think they must have come out and taken him; but I admire his spirit and resolution to attack her under all the disadvantages of situation, and such conduct will, some happy day, meet its reward.

We have not a sick man in the fleet, except Kent, who has been to Malta.

Memo, 23 Feb.

As it is my intention to engage the enemy as soon as possible, should we fall in with them during the night, the fleet may expect that signal No. 63 or 64 will be made. Lord Nelson has no doubt but that great attention will be paid, that none but ships of the enemy will be fired into, for which purpose it is recommended not only to be careful that the signal-lights for knowing each other are clear, and well placed on the signal-staff, but also that the ship should be hailed, if there is the smallest doubt of her being a French ship.

Lord St. Vincent, 26 Feb.

I feel confident that there is not an officer in the service that bows with more respect to the orders of the Admiralty than myself; but I am sure you will agree with me, that if I form plans for the sending home our convoys, and the clearing the different parts of the station from privateers, and the other services requisite, and that the Admiralty in some respects makes their arrangements, we must clash. For instance, I judged it necessary, from the force of the enemy in Toulon, to call the Donegal from watching L'Aigle at Cadiz, and I directed Captain Gore to take the Agincourt, and with her to attend to the French ship; for although the Agincourt could not catch her in running, yet she would protect the trade coming to and from the Mediterranean; but [her] being taken away, I admit on an important service, has left L'Aigle at liberty, although Gore has collected the three frigates, Medusa, Amphion, and Maidstone, and means to attack her if she puts to sea. But this laudable purpose interferes with the protection it is necessary to give to the mouth of the Tagus; and I much fear the Amphion, who was ordered to Lisbon, not going, has exposed our commerce to the depredations of a large French privateer. Lord Robert Fitz-Gerald calls out, but I have not the means of doing all that is necessary.

He then goes on to speak of other instances in which the Admiralty arrangements had clashed with his; and concludes:

I hope the Gibraltar when fitted will answer the Board's expectation, but I firmly believe, when done, she will only be fit for a summer's passage to England. I shall send her to Otway when she can be spared from Naples. She is a very fine ship, and in excellent order. My letter to Sir Evan Nepean, on my first arrival, I find every day was perfectly correct. The Kent is under jury-masts. I had rather have bestowed new masts upon her than the other. However, we must very soon have a battle, and then we shall all want new masts, &c.

Yesterday I received the favour of the fourth edition of your invaluable work on tropical diseases,[1] and with it your most kind letter; and though I know myself not equal to your praises, yet I feel that my honest intentions for the good of the service have ever been the same, and as I rise in rank, so do my exertions. The great thing in all military service is health; and you will agree with me that it is easier for an officer to keep men healthy, than for a physician to cure them. Situated as this fleet has been, without a friendly port where we could get all the things so necessary for us, yet I have, by changing the cruising ground, not allowed the sameness of prospect to satiate the mind—sometimes by looking at Toulon, Villafranca, Barcelona, and Rosas, then running round Minorca, Majorca, Sardinia, and Corsica: and two or three times anchoring for a few days, and sending a ship to the last place for onions, which I find the best thing that can be given to seamen; having always good mutton for the sick, cattle when we can get them, and plenty of fresh water. In the winter it is the best plan to give half the allowance of grog, instead of all wine. These things are for the commander-in-chief to look to, but shut very nearly out from Spain, and only getting refreshments by stealth from other places, my command has been an arduous one.

Cornwallis has great merit for his persevering cruise, but he has everything sent him, we have nothing. We seem forgotten by the great folks at home. Our men's minds, however, are always kept up with the daily hopes of meeting the enemy. I send you, as a curiosity, an account of our deaths, and sent to the hospital, out of six thousand men. The fleet put to sea on 18 May, 1803, and is still at sea; not a ship has been refitted or recruited, excepting what has been done at sea. You will readily believe that all this must have shaken me. My sight is getting very bad, but *I* must not be sick until after the French fleet is taken.

I regret that I did not know of the Diana's being ordered to

[1] See *ante*, pp. 4, 11.

Capt. Gore, Medusa, 17 March.

England with the trade, as I would have detained the Braakel to have assisted in the blockade of L'Aigle. Your intentions of attacking that ship with the small squadron under your command are certainly very laudable, but I do not consider your force by any means equal to it. I must, however, leave your judgment to determine upon this point, as well as with regard to the future arrangement of the ships under your orders; and only observe that the protection of our commerce, and the destruction of the enemy's privateers and cruisers, are most essential objects for your consideration.

Sir J. T. Duckworth, 19 March.

I hope to hold out, to beat your friend Admiral la Touche Tréville, who took the command at Toulon the moment of his arrival there. He was sent for on purpose, as he beat me at Boulogne, to beat me again, but he seems very loth to try.

Dr. Baird, 19 March.

I am sure no man is more able to place our hospitals in a proper state than yourself, and that you always bear in mind not to be penny-wise and pound-foolish. A small sum, well laid out, will keep fleets healthy, but it requires large sums to make a sickly fleet healthy, besides the immense loss of personal services. Health cannot be dearly bought at any price, if the fleet is never sickly. By general exertions we have done well, but we have not a place that we can be sure of supplies from. Spain will not give us a live animal; Naples dare not; and Sardinia ought not: but that is the only place we have a chance for fresh provisions. God knows how many days—it will not be many—that island will be out of the hands of the French.

Lieut. Woodman, 21 March.

Admiral Holloway having acquainted me by letter of your arrival in this country as an agent of transports, and also of your being very equal to any important service, from your intelligence and observation; and the Lords Commissioners of the Admiralty having recommended me to send an officer of that description in charge of the transports, I have therefore thought proper to send you, and must recommend to your serious attention the circumstances in general that are passing in the Black Sea on the part of Russia, who, it is said, is forming an armament to a very considerable extent; and although there is not the most distant idea that this armament will direct its operations against the interests of Great Britain, yet it is essentially necessary that its real intentions should be discovered as early as possible, and therefore you will let no opportunity escape you of obtaining all the information you may be able to collect on this important subject.

And I must desire you will endeavour to gain a particular account of the naval force which Russia may have at Sebastopol and Cherson (their two principal naval ports in the Black Sea), and to what extent they are arming there. You will likewise endeavour to obtain a knowledge of their fortifications, and what number of guns is mounted on their different batteries, and whether they are able to protect their trade. It will be advisable to ascertain whether these armaments are with a view to check and oppose the measures of the French, should they attempt to possess themselves of the Morea. You will also endeavour to gain information of the trade and manufactures carried on by the Russians in the ports above mentioned—what supplies of provisions and naval stores might be drawn from that country, and upon what terms. In order to obtain a perfect knowledge of the local situation of the Russian territory in the Black Sea, you are to procure a chart of their country, which will assist you in forming a more clear idea of the places of principal importance, and endeavour by every means to obtain information of their present and future intentions with regard to England, transmitting me a very full and correct account of your observations on your return to Malta.

My reports say that the French have taken up at Leghorn a number of Greek vessels as transports. If they leave Leghorn without troops, it is natural to suppose they are destined to take the French troops from the coast of the Adriatic. If so, they must either be destined for the Morea or Egypt. Information upon these points is so important, to enable me to form a probable guess at the destination of the Toulon fleet, that no money or trouble ought to be spared to obtain it. At eight o'clock yesterday morning, our frigates saw the French fleet quite safe. I am going to Madalena to get some refreshments, for I am sorry to say the scurvy has made its appearance in several ships. H. Elliot, 23 March.

We are on the eve of great events. Last week, at different times, two sail of the line put their heads outside Toulon; and on Thursday the 5th, in the afternoon, they all came out. We have had a gale of wind and calm since; therefore I do not know whether they are returned to port or have kept the sea. I have only to wish to get alongside of them with the present fleet under my command; so highly officered and manned, the event ought not to be doubted. Geo. Rose, 8 April.

If we go on playing out and in, we shall some day get at them. J. H. Frere.

Sir R. Bickerton, 7 April.

As the enemy's fleet has been out, and may still be at sea, and as I should be very sorry to baulk their inclinations of a battle by your superiority of numbers, you will, therefore, whenever I make the signal, haul from us, to the southward, furl your top-gallant sails so as not to be discovered from the shore, and just keep sight of us from the masthead; and make the signal for your division (except Excellent, who is going towards Toulon), and do you call in Belleisle, unless I should call her by signal to me.

The Hindostan store-ship, commanded by Commander Le Gros, caught fire, and was totally destroyed in the Bay of Rosas on 2 April; and on the next day, 3 April, the Swift hired cutter, of eight 4-pounders and 23 men, commanded by Lieutenant Leake, was captured by the French privateer L'Espérance. Mr. Leake was killed in the action, but the bulk of the despatches seem to have been thrown overboard, though uncertainty as to their fate gave Nelson great anxiety.

A. Davison, 19 April.

Whatever I might have had in the Hindostan is gone, and also all our letters in the Swift cutter. She was taken the 5th, and all our despatches, letters, &c. &c., are gone to Paris. I have only had two despatches sent me since my leaving England. One, the British Fair, was very near taken in the Gut. The Swift, of the force of twenty-three men and boys, is taken by a thing of fifty-three men and boys. How Government can think of sending papers of consequence in such a vessel I cannot imagine. I suppose we shall have a book of intercepted correspondence, with such additions as the ingenious head of a Frenchman can invent.

Lord St. Vincent, 19 April.

The loss of the Hindostan has been great; but from our care and attention, I may truly say of every captain in the fleet, we shall get on for the summer. It is an accident such a ship must be liable to; and if Captain Le Gros' account is correct (he is now on his trial) he had great merit in the order in which the ship was kept, and it must have arose from either some of the medicine-chests breaking, or from wet getting down, which caused things to heat. The preservation of the crew seems little short of a miracle: I never read such a journal of exertions.

Misfortunes seldom come alone. The Juno very properly, hearing of the accident, quitted her station off Cape St. Sebastian the very day the Swift was taken, or that would have been prevented. I send the account I have of that event to the Admiralty. I only hope that no despatches of any consequence were entrusted in such a vessel. Whatever they are, they are this day before Bonaparte.

I rely with confidence that, although the Admiralty for ever send their despatches, of whatever consequence, without the use of cipher, and trust to their being thrown overboard in case of capture, yet, as I know the other departments of Government always use cipher if of importance, and although admirals are never entrusted with ciphers, yet I rely that your Lordship would not trust any despatch of consequence in a vessel with twenty-three men, much less commit the interests and schemes of other powers to such a conveyance. This is the only consolation I derive from all the despatches being this day read by the First Consul; I wish they were in his throat. I think a great deal on this matter, but it may be prudent to hold my tongue.

Lord Hobart, 19 April.

In transmitting to the Admiralty the minutes of the court-martial on Captain Le Gros, who was honourably acquitted, Nelson added:

From every information which I have received, the exertions of Captain Le Gros, his officers and ship's company, in the late unfortunate business, deserve great commendation, and that to the cool and collected conduct of Captain Le Gros is to be attributed the preservation of their lives.

W. Marsden, 19 April.

I expect the French ships from Ferrol, if they can escape our squadron, and then, probably, they will fight us. Till then they will only try to escape this squadron—certainly, I believe, the finest we have at sea. You will have heard they have been playing in and out of Toulon. They may carry their play further some day than they intend.

Lord Radstock, 20 April.

As it is my determination to attack the French fleet in any place where there is a reasonable prospect of getting fairly alongside of them, and as I think that in Hières Bay, Golfe Jouan, Spezia, Leghorn Roads, Ajaccio, and many other places, opportunities may offer of attacking them, I therefore recommend that every captain will make himself, by inquiries, as fully acquainted with the above-mentioned places as possible—viz. for Hières Bay, the Petite Passe, Grande Passe, and passage from the eastward; Golfe Jouan (of which I send a chart from the latest surveys made), Spezia, and, in particular, the northern passage into Leghorn Roads, from which side it is only, in my opinion, possible to attack an enemy's fleet to advantage; and with the Gulf of Ajaccio.

In going in to attack an enemy's fleet, it is recommended, if possible, to have the launch out, and hawsers and stream-anchors in her; and, with any other boats, to lay out of gun-shot, ready to act as circumstances may require. Ships, in bringing up, will

Memorandum, 28 April.

anchor as the captains may think best, from circumstances of wind and weather, and the position of the enemy; but I would recommend strongly having the four large anchors clear for letting go, because I know, from experience, the great difficulty, with crippled masts and yards, getting an anchor over the side; and it is probable that it may be necessary to remove the ship after an action, and to leave some of her anchors behind. The ships will anchor in such a manner as to give each other mutual support for the destruction of the enemy.

A chart of Golfe Jouan to be delivered to each line-of-battle ship.

Sir Ed. Pellew,[1] 1 May.

Your letter of 10 April, notwithstanding it has been afloat in the Mediterranean six days, conveys to us very late news. I wish our Government in their important communications with me would direct their despatches to Mr. Frere at Madrid, and direct him to forward them by a confidential person to Barcelona, where almost every week I send a frigate for information : then such distressing circumstances as have happened to the cutter could not take place. Bonaparte read all the public despatches on 16 April. I wish they had choked him.

I wish I was sure that our letters are not read by the way; however, what I am going to say cannot do much harm. The French have 14,000 men ready for embarkation at Toulon ; as many more in the heel of Italy. They only want more ships; and my information leads me to suppose that certainly the [? Rochefort] squadron is destined for the Mediterranean, and also the Brest fleet, either before or after they may have thrown their cargo of troops on shore in Ireland. Egypt and the Morea supposed to be their next object after their English and Irish schemes. Our force here is not equal to such a force united to the Toulon fleet, which is ten sail of the line, seven of which are full manned. . . . Our ships, hulks many of them, are but in a very indifferent state ; however, we can [? muster] nine sail of the line at sea. I do not choose to say more upon this subject, but this I may pride myself upon, that no man ever commanded a fleet better manned, more healthy, or where greater unanimity prevailed, than the one I have the honour of commanding. I believe the Russian fleet from the Black Sea is by this time in the Mediterranean : their object I can only guess at, for I have not a word of information or a scrap of a pen from England since the end of January.

[1] Of this letter, Nicolas has given only a short extract. It is printed at full length in Lady Chatterton's *Life of Lord Gambier*, vol. ii. p. 2.

I am truly sensible of the honour you do me in expressing a wish to serve under me, but you have always proved yourself so equal to command a fleet, that it would be a sin to place you in any other situation; and my services are very nearly at an end, for in addition to other infirmities, I am nearly blind. However, I hope to fight one more battle, and then, unless my health and sight mend, which is not very likely, I ought, perhaps, to lay down the cudgels, and console myself with the idea that there are so many more able officers than ever I could pretend to be, ready to take them up.

On 3 May, Sir William Bolton in the Childers, with the Swift sloop, was ordered to cruise off Tunis for three French privateers reported as in that neighbourhood. To the orders was added the following memorandum, the draught of which was written by Lord Nelson's own hand:

In looking for these privateers mentioned in my order of this date, I would recommend, if the wind is favourable, sending a boat into S. Pietro, south-west end of Sardinia, for information, as last year that was their place of great resort; but it is possible they may lay under the Isle of Vacca or Toro, and keep people on the top to give them information.

From S. Pietro, or Toro, I would advise making Galita, running close round it. This island I do not consider as belonging to any state which can give it neutrality. From thence, passing under the Cannes, and either pass between Plane Island and the point of Porto Farina, or outside of it, steer for the islands of Zembra, from which place last year one of these captains of French privateers made captures of our ships passing, using the Tunisian flag, and dressing their men with turbans, &c.; and on representing the capture to the Bey of Tunis, his answer was that the islands of Zembra were rocks in the sea, from which the English might look out, as well as the French, but that prizes must not be taken within gun-shot of his coast. It is therefore evident that the Bey did not consider the Zembras as part of his coast, and therefore that you may take vessels close to Zembra, and you may do the same close to the rocks called Cannes, which are several miles from the shore; but you will be very careful not to infringe the neutrality of Tunis by making captures within cannon-shot of the shore.

Should you gain no information of the privateers, you will stand over to Pantellaria, and from thence to Maritimo, inquiring at those places, and Trapani, for information; and not being able to get such information as may lead you to suppose it in your power to get at them, you will return and join me.

I would recommend disguising both the brigs from the moment

of separation, and I rely upon your exertions in getting hold of these gentry; and if you do, take them to Malta, and take care the captains and officers of the privateers are not liberated upon any account.

On 10 May Nelson sailed with the squadron for the Madalena Islands, leaving Captain Moubray of the Active with a squadron of four frigates to keep watch on Toulon. Captain Moubray's instructions were very detailed; but the following sentences contain the gist of the whole:

Capt. Moubray, 10 May.

You will take an early opportunity of reconnoitring the enemy's force at the above-mentioned place, and as they are occasionally in the habit of sending out two or three of their frigates (sometimes under cover of a ship of the line), you will perform this service with proper caution, so as to enable you to ascertain their real situation without the risk of being captured. And you will on the first examination of Toulon, after my leaving you, send a frigate to Madalena with an account [of the enemy's motions], and continue frequently with the rest of your ships to reconnoitre them during my absence.

Memo, 13 May.

It is my directions that the artillery embarked on board the bomb-ships do, when in port, keep watch as sentinels, and when at sea, in the same manner as the ship's company.

Capt. L. Shepheard, 16 May.

I am to desire you will proceed with his Majesty's ship Thisbe, together with the victuallers under your charge, and join me on rendezvous No. 102 [off Toulon]. In joining I must recommend you will proceed through the Straits of Bonifacio, passing on the west side of the island of Corsica, and not attempt to go round Cape Corse, as in the event of the wind coming strong from the NW, it would be an awkward passage for a stranger, particularly with victuallers under his charge.

Capt. Cocks, Thunder, 19 May.

From representations made to me, it appears that the officers of artillery embarked on board his Majesty's bombs Thunder, Etna, and Acheron, are entirely ignorant of the Act of Parliament for the regulation of his Majesty's ships, vessels, and forces by sea. It is therefore my directions that you deliver to the officer of artillery embarked to serve on board his Majesty's bomb Thunder, under your command, the Act of Parliament inclosed in a letter, in order that in future he may not plead ignorance of the Act above mentioned, as he will be made answerable for a breach of it.

You will direct the officer of artillery to muster, when you think necessary, the clothes of the artillery, and direct him to take care that the men are kept in cleanliness and discipline, becoming such a fine body of men. You will give directions that the mortars and artillery stores are examined occasionally, in order that they may be always fit for service, and direct the officer of artillery to report to you any defect in them, that such directions may be given as the case shall require. And in every respect you will pay the same attention to the artillery embarked on board the bomb under your command as is paid to officers and men of the navy of like rank.

N.B.—A letter of the above tenor and date was delivered to the commanders of the Etna and Acheron bomb-vessels.

On being joined by the bomb-vessels [Thunder, Etna, and Acheron], I was informed that on coming to sea, the artillerymen were ordered to keep watch the same as the people composing their companies, but were prevented from it by their officers, who had directed them not to keep watch. The commanders of these vessels not judging it prudent to enforce their compliance, in consequence, I presume, of their Lordships' instructions to them respecting the artillery, allowed this measure, so subversive of discipline, to remain for my directions; and in consequence of such communication, I gave out an order, dated the 13th inst., a copy of which is herewith transmitted. [On the 19th], I found [it] necessary, from the conduct of the artillery officers, to give [an order] to the respective commanders of the said bomb-vessels, [a copy of] which I desire you will please to lay before the Lords Commissioners of the Admiralty for their information; and at the same time acquaint their Lordships that I have read their instructions which have been given to the commanders of the bombs, which may be interpreted as not rendering the officers and soldiers embarked in the bomb-vessels liable to be tried by court-martial. I am, however, decidedly of opinion that nothing short of an Act of the Legislature can lay aside the Acts of Parliament by which our naval service is directed to be governed; and as these Acts clearly point out that soldiers are (with the exception of their being embarked in transport ships) as liable to the regulations of that Act of Parliament as any seaman, and as it is impossible that two commanders can exist in the same ship, and the very salvation of our navy, perhaps of our country, depends upon the perfect subordination of every individual to the commander thereof, I have to request their Lordships will take this most important subject into their serious consideration, that such directions may be given thereupon as the wisdom of Parliament shall think proper; for, until the Act of Parliament is altered, I

Wm. Marsden, 22 May.

shall hold it my indispensable duty to enforce obedience from the artillery officers before mentioned to the orders of their respective commanders, be it by court-martial or otherwise, and communicate the result to the commander-in-chief of the army in the Mediterranean, in order that it may be laid before the king.

I lament that it is necessary for me to call their Lordships' attention to this very recent circumstance of the army serving on board his Majesty's fleet; the sea-lords, to whom I particularly address myself on this most serious subject, are well aware of the dangerous tendency of insubordination, and of the consequences which would result from placing the army, who serve in the different ships, independent of the officers who command them.

On 24 May, as Rear-Admiral Campbell in the Canopus, with Donegal and Amazon frigate, was close in with Cape Sepet, the main body of the fleet being out of sight to seaward, five French ships of the line, three frigates, and several gunboats came out of the harbour with the evident intention of cutting off the small reconnoitring squadron. Campbell of course made sail away from them; and the French, unwilling to risk even the possibility of being drawn too far from the shelter of their port, gave up the pursuit at 3.30 P.M. It was not till six hours later that the Canopus and her consorts rejoined the fleet.

R.-Admiral Campbell, 24 May.

I am more obliged to you than I can express, for your not allowing the very superior force of the enemy to bring you to action. Whatever credit would have accrued to your own and your gallant companions' exertions, no sound advantages could have arisen to our country; for so close to their own harbour they could always have returned, and left your ships unfit, probably, to keep the sea. I again, my dear admiral, thank you for your conduct. Some day, very soon, I have no doubt but an opportunity will offer of giving them fair battle.

G. Rose, 25 May.

I have read with attention Mr. Pitt's speech respecting the Admiralty. My mind has been long formed upon that subject; and with all my personal regard for Lord St. Vincent, I am sorry to see that he has been led astray by the opinion of ignorant people. There is scarcely a thing he has done since he has been at the Admiralty that I have not heard him reprobate before he came to the Board. I do not mean but that the attempt to prevent the gross abuses in our dockyards, &c. &c., was laudable, but it is the mode of reforming those abuses which I disapprove of; but this is too long a subject for me to enter into upon paper.

I had wrote a memoir, many months ago, upon the propriety

of a flotilla. I had that command at the end of last war, and I know the necessity of it, even had you, and which you ought to have, thirty or forty sail of the line in the Downs and North Sea, besides frigates, &c.; but having failed so entirely in submitting my thoughts upon three points, I was disheartened. They were upon the speedy manning the navy at the commencement of a war—the inducing the seamen to fly into the naval service instead of from it—and for the better payment of prize-money. I have not the vanity to think that any of my plans were perfect; but they were intended, by contradicting my plans, to bring forth better: but nothing has been done, and something was and is necessary.

There is no real happiness in this world. With all content and smiles around me, up start these artillery boys, I understand they are not beyond that age, and set us all at defiance—speaking in the most disrespectful manner of the navy and its commanders, &c. With your quickness, the matter would have been settled, and perhaps some of them been broke. I am perhaps more patient, but I do assure you not less resolved, if my plan of conciliation is not attended to. You and I are on the eve of quitting the theatre of our exploits, but we owe it to our successors, never, whilst we have a tongue to speak, or a hand to write, to allow the navy to be in the smallest degree injured in its discipline by our conduct. If these continued attacks upon the navy are to be carried on every two or three years, it would be much better for the navy to have its own corps of artillery. *Lord St. Vincent, 25 May.*

I have been obliged to write a letter to the Admiralty on the subject of soldiers embarked on board ships of war; and I have written it strong, as I know it must go further than your Board. It is the old history—trying to do away the Act of Parliament. But I trust they will never succeed, for when they do, farewell to our naval superiority! We should be prettily commanded! You may say, 'they are not intended to command the navy, but that the navy is not to command soldiers on board a ship.' Let them once gain the step of being independent of the navy on board a ship, and they will soon have the other, and command us. It may be said, 'if the soldiers behave improperly, they would be tried by a court-martial on shore.' Were that possible, of what members could that court be composed? Mostly subalterns, I fancy, who although we might think the officer had behaved very improperly, might, and probably would, think that he had behaved very properly, *Sir T. Troubridge, (?)25 May.*

to us sea-brutes. But thank God, my dear Troubridge, the king himself cannot do away the Act of Parliament. Although my career is nearly run, yet it would embitter my future days and expiring moments to hear of our navy being sacrificed to the army. I can readily conceive the attempts of the army at this moment, when they think themselves of such great importance. The Admiralty order might lead those wrong who do not know that nothing but an Act of Parliament can do away an Act of Parliament.

Sir C. M. Pole, 25 May.

I assure you that I most sincerely wish to promote Brown, who is an ornament to our service; but alas! nobody will be so good as to die, nor will the French kill us. What can I do? But I live in hopes, as the French keep playing about the mouth of Toulon harbour, that some happy day I shall be able to get a blow at them. My system is the very contrary of blockading, therefore I for one shall not be entitled to those thanks which the newspapers say the City of London mean to give the blockading squadrons. I would no more accept thanks for what I was conscious I did not merit, than I would refuse them, and feel hurt at their not being given for a great victory, and it is curious I am likely to be placed in both situations; but such things are.

I am sure Lord St. Vincent ought to feel grateful for your zealous support of his measures; and I hope you will stand by the navy against all attempts to have soldiers placed in our ships independent of the naval Act of Parliament, from whatever quarter it may be attempted. When that takes place there is an end of our navy—there cannot be two commanders in one ship.

W. Marsden, 29 May.

His Majesty's ship Victory, on her passage to the Mediterranean, captured the Ambuscade French frigate, manned her with a sufficient number of officers and seamen, and directed her to proceed to Gibraltar. On her way there, and after she had parted company with the Victory, she fell in with and captured the Marie Thérèse, a French merchantman, and carried her with her to that place. On the Ambuscade's arrival off the mole with her prize, as above, the Revolutionnaire and Bittern, who were lying there, sent out their boats to the said merchant ship (knowing her to be the Ambuscade's prize), and afterwards laid in their claim as joint captors in the Vice-Admiralty Court at Gibraltar; but upon trial of the said vessel, their claim was thrown out, and the Marie Thérèse condemned as sole and legal prize to the Victory. The agent consequently (after keeping the proceeds a considerable time in his possession to meet the claims of those ships, in the event of any having been established by them in England), not hearing of any claim being made, sent the prize-money to the Victory for distribution, but has since acquainted the captain of that ship that the Marie Thérèse is claimed as a droit of Admiralty. I therefore request you will be pleased to lay this particular case before the Lords Commissioners of the Admiralty, and move their Lordships, under the circumstances before mentioned, to order the Admiralty claim (if any has been made) to be withdrawn, as I consider it a very great hardship upon the officers and seamen of the Victory.[1]

The health of this fleet cannot be exceeded; and I really believe that my shattered carcase is in the worst plight of the whole fleet. I have had a sort of rheumatic fever, they tell me; but I have felt the blood gushing up the left side of my head, and the moment it covers the brain, I am fast asleep. I am now better of that; and with violent pain in my side, and night-sweats, with heat in the evening, and quite flushed. The pain in my head, nor spasms, I have not had for some time. Mr. Magrath, whom I admire for his great abilities every day I live, gives me excellent remedies, but we must lose such men from our service if the army goes on in encouraging medical men whilst we do nothing. I am sure much ought to be done for our naval surgeons, or how can we expect to keep valuable men?

Dr. Baird.
30 May.

Expecting your Lordship's answer, I did not, of course, commence hostilities against the Dey's cruisers. I meant that the 28th of April was about the time of their sailing, and when an effective blow might be struck. I do not think the Dey has ventured to send his cruisers to sea. I have sent Captain Keats to Algiers; and unless the Dey is set on, and supported by the French against us, I have every hope, that now Mr. Falcon is out of the question, matters will be amicably settled. As for three bombs going against Algiers, I could as soon whistle the walls down. If force is to be used, not less than ten or twelve sail of the line, and as many bombs as possible, could, in my opinion, produce the proper effect of humbling him; and I feel that a fleet is not at this moment to be crippled on such a service.

Lord Hobart,
31 May.

---

[1] Nelson's opinion on this point was not held good in a court of law. On 5 April, 1805, the Lords of Appeal reversed the sentence by which the Marie Thérèse had been adjudged a prize to the Victory, and condemned the ship and cargo as a droit of Admiralty.

H. Elliot,
1 June.

You may safely rely that I never trust a Corsican or a Frenchman. I would give the devil all the good ones to take the remainder.

I wonder that General Acton should for one moment believe the professions of General St. Cyr, more especially coming through the mouth of Micheroux, who I know of old. Did the French ever appear friendly but for the purpose of more readily destroying those whom they can cajole? This word is English, although it writes very bad.

Sir A. J.
Ball,
7 June.

The going on in the routine of a station, if interrupted, is like stopping a watch—the whole machine gets wrong. . . . Mr. Elliot wanted to send me a *good* Frenchman, that I might land and take on board occasionally. My answer was, No! I knew the force at Toulon, and that nothing would be of any use to me but a copy of the French admiral's sailing orders. . . .

I send you our last Paris papers; in addition to their contents, the French fleet in Toulon fired a *feu-de-joie*, dressed ship, &c. on the 3rd, for his taking upon himself the title of emperor. At Marseilles they talk of peace, and you will see the probability of a change of administration. . . .

The Victory, in June 1803, captured a French tartan; and, to avoid being put into quarantine, he sunk her, and, as the captain conceived, French property to the amount of several thousand pounds. It was so truly disinterested a measure that it met my most sincere approbation. . . .

Do not think I am tired of watching Mr. La Touche Tréville. I have now taken up a method of making him angry. I have left Sir Richard Bickerton, with part of the fleet, twenty leagues from hence, and, with five of the line, am preventing his cutting capers, which he had done for some time past, off Cape Sicie. Mr. La Touche has several times hoisted his topsail-yards up; and on 4 June, we having hoisted the standard and saluted, he sent outside Sepet, about one mile, five sail of the line and two frigates, and kept three sail and three frigates with their yards aloft, himself one of them and the rear-admiral another, therefore I did not believe him in earnest; however, we run as near as was proper, and brought to. They formed a pretty line at sunset, and then stood into the harbour. A ship of the line and frigate every morning weigh, and stand between Sepet and La Malgue. Some happy day I expect to see his eight sail, which are in the outer road, come out; and if he will get abreast of Porquerolle, I will try what stuff he is made of; therefore you see I have no occasion to be fretful; on the contrary, I am full of hopes, and command a fleet which never gives me an uneasy moment.

In October 1803, a complaint had been made by the Neapolitan minister in London, that Lieutenant Shaw, commanding the Spider brig, had violated the neutrality of Girgenti, by recapturing there three English merchant ships, prizes of two French privateers. The case was referred to Nelson for investigation, but it was not till 8 June that he was able fully to report on it; when, inclosing the several letters and affidavits, he added :

I consider Lieutenant Shaw's conduct on this occasion very meritorious and praiseworthy; and I have to hope that their Lordships' approbation of his conduct will be signified to him; for while the Sicilian Government and that of the Republic of the Seven Isles hold forth such retreats, and allow such piratical proceedings by the enemy's privateers, from their ports, in violation of the laws of neutrality, it certainly becomes the duty of every British officer to capture or destroy any enemy's vessel that attacks him, wherever the attack is made. The piratical conduct of the enemy's privateers, which are allowed to use the harbours, bays, creeks, &c., of the Republic of the Seven Isles, from whence they capture our trade, and, when attacked, complain of a violation of the neutrality, is so notoriously practised, to the great annoyance and destruction of our trade, that I submit to their Lordships the necessity of a very strong remonstrance being made to the government of the Seven Islands, in order to prevent those privateers the use of their harbours and ports, &c., for such piratical purposes.

W. Marsden, 8 June.

It was not only the enemy's privateers whose conduct Nelson thus stigmatised. An English privateer had apparently violated the neutrality of Tunis. In forwarding the Bey's letter, Nelson wrote :

The disgraceful conduct of the privateer in question calls loudly for redress, and may involve unpleasant consequences between our country and the Bey of Tunis, who very justly demands redress, and considers that my power is not only equal to this measure, but to prevent similar conduct in these pirates in future. I have exceedingly to lament that this line of conduct, so disgraceful to the character of the British nation, is practised by the Gibraltar privateers in these seas every day, as complaints are constantly laid before me from the government of Sardinia of their nefarious conduct, which I have transmitted to the governor of Gibraltar for his interference, as naval commanders have no authority whatever over those pirates.

Lord Hobart, 8 June.

A A

Capt. Lamb, Transport Agent, Malta, 8 June.

With respect to sending prisoners of war to England in ships charged with convoys, or in unoccupied transports, as mentioned in your letter, I must desire to observe that but very few could be sent in the ships of war; and certainly a very small number of determined prisoners, on board of any transport, might at pleasure, by taking advantage of the night, rise upon her company and run away with her. It therefore strikes me as a very improper way of sending them to England, and I do not feel justified in acquiescing in it without directions from the Admiralty for that purpose. But should Sir Alexander Ball wish to have any of the officers sent from Malta to England in the manner before mentioned, I have no objections to your doing so, as there cannot be any consequences apprehended from two or three, under strict watchfulness, being sent in any of the ships of war or transports.

Sir J. Acton, (?) 8 June.

I am in hopes to shame La Touche out of his nest; and when I reflect on his insult to my sovereigns, at Naples, in 1793, it will add vigour to my attack. My first object must ever be to keep the French fleet in check, and if they put to sea, to have force enough with me to annihilate them; and that, with God's blessing, I have no fear of being able to perform. That would keep the Two Sicilies free from any attack from sea. If the French fleet could carry 12,000 men into the Bay of Naples, whilst their army was marching by land, the consequences would be fatal to that capital. . . . I am glad to find Russia thinks properly, and I trust there will be no jealousies, but that both countries will try who can best serve and save the Two Sicilies. Temporising may be necessary in small states, in large ones it ought not to happen—it is humiliating. Either peace, or 100,000 Russians and as many Austrians in Italy; but I cannot help thinking that Bonaparte will wish for peace rather than a war with two empires.

H. Elliot, 18 June.

We are as usual: the French fleet safe in Toulon, but, upon the 14th, Monsieur La Touche came out with eight sail of the line and six frigates, cut a caper off Sepet, and went in again. I was off with five ships of the line, and brought to for his attack, although I did not believe that anything was meant serious, but merely a gasconade.

The French admiral's account of this 'caper' was curiously different, and on being published, not unnaturally drew some angry comments from Lord Nelson. The letter, dated 'le 26 prairial' (15 June) 'à bord du Bucentaure,' ran :

'Général,—J'ai l'honneur de vous rendre compte de la sortie de toute l'escadre à mes ordres. Sur l'avis que j'avais reçu que plusieurs corsaires anglais infestaient la côte et les îles d'Hières, je donnai l'ordre, il y a trois jours, aux frégates l'Incorruptible et la Syrène, et le brick le Furet, de se rendre dans la baie d'Hières. Le vent d'est les ayant contrariées, elles mouillèrent sous le château de Porqueroles. Hier matin, les ennemis en eurent connaissance. Vers midi, ils détachèrent deux frégates et un vaisseau, qui entrèrent par la grande passe, dans l'intention de couper la retraite à nos frégates. Du moment où je m'aperçus de sa manœuvre, je fis signal d'appareiller à toute l'escadre ; ce qui fut exécuté. En 14 minutes, tout était sous voiles, et je fis porter sur l'ennemi pour lui couper le chemin de la petite passe, et dans le dessein de l'y suivre, s'il avait tenté d'y passer ; mais l'amiral anglais ne tarda pas à renoncer à son projet, rappela son vaisseau et ses deux frégates engagés dans les îles et prit chasse. Je l'ai poursuivi jusqu'à la nuit ; il courait au sud-est. Le matin, au jour, je n'en ai eu aucune connaissance. Je vous salue avec respect, LA TOUCHE TRÉVILLE.'

The conduct of all privateers is, as far as I have seen, so near piracy, that I only wonder any civilised nation can allow them. The lawful as well as unlawful commerce of the neutral flag is subject to every violation and spoliation. *T. Jackson, 20 June.*

In case Earl St. Vincent and Sir Thomas Troubridge should not send you my letters to them respecting the conduct of soldiers embarked to serve in his Majesty's ships, I think it of great consequence to the naval service you should be informed of my sentiments upon that subject. It requires not the gift of prescience to assert, if soldiers embarked in ships of war are not, as heretofore, left subject to the Act of Parliament for the government of his Majesty's ships, vessels, and forces by sea, whereon, as our forefathers said, 'the safety, wealth, and prosperity of the kingdom chiefly depend,' that the navy, which we have all heretofore looked up to, will be ruined. The absolute power must remain; there cannot be two commanders in one ship, nor two sets of laws to regulate the conduct of those embarked in the same bottom. I will not, my Lord, take up your time in debating, whether it would be better for the navy to be subject to the same Articles of War as the army, but we may take a lesson from the epitaph, 'I was well; I would be better, and here I am.' My opinion is, 'Let well alone.' *Lord Melville, 21 June.*

The loss [of Sardinia] to us will be great indeed. I do not think that the fleet can then be kept at sea. From Sardinia we get water and fresh provisions; the loss of it would cut us off from Naples except by a circuitous route, for all the purposes of getting refreshments, even were Naples able to supply us. I have hitherto watched Sardinia; but at this moment, when from the bad condition of many of the ships under my command, I can barely *Lord Hawkesbury, 22 June.*

keep a sufficient force at sea to attend to the French fleet, I have not ships to send to Madalena: not less, my Lord, than ten frigates, and as many good sloops, would enable me to do what I wish, and what, of course, I think absolutely necessary. But I am aware of the great want of them in England, and that other services must be starved to take care of home. If I were at your Lordship's elbow, I think I could say so much upon the subject of Sardinia, that attempts would be made to obtain it; for this I hold as clear, that the King of Sardinia cannot keep it, and, if he could, that it is of no use to him; that if France gets it, she commands the Mediterranean; and that by us it would be kept at a much smaller expense than Malta: from its position, it is worth fifty Maltas. Should the war continue, the blockade of Marseilles is a measure absolutely essential, and the points necessary for us to occupy are to be considered, and I think I could satisfy your Lordship of the probability of holding those positions: nothing could distress France so much, and make her wish for peace with us at present. Not less than forty sail a week go into Marseilles.

W. Marsden, 30 June.

Commissioner Otway having informed me that by the present plan of having the mail brought from Lisbon to Faro by land, the letters become liable to a very heavy postage, and that there are now many letters in the post-office for the seamen and petty officers of the fleet unredeemed, I therefore request you will please to communicate to the Lords Commissioners of the Admiralty, that from the very high charge of postage from Lisbon, it is impossible that the seamen and petty officers can redeem their letters, and submit to their Lordships the propriety of directing the postage thereof being paid by Government, as I understand has been done on some former occasions.[1]

Capt. Donnelly, Narcissus, 2 July.

I believe your orders are to cruise or anchor as you may judge best for carrying on the service entrusted to you, therefore you will act as you see best. Your boats can be inside at night in moderate weather, and in day-time you can work between the islands, but I should wish you not to be out of the reach of the fleet in case Monsieur La Touche should come out of his nest. I am obliged by your accounts of Hières Bay. When

---

[1] On 27 April, 1779, Rear-Admiral Barrington, in forwarding a memorial to a similar effect, from the seamen of the West India fleet, said that the indulgence had been granted in North America. At his request it was then also granted in the West Indies. No doubt there were later instances to which Nelson here more immediately alludes.

our fleets occupied it, the islands were not fortified. The enemy, I am sure, want to get some small ships of war to the eastward, probably for the invasion of Sardinia; and by disappointment for some time, I think the fleet will be ordered out to fight close to Toulon, that they may get their crippled ships in again, and that we must then quit the coast to repair our damages, and thus leave the coast clear; but my mind is fixed not to fight them, unless with a westerly wind, outside the Hières, and with an easterly wind to the westward of Sicie. I am sure one of these days they will come out; for, besides their degradation to all Europe, Marseilles must suffer for want of her usual commerce. I have only again to repeat that you will keep under sail or anchor as you please, and I am sure you will always be upon your guard against a surprise from a superior force.

We have nothing but incessant gales of wind, and I am absolutely worn out. From Gantheaume's having hoisted his flag at Brest, I have no doubt but that an attempt will be made to get a superiority of force into the Mediterranean. However, our force is diminishing daily. Kent, Renown, and Gibraltar are gone for any further use; Superb and Triumph must go. Several of the ships want to go into port to refit, and if I was to do as they do in the Channel, I have not, by that mode of judging, four sail fit to keep the sea. I absolutely keep them out by management; but the time must come when we shall break up, unless the new Admiralty act very differently from the old, and send out six sail of the line and fifteen frigates and sloops; and I do not believe that the late Admiralty have left them one to send. But I must not indulge these thoughts, or I should say much more, but I pay it off with thinking. *H. Elliot, 7 July.*

If Russia goes to war with France, I hope it will be her own war, and not joined with us. Such alliances have never benefited our country. If the Emperor of Germany joins against France, something good may arise. If not, Russia's going to war in the way I am sure she will, will cause the loss of Naples and Sardinia, for that court will not send 100,000 men into Italy, and less are useless for any grand purpose. No; Russia will take care of the Ionian Republic, the Morea, and, in the end, Constantinople. The views of Russia are perfectly clear. *8 July.*

The French navy is daily increasing, both at Toulon and Brest, whilst ours is as clearly going down-hill. It will require all Lord Melville's abilities to get our fleet ahead of that of the French. We made use of the peace, not to recruit our navy, but to be the cause of its ruin. Nothing but a speedy battle, a complete annihilation of the enemy's fleets, and a seven years' peace, can get our fleet in the order it ought to be; therefore I, for one, do not wish to be shackled with allies. I am for assisting Europe to the utmost of our power, but no treaties, which England only keeps.

I hope your next letters from Naples will give me the news to alter my opinion of degenerate Europe, for I am sick at heart at the miserable cringing conduct of the great powers.

The fleet is as healthy as usual, but if the Admiralty do not very largely reinforce this fleet, so as to enable me to send some ships home and others into port to refit, it cannot be kept at sea another winter.

9 July. I had a letter yesterday from Rear-Admiral Cochrane, who commands off Ferrol. The French fleet at Brest, Rochefort, and Ferrol are perfectly ready for sea, and we know they are ready at Toulon, and I have no doubt but that the Mediterranean will be the scene of action. I only hope that it will very soon happen, or I shall have nothing to do with it, for I do assure you that every part of my constitution is broke up. . . . A great expedition seems fitting out. I fear it is to send abroad, when I think it might be much more usefully employed in the Mediterranean, and in taking Belleisle.

Q. of Naples, 10 July It would be presumptuous on my part to venture to speak of political matters in a letter to your Majesty, but I cannot help wishing that Europe was like a handful of rods against France. If it be proper to give way to the times, let us temporise : if to make war, let us all make it. On this principle I could have wished that Russia had avoided war, unless she had been joined by Austria. Then, acting honourably side by side, there would have been some hope from such a coalition. If Russia sends men and vessels to the Ionian Republic, and into the Morea only, I have no hesitation in saying that she compromises Naples much more than if she had, for the moment, bent to the storm. At least 50,000 troops (it should be 100,000) are necessary to answer for the safety of Italy. To say the truth, I do not believe we had in the last war, and, according to all appearance, we shall not have in the present one either, plans of a sufficiently grand scale to force France to keep within her proper limits. Small measures produce only small results. I dare not let my pen run on. The intelligent mind of your Majesty will readily comprehend the great things which might be effected in the Mediterranean. On this side Bonaparte is the most vulnerable. It is from here that it would be most easy to mortify his pride, and so far humble him as to make him accept reasonable conditions of peace.

I have received your letter of 5 June, giving an account of your having, on the 3rd of that month, destroyed, and set fire to a French privateer under the island of Fano. The destruction of the enemy's privateers, who are so numerous in these seas (and contrary to all known laws of neutrality, shelter themselves, and make a convenience of the neutral territory of the powers at amity with Great Britain, from whence they commit the most unwarrantable depredations on our commerce), becomes an object of serious consideration, and certainly justifies an attack upon these pirates. I therefore feel pleased with your conduct in the destruction of the privateer before mentioned, and shall write Mr. Foresti, his Majesty's minister at Corfu, to remonstrate against the conduct of those unprecedented and sanctioned pirates, as I did in the instance of the Thisbe; for certainly the neutral territory that does not afford protection cannot be allowed to give it to the original breaker of the neutrality, and therefore, from the offensive state of the privateer in question, and her firing upon the Arrow's boats, I cannot but approve of your having destroyed her; but I must beg to be perfectly understood, that I would on no account have the neutrality broken or disturbed by his Majesty's ships or vessels, under my command, firing upon any of the enemy's privateers or endeavouring to destroy them under the protection of a neutral port, unless such privateers shall first use such offensive measures and fire upon his Majesty's subjects, in which case they forfeit the protection of the neutral port, and ought to be destroyed, if possible.

Capt. Vincent, Arrow, 28 July.

As canvas was to be had at Naples, I cannot account for your having ordered such a quantity of it, and other stores, from Fiume, on your return to Naples from Malta, as there appears no necessity for such a measure, and my instructions only justify your making inquiry where naval stores may be had in case of emergency, and not to purchase, except small quantities, and that in cases only of absolute necessity, with the concurrence and authority of the senior officer. I hope your conduct on this occasion will meet the approbation of the Navy Board, and that the disbursement of the public money in your department for every article purchased may be perfectly correct, and entirely to their satisfaction.

N. Taylor, Naval Officer, Malta, 28 July.

In future, it is my directions that previous to the purchase of any description of stores, you consult with the senior officer on the necessity thereof, as well as to the exact quantity of every article wanted; and upon his being perfectly and fully satisfied of the absolute and indispensable necessity of such temporary purchase, you are to obtain from him an order for that purpose, which must specify the particular quantity of every article intended to be procured, a copy of which order &c. you will transmit to me immediately (in the event of there not being time to make application to me in the first instance, which is always to be done when practicable), and also an account from the person of whom the purchase is made, setting forth the quantity and price of every article, in order that I may, on any future occasion, satisfy myself with the correctness thereof.

The jolly-boat for the Childers has been received, and also the Victory's hammock-cloths, but I am extremely concerned to observe the inattention which they have met with in Malta yard. They have been badly painted (if it may be called painting), as it is all run in flecks, and peels off with the least touch. In addition to this, a considerable part of one of them is entirely rotten. The want of these hammock cloths will be severely felt, and there is none on board to cover the men's bedding. A survey shall be ordered upon them, and a report thereof sent to the Admiralty for their Lordships' consideration.

On 31 July, Lord Nelson changed his flag from blue at the fore to white.

The Lord Mayor, 1 August.

My Lord,—This day I am honoured with your Lordship's letter of 9 April, transmitting me the resolutions of the Corporation of London, thanking me as commanding the fleet blockading Toulon. I do assure your Lordship that there is not a man breathing who sets a higher value upon the thanks of his fellow-citizens of London than myself, but I should feel as much ashamed to receive them for a particular service marked in the resolution, if I felt that I did not come within that line of service, as I should feel hurt at having a great victory passed over without notice. I beg to inform your Lordship that the port of Toulon has never been blockaded by me, quite the reverse; every opportunity has been offered the enemy to put to sea, for it is there that we hope to realise the hopes and expectations of our country, and I trust that they will not be disappointed.

Your Lordship will judge of my feelings upon seeing that all the junior flag-officers of other fleets, and even some of the captains, have received the thanks of the Corporation of London, whilst the junior flag-officers of the Mediterranean fleet are entirely omitted. I own it has struck me very forcibly; for, where the information of the junior flag-officers and captains of other fleets was obtained, the same information could have been given of the flag-officers of this fleet and the captains; and it is my duty to state, that more able and zealous flag-officers and captains do not grace the British navy than those I have the honour and happiness to command.

It likewise appears, my Lord, a most extraordinary circumstance, that Sir Richard Bickerton should have been, as second in command in the Mediterranean fleets, twice passed over by the Corporation of London : once after the Egyptian expedition, when the first and third in command were thanked, and now again! Conscious of high desert instead of neglect, the rear-admiral resolved to let the matter rest until he could have an opportunity personally to call upon the Lord Mayor to account for such an extraordinary omission, but from this second omission I owe it to that excellent officer not to pass it by. I do assure your Lordship, that the constant, zealous, and cordial support I have had in my command, from both Rear-Admiral Sir Richard Bickerton and Rear-Admiral Campbell, has been such as calls forth all my thanks and admiration. We have shared together the constant attention of being fourteen months at sea, and are ready to share the dangers and glory of a day of battle; therefore it is impossible that I can ever allow myself to be separated in thanks from such supporters.

My opinion of the views of Russia has long been formed, and to this moment I see everything she does works to the same end— the possession of all European Turkey. I have delivered my opinion when in England how this plan of Russia might be turned to much advantage for us, and how it would operate against France. I know the importance of Malta, but I fancy I also know how far its importance extends. On this point we may differ, but we both agree that it never must be even risked falling into the hands of France. . . . Look at the position of Sardinia ; I have touched, I recollect, before upon that subject, and you should be viceroy. I have warned the folks at home, but I fear in vain. Algiers will be French in one year after a peace : you see it, and a man may run and read, that is the plan of Bonaparte. And now I will not plague you with my nonsensical ideas any more, and have only to hope Monsieur La Touche, who says, in his letter to Paris,[1] that I ran away from him on June 14, will give me an opportunity of

Sir A. J. Ball. 8 August.

---

[1] See *ante*, p. 355.

settling my account before I go home, which cannot be much longer deferred.

<small>Sir R. Kingsmill, 4 August.</small>

I am sorry to tell you that my health, or rather constitution, is so much shook, that I doubt the possibility of my holding out another winter without asses' milk and some months' quiet; then I may get on another campaign or two. But when I run over the undermentioned wounds, eye in Corsica, belly off Cape St. Vincent, arm at Teneriffe, head in Egypt, I ought to be thankful that I am what I am. If Monsieur La Touche will give me the meeting before I go home, it will probably finish my naval career. He is ready, and, by their handling their ships, apparently well manned; but I command, for captains and crews, such a fleet as I never have before seen, and it is impossible that any admiral can be happier situated. Rotten ships neither rests with me nor them.

<small>W. Marsden, 7 August.</small>

Two pursers who have been dismissed their situations for improper conduct are both employed at Malta; one as agent to the hospital, and the other as agent to the contractors for prisoners of war. The conduct of the former has already been extremely improper, as represented by Dr. Snipe to the sick and hurt board, and it will naturally occur to their Lordships the impropriety of appointing such characters to public situations abroad.

I am informed it is the intention of the agent to the contractor for prisoners of war to discontinue giving them fresh beef, and to supply them with salt in lieu, on account of the latter being so much more reasonable than the former. I must therefore beg to observe to their Lordships, that as prisoners of war are not allowed wine, the giving them salt beef instead of fresh will, from their long and close confinement, naturally produce disease and very dangerous consequences; and it is with much deference I take the liberty of mentioning to their Lordships (as Frenchmen are in the habit of drinking small wine in their own country) the propriety of allowing prisoners of war a certain quantity each per day.

In another letter of the same date, after acknowledging a complaint made by the Spanish minister of the misconduct of an English privateer, he added:

<small>W. Marsden, 7 August.</small>

If I had the least authority whatever in controlling the privateers, whose conduct is so disgraceful to the British nation, I would instantly take their commissions from them, but as naval commanders have no power over them whatever, I am obliged to hear from the Sardinian Government and others of their daily depredations, without being able either to check or put a stop to it. The only thing I can, therefore, do in the present instance (as I have in several other similar ones) is to transmit your letter and its inclosure to the Governor of Gibraltar, that he may take such steps as may appear to him proper to put a stop to the piratical proceedings of such a horde of sanctioned robbers.

It is not necessary for me to point out the disgraceful conduct of the Gibraltar privateers in these seas, as so many circumstances must long ago have satisfied you with this truth. I shall therefore say no more on the subject, and only beg to express a hope that the most exemplary punishment may be inflicted upon the delinquents, when the enormity of their crimes can be proved to conviction, in order to deter them from future depredations. Sir T. Trigge, 7 August.

I sincerely hope, now a change has taken place, that you will get a ship. I attribute none of the tyrannical conduct of the late Board to Lord St. Vincent. For the earl I have a sincere regard, but he was dreadfully ill-advised, and I fear the service has suffered much from their conduct. Sir E. Berry, 8 August.

I have been expecting Monsieur La Touche to give me the meeting every day for this year past, and only hope he will come out before I go hence. . . . You will have seen his letter of how he chased me and how I ran. I keep it; and, by God, if I take him he shall eat it! Rev. W. Nelson, 8 August.

Although I most certainly never thought of writing a line upon Monsieur La Touche's having cut a caper a few miles outside of Toulon on 14 June, where he well knew I could not get at him without placing the ships under the batteries which surround that port, and that, had I attacked him in that position, he could retire into his secure nest whenever he pleased, yet as that gentleman has thought proper to write a letter stating that the fleet under my command ran away, and that he pursued it, perhaps it may be thought necessary for me to say something. But I do assure you that I know not what to say, except by a flat contradiction, for if my character is not established by this time for not being apt to run away, it is not worth my time to attempt to put the world right. It is not, therefore, with any such intention that I stain my paper with a vaunting man's name, and therefore I shall only state that the fleet I have the honour and happiness to command is in the highest state of discipline, good order, good W. Marsden, 12 August.

humour, and good health, and that the united wishes of all are, I am sure, to meet Monsieur La Touche at sea: then I ought not to doubt that I should be able to write a letter equally satisfactory to my king, my country, and myself.

I send you a copy of the ship's log. I observe that even the return of Monsieur La Touche into Toulon is not noticed, so little must have been thought of the French returning into port that day more than any other. I send you the bearings of the land for the 14th and 15th, and the movements of the squadron on the evening of the 14th June.

French fleet under Monsieur La Touche, eight sail of the line and four frigates; two frigates and a brig in Hières Bay, who joined in the night.

British fleet—five sail of the line and two frigates, one of which, the Excellent, 74, and two frigates, did not join till the middle of the night, having been sent into Hières Bay.

From 6.10 to 7.28 P.M. the British formed in a line to receive Monsieur La Touche, maintopsail to the mast,
{ Canopus,
Belleisle,
Donegal,
Victory.

Movements of the squadron on the evening of 14 June, 1804.

At 5.43 P.M.—Prepared for battle.
    5.49 . . Recalled the Excellent.
Laying to { 6.10 . . Formed the line of battle.
7.28 . . Came to the wind together on the larboard tack.
    7.45 . . Tacked together.
    7.59 . . Formed the order of sailing.

With which was inclosed the copy of the log:

'At 5 observed the enemy's ships coming out of Toulon. In steering sails and royals and hauled in a line of battle on the starboard tack (wind WNW). The enemy's ships consisting of eight sail of the line and four frigates. (6–8; wind SW by W: up S by E, off SE by S.) Wore ship. At 7.35 in 1st and 2d reefs of topsails. Moderate breezes and clear. At 8 Cape Sicie bore NW by W 7 leagues: NW end of Porquerolle, N 7 miles; SE end of do. NE by E ½ E 7 miles. . . . At noon, NW end of Porquerolle, E by N ¼ N 11 miles.

W. Marsden, 12 August.

The Diligent transport has brought out frocks and trowsers for the use of the fleet under my command, but instead of their being made of good Russia duck, as was formerly supplied the seamen of his Majesty's navy, the frocks at 4s. 8d. each, and the trowsers at 4s. per pair, those sent out are made of coarse wrapper-stuff, and the price increased—the frocks twopence each, and the trowsers threepence per pair, which makes the former 4s. 10d. and the latter 4s. 3d. I therefore think it necessary to send you one of each, in order that their Lordships may judge of their quality and price, and at the same time beg to observe, for their information, that the issuing such coarse stuff to the people, who have been accustomed to good Russia duck cheaper, will no doubt occasion murmur and discontent, and may serious consequences. I therefore am most decidedly of opinion that the contractor who furnished such stuff ought to be hanged; and little less, if anything, is due to those who have received them from him. I shall say no more on the subject, as their Lordships will naturally see the propriety of this evil being remedied as early as possible.

We have an uniform sameness, day after day and month after month—gales of wind for ever; in July we had seventeen days very severe weather. The Mediterranean seems altered. However, with nursing our ships, we have roughed it out better than could have been expected. I have always made it a rule never to contend with the gales, and either run to the southward to escape its violence, or furl all the sails and make the ships as easy as possible. Duke of Clarence, 15 August.

It is with much uneasiness of mind that I feel it my duty to state to you, for the information of their Lordships, that I consider my state of health to be such as to make it absolutely necessary that I should return to England to re-establish it. Another winter such as the last I feel myself unable to stand against. A few months of quiet may enable me to serve again next spring, and I believe that no officer is more anxious to serve than myself. No officer could be placed in a more enviable command than the one I have the honour of being placed in, and no command ever produced so much happiness to a commander-in-chief, whether in the flag-officers, the captains, or the good conduct of the crews of every ship in this fleet; and the constant marks of approbation for my conduct which I have received from every court in the Mediterranean leave me nothing to wish for but a better state of health. W. Marsden, 15 August.

I have thought it necessary to state thus much, that their Lordships might not for a moment suppose that I had any uneasiness of mind upon any account. On the contrary, every person, of all ranks and descriptions, seems only desirous to meet my wishes and to give me satisfaction. I must therefore entreat their Lordships' permission to return to England for the re-establishment of my health, and that their consent may reach me as soon as possible, for I have deferred my application already too long.

Lord Melville, (?)16Aug.

I know there are many admirals desirous of this command, with better health and probably with greater abilities than myself, but none who will serve with more zeal; therefore I can hardly expect, should even my health be perfect, to be allowed to return to this, my favourite command. But should any such plan occur to your Lordship, it is my duty to state, and it is well known to the Board, that the second in command here, who has held that post, and the command of the fleet, for four years, Sir Richard Bickerton, is an officer of not only distinguished merit, but also a most perfectly correct and safe officer, and fit to command any fleet.

Sir E. Nepean, (?)16Aug.

You will, I am sure, see with regret, that my shattered carcase requires rest. The leaving this fleet, where everyone wishes to please me, and where I am as happy as it is possible for a man to be in a command, must make me feel; but I owe to my king and country, and to myself, not to let the service suffer upon my account. I have not interest, nor can I expect to be permitted to return in the spring to this command. Yet is this place, perhaps, more fitted for me than any other—but I submit. All my wishes now rest that I may meet Monsieur La Touche before October is over.

Sir A. J. Ball, 19 August.

The French ships have been out a few miles, but they see so far that the coast is clear, that there is but very little prospect of getting at them. They are now reported nine sail of the line in the outer road, and seven or eight frigates. I am keeping as many frigates as possible round me, for I know the value of them on the day of battle, and compared with that day, what signifies any prizes they might take? I yet hope to get hold of them before my successor arrives, then ten years will be added to my life. Although I have no particular complaint, my general constitution has suffered much the last winter, and I ought not, in justice to myself, to encounter another. I think either Sir Roger Curtis or Young are likely to come here: either will do well, but they may leave the command with Sir Richard Bickerton. . . .

I send you, in confidence, a copy of my letter to the Admiralty about Monsieur La Touche: they may do as they please, I care not. Such a liar is below my notice, except to thrash him, which will be done, if in the power of, my dear Ball, your sincere friend,
NELSON AND BRONTE.

I have every reason to think, that if this fleet gets fairly up with Monsieur La Touche, his letter, with all his ingenuity, must be different from his last. We had fancied that we had chased him into Toulon; for blind as I am, I could see his water-line when he clued his topsails up, shutting in Sepet; but from the time of his meeting Captain Hawker in the Iris, I never heard of his acting otherwise than as a poltroon and a liar.[1] Contempt is the best mode of treating such a miscreant.

Capt. Sutton, (?)20 Aug.

I dare say Monsieur La Touche will have a different sort of letter to write, if I can once get a shake at him. Whether the world thinks that I ran away or no, is to me a matter of great indifference. If my character is not fixed by this time, it is useless for me to try to fix it at my time of life.

A. Davison, 22 August.

I have wrote to Lord Melville my desire to return to this command in March, or April, if I am removed, but the Administration may have so many other admirals looking to them, that I may very possibly be laid upon the shelf. I dare not presume to think that with all my zeal and attachment to their Sicilian Majesties, that I am of sufficient importance for the king to express his wish to England for my return. That must be for him to consider; and if he thinks proper to do it, nothing, I suppose, but a letter to his brother George can do it, and that must not go through me, but through his minister Castelcicala.

H. Elliot, 28 August.

With respect to the line of conduct necessary to be observed with the enemy's privateers under similar circumstances, it is impossible for me to name any precise mode of proceeding; for if the laws of neutrality are not adhered to and enforced by the powers in amity with all the world, it will, I fear, if remonstrances are not attended to by those powers, become necessary to destroy the enemy's privateers wherever they may be found. But this measure must not be resorted to until proofs of misconduct on the part of our enemies have been made manifest. In that case I am clearly

Capt. Raynsford, 2 Sept.

---

[1] *Beatson's Naval and Military Memoirs*, vol. v. p. 47. Perhaps the most accurate account of the affair now attainable is the following extract from the Iris's log, 7 June, 1780, Sandy Hook, West, 28 leagues. 'At 7 A.M. saw a frigate bearing NW. Left off chasing the above vessels and chased the frigate. Soon after, she tacked and stood towards us. Cleared ship for action. At about a musket shot she hoisted French colours. Proved to be La Hermione, of 36 guns. At 9 we began a close action, which continued an hour and twenty minutes, when the French frigate made sail from us, with all the sail she could make. We followed her for three-quarters of an hour, when another sail was seen ahead, and we were obliged to haul our wind, when our fore-topsail-yard went away, and being very much damaged in our sails and rigging. We had 7 men killed and 9 wounded. Employed knotting, splicing, and reeving running rigging.' 'Thursday, 8th, fresh breezes, &c., &c.' 'Friday, 9th, ditto.' 'Saturday, 10th. Inside the Hook. Unbent sails, and moored ship.'

of opinion, that on the spot where the breach of neutrality has been committed by the French, the enemy has no right to claim the protection of neutrality if he should be overpowered. I am sure it is the furthest from the wish of our Government to break the neutrality of any state, although the French may; but it is no longer a neutral spot if the French are permitted to commit hostilities against us.

The Sardinian Government had claimed as a deserter a man who had enlisted at Madalena. Nelson at once sent back the man, with a request that, if found not to be a deserter, he might be returned. And to General Villettes he wrote:

M.-General Villettes, 6 Sept.

It is but an act of common justice, as they give up all ours. And, to say the truth, I had rather that not one Corsican or Italian was raised, if it is to be at the expense of perhaps losing double the number of English seamen, for such is the love for roaming of our men, that I am sure they would desert from heaven to hell, merely for the sake of change. . . .

I never wish to see an Italian recruit. If they come, I must receive them; but I give no encouragement to the raising Italians. Good Germans I cannot have any objections to. If the Russians continue increasing their naval force in this country, I do not think the French will venture to the eastward; therefore I rather expect they will, as the year advances, try to get out of the Straits, and should they accomplish it with 7,000 troops on board, I am sure we should lose half our West India Islands, for I think they would go there, and not to Ireland. Whatever may be their destination, I shall certainly follow, be it even to the East Indies. Such a pursuit would do more, perhaps, towards restoring me to health than all the doctors; but I fear this is reserved for some happier man. Not that I can complain; I have had a good race of glory, but we are never satisfied, although I hope I am duly thankful for the past, but one cannot help, being at sea, longing for a little more. La Touche has given me the slip—he died of the colic; perhaps Bonaparte's, for they say he was a rank republican. Dumanoir is the rear-admiral at present in Toulon.

Sir A. J. Ball, 6 Sept.

I cannot bring myself to suppose but that one half of the admirals on the list will perform the duty of the Mediterranean command as well, at least, as myself, and if the other half of the admiral's list was to hear of my vanity they would think me a fool; but be that as it may, I am very far from well. At the same time, if I was to get better, nothing could please me so

much as returning to this command; but I have no interest and
another will come, and I think very probably Orde or Curtis—
Young seems fixed at Plymouth.

I have read the account of the Marquis Dasserto. I never intended to hold any communication with him. I considered him as
a French spy, and for that reason referred him to diplomatic characters if he had anything to communicate. Mr. Elliot wanted to
send me some good Frenchmen[1] to go ashore and to get me information. My [answer] to all these offers [is], 'I can be told nothing
of any consequence to me; but a copy of the French admiral's
orders, when he is to put to sea, and where he is destined to, is the
only useful information I can care about. I can see the number
and force at Toulon any day I please, and as for the names of the
captains or admirals, I care not what they are called;' therefore,
as you may suppose, I have none of these 'good Frenchmen'
about me.

I wish I had any sloops of war; but you have them all to the
eastward and at Gibraltar; the Childers is the only one I can call
upon. The Termagant is going to Gibraltar to be hove down. I
wrote to the Admiralty until I am tired, and they have left off
answering those parts of my letters. The late Admiralty thought I
kept too many to the eastward of Sicily; the Smyrna folks complain
of me, so do the Adriatic, so they do between Cape Gata and Gibraltar. If I had them, I do assure you not one of them should go prize-hunting—that I never have done; and to this day, I can solemnly
assure you, that I am a poorer man than the day I was ordered to
the Mediterranean command, by upwards of 1,000*l.*; but money
I despise, except as it is useful, and I expect my prize-money is
embarked in the Toulon fleet. I should think, now the Russians
are getting so large a naval force into the Mediterranean, that the
Toulon fleet will not think of going to the eastward. I should
rather think the West Indies more likely for them to succeed in.
Suppose this fleet escapes, and gets out of the Straits, I rather
think I should bend my course to the westward; for if they carry
7,000 men—with what they have at Martinique and Guadeloupe—
St. Lucia, Grenada, St. Vincent, Antigua, and St. Kitts would fall,
and in that case England would be so clamorous for peace that
we should humble ourselves. What do you think? Tell me. I
have weighed Ireland against the West Indies. With me the
latter throws the beam up to the ceiling; but I may be wrong. It

---

[1] See *ante*, pp. 324, 352.

is at best but a guess, and the world attaches wisdom to him that guesses right.

Capt.
Duibrn,
11 Sept.

Whereas I wish very much to be made acquainted with the anchorage and Gulf of Palma, in the island of Majorca, and as a most favourable opportunity now presents itself by the circumstance of the Cardinal Despuig wanting a passport from me, and as he is brother to the viceroy, the Marquis de Monte Negro, you are therefore hereby required and directed to proceed to Palma, and first by offering to salute the place upon the assurance of an equal number of guns being returned, deliver my letter to the cardinal, and personally assure his eminence of my earnest desire to meet his wishes; so much so, that even should he wish to go to Italy in the Ambuscade, that you are at liberty to carry him to either Civitá Vecchia or Naples without any further order from me, provided his eminence is ready to embark in forty-eight hours, to which time I must limit your stay; during which time you are to examine not only everything laid down in the printed orders of the Admiralty, but examine the general state of the island, its forts, and the probability of its being taken in case of a Spanish war. You will examine in the environs of Palma the best place for landing troops, the situation of the forts or towers which are in the gulf, the best mode of approaching the town, the strength of its fortifications, both on the land and sea side; whether there is a ditch; how deep; and what is the probable height of the wall; whether ships could approach near enough to batter the fortifications; how bomb-vessels could act; what is the general garrison; in short, everything which my opinion of your good sense and abilities leads me to expect from you. Whether, if the fleet was to anchor there, that it would be ill or well received; the cattle or other refreshments it could obtain. Having made the observations &c. at Palma as before mentioned, which must not detain the Ambuscade more than two or three days, you will leave that place, and return and join the squadron on Rendezvous No. 97, under Cape St. Sebastian, with all possible despatch, where you will find me, or orders for your further proceedings. But should Cardinal Despuig express a desire to be conveyed to Italy in the Ambuscade, you will receive his eminence and suite on board, and proceed with them, with all convenient expedition, either to Civitá Vecchia or Naples, where you will land them, and afterwards return and join me on Rendezvous No. 97 without delay, as before directed. You are not to wait for his eminence at Palma, in the event of his going with you, longer than the time above mentioned.

My complaints have not been so violent, but are sufficient to make me require a few months' rest. Since 16 June, 1803, I have never set my foot outside the ship. Experience teaches us that this climate is the worst in the world for hectic complaints— at least it is so at sea. Of the few men we have lost, nine in ten are dead of consumption. Upon the best mode of keeping a fleet healthy much may be said and much must be done—there are various opinions; suffice it for me, that although other places may be better, yet that we have no sick. We shall talk of this and many other matters before any great length of time.

<small>Dr. Baird 22 Sept.</small>

The measure of paying for such provisions which the seamen do not either take up, or which is not issued to them, either from scarcity or from its not being in the fleet, is so just that it cannot be controverted, but upon the present case there seems doubts whether the men have a right to be paid for the half allowance of oatmeal when no molasses is to be procured. I am sure their Lordships will see the justness of the case as plainly as I do. Each man was formerly allowed a pint of oatmeal on certain days. As it was found that generally a man could not get a pint of dry oatmeal down his throat, and, I suppose, thinking it no longer necessary to present this saving to the purser, half a pint of oatmeal was issued instead of the pint, and in lieu of the other half-pint, a proportion of molasses. It has sometimes occurred in the Channel fleet that no molasses could be procured, nor was there any allowance made for such temporary omissions. In the West Indies cocoa and sugar are allowed; in the Channel, I hear, tea and sugar. In the Mediterranean we have no molasses, nor any substitute, nor is our want of molasses temporary, but lasting.

<small>W. Marsden, 22 Sept.</small>

I beg, therefore, with all due respect, to call their Lordships' attention to the circumstance, and to propose that when molasses cannot be obtained, a proportion of sugar should be allowed to bo mixed with the oatmeal in lieu of molasses; and that if sugar cannot be obtained, the men having no substitute in lieu, should be paid the saving, as in all other species of provisions.

I have received your letter of the 6th ultimo, acquainting me with the circumstance of your having flogged John Carter, seaman, belonging to the Spider, on the 5th of that month; that soon after a shot was flung from forward by some of the people, which fell

<small>Lieut. Shaw, Spider, 4 October.</small>

close by you and Mr. Langdon, the master; and in order to discover the offender you judged it necessary to threaten them with individual punishment, which, as they would not confess, you had inflicted upon each of your company, by calling them over by the watch-bill, and giving them a dozen each. In answer to which, I cannot approve of a measure so foreign to the rules of good discipline and the accustomed practice of his Majesty's navy, and therefore caution you against a similar line of conduct. Had you fixed upon one or more guilty individuals, and punished them severely, it might have had the desired effect, or put them into confinement and brought them to a court-martial. I trust your watchful conduct will prevent any such confusion or disposition to riot from happening again.

Sir A. J. Ball, 4 October.

I sincerely hope that the Russians will not act so as to have the Austrians united with the French and Turks against them and us; but Russia must be careful how she conducts herself in the Ionian Republic and the Morea. I have great fears; I think I see much too close a connection between France and Austria, and we know the Turks would jump to join such an alliance. The times are big with great events. I wish my health was better. I have mentioned to Lord Melville what you have thought about Sir Richard Bickerton in case I should be able to return, but I do not expect such a compliance. Time will show. Toulon was safe on Sunday last, as Boyle will tell you. No admiral has hoisted his flag in the room of La Touche;[1] he is gone, and all his lies with him. The French papers say he died in consequence of walking so often up to the signal-post upon Sepet to watch us; I always pronounced that that would be his death.

Lieut. R. Spencer, 4 October.

I have received your letter of 30 July, acquainting me that, on account of the weather, you judged it necessary to let the four small vessels under your convoy on the 28th of that month anchor to the southward of Cape Murro di Porco, and took that occasion to reconnoitre a vessel to leeward. In the meantime a strange vessel came round the cape from Syracuse, which the masters of those four vessels judging to be a privateer, cut their cable, and ran down to you; that on the said privateer observing you stand towards her, she ran upon the rocks and landed her men; and that, from the frequent violations of neutrality which

[1] Died, 18 August.

the enemy's privateers had been guilty of, you judged it a good occasion to chastise them. In answer to which, however much the destruction of the enemy's privateers under the violation of the laws of neutrality may be desired, I cannot, in the present instance, justify your leaving the vessels under your convoy exposed to the risk of capture, under any circumstances whatever. Had you been in company with your convoy, a legal opportunity might have offered for capturing or destroying the privateer alluded to. The instructions for officers charged with convoys are so strict and well known, that I am sorry it becomes necessary for me to call your most strict attention to them in future.

There is no man who more sincerely laments the heavy loss you have sustained than myself; but the name of Duncan will never be forgot by Britain, and in particular by its navy, in which service the remembrance of your worthy father will, I am sure, grow up in you. I am sorry not to have a good sloop to give you, but still an opening offers which I think will insure your confirmation as a commander. It is occasioned by the very ill state of health of Captain Corbet of the Bittern, who has requested a few weeks' leave to reside on shore at the hospital. You will be confirmed before he resumes his command.

Lieut. H. Duncan,[1] 4 Oct.

Mr. Elliot had written to Lord Nelson under date 8 September :

'My Lord,—I cannot sufficiently express the infinite regret with which their Sicilian Majesties have learnt your determination of quitting your command in the Mediterranean, and of going to England this winter for the re-establishment of your health. Their Sicilian Majesties are in this not more concerned for your indisposition, than they are anxious from the evil effects which they apprehend must ensue to their interest, in consequence of your Lordship's absence from the Mediterranean. I know it is the king's intention to write to the Prince of Castelcicala, to apply to the British Government for your Lordship's speedy return to these seas, in order to resume the high command you have hitherto exercised, with no less credit to yourself than advantage to the many countries whose future security rests entirely upon the skill by which a British admiral may be enabled to maintain the superiority of the British fleet over that of the enemy in the Mediterranean. When such great interests are concerned, I shall not presume to dwell upon my own feelings, although I cannot but recall to your Lordship, that I only consented to depart as abruptly as I did from England, to undertake this arduous and ruinous mission, from the expectation that my efforts to direct the councils of this kingdom would have been seconded by your pre-eminent talents and judgment. Allow me, however, my Lord, in this emergency, to propose to your consideration a

---

[1] Second son of Admiral Lord Duncan. The letter was accompanied by a newspaper announcing the death of Lord Duncan on 4 August.

plan, concerning which I have already had much conversation with the queen, and which, if it can be adopted, will obviate many of the misfortunes to which we should be exposed by your absence. As your Lordship's health requires that you should not be exposed to the rigours of another winter's cruise in the Gulf of Lyons, it is the sincere wish of this court that you would spend the severe months of the year either here or at Palermo, without abandoning your chief command in the Mediterranean. I only do my duty in suggesting this idea to your Lordship, without venturing to press upon you the many arguments by which, I think, I could prove its expediency. You must be sensible, my Lord, that no admiral who is not as well acquainted as yourself with the political state of these kingdoms, or other eastern countries, and of Russia, can possibly act with the same effect that you can do, when there is every reason to expect that the Emperor of Russia, and perhaps even the Ottoman Porte, will ultimately co-operate with us in our endeavours to set bounds to the lawless ambition of France. May my representations upon this subject not come too late, as I am certain that your departure from the Mediterranean will not less tend to encourage our enemies, than to diminish the confidence of those friendly powers who look towards your Lordship's abilities as to the surest means of success.'

H. Elliot,
7 October.

I am truly sensible of the kind concern you express for the state of my health; but you might be sure that, if I had not found it indispensably necessary, I should not have made the application for a few months' rest. If I am able, it is my wish to return; for where such unbounded confidence is placed, I should feel a beast not to exert myself. Long before this time, Lord Melville has fixed upon whether I am to return; or another admiral is, most probably, at this moment upon his passage. Being on shore, either in Sicily or Naples, would not relieve my mind of the charge entrusted to me, for my thoughts would always be off Toulon, and I should feel answerable for measures which I do not direct. If the Admiralty choose to leave Sir Richard Bickerton, the Mediterranean cannot be left in the hands of a more correct and discreet officer. I beg you will express to their Majesties my true sense of all their gracious goodness towards me.

On the afternoon of 23 August, an officer and boat's crew from the Bittern boarded three Dutch vessels in the mole at Naples, in search of four deserters. Not finding them, they proceeded to a French brig, the master of which positively refused to allow his vessel to be examined without an order from the French ambassador. The officer on this returned to the Bittern for further orders. Nothing more, however, took place; but the Neapolitan Government made a formal complaint to Nelson, which drew from him the following reply:

The trivial, although certainly irregular conduct of the Bittern's boat, was not worth the time of your Excellency to write to a public minister. In the first instance, if the captain of the port, or naval officer, had gone with the complaint to Captain Malcolm, he would, in the first instance, have not only disapproved the proceeding, but reprimanded the officer, as he has done when communicated to him, for his conduct. The searching for deserters, or for men absent from their ships, has in all countries been tolerated. If improper conduct is pursued, certainly it is cause for just offence; but none is stated to have happened. All vessels in the mole of Naples are neutrals, as far as relates to any of the belligerent powers; therefore no offence could be given to either French or Dutch. It may be an irregularity searching for absent seamen, but it is tolerated by all nations. Do not other nations look for their men every day at Naples? Certainly they do. But it is my wish to have our conduct so correct, that envy and malice itself should not be able to find fault with us, and to contrast our conduct with that of French armed vessels in the mole of Naples to the British officers and men.

<small>Chev. Micheroux, 7 October.</small>

I have sent Mr. Elliot the officer's [1] report of his destroying the privateer upon the coast of Sicily, and I have already directed a strict inquiry into the transaction; for although the conduct of the enemy's privateers is so infamous, and in defiance of all laws of neutrality, yet their doing wrong is no rule why we should. There is a general principle which I have laid down for the regulation of the officers' conduct under my command—which is never to break the neutrality of any port or place. But never to consider as neutral any place from whence an attack is allowed to be made—the attacker forfeits all neutrality.

The result of this inquiry shall be sent to Naples as soon as possible; and I beg leave to request that your Excellency will assure his Sicilian Majesty that the strictest justice shall be done, as far as is in the power of your Excellency's most obedient, humble servant,
NELSON AND BRONTE.

The fault of the Bittern's officer was nothing if he conducted himself properly. It is an irregularity committed by all nations, every day, in every port. But certainly Captain Malcolm's reprimand was full and ample for every hurt which the foot of a British officer could do in trampling upon the deck of a French or Dutch ship. I certainly wish nothing to be done which could in any

<small>H. Elliot, 7 October.</small>

---

[1] Lieutenant Robert Spencer, commanding the Renard schooner. See *ante*, p. 372.

manner commit the good King of Naples with the French. They wish for nothing better. I send your Excellency Lieutenant Spencer's letter. I have not approved of his conduct, for although I have no doubt but that this vessel would have committed herself, yet as she does not appear to have done it, under that presumption Mr. Spencer was hasty. This privateer has before, I dare say, broke the neutrality; at least, I hope, for Mr. Spencer's sake, that it will appear so in the inquiry I have ordered. The conduct of the French in Sicily, and of many of the governors, has been shameful. Nothing would prevent their being complained of but the consideration of the very delicate situation of his Sicilian Majesty.

Capt. Gore, Medusa, 13 Oct.

Last night I received your letter of 1 October, with a copy of Captain Graham Moore's orders from Admiral Cornwallis, which has filled me with astonishment. But without presuming to set myself in opposition to the Honourable Admiral's orders, there is a duty which I owe my country that, although I risk the most precious thing to me in the world—my commission—I feel it my duty to give you my full opinion of the line of conduct you ought to pursue on this most extraordinary occasion; and to enable you to form a complete judgment of the conclusion I shall draw for your guidance, I shall detail to you what I think may have led Admiral Cornwallis to have given this most extraordinary order of sending a frigate to cruise upon this station.

It is reported to me by Mr. Hunter, consul-general at Madrid, that [? 13] September, the Spanish squadron at Ferrol dropped down the harbour, having on board a number of Spanish troops, intending to carry them to the province of Biscay, then in insurrection. (N.B. The passes by land into Biscay are very difficult, and probably in the hands of the insurgents.) On 14 September Admiral Cochrane wrote the Spanish admiral, that as the French openly declared that they should sail with the Spanish squadron, that he should attack [them], and that he hoped nothing would happen to interrupt the neutrality, &c. Admiral Cochrane, in his letter to Mr. Hunter of the 15th [said], 'the pretext to carry troops to Biscay is too flimsy to go down' (I use Mr. Hunter's own words). Mr. Hunter goes on to say, in consequence of what he has written by the Naiad, and what, of course, Mr. Frere will represent personally, the admiral expects instructions and a reinforcement. This letter is dated Madrid, 22 September. On the 26th Mr. H. writes, 'Admiral Cochrane's letter seems to have had an almost instantaneous effect.' It was dated the 14th, and on the 17th the ships returned to the arsenal, or inner harbour, and the troops were landed and ordered to go by land. Now, supposing the Naiad left Ferrol the 14th, she could not have got to England, and orders be sent out to Admiral Cornwallis by the 22nd; therefore it is my decided opinion that the orders emanated from Admiral Cornwallis in consequence of Admiral Cochrane's letter. But, upon the whole proceedings of Spain, as far as have come to my knowledge, and from the best consideration which my abilities enable me to give to this most important subject, I am clearly of opinion that Spain has no wish to go to war with England, nor can I think that England has any wish to go to war unnecessarily with Spain. Therefore, unless you have much weightier reasons than the order of Admiral Cornwallis, or that you receive orders from the Admiralty, it is my most positive directions that neither you, or any ship under your orders, do molest or interrupt in any manner the lawful commerce of Spain, with whom we are at perfect peace and amity.

This letter, which is interesting as showing the writer's correct views of the circumstances preceding the seizure of the Spanish treasure ships on 5 October and the war with Spain, was not forwarded, Nelson having received Marsden's letter, dated 19 September, a few hours later. It ran:

'My Lord,—I have it in command from my Lords Commissioners of the Admiralty, to send you herewith a copy of their Lordships' order, of yesterday's date, to Admiral Cornwallis, respecting the blockade of the port of Ferrol, and to signify their direction to you to take such measures of precaution as may be necessary for opposing or counteracting any hostile attempts of the government or subjects of Spain against his Majesty's dominions, or the trade of his Majesty's subjects, within the limits of your command. Your Lordship is, however, not to suffer any act of hostility or aggression (with the exception of detaining for further orders ships having treasure on board belonging to the Spanish Government) to be committed by the ships under your command towards the dominions or subjects of Spain, until you receive further orders, or until your Lordship shall have received, from unquestionable authority, positive information of hostilities having been committed by the subjects of Spain against his Majesty's interests.'

And this inclosed a copy of the orders which had been sent to Cornwallis.

'Most Secret :—You are hereby required and directed to give immediate orders to Rear-Admiral Cochrane, to continue the blockade of the port of Ferrol with the utmost vigilance, not only with the view of preventing the French squadron from escaping from that port, but likewise with a view of preventing any of the Spanish ships of war from sailing from Ferrol, or any additional ships of war from entering that port : and if, in consequence of your correspondence with Rear-Admiral Cochrane, you should be of opinion that the force under the rear-admiral is not adequate to the purposes above mentioned, you are without delay to reinforce the squadron under his command, and measures will be taken with all possible expedition to send out to you a sufficient number of ships to replace the force which you may so detach. You are to send intimation to the Spanish Government, through Rear-Admiral Cochrane, of the instructions you have given to the rear-admiral, and of your determination, in consequence thereof, to resist, under the present circumstances, the sailing either of the French or Spanish fleets, if any attempt for that purpose should be made by either of them. And whereas information has been received that some frigates are speedily expected to arrive at Cadiz, loaded with treasure from South America, you are to lose no time in detaching two of the frigates under your command, with orders to their captains to proceed with all possible despatch off Cadiz, and the entrance of the Straits, and to use their best endeavours, in conjunction with any of his Majesty's ships they may find there, to intercept, if possible, the vessels in which the above-mentioned treasure may be contained, and to detain them until his Majesty's pleasure shall be further known. Given under our hands, the 18th September, 1804.   J. GAMBIER, JNO. COLPOYS, PH. PATTON.'

And thus instead of the cancelled letter to Captain Gore, a letter was sent to Sir Richard Strachan inclosing a copy of these papers, and directing him to attend to them.

Lieut. H. F. Woodman,¹ 20 Oct.

I have read with much satisfaction your letter of 8 October, 1804, giving the account of the Black Sea, of its ports, and what you think may be procured from thence; the clearness with which everything is stated does you the greatest credit.

I shall not fail to transmit your very interesting letter to Lord Melville, and from his Lordship's liberal way of thinking, I flatter myself he will be induced to notice, in a satisfactory manner, your indefatigable and important exertions. For myself, I selected you for this service of observation from the character I had heard of you, and which your conduct has most fully justified, and I beg you will accept my sincere thanks for your services. As you must necessarily have been at some expenses, I desire you will send me an account of them, that they may be paid. In addition to your other interesting papers, I beg you will send me a copy of your log-book, that courses, distances, marks for anchorage &c. &c. may be known.

Sir A. J. Ball, 22 Oct.

Hallowell thinks the ministers will not name another commander-in-chief, but see if I am able to return. I do not think so, for they are so beset by admirals. Sir John Orde, I am told, is likely. Lord Radstock is trying, so is Sir Roger Curtis; and if a Spanish war comes, Lord Keith loves a little money, and a great deal much better. Time will bring many strange things to

¹ See *ante*, p. 340.

pass, but I believe can never alter the sincere, affectionate regard of your most attached and sincere friend, NELSON AND BRONTE.

The weather was very thick when I looked into Toulon, but I believe a vice-admiral has hoisted his flag, his name I have not yet heard. They now amuse themselves with night-signals, and by the quantity of rockets and blue lights they show with every signal, they plainly mark their position. These gentlemen must soon be so perfect in theory, that they will come to sea to put their knowledge into practice. Could I see that day, it would make me happy.

Lord Melville, 30 Oct.

On 5 November, Mr. Frere demanded his passports: on the 27th, the Court of Madrid issued a decree, stating that the English having attacked Spanish ships of war, and detained merchant vessels, reprisals were to be made on British property; and on 12 December, Spain declared war against England.

The appearances of a rupture with Spain induced me to proceed off this place, in hopes of hearing from his Majesty's minister at the Court of Madrid; or, should he not think it proper to write to me, that I might be able to form a judgment whether war or peace was likely to take place of the uncertainty which for some weeks past has prevailed. For this purpose I sent the Fisgard to Rosas for the purpose of watching, and desiring water and refreshments. The governor seemed very anxious that he should anchor between the forts, when he told the officer the ship should be furnished with whatever she wanted. In short, his conduct, from rudeness, was so polite, that no doubt was entertained in Lord Mark Kerr's mind of the views of the Spanish governor, and he joined me last night.

W. Marsden, 15 Nov. Off Barcelona.

The Ambuscade, which I stationed off Barcelona, joined me this morning, with a merchant brig which was lying in Barcelona roads. She was yesterday, on her attempting to join the Ambuscade, fired at by the batteries, and very much damaged, but she escaped.

The fleet is perfection itself. We have just captured a complete regiment going to Minorca.

In consequence of this firing at the brig by the Barcelona batteries, Nelson at once issued a general order to 'The respective Captains and Commanders,' which, premising that hostilities had commenced between Great Britain and Spain, required and directed them on falling in with any Spanish ship or vessel of war, or merchantman belonging to the subjects of his Catholic Majesty, or having Spanish property on board, to use their utmost endeavour to capture, seize, burn, sink, or destroy them. Merchant ships, if captured, were to be sent in to await his Majesty's pleasure. The order was premature; for it afterwards appeared that the information was inexact, and Nelson wrote a few days later:

W. Marsden, 23 Nov.

I have since been informed that the English vessel alluded to was sent from Barcelona to perform quarantine at Mahon, but on her attempting to enter that place, she was fired upon by the batteries and very much damaged—perhaps from its being considered she had the plague aboard, or come from some place where it was raging. The said vessel afterwards fell in with the Ambuscade, and joined the squadron in company with her. I judge it proper to clear up this mistake, lest hereafter it may become a matter of public discussion with Spain.

Commissr. Otway, Gibraltar, 24 Nov.

You are so attentive to all our wants, that I am sure you will very soon procure canvas for us. Captain Hardy has a mizen-topsail made of Neapolitan canvas. It has been five months in wear, and as we have the custom of laying-to with that sail, it has had much wear, and we find it very excellent, and far preferable to English canvas; for as there is no gum or size to fill up the pores, it does not mildew. Captain Hardy desires me to say that our top-lining is of Neapolitan canvas, which bears the beating much better than the harsh English canvas.

Sir A. J. Ball, 25 Nov.

A lieutenant, late of the Bittern, who came down in the Childers, told me, that in the mouth of the Adriatic they fell in with the Algerine fleet, consisting of three frigates and nine corvettes; but as Captain Corbet has not mentioned it, I should almost doubt it but from the circumstantial account Lieutenant Nicholas gave. Now, if this is really so, I should like to know it, and if they are still at sea, for I have the very greatest inclination, if I could lay my hands upon the whole fleet, to waylay them, for they have, in my opinion, insulted us beyond what we ought to have suffered. I never would have given up a single point, for it only encourages them in their more insolent demands. But if you can tell me that his cruisers have this year taken a single Maltese vessel, I will try and take or destroy his whole fleet, for I can stretch over to the coast of Barbary, between Tunis and Algiers; but I will not strike unless I can hit him hard, for I would sooner allow two or three of his small cruisers to pass unmolested than to give the scoundrel an idea of my intentions.

5 Dec.

No Sir John Orde, no orders, no letters from England; very extraordinary. I almost begin to think that he is sent off Cadiz to reap the golden harvest, as Campbell was sent off Cadiz by Cornwallis (by orders from England) to reap my sugar harvest. It's very odd, two Admiralties to treat me so: surely I have dreamt that I have 'done the State some service.' But never mind; I am superior to those who could treat me so. When am I to be relieved? Seventy-six days since my last letter from the Admiralty. Poor Admiral Campbell sailed yesterday for England, very ill with debility, hectic fever, &c., but he cheered up on going away. I shall not trouble you with all my conjectures about Sir John Orde's never communicating with me for the three weeks he has been off Cadiz.

Sir John Orde had in fact written on 17 November, announcing his arrival in command of a squadron off Cadiz. The letter, however, did not reach Nelson till 15 December.

Since the Spanish hostilities—for I hardly know whether I am to call it war—I have not had the smallest communication with the continent; therefore I am in most total darkness. I received yesterday the inclosed from Sir John Orde. I have learnt not to be surprised at anything; but the sending an officer to such a point, to take, if it is a Spanish war, the whole harvest, after all my toils (God knows unprofitable enough! for I am a much poorer man than when we started in the Amphion), seems a little hard; but pazienza. I suppose Sir John, in the end, will command here. I am but very very so-so. My cough, if not soon removed, will stay by me for ever. On the 12th, the French fleet were safe in Toulon, but I am firmly of opinion before this day fortnight they will be at sea. What would I give to know their destination! But I must take my chance, and I hope my usual good fortune will attend me. On 14 January I shall be at Madalena; therefore if you want to send over in a Neapolitan corvette any despatches, it will be sure to find me there for some days—perhaps a fortnight or upwards. That position secures Sicily and Naples, and you will assure their Majesties that must be an object ever most near my heart. It is now ninety days since I have heard from England; it is rather long at these critical times. Sir John Orde has three cutters and four or five fine brigs attached to his squadron; but no—not one for me. Such things are. [H. Elliot, 19 Dec.]

The Swiftsure joined the squadron yesterday evening, off Cape St. Sebastian, in my way to reconnoitre the enemy's force at Toulon, which, from every information I have received, are embarking troops and preparing for some immediate expedition. [W. Marsden, 26 Dec.]

I shall, agreeable to their Lordships' orders, take the said ship under my command, and also the Tribune on her joining the squadron from Malta, to which place she has proceeded with the convoy from England. The fleet is in perfect good health and good humour, unequalled by anything which has ever come within my knowledge, and equal to the most active service which the times may call for or the country expect of them.[1]

A. Davison, 29 Dec.

I believe you could have hardly thought it possible that any man could have been sent to take the chance of a few pounds prize-money from me, in return for all my hard service. At this moment, I am as poor as when I left you at Portsmouth; but my spirit is above riches, and nothing can shake my firm resolution to do my duty to my country. I respect Lord Melville, and shall probably give him my support, when the great Sir John Orde will not thank him for his great favour. Lord Melville is a liberal-minded man, and he may oblige me some other way, in giving me something for some of my relations. God knows, in my own person I spend as little money as any man; but you know I love to give away. The moment an admiral arrives in the room of Admiral Campbell, I shall sail; for although this winter is hitherto so much milder than the last, yet I feel it pretty severely.

Memorandum, (?) June–August 1804.[2]

The business of an English commander-in-chief being first to bring an enemy's fleet to battle on the most advantageous terms to himself (I mean that of laying his ships close on board the enemy as expeditiously as possible), and secondly to continue them there, without separating, until the business is decided; I am sensible beyond this object it is not necessary that I should say a word, being fully assured that the admirals and captains of the fleet I have the honour to command will, knowing my precise object, that of a close and decisive battle, supply any deficiency in

[1] It is not uninteresting to notice this use of this phrase.
[2] The exact date of this memorandum is quite uncertain. Clarke and McArthur, from whose work it is taken (vol. ii. p. 427), assign it to the period of the West Indian voyage, May—July 1805. But as at that time the enemy's fleet consisted of 18 ships of the line, and even in the earlier outbreak from Toulon in January it consisted of 11, whilst this memorandum provides specially for the attack on an enemy's fleet of 8, it must be referred to a date at which a battle with a fleet of 8 seemed imminent. Now it was with 8 ships of the line that La Touche 'cut his caper' outside Toulon on 14 June, 1804; and for two months after that the strength of the French fleet in Toulon rested at 8. The memorandum therefore probably belongs to June—August 1804; possibly earlier; certainly not later. On 9 August, 1804, the French were reported as having a ninth ship ready for sea; nor does their number, after that date, seem to have been ever smaller. Clarke and McArthur speak of several copies of the paper, and of one especially sent to Lord Barham, at the Admiralty; but search in the Public Record Office has failed to discover either this or any other copy.

my not making signals; which may, if not extended beyond these objects, either be misunderstood, or, if waited for, very probably, from various causes, be impossible for the commander-in-chief to make. Therefore it will only be requisite for me to state, in as few words as possible, the various modes in which it may be necessary for me to obtain my object, on which depends not only the honour and glory of our country, but possibly its safety, and with it that of all Europe, from French tyranny and oppression.

If the two fleets are both willing to fight, but little manœuvring is necessary; the less the better—a day is soon lost in that business. Therefore I will only suppose that the enemy's fleet being to leeward, standing close upon a wind on the starboard tack, and that I am nearly ahead of them, standing on the larboard tack; of course I should weather them. The weather must be supposed to be moderate, for if it be a gale of wind, the manœuvring of both fleets is but of little avail, and probably no decisive action would take place with the whole fleet. Two modes present themselves. One to stand on, just out of gun-shot, until the van-ship of my line would be about the centre ship of the enemy, then make the signal to wear together, then bear up, engage with all our force the six or five van-ships of the enemy, passing, certainly, if opportunity offered, through their line. This would prevent their bearing up, and the action, from the known bravery and conduct of the admirals and captains, would certainly be decisive; the [two or three] rear-ships of the enemy would act as they please, and our ships would give a good account of them should they persist in mixing with our ships. The other mode would be to stand under an easy but commanding sail, directly for their headmost ship, so as to prevent the enemy from knowing whether I should pass to leeward or windward of him. In that situation I would make the signal to engage the enemy to leeward, and to cut through their fleet about the sixth ship from the van, passing very close; they being on a wind and you going large, could cut their line when you please. The van-ships of the enemy would, by the time our rear came abreast of the van-ship, be severely cut up, and our van could not expect to escape damage. I would then have our rear-ship, and every ship in succession, wear, continue the action with either the van-ship or second ship, as it might appear most eligible from her crippled state; and this mode pursued, I see nothing to prevent the capture of the five or six ships of the enemy's van. The two or three ships of the enemy's rear must either bear up or wear, and in either case, although they would be in a better plight probably than our two van-ships (now the rear) yet they would be separated, and at a distance to leeward, so as to give our ships time to refit; and by that time, I believe, the battle would, from the judgment of the admiral and captains, be over with the rest of them. Signals from these moments are useless, when every man is disposed to do his duty. The great object is for us to support each other, and to keep close to the enemy, and to leeward of him.

If the enemy are running away, then the only signals necessary will be, to engage the enemy as arriving up with them; and the other ships to pass on for the second, third, &c., giving, if possible, a close fire into the enemy in passing, taking care to give our ships engaged notice of your intention.

H. Elliot, 13 Jan. 1805.

Sir John Orde brought me out my leave to go to England for the re-establishment of my health, and many suppose that, the moment I had passed the Straits, he would take upon him the command. Others suppose Sir John Colpoys will be my successor, and there are others that think I shall return, if my health permits, and that my services will continue to be acceptable. However, I have kept my permission a profound secret in the fleet. Everybody expects that it will come, therefore do not mention my having received it to either Captain Sotheron or Captain Malcolm, although you may to the king and queen. I do assure you that nothing has kept me here but the fear for the escape of the French fleet, and that they should get to either Naples or Sicily in the short days; and that when I go I shall leave such instructions with Sir Richard Bickerton (who I am sure will follow them well up) to guard the Two Sicilies as he would the apple of his eye; and nothing but gratitude to those good sovereigns could have induced me to stay one moment after Sir John Orde's extraordinary command, for his general conduct towards me is not such as I had a right to expect.

Sir J. Acton, 22 Jan.

The French fleet sailed from Toulon on Friday last, the 18th. Our frigates saw part of them all day, and were chased by some of the ships. At ten o'clock the same night they were in the French fleet, then nearly in the latitude of Ajaccio, steering south, or S by W, the direct course for the island of Toro, south end of Sardinia, it blowing a strong gale at NW and a heavy sea. The French were then, by Captain Moubray's account, carrying a heavy press of sail. At three o'clock in the afternoon of the 19th, Captain Moubray made his report to me at Madalena, and at six the whole fleet was at sea, with a fresh breeze at WNW, steering to the southward along the Sardinian shore, intending to push for the south end of Sardinia, where I could have little fear but that I should meet them; for, from all I have heard from the captains of the frigates, the enemy must be bound round the south end of Sardinia, but whether to Cagliari, Sicily, the Morea, or Egypt, I am most completely in ignorance. I believe they have six or seven thousand troops on board. On the 20th we were taken with a heavy gale at SSW, which has arrested our progress. It is now (eight o'clock on the morning of the 22nd) at W by S, and we are sixteen leagues east from Cape Carbonara, blowing fresh, with a heavy sea, so that I stand no chance of closing with Sardinia to-day. I have sent a frigate to both Cagliari and the island of St. Pierre, to try and get information; and although I have only one frigate with me, I send her to your Excellency, that you may be put upon your guard in case the enemy are bound to Sicily; and I beg that you will send likewise to Naples, in case their passing the south end of Sardinia should be a feint in order to deceive me. But I rather think they believe I am off Cape St. Sebastian, where I am often forced to take shelter. If the French have had similar winds to us, it was impossible they could be round Toro before the morning of the 20th; and since that time, till this morning, they have had no winds which would allow them to weather Maritimo, if they are destined for either Egypt or the Morea. It is almost impossible they can have passed us and gone to Naples, and I am at this moment in the best possible position for intercepting them, should that be their destination.

I must be guided in all my future movements by information which I may receive; therefore I can only assure your Excellency of my ardent desire to fall in with them, and that no exertion of mine shall be wanting to annihilate them.

From the middle of December, I had information from various places, and amongst others from the King of Sardinia, that the French were assembling troops near Toulon, and had taken some of the best troops and a corps of cavalry from the Riviera of Genoa. Captain Capel obtained information that every seaman was pressed and sent to Toulon. On the 16th the Active spoke a vessel from Marseilles, who reported that seven thousand troops were embarked on board the French fleet. The wind had been near fourteen days easterly, from NE to SE; therefore, if the enemy had been bound to the westward, they could have gone with a fair wind. On the 18th the enemy put to sea, steering for the south end of Sardinia. On the 19th I was informed of it, and put to sea

W. Marsden, 29 Jan. Faro of Messina.

from the Madalena Islands that evening. On the 21st a French frigate was seen off the south end of Sardinia by the Seahorse, but the weather was so thick and gale so strong, that Captain Boyle could not see their fleet, and she joined me the 22nd with the information; but it was, from heavy gales, the 26th before I could communicate with Cagliari, at which place they knew nothing of the enemy. On the same day the Phœbe joined with information that a French ship of eighty guns had put into Ajaccio on the 19th, in the evening, with the loss of her topmasts and otherwise much crippled. The Seahorse was detached to Naples the 25th with information. On the 27th I was off Palermo and communicated with Sir John Acton; and the news which the Court of Naples has from Paris of 5 January makes them fear that Sicily might be the object of the enemy's armament.

One of two things must have happened, that either the French fleet must have put back crippled, or that they are gone to the eastward, probably to Egypt, therefore I find no difficulty in pursuing the line of conduct I have adopted. If the enemy have put back crippled, I could never overtake them, and therefore I can do no harm in going to the eastward; and if the enemy are gone to the eastward, I am right.

12 Feb.

I now know that the enemy's fleet came out of Toulon on 17 January, with a gentle breeze from the NW, and waited between that and the Hières Islands until the breeze freshened on the 18th, when they proceeded with a strong gale.

Sir A. J. Ball,
31 Jan.

The French fleet may possibly be severely crippled, and put into various ports. On the 22nd, in the evening, in a gale WSW, the Hydra saw three large ships running along shore toward St. Fiorenzo, but as Captain Mundy did not know the enemy's fleet had sailed, he thought they might be some of our ships.

I have sent Morgiana to look into Elba and St. Fiorenzo, then to drop a letter for me either at Madalena, St. Pierre, or Cagliari, and proceed to Malta; Bittern to Tunis and Pantellaria, then to Malta; Seahorse round Cape Corse, or through the Madalena Islands, off Toulon. Hydra round the south end of Sardinia, or Madalena off Toulon. Active, orders left at Messina, round either end of the islands or through Bonifacio, off Toulon. Each ordered to send letters for me to St. Pierre, Madalena, and Cagliari, and to Malta. Termagant to cruise off Toro fourteen days; Phœbe to Coron, round by Gozo of Candia. I shall proceed as winds, or information, or the getting no information may make me judge proper; you shall hear of me. If I return I shall call perhaps off

Malta, but that must be very uncertain. Celerity in my movements may catch these fellows yet. By reports of vessels from Toulon, taken by Termagant, eleven sail of the line and nine frigates and corvettes—twenty sail of ships in the whole. I shall only hope to fall in with them. I should be unworthy of my command if I dared to doubt the event with such a fine fleet as I have the happiness of commanding.

On the evening of 7 February the fleet was off Alexandria, but did not anchor.

Although I have not yet heard of the French fleet and remain in total ignorance where they are got to, yet to this moment I am more confirmed in my opinion, from communicating with Alexandria, that Egypt was the destination of the French armament from Toulon; and when I call all the circumstances which I know at this moment, I approve (if nobody else does) of my own conduct in acting as I have done. We know the success of a man's measures is the criterion by which we judge of the wisdom or folly of his measures. I have done my best. I feel I have done right; and should ministers think otherwise, they must get somebody else of more wisdom; for greater zeal I will turn my back on no man. The following are the circumstances which made me form my opinion, and the situation in which I found Egypt warrants the judgment I had formed. On these points it is fair to judge me, and not upon what it is now known the French fleet have done. The winds had blown from NE to SE for a fortnight before they sailed: therefore it was fair to presume they were not bound to the westward. On the 17th they came out of Toulon with gentle breezes at NNW, and lay between Giens and the Hières Islands till the gale set in on the 18th, in the afternoon. Had they been bound to Naples, it would have been better for them to have gone to the eastward, along their own coast, in fine weather, with friendly ports open to them. If Cagliari was their object, although I think of very great importance, yet their fleet ran the risk of a battle, and the event, I fancy, they hardly doubt. Almost as much might be said of Sicily, for if the French army took Naples, the king would, I think, subscribe to such terms as Bonaparte would dictate: however, I did not choose to run that risk, but assured myself they had neither gone to Sardinia, Naples, nor Sicily. The French sailed with a strong gale at NW and NNW, steering south or SW, on the 19th. One of their ships put into Ajaccio, crippled. On the 21st Boyle saw a French frigate off the south end of

11 Feb.
Off Gozo
of Candia.

Sardinia, probably looking for stragglers; they might have been crippled and dispersed in the very heavy gale in which they left their own shore. On the 25th I was off Cagliari; on the 30th the Seahorse joined from Naples; the same day I passed the Faro. On 2 February was off the Morea; on the 7th was off Alexandria, where we found three Turkish frigates, not more than 300 bad soldiers, and, in short, not the least probability of making a defence had they been so inclined, but 600 troops would, without any difficulty, have taken the place. The consul told Captain Hallowell that, taking us for the French fleet, the Governor and Capitan Bey gave all up for lost. The frigates intended to fire their guns. The works are precisely in the state we left them, and one week's work of the French would make it as strong as ever. The Turks and Mamelukes are at war in Upper Egypt; and the Albanians have left the Mamelukes, who would not pay them, and are now with the Turks. These troops would certainly join (at least, the greater number) the French army. Thus, the Mamelukes for their friends (at least for the moment), no Turkish army which would oppose them, Cairo would fall as easily as Alexandria, and I calculate the French, with the junction of part of the Albanians, would, within a week, have an army of 13,000 men; and we know there would be no difficulty for single polaccas to sail from the shores of Italy with 300 or 400 men in each (single ships); and that, in the northerly winds, they would have a fair chance of not being seen, and even if seen, not be overtaken by the Russian ships. Thus, 20,000 men would be fixed again in Egypt, with the whole people in their favour. Who would turn them out? Therefore, from the whole which I know, I have not a shade of doubt but that Egypt was the original destination of the Toulon fleet, when they sailed 17 January, 1805. You are tired of my reasoning, but I naturally am anxious that my friends should see fairly before them what has guided my proceedings, and be I right or wrong, I have acted to the best of my judgment.

Lord Melville, 14 Feb.

I have consulted no man, therefore the whole blame of ignorance in forming my judgment must rest with me. I would allow no man to take from me an atom of my glory had I fallen in with the French fleet, nor do I désire any man to partake of any of the responsibility—all is mine, right or wrong. Therefore I shall now state my reasons, after seeing that Sardinia, Naples, and Sicily were safe, for believing that Egypt was the destination of the French fleet, and at this moment of sorrow I still feel that I have acted right.

1. The wind had blown from NE to SE for fourteen days before they sailed; therefore they might without difficulty have gone to the westward. 2. They came out with gentle broezes at NW and NNW. Had they been bound to Naples, the most natural thing for them to have done would have been to run along their own shore to the eastward, where they would have had ports every twenty leagues of coast to take shelter in. 3. They bore away in the evening of the 18th, with a strong gale at NW or NNW, steering S or S by W. It blew so hard that the Seahorse went more than thirteen knots an hour to get out of their way. Desirable as Sardinia is for them, they could get it without risking their fleet, although certainly not so quickly as by attacking Cagliari. . . . However, I left nothing to chance in that respect, and therefore went off Cagliari. . . . Having afterwards gone to Sicily, both to Palermo and Messina, and thereby given encouragement for a defence, and knowing all was safe at Naples, I had only the Morea and Egypt to look to: for although I knew one of the French ships was crippled, yet I considered the character of Bonaparte, and that the orders given by him on the banks of the Seine would not take into consideration winds or weather; nor indeed could the accident of even three or four ships alter, in my opinion, a destination of importance: therefore such an accident did not weigh in my mind, and I went first to the Morea and then to Egypt. The result of my inquiries at Coron and Alexandria confirms me in my former opinion, and therefore, my Lord, if my obstinacy or ignorance is so gross, I should be the first to recommend your superseding me; but on the contrary, if, as I flatter myself, it should be found that my ideas of the probable destination of the French fleet were well founded, in the opinion of his Majesty's ministers, then I shall hope for the consolation of having my conduct approved by his Majesty, who will, I am sure, weigh my whole proceedings in the scale of justice.

I arrived with the fleet off Malta on the morning of the 19th instant, and received information from Captain Schomberg of the enemy's fleet having put back to Toulon in a very crippled state.

W. Marsden, 22 Feb.

The fleet under my command is in excellent good health, and the ships, although we have experienced a great deal of bad weather, have received no damage, and not a yard or mast sprung or crippled, or scarcely a sail split.

I herewith transmit you the sentence of a court-martial, held on Captain Layman, the officers and the company of his Majesty's

10 March.

late sloop Raven, for the loss of the said sloop on 30 January last, which I request you will be pleased to lay before the Lords Commissioners of the Admiralty for their information; and at same time acquaint their Lordships that I feel it my duty, in justice to Captain Layman, to state, from the information I have received of this unfortunate circumstance from Mr. Duff, consul at Cadiz, and also the Marquis de la Solano, captain-general at that place, that the exertions of Captain Layman, after the Raven was in a dangerous situation, were unequalled by anything they ever witnessed; and that, notwithstanding the heavy gale of wind which she encountered, the Raven would have twice got clear off, had she not, in the first instance, carried away her mainyard, and afterwards parted from her anchors. I have exceedingly to lament Captain Layman's misfortune, as I consider his present loss to the service a very great one indeed, knowing from experience the abilities and exertions of that officer.

Lord Melville, 10 March.

I inclose some remarks made by Captain Layman whilst he was in Spain, after the very unfortunate loss of that fine sloop which your Lordship was so good as to give him the command of. Your Lordship will find the remarks flow from a most intelligent and active mind, and may be useful should any expedition take place against Cadiz; and, my dear Lord, give me leave to recommend Captain Layman to your kind protection; for, notwithstanding the court-martial has thought him deserving of censure for his running in with the land, yet, my Lord, allow me to say that Captain Layman's misfortune was, perhaps, conceiving that other people's abilities were equal to his own, which indeed very few people's are.

I own myself one of those who do not fear the shore, for hardly any great things are done in a small ship by a man that is; therefore I make very great allowance for him. Indeed his station was intended never to be from the shore in the Straits; and if he did not every day risk his sloop, he would be useless upon that station. Captain Layman has served with me in three ships, and I am well acquainted with his bravery, zeal, judgment, and activity; nor do I regret the loss of the Raven compared to the value of Captain Layman's services, which are a national loss.

You must, my dear Lord, forgive the warmth which I express for Captain Layman, but he is in adversity, and therefore has the more claim to my attention and regard. If I had been censured every time I have run my ship, or fleets under my command, into great danger, I should long ago have been out of the service, and never in the House of Peers.

The French fleet are reported not to have disembarked their troops, and I am in hourly hopes of getting at them; after which, I shall certainly return to England. But I shall never quit my post when the French fleet is at sea, as a commander-in-chief of great celebrity once did.[1] I would sooner die at my post than have such a stigma upon my memory. To mend matters, poor Captain Layman came to me in a cartel, having lost his fine sloop, and I only hope that all despatches are lost; but I much fear, as they were not thrown overboard till the vessel struck, that they may wash on shore. Layman says it is impossible. He was tried by a court-martial the day before yesterday, and, to my great surprise, severely censured, for running incautiously in with the land. The testimonies of his exertions to save the sloop are incontrovertible, and were never exceeded. I know too well to comment upon a sentence, but if running in with the land, to rocks, passing narrow and dangerous passages, where my ship, or fleets entrusted to my care, might have been lost, is a fault, I have been guilty of a thousand. I would employ Layman to-morrow if I could.

<small>A. Davison, 11 March.</small>

I shall, if possible, make my appearance off Barcelona, in order to induce the enemy to believe that I am fixed upon the coast of Spain, when I have every reason to believe they will put to sea, as I am told the troops are still embarked. From off Barcelona I shall proceed direct to Rendezvous 98. Should the Leviathan be at 98 before me, and find there either Termagant or Bittern, it would be very desirable to have a vessel fixed ten leagues west of St. Pierre, in case the French fleet should not steer close to the island, for I think Egypt is still their object.

<small>Capt. Bayntun, Leviathan, 11 March.</small>

Their Lordships are fully aware of my reasons for not attending to my own health since I received their permission to return to England for its re-establishment. I do assure you that no consideration for self could come into my mind when the enemy's fleet was sure of putting to sea, and they are now perfectly ready in appearance to put to sea again. Therefore, although I have suffered very much from anxiety and a very stormy winter, yet I shall either stay to fight them, which I expect every hour, or until I believe they will not come to sea for the summer, when I shall embrace their Lordships' permission and return to England for a few months for the re-establishment of a very shattered constitution.

<small>W. Marsden, 13 March. Off Toulon.</small>

---

[1] The reference is probably to Rodney's going home from the West Indies, in the summer of 1781.

V.-Adml. Collingwood, 13 March.

My constitution is much shook, and nothing has kept me here so long but the expectation of getting at the French fleet. I am told the Rochefort squadron sailed the same day as that from Toulon. Bonaparte has often made his brags that our fleet would be worn out by keeping the sea—that his was kept in order, and increasing by staying in port; but he now finds, I fancy, if emperors hear truth, that his fleet suffers more in one night than ours in one year. However, thank God, the Toulon fleet is got in order again, and, I hear, the troops embarked; and I hope they will come to sea in fine weather. The moment the battle is over, I shall cut; and I must do the same if I think, after some weeks, that they do not intend to come out for the summer. We have had a very dull war, but I agree with you that it must change for a more active one. We are in a sad jumble with Sir John Orde off Cadiz; but let him do as absurd things as he pleases about blockading the ships under my command—even to be angry at my sending ships to Lisbon with my despatches, and angry at my sending ships to a part of the station under my orders, before I knew of his arrival to take that lucrative part of my station from me—I shall never enter into a paper war with him or any one else. We have lost one convoy, I think, by it, and we shall lose more; between two stools, &c. &c. &c.

W. Marsden, 14 March.

The fleet under my command arrived off Toulon yesterday evening, and by the information I have received from the frigates stationed to watch the enemy, their fleet is all in the above harbour, apparently in perfect readiness to put to sea. Whether their troops, who were disembarked on their late return, are again put on board, has not been learnt, but there is reason to believe they are. Their Lordships may rest assured, in the event of the enemy putting to sea again, that I shall use every possible means to fall in with them and bring them to action.

Capt. Sutton, 14 March.

I hope your expectations of gain by the galleons will be realised; and I hope you will get enormously rich, for your own and good Captain Hardy's sake, although an admiral of more interest than I have will take what ought to belong to me. I should think that the whole of this fleet will be put under Sir John Orde's command; or, when he has made money enough, he will be removed, and the responsibility left where it was before.

We have had a long run to Egypt and back; but as the French fleet are now ready for sea again, I fully expect we shall meet them; and then I would change with no man living. My health is but so-so, and the moment after the battle I shall go home for a few months. I think you will soon be drove off your cruising ground; the Rochefort squadron will be with you before long, therefore make hay whilst the sun shines.

If Sir John Orde condescends to ask after me, make my respectful compliments.

The affairs of the Renard and Bittern[1] continued to be the subject of complaint and misrepresentation; and a fresh letter from Mr. Marsden drew from Nelson:

The neutrality of his Sicilian Majesty's dominions has been most shamefully violated by the French privateers and row-boats, which have been suffered to shelter themselves in the different ports of his kingdom, from whence they have issued forth and captured our coasting trade under their forts. I am perfectly aware of the delicate situation of the king of Naples, and, consequently, gave the most strict orders to the commanders of his Majesty's ships on no account to commit the least violation of neutrality in any part of his kingdoms; but where French privateers have so daringly and piratically captured our trade, his Majesty's officers would have been highly reprehensible to have witnessed it without attempting to destroy the unwarrantable offenders. It is but justice for me to repeat, what I have frequently mentioned, that the ships under my command have invariably adhered to the strictest neutrality, and that they cannot, without being guilty of a breach of my most positive orders, commit the least violation of neutrality in any place.

W. Marsden, 14 March.

It is worthy of remark, that the French minister's complaint relative to the Bittern (even by his own account) has no foundation, as no French vessel was boarded by any of her boats. This circumstance would have been noticed by me to Mr. Elliot had I been in possession of Captain Corbet's statement, which was perfectly correct, and shows his conduct to have been officer-like and regular in the search for the seamen who had deserted from the Bittern at Naples, so that the French minister has taken up the affairs of those of other courts which he had nothing to do with, and made the concern his own.

The original destination of the French fleet, I am every day more and more confirmed, was Egypt. To what other country should they carry 5,000 saddles &c. &c. and flying artillery? The commander of the bomb, who was a prisoner on board the Hortensia (one of the ships who might, but did not, take our convoy—only six sail being taken and destroyed), says the frigates had each

H. Elliot, 27 March.

[1] See *ante*, pp. 372, 374.

300 troops, Swiss, on board. He could never learn their destination. However, they are ready for sea again, and I hope they will come forth; for, if they defer it one month from this time, they will not come forth this summer, unless the Brest fleet comes into the Mediterranean. I shall, therefore, when I believe the danger from the fleet is passed, take the opportunity of getting a few months' rest, and return here before the next winter, which is the dangerous time for a run. Rear-Admiral Louis, who was in the Minotaur, and is known to their Majesties, is arrived in the room of Admiral Campbell.

I write a line to their Majesties to tell them that, from October, when I got my permission to go home for a few months' rest, I had, in consequence of my belief of the French fleet intending to put to sea, and afterwards their having come to sea, and my belief that they may this spring put to sea again, deferred my departure through all the winter months. I can solemnly declare that nothing but my most particular gratitude to their Sicilian Majesties, with a due sense of what I owe to my own character, could have induced me to remain in the Mediterranean after my leave arrived; and I believe the French fleet will not move until my return in the autumn, should my health permit. I leave the finest fleet in the world, with every officer and man attached to me; therefore you may easily believe that nothing but absolute necessity could induce me to go home for one instant. Sir Richard Bickerton will take a most active interest in the safety of their Majesties and their kingdoms, and I feel confident that I may very essentially serve the good cause by my personal communications in England.

Sir A. J. Ball, 29 March.

I am glad you approved of my voyage to Egypt, and that may be their future destination. I shall remain here a very few weeks longer, when, if the French do not put to sea, I think it very probable they will lay up for the summer, unless the Brest or Ferrol and Cadiz fleet should come into the Mediterranean. I am fully aware that more sloops of war are wanted for the service of Malta and the convoys to the eastward than I have in the Mediterranean; but none are sent me, and my force decreases every day. Gibraltar is in absolute distress; they have not force sufficient to convoy over their bullock-vessels. Fox has called upon Sir John Orde, who tells him he must refer to me, which he has done, and I have been forced to answer him, that I regretted the officer at the Straits' mouth was not junior to me, when I should order him to take care of Gibraltar. But this cannot go on. I have, on 7 January, wrote home of what would happen; and I dare say

Orde has a trimmer before this time. He will not be suffered to remain much longer; he will go to the Channel; he will be the richest admiral that England ever had, and I one of the poorest.

Sir John Orde did, in fact, write on 27 March, requesting permission to resign his command, as he felt unequal to perform its arduous duties with satisfaction to his employers and to his own feelings, extremely hurt by recent treatment.

The arrival of Admiral Louis will enable me to get a little rest, which I shall take as soon as I am satisfied in my own mind that the French will not put to sea. On 25 March they either entirely disembarked their troops, or re-embarked them: I sincerely hope the latter, and if so, I think a few days will settle all my business in the Mediterranean. W. Marsden, 30 March.

Report says that Sir John Orde will be the richest admiral that England ever saw. It cannot be pleasing to me to have every person tell me this; but my soul soars above this consideration, although I cannot help thinking that I could have made as good a use of a large fortune as Sir John Orde or any other admiral. I should like to have tried. Lord Radstock, 1 April.

The French fleet is at sea, steering to the southward. Proceed off Cagliari, fire guns, and call out the Seahorse, and desire Captain Boyle to join me. I am now standing to the westward, as I do not think the French will make Toro. I can tell him no more, as my movements must be very uncertain; but I believe the French, if they do not make Toro, will make Galita. Capt. Thomas, Etna, 4 April.

The French fleet put to sea in the night of Saturday, 30 March, and on Sunday morning, the 31st, at eight o'clock, they were seen by the Active and Phœbe, with a light breeze at NE, steering SSW, with all sail set; their force is supposed by the frigates to be eleven sail of the line, seven frigates, and two brigs. At eight o'clock in the evening Captain Moubray detached the Phœbe (Cape Sicie then bearing N by E, true bearing, twenty leagues) to join me, which she did off Toro yesterday morning, 4 April, and the Active joined at three o'clock in the afternoon. Captain Moubray, the night of the 31st ultimo, having kept his wind, with fresh breezes from the WNW, lost sight of the enemy; and therefore thinks they either bore away to the eastward or steered SSW, as they were going when first seen. From the morning of 1 April, the winds have been very variable and mostly southerly and easterly, till the night of the 3rd, when it set in fresh at NW. I have placed frigates on the coast of Barbary and off Toro, and am W. Marsden, 5 April.

lying half-way between Galita and Sardinia; for I am sure, if they are bound this route, that they could not pass before this day. The Minister of the Marine is said to command them. . . .

Lord Melville, 5 April.

Although I feel so far comfortable that the French fleet is at sea, yet I must have a natural, and I hope a laudable anxiety of mind, until I have the happiness of seeing them. However, I have covered the Channel from Barbary to Toro with frigates and the fleet. The French could not pass before to-day, if this be their route. I must leave as little as possible to chance, and I shall make sure they are to the eastward of me before I risk either Sardinia, Sicily, or Naples; for they may delay their time of coming even this distance, from an expectation that I shall push for Egypt, and thus leave them at liberty to act against Sardinia, Sicily, or Naples.

H. Elliot, 7 April.

I must be guided in my further movements by such information as I may be able to obtain, but I shall neither go to the eastward of Sicily or to the westward of Sardinia until I know something positive. I am uneasy enough, but I must bear it as well as I can.

Capt. Thomas, 16 April.

We have a report from the vessel spoke by Leviathan, that the French fleet (at least a fleet) was seen on Sunday, 7 April, off Cape Gata, with the wind easterly, steering to the westward; therefore you must tell any ships in search of me that I am going to ascertain that the French fleet is not in Toulon, and then to proceed to the westward, and this is all I can tell at present. I would have you continue until further orders on the station off Toro, to which place I shall send information, when I am sure where the French fleet is gone, or that I am likely to leave the Mediterranean after them.

H. Elliot, 18 April, off Toro.

I am going out of the Mediterranean after the French fleet. It may be thought that I have protected too well Sardinia, Naples, Sicily, the Morea, and Egypt, from the French; but I feel I have done right, and am therefore easy about any fate which may await me for having missed the French fleet. I have left five frigates, besides the sloops &c., stationed at Malta for the present service of the Mediterranean, and with the Neapolitan squadron will, of course, be fully able to prevent any force the French have left to convoy troops to Sicily.

W. Marsden, 18 April.

Under the severe affliction which I feel at the escape of the French fleet out of the Mediterranean, I hope that their Lordships will not impute it to any want of due attention on my part; but on the contrary, that by my vigilance the enemy found it was impossible to undertake any expedition in the Mediterranean. I was obliged to come to Palma to meet the transports with provisions, and by the report of the first captain, I trust it could not with propriety be longer deferred; however, I showed myself off Barcelona and the coast of Spain, and the islands of Majorca and Minorca, till 21 March. The frigates which I appointed to watch them unfortunately lost sight of them the night of 31 March; and from 4 April, when they joined, we have had nothing but strong and sometimes hard gales of westerly and NW winds (and it appears that the French fleet must have had strong gales easterly). After allowing forty-eight hours for the possibility of the enemy passing round the south end of Sardinia, I proceeded off Sicily, sending ships to Palermo and Naples for information.

On Tuesday the 9th I made sail from the west end of Sicily for the westward, but to this moment I have only advanced sixty-five leagues, being only off Toro, owing to very bad weather, and have just received the account of the enemy having passed the Straits on 8 April. I am pursuing my route to the westward, and must be guided by what I hear when I get off Gibraltar.

Whereas, from the information I have received that the enemy's fleet, which was seen off Cape Gata on the 7th inst., passed through the Straits on the day following, I am proceeding with the fleet under my command as expeditiously as possible to the westward in pursuit of them; and it being very probable that they may have left some frigates and other vessels of war at Toulon, for the purpose of convoying troops either to Sardinia, Naples, Sicily, or Egypt, you are hereby required and directed to take his Majesty's ships [Hydra, Juno, Ambuscade, Niger, Thunder] under your command, and station yourself off the island of Toro, and between that and Maritimo, for the purpose of intercepting any expedition which the enemy may attempt against Sardinia, Sicily, or Egypt. With regard to the limitation of your squadron between Toro and Maritimo, I only mention it as the most likely place to fall in with any expedition which the enemy may attempt against those places from Toulon, but must leave this important trust to your judgment, and to act as from certain circumstances of information you shall judge best, to prevent their effecting a landing at Sardinia, Sicily, or Egypt. ^{Capt. Capel, 18 April.}

You will guess at my uneasiness at not having met the French fleet, but I could not quit my charge of Egypt, Morea, Sicily, Naples, and Sardinia, until I was sure that the enemy were gone to the westward; for any of these countries would have been lost ^{Commr. Otway, 19 April.}

for ever if the French had twenty-four hours' start of me. We have been nine days coming sixty-five leagues. We have had nothing but gales of westerly winds. I now hope that you will soon see us pass the Rock.

Sir A. J. Ball, 19 April.

My good fortune seems flown away. I cannot get a fair wind, or even a side wind. Dead foul!—dead foul! But my mind is fully made up what to do when I leave the Straits, supposing there is no certain information of the enemy's destination.

W. Marsden, 19 April. 10 lgs. W of Toro.

The enemy's fleet having so very long ago passed the Straits, and formed a junction with some Spanish ships from Cadiz, I think it my duty, which must be satisfactory to their Lordships, to [let them] know exactly my intentions. I have detached the Amazon to Lisbon for information, and I am proceeding off Cape St. Vincent as expeditiously as possible, and I hope the Amazon will join me there, or that I shall obtain some positive information of the destination of the enemy. The circumstance of their having taken the Spanish ships which were [ready] for sea from Cadiz, satisfies my mind that they are not bound to the West Indies (nor probably the Brazils); but intend forming a junction with the squadron at Ferrol, and pushing direct for Ireland or Brest, as I believe the French have troops on board; therefore, if I receive no intelligence to do away my present belief, I shall proceed from Cape St. Vincent, and take my position fifty leagues west from Scilly, approaching that island slowly, that I may not miss any vessels sent in search of the squadron with orders. My reason for this position is, that it is equally easy to get to either the fleet off Brest or to go to Ireland, should the fleet be wanted at either station. I trust this plan will meet their Lordships' approbation, and I have the pleasure to say that I shall bring with me eleven as fine ships of war, as ably commanded, and in as perfect order, and in health, as ever went to sea.

I shall send to both Ireland and the Channel fleet an extract of this letter, acquainting the commander-in-chief where to find me.

Commr. Otway, 4 May. Off Tetuan.

I believe my ill-luck is to go on for a longer time, and I now much fear that Sir John Orde has not sent his small ships to watch the enemy's fleet, and ordered them to return to the Straits' mouth to give me information, that I might know how to direct my proceedings; for I cannot very properly run to the West Indies without something beyond mere surmise; and if I defer my departure, Jamaica may be lost. Indeed, as they have a month's start of me, I see no prospect of getting out time enough to prevent much mischief from being done.

Accordingly, on the following day, 5 May, he gave Sir Richard Bickerton an order to remain behind, in order to carry on the business of the station, in the event of his having to leave it, and pushed out to sea, hoping to get more definite information from some of the frigates.

God only knows, my dear friend, what I have suffered by not getting at the enemy's fleet; and when I naturally consoled myself that, at least, time would be given for Sir John Orde's frigates, who were naturally sent after them, to return to Gibraltar with information for me, I had the mortification yesterday to find that none had been sent there. Nor was it generally believed that Sir John Orde had sent after them; but this I cannot believe, and I must suppose that they have all been unfortunately captured. I think it more than probable I shall go to the West Indies; for I believe from what I have yet heard of their course &c. that is their destination, and there I hope to get hold of them, and to save our valuable West India possessions, and then I shall immediately return to England. But my health, or even my life, must not come into consideration at this important crisis; for, however I may be called unfortunate, it never shall be said that I have been neglectful of my duty or spared myself.

<small>A. Davison, 7 May.</small>

I have just heard that Lord Melville has left the Admiralty, owing to the tenth report of the navy inquiries. His Lordship was doing much for the service, and now we have to look forward to some one else.

All my letters by Niger and Avenger are gone up the Mediterranean, and will never be received by me. But salt beef and the French fleet is far preferable to roast beef and champagne without them.

After a heavy beat down the Mediterranean I reached Tetuan Bay on the 4th, and completed the water of the fleet, and cleared a transport with wine, and sailed on the 5th. Yesterday at 2 P.M. we anchored in Gibraltar Bay, with fresh breezes westerly, and began to clear transports with fuel and provisions; but before the whole fleet had anchored, there was every appearance of a Levanter coming on. The fleet was unmoored, the transports taken in tow, and at 6 o'clock the whole fleet was under sail, steering through the Gut. I was in great hopes that some of Sir John Orde's frigates would have arrived at Gibraltar from watching the destination of the enemy, from whom I should have derived information of the route the enemy had taken, but none had arrived. The Halcyon, which left Lisbon on 27 April in the evening, reports to me that nothing had been heard of them at Lisbon when the

<small>W. Marsden, 7 May.</small>

Halcyon sailed. I am now pushing off Cape St. Vincent, and hope that is the station to which Sir John Orde may have directed his frigates to return from watching the route of the enemy, and I shall also join the Amazon from Lisbon. If nothing is heard of them from Lisbon or from the frigates I may find off Cape St. Vincent, I shall probably think the rumours which are spread are true, that their destination is the West Indies, and in that case think it my duty to follow them, or to the antipodes, should I believe that to be their destination. I shall detach a sloop of war to England from off the Cape, when my mind is made up from either information or the want of it.

Off Cape St. Vincent he received intelligence from different quarters, including, amongst others, his old acquaintance at Naples, Commodore now Rear-Admiral Campbell, of the Portuguese navy, and all agreeing that the combined French-Spanish fleet had gone to the West Indies. His mind was already made up, and on 9 May he wrote:

<small>W. Marsden, 9 May. Off C. St. Vincent.</small>

I shall wait here until Admiral Knight joins, and then proceed to Barbadoes. I am now clearing transports and victualling the fleet to five months, and shall bear away the moment I can get hold of the convoy. Should the enemy not have gone to the West Indies, I shall return off Cape St. Vincent's and then act as I may find orders; or, if I receive none, according to the best of my judgment.

<small>Sir A. J. Ball, 10 May. Lagos Bay.</small>

My lot is cast, and I am going to the West Indies, where, although I am late, yet chance may have given them a bad passage and me a good one. I must hope the best.

And so with a squadron consisting of ten sail of the line, Nelson weighed from Lagos Bay on the 4th, leaving the following order addressed to 'The Commander of any of his Majesty's ships or vessels in search of the Mediterranean squadron:'

<small>10 May.</small>

Most Secret—I desire to acquaint you that I am proceeding, with the squadron under my command, to the West Indies, in search of the enemy's fleet; and request that you will, without a moment's loss of time, communicate the same to the Lords Commissioners of the Admiralty, and to the commander-in-chief of the Channel fleet, in the event of your falling in with him.

<small>Capt. Keats 19 May.</small>

I am fearful that you may think that the Superb does not go so fast as I could wish. However that may be (for if we all went ten knots, I should not think it fast enough), yet I would have you be assured that I know and feel that the Superb does all which is possible for a ship to accomplish; and I desire that you will not fret upon the occasion. . . . I think we have been from Cape St.

Vincent very fortunate, and shall be in the West Indies time enough to secure Jamaica, which I think is their object.

27 May. We shall be at Barbadoes on 3 or 4 June; and I hope Cochrane will be able to give us every information about the enemy. I still think Jamaica is their object, but many think Surinam or Trinidad; and Bayntun, that they will land their troops at the city of San Domingo. In short, everyone has an opinion, but it will soon be beyond doubt. Our passage, although not very quick, has been far from a bad one. They started from Cadiz thirty-one days before we did from St. Vincent, and I think we shall gain fourteen days upon them in the passage; therefore they will only arrive seventeen days before us at Martinique, for I suppose them bound there. I shall not anchor at Barbadoes. Martin, you know, is gone there; and I have prayed Lord Seaforth to lay an embargo, that the French may not know of my approach, and thus again elude our vigilance. My mind is not altered that Egypt was their destination last January.

W. Marsden, 4 June. Carlisle Bay. I arrived off here at noon this day, where I found Rear-Admiral Cochrane in the Northumberland, and the Spartiate is just joining. I send you some letters of information, which the rear-admiral and Sir William Myers have received from Dominica and from St. Lucia. There is not a doubt in any of the admirals' or generals' minds, but that Tobago and Trinidad are the enemy's objects; and although I am anxious in the extreme to get at their eighteen sail of the line, yet, as Sir William Myers has offered to embark himself with 2,000 troops, I cannot refuse such a handsome offer; and, with the blessing of God on a just cause, I see no cause to doubt of the annihilation of both the enemy's fleet and army.

In this letter Lord Nelson inclosed the following extract from a letter from Brigadier-General Brereton to Sir William Myers, dated St. Lucia, 29 May, 11 A.M. 'I have this moment received a report from the windward side of Gros Islet that the enemy's fleet, of 28 sail in all, passed there last night. Their destination, I should suppose, must be either Barbadoes or Trinidad.' On which Nelson added in his own hand:

4 June. Written by Major Myers, Sir William Myers's secretary, and extracted from the general's letter; and Major Myers has no doubt but that the intelligence may be relied upon.

Lord Seaforth. Barbadoes, 8 June. The information from St. Lucia of the combined squadron having been off that island to windward must have been very incorrect.[1]

[1] It is a curious coincidence that in 1778 Dominica was lost by the governor's sending to Rear-Admiral Barrington at Barbadoes similar false intelligence of an imaginary French fleet.

I have my doubts respecting the certainty of the arrival of the Ferrol squadron, as I have always understood that nothing could pass in or out of Fort Royal without being seen; but powerful as their force may be, they shall not with impunity make any great attacks. Mine is compact, theirs must be unwieldy; and although a very pretty fiddle, I don't believe that either Gravina or Villeneuve know how to play upon it.

Lord R. Fitz-Gerald, Lisbon, 15 June.

The combined squadrons passed to leeward of Antigua on the 8th, standing to the northward, and when I left St. John's Road in that island on the 13th, nothing had been heard of them; therefore I believe they are on their return to Europe.

As my trip to the West Indies must have greatly interested your Lordship, I shall briefly run over the occurrences. I arrived at Barbadoes 4 June, where I found Lieutenant-General Sir William Myers, who the night before had received information from Brigadier-General Brereton, at St. Lucia, that twenty-eight sail of the enemy's fleet had been seen to windward of St. Lucia, steering to the southward. As there was no reason to doubt this information, the general offered to embark himself with 2,000 troops, for the relief of either Tobago or Trinidad, which were supposed to be the intended objects of the enemy's attack. On the 6th we were off Tobago, on the 7th at Trinidad, on the 8th I received an account that the enemy had not moved on the 4th from Fort Royal, but were expected to sail that night for the attack of Grenada. On the 9th I was at Grenada, when I received a letter from General Prevost to say, that the enemy had passed Dominica on the 6th, standing to the northward, to the leeward of Antigua, and took that day a convoy of fourteen sail of sugar-loaded ships, which unfortunately left St. John's in the night for England. On the 11th I was at Montserrat, and at sunset on the 12th anchored at St. John's, Antigua, to land the troops, which was done on the morning of the 13th, and at noon I sailed in my pursuit of the enemy; and I do not yet despair of getting up with them before they arrive at Cadiz or Toulon, to which ports I think they are bound, or at least in time to prevent them from having a moment's superiority. I have no reason to blame Dame Fortune. If either General Brereton could not have wrote, or his look-out man had been blind, nothing could have prevented my fighting them on 6 June; but such information, and from such a quarter, close to the enemy, could not be doubted. The frigate is directed to join me off Cape St. Vincent; and if Sir John Orde, my senior officer, is not off Cadiz, I shall anchor in Lagos Bay, and try to get both water and refreshments. If he has resumed his former station, I must go inside the Mediterranean, as I know he is exceedingly displeased if any of the Mediterranean ships are a moment upon his station, and I have too great a respect for the wishes of my superiors to act contrary to them.

So far from being infallible, like the Pope, I believe my opinions to be very fallible, and therefore I may be mistaken that the enemy's fleet is gone to Europe, but I cannot bring myself to think otherwise, notwithstanding the variety of opinions which different people of good judgment form. But I have called every circumstance which I have heard of their proceedings before me— I have considered the approaching season, the sickly state of their troops and ships, the means and time for defence which have been given to our islands, and the certainty the enemy must expect of our reinforcements' arrival; and therefore, if they were not able to make an attack for the first three weeks after their arrival, they could not hope for greater success after our means of resistance increased, and their means of offence were diminished; and it is to be considered that the enemy will not give me credit for quitting the West Indies for this month to come. As this is a letter of reasoning for my conduct, I may perhaps be prolix, but I am anxious to stand well in your opinion; and if my conduct is taken into consideration by Mr. Pitt, I will thank you to show him this letter. A frigate certainly arrived from France 31 May—from that moment all was hurry: on 1 June, I believe, the Furet arrived with an account of my being on the passage.—N.B. A corvette watched us two days, when 150 leagues to the westward of Madeira. If Barbadoes is the object of the enemy's attack, a fleet of men-of-war could get there, on the average, in four or five days from Martinique; therefore why should they make a passage of at least fifteen or sixteen days, by going to the northward? If Tobago or Trinidad was their object, they had only to weather St. Lucia, and they could fetch them with ease; to St. Lucia, St. Vincent, and Grenada they had a fair wind, therefore it must be unnecessary to go to the northward. If, therefore, any of those islands are the objects of their attack, as some people suppose, they are playing a game which, I own, is incomprehensible to my weak understanding, and I am completely deceived.

What impression could they expect to make upon Jamaica with 4,000 or 5,000 men; and if that was their object, why not steer direct from Martinique? Some think they may be going to St. John's, Porto Rico, and wait to be joined there by reinforcements,

Sir E. Nepean, 16 June.

but the season is passed; nor, if fifteen sail of the line are coming out to join them, is there occasion to hide themselves from our observations. My opinion is firm as a rock, that some cause, orders, or inability to perform any service in these seas, has made them resolve to proceed direct for Europe, sending the Spanish ships to the Havana.

There would have been no occasion for opinions, had not General Brereton sent his damned intelligence from St. Lucia; nor would I have received it to have acted by it, but I was assured that his information was very correct. It has almost broke my heart, but I must not despair.

W. Marsden, 19 June.

I send you a report of a vessel spoke, which, with the circumstances attending it, can leave me no room to doubt but that I am hard upon the heels of the enemy's fleet. In addition, Captain Parker reports to me that there was a note in the American's log, that they supposed them the French fleet from Martinique. The master was anxious to know if the French had taken Antigua, as he was bound there, and had traded to that island many years. The remark of seeing this fleet in the log of the vessel, with the difference of the course the master and mate supposed the fleet to be steering, satisfies my mind that there could be no intended deceit in the information (which sometimes happens); nor did the vessel see our fleet until she had been spoke by the Amazon. I think we cannot be more than eighty leagues from them at this moment, and by carrying every sail, and using my utmost efforts, I shall hope to close with them before they get to either Cadiz or Toulon.

Inclosed in which was :—The vessel Sally, of North Carolina, bound to Antigua, boarded on 17 June 1805, by Captain Parker, H.M.S. Amazon, 17 days out, gave the following intelligence:—" At 7 P.M., on Sunday evening last, saw about 22 sail of large ships steering, master's account, NNE ; mate's account, NNW, in latitude, on Saturday noon, 27° 28', longitude, 60° 58' W." [1]

Diary, 17 July.

Our whole run from Barbuda, day by day, was 3459 miles; our run from Cape St. Vincent to Barbadoes was 3,227 miles, so that our run back was only 232 miles more than our run out—allowance being made for the difference of the latitudes and longitudes of Barbadoes and Barbuda ; average per day, thirty-four leagues, wanting nine miles.

[1] I see no reason to doubt that this is the very slight foundation for the romantic and certainly fictitious story of a half-burnt privateer related by Clarke and McArthur (vol. ii. p. 417); and after them by Southey, by James, and many others.

Cape Spartel in sight, but no French fleet, nor any information 18 July. about them: how sorrowful this makes me, but I cannot help myself!

The same day he fell in with the squadron before Cadiz, commanded by Vice-Admiral Collingwood, to whom he wrote:

I am, as you may suppose, miserable at not having fallen in 18 July. with the enemy's fleet. The name of General Brereton will not soon be forgot. But for his false information, the battle would have been fought where Rodney fought his, on 6 June. I must now only hope that the enemy have not tricked me, and gone to Jamaica; but if the account, of which I send you a copy, is correct, it is more than probable they are either gone to the northward, or, if bound to the Mediterranean, not yet arrived. The Spaniards, or the greatest part of them, I take for granted, are gone to the Havana, and I suppose have taken fourteen sail of Antigua sugar-loaded ships with them. The moment the fleet is watered and got some refreshments, of which we are in great want, I shall come out and make you a visit; not, my dear friend, to take your command from you (for I may probably add mine to you), but to consult how we can best serve our country by detaching a part of this large force.

Collingwood had meantime written to Nelson:
'I congratulate your Lordship on your return from the long chase you have had to the West Indies, and wished sincerely I could have had the pleasure of seeing you, and of telling you how truly dear you are to my friendship. We approached you with caution, not knowing whether we were to expect your Lordship or the Frenchmen first.

'I had been for some time under orders for foreign service before the Toulon ships sailed, and my ships were increased or diminished as the apparent service seemed to require. The sailing of the Toulon ships determined my route. But I have always had an idea that Ireland alone was the object they have in view, and still believe that to be their ultimate destination—that they will now liberate the Ferrol squadron from Calder, make the round of the bay, and, taking the Rochefort people with them, appear off Ushant—perhaps, with thirty-four sail, there to be joined by twenty more. Admiral Cornwallis collecting his out squadrons may have thirty and upwards. This appears to be a probable plan: for unless it is to bring their great fleets and armies to some point of service—some rash attempt at conquest—they have been only subjecting them to chance of loss, which I do not believe the Corsican would do, without the hope of an adequate reward. This summer is big with events. We may all, perhaps, have an active share in them, and sincerely I wish your Lordship strength of body to go through— and to all others, your strength of mind.'

I have to acquaint you that I anchored in this bay yesterday

W. Marsden, 20 July.

morning, without having obtained the smallest intelligence of the enemy's fleet, except what is contained in the inclosed paper.[1] The squadron is in the most perfect health, except some symptoms of scurvy which I hope to eradicate by bullocks and refreshments from Tetuan, to which I shall proceed to-morrow.

Diary, 20 July.

I went on shore for the first time since 16 June, 1803; and from having my foot out of the Victory, two years, wanting ten days.

On 19 July Collingwood wrote in reply to Nelson's letter of the 18th:

'I well know what your Lordship's disappointment is, and share the mortification of it. It would have been a happy day for England, could you have met them; small as your force was, I trust it would have been found enough. Truly glad will I be to see you, my dear friend, and to give you my best opinion on the present state of affairs, which are in the highest degree intricate; but reasoning on the policy of the present French Government, who never aim at little things while great objects are in view, I have considered the invasion of Ireland as the real mark and butt of all their operations. The flight to the West Indies was to take off the naval force, which is the great impediment to their undertaking. The Rochefort squadron's return confirmed me. I think they will now collect their force at Ferrol, which Calder tells me are in motion—pick up those at Rochefort, who, I am told, are equally ready, and will make them above thirty sail; and then, without going near Ushant, or the Channel fleet, proceed to Ireland. Detachments must go from the Channel fleet to succour Ireland, when the Brest fleet—twenty-one, I believe, of them, will sail, either to another part of Ireland, or up the Channel—a sort of force that has not been seen in those seas, perhaps, ever.'

Q. of Naples, 21 July.

I rather think most of the Spanish ships are gone to the Havana. Both French and Spaniards are dreadfully sickly. They landed 1000 sick when they arrived at Martinique, and buried full that number during their stay. The fleet under my command, thank God, has lost neither officer or man by sickness since I left the Mediterranean.

Lord Barham, 23 July. Tetuan.

The fleet is complete, and the first easterly wind I shall pass the Straits. I have yet not a word of information of the enemy's fleet; it has almost broke my heart. But the name of General Brereton will never be forgot by this generation; but for him our battle would have been fought on 6 June. The event would have been in the hands of Providence; but we may without, I hope, vanity, believe that the enemy would have been fit for no active

---

[1] The Sally's boarding report; *ante*, p. 404: therefore, the half-burnt privateer had not been seen up to 20 July.

service after such a battle. All our losses which have happened, or may happen, are entirely to be attributed to his information. I shall take my position most convenient for receiving intelligence; and if I find the enemy gone to the bay, I shall go off Ferrol or Ushant, as the case appears to me to require.

<small>A. Davison, 24 July.</small>

I am as miserable as you can conceive. But for General Brereton's damned information, Nelson would have been, living or dead, the greatest man in his profession that England ever saw. Now, alas! I am nothing—perhaps shall incur censure for misfortunes which may happen and have happened. When I follow my own head, I am, in general, much more correct in my judgment than following the opinion of others. I resisted the opinion of General Brereton's information till it would have been the height of presumption to have carried my disbelief further. I could not, in the face of generals and admirals, go NW, when it was apparently clear that the enemy had gone south. But I am miserable. I now long to hear that they are arrived in some port in the bay; for until they are arrived somewhere, I can do nothing but fret. Then I shall proceed to England. I can say nothing, or think of anything, but the loss my country has sustained by General Brereton's unfortunate, ill-timed, false information.

<small>Capt. Parker, 25 July.</small>

Having received information that the combined fleet was seen on the 19th ult., steering to the northward, I am proceeding with the fleet in pursuit of them with all despatch. You are therefore hereby required and directed to repair immediately in search of me off Cape St. Vincent; or, not finding me there, you will make the best of your way off Ferrol, if you shall judge, from information, that I have gone there; otherwise you will proceed direct off Ushant or Ireland, where you will fall in with me, or gain intelligence where I am gone to.

On 24 July, the Decade frigate joined from Admiral Collingwood, yet still no information of the enemy. On the 25th the Termagant joined with an account that the combined fleet had been seen by the Curieux brig on 19 June, standing to the northward.[1]

<small>Adml. Cornwallis, 27 July.</small>

The enemy's fleet from the West Indies being certainly gone to some port in the bay, I am proceeding to the northward with eleven sail of the line. I shall either call off Cape Clear, or proceed direct off Ushant, to form a junction with you, as circum-

---

[1] The first news of the enemy's fleet since the Sally. I call attention to this because the half-burnt privateer story is one of the many silly galley yarns which have been accepted as history, and it is satisfactory to demolish it thus utterly.

stances may, in my judgment, (from intelligence,) require. I shall only hope, after all my long pursuit of my enemy, that I may arrive at the moment they are meeting you; for my very wretched state of health will force me to get on shore for a little while.

W. Marsden, 12 Aug.

The Lords Commissioners of the Admiralty having directed me, by their order dated 26 October 1804, to take the Tribune under my command, I beg leave to acquaint you for their Lordships' information, that Captain Bennett arrived at Gibraltar in December following; that after giving orders to the ships at that place under my command, directing them to perform different services, he judged proper to proceed and cruise, and afterwards to proceed to England; and their Lordships, by your letter of 15 February last, having disapproved of his conduct, and acquainted me that it was their intention to bring him to a court-martial for not proceeding and putting himself under my command (which afterwards took place), I must, in justice to myself and the other flag officers concerned, beg to represent to their Lordships that the Tribune captured some valuable prizes on her cruise from Gibraltar to England, three-eighths of which, I understand, Captain Bennett has claimed as his own exclusive right, by which means myself, and the other flag officers on the Mediterranean station, are excluded from what certainly justice, and as far as I interpret [it], the proclamation for the distribution of prize-money, entitle us to.

I need not point out to their Lordships the serious ill-consequences that may arise to the service, if junior officers, in disobedience of their orders to join a commander-in-chief, judge proper to consider the performance of any other service necessary, in preference to that on which they are particularly ordered, (and that they are to receive a reward of one-eighth of all the captures they may make, for such disobedience of their orders,) as they are too evident to escape their notice; and if, in one instance, the point is given up, a private captain may find many excuses, and cruise for any length of time without joining his commander-in-chief.

I am not much in the habit of interfering in prize concerns, but the present appears a proper instance for flag officers doing justice to the service, as well as for preventing junior officers from being guilty of a similar line of imprudence. This case coming so perfectly within the spirit of the proclamation and their Lordships' particular cognisance, affords me reason to hope that they will be pleased to give such directions as will make any interference of the law unnecessary.

I could not last night sit down to thank you for your truly kind letter, and for your large packet of newspapers, for I was in truth bewildered by the account of Sir Robert Calder's victory, and the joy of the event; together with the hearing that John Bull was not content, which I am sorry for. Who can, my dear Fremantle, command all the success which our country may wish? We have fought together, and therefore well know what it is. I have had the best disposed fleet of friends, but who can say what will be the event of a battle? and it most sincerely grieves me, that in any of the papers it should be insinuated that Lord Nelson could have done better. I should have fought the enemy; so did my friend Calder; but who can say that he will be more successful than another? I only wish to stand upon my own merits, and not by comparison, one way or the other, upon the conduct of a brother officer. *Capt. Fremantle, 16 Aug.*

You will be pleased to acquaint the Lords Commissioners of the Admiralty, that on the evening of the 15th inst., I joined the Honourable Admiral Cornwallis off Ushant, with [the Victory, Canopus, Superb, Spencer, Belleisle, Spartiate, Conqueror, Tigre, Leviathan, Donegal, Swiftsure]; that on doing so I received an order from him to proceed immediately with the Victory and Superb to Spithead, where I arrived this morning. *W. Marsden, 18 Aug. Spithead.*

Another letter,[1] of the same date, inclosed:

'Abstract of the weekly returns of the physician to the fleet (under the command of Lord Nelson) between 13 August 1803 and 4 August 1805, during which time the said fleet generally consisted of ten or twelve ships of the line and two or three frigates, manned by from 6,000 to 8,000 seamen and marines. *Report of the Physician to the Fleet, 14 Aug.*

    1803— From 13 August until the end of the year:
        Number of men deceased on board . . . 18
        Number sent to hospitals 19
        Medium number of men on the sick lists . . 185
    1804—Number deceased on board 43
        Number sent to hospitals 46
        Medium number of men on the sick lists . . 190
    1805—To 4 August:
        Number deceased on board 49
        Number sent to hospitals 76
        Medium number of men on the sick lists . . 200

        Total number of deaths on board 110
        Total number sent to hospitals . . . 141
        Medium number of men on the sick lists . . 190
        or 18 to each ship, nearly.

---

[1] Not given by Nicolas. P. R. O.; Admiral's Despatches, Mediterranean, xxxi. 272.

'The above statement exhibits the most convincing and satisfactory proofs of the advantages arising from the practice of the improvements adopted in this fleet for the purpose of preserving the crews in good health and the ships wholesome; and if compared with the accounts of the state of health of fleets or squadrons on foreign stations in former wars, the result will be found to show the importance of the regulations now used in preserving the health and lives of British seamen.

'Thus we find Dr. Blane, physician to the fleet in the West Indies in the year 1781, in a memorial presented by him, in October of that year, to the Lords of the Admiralty, on the health of seamen, deploring the rapid expenditure of seamen in the navy, and stating that during one year, in a fleet of twenty sail of the line, manned by 12,000 seamen, there died on board 715 men; and in the hospitals 862 men; forming a total of 1,577 men, of which number only fifty men died in consequence of wounds. During the same period 350 men were invalided. . . .

'The following causes may be assigned for the high state of health in which the fleet under the command of Lord Nelson has been preserved, for upwards of two years, unexampled perhaps in any fleet or squadron heretofore employed on a foreign station.

'1. The attention paid by his Lordship to the victualling and purveying for the fleet; in causing good wholesome wine to be used in room of spirits; fresh beef as often as it could possibly be procured; vegetables and fruit were always provided in sufficient quantity, when they could be purchased, and an abundant supply of excellent sweet water was always allowed to the ships' companies.

'2. The ships were preserved as free as possible from the baneful effects of humidity, by avoiding the wetting decks (at least between the decks) and by the use of stoves and ventilation below.

'3. The constant activity and motion in which the fleet was preserved, being always at sea and never exposed to the consequences of the idleness and intemperance which too often take place on board of ships lying in harbour, may doubtless be assigned as a principal cause of the good state of health of the crews of this fleet.

'4. Intemperance and skulking were never perhaps so little practised in any fleet as in this. As ships were never in port, the opportunity of procuring spirits or of going to an hospital by imposing on the surgeons, was difficult or impossible. Hence these causes of disease were subtracted.

'5. The promoting cheerfulness amongst the men was encouraged by music, dancing, and theatrical amusements, the example of which was given by the commander-in-chief in the Victory, and may with reason be reckoned amongst the causes of the preservation of the health of the men.

'6. The sick were in general very comfortably accommodated, lodged in airy sick-berths, in many ships placed on a regular sick diet, and supplied with live stock, vegetables, fruit, soft bread, maccaroni, and other articles of diet and refreshment, whenever the circumstances of the service would admit of these supplies being furnished.

'7. By a standing order of the commander-in-chief, Peruvian bark, mixed in wine or spirits, was regularly served to the men employed on the service of wooding and watering. . . . By the returns made by the surgeons to the physician to the fleet . . . it fully appears that this practice entirely obviated any ill effects which might have been occasioned with regard to the health of the wooding and watering parties, and that it effectually prevented the occurrence of fevers, whether intermittent or continued.

'LEONARD GILLESPIE, Physician to the Fleet.'

On 19 August, Lord Nelson struck his flag and went to Merton, where he resided during the few weeks he remained ashore.

I cannot rest until the importance of Sardinia, in every point of view, is taken into consideration. If my letters to the different Secretaries of State cannot be found, I can bring them with me. My belief is, that if France possesses Sardinia, which she may do any moment she pleases, our commerce must suffer most severely, if possible to be carried on when France possesses that island. Many and many most important reasons could be given why the French must not be suffered to possess Sardinia, but your time is too precious to read more words than is necessary; therefore I have only stated two strong points to call your attention to the subject; that I am [sure] our fleet would find a difficulty, if not impossibility, of keeping any station off Toulon for want of that island to supply cattle, water, and refreshments, in the present state of the Mediterranean, and that we can have no certainty of commerce at any time but what France chooses to allow us, to either Italy or the Levant.

W. Pitt, 29 Aug.

My time and movements must depend upon Bonaparte. We are at present ignorant of his intentions, and whether the squadrons from Ferrol are coming to join the Brest fleet, going to the Mediterranean, or cruising for our homeward-bound fleets. With respect to your kind offer of money, I shall try and settle my account with you, even should I feel it necessary to begin a new one; for long accounts ought to be closed between the dearest friends.

A. Davison, 31 Aug.

On 1 September Captain Blackwood of the Euryalus arrived with intelligence that the combined fleet had put into Cadiz. On his way to London, at 5 A.M. on the 2nd, he called on Lord Nelson at Merton, and found him already up and dressed. Immediately on seeing Captain Blackwood, he exclaimed, 'I am sure you bring me news of the French and Spanish fleets, and I think I shall yet have to beat them.' Later in the day Nelson followed him to London, and in talking over the operations that were intended, on returning to the Mediterranean, is said to have repeated, 'Depend upon it, Blackwood, I shall yet give Mr. Villeneuve a drubbing.' It was at once arranged that he should go out in the Victory and resume the command of the fleet off Cadiz.

**A. Davison,
6 Sept.**

I much fear that I shall not have the pleasure of seeing you before my departure, and to thank you for all your kind attentions. . . . I hope my absence will not be long, and that I shall soon meet the combined fleets, with a force sufficient to do the job well; for half a victory would but half content me. But I do not believe the Admiralty can give me a force within fifteen or sixteen sail of the line of the enemy; and therefore, if every ship took her opponent, we should have to contend with a fresh fleet of fifteen or sixteen sail of the line. But I will do my best; and I hope God Almighty will go with me. I have much to lose, but little to gain; and I go because it's right, and I will serve the country faithfully.

**V.-Admiral Collingwood,
7 Sept.**

I shall be with you in a very few days, and I hope you will remain second in command. You will change the Dreadnought for Royal Sovereign, which I hope you will like.

**Diary,
13 Sept.**

At half-past ten drove from dear dear Merton, where I left all which I hold dear in this world, to go to serve my king and country. May the great God whom I adore enable me to fulfil the expectations of my country; and if it is His good pleasure that I should return, my thanks will never cease being offered up to the throne of His mercy. If it is His good providence to cut short my days upon earth, I bow with the greatest submission, relying that He will protect those so dear to me that I may leave behind. His will be done: Amen, Amen, Amen.

14 Sept.

At six o'clock arrived at Portsmouth, and having arranged all my business, embarked at the bathing machines with Mr. Rose and Mr. Canning at two; got on board the Victory at St. Helens, who dined with me; preparing for sea.

The Victory, with the Euryalus in company, sailed at 8 A.M. on Sunday, 15 September.

**A. Davison,
16 Sept.**

I am, my dear friend, so truly sensible of all your goodness to me, that I can only say, thanks, thanks: therefore I will to business. I wish I could have been rich enough, with ease to myself, to have settled my account with you; but as that is not done, I wish for my sake that you would have it closed, and receipts pass between us; and then I will give you a bond for the balance, as for money lent. Those bonds relative to Tucker, being all settled, should be returned to me. Be so good as to give them to Haslewood. If you and I live, no harm can happen; but should either of us drop, much confusion may arise to those we may leave behind. I have said enough. Haslewood will settle the account with all legal exactness.

With respect to your petitioning for your rank on the list of admirals, I shall answer you, my dear Sir Andrew, to the best of my opinion; and if it should not meet exactly your ideas, yet I trust you will believe that no one has a higher opinion of your naval abilities, as a captain or admiral, than myself.

If my memory serves me right, when you passed your flag, I wrote my regret that the service was to lose your abilities at sea. You would long since have commanded the fleets of Britain, with the whole service looking up to your abilities. But, with what you may deem precedents, Lord Barham, Sir John Laforey, Lord Hood, Admiral Gambier, and lately, Admiral Sterling, yet these gentlemen contended for their flags. We will not [they said] hold our civil employments (Lord Barham, Sir John Laforey, and Admiral Sterling, in a stronger degree than the other two). You allowed it to pass over, and holding your civil employment for many years, desire to take your place on the list of admirals. Your pension ought to be equal to your wishes, and much more, in addition to your comptroller's pension, than an admiral's half-pay. But I fear, that if the precedent was established, however properly in your person, that such a field would be opened for officers getting on the list of admirals, after being long out of the service, that the ministry would never get clear of applications; nor could the service know who were likely to command them. Having given you, my dear Sir Andrew, my full opinion, allow me to say, and to offer, that if the king is pleased to place you on the list of admirals, that I shall be ready, and offer myself to serve as second under you for a given time, to mark, at least in myself, to the service, that I receive you with open arms as a most valuable officer restored to us.

<small>Sir A. S. Hamond, 17 Sept.</small>

I send [the Euryalus] forward to announce my approach; and to request that if you are in sight of Cadiz, that not only no salute may take place, but also that no colours may be hoisted, for it is as well not to proclaim to the enemy every ship which may join the fleet.

I would not have any salute even if you are out of sight of land.

<small>V.-Admiral Collingwood, 25 Sept.</small>

It is my particular directions that no junior flag officer salutes on joining the fleet under my command, nor any ship show their colours.

<small>General Memo, 28 Sept.</small>

I got fairly into the fleet yesterday, and under all circumstances I find them as perfect as could be expected. . . . The force is at

<small>Sir A. J. Ball, 30 Sept.</small>

present not so large as might be wished, but I will do my best with it; they will give me more when they can, and I am not come forth to find difficulties, but to remove them. I know not a word of Sir James Craig or his troops, or what they are going about, except as the man said of the parson, 'he preached about doing good,' and so ministers talked of our troops doing good to the common cause; but I was so little a time in England, and not more than four times in London, that really I could hardly talk of anything seriously but naval matters.

Lord Barham, 30 Sept.

I did not fail, immediately on my arrival, to deliver your message to Sir Robert Calder; and it will give your Lordship pleasure to find, as it has me, that an inquiry is what the vice-admiral wishes, and that he had written to you by the Nautilus, which I detained, to say so. Sir Robert thinks that he can clearly prove, that it was not in his power to bring the combined squadrons again to battle. It would be only taking up your time, were I to enter more at large on all our conversation; but Sir Robert felt so much, even at the idea of being removed from his own ship which he commanded, in the face of the fleet, that I much fear I shall incur the censure of the Board of Admiralty, without your Lordship's influence with the members of it. I may be thought wrong, as an officer, to disobey the orders of the Admiralty, by not insisting on Sir Robert Calder's quitting the Prince of Wales for the Dreadnought, and for parting with a 90-gun ship, before the force arrives which their Lordships have judged necessary; but I trust that I shall be considered to have done right as a man, and to a brother officer in affliction—my heart could not stand it, and so the thing must rest. I shall submit to the wisdom of the Board to censure me or not, as to them may seem best for the service; I shall bow with all due respect to their decision.

V.-Admiral Collingwood, 30 Sept.

I had rather that all the ships burnt a blue light or false fire; for it must often happen that the cause of wearing is change of wind, and often a very confused sea, and ships may be very anxious, from various circumstances, to be assured that her neighbour astern has wore, as the line from the above circumstances would be entirely broke. It is perfectly understood that, unless in very fine weather, or extraordinary circumstances, the fleet will not be directed to wear in succession. We have found the comfort of blue lights and false fires in the Mediterranean, where the wind changes so often.

The far greater part of the combined fleets is in the harbour, and indeed none can be called in the Bay of Cadiz; they lie in such a position abreast of the town, and many entirely open, over the narrow strip of land, that Congreve's rockets, if they will go one mile and a half, must do execution. Even should no ships be burnt, yet it would make Cadiz so very disagreeable, that they would rather risk an action than remain in port. I do assure your Lordship, that myself and many thousands in the fleet will feel under the greatest obligations to Colonel Congreve. But I think, with your Lordship's assistance, we have a better chance of forcing them out by want of provisions: it is said hunger will break through stone walls—ours is only a wall of wood. The French are sending provisions of all kinds from Nantes, Bordeaux, and other ports in the bay, in Danish vessels, called of course Danish property, to Ayamonte, Conil, Algeziras, and other little ports from Cape St. Mary's to Algeziras; whence it would be conveyed in their coasting boats without the smallest interruption to Cadiz, and thus the fleets be supplied with provisions for any expedition. Vice-Admiral Collingwood has most properly directed their being detained and sent to Gibraltar, to be libelled in the Vice-Court of Admiralty. I have followed so good an example. I am able enough to see the propriety and necessity of the measure, without which the blockade of Cadiz is nugatory, and we should only have the odium of the measure, without any benefit to us or real distress to our enemies. There never was a place so proper to be blockaded, at this moment, as Cadiz. I have therefore to request that your Lordship will take the proper measures, that the officers under my orders may not get into any pecuniary scrape by their obedience; and, should it be thought proper to allow the enemy's fleet to be victualled, that I may be informed as soon as possible. . . . I can have nothing, as an admiral, to say upon the propriety of granting licences; but from what your Lordship told me of the intentions of ministers respecting the neutral trade, it strikes me, some day it may be urged that it was not for the sake of blockade, but for the purpose of taking all the trade into our own hands, that Great Britain excluded the neutrals. Your Lordship's wisdom will readily conceive all that neutral courts may urge at this apparent injustice, and of might overcoming right.

<small>Lord Castlereagh, 1 Oct.</small>

The ships are getting short in their water and provisions: I shall therefore send Rear-Admiral Louis with six sail of the line immediately to Gibraltar and Tetuan to complete in everything;

<small>W. Marsden, 2 Oct.</small>

and the moment he returns, I shall send others to those places, in order that the fleet may be all prepared for service before the winter sets in. The Zealous having come out from England with a bad mainmast, which has been found, upon survey, to be sprung, and decayed in several places, is just ordered to Gibraltar to get a new one, and otherwise completed for immediate service. The Endymion must also go into Gibraltar, having this day joined the fleet with her mainmast badly sprung.

The fleet is in very fair condition and good humour, and their Lordships may be assured that every exertion of mine shall be used to keep it so, and in a state to meet the combined fleet in Cadiz whenever they come out.

On the evening of 3 October, the Queen, Canopus, Spencer, Zealous, Tigre, and Endymion, parted company. Louis had dined on board the Victory, and on taking leave said, 'You are sending us away, my Lord—the enemy will come out, and we shall have no share in the battle.' Nelson replied, 'My dear Louis, I have no other means of keeping my fleet complete in provisions and water, but by sending them in detachments to Gibraltar. The enemy will come out, and we shall fight them; but there will be time for you to get back first. I look upon Canopus as my right hand and I send you first to insure your being here to help to beat them.' The story is told on the authority of Sir Francis Austen, then Louis's flag-captain, and one of the party at dinner.

W. Marsden, 2 Oct.

In consequence of the inclosed letter from Vice-Admiral Sir Robert Calder, requesting, for the reasons therein mentioned, that I will allow the captains of his Majesty's ships named to return to England, you will please to acquaint the Lords Commissioners of the Admiralty, that the captains of the Thunderer and Ajax having signified to me their willingness to attend as evidences at the court-martial required by the vice-admiral, I shall permit them to return with him to England, and appoint acting captains to their ships till they rejoin them; and should Captain Durham, on the Defiance joining the fleet, wish to return to England for the above purpose, I shall also permit him, and appoint an acting captain during his absence; but I do not feel authorised to order him, or any others, who may not wish to go home on this service, without their Lordships' direction, although I am at the same time satisfied that they would not deprive Sir Robert Calder of any evidence he might think necessary to have on the occasion. I trust their Lordships will approve of this measure.

The officers who came on board to welcome my return forgot

my rank as commander-in-chief in the enthusiasm with which they greeted me. As soon as these emotions were past, I laid before them the plan I had previously arranged for attacking the enemy; and it was not only my pleasure to find it generally approved, but clearly perceived and understood. The enemy are still in port, but something must immediately be done to provoke or lure them to a battle. My duty to my country demands it, and the hopes centred in me, I hope in God, will be realised. In less than a fortnight expect to hear from me, or of me; for who can foresee the fate of battle? *(?) 3 Oct.[1]*

I have the honour to inform you that I have taken the command of his Majesty's fleet in the Mediterranean station; and I am very sorry that I must begin my correspondence by a complaint against the conduct of the Portuguese government at Lagos. They say, at least by their conduct, that, by their secret treaty with Spain, they are to throw every obstacle in the way of our remaining in their ports or on their coasts, by refusing us water and refreshments, [except] in such a manner as is disgraceful to the Portuguese government which offers, or the British government which allows. Great Britain can have nothing to do with their infamous or degrading treaties: she looks to her treaty being fulfilled in the most liberal manner. *Lord Strangford. Lisbon, 3 Oct.*

I shall state my complaint of the circumstances which generally happen at Lagos. A ship of war goes there for water and refreshments, which, by treaty, she has a right to: from her communications, she seems placed under the direction of the consul of one of our enemies, and very improper language is held by our enemies to the British officers and seamen, and inducements held out to them to desert. The enemy's consul then directs that only so many cabbages, or bullocks, or sheep, shall go on board—and, at his will and pleasure, so much water: and it has been carried so

---

[1] This letter was published anonymously in the *Naval Chronicle*, vol. xv. p. 37. Whatever credit it may be entitled to, as far as its matter goes, it needs but a very slight acquaintance with Nelson's epistolary style, to see that as to its language, it is none of his. The plan of attack was not issued until 9 October, but it may have been talked of some days before. Twenty-four years later it was said by Sir Richard Keats to have been discussed at Merton; and that some conversation on the subject did then take place is highly probable; but the details, related from memory after twenty-four years, cannot be trusted. I would equally refuse to accept the story that, when dining with Lord Sidmouth, shortly before leaving England, Nelson drew his plan on the table and said, 'I shall attack in two lines, led by myself and Collingwood, and I am confident I shall capture either their van and centre or their centre and rear,' Sidney's *Life of Lord Hill*, p. 368. Rodney is said to have done something of the same kind. My own opinion is that neither of them did it.

E E

far that a captain, whose ship was complete with water, giving his people water to wash the linen, on sending ashore for more, was threatened by the Portuguese sentry to be fired upon if they presumed to attempt to take a drop. To this degradation no nation can submit. Now, what I demand is, that our officers and men, whilst in the neutral port, shall be under the protection of the neutral flag, and not be permitted to be insulted by the interference, either secret or open, of our enemies; and that every ship which goes into Lagos, or other ports, shall have such refreshments as are reasonable. And as to water, I never before heard that any limited quantity was allowed, much less that if a dirty shirt was washed, any French or Spanish consul should be allowed to say, 'You English shall either wear a dirty shirt, or go without water to drink: and that a sentinel of a neutral power should presume to threaten to fire, if an ally presumed to take water! I shall send a ship or ships to take in water at Lagos. They shall wash, or let it run overboard, if they please; and I rely that the Portuguese government will direct that our enemies shall not insult our people, much less dictate to the Portuguese governor for his treatment of us. However degraded the Portuguese may allow themselves to become, it is hardly fair that they should expect us to be insulted by our enemies on their neutral ground; for if, by words, or any other mode of warfare, they do permit it, I shall certainly retaliate. I should get warm was I to go any farther, therefore I shall leave the business in much better hands—those of your Lordship; only repeating, that all we want is, that when our ships go to Lagos, we may not be allowed to be insulted by our enemies (unless we have permission to retaliate); that we shall take either one ton, or one thousand tons of water, as we please, and be allowed the free use of the markets, as by friendship we had a most unquestionable right to expect; and that the Portuguese governor may be called to a most severe account for his conduct in allowing a sentinel to threaten to fire on an English boat going for water, or any other purpose, to the shore of friendly powers.

Capt. Duff,[1] Mars, 4 Oct.

As the enemy's fleets may be hourly expected to put to sea from Cadiz, I have to desire that you will keep, with the Mars, Defence, and Colossus, from three to four leagues between the fleet and

---

[1] It is an interesting coincidence that Captain Duff's great-uncle, Robert Duff, then in the Rochester of 50 guns, commanded the inshore squadron at Quiberon Bay (20 Nov. 1759); the only battle in modern English naval history which for its magnitude, its importance, and its results can be compared with Trafalgar.

Cadiz, in order that I may get the information from the frigates stationed off that port as expeditiously as possible. Distant signals to be used, when flags, from the state of the weather, may not readily be distinguished in their colours. If the enemy be out, or coming out, fire guns by day or night, in order to draw my attention. In thick weather, the ships are to close within signal of the Victory: one of the ships to be placed to windward, or rather to the eastward of the other two, to extend the distance of seeing; and I have desired Captain Blackwood to throw a frigate to the westward of Cadiz, for the purpose of an easy and early communication.

I have received from Rear-Admiral Louis your information respecting the intended movements of the enemy, which strengthens my conviction that you estimate as I do the importance of not letting these rogues escape us without a fair fight, which I pant for by day and dream of by night. I am momentarily expecting the Phœbe, Sirius, Naiad, and Niger, from Gibraltar; two of them shall be with you directly, as I get hold of them; and if you meet them, and there is any way of sending information and their despatches from Gibraltar, keep Naiad and Phœbe. Juno is a fixture between Cape Spartel and Gibraltar; Mars, Colossus, and Defence will be stationed four leagues east from the fleet, and one of them advanced to the east towards Cadiz, and as near as possible in the latitude. The fleet will be from sixteen to eighteen leagues west of Cadiz; therefore, if you throw a frigate west from you, most probably in fine weather we shall communicate daily. In fresh breezes easterly, I shall work up for Cadiz, never getting to the northward of it: and in the event of hearing they are standing out of Cadiz I shall carry a press of sail to the southward towards Cape Spartel and Larache, so that you will always know where to find me. I am writing out regular instructions for the frigates under your orders, but I am confident you will not let these gentry slip through our fingers, and then we shall give a good account of them, although they may be very superior in numbers. The Royal Sovereign and Defiance were to sail after the 24th. Belleisle, too, is ordered here.

Capt. Blackwood, 4 Oct. Cadiz, East 17 lgs.

The French and Spanish ships have taken the troops on board which had been landed on their arrival, and it is said that they mean to sail the first fresh Levant wind; and as the Cartagena ships are ready, and when seen a few days ago had their topsailyards hoisted up, it looks like a junction. The position I have taken for this month is from sixteen to eighteen leagues west of Cadiz;

Lord Barham, 5 Oct.

for although it is most desirable that the fleet should be well up in the easterly winds, yet I must guard against being caught with a westerly wind near Cadiz, as a fleet of ships with so many three-deckers would inevitably be forced into the Straits, and then Cadiz would be perfectly free for the enemy to come out with a westerly wind, as they served Lord Keith in the late war. I am most anxious for the arrival of frigates; less than eight, with the brigs &c., as we settled, I find are absolutely inadequate for this service and to be with the fleet, and Capes Spartel, Cantin, or Blanco, and the Salvages, must be watched by fast-sailing vessels, in case any squadron should escape. I have been obliged to send six sail of the line to water and get stores at Tetuan and Gibraltar, for if I did not begin, I should be very soon obliged to take the whole fleet into the Straits. I have twenty-three sail with me, and should they come out I shall immediately bring them to battle. But although I should not doubt of spoiling any voyage they may attempt, yet I hope for the arrival of the ships from England, that as an enemy's fleet they may be annihilated.

G. Rose,
6 Oct.

I verily believe the country will soon be put to some expense for my account, either a monument, or a new pension and honours; for I have not the very smallest doubt but that a very few days, almost hours, will put us in battle; the success no man can ensure, but the fighting them, if they are to be got at, I pledge myself, and if the force arrives which is intended. I am very, very, very anxious for its arrival, for the thing will be done if a few more days elapse; and I want for the sake of our country that it should be done so effectually as to have nothing to wish for; and what will signify the force the day after the battle? It is, as Mr. Pitt knows, annihilation that the country wants, and not merely a splendid victory of twenty-three to thirty-six,—honourable to the parties concerned, but absolutely useless in the extended scale to bring Bonaparte to his marrow-bones: numbers can only annihilate. I think, not for myself but the country; therefore I hope the Admiralty will send the fixed force as soon as possible, and frigates and sloops of war, for I am very destitute. I do not mean this as any complaint, quite the contrary; I believe they are doing all they can, if interest does not interfere; therefore, if Mr. Pitt would hint to Lord Barham that he shall be anxious until I get the force proposed, and plenty of frigates and sloops in order to watch them closely, it may be advantageous to the country. You are at liberty to mention this to Mr. Pitt, but I would not wish it to go farther.

Thinking it almost impossible to bring a fleet of forty sail of the line into a line of battle in variable winds, thick weather, and other circumstances which must occur, without such a loss of time that the opportunity would probably be lost of bringing the enemy to battle in such a manner as to make the business decisive, I have therefore made up my mind to keep the fleet in that position of sailing (with the exception of the first and second in command) that the order of sailing is to be the order of battle, placing the fleet in two lines of sixteen ships each, with an advanced squadron of eight of the fastest sailing two-decked ships, which will always make, if wanted, a line of twenty-four sail, on whichever line the commander-in-chief may direct.

Memorandum, 9 Oct.

The second in command will, after my intentions are made known to him, have the entire direction of his line to make the attack upon the enemy, and to follow up the blow until they are captured or destroyed.

If the enemy's fleet should be seen to windward in line of battle, and that the two lines and the advanced squadron can fetch them, they will probably be so extended that their van could not succour their rear. I should therefore probably make the second in command's signal to lead through about their twelfth ship from their rear (or wherever he could fetch, if not able to get so far advanced); my line would lead through about their centre, and the advanced squadron to cut two or three or four ships ahead of their centre, so as to ensure getting at their commander-in-chief, on whom every effort must be made to capture.

The whole impression of the British fleet must be to overpower from two or three ships ahead of their commander-in-chief, supposed to be in the centre, to the rear of their fleet. I will suppose twenty sail of the enemy's line to be untouched; it must be some time before they could perform a manœuvre to bring their force compact to attack any part of the British fleet engaged, or to succour their own ships, which indeed would be impossible without mixing with the ships engaged. The enemy's fleet is supposed to consist of forty-six sail of the line, British fleet of forty. If either is less, only a proportionate number of enemy's ships are to be cut off; British to be one-fourth superior to the enemy cut off.

Something must be left to chance; nothing is sure in a sea fight beyond all others. Shot will carry away the masts and yards of friends as well as foes, but I look with confidence to a victory before the van of the enemy could succour their rear, and then that the British fleet would most of them be ready to receive their twenty sail of the line or to pursue them should they endeavour to make off.

If the van of the enemy tacks, the captured ships must run to leeward of the British fleet; if the enemy wears, the British must place themselves between the enemy and the captured and disabled British ships; and should the enemy close, I have no fears as to the result.

The second in command will in all possible things direct the movements of his line by keeping them as compact as the nature of the circumstances will admit. Captains are to look to their particular line as their rallying point. But, in case signals can neither be seen or perfectly understood, no captain can do very wrong if he places his ship alongside that of an enemy.

Of the intended attack from to windward, the enemy in line of battle ready to receive an attack:

The divisions of the British fleet will be brought nearly within gunshot of the enemy's centre. The signal will most probably then be made for the lee line to bear up together, to set all their sails, even steering sails, in order to get as quickly as possible to the enemy's line, and to cut through, beginning from the twelfth ship from the enemy's rear. Some ships may not get through their exact place, but they will always be at hand to assist their friends, and if any are thrown round the rear of the enemy, they will effectually complete the business of twelve sail of the enemy.

Should the enemy wear together, or bear up and sail large, still the twelve ships composing, in the first position, the enemy's rear, are to be the object of attack of the lee line, unless otherwise directed from the commander-in-chief, which is scarcely to be expected, as the entire management of the lee line, after the intentions of the commander-in-chief [are] signified, is intended to be left to the judgment of the admiral commanding that line.

The remainder of the enemy's fleet, thirty-four sail, are to be left to the management of the commander-in-chief, who will endeavour to take care that the movements of the second in command are as little interrupted as is possible.[1]

V.-Adml. Collingwood, 8 Oct.

The Royal Sovereign is very deep. She has eleven cables,

---

[1] It can scarcely be doubted that the leading idea of this 'intended attack from to windward' is taken from Clerk's Essay; but it seems to have escaped observation that in the battle of Trafalgar, the attack, though made from the position to windward, was made rather in the manner here prescribed for the attack from the position to leeward. We must suppose that this alternative method had been discussed *virâ voce* with the several officers who so gloriously carried it into execution.

three of which shall go to Gibraltar, and the money will go on board of a frigate. I am sure you will admire her as a far better ship than the Victory. You need not hurry yourself, but change at your leisure.

I shall be glad to see you mounted in her. I send you my plan of attack, as far as a man dare venture to guess at the very uncertain position the enemy may be found in. But, my dear friend, it is to place you perfectly at ease respecting my intentions, and to give full scope to your judgment for carrying them into effect. We can, my dear Coll., have no little jealousies. We have only one great object in view, that of annihilating our enemies, and getting a glorious peace for our country. No man has more confidence in another than I have in you: and no man will render your services more justice than your very old friend,

NELSON AND BRONTE.

9 Oct.

Keep the schooner; she will be useful in the night close in shore; and as Weasel sails faster, you can send her to me with accounts when you can't communicate by signals; I should never wish to be more than forty-eight hours without hearing from you. Hydra you can victual and water out of the other frigates, who are all full.

Capt. Blackwood, 9 Oct. Cadiz, East 19 lgs.

Those who know more of Cadiz than either you or I do say, that after those Levanters come several days of fine weather, sea-breezes westerly, land wind at night; and that if the enemy are bound into the Mediterranean they would come out at night, which they have always done, placing frigates on the Porpoises and Diamond, and the shoal off Cadiz, run to the southward, and catch the sea-breezes at the mouth of the Gut, and push through whilst we might have little wind in the offing. In short, watch all points, and all winds and weathers, for I shall depend upon you.

Fresh breezes easterly. Received an account from Blackwood, that the French ships had all bent their top-gallant sails. Sent the Pickle to him, with orders to keep a good look-out. Sent Admiral Collingwood the Nelson touch. At night, wind westerly.

Diary, 9 Oct.

The ships and vessels of the fleet under my command are directed not to show their colours on joining, unless the commander-in-chief should show his.

General Memo, 10 Oct.

When in presence of an enemy, all the ships under my command are to bear white colours, and a union jack is to be suspended from the fore top-gallant stay.

It is expected in fine weather that the ships in order of sailing do not keep more than two cables' length from each other.

As gales of wind increase so suddenly in this country, the ships of the fleet are directed, particularly in the night, to shorten sail, and get top-gallant yards and masts down, and take such other precautions as the captains may judge necessary, without waiting for the admiral's motions.

V.-Adml. Collingwood, 10 Oct.

I think we are near enough, for the weather if it is fine, [the wind] serves, and we are in sight, they never will move; and should it turn bad, we may be forced into the Mediterranean, and thus leave them at liberty to go to the westward, although at present I am sure Mediterranean is their destination. I shall make the signal at half-past four or five for boats to repair on board, and make sail under top-sails, and perhaps fore-sail; supposing the wind to remain, stand into the latitude of Cadiz, and then wear to the southward for the night.

Should the enemy move, I have directed the vessels coming with the information to fire a gun every three minutes, and burn a rocket from the mast-head every half-hour. It is then probable that I shall make the signal, bear up, and steer for the entrance of the Straits.

Capt. Blackwood, 10 Oct.

I rely on you that we can't miss getting hold of them, and I will give them such a shaking as they never yet experienced; at least I will lay down my life in the attempt. We are a very powerful fleet, and not to be held cheap.

Sir A. J. Ball, 11 Oct.

I have five frigates, a brig, and a schooner watching them closely, an advanced squadron of fast-sailing ships between me and the frigates, and the body of the fleet from fifteen to eighteen leagues west of Cadiz. I am aware there will be moments when it might be wished we were closer; but I have considered all possible circumstances, and believe there will often be times, in strong gales of westerly wind, when we may often wish ourselves farther off, as we shall be in danger of being driven into the Mediterranean; when, if they choose to go westward, they will have no interruption. However, whether I am right or wrong, I act from the best of my judgment. Admiral Murray is in England, settling the affairs of his father-in-law, lately dead: he might have had his flag, if he pleased, in this fleet.

W. Marsden, 13 Oct.

His Majesty's ships Agamemnon and L'Aimable joined this forenoon, and the Prince of Wales, bearing the flag of Vice-Admiral Sir Robert Calder, leaves the fleet this evening with orders to proceed direct to Spithead. The vice-admiral takes with him the captains of his Majesty's ships Thunderer and Ajax, whom I have permitted to accompany him, for the purpose of attending the court requested by that officer on his late conduct between the 22nd and 25th of July last, which I hope, for the reasons I have before stated, their Lordships will be pleased to approve of.

I hope we shall soon get our Cadiz friends out, and then we may (I hope) flatter ourselves that some of them will cruise on our side; but if they do not come forth soon, I shall then rather incline to think they will detach squadrons; but I trust, either in the whole or in part, we shall get at them. *Capt. Blackwood, 14 Oct.*

I am confident in your look-out upon them. I expect three stout fire-ships from England; then, with a good breeze, so that the gun-boats cannot move, and yet not so much but that a gig can with ease row out, I should hope that at the least the gentry may be disturbed; and I should not be surprised if Mr. Francis and his catamarans were sent, and Colonel Congreve and his rockets. But all this keep to yourself, for officers will talk, and there is no occasion for putting the enemy on their guard. When these arrive, we will consult how to manage them, and I shall have the two bombs ready by that time.

You will, with the Agamemnon, take a station west from Cadiz from seven to ten leagues, by which means, if the enemy should move, I hope to have instant information, as two or three ships will be kept, as at present, between the fleet and your two ships; and it seems thought by Captain Blackwood that a ship or two may attempt to drive the frigates off, and if that should be the case you will be at hand to assist. *Capt. Hope, Defence, 15 Oct.*

I want to send ten sail of the line, two frigates and two sloops, off Toulon, Genoa, and that coast, to cover our army and to prevent any stores, provisions, &c., from moving alongshore, and to save Sardinia; but as yet I have not the means. But when the ships are released from the expedition, and the frigates carrying the money return, I shall have a very respectable squadron in that part of the Mediterranean—probably under our friend Keats, if he will accept it, and give up the certainty of fighting with the fleet, as my second. *Sir A. J. Ball, 15 Oct.*

Sir Robert Calder has just left us to stand his trial, which I think of a very serious nature. God send him a good deliverance. *Capt. Hamond, 15 Oct.*

Diary, 19 Oct.

Fine weather, wind easterly. At half-past nine, the Mars being one of the look-out ships, repeated the signal, 'that the enemy was coming out of port.' Made the signal for a 'general chase SE;' wind at south, Cadiz bearing ENE by compass, distant sixteen leagues. At three the Colossus made the signal, 'that the enemy's fleet was at sea.' In the evening directed the fleet to observe my motions during the night, and for Britannia, Prince, and Dreadnought, they being heavy sailers, to take their stations as convenient; and for Mars, Orion, Belleisle, Leviathan, Bellerophon, and Polyphemus to go ahead during the night, and to carry a light, standing for the Straits' mouth.

Lady Hamilton, 19 Oct.

My dearest beloved Emma, the dear friend of my bosom,—The signal has been made that the enemy's combined fleet are coming out of port. We have very little wind, so that I have no hopes of seeing them before to-morrow. May the God of battles crown my endeavours with success; at all events I will take care that my name shall ever be most dear to you and Horatia, both of whom I love as much as my own life. And as my last writing before the battle will be to you, so I hope in God that I shall live to finish my letter after the battle. May Heaven bless you prays your   NELSON AND BRONTE.

Miss Horatia Nelson Thompson, 19 Oct.

My dearest angel,—I was made happy by the pleasure of receiving your letter of 19 September, and I rejoice to hear that you are so very good a girl, and love my dear Lady Hamilton, who most dearly loves you. Give her a kiss for me. The combined fleets of the enemy are now reported to be coming out of Cadiz; and therefore I answer your letter, my dearest Horatia, to mark to you that you are ever uppermost in my thoughts. I shall be sure of your prayers for my safety, conquest, and speedy return to dear Merton, and our dearest good Lady Hamilton. Be a good girl; mind what Miss Connor says to you. Receive, my dearest Horatia, the affectionate parental blessing of your father,
                                  NELSON AND BRONTE.

Memorandum, 20 Oct.

Captain Blackwood to keep with two frigates in sight of the enemy in the night. Two other frigates to be placed between him and the Defence, Captain Hope. Colossus will take her station between Defence and Mars. Mars to communicate with the Victory.

Signals by night—If the enemy are standing to the southward, or towards the Straits, burn two blue lights together every hour, in order to make the greater blaze. If the enemy are standing to the westward three guns, quick, every hour.

Fresh breezes SSW, and rainy. Communicated with Phœbe, Defence, and Colossus, who saw near forty sail of ships of war outside of Cadiz yesterday evening; but the wind being southerly, they could not get to the mouth of the Straits. We were between Trafalgar and Cape Spartel. The frigates made the signal that they saw nine sail outside the harbour; gave the frigates instructions for their guidance, and placed Defence, Colossus, and Mars between me and the frigates. At noon fresh gales and heavy rain; Cadiz, NE 9 leagues. In the afternoon Captain Blackwood telegraphed that the enemy seemed determined to go to the westward; and that they shall *not* do if in the power of Nelson and Bronte to prevent them. At 5, telegraphed Captain Blackwood that I relied upon his keeping sight of the enemy. At 6 o'clock Naiad made the signal for 31 sail of the enemy NNE. The frigates and look-out ships kept sight of the enemy most admirably all night, and told me by signals which tack they were upon. At 8 we wore, and stood to SW, and at 4 A.M. wore, stood to the NE. Diary, 20 Oct.

At daylight saw the enemy's combined fleet from east to ESE; bore away; made the signal for order of sailing, and to prepare for battle; the enemy with their heads to the southward: at seven the enemy wearing in succession. May the great God, whom I worship, grant to my country, and for the benefit of Europe in general, a great and glorious victory; and may no misconduct in any one tarnish it; and may humanity after victory be the predominant feature in the British fleet. For myself individually, I commit my life to Him who made me, and may His blessing light upon my endeavours for serving my country faithfully. To Him I resign myself and the just cause which is entrusted to me to defend. Amen. Amen. Amen. 21 Oct.

> October the twenty-first, one thousand eight hundred and five, then in sight of the combined fleets of France and Spain, distant about ten miles.

Whereas the eminent services of Emma Hamilton, widow of the Right Honourable Sir William Hamilton, have been of the very greatest service to our king and country, to my knowledge, without her receiving any reward from either our king or country;—first, that she obtained the King of Spain's letter, in 1796, to his brother, the King of Naples, acquainting him of his intention to declare war against England; from which letter the ministry sent out orders to then Sir John Jervis, to strike a stroke, if opportunity offered, against either the arsenals of Spain or her fleets. That neither of these was done is not the fault of Lady Hamilton. The opportunity might have been offered. Secondly, the British fleet under my command could never have returned the second time to Egypt, had not Lady Hamilton's influence with the Queen of Naples caused letters to be wrote to the Governor of Syracuse,[1] that he was to encourage the fleet being supplied with everything should they put into any port in Sicily. We put into Syracuse, and received every supply, went to Egypt, and destroyed the French fleet. Could I have rewarded these services I would not now call upon my country; but as that has not been in my power, I leave Emma Lady Hamilton, therefore, a legacy to my king and country, that they will give her an ample provision to maintain her rank in life. I also leave to the beneficence of my country my adopted daughter, Horatia Nelson Thompson; and I desire she will use in future the name of Nelson only.[2] These are the only favours I ask of my king and country at this moment when I am going to fight their battle. May God bless my king and country, and all those who I hold dear. My relations it is needless to mention: they will of course be amply provided for.

NELSON AND BRONTE.

Witness—Henry Blackwood.
T. M. Hardy.

The rest of the story must be told by other pens.

Victory's Log, 21 Oct.[3]

'A.M. Moderate breezes. At 4 wore ship. At 6 observed the enemy's fleet bearing E by S, distant ten or twelve miles—bore up to the eastward and made all possible sail, out reefs, topsails, set steering sails, and royals and stay sails—cleared for quarters. At 8 light breezes and

---

[1] If such letters were written, they did not arrive in time to be of any use, (see *ante*, p. 145); but in fact there is no evidence, except the word of a vain woman, that they were written. Nelson knew nothing about the matter, but believed what Lady Hamilton told him.

[2] How disgracefully these, Nelson's last wishes, were ignored, is matter of painful notoriety. Lady Hamilton was left to die in the extreme of penury and want, in a wretched lodging at Calais; Horatia Nelson, then still a mere child, afterwards lived with the Boltons or Matchams, till she married in 1822; but not one penny was given to either of them by that king or that country to which Nelson, in his last hours, so touchingly bequeathed them. It matters not in the least who or what this woman and this child were: it is sufficient that they were the objects of Nelson's love, and that he left them a legacy to his king and country.

[3] This and the other logs are here given from the official originals in the P.R.O. Many of those given by Nicolas seem to have been taken from other copies, and are often very inaccurate.

cloudy. Body of the enemy's fleet E by S, nine or ten miles - enemy's line from NNE to SSW, consisting of 33 sail of the line, 6 frigates, and 2 brigs—still standing for the enemy's van—the Royal Sovereign and her line of battle steering for the centre of the enemy's line. At 11.30 the enemy opened upon the Royal Sovereign. At 11.40 the Royal Sovereign commenced firing on the enemy. At 11.50 the enemy began firing upon us and the Téméraire. At noon, standing for the enemy's tenth ship with all possible [sail] set. Light breezes and hazy weather. Swell from the WNW.

'Light airs and cloudy, standing towards the enemy's van with all sail set. At 4 minutes past 12 opened our fire on the enemy's van, in keeping down their line. At 20 minutes past 12, in attempting to pass through the enemy's line we fell on board the tenth and eleventh ship, when the action became general. About 1.15 [Lord Nelson] was wounded in the shoulder. At 1.30, the Redoutable having struck her colours, we ceased firing our starboard guns but continued engaged with the Santissima Trinidad and some of the enemy's ships on the larboard side. Observed the Téméraire between the Redoutable and another French ship of the line, both of which had struck. The action continued general until 3 o'clock, when several of the enemy's ships around us had struck. Observed the Royal Sovereign with the loss of her main and mizen-masts, and some of the enemy's ships around her dismasted. At 3.10 observed 4 sail of the enemy's van tack, and stood along our line to windward, fired our larboard guns at those which could reach them. At 3.40 made the signal for our ships to keep their wind and engage the enemy's van coming along our weather line. At 4.15, the Spanish rear-admiral to windward struck to some of our ships which had tacked after them. Observed one of the enemy's ships blow up and fourteen sail of the enemy's ships standing towards Cadiz, and three sail of the enemy's ships standing to the southward. Partial firing continued until 4.30, when a victory being reported to [Lord Nelson], he then died of his wounds. . . .

22 Oct.

'P.M. 2.57 cut away our lower and topmast studding-sails, observing the van of the enemy's ships had wore to form a junction with their centre. At 3 hailed the Minotaur to allow us to pass ahead of her, hauled our wind to prevent the enemy's design, five of them bore up, and five of them kept their wind to engage us and the Minotaur, four French and one Spanish. At 3.7 the Minotaur and Spartiate commenced close action with their headmost ships, received and returned the fire of the five ships, with our topsails to the mast, occasionally filled to pass enemy's ships that had struck. 3.40 observed the sternmost (a Spaniard) with her rigging and sails very much cut up, lay to on her quarter, with our fore and main topsails to the mast, all our after sail set, firing obliquely through her, she only returning at times from her sternchase and quarter guns. 4.10 wore ship to engage her on the other tack, the other four ships having left her on seeing some of our ships coming to our assistance. 4.27 observed an enemy's ship on fire (L'Achille) in the SE quarter, a frigate, the Pickle schooner, and Entreprenante cutter, taking up their men. 4.42 the Spanish ship engaged by the Spartiate and Minotaur had her mizen-mast shot away. 5.10 she struck, after being very much disabled—she proved to be the El Neptuno, 80 guns. 5.20 the firing ceased—observed fourteen ships of the

Spartiate's Log, 22 Oct.

enemy in our possession, including the Santissima Trinidad and Santa Anna, three-deckers, two admiral's ships, and the Bucentaure, Admiral Villeneuve.'

Orion's Log, 21 Oct.

22 Oct.

'A.M. At 6.15 answered the general signal 76 [bear up and sail large]; saw the enemy's fleet to the eastward, 33 sail of the line . . . .; hove several things overboard and cleared ship for action.

'P.M. The signal was made to prepare to anchor if necessary. 12.15, general signal to engage more closely; Victory made the Leviathan's signal to lead the van and Mars's to lead the lee line.¹ 12.35 the Royal Sovereign broke through the enemy's rear and ranged up under the lee of the Santa Anna, three-decker, Spanish ship; the larboard² division attacking the remainder of their rear as they arrived up in succession. The Victory, after making a feint of attacking their van, hauled to starboard, so as to reach their centre, and then wore round to pass under the lee of the Bucentaure. Each ship of our fleet passed through the enemy's line with studding-sails set, as she arrived up in succession; passed the Santa Anna dismasted at 1.30, and had struck, the Royal Sovereign under her lee, with her foremast only standing; passed the Mars, Colossus, and Tonnant, aboard and surrounded by several of the enemy's ships, all dismasted or nearly so.' . . .

In confirmation or illustration of a very important statement in the Orion's log, is a letter to Sir Harris Nicolas from Sir Edward Codrington, then captain of the Orion, and which, though written forty years after the date, is shown by the log not to be a mere fancy of after meditation.

Sir Ed. Codrington to Sir H. Nicolas, (?) 1845.

'In Lord Nelson's memorandum of 9 October 1805, he refers to "an advanced squadron of eight of the fastest sailing two-decked ships," to be added to either of the two lines of the order of sailing as may be required; and says that this advanced squadron would probably have to cut through "two, three, or four ships of the enemy's centre, so as to ensure getting at their commander-in-chief, on whom every effort must be made to capture;" and he afterwards twice speaks of the enemy's van coming to succour their rear. Now I am under the impression that I was expressly instructed by Lord Nelson (referring to the probability of the enemy's van coming down upon us), being in the Orion, one of the eight ships named, that he himself would probably make a feint of attacking their van in order to prevent or retard it. I have no doubt of the Victory having hauled out to port for a short space, and of my calling the attention of my first lieutenant, Croft, to the circumstance of her having taken her larboard and weather studding-sails in, whilst she kept her starboard and lee studding-sails set and shaking, in order to make it clear to the fleet that his movement was merely a feint, and that the Victory would speedily resume her course and fulfil his intention of cutting through at the centre. In admiration of this movement I observed to Lieutenant Croft, "how beautifully the admiral is carrying into effect his intentions," and it was this exposure to the raking fire of several of the ships ahead of the French centre, that occasioned

---

¹ This is only one of the many signals casually reported which there is no reason to believe were really made.
² Clearly a slip of the writer's pen for starboard, or lee.

the Victory being so much cut up before she reached her proposed position.'

'Noon, running down for the enemy.

'P.M. Light winds, running down with lower topmast and top- gallant studding-sails set on the larboard side, within a ship's length of the Victory, running for the 14th ship of the enemy's line from the van. 15 min. past noon, cut away the studding-sails and hauled to the wind. At 18 min. past noon, the enemy began to fire ; 20 min. past noon, the Victory opened her fire; immediately put our helm a-port to shear clear of the Victory and opened our fire against the Santissima Trinidad, and two ships ahead of her, when the action became general. Some time after, the Victory falling on board her opponent, the Téméraire being closely engaged on both sides, the ship on the larboard side, engaging the Victory, fell alongside of us, the Victory on her larboard side, the yard-arms locked, and immediately after struck and was boarded by some of the officers and part of the crew of us, at the same time being engaged with one of the enemy on the starboard side, a Spanish three-deck ship being on the larboard bow or nearly ahead, who had raked us during great part of the action. About 10 or 15 minutes past 2, the enemy's ship on the starboard side fell alongside of us, on which we immediately boarded her and struck her colours.' — Téméraire's Log, 22 Oct.

'A.M. At daylight saw the enemy in line of battle bearing from SSE to E—our fleet ahead, steering towards the enemy. At 8 light winds, still continuing the same under all sail. At noon the centre of the enemy's fleet, bearing ESE, about six miles, consisting of one four-decker, two three-deckers, 30 two-deckers, six frigates, and two brigs, under the command of the French Admiral Villeneuve and Spanish Admiral Gravina. — Naiad's Log, 21 Oct.

'P.M. At 12.10 light breezes ; observed the Royal Sovereign commencing the action, as did several other ships of the lee line at 12.30. At 12.50 the Spanish admiral commenced firing, and the action became very general. At 1 a Spanish three-decker hauled down her colours to the Royal Sovereign. At 1.30 all the same three-decker's masts went over the side. At 1.35 observed a Spanish two-decker haul down her colours. At 1.50 a French two-deck ship and the French admiral both struck to the Victory and Téméraire. At 2 observed the main and mizen-mast of a French two-decker go over the side. At 2.10 observed several of the enemy's ships dismasted, and one of ours with her fore and mizen-mast gone. At 2.20 observed the Neptune dismast a Spanish four-deck ship, and likewise several of ditto strike their colours. At 2.40 the action became general from the van to rear. At 2.45 the main and mizen-masts of the Royal Sovereign went by the board. At 3.35 bore up to take one of our ships in tow. At 4 took the Bellcisle in tow, she being without a mast or bowsprit; observed one of the French line-of-battle ships on fire. At 4.20 out boats and sent them to take men from ditto. At 5 the firing ceased from all the ships. At 5.10 observed the ship that was on fire to blow up.' — 22 Oct.

The Naiad's log is the only one which has entered the signals with any degree of fulness. The Victory's signal log, if in existence, cannot be found ; the log of the Euryalus merely notes 'repeated several signals.'

Naiad's Log : 21 October.

No. Signal.	Telegraph, Admiralty, or accompanying Telegraph, or Pennants.	Purport.	By whom made.	To whom made.	At what time made.	Remarks.
					A.M.	
13	Admiralty	Prepare for battle	Commander-in-chief	General	6h 40m	Answered by the Fleet immediately, and complied with
76	Admiralty	Bear up, sail large on the course steered by Admiral	Victory	General	6 50	Answered and complied with immediately
	Naiad's pennants	Signal for Captain Dundas	Victory	—	7 50	Ditto
76	Admiralty and Prince's pennants	As before	Victory	Prince	8 40	Answered by the Prince immediately
92	Admiralty and S. pennants	Shorten sail, and carry as little sail as possible [1]	Victory	General	10 0	Answered and complied with immediately
420 [2]	Admiralty and R.Sovereign's pennants	—	Victory	R.Sovereign	10 50	Ditto
642	Admiralty	The strange sail is a vessel of war	Victory	R.Sovereign	10 50	Ditto
307	Admiralty & [Africa's] pennants	Make all sail possible with safety to the masts	Victory	[Africa]	11 5	—
	Telegraph	England expects that every man will do his duty	Victory	General	11 35	Repeated by the Naiad immediately
63	Admiralty and preparative	Prepare to anchor	Victory	General	12 0	Repeated by the Naiad immediately, and complied with
8	. .	The above signal to take place immediately after the close of day				

22 October.

					P.M.	
16	Admiralty	Engage more closely	Victory	General	12h 20m	Repeated by the Naiad immediately
307	Admiralty & [Africa's] pennants	Make all sail possible with safety to the masts	Victory	Africa	12 30	Repeated twice by the Naiad
	Naiad's pennants and Compass Signal	To take a disabled ship in tow	Euryalus	Naiad	3 0	Answered and complied with immediately
101	Admiralty	Come to the wind on the larboard tack	Euryalus	General	3 20	Repeated by the Naiad immediately
99	Admiralty	Come to the wind on the starboard tack	Euryalus	General	3 30	Ditto
101	Admiralty	As before	Phœbe	General	4 0	Ditto
101	Admiralty	As before	Phœbe	General	4 35	Ditto
99	Admiralty	As before	Admiral on board the Euryalus	General	5 25	Ditto
58	Admiralty	Take possession of ships that have struck	Admiral on board the Euryalus	General	5 40	Ditto

[1] This, under the circumstances, is utter nonsense; but it stands so in the log.
[2] No interpretation of this signal is given in the log. Nicolas has added, 'The enemy are coming out of port,' which, addressed at that time to Collingwood, is nonsense. If not a simple mistake, it must have been a private signal between the two admirals.

1805 BATTLE OF TRAFALGAR

'A.M. At 10 observed the enemy wearing, and coming to the wind on the larboard tack. At 11.40 repeated Lord Nelson's telegraph message, "I intend to push or go through the end of the enemy's line, to prevent them from getting into Cadiz." Saw the land bearing E by N five or six leagues. At 11.56 repeated Lord Nelson's telegraph message, "England expects that every man will do his duty." At noon light winds and a great swell from the westward; observed the Royal Sovereign, Admiral Collingwood, leading the lee line, bearing down on the enemy's rear line, being then nearly within gun-shot of them; Lord Nelson leading the weather line, bore down on the enemy's centre. Captain Blackwood returned from the Victory—Cape Trafalgar SE by E about five leagues.

'P.M. Light winds and hazy; British fleet bearing down in two lines on the enemy's, which was formed in one line from NNE to SSE. . . . At 12.15 the British fleet bearing down on the enemy; Vice-Admiral Lord Viscount Nelson leading the weather line in the Victory, and Vice-Admiral Collingwood the lee line. At 12.15 the enemy opened a heavy fire on the Royal Sovereign. At 12.16 the English admirals hoisted their respective flags, and the British fleet the British ensign (white). At 12.17 Admiral Collingwood returned the enemy's fire in a brave and steady manner. At 12.20 we repeated Lord Nelson's signal for the British fleet to engage close, which was answered by the whole fleet. At 12.21 the van and centre of the enemy's line opened a heavy fire upon the Victory, and the ships she was leading into action. At 12.22 Admiral Collingwood and the headmost ships of his line broke through the rear of the enemy's, when the action commenced in a most severe and determined manner. At 12.23 Lord Nelson returned the enemy's fire in the centre and van in a determined, cool, and steady manner. At 12.24 Lord Nelson and the headmost of the line he led into action broke into the van and centre of the enemy's line, and commenced the action in that quarter in a steady and gallant manner—observed the Africa coming into the line, she being to leeward with all sail set, on the starboard tack (free), we kept Lord Nelson's signal flying at the main royal masthead, for the British fleet to engage close. At 12.26 observed one of the French ships totally dismasted about the centre of the line, by some of the ships of our lee line, and another of them with her foreyard and mizen topmast shot away. At 1.15 observed the Tonnant's fore topmast shot away; at 1.20 a Spanish three-decked ship with her mizen mast shot away; at 1.25 observed an English ship with her fore and mizen mast shot away; at 1.32 her main yard shot away; the centre and rear of the enemy's line hard pressed in action. At 2 the Africa engaged very close a French two-decked ship, and in about 5 minutes time shot away her main and mizen masts; at 2.10 observed the Mars hard pressed in action. The remainder of the British fleet, which were come into action, kept up a well-directed fire on the enemy. At 2.15 the Neptune, supported by the Colossus, opened a heavy fire on the Santissima Trinidad, and two other of the enemy's line which were next her; at 2.20 the Trinidad's main and mizen masts shot away; at 2.30 the Africa shot away the fore mast of the two-decked ship she was engaged with, and left her a complete wreck; she then bore up under the Trinidad's stern, and raked her fore and aft; Colossus and Neptune still engaged with her, and the other two ships, which appeared by their

Euryalus's Log, 21 Oct.

22 Oct.

colours to be French. At 2.34 the Trinidad's fore mast shot away, and one of the French ship's main and mizen masts; observed nine of the enemy's van wear and stand down towards the centre; observed the Royal Sovereign with her main and mizen mast gone. At 2.36 answered Lord Nelson's signal to pass within hail; made all possible sail, and made the signal to the Sirius, Phœbe, and Naiad, to take ships in tow which were disabled ENE, which they answered ; sounded in 50 fms. At 2.40 observed a French two-deck ship on fire and dismasted in the SSE quarter; passed the Spartiate and another two-deck ship standing towards the enemy's van, and opened a heavy fire, when the action in that quarter commenced very severe. At 2.50 passed by the Mars, who hailed us to take them in tow; Captain Blackwood answered that he would do it with pleasure, but that he was going to take the second in command, the Royal Sovereign; the officer that hailed us from the Mars said that Captain Duff was no more. At 3 came alongside the Royal Sovereign and took her in tow; Captain Blackwood was hailed by Admiral Collingwood, and ordered to go on board the St. Anna, Spanish three-deck ship, and bring him the admiral, which Captain Blackwood obeyed. At 3.30 the enemy's van approached as far as the centre, and opened a heavy fire on the Victory, Neptune, Spartiate, Colossus, Mars, Africa, Agamemnon, and Royal Sovereign, which we had in tow, and was most nobly returned. We had several of our main and topmast rigging cut away, and backstays, by the enemy's shot, and there being no time to haul down the studding-sails, as the enemy's van ships hauled up for us, we cut them away, and let them go overboard, at which time one of the enemy's nearest ships to us was totally dismasted. At 4 light variable winds; not possible to manage the Royal Sovereign so as to bring her broadside to bear on the enemy's ships. At 4.10 we had the stream cable by which the Royal Sovereign was towed shot away, and a cutter from the quarter ; wore ship, and stood for the Victory; observed the Phœbe, and Sirius, and Naiad coming into the centre and taking some of the disabled ships in tow; at this time the firing ceased a little. At 4.20 observed a Spanish two-deck ship dismasted and struck to one of our ships ; observed several of the enemy's ships still hard engaged. At 5   of the enemy's van and   of their rear, bore up and made all sail to the northward ; were closely followed by the English, which opened a heavy fire upon them, and dismasted a French two-deck ship and a Spanish two-deck ship. At 5.20 the Achille, French two-deck ship, which was on fire, blew up with a great explosion. At 5.25 made sail for the Royal Sovereign; observed the Victory's mizen-mast go overboard, about which time the firing ceased, leaving the English fleet conquerors, with   sail of the enemy's ships in our possession, and one blown up, two of which were first-rates, and all dismasted. At 5.55 Admiral Collingwood came on board and hoisted his flag (blue at the fore).'

It is unnecessary to give more extracts from the several logs; the others but repeat the same story, with more or less exaggerated inaccuracies and discrepancies, more especially in point of time. In the confusion and excitement of the day, the masters in writing up the logs have made the most astounding and perplexing mistakes; have written lee when they meant weather, larboard when they meant starboard, and apparently noted the times at wild guess. The Royal Sovereign noted that she was in close action for 40 minutes before she received any support from the Belleisle: the Belleisle, on the other hand, has recorded that she was two cables astern of the Royal Sovereign, and began the action just one minute after her. The recorded differences in the interval between the Royal Sovereign's and the Victory's breaking through the enemy's line are equally great and more remarkable. They vary from two minutes to forty: probably 10, as recorded by the Britannia, Lord Northesk's flagship, is the nearest approach to correctness that can be made. We must however be content to recognise the fact that questions of exact time cannot possibly be answered; but that the Phœbe had made it noon by the sun (latitude 36° 15′) a few minutes before the Royal Sovereign began her work, and that somewhere about 5 the firing ceased.

The exact wording of the celebrated telegraph has often been warmly and angrily discussed. It is not a question for discussion at all, but one of simple evidence. The Naiad and Euryalus, the repeating frigates, noted it in their log, and that they repeated it. Other ships also noted it. The Orion noted the code numbers. There is thus no possible doubt about the matter. The words were 'England expects that every man will do his duty.' Many inaccurate versions were, of course, quoted from memory by the several officers of the fleet, and these have been repeated till people have begun to doubt whether they are not the real thing. The most extraordinary, and in a way, the best authenticated of all of these is the inscription on a ring which belonged to Collingwood and was presumably engraved by his order. It reads: 'England expects everything: men, do your duty.' Whether this version is Collingwood's or not, it is very certainly not Nelson's; it is not the signal which was made at Trafalgar.

'The ever-to-be-lamented death of Vice-Admiral Lord Viscount Nelson, who, in the late conflict with the enemy, fell in the hour of victory, leaves to me the duty of informing my Lords Commissioners of the Admiralty, that on the 19th instant it was communicated to the commander-in-chief from the ships watching the motions of the enemy in Cadiz, that the combined fleet had put to sea. As they sailed with light winds westerly, his Lordship concluded their destination was the Mediterranean, and immediately made all sail for the Straits' entrance with the British squadron, consisting of twenty-seven ships, three of them sixty-fours, where his Lordship was informed by Captain Blackwood (whose vigilance in watching, and giving notice of the enemy's movements has been highly meritorious), that they had not yet passed the Straits.

'On Monday the 21st instant, at daylight, when Cape Trafalgar bore E by S about seven leagues, the enemy was discovered six or seven miles to the eastward, the wind about west, and very light; the commander-in-chief immediately made the signal for the fleet to bear up in two columns, as they are formed in order of sailing; a mode of attack his Lordship had previously directed, to avoid the inconvenience and delay in forming a line of battle in the usual manner. The enemy's line consisted of thirty-three ships (of which eighteen were French and fifteen Spanish), commanded in chief by Admiral Villeneuve; the Spaniards, under the direction of Gravina, wore, with their heads to the northward, and formed their line of battle with great closeness and correctness; but as

V.-Adml. Collingwood to W. Marsden, 22 Oct.

the mode of attack was unusual, so the structure of their line was new —it formed a crescent convexing to leeward—so that, in leading down to their centre, I had both their van and rear abaft the beam. Before the fire opened, every alternate ship was about a cable's length to windward of her second ahead and astern, forming a kind of double line, and appeared, when on their beam, to leave a very little interval between them; and this without crowding their ships. Admiral Villeneuve was in the Bucentaure in the centre, and the Prince of Asturias bore Gravina's flag in the rear; but the French and Spanish ships were mixed without any apparent regard to order of national squadron.

'As the mode of attack had been previously determined on and communicated to the flag officers and captains, few signals were necessary, and none were made except to direct close order as the lines bore down.

'The commander-in-chief in the Victory led the weather column; and the Royal Sovereign, which bore my flag, the lee.

'The action began at twelve o'clock, by the leading ships of the columns breaking through the enemy's line, the commander-in-chief about the tenth ship from the van, the second in command about the twelfth from the rear, leaving the van of the enemy unoccupied; the succeeding ships breaking through in all parts, astern of their leaders, and engaging the enemy at the muzzles of their guns, the conflict was severe. The enemy's ships were fought with a gallantry highly honourable to their officers, but the attack on them was irresistible; and it pleased the Almighty Disposer of all events to grant his Majesty's arms a complete and glorious victory. About 3 P.M., many of the enemy's ships having struck their colours, their line gave way; Admiral Gravina, with ten ships, joining their frigates to leeward, stood towards Cadiz. The five headmost ships in their van tacked, and standing to the southward to windward of the British line, were engaged, and the sternmost of them taken; the others went off, leaving to his Majesty's squadron nineteen ships of the line (of which two are first-rates, the Santissima Trinidad and the Santa Anna), with three flag officers; viz. Admiral Villeneuve, the commander-in-chief; Don Ignatio Maria d'Alava, vice-admiral; and the Spanish rear-admiral, Don Baltazar Hidalgo Cisneros.

'After such a victory it may appear unnecessary to enter into encomiums on the particular parts taken by the several commanders; the conclusion says more on the subject than I have language to express; the spirit which animated all was the same. When all exert themselves zealously in their country's service, all deserve that their high merits should stand recorded; and never was high merit more conspicuous than in the battle I have described.

'Such a battle could not be fought without sustaining a great loss of men. I have not only to lament, in common with the British navy and the British nation, in the fall of the commander-in-chief, the loss of a hero whose name will be immortal, and his memory ever dear to his country, but my heart is rent with the most poignant grief for the death of a friend to whom, by many years' intimacy and a perfect knowledge of the virtues of his mind, which inspired ideas superior to the common race of men, I was bound by the strongest ties of affection ;—a grief to which even the glorious occasion in which he fell does not bring the consolation which perhaps it ought : his Lordship received a musket ball in his left breast about the middle of the action, and sent an officer to me immediately with his last farewell, and soon after expired.

'I have also to lament the loss of those excellent officers, Captains Duff of the Mars and Cooke of the Bellerophon: I have yet heard of none others.

'I fear the numbers that have fallen will be found very great when the returns come to me; but it having blown a gale of wind ever since the action, I have not yet had it in my power to collect any reports from the ships.

'The Royal Sovereign having lost her masts, except the tottering foremast, I called the Euryalus to me, while the action continued, which ship lying within hail, made my signals, a service Captain Blackwood performed with great attention. After the action I shifted my flag to her, that I might more easily communicate my orders to, and collect the ships, and towed the Royal Sovereign out to seaward. The whole fleet were now in a very perilous situation; many dismasted, all shattered; in thirteen fathoms water, off the shoals of Trafalgar; and when I made the signal to prepare to anchor, few of the ships had an anchor to let go, their cables being shot. But the same good Providence which aided us through such a day preserved us in the night, by the wind shifting a few points, and drifting the ships off the land, except four of the captured dismasted ships, which are now at anchor off Trafalgar, and I hope will ride safe until those gales are over.'

'In my letter of the 22nd, I detailed to you, for the information of my Lords Commissioners of the Admiralty, the proceedings of his Majesty's squadron on the day of the action, and that preceding it, since which I have had a continued series of misfortunes, but they are of a kind that human prudence could not possibly provide against, or my skill prevent.

24 Oct.

'On the 22nd, in the morning, a strong southerly wind blew, with squally weather, which however did not prevent the activity of the officers and seamen of such ships as were manageable from getting hold of many of the prizes (thirteen or fourteen), and towing them off to the westward, where I ordered them to rendezvous round the Royal Sovereign, in tow by the Neptune; but on the 23rd the gale increased, and the sea ran so high that many of them broke the tow-rope and drifted far to leeward before they were got hold of again; and some of them, taking advantage of the dark and boisterous night, got before the wind, and have perhaps drifted upon the shore and sunk. On the afternoon of that day the remnant of the combined fleet, ten sail of ships, who had not been much engaged, stood up to leeward of my shattered and straggled charge, as if meaning to attack them, which obliged me to collect a force out of the least injured ships, and form to leeward for their defence. All this retarded the progress of the hulks, and the bad weather continuing, determined me to destroy all the leewardmost that could be cleared of the men, considering that keeping possession of the ships was a matter of little consequence compared with the chance of their falling again into the hands of the enemy. But even this was an arduous task in the high sea which was running. I hope, however, it has been accomplished to a considerable extent. I entrusted it to skilful officers, who would spare no pains to execute what was possible. The captains of the Prince and Neptune cleared the Trinidad and sunk her. Captains Hope, Bayntun, and Malcolm, who joined the fleet this moment from Gibraltar, had the charge of destroying four others. The Redoutable sunk astern of the Swiftsure while in tow. The Santa Anna, I have no doubt, is sunk, as her side was almost entirely beat in; and such is the shattered condition of the whole of them, that unless the weather moderates, I doubt whether I shall be able to carry a ship of them into port. I hope their Lordships will approve of what I (having only in consideration the destruction of the enemy's fleet) have thought a measure of absolute necessity.

'I have taken Admiral Villeneuve into this ship; Vice-Admiral Don Alava is dead. Whenever the temper of the weather will permit, and I can spare a frigate, (for there were only four in the action with the fleet, Euryalus, Sirius, Phœbe, and Naiad; the Melpomene joined the 22nd, and the Eurydice and Scout the 23rd,) I shall collect the other flag officers and send them to England with their flags, (if they do not all go to the bottom,) to be laid at his Majesty's feet.

'There were four thousand troops embarked, under the command of General Contamin, who was taken with Admiral Villeneuve in the Bucentaure.'

28 Oct.

'Since my letter to you of the 24th, stating the proceedings of his Majesty's squadron, our situation has been the most critical, and our employment the most arduous, that ever a fleet was engaged in. On the 24th and 25th it blew a most violent gale of wind, which completely dispersed the ships and drove the captured hulls in all directions.

'I have since been employed in collecting and destroying them, where they are at anchor upon the coast between Cadiz and six leagues westward of San Lucar, without the prospect of saving one to bring into port. I mentioned in my former letter the joining of the Donegal and Melpomene, after the action; I cannot sufficiently praise the activity of their commanders in giving assistance to the squadron in destroying the enemy's ships. The Defiance, after having stuck to the Aigle as long as it was possible, in hope of saving her from wreck, which separated her for some time from the squadron, was obliged to abandon her to her fate, and she went on shore. Captain Durham's exertions have been very great. I hope I shall get them all destroyed by tomorrow, if the weather keeps moderate. In the gale the Royal Sovereign and Mars lost their foremasts, and are now rigging anew where the body of the squadron is at anchor to the NW of San Lucar.

'I find that on the return of Gravina to Cadiz he was immediately ordered to sea again, and came out, which made it necessary for me to form a line to cover the disabled hulls: that night it blew hard, and his ship, the Prince of Asturias, was dismasted and returned into port; the Rayo was also dismasted and fell into our hands; Don Enrique M'Donel had his broad pennant in the Rayo, and from him I find the Santa Anna was driven near Cadiz, and towed in by a frigate.'

4 Nov.

'Rear-Admiral Louis in the Canopus, who had been detached with the Queen, Spencer, and Tigre, to complete the water &c. of these ships, and to see the convoy in safety a certain distance up the Mediterranean, joined me on the 30th.

'In clearing the captured ships of prisoners, I found so many wounded men, that to alleviate human misery as much as was in my power, I sent to the Marquis de Solana, governor-general of Andalusia, to offer him the wounded to the care of their country, on receipts being given;— a proposal which was received with the greatest thankfulness, not only by the governor, but the whole country resounds with expressions of gratitude. Two French frigates were sent out to receive them, with a proper officer to give receipts, bringing with them all the English who had been wrecked in several of the ships, and an offer from the Marquis de Solana of the use of their hospitals for our wounded, pledging the honour of Spain for their being carefully attended.

'I have ordered most of the Spanish prisoners to be released; the officers on parole, the men for receipts given, and a condition that they do not serve in war, by sea or land, until exchanged. By my correspondence with the Marquis, I find that Vice-Admiral d'Alava is not dead, but dangerously wounded.'

Abstract of English Loss.

	Killed.	Wounded.
Officers	21	43
Seamen	315	959
Marines	113	212
Total	449	1,214

Abstract of State of Combined Fleet.

At Gibraltar	4
Destroyed	16
In Cadiz, wrecks	6
„ serviceable	3
Escaped to the southward	4
	33

And it may be noted that these four which 'escaped to the southward' were captured by Sir Richard Strachan on 4 November.

It only remains to add, as personal to Lord Nelson, that his body was sent to England, was landed at Greenwich on 23 December; and after lying in state for three days in the Painted Hall, was, on 8 January 1806, conveyed by water, with great state, to Whitehall Stairs, whence it was carried to the Admiralty, and on the next day, 9 January, to St. Paul's Cathedral, where it was deposited in the crypt. At a later date were laid, one on each side of it, the bodies of Lord Collingwood and the Earl of Northesk, Nelson's companions in arms at Trafalgar.

INDEX.

[*The biographical references in small capitals are to Charnock's* 'Biographia Navalis;' *Marshall's* 'Royal Naval Biography;' *O'Byrne's* 'Dictionary of Naval Biography;' *Ralfe's* 'Naval Biography;' *Stephen's* 'Dictionary of National Biography,' *now in course of publication; and to special memoirs by the authors named.*]

ACRE; defence of, by Sir Sidney Smith, 209, 211
Acton, Sir John Francis Edward, Bart., Neapolitan prime minister [STEPHEN]; letters to, 306, 354, 384
Addington, Right Hon. Henry, First Lord of the Treasury 1801-4; [afterwards Viscount Sidmouth, STEPHEN]; letters to, 261-6, 271-2, 278, 285, 288, 291, 308-11, 316, 322, 324
Admiralty; complaints against, 80; reprimand Nelson for disobedience of orders, 206; seamen suspicious of, 285; interfere with Nelson's dispositions, 338; tyrannical conduct, 363
Agamemnon; Nelson commissions, 6, 47; cruises in the Channel, 48; goes out to the Mediterranean, 49; is sent to Naples for troops, 51; blockades a French frigate in Leghorn, 52; engagement with Melpomene, 54; first action off Toulon, 74-9; second ditto, 83, 85; is chased by the French fleet, 82; is quite rotten, 94; captures a number of storeships, 100; Nelson moves into Captain, 102; joins the fleet off Cadiz, 424. *See* Nelson, Horatio, Viscount
Agincourt Sound; surveyed by Captain Ryves, 327; [cf. James, iii. 178]
Albemarle; Nelson commissions, 4, 13; captures a mast ship, 17; unsuccessful attack on Turk's Island, *ib.*; is paid off, 5, 18. *See* Nelson, Horatio, Viscount
Alcide; burning of, 83
Algiers; insolence of, 225; the Dey ought to be punished, 226; decisive measures recommended, 226, 307-8; Nelson instructed to take vigorous measures, 323; proposes to seize all his cruisers, 335; the Dey did not send his cruisers to sea, 351; doubtful news of his fleet being at sea, 380
Alliances, continental; futility of, 89, 99
Ambuscade; recaptured by Victory, 350; captures a merchant ship, held to be a droit of Admiralty, 350-1
Amphion; Nelson hoists his flag on board, 306; goes back to Victory, 315
Anchoring; directions for, in an attack on the enemy at anchor, 344; signal to prepare for, 432
Andrews, George; midshipman of Boreas, wounded in a duel, 32; lieutenant of Agamemnon, 88. [Captain, 1796; died 1810]
Andrews, Miss [sister of George]; Nelson wishes to marry, 21
Armistice; at Naples, opinion on the, 197; is infamous, 197, 200; is annulled by signal, 198; and by declaration sent to the rebels and Jacobins, *ib.*; was fully annulled and known to be so by the rebels when they came out unconditionally, 202; at Copenhagen, 265; its advantages, 265, 271, 273; not fairly kept by the Danes, 279-81
Austrians; Nelson co-operates with the, on coast of Genoa, 83-99; deceitful conduct of their court, 89; are defeated by the French, 92-4, 97, 99, 105; complain of want of effective co-operation by the fleet, 93; prisoners of war sold to the

442   INDEX

BAI

Spaniards, 101; are recaptured by Agamemnon and squadron, 100-1

BAIRD, ANDREW, Dr.; letters to, 295, 316, 340, 351, 371

Baldwin, George, consul at Alexandria; letter to, 139

Ball, Sir Alexander John, captain of Alexander, later Rear-Admiral and Governor of Malta [STEPHEN]; wears epaulettes in France, 21; a great coxcomb, *ib.*; takes Vanguard in tow, 134; Nelson's warm affection for, 279; letters to, 168, 181-2, 192, 211, 279, 320, 324, 328, 337, 352, 361, 366, 368, 372, 378, 380, 386-8, 394, 398, 400, 413, 424-5

Baltic; orders to Sir Hyde Parker to proceed to the, 247; Nelson's scheme of operations in, 248-9; is appointed commander-in-chief in, 271; returns from, 281

Barham, Lord, First Lord of the Admiralty, 30 April 1805; letters to, 406, 414, 419. *See* Middleton, Sir Charles

Barrington, Samuel, Admiral the Hon. [STEPHEN]; 'gets amongst the youngsters,' 15; advocates the free postage of seamen's letters, 356 *n*; gets false news from Dominica, 401 *n*

Bastia; report on strength of, 57; Hood determines to lay siege to, 59; General Dundas refuses to co-operate, *ib.*; so also General d'Aubant, 60; Nelson landed for siege of, 61; siege of, 61-3; capitulation of, 62; Nelson discontented with Hood's despatch, 63

Bayntun, Henry William, captain of Leviathan [STEPHEN]; letter to, 391

Beckford, William [of Fonthill; STEPHEN]; letter to, 277

Berry, Sir Edward, lieutenant of Agamemnon, captain of Vanguard, Foudroyant, and of Agamemnon at Trafalgar [STEPHEN]; a volunteer at St. Vincent, 115 and *note*; his marriage, 131 and *note*; his narrative of the battle of the Nile, 146-155; is sent home with despatches, 146, 155; captured in the Leander, 155 *n*; captures the Guillaume Tell, 237. Letters to, 131, 145, 233, 244, 246, 287, 293, 303, 363. Letter from, 237

Bertie, Thomas, Captain [afterwards Vice-Admiral Sir Thomas, an early

BYR

shipmate of Nelson in Seahorse; STEPHEN]; letter to, 131

Bickerton, Sir Richard [STEPHEN]; twice passed over by the City of London, 361; recommended for the command of the Mediterranean, 366; left in temporary command, 399. Letter to, 342

Bighi; establishment of naval hospital at, 332

Black Sea; Nelson desires intelligence concerning, 340; receives a report concerning, 378

Blackwood, Hon. Sir Henry, captain of Penelope and Euryalus [STEPHEN]; brings the Guillaume Tell to action, 238; brings news of the French fleet, 411; commands the frigates inshore, 419; to keep in sight of the enemy, 426; witness to Nelson's last wishes, 428. Letters to, 238, 419, 423-5. *See* Euryalus

Bolton, Sir William, commander of Childers brig [nephew, by her marriage, of Nelson's sister Susannah, wife of Thomas Bolton, whose daughter Catherine he married; knighted in May 1803, as proxy for Lord Nelson at his installation as K.B.; posted 10 April 1805; died Dec. 1830]; letter to, 345

Bombay; letter to the governor of, 162; supposed design of the French on, 163

Bonaparte; capture of maps and books for, 101; capture of his despatches, 162-3; his first experience of an English officer, 163; returns to France, 227; his staff and despatches captured, 228

Boreas; Nelson commissions, 5, 23; and commands in the West Indies, 25-40; is paid off, 41

Boulogne; projects for an attack on, 285; repulse at, 289-91; proposal to keep it 'in hot water,' 295

Bowen, Richard, captain of Terpsichore; slain at Santa Cruz, 127

Brereton, Robert, Brig.-General; sends false news from St. Lucia, 401, 404-7

Bronte; Nelson, Duke of, 7; estate of, 315

Burgh, John Thomas de, Lieut.-General [afterwards Earl of Clanricarde]; commands the garrison at Porto Ferrajo, 112; refuses to abandon the place, *ib.* Letter to, *ib.*

Byron, William, lieutenant in the army, heir to the title of Lord Byron; slain at Calvi, 70

ÇA

ÇA IRA; capture of the, 78-9
Cadiz; Nelson visits the dockyard at, 49; commands the inshore squadron off, 6, 122-5; is bombarded, 123; squadron from —, joins the French, 398; Nelson joins Collingwood off —, 405; Nelson resumes the command before, 413; combined fleet in —, preparing for sea, 419; puts to sea, 426
Calder, Sir Robert, First Captain to Sir John Jervis, later Vice-Admiral [STEPHEN]; anecdote of, 120; action off Cape Finisterre, 409; applies for a court-martial, 414; returns to England in Prince of Wales, 414, 416, 424; charge 'of a very serious nature,' 425. Letter to, 125
Calvi; siege of, 65-70; danger from climate, 69-70; surrender of, 70
Campbell, Donald, Commodore, and later Rear-Admiral in the Portuguese service; too hastily burns the Neapolitan ships of war, 181; is sent to Tripoli, 191; gives intelligence of the French fleet, 400
Campbell, George, Rear-Admiral; letter to, 348
Capel, Hon. Thomas Bladen, flag-lieutenant at the Nile, promoted to the command of the Mutine brig and sent home with duplicate despatches, 162; later, captain of Phœbe. Letter to, 397
Captain; Nelson hoists his broad pennant on board, 6, 102; and commands her at St. Vincent, 114; she is severely damaged, 117; Nelson removes to Theseus, 122.
Capua; surrenders to Troubridge, 209
Caracciolo, Francisco, Prince [commodore in the Neapolitan navy]; is serving as a common soldier, 190; is a Jacobin, 193; in the gunboats at Castellamare, ib.; ordered to be tried by court-martial, 201; is tried and condemned to death, 202; ordered to be hanged, ib.; and hanged accordingly, 201
Carysfort, Lord, Envoy Extraordinary to the King of Prussia; letter to, 273
Castlereagh, Viscount [Foreign Secretary 1805]; letter to, 415
Censeur; capture of, 78-9
Clarence, H.R.H. the Duke of [afterwards William IV.]; letters to; revolutionary feeling among the peasantry, 45-6; the French in Golfe Jouan, 70, 73, 79, 80; Ho-

COR

tham's second action, 83; affairs in Genoa, 90-1; in Corsica, 104, 106, 110; the fleet off Cadiz, 119; affairs in Sicily, 190; in the Mediterranean, 216; soldiers and sailors, 222; 'the name of Rodney,' 303; French designs in the Mediterranean, 312; severe gales in Gulf of Lion, 330, 365. *See* William Henry, Prince
Climate; of Corsica, 69; the lion sun, 70; intense cold above Genoa, 90
Cochrane, Hon. Sir Alexander F. I., Rear-Admiral [STEPHEN]; in command off Ferrol, 376; sends news of the Spanish ships having dropped down the harbour, ib.; which leads to the seizure of the treasure ships, 377; and war with Spain, 379; joins Nelson in the West Indies, 401
Cocks, George, commander of the Thunder bomb; letter to, 346
Codrington, Sir Edward, Admiral, captain of Orion at Trafalgar [BOURCHIER]; letter from, 430
Collingwood, Cuthbert, Lord, captain of Mediator and Excellent; later, vice-admiral [COLLINGWOOD]; 'an amiable good man,' 25; commands the Excellent at St. Vincent, 115, 117; his firm discipline, 245; falls in with Nelson off Cadiz, 405; his judgment of the French plans, 405-6. Letters to, 87, 99, 110, 117, 392, 405, 412-14, 422, 424. Letters from, 117, 405-6, 435-9
Colours; Irish, with thirteen stripes, hoisted at St. Kitts, 32; national —, struck at Rogliano, 56; of Vesuvian Republic, 182; neutral —, abuses of, 326-7; none to be shown by the ships off Cadiz, 413; white ensign to be worn in presence of the enemy, 153 n, 329, 423, 433
Combustibles; used by the French, 80, 83; Nelson will not use shell at sea, 319; fireships and rockets off Cadiz, 415, 425
Connor, Charles [Lady Hamilton's cousin]; letter to, 331
Copenhagen; battle of, 250-61, 266-70; English loss in, 259; question of medal for, 295; and thanks of the City of London, 296-7, 300
Corbet, Robert, commander of Bittern [STEPHEN]; complaints against for violation of neutrality, 375, 393
Cork, Earl of; letter to, relative to his son's education, 40
Cornwallis, Hon. William, Admiral [STEPHEN]; captain of Lion, 4, 11;

COR

tried by court-martial, 99; commander-in-chief off Brest, 306, 409; Admiralty orders to, 377; sends the Indefatigable frigate off Cadiz, 376

Corsica; operations on coast of, 55–71; produces very fine timber, 74; French reaction in, 99, 104–5, 108; evacuation of, 109

Courage; conspicuous, 6; political as necessary as military, 84

Culloden; at St. Vincent, 115, 119; sent into Mediterranean and joins the squadron under Nelson, 137, 140, 147; gets ashore at the battle of the Nile, 154, 157; refitted at Naples, 167; ashore in Marsa Scirocco, 228–9. *See* Troubridge, Sir Thomas

DARBY, HENRY D'ESTERRE, captain of Bellerophon at the Nile; letter to, 213

Davison, Alexander, Nelson's agent, banker and confidential friend; letters to, 164, 214, 239–40, 245–6, 270–1, 275, 293, 295, 297, 313, 315, 330, 342, 367, 382, 391, 399, 407, 411–12

Dean, Forest of; state of, 297–300

Defence flotilla; Nelson appointed to command, 281; memorandum respecting, 282–4

Denmark, Crown Prince of; Nelson dines and has a long conversation with, 261; armistice concluded with, 265. Letters to, 257, 259

Deserters; return of —, by Spain shall be reciprocal, 318; punishment of —, left to their own feelings, 319; in future — will be tried by court-martial, 329; Sardinian — restored, 368; complaint of a search made for —, 374; which has in all countries been tolerated, 375

Desertion; loss by — during the war, 301; memo respecting, 319, 328

Discipline; as established by the commander-in-chief punctually attended to, 167; question of foreign officers commanding English, 170–1, 172, 179, 190; — of Vanguard, 195; 'young men will be young men,' 233; soldiers serving on board ship subject to naval —, 346–50, 355; Spider's ship's company flogged by the watch bill, 372

Disobedience of orders, 203–7; Nelson is reprimanded for, 206; he defends his conduct, accepting the

EPA

responsibility, 214; his views on, 221; reputed — at Copenhagen, 256 and *note*; 'if the king's service clearly marks what ought to be done,' 324

Donnelly, Ross, captain of Narcissus [afterwards Admiral Sir Ross]; letters to, 317, 356

Drake, François, Minister at Genoa; report of conference with, 95. Letters to, 84, 86, 90, 97–8, 106. Letter from, 93

Droit of Admiralty; Ambuscade's prize held to be a —, 350–1

Duckworth, Sir John Thomas, Commodore, later Rear-Admiral; letters to, 173–4, 182, 191, 197–8, 207, 210, 212, 340

Duff, George, captain of Mars; commands the inshore squadron off Cadiz, 418 and *note*; slain at Trafalgar, 434, 437. Letter to, 418

Duncan, the Hon. Henry, Lieutenant [afterwards Captain]; a legacy to the service, 334. Letter to, 373

Dundas, Sir David, General; retires from before Bastia, 58; considers the siege 'a visionary and rash attempt,' 59; refuses to co-operate, *ib.*; gives up the command of the troops, 60

Durban, William, captain of Ambuscade; letter to, 370

Dutch East Indiaman; dispute with a, 23–4

EDEN, SIR MORTON, Minister at Vienna; letter to, 173

Education of a young naval officer, 40

Elephant; Nelson hoists his flag on board, 251; his flagship in the battle of Copenhagen, 255

Elgin, Earl of, Minister at Constantinople; wishes a larger squadron in the Levant, 227. Letter to, 228

Elliot, Sir Gilbert, Viceroy of Corsica; later, Earl of Minto [afterwards Governor-General of India]; a spectator at St. Vincent, 113. Letters to, 64, 69, 85–6, 88, 92, 99, 103–4, 106, 108, 117. *See* Minto, Lord

Elliot, Hugh [brother of Sir Gilbert], Minister at Naples; letters to, 307, 313–14, 327, 329, 333, 341, 352, 354, 357–8, 367, 374–5, 381, 384, 393, 396

Epaulettes; worn by Captains Ball and Shepard, 21; first worn in the English navy, *ib. n.*

INDEX 445

Erskine, Sir James St. Clair, Lieut.-General, commandant at Minorca [afterwards Earl of Rosslyn]; refuses to send troops to Malta, 219, 232. Letters to, 213, 216, 218. Letter from, 219
Euryalus; sails from St. Helens in company with Victory, 412; her log at Trafalgar, 433-4; Collingwood hoists his flag on board, 434, 437. *See* Blackwood, Hon. Sir Henry
Excellent; at St. Vincent, 115, 117, 119
Extortion; attempt at, 293

FARMER, GEORGE, captain of Seahorse [slain in fight, when in command of Quebec, 1779], 2
Fees for honours conferred by the king; Nelson refuses to pay, 245
Fencibles; *see* Sea-fencibles
Fischer, Johan Olfert, commodore [born 1747; died, vice-admiral, 1829]; commands the Danish fleet at Copenhagen, 255; his account of the battle, 259-261; Nelson's reply, 266-8
FitzGerald, Lord Robert, Minister at Lisbon; letter to, 402
Flag of truce at Copenhagen, 258, 270, 272-3
Fleet; well manned and healthy, 344; needs large reinforcements, 358; the finest — in the world, 394; a very powerful —, 424. The combined —, 'a very pretty fiddle,' 402; must be unwieldy, *ib.*; in a sickly state, 403, 406; must be annihilated, 420. *See* French; Health; Sickness
Flushing; proposed attack on, 291; is not feasible, 292
Foote, Edward James, captain of Seahorse [afterwards Vice-Admiral Sir E. J.; author of 'Vindication of his Conduct']; senior officer in the Bay of Naples, 196; signed a treaty with the rebels, 197. Letter to, 196
Foreign; question of English rank for — officers, *see* Discipline; troops in garrison at Gibraltar, 308
Foudroyant; Nelson hoists his flag on board, 196; captures Généreux, 234-5; captures Guillaume Tell, 237-8; has many defects and ought to go to England, 242; carries the Queen of Naples and suite to Leghorn, *ib.*; must be refitted at Ma-

hon, 243; letter from barge's crew, *ib.*; Nelson strikes his flag, *ib.*
Fox, Charles James; attack by — on Nelson, in the House of Commons, 239
Fox, Hon. Edward Henry, Lieut.-General; letter to, 227
Frauds on Government; *see* Wilkinson. Alleged, 208-9; correspondence with Victualling Board concerning, 223-4
Fremantle, Thomas Francis, captain of Inconstant, Ganges, and Neptune [afterwards Vice-Admiral Sir T. F.]; conducts the evacuation of Leghorn, 103 and *note*. Letter to, 409
French; extreme youth of — soldiers, 94; — will make a great effort to get into Italy, *ib.*; Nelson grieves when they have any good fortune by sea, 97; believes accounts of their victories, 99. Expedition to Egypt sails from Toulon, 137; captures Malta, 139; — fleet destroyed at the Nile, 145-6; — army not to be permitted to leave Egypt, 186-7, 232, 237; to be hoped they will all die there, 228; Western fleet comes into the Mediterranean, 192; danger to Minorca, *ib.*; checks the operations at Naples, 194-7; probable designs on Sicily, 194-7; force in Toulon is equal if not superior, 312; the fleet from St. Domingo may come to the Mediterranean, 314; a 74-gun ship at Cadiz, 315; fleet at Toulon ready for sea, 317; appears as if near putting to sea, 324; Nelson would like a copy of the — admiral's instructions, 324, 352, 369; speculations on the destination of the fleet, 325; fleets at all the ports ready for sea, 358; they probably mean to go to the West Indies, 369; sailed from Toulon, 384, 387; put back in a very crippled state, 389; again put to sea, 395; pass Gibraltar, 397; join the Spaniards at Cadiz, 398; and sail for the West Indies, 400; their object in the West Indies is incomprehensible, 403; Nelson thinks they are returning to Europe, 404
Frenchman; 'lay a — close and you will beat him,' 183; the only way of dealing with a, 210; 'close with a —,' 253; the London mob drag a —'s carriage, 295; will not have one in the fleet, 324, 352, 369
Frere, John Hookham, Minister at Madrid; letters to, 329, 341

FRI

Frigates; leave Nelson's squadron in the Mediterranean, 137; want of —, 163; want of — has permitted Bonaparte to return to France, 227; Nelson much distressed for want of, 333; and of small craft, 369; narrow escape of French —, 324

GAETA; capitulates, 209
Gales; frequent in the Gulf of Lion, 330; shelter from, *ib.*
Gardner, Alan, commodore at Jamaica [afterwards Admiral Lord —; died 1809]; letter to, 38
Gazette; 'one day I will have a — to myself,' 104
Généreux; escapes from the battle of the Nile, 153, 160; captures Leander, 155 *n*; escapes from the Russians at Ancona, 195; at Toulon, heaving down, 214; capture of, 234-5
Genoa; Nelson commands a squadron on the coast, 83-107; complaints of his conduct, 86; breaches of neutrality, 91, 102, 106-7; it has not even a name of independence, 310; should be blockaded, 311; ordered to be blockaded, 323
Gibbs, Abraham, Nelson's agent in Sicily; letter to, 315
Gibert, J. B., consul at Barcelona, letter to, 318. [The name in the text is erroneously printed Gilbert]
Gibraltar; imprudence of garrisoning with foreign regiments, 308
Glasgow; burning of the, 4, 10
Gore, John, captain of Medusa; letters to, 314, 340, 376
Graham, Thomas, Brig.-General [afterwards Lord Lynedoch]; letters to, 224, 236
Guillaume Tell; escapes from the battle of the Nile, 153, 160; is captured, 237-8
Guns; method of pointing, 246

HALLOWELL, BENJAMIN, captain of Swiftsure [afterwards Admiral Sir B. Hallowell Carew; STEPHEN]; a volunteer at the siege of Calvi, 67
Hamilton, Emma, Lady; of great assistance to the royal family on leaving Naples, 176-7; is granted the cross of Malta, 235; her eminent services, 427; 'a legacy to my king and country,' 428. Letters to, 167, 426
Hamilton, Sir William, Minister at

HOO

Naples; letters to, 137-9, 143-5, 162, 171, 174, 238
Hamond, Sir Andrew Snape, Bart., Comptroller of the Navy; letters to, 130, 413
Hamond, Graham Eden, captain of Lively [son of Sir Andrew, afterwards Admiral Sir G. E.; O'BYRNE]; letter to, 425
Hardy, Thomas Masterman, commander of Mutine brig at the Nile, posted to Vanguard; later, captain of Foudroyant and Victory [afterwards Vice-Admiral, Sir T. M.; died 1839. MARSHALL, iii. 153]; witness to Nelson's last will, 428
Hawkesbury, Lord, Foreign Secretary 1801-4; letter to, 355
Health, of the fleet; is good, 316; beyond what I have ever seen, 320, 322-3; not a sick man in the fleet, 338; measures for insuring, 339, 371; we have no sick, 371; lost neither officer nor man, 406; report of the physician of the fleet, 409-11
Health, Nelson's personal; will suffer from a cold damp climate, 15; excellent in Canada, 16; he is worn to a skeleton, 34; feels the effect of his wound at the Nile, 163, 165; very weak with cough and fever, 167; has been nursed by Sir William and Lady Hamilton, 182; — is much broken, 234-7; necessitates his giving up his command, 241-3; is re-established, 243; much tried by the Baltic, 271; much broken, 275-7; he requires nursing like a child, 289; suffers from sea-sickness, 291; in the worst plight of the whole fleet, 351; compelled to apply for leave to return to England, 365; requires a few months' rest, 371-4
Heard, Sir Isaac, Garter King at Arms; his fees have been paid, 245. Letter to, 221
Herbert, Mr., President of Nevis, uncle of Mrs. Nisbet, 33
Higgins, *see* Wilkinson
Hill, a scoundrel; threatens to libel Nelson, 293; escapes, *ib.* Letter to, 293
Hinchingbrook; Nelson posted to, 4, 10; his services in, 4, 18
Hindostan storeship; burnt, 342
Hobart, Lord; letters to, 325, 332-3, 335, 343, 351, 353. Letter from, 323
Hood, Samuel, Viscount [RALFE, 1.

INDEX   447

HOO

242]; commands in the West Indies, 16; 'his house always open to me,' 22; coolness between — and Nelson, 46; 'after clouds, sunshine,' 47; commander-in-chief in Mediterranean, 6, 48-74; chases the French fleet into Golfe Jouan, 64, 71-2; leaves the fleet, 72; Nelson's high opinion of, 71, 82; resigns the command of the Mediterranean, 82. Letters to, 17, 56-9, 61, 64-5, 67-70. Letters from, 59, 62, 67, 68

Hood, Samuel, captain of Zealous at the Nile [afterwards Vice-Admiral Sir S. Hood, Bart.; died commander-in-chief in the East Indies, 1814, cousin of Lord Hood. RALFE, iv. 55]; commands the squadron on coast of Egypt, 164, 167. Letters to, 164, 166

Hope, George, captain of Defence; letter to, 425

Hotham, William, Admiral [afterwards Lord; RALFE, i. 261]; commands in chief in the Mediterranean, 6, 72-90; mistaken as to French force, 71; his two actions off Toulon, 6, 74-83; Nelson's opinion of, 81-2, 85; has struck his flag, 90. Letters to, 84, 87

Hoste, Rev. Dixon [father of William Hoste, then a midshipman of Agamemnon, afterwards Captain Sir W. Hoste, Bart.; HOSTE; MARSHALL, iii. 470]; letters to, 81, 123

Howe, Richard, Earl [BARROW]; Nelson calls on, 22 and *note*; 'a great officer in the management of a fleet,' 82. Letter from, 179. Letter to, 180

Hughes, Lady, wife of Sir Richard; goes out in Boreas, 23; 'a fine talkative lady,' 24; 'has an eternal clack,' 25

Hughes, Sir Richard, commander-in-chief in the West Indies [CHARNOCK, vi. 180]; bows and scrapes too much, 25; not sufficiently firm, *ib.*; gives orders to see the Navigation Act carried out, 27; gives contrary orders, *ib.*; Nelson refuses to obey, *ib.*; he thanks Nelson for having put him right, 28; is thanked by the Treasury, *ib.*; authorises the commissioner at Antigua to hoist a broad pennant, 29; Nelson refuses to acknowledge it, 29-31; Nelson's opinion of, 33, 35. Letter to, 29

INGLEFIELD, JOHN NICHOLSON, captain of l'Aigle; later, commissioner

LAY

at Gibraltar [MARSHALL, iii. 62]; letter to, 125

Irresistible; Nelson hoists his broad pennant on board of, 117

Italinsky, Chevalier, Russian Minister at Naples; letter to, 218

Italy; a gold mine for the French, 94-5

JACKSON, THOMAS, Minister at Court of Sardinia; letters to, 336, 355

Jacobins; thirteen hanged, 196; declaration and proclamation to, 198, 201; their lying reports, 197; they came out of the castles with full knowledge and understanding, 202, 239

Jamaica; expected attack on, 4, 11; the probable object of the combined fleet, 401

Janus; Nelson captain of, 4, 12

Jervis, Sir John, later Earl of St. Vincent [BRENTON; TUCKER]; commander-in-chief in the Mediterranean, 94-196; Nelson's first interview with, 94; Nelson's high opinion of, 106; his despatch after the battle of St. Vincent, 113. Letters to, 94-109, 113, 120-8, 130. *See* St. Vincent, Earl of

Jouan, Golfe; the French fleet in, 71-2

KEATS, RICHARD GOODWIN, captain of Superb [afterwards Admiral Sir Richard; RALFE, iii. 487; MARSHALL, i. 342]; 'one of the very best officers in his Majesty's navy,' 313; his reminiscence of a conversation at Merton, 417. Letter to, 400

Keith, Viscount [ALLARDYCE]; succeeds Lord St. Vincent as commander-in-chief in the Mediterranean, 196; orders Nelson to send all the ships he could spare to Minorca, which Nelson at first refuses to do, 203-7; leaves the Mediterranean, 210; comes out again as commander-in-chief, 234; superseding Nelson, 234. Letters to, 196, 199, 203, 205, 230, 234-6, 238, 242-3. Letters from, 204, 207, 243

Kingsmill, Sir Robert Brice, Admiral [RALFE, i. 354]; letter to, 362.

LAMB, PHILIP, Captain, transport agent, letter to, 354

Layman, William, commander of

448 INDEX

LEG

Raven sloop [MARSHALL, x. 323]; court-martial on, 389; Nelson's high opinion of, 390-1
Le Gros, John; commander of Hindostan when burnt, 342; tried and honourably acquitted, 343
Leander; position of in the battle of the Nile, 152, 157; is captured, 155
Legacies to the service; the near relations of brother officers are, 303, 334
Leghorn; blockade of French frigate in, 52; taken by the French, 103; blockade of, ib.; intended attack on, 105; prevented by the defeats of the Austrians, 105
Letters from England; delay in receiving, 321; suggestion for free postage of seamen's —, 356
Lindholm, Danish adjutant-general; goes on board Elephant, 258; and London, 259. Letters to, 266, 270, 280. Letter from, 268
Lock, Charles, consul-general at Naples; lays a vague information of frauds on the government, 208; his accusation is 'malicious and scandalous,' 223; his conduct has been highly improper, 226; his ruin not sought for, ib. Letter to, 208
Locker, William, captain of Lowestoft, commodore at the Nore, lieut.-governor of Greenwich Hospital; died 1800; first lieutenant of Experiment, 183 n. Letters to, 10-16, 18-29, 32, 34-6, 41, 47, 50, 72, 78, 81-2, 95, 102, 110, 118, 183
Louis, Thomas, captain of Minotaur at the Nile; later, Rear-Admiral Sir Thomas; receives the capitulation of Gaeta, 209-10; joins the fleet before Toulon, 394; sent to Gibraltar for water and provisions, 415-6. Letters to, 209-10
Lowestoft; Nelson lieutenant of, 3, 9
Lutwidge, Skeffington; captain of Carcass, 2; admiral commanding in the Downs, 281; his command divided with Nelson, 282. Letter to, 292

MCARTHUR, JOHN, purser; secretary to Lord Hood in the Mediterranean; joint editor of 'Naval Chronicle;' joint author of 'Life of Nelson.' Letters to, 1, 73, 122
Majorca; Captain Durban sent to gain intelligence concerning, 370
Malta; taken possession of by the French, 138; is blockaded, 168;

MIN

shameful neglect of the Neapolitan ministers to send provisions and stores, 171, 229-32; failure of attempt to storm, 182; Graham commands the troops on shore, 224, 236; French ships at — ready to put to sea, 235; Nelson ordered to take personal command of the squadron off, 234; which he refuses to do, 234-5; [the French garrison surrendered, 5 Sept. 1800]; an important outwork to India, 309; of no use to the fleet off Toulon, 309, 322, 331
Marines; want a serious inspection, 245
Marsden, William, secretary to the Admiralty; letters to, 343, 347, 350, 353, 356, 362-5, 371, 379-81, 385-6, 389, 391-3, 395-401, 404, 408-9, 415-6. Letter from, communicating instructions to Cornwallis, 377
Marseilles; blockade of, essential, 356
Mayor, Lord; reference to, 297; Nelson declines to dine with, 300. Letters to, 296, 300, 360
Mediterranean; question of keeping the fleet in, 99; preparing to leave, 109; the fleet withdrawn from, 110; duties of the fleet in, 169; Lord Keith withdraws the fleet from, 210; Nelson appointed commander-in-chief in, 304; his instructions, 304-6; danger of being driven into, 424
Melpomene; engagement with, 54; is captured, 70
Melville, Lord, First Lord of the Admiralty 1804-5; leaves the Admiralty, 399; 'was doing much for the service,' ib. Letters to, 355, 366, 379, 388-90, 396
Merchants in the West Indies; are opposed to Nelson's carrying out the Navigation Act, 5, 26-8
Micheroux, Chevalier, Neapolitan minister; letter to, 375
Middleton, Sir Charles, Comptroller of the Navy; letters to, 40, 41. See Barham, Lord
Miller, Ralph Willett, captain of Theseus; a 'most exceeding good officer,' 102; narrative of the battle of the Nile, 155-162; his death, 207 n, 211; monument in memory of, 244
Minerve; capture of, 82 n; Nelson goes up the Mediterranean in, 6, 110; captures Sabina (Sabina retaken), 111; rejoins the fleet off Cape St. Vincent, 113
Minorca; capture of, 173; expected

INDEX 449

MIN

attack on, 192; arrangements for defence of, *ib.*; more troops there than they know what to do with, 213; French intrigues in, 322
Minto, Lord [*Life and Letters of*]; letters to, 165, 235, 335. *See* Elliot, Sir Gilbert
Mitchell, Sampson, commodore in Portuguese service; letters to, 179, 190
Moira, Lord; letter to, 311
Money; the great object at New York, 16; Nelson consults his uncle about, 21, 32; gives to his relations, 203; grant from the E.I.C., 214; settlement of affairs, 411-12
Moore, Graham, captain of Indefatigable [MARSHALL, ii. 533]; sent off Cadiz, 376; captures the Spanish treasure ships, 377
Morea; French designs on the, 311-12, 337, 341
Morocco; contemplated expedition against, 42
Moseley, Dr., author of 'Treatise on Tropical Diseases;' letter to, 339
Motto; *Fides et opera*, 104 and *note*
Moubray, Richard Hussey, captain of Active [RALFE, iv. 116]; letter to, 346
Moutray, John, commissioner at Antigua [CHARNOCK, vi. 331], hoists a broad pennant, 29; Nelson refuses to acknowledge it, *ib.*; and states the case to the Admiralty, 29-31; the commissioner recalled, 31; Nelson's great regard for Mrs. Moutray, 32
Murray, George, first captain of Victory in the Mediterranean; absent from Trafalgar on family business, 424
Mutiny in the fleet off Cadiz, 124-5

NAIAD; her log at Trafalgar, 431-2
Naples, a country of 'whores and scoundrels,' 167; English residents may send their valuables on board the fleet, 174; the king leaves, 174-7; a republic under French protection, 179, 182; Troubridge commands in the Bay of, 189-90; Foote is left senior officer in, 196; Nelson arrives in, 197; entire liberation of, 209; the foulest corruption everywhere, 235; Mr. Elliot minister at, 307, is directed to correspond directly with Nelson, 323; letter to king of, 333; to queen of, 333, 358, 406

NEL

National; colours struck at Rogliano 56; letter to the commander of — corvette, 86; seizure of corvette, 87
Navigation Act enforced, 5, 25-9
Navy; ruined during the peace, 357; letter to — Board, 333
Nayler, George [afterwards Sir], York Herald; letter to, 327
Neapolitan; misconduct of officials, 172; cowardice of officers, 173; and of troops, 179; general shot by his own men, 174; provisional order to burn ships of war, 176; too hastily carried out by Portuguese officers, 181; officers of the — republic to surrender on pain of being considered rebels, 201; neglect to send supplies to Malta, 229-32; — troops ordered to Malta, 232; — canvas better than English, 380
Nelson, Rev. Edmund, Lord Nelson's father; letters to, 16, 105, 112
Nelson, Horatio, Viscount; birth and parentage, 1; enters the navy, 1; early service, 2-3; is made lieutenant, and appointed to the Lowestoft, 3, 9; lieutenant of Bristol, 3; promoted to be commander of Badger, 3, 10; posted to the Hinchingbrook, 4, 10; has naval command of an expedition against San Juan, 4, 11; is appointed to Janus, but invalids, 4, 12; commissions the Albemarle, 13; and commands her in the North Sea, 14; in Canada, 16; and in the West Indies, 17; pays off the Albemarle, and visits France, 19-21; entertains thoughts of marriage, 21; which do not lead to any result, 22; commissions the Boreas, 23; commands her in the West Indies, 25-40; adventure with a runaway horse, 24; his opinion of the Admiral, 25, 33, 35; and of the Admiral's wife, 24, 25; enforces the Navigation Act, 25-9; for which the Admiral is thanked, 29; declines to recognise the broad pennant of Commissioner Moubray, 29-31; his doing so disapproved of by the Admiralty, 31; becomes engaged to Mrs. Nisbet, 32; whom he marries, 40; places Mr. Schomberg under arrest, 36; sends him to Jamaica to be tried, 38; his sending the Pegasus to Jamaica disapproved of, 39; exposure of frauds on the government, 40-4; pays off the Boreas, 41; commissions the Agamemnon, 6, 47; commands her in the Mediterranean, 49-102; engagement

G G

NEL

with the Melpomene, 54; on shore at Bastia, 61-3; and at Calvi, 65-70; loses the sight of right eye, 66-7, 69, 71; Hotham's first action, 74-9; and second action, 83, 85; his opinion of Lord Hood, 71, 82, 86; of Howe, 82; of Hotham, 79, 82, 85; commands a squadron in the Gulf of Genoa, 84-107; is authorised to wear a distinguishing pennant, 6, 100; removes to the Captain, 102; hoists his broad pennant temporarily in the Minerve, 110; captures the Sabina, 111; returns to the Captain, 113; which he commands in the battle off Cape St. Vincent, 114; is wounded in the belly, 117; hoists his pennant temporarily in the Irresistible, 116; promoted to be Rear-Admiral, 118; appointed a K.B., 119; hoists his flag in the Theseus, 122; mischief 'hatched by a Sunday's grog,' 125; commands the inshore squadron off Cadiz, 122-6; commands a detached squadron against Santa Cruz, 126-30; loses his right arm, 128, 130; returns to England in Seahorse, 130; hoists his flag in the Vanguard, 132; joins the fleet off Cadiz, *ib.*; and is sent into the Mediterranean with a small squadron, 133; which is afterwards reinforced, 137; but is deserted by the frigates, *ib.*; searches for the French fleet, 137-45; and finds it off the mouth of the Nile, 145; where he destroys it, 145-162; receives a severe wound in the head, 152; from the effects of which he suffers [apparently for the rest of his life], 163; [is created Baron Nelson of the Nile, 6 Oct. 1798]; arrives at Naples, 167; 'a country of fiddlers and poets, whores and scoundrels,' *ib.*; takes the royal family to Palermo, 176; is much annoyed by the pretensions of Sir Sidney Smith [q. v.], 178, 184, 186; is congratulated by Lord Howe on the victory at the Nile, 179; to whom he writes a tactical account of the battle, 180; is a 'good scholar' of Captain Locker, 183; sends Troubridge with a squadron to the Bay of Naples, 189; but is obliged to recall him and the ships of the line, 193; leaving Foote senior officer, 196; hoists his flag in Foudroyant, 196; takes the squadron to Naples, 197; annuls the treaty which Foote had signed,

NEL

198; compels the rebels to surrender at discretion, 199, 201-2, 239; issues a proclamation to the rebel officers, 201; orders Caracciolo to be tried by court-martial, 201; and to be hanged, 202; reduces St. Elmo, 204; Capua and Gaeta, 209; disobeys Lord Keith's order to send ships to Minorca, 205-6; for which he is reprimanded by the Admiralty, 206. [Created Duke of Bronte, 13 Aug. 1799.] Is anxious to chastise the insolence of the Dey of Algiers [q. v.], 226, 307-8, 335; joins Lord Keith at Leghorn, 233; captures the Généreux, 234-5; strikes his flag, and goes home overland, 243; separates from his wife, 270. [Promoted to be Vice-Admiral, 1 Jan. 1801.] Hoists his flag in the San Josef, 243; moves to the St. George on being appointed second in command of the fleet for the Baltic, 240; transfers his flag temporarily to the Elephant, 251; and in command of a detachment of the fleet, fights the battle of Copenhagen, 254-9; his alleged disobedience of a signal, 256 and *note*; succeeds to the command-in-chief, 271; and takes the fleet into the Gulf of Finland, 275; but withdraws, on the representation of Count Pahlen, 276. [Created Viscount Nelson of the Nile, 22 May 1801.] Is compelled by his health to return to England [in the Kite brig], 281 [arrived at Yarmouth, 1 July, 1801]. Appointed to command the defence flotilla, 281; hoists his flag in the Unité, 282; attack on French flotilla at Boulogne fails, 289; a scoundrel threatens to publish an abusive article in the papers, 293; he is discontented at the want of proper recognition of Copenhagen, 295-7, 300; is appointed commander-in-chief in the Mediterranean, 304; hoists his flag in the Victory, *ib.*; moves into the Amphion, 306; joins the fleet under Sir R. Bickerton off Toulon, 311; returns to Victory, 315; keeps watch on Toulon, 312-95; but does not blockade it, 360; is indignant at a false despatch of La Touche Tréville [q. v.], 361, 363-4, 366-7; searches for the French fleet, 384-9; and again, 395; follows it to the West Indies, 400; and back to Europe, 404; receives definite news of it, 407;

INDEX

NEL

joins Cornwallis off Ushant, 409; returns to England, *ib.*; and strikes his flag, 411; again hoists his flag in the Victory, 412; joins the fleet off Cadiz, 413; engages the combined fleet off Trafalgar, 429-37; is mortally wounded, 429; and dies, *ib.*; his body is sent to England, 439; and buried in St. Paul's, *ib.*

Nelson, Maurice, brother of Lord Nelson; letter to, 234

Nelson, Mrs., later Lady, Lord Nelson is separated from, 270; has made her a liberal allowance, *ib.* Letters to, 47-53, 55-6, 58, 61-2, 71-2, 74, 79, 82, 84, 88-9, 94-5, 104, 109, 118, 123, 132, 134, 144, 203

Nelson, Rev. William, later Dr. [brother and successor of Lord Nelson; created Earl Nelson, 9 Nov. 1805]; wishes to enter the navy as chaplain, 13; chaplain of the Boreas, 24. Letters to, 9, 12-14, 22-4, 32, 34-5, 47-9, 60, 63, 72, 79, 80-2, 102, 119, 326, 363

Nepean, Evan, later Sir, Secretary to and one of the Lords of the Admiralty; letters to, 90, 130, 162, 164, 199, 204, 206, 209, 211, 213-15, 222, 227-8, 237, 243, 272, 280, 285, 287, 289, 292-3, 304, 307, 320, 330, 366, 403. Letter from, 206

Neutral; flag, abuse of, 326-7; trade, 415

Neutrality; laws of —, constantly violated by privateers, 372; must be respected, 373, 375; violation of — complained of, 375, 393; complaint against Spanish, 329; against Portuguese, 417-18

Nile, battle of the, 145-62, 180

Nisbet, Mrs.; Nelson becomes engaged to, 32-3; marries, 5, 40; letter to, 35. *See* Nelson, Mrs.

Niza, Marquis de, rear-admiral and commander-in-chief of the Portuguese squadron at Naples and Malta; wishes to have rank in the English squadron, 170; completely ignorant of sea affairs, 172; is urged to remain at Malta, notwithstanding his orders to return to Portugal, 215, 217, 219; receives Nelson's permission to return, 227; letters to, 166, 170-1, 212, 215, 217, 219, 227

Nootka Sound; dispute with Spain concerning, 5, 45

Nuovo, Castle, *see* Uovo

Oak trees in Forest of Dean, 297-300

PIL

Orde, Sir John [RALFE, ii. 57]; commands a squadron off Cadiz, 381; Nelson's disgust thereat, *ib.*; is in a sad jumble, 392; begs to resign his command, 395; will be the richest admiral England ever saw, *ib.*

Orient, L' [of 120 guns, formerly Sans Culotte, originally Dauphin Royal]; flagship at the Nile, burnt and blown up, 153, 158; had struck before she blew up, 165-6; had 600,000*l.* on board, 166

Orion; her log at Trafalgar, 430

Otway, Robert Waller, Sir Hyde Parker's flag captain in the Baltic; later, commissioner at Gibraltar [RALFE, iv. 1]; letters to, 380, 397-8

PAHLEN, COUNT, Russian minister; letters to, 274, 276, 278; letters from, 275, 277

Parker, Sir Hyde [RALFE, i. 377]; commands in the Mediterranean, 90; in the North Sea and Baltic, 244; a little nervous about dark nights and fields of ice, 246; his instructions, 247. Letter to, 248

Parker, Lady, wife of Sir Peter; letter to, 182

Parker, Sir Peter, commander-in-chief at Jamaica, later at Portsmouth, chief mourner at Nelson's funeral [RALFE, i. 114]

Parker, William, captain of Amazon [PHILLIMORE]; dashing conduct of, 337. Letters to, 333, 407

Pegasus; commanded by Prince William, bad state of, 36; Nelson sends her to Jamaica, 38; which the Admiralty disapprove of, 39

Pellew, Sir Edward [afterwards Lord Exmouth; OSLER]; in command off Ferrol, 337; wishes to serve under Nelson, 345. Letter to, 344

Pennant; Nelson dissatisfied at not having a distinguishing —, 90; is ordered to hoist a distinguishing —, 100; order to Troubridge to bear a broad —, 210; Fischer's broad —, 260, 267, 269

Pilot; Nelson, a good Thames —, 2, 287; the — ran the Albemarle aground, 24

Pilotage; captains to make themselves acquainted with, 343; notes on the coast of Africa, 345; inquiry about the Black Sea, 340, 378 and Majorca, 370

PIT

Pitt, William, First Lord of the Treasury; letters to, ?40, 411
Pole, Sir Charles Morice, Vice-Admiral [RALFE, ii. 129]; letter to, 350
Porto Ferrajo; taken by the English, 103; De Burgh refuses to evacuate the place, 112-3; he does evacuate it, 122
Portuguese neutrality, complaint of, 417-18
Postage of seamen's letters should be remitted, 356
Presents; an imperfect list of, 8
Prince of Wales; sent home with Sir Robert Calder, 414
Prisoners of war; not to be sent to England in transports, 254; ought not to be fed on salt beef, 362; should have a ration of wine, ib.
Privateer; destroyed by Renard, 372, 375, 393; story of the half-burnt — confuted, 404 n, 406 n, 407 n
Privateers; Nelson's strong opinion of, 278, 336, 353, 359, 362, 363, 375
Prize; Nelson boards a —, 3; question of burning the Nile prizes, 164-5
Prize-money; for Bastia and Calvi, 73; suit with Lord St. Vincent respecting, 239-41, 246; for Copenhagen, 264; question of — made by a ship in disobedience of orders, 408
Promotion; ought to rest with the commander-in-chief, 334

RADSTOCK, Lord, Admiral [MARSHALL, i. 56]; letters to, 316, 343, 395
Raynsford, Robert, commander of Morgiana sloop; letter to, 367
Rebels; *see* Jacobins
Redhot shot; used by the French, 78, 80
Republic; the Vesuvian, 182; its flag, ib.; the Italian, 310
Reval, Nelson brings a squadron to, 274; withdraws it at Count Pahlen's request, 276
Richardson, Henry, captain of Juno; letter to, 308
Riou, Edward, 'the gallant good Riou;' commands the Amazon at Copenhagen, 252; his introduction to Nelson, ib.; assists Nelson in drawing up the detailed instructions, 254; is slain, 257

SAR

Rodney; claims of the son of, 303
Rose, Right Hon. George; letters to, 341, 348, 420
Ross, Hercules [a West-India merchant, with whom Nelson had contracted an intimate friendship, and to whose son, Horatio Ross, he was afterwards godfather]; letter to, 42
Russia, Emperor of; letter to, 220; death of, 271
Russian; co-operation, 169; is worthless, 227, 229; 'out-manœuvre a —,' 253
Russians; their selfish policy in the Mediterranean, 173, 211, 357-8, 361, 372; Nelson suspects them, 181, 212; their carelessness has retarded the fall of Malta, 228; they deserved punishment, 273; are miserable seamen, 277
Ryves, George Frederick, captain of Agincourt, later of Gibraltar; letter to, 327

ST. ELMO; summons to governor of, 198; capitulates, 204
St. Fiorenzo; occupied, 57
St. John's; survey of harbour at, 25
St. Omer; residence at, 19-21
St. Vincent; battle of, 6, 113-17
St. Vincent, Earl of; invalided from the command of the Mediterranean, 196; in command of the Channel fleet, 244; First Lord of the Admiralty, 246; led astray by the opinion of ignorant people, 348. Letters to, 131, 133, 137, 140-5, 163-5, 167, 169-70, 173, 175-8, 180, 182, 184-6, 191-2, 194-6, 233, 244-6, 275-6, 281, 284-8, 290-1, 294-5, 304, 306, 312-13, 321, 330, 334, 337-8, 342, 349. *See* Jervis, Sir John
Salutes; not to be fired, 413
San Josef; capture of, 114, 116; Nelson hoists his flag on board, 243; 'the finest ship in the world,' 244; Nelson leaves, 245
San Juan; expedition to, 4, 11; heavy loss in, 12
Santa Cruz; proposal for an attack on, 120-2; expedition against, 126; its failure, 126-7; detailed proceedings of, 127-30
Sardinia; declared neutral, 310; expected invasion of, 317, 333; a very desirable possession, 332; most important as a naval station, 335, 355,

SAV

411; measures for defence of, 336

Savings; should be allowed for oatmeal, 371

Schomberg, Charles Marsh, captain of Madras; letter to, 324

Schomberg, Isaac, first lieutenant of Pegasus [afterwards captain, author of 'Naval Chronology']; applies for a court-martial, 36; is put under arrest, *ib.*; sent to Jamaica, 38; the affair arranged, 39. Letter to, 37

Scott, Sir William [afterwards Lord Stowell]; letter to, 303

Sea-fencibles; cannot be employed for any length of time, 286-8; the establishment was bad, 293

Sea officer, a, cannot form plans like a land officer, 99

Seaforth, Lord, governor of Barbadoes; letter to, 401

Seahorse; Nelson serves in, 2; in Bay of Naples, *see* Foote, E. J.

Seamen; work the guns at Calvi, 69; always afraid of some trick of the Admiralty, 285; proposal for registering, 301-4

Shaw, Harding, lieutenant commanding Spider brig; complaint against, for violating the neutrality of Girgenti, 353; his conduct very meritorious and praiseworthy, 353; letter to, disapproving his flogging the whole ship's company, 371

Shepheard, Lewis, commander of Thisbe; letter to, 346

Ships; 'half-fit — drain us of stores,' 212; 'if not fit to stand bad weather they are useless,' 330; several are in a very bad condition, 312-14, 321; in a very indifferent state, 344, 355; very crazy, 357; rotten, 362

Sicily; question as to security of, 307; in a very bad state, 309; French intrigues in, 310; active measures for security of, 325

Sickness; serious outbreak of — on board Northumberland, 236; several of the ships have much scurvy, 313, 316; scurvy has made its appearance in several ships, 341; some symptoms of scurvy, 406; much — in combined fleet, 403, 406

Signal; Nelson's last, 382 *n*, 435

Signals; to engage, their meaning, 329; by night, to be careful the lights are clear, 338; may be misunderstood, 383; if not perfectly understood, 422

Signature, 237, 258

STE

Smith, John Spencer, Minister at Constantinople [brother of Sir W. S. Smith]; letters to, 169, 209, 228

Smith, Sir William Sidney, captain of Tigre and, in conjunction with his brother, J. S. Smith, Minister at Constantinople [BARROW; HOWARD]; 'Great talkers do the least, we see,' 81; senior officer in the Levant, 177; Nelson offended by his conduct and assumption, 178, 184, 186; he is admonished by Lord St. Vincent, 181; explanation by Lord Spencer, 185; passport issued by, 186-7; Nelson's wrath is appeased, 209, 211; his defence of Acre, 211. Letters to, 177, 184-5, 207, 211, 217, 226, 232

Soldiers; on board ship subject to naval discipline, 346-50, 355

Spain; war with — expected, 105, 320, 322; war declared, 107, 379

Spanish; fleet joins Hood off Alicant, 49; its inefficiency, *ib.*; joins the French at Toulon, 110; and off Cadiz, 398;— frigate, correspondence with captain of, 107-8; ships of war at Palermo cannot be allowed to go to sea, 239; probable junction of — with French, 320-1, and *note*; — neutrality is gross partiality, 329; treasure ships seized, 377

Spartiate; capture of, 156-7; joins the fleet in the West Indies, 401; log of, at Trafalgar, 429

Spencer, Lord, First Lord of the Admiralty 1797-1801; suggests that Nelson should command the detached squadron, 135; explains the sending Sir W. S. Smith into the Levant, 185; advises Nelson to return to England for his health, 241. Letters to, 130, 138, 163, 169, 172-3, 178, 188, 190, 202, 205, 214, 221, 225, 227, 229, 232, 242, 244. Letters from, 185, 241

Spencer, Hon. Robert Cavendish, commander of Renard schooner [son of Lord Spencer; MARSHALL, vii. 256]; destroys a privateer on the coast of Sicily, 372, 375, 393. Letter to, 372

Stephens, Alexander, author of 'History of the Wars of the French Revolution;' letter to, 300

Stephens, Sir Philip, secretary to, and later, one of the Lords of the Admiralty; letters to, 13, 14, 23, 29, 36, 54

STE

Stewart, Hon. William, Lieut.-Colonel; commands the troops embarked in the Baltic fleet, 250; his narrative of the battle of Copenhagen, 250-9, 271, 276-7

Stores; economy of, 276; great want of, 320, 331, 333; unwarranted purchase of, 359; measures to be observed in future, 360; hammock cloths rotten, *ib.*

Strachan, Sir Richard John, captain of Donegal [RALFE, ii. 456]; letters to, 315, 317, 320; sent to, 378

Strangford, Lord, Minister at Lisbon; letter to, 417

Stuart, Hon. Sir Charles, Lieut.-General; commanding at Minorca, 179; brings 1,000 men to Palermo, 185. Letter to, 179

Stuart, Don Jacobo, a descendant of the Duke of Berwick; captain of La Sabina, 112; Nelson returns his sword, *ib.*; he is exchanged, *ib.*

Suckling, Maurice, Comptroller of the Navy [CHARNOCK, vi. 149]; Nelson's uncle and captain in Raisonable, 1; his recommendations to Nelson, 9, 10; his legacy to Nelson, 34

Suckling, William, Nelson's uncle [in the custom-house; died Nov. 1798]; letters to, 21, 32, 34, 53-4, 60-1, 63, 71, 73-4, 80-1, 89

Sutton, Evelyn, captain of Isis; court-martial on, 12 and *note*

Sutton, Samuel, captain of Amazon and Amphion; fits out Victory, 303-4. Letters to, 279, 367, 392

Surgeons; different treatment of in army and navy, 351

Swedes; a battle with the — to be avoided, 273

Swedish Admiral, letter to the, 273

Swift, cutter, with despatches, taken by a privateer, 342

Syracuse; the squadron waters at, 144-5; no private orders given to the governor, 145

TACTICS; Nelson's early study of, 17; notice of, 150-1; account of — at the Nile, 180; memo on, 382, 421

Taylor, Nathaniel, storekeeper at Malta; letter to, 359

Téméraire; log of, at Trafalgar, 431

Teneriffe; *see* Santa Cruz

Theseus; Nelson hoists his flag on

TRO

board, 6, 122; satisfaction of the ship's company, 123; with the inshore squadron off Cadiz, 122-5; expedition against Santa Cruz, 126. *See* Miller, R. W.

Thomas, Richard, commander of Ætna bomb [MARSHALL, iv. 953]; letters to, 395-6

Thompson, Miss Horatia Nelson [afterwards Mrs. Philip Ward; died 6 March 1881]; left by Nelson to the 'beneficence of his country,' 428; a bequest which was scandalously ignored, *ib. n.* Letter to, 426

Time; value of, 246 and *note*

Toulon; occupied by Lord Hood, 51; evacuation of, 54-5; might have been re-occupied by Hotham, 86; Nelson joins the fleet off, 311; La Touche Tréville in command at, 340; fleet is ready for sea, 317, 324; 'playing in and out,' 341, 343, 348, 352, 354; 14,000 men ready for embarkation at, 344; constant watch kept on, 346; has never been blockaded, 360; a vice-admiral has hoisted his flag at, 379; troops are embarking, 381; fleet sailed from, 384, 395; put back in a very crippled state, 389

Tour in France, 19

Trafalgar, battle of, 429-39

Treaty; with the Neapolitan rebels cannot be carried out, 199

Tréville, La Touche, commands the French fleet at Toulon, 340; has several times hoisted his topsail-yards up, 352; Nelson 'hopes to shame him out of his nest,' 354; he 'cut a caper' off Sepet, 354; his letter describing 'the caper,' 355; Nelson's extreme indignation and disgust, 361, 363-4, 366-7; his death, 368, 372

Trevor, Hon. John, Minister at Turin; letter to, 98

Trigge, Sir Thomas, Lieut.-General, governor of Gibraltar; letter to, 363

Tripoli; negotiations with, 188; the bashaw's dispositions most friendly, 325

Troubridge, Sir Thomas, captain of Culloden, later one of the Lords of the Admiralty, 1801-4 [afterwards Rear-Admiral and Commander-in-Chief in the East Indies; lost in the Blenheim, Feb. 1807; RALFE, iv. 397]; leads the line at St. Vincent, 115; nobly supports Nelson, *ib.*; commands the landing party at

INDEX 455

TUN

Santa Cruz, 126; his report of the proceedings, 129 joins Nelson in the Mediterranean, 137, 140, 147; goes to Naples in quest of news, 138, 148; and to Coron, 150; gets his ship ashore at the Nile, 154, 157; equally entitled to honours and rewards, 170; his ability and activity, *ib.*; commands expedition to Leghorn, 172; is recalled to Naples, 174; ordered to command the operations in the Bay of Naples, 187; is presented with the head of a Jacobin, 191; 'eight or ten of the villains ought to be hung,' 190; is quite willing to confirm the sentence if Yauch is ordered to be shot, 194; English officers ought not to sit on Neapolitan courts-martial, *ib.*; he is called away from Naples, 193, 195; commands the attack on St. Elmo, 222; is sent to attack Capua and Gaeta, 204; he reduces them, 209; is ordered to bear a broad pennant, 210; ordered to command off Malta, 224; his complaints of the neglect of the Neapolitan government, 230; seizes provision ships at Girgenti, 231; is 'full of resources,' 233; signs Sir Hyde Parker's orders for the Baltic, 248; and Nelson's for the Mediterranean, 306. Letters to, 173-4, 183, 187, 191-3, 204, 210-13, 215, 229, 231-2, 236-7, 331, 349. Letters from, 189-90, 193-4

Tunis, Bey of; complaint by, of the conduct of a privateer, 353

Turkish co-operation, 169

Turks; 'good people, but perfectly useless,' 212

Turk's Island; unsuccessful attack on, 17

Tuscany; virtually French territory, 310

Tyson, John, Nelson's secretary in Vanguard and Foudroyant; later, Clerk of the Survey at Chatham; letter to, 331

UNITÉ frigate; Nelson hoists his flag on board, 282

Uovo, Castle of; the rebels in — must surrender to his Majesty's mercy, 198; the rebels surrender accordingly, 199, 201-2, 239

VADO BAY, an open anchorage, 84
Vanguard; commissioned for Nelson's

WIL

flag, 7, 132; joins the fleet off Cadiz, 132; is sent up the Mediterranean, 133; dismasted in a gale, 133-5; puts into S. Pietro, 134, 147; is joined by reinforcement under Troubridge, 137; pursuit of the French, 138-45; battle of the Nile 145-62; arrives at Naples, 167; king of Naples and family take refuge on board of, 174-7; and are conveyed to Palermo, 177; the 'real good discipline of,' 195; Nelson moves into Foudroyant, 7, 196. *See* Nelson, Horatio, Viscount

Vansittart, Nicholas, Ambassador to Copenhagen [afterwards Lord Bexley]; letter to, 274

Vesuvian Republic; its flag, 182; its officers proclaimed rebels, 201

Victory, Nelson hoists his flag on board, 304; he quits her off Ushant and goes to Amphion, 306; she joins the fleet, and Nelson again hoists his flag in her, 315; he hopes to do better with her than Keppel did, 326; arrives at Spithead, 409; Nelson again hoists his flag on board, 412; she sails from St. Helens, *ib.*; joins the fleet off Cadiz, 413; her log at Trafalgar, 428-9. *See* Nelson, Horatio, Viscount

Victualling Board; letters to, 223, 226; letter from, 224

Vienna; the conduct of the Court of — is deception, 89

Villettes, William Anne, Major-General, commanding the garrison at Malta; letters to, 319, 368

Vincent, Richard Budd, captain of Arrow; letter to, 359

Vizir, the Grand; letter to, 337

WEST INDIA merchants; Nelson's dispute with, 26-8

Westcott, George Blagdon, captain of Majestic; is slain at the Nile, 145, 157

Wilkinson and Higgins; frauds discovered by, 40-1, 43-4; imprisoned at Antigua, 43. Letters to, 43-4

William Henry, H.R.H. Prince; Nelson is introduced to, 17; commands Pegasus in the West Indies, 36; is a good officer, *ib.*; promises to give Mrs. Nisbet away, 35; and does so, 40; commands Andromeda, 42 Letter from, concerning Mr. Schomberg [q. v.], 37-8. Letter to, asking for his interest to procure for Mrs. Nelson a situation in the Princess Royal's household, 42-3

Williams, Miss Helen Maria, author of 'Sketches of Manners,' &c.; falsehood of her book, 301

Williamson, John, captain of Agincourt at Camperdown; court-martial on, 131 and *note*

Woodman, Henry Frederick, lieutenant; letters to, 340, 378

Woronzow, Count; letter to, 326

Wyndham, Hon. William Frederick, Minister at Florence; letters to, 166, 224

YAUCH, Neapolitan General; infamous conduct of, 191, 194; court-martial ordered on, 194; will probably be shot, *ib.*

www.ingramcontent.com/pod-product-compliance
Lightning Source LLC
Chambersburg PA
CBHW051858300426
44117CB00006B/440